The Presbyterian Valley

Showing the location of the early itinerating preaching points and historic churches referred to in this book.

SCALE 1″= 22½ MILES

ROLLINS · COLLEGE ·
FIAT LUX
MDCCCLXXXV

THE PRESBYTERIAN VALLEY

TO

ALLEN STEWART DAVISON

AN ENTHUSIASTIC CONSERVER OF RECORDS

A KEEN STUDENT OF LOCAL HISTORY

AN OUTSTANDING CLERK OF SESSION

THIS HISTORY OF PRESBYTERIANISM IN THE

UPPER OHIO VALLEY

IS AFFECTIONATELY

DEDICATED

As an officer of The Presbyterian Historical Society of The Upper Ohio Valley, and one of its most loyal supporters, the present undertaking was close to his heart, as it is to

his wife

REBECCA PAULL MILLER DAVISON

This book is published as a religious feature of the Pittsburgh Bicentennial Year 1958-1959 in recognition of the continued influence of Presbyterianism throughout the two hundred years of Pittsburgh's growth and expansion.

ALLEN STEWART DAVISON
November 6, 1874–December 2, 1954

The Presbyterian Valley

WILLIAM WILSON McKINNEY

EDITOR

FOREWORD BY

EUGENE CARSON BLAKE

PITTSBURGH

DAVIS & WARDE, INC.

1958

Library of Congress Catalog Card Number: 58-14156

PRINTED IN THE UNITED STATES OF AMERICA
BY DAVIS & WARDE, INC.
704 SECOND AVE., PITTSBURGH 19, PA.

Contents

The Years of Fruitage, 1870–1958

Illustrations

Foreword

I SUPPOSE there are many reasons why history is written and read. To recreate the past by putting together with imaginative insight bits and pieces from old letters, lines from minute books, articles from yellowed journals, is a rewarding task for the writer even if no one read the story or was really benefited by it. To read authentic history is for the reader to live again in an era that is past.

It has been argued that men learn little from others' experiences and, therefore, reap small benefit from history. Though our own experiences are more eloquent teachers, I am convinced that the reading of authentic history is one of the few ways that wisdom comes to men in time to be useful.

In the past few years there has been a renewed interest in Presbyterian history. Part of the reason for an upsurge of our historical activity is the pressure to fill the vacuum in secular history which has too often been written as if the Churches did not really influence the course of our past. Part of the reason is the present revitalization of the Presbyterian Churches in the United States. The two decades from 1920 to 1940 formed a comparatively dark period for the Presbyterian Church. The aftermath of World War I, the collapse of grandiose plans of expansion, bitter theological controversy leading to schism, and a financial depression left Presbyterians in 1940 weak and frustrated.

Since that year the story has been one of renewed theological vitality and dynamic unity, expansion of churches and programs, new devotion and renewed hope. Presbyterians are proud again to be Presbyterians even though they have never been so co-operative and catholic as today.

For these reasons, I am sure that the pages of this book will be of special interest and benefit to the members of the new United Presbyterian Church in the United States of America. If we really understand and appreciate the strength and weaknesses of our

Church in its two hundred years of development in the Upper Ohio Valley, we will be better able to make the decisions that our present opportunities demand from us.

I hope further that *The Presbyterian Valley* will be of wide interest to all American historians helping them see the part that Presbyterians played in the building up of the culture and civilization of this early frontier of the nation.

I hope finally that this book may be only one of many scholarly works which will preserve and delineate our history as the foundation of a greater future than our past.

EUGENE CARSON BLAKE

Introduction

THIS REGIONAL HISTORY is the second volume which has been prepared for publication by the Presbyterian Historical Society of the Upper Ohio Valley, an Auxiliary of the Historical Society of the Presbyterian Church in the United States of America. The Stated Clerk of the General Assembly, Dr. Eugene Carson Blake, has written an appropriate foreword to this semi-official history of an important area of Presbyterian influence where reside more Presbyterians than in any other section of the country.

The book is the matured result of a motion which was presented by Dr. Gaius J. Slosser who at that time was Professor of Ecclesiastical History in Western Theological Seminary in Pittsburgh, Pennsylvania. During the annual meeting of the Upper Ohio Valley Historical Society in 1949, favorable action was taken upon his motion that "a committee on Publication be named to prepare and subsequently publish an interesting and definitive history, recording the development of Presbyterianism west of the Allegheny Mountains and throughout the Upper Ohio Valley. This history would be written on a co-operative basis by various members of our Historical Society who would write the portions assigned to them by this committee." Dr. W. W. McKinney was chosen chairman of the Publication Committee and later asked to edit the various chapters for publication in their present form.

After nine years of careful research and mutual criticism and guidance, the members of the committee present to the public the fruits of their study under the title, *The Presbyterian Valley*. It is the comprehensive story of the development and expansion in service to the community and nation of the Presbyterian Church U.S.A. throughout western Pennsylvania, eastern Ohio, and northern West Virginia. It includes a more detailed survey of the Pittsburgh district, which *Presbyterian Life* has recently described as "The Presbyterian Heartland." This great Presbyterian valley has been a fertile seedbed of pioneering personalities, policies, and programs that have made the Presbyterian church a dynamic and efficient force in American life.

The period covered is the entire two centuries of Presbyterian activity, beginning with the building of Fort Pitt in 1758 and culminating in the historic merger in Pittsburgh on May 28, 1958, of the Presbyterian and United Presbyterian denominations, the two religious forces which have largely moulded the culture and ideals of the Upper Ohio Valley.

The year 1958 was chosen as the strategic date of publication since this historic year brings to a close two hundred years of separate service of the two branches of Presbyterianism which are now merged to form the United Presbyterian Church in the U.S.A. Moreover, the city of Pittsburgh is giving widespread emphasis to its Bicentennial Celebration which begins on Thanksgiving Day of November, 1958, and which commemorates the erecting of Fort Pitt and the subsequent development of Pittsburgh into a leading metropolitan area.

The former United Presbyterian Church has published this same year a similar history—*The United Presbyterian Story.** The two volumes have been designed to supplement each other and thus give to the merged denominations a composite picture of Presbyterianism in its area of greatest growth and influence.

The Publication Committee would record its obligation to Dr. G. J. Slosser, Dr. C. R. Zahniser, and Dr. H. G. Harold, former members of the committee who placed their researches in the possession of the men who have written the assigned chapters on a co-operative basis. Also a word of appreciation is expressed to Professor Elwyn A. Smyth and Dr. John Hare for their helpful counsel as consultants to the committee.

In a book of composite authorship, it may be advisable to intro-

*Jamison, Wallace N. *The United Presbyterian Story,* a Centennial Study, 1858-1958. Pittsburgh: The Geneva Press, 1958.

duce the different writers with a brief summary of their background and interest in church history.

Dwight Raymond Guthrie, Ph.D., D.D., is Samuel P. Harbison Professor of Religion at Grove City College, Pennsylvania. Formerly he served as Presbyterian pastor at Oil City and Johnstown in Pennsylvania. He is author of *John McMillan, The Apostle of Presbyterianism in the West, 1752–1833,* and a former president of our Historical Society.

Frank Dixon McCloy, Jr., M.A., D.D., until recently Librarian and Dean of Western Theological Seminary, Pittsburgh, is now associate professor of Ecclesiastical History in that institution. He is chairman of the Curriculum Committee of the Council of Theological Education, Presbyterian Church U.S.A., and of the Curriculum Survey Committee of the Council, 1954–1958.

William Wilson McKinney, Ph.D., D.D., LL.D., has had only two pastorates, Round Hill Presbyterian Church, Elizabeth, Pennsylvania, and since 1928, the First Presbyterian Church of Ambridge, Pennsylvania. He is the present president of our Historical Society and a former moderator of the Presbyterian Synod of Pennsylvania (1940). He has contributed frequently to numerous periodicals and is the author of *Early Pittsburgh Presbyterianism* and of the second chapter of *They Seek A Country*. He is president also of the National Reform Association.

Walter Lysander Moser, Ph.D., D.D., was pastor of the First Presbyterian Churches of Apollo and Greenville, Pennsylvania, and has been serving for more than twenty-five years as pastor of the Edgewood Community (Presbyterian) Church in Pittsburgh. During World Wars I and II he was a chaplain with rank of Lieutenant Colonel. He is Stated Clerk of the Presbytery of Pittsburgh, a former Marvin Fellow and instructor in Ecclesiastical History at Western Theological Seminary. He is the present moderator of the Presbyterian Synod of Pennsylvania (1958) and vice-president of our Historical Society.

George Francis Swetnam, Ph.D., served pastorates in the Presbyterian Church U.S. and was professor of English and German at the University of Alabama. Since 1943 he has been a feature writer for *The Pittsburgh Press.* His published books include *Pittsylvania Country, Bicentennial History of Pittsburgh,* in three volumes, *So Stand Through the Years,* and *Where Else But Pittsburgh!* He was supply pastor at Dunlap's Creek (1942–1949) and at Youngwood (1949–1951) in Redstone Presbytery.

Edward Burgett Welsh, D.D., recently retired, has served pastorates at Wilmington, Delaware; Oil City, Ridgway, and Coraopolis in Pennsylvania; and New Concord and Norwich in Ohio. Graduate study at Erlangen and Basle, Switzerland, and Columbia University where he completed residence requirements for Ph.D. degree. He was the first president of our Historical Society and still is its guiding spirit. Author of a chapter in *They Seek A Country* and of numerous articles in *Princeton Theological Review, Journal of Presbyterian Historical Society,* and *Western Pennsylvania Historical Society Magazine.* Editor, *The Bulletin* of the Presbyterian Historical Society of the Upper Ohio Valley.

Daniel James Yolton, Th.M., is the youngest of the seven writers. Majored in Ecclesiastical History at Western Theological Seminary. Wrote as his graduate thesis *The Whiskey Rebellion in Western Pennsylvania.* Since 1957 he is the pastor of the English Congregational Church, Lansford, Pennsylvania. Previously he had served the Evangelical Protestant Church of Spring Hill, Pittsburgh, 1954–1957.

The generosity of interested friends has partially subsidized publication costs so that the book can be offered to the public at a popular price as a service to the Presbyterian church. In gratitude the Publication Committee acknowledges its debt to Mrs. Allen S. Davison, who has given the major share of the sustaining subsidy, and to Mrs. J. Harry Gorley, Dr. Roy R. Snowden, and the Pitcairn-Crabbe Foundation for added financial assistance.

The editor would also express his personal appreciation of the hearty co-operation of the other members of the Publication Committee and his indebtedness to Dr. Guy S. Klett who was the soul of helpfulness during the summers the editor searched the tremendous resources of the library of the Presbyterian Historical Society in the Witherspoon Building; to Dr. Gill I. Wilson of Parkersburg, West Virginia, who graciously made available his previous researches in the preparation of Chapter VIII; to Mrs. Walter Wilkening, the editor's secretary, who diligently typed and retyped the entire manuscript; and to Miss Mary Dickson of Davis & Warde, Inc., who carefully re-edited the manuscript in course of printing. The co-operation of those and other friends has improved the book and made the editor's task a pleasant diversion.

WILLIAM W. MCKINNEY

823 Maplewood Avenue
Ambridge, Pa.
July 1, 1958

COURTESY OF REVEREND HARRY CLAWSON

HOME OF THE REVEREND JAMES POWER, D.D.

The first minister to bring his family west of the Allegheny Mountains. Settled at Dunlap's Creek with wife and four daughters in 1776. Pastor of Sewickley and Mt. Pleasant Presbyterian churches in Westmoreland County.

COURTESY OF HELEN A. WRAGG, GREAT-, GREAT-, GREAT-GRAND-DAUGHTER OF DR. MCMILLAN

DR. JOHN McMILLAN

Only oil portrait available of any of "The Four Horsemen." Pioneer Preacher and Educator, 1752–1833. First Moderator of Redstone Presbytery in 1781.

REAR OF HILL CHURCH (CHARTIERS) AND CEMETERY SHOWING OLDER STONES

Dr. McMillan served as pastor, 1776–1793.

PHOTOGRAPH BY REVEREND JAMES YOLTON

CHAPTER I The Organizational Foundations

THE REVEREND JOHN MCMILLAN was a serious but cordial host as he stood in the doorway of John Stevenson's log cabin that brisk morning of September 19, 1781.[1] He was welcoming his two fellow Presbyterian ministers and three elders from widely scattered Presbyterian churches. They had braved the dangers of wilderness travel on horseback to respond to the call of the Synod of New York and Philadelphia to organize themselves into the Presbytery of Redstone.[2] John Stevenson was a member of the Pigeon Creek congregation in what is now Washington County. His rather commodious cabin was only three-quarters of a mile from the church of which John McMillan was pastor.[3]

The austere parson was delightfully genial as he congratulated his travel-stained guests on their safe journey through the trail-marked forests, and as he thought of the important business which the little group had assembled to discuss. After a glass of refreshment and a brief exchange of travel experiences, the conversation centered around the encouraging news of the progress of the War of the Revolution. Critical battles were raging as the colonists struggled bravely to achieve the victory over the British which culminated one month later in the surrender of Lord Cornwallis at Yorktown.[4]

Talk soon shifted to heart-rending stories of recent raids of the hostile Indians who resented the encroachment of the white settlers upon their hunting grounds. These raids increased in ferocity following the savage massacre by white intruders of the Christian Indians on March 8, 1782, at the Moravian settlement of Gnadenhuetten along the Tuscarawas River.[5] Many a frontier home went up in flames amid the shrieks of the tomahawked families and the captured women and children during that terrible year.

Calling the Roll of Presbytery

These perilous conditions made it impossible for Reverend Joseph Smith to share in the organizing fellowship of the Redstone Presbytery.[6] He was the pioneer pastor of the Buffalo and Cross Creek congregations in Washington County where he had been serving since 1779.[7] His fiery preaching had won for him the nickname, "hell-fire" Smith. He was particularly gifted as a revival preacher. Many notable revivals took place under his ministry both in his own and in neighboring Presbyterian churches. He also was one of the four ministers whom the Synod in May of 1781 had commissioned to form the Presbytery of Redstone with ecclesiastical jurisdiction over the entire frontier west of the Allegheny Mountains.[8] We listen as the roll is called following a prolonged period of prayer.

The oldest of the three ministers responding was Reverend James Power, a comparatively young man of thirty-five years. Synod had ordered that this first meeting of the newly formed Presbytery of Redstone be in his former parish at Laurel Hill, but the Indian raids in that area necessitated the change to Pigeon Creek. With his wife and four young daughters, he was the first Presbyterian minister to settle in Western Pennsylvania.[9] One month after his arrival in November of 1776, a fifth daughter graced their pioneer cabin, the first child to be born in a Presbyterian manse in Western Pennsylvania.[10] Mr. Power's home was near Brownsville on Dunlap's Creek. His missionary parish included preaching stations at Laurel Hill, Mt. Pleasant, Sewickley, Tyrone, and Unity. This circuit riding exposed him to the lurking savages who raided that area with deadly frequency. On several occasions he was reported killed by the Indians.[11] Miraculous escapes seemed to justify his faith in the protecting hand of Almighty God as he continued to reappear in the scattered churches. After three years of this itinerating ministry, he became the settled pastor of the Sewickley and Mt. Pleasant congregations in Westmoreland County. He was graceful in manner, neat in appearance, and with a rich capacity for enduring friendship. In a voice of remarkable clarity and distinct enunciation, he answered "present" during the organizational roll call.[12]

The second voice to be heard in response to the first roll call was that of the Reverend Thaddeus Dod, another resident of Washington County. His sallow complexion and slender frame might well indicate he was better equipped for the scholarly pursuits which interested him rather than the rugged life of a frontier preacher. He had come westward at the invitation of a group of the cultured families who, four years previous to his coming, had made the same perilous trip from Mr. Dod's native community of Mendham, New Jersey.[13] The severity of the Indian raids throughout the tragic months of the Fall of 1777 made it necessary for him to leave his family at Patterson's Creek in Virginia while he journeyed alone and undaunted. He found his future congregation huddled together for safety around Fort Lindley, eager to welcome him and to hear the news from home and of the early struggles of the colonists for independence.[14] When he responded to the roll call of Presbytery four years after his arrival in Western Pennsylvania, he was still a young man of thirty-one years of age and the pastor of two flourishing churches at Upper and Lower Ten Mile. He was a gifted preacher, teacher, poet and musician, with outstanding attainments in the broad field of scholarship.[15]

When the name of the host pastor was next called, John McMillan responded in that loud voice which was capable of being heard distinctly almost a mile away. He was a powerfully built young man of less than twenty-nine years. He seemed ideally endowed by nature for leadship in the development of the frontier where courage, strength, endurance, and a dominating will were essential qualifications. He was the second Presbyterian minister to establish his permanent home in Western Pennsylvania. He was only twenty-three years of age when he made his memorable tour of the Presbyterian settlers scattered through Western Pennsylvania in 1775.[16] The following year he returned to accept the call of the Pigeon Creek and Chartiers churches, where some of his relatives had already settled. Throughout a marvelous ministry of sixty years, he was the crusading leader and dominating personality among the founders of Western Pennsylvania Presbyterianism. He merits the honored title, "The Apostle of the West."[17]

Each of these three ministers brought with him an elder from one of his churches. They also were enrolled as commissioners to this initial meeting of Redstone Presbytery since the Presbyterian church has always placed equal responsibility upon the elders in the courts of the church. The Ten Mile Church was represented by Elder Demas Lindley, a tall powerful man of forty-six years. He was a spiritual product of the Whitefield revival. He had moved from Mendham, New Jersey, to Washington County two years before McMillan made his tour of the West. Along the bank of Ten Mile Creek, he had established his home. Here he erected a fort and a blockhouse for the protection of his family and the other settlers who had come from the same county in New Jersey.[18]

Fort Lindley was an almost constantly needed refuge of protection since Lindley's Settlement, or Ten Mile, was the most westerly portion of the frontier at that time and frequently exposed to the recurring Indian raids. It was to this fort that Thaddeus Dod came when he first accepted the call of the Ten Mile congregation. In that same point of refuge, Lindley's pastor directed the thoughts of the harassed settlers to God in his first revival and won some forty converts. Lindley was a pillar in his church and one of the first magistrates in Washington County.[19]

Patrick Scott was Dr. McMillan's elder, representing the host congregation of Pigeon Creek. He was a vigorous man of forty-seven years and devoted to the church. He was typical of the devout laymen who upheld the hands of the pioneer ministers and whose supporting devotion was essential to the minister's success. Elder John Neel accompanied his pastor as the lay representative of the Mt. Pleasant Church.[20] Thus six men, three ministers and an equal number of elders, constituted the first meeting of Redstone Presbytery.[21] In the ensuing years, this mother Presbytery was to give birth to churches, presbyteries, and synods throughout that vast area of ecclesiastical jurisdiction extending from the Laurel Ridge of the Allegheny Mountains on the east, to Lake Erie on the north, Virginia on the south, and the setting sun as the westerly border.[22]

In addition to these six chosen leaders, a number of guests probably were present as visitors but not as members. Doubtless the home of John Stevenson was crowded with neighboring families who had gathered to hear Reverend Thaddeus Dod preach the opening sermon on this historic occasion. Mr. Dod chose as his text these words from the Book of Job: "I have heard of Thee by the hearing of the ear; but now mine eye seeth Thee. Wherefore I abhor myself and repent in dust and ashes."[23] With scholarly penetration and a quiet persuasive appeal, he dramatized the majesty of Almighty God and the necessity of sincere repentance and humble fidelity on the part of those who would be used of God as His courageous servants and worthy representatives in building the frontier into a "Western Zion." Following the sermon, John McMillan was chosen to serve as the first moderator of this newly constituted Redstone Presbytery and James Power as its first Stated Clerk.[24]

The minutes fail to record the transaction of any further business. The two-day meeting was devoted largely to prayer, fellowship, and conference as each sought the power and guidance of the Heavenly Father and rejoiced to go forth in the triumphant name of Him "who is above every name." They adjourned with renewed faith and clarified vision and departed to their isolated fields of labor in the full realization that "it has been good for us to have been here."[25] They had discharged the duty laid upon them by the Synod. They had laid the organizational foundation for the subsequent growth of Presbyterianism throughout an ever-expanding frontier, peopled by a rapidly increasing population of Scotch-Irish settlers. September 19 of the year 1781 was a memorable day in the religious history of Western Pennsylvania. "Despise not the day of small beginnings."

Missionaries Scatter the Seeds of Presbyterianism

The organization of this rather small Presbytery of Redstone was more than the grateful fulfillment of the dreams of the four ministers who had made their permanent homes in Western Pennsylvania and who had asked Synod's permission to organize themselves into a separate presbytery. It was just another of the organizational results of the long-established policy of the Presbyterian church to send its ministers on missionary tours among the venturesome pioneers who were carving homes for themselves on the frontiers of American civilization. When seven Presbyterian ministers had responded to the call of the Reverend Francis Makemie and organized at Philadelphia in 1706 the first Presbytery on American soil, one of their acts at their second meeting was to pledge themselves "to set on foot and encourage private Christian societies (new churches) and to supply neighboring desolate places where a minister is wanting and opportunity of doing good offers."[26] The Presbyterian church at its very beginning thus determined to be a growing missionary church.

Doubtless this missionary policy was born of necessity. Presbyterians at that time were sparsely scattered throughout most of the colonies. They were not grouped together in a few colonies as were the Episcopalians in New York and Virginia, the Congregationalists in New England, and the Quakers in Pennsylvania and Delaware. Nor were they localized in towns and cities but isolated on farms. Makemie bemoaned that these widely diffused Presbyterians seemed never to collect themselves into towns, which he attributed "to some strange unaccountable humor."[27] This scattering trait of colonial Presbyterians proved to be a determining blessing. It made necessary an aggressive missionary program and the development of new presbyteries for closer supervision, and the resulting organization of a general Synod of Philadelphia in 1717.[28] Presbyterians now numbered nineteen ministers, forty churches, and three thousand communicants.[29]

Scotch-Irish Migration

But even the missionary zeal of these nineteen ministers proved unequal to the task of ministering to the Scotch and Scotch-Irish who were beginning to migrate to America in increasing numbers as they sought to escape religious persecution and economic hardship. Beginning with the second decade of the eighteenth century, this tide of migration annually carried from three to six thousand refugees to the colonies. It reached its peak from 1740 to the outbreak of the Revolutionary War. In some years, from Ulster alone, came as many as twelve thousand immigrants in search of new homes and religious freedom along the retreating western frontier.[30] They spread throughout all the middle colonies.

Pennsylvania especially, with its Quaker tradition of religious toleration and its broad unoccupied valleys, seemed to be the logical promised land for these Scotch-Irish immigrants. Ever westerly they rolled onward. Even the Allegheny Mountains proved to be no insuperable barrier as they searched for arable farm land in disregard of Indian ownership and the conflicting title claims of Pennsylvania and Virginia. "It is against the laws of God and nature," they reasoned, "that so much land should be idle while so many Christians wanted it to labor on and to raise their bread."[31]

The great majority of these new settlers were of Presbyterian heritage. They brought with them the prejudices and hatreds born of persecution. As a result, they cherished a passionate yearning for liberty and self-government both in civil and religious affairs. Quick to respond to the call of patriotism, they became zealous advocates of freedom from British rule and Episcopalian prelacy. They were the leaders in the early agitation for colonial independence and the aggressive fighters throughout the Revolutionary War.[32]

Missionaries Move Westward

Toward these determined Scotch-Irish settlers, the Presbyterian church naturally felt an inescapable responsibility. The minutes of Synod and of the various presbyteries abound with assignments of missionary tours and months of itineration by the ministers who willingly left their own churches to carry the restraints and comforts of religion throughout the westward-moving frontier. Appeals for additional ministers were sent to Scotland, Ireland, Wales, and England. Reverend William Tennent organized his famous Log College in 1726 to provide a needed opportunity to train young men for the ministry.[33] Donegal Presbytery was constituted in 1732 to give better supervision throughout Lancaster County and on to the foothills of the Allegheny Mountains.[34]

Western Pennsylvania Presbyterians owe a tremendous debt of gratitude to the members of this faithful Presbytery of Donegal whose vision of the missionary opportunity along the western frontier never faded. Their zeal and consecration were indicated in the repeated commissioning of various ministers and licentiates to bring the message of the church to the venturesome settlers throughout the area which was later to be the Presbytery of Redstone. The fires of revivalism added enthusiasm to these missionary efforts among the new settlers as The Great Awakening multiplied the number of Presbyterian converts.

With this rapid growth came also discord and disagreement. The zeal of Reverend Gilbert Tennent and his associates in the revival exceeded their good judgment.[35] Soon the Presbyterian church was experiencing the pains of growth and controversy. Convictions had differed as to the best methods of rapidly equipping ministers to carry the gospel to the new settlers and at the same time not lowering the high standards of education and doctrinal purity which have always been two of the most cherished Presbyterian ideals. The resulting fraternal quarrels temporarily divided the Presbyterian church into the New Side and Old Side Schism of 1741, with the rival Synods of Philadelphia and New York competing for growth and prestige.[36] But Presbyterian brethren, who had so much in common, could not long remain apart. After seventeen years of broadened experience, the two Synods merged in 1758 to form the united Synod of New York and Philadelphia.[37] This united Synod remained the supreme judicatory of the Presbyterian church until the General Assembly was organized thirty years later.[38]

The Significance of the Year 1758

The year 1758 was the turning point in the developing history of Western Pennsylvania both from the religious and the political viewpoints. The healing of the schism between the New Side and Old Side branches of the church was the signal for increased missionary efforts and united zeal for the westward expansion of Presbyterianism among the Scotch-Irish settlers who were coming to America in steadily increasing numbers and who were seeking homes on the western frontier. The year 1758 also witnessed the burning of Fort Duquesne on November 28 by the Indians and French who had retreated before the advance of General John Forbes's army. This withdrawal by the French gave to the English crown possession of the entire Upper Ohio Valley which was drained by the Monongahela and Allegheny rivers.[39]

The fall of Fort Duquesne and the subsequent erection of Fort Pitt also shifted from the Roman Catholic church to the Protestant church religious responsibility for this vast frontier area. The future city of Pittsburgh was thus destined to become for many years a Presbyterian city. Very appropriately then it was the Reverend Charles C. Beatty, the Presbyterian chaplain in General Forbes's army, who preached the Thanksgiving sermon, thanking God that

Fort Duquesne had fallen to the British without further loss of precious Protestant lives.[40]

Tradition indicates that this sermon of Chaplain Beatty's was the first Protestant sermon preached in Pittsburgh. But it was not Beatty's last sermon in that area nor the end of his interest in the spiritual welfare of the venturesome settlers who were beginning to cross the Laurel Ridge into Western Pennsylvania. In 1763 Synod commissioned the Reverend Charles Beatty, along with Reverend John Brainerd, to "preach to the distressed frontier inhabitants and to report their distresses and to let us know where new congregations are a forming and what is necessary to be done to promote the gospel among them and that they inform us what opportunities there may be of preaching the gospel to the Indian nations in that neighborhood."[41]

Journey of Beatty and Duffield

This resolution was well intentioned but poorly timed. Unfortunately, in that year the settlers west of the Allegheny Mountains were to experience the worst horrors of Indian warfare. Pontiac and Guyasuta attacked in a united determination to drive out the English settlers and exterminate those who sought to remain on territory still claimed by the Indians.[42] Fort after fort fell before the Indian onslaughts. Fort Pitt, Detroit, and Fort Ligonier alone were left standing when the Battle of Bushy Run brought a temporary safety to the few remaining survivors. The unstable peace became more secure when a year later Bouquet led his army westward into Ohio. Here he attacked the Indian villages along the Muskingum River and compelled the Indian chiefs to accept his terms of surrender.[43]

That conquest of the Indians encouraged the Synod three years later to recommission Reverend Charles Beatty, with Reverend George Duffield as his newly appointed companion, to tour the western frontier with the joint objective of evangelizing the Indians and preaching to the settlers. In an epoch-making journey, the two missionaries traveled among the settlers and on to the rebuilt Indian villages on the Muskingum. At Fort Pitt, Beatty preached on several occasions.[44] Their mission to the Indians was unsuccessful due to the hatreds engendered by Bouquet's victory over them. But the tour itself proved to be a permanent blessing to the settlers who were hungry for spiritual food.

Beatty and Duffield reported to the Synod that they "had found on the frontiers numbers of people, earnestly desirous of forming themselves into congregations but in circumstances exceedingly necessitous from the late calamities of war in these parts."[45] Their report was received with approval. Synod determined to send more ministers to assist in the spiritual development of the frontier. A definite missionary program was adopted, with the happy result that every year either the Synod or the Presbytery of Donegal sent at least one minister, oftentimes several ministers, to preach beyond the Allegheny Mountains.[46] The treaty of Fort Stanwix in 1768 had opened the territory west of the mountains to settlers who were establishing homes in the fertile valleys along the tributaries of the Youghiogheny and Monongahela valleys. Population was increasing steadily and in sufficient numbers to necessitate the formation of the County of Westmoreland in 1773 with Hannastown as the county seat.[47] The calls for missionaries were increasing in numbers and earnestness.

McClure and Frisbee on a Ten-Month Tour

Of the numerous missionaries who were commissioned to go on these tours of visitation among the western settlers, the most notable were Reverend Levi Frisbee and Reverend David McClure. They spent a longer period of time west of the mountains and visited the settlers more frequently than any of the men who had previously gone forth under the direction of the Synod. We see them crossing the mountains on horseback early in August of 1772. Their purpose was to preach to the Indians along the Muskingum River. But the Indians were in no mood to hear the white man's gospel.[48]

The two men established their headquarters at Pittsburgh during their ten-month tour. They were unable to find a settled minister of any church in all the country west of the Appalachian Mountains.[49] The settlers, they discovered, were "generally Presbyterians" who welcomed them eagerly and "expressed an earnest desire that they should preach to them."[50] The invitation was accepted.

Ill health prevented Levi Frisbee from traveling extensively. He spent most of his time preaching regularly at Pittsburgh and Long Run, near the present town of Irwin, where a meeting house for public worship had already been erected. David McClure itinerated widely throughout a five-point preaching field. Later, when Frisbee regained his strength, the two men exchanged their fields of preaching for a little variety and perhaps repetition of their sermons.

Listen as the names of these preaching points are called. Note the permanent results of the missionary labor of these two evangelists. Long Run is a thriving rural church eighteen miles east of Pittsburgh in the present Presbytery of Redstone. Ligonier, now called Pleasant Grove, is still enrolled in the Blairsville Presbytery. Squirrel Hill, which embraced the two churches of Fairfield and Armagh, is likewise a part of that same Presbytery. The other churches are located in the bounds of Redstone Presbytery. They included Jacob's Swamp, now euphonized to read Mount Pleasant; Stewart's Crossing, which grew into the historic churches of Laurel Hill and Tyrone; and Proctor's Tent, later known as Unity, which has rather recently been disbanded because its members had joined other churches. In addition, these two men preached occasionally at several other places, including Round Hill, where flourishing churches developed which can reasonably date their origin to the work of these two traveling missionaries.[51]

Their task of itineration being completed, the two young preachers rode back across the mountains. As they journeyed, they reviewed their experiences. "In each of the places where I preached," said McClure, "there were some zealous and pious persons who came forward and willingly devoted their time and labor to form the people into a society for the public worship of God."[52] "Yes," observed his companion, "these Presbyterians are well indoctrinated in the principles of the Christian religion. The young people are taught by their parents and school masters the Larger and Shorter Catechisms and almost every family has the Westminster Confession of Faith which they carefully study."[53]

After a reflective pause, McClure replied: "A great proportion of these people manifest a desire for the gospel and would gladly make provision for the support of ministers according to their ability. For example, at Ligonier Captain Arthur St. Clair informed me that the settlement in the valley of Ligonier consisted of about 100 families, principally Scotch and Irish, and that they had purchased a parsonage for a minister and subscribed 100 pounds currency as salary and wished to obtain a settled clergyman."[54] "Truly," sighed McClure, "the people here in this new country are as sheep scattered upon the mountains without a shepherd. May the good Lord raise up and send forth faithful laborers into this part of His vineyard."[55]

With this prayer inscribed in our memory, we bid farewell to our visiting friends, David McClure and Levi Frisbee, as they continue their solitary journey to report back to the Synod of New York and Philadelphia. Thence they returned to their native New England where they spent their entire ministry, never, as far as the records reveal, to return to the scene of their creative labors in Western Pennsylvania. But God heard their prayers. The answer came speedily in the arrival of the four men who made their permanent homes in widely scattered parts of Western Pennsylvania and who petitioned the Synod to be permitted to organize themselves into the Presbytery of Redstone. That historic meeting in 1781, when the mother Presbytery of the West was formed, was thus the long-cherished harvest of many years of missionary zeal on the part of a missionary church, working through its Synod and the Presbytery of Donegal. Men of vision and consecration reaped in due season because they fainted not amid the discouragements of hardships and Indian devastations.

When the Presbytery of Redstone adjourned its first meeting, the interval before the next meeting was much longer than the members imagined or had anticipated. The little group had planned to meet at Mount Pleasant in November of that year. Then they set April 7 of the next year as the meeting day at Sewickley. Again they were disappointed. The reason was obvious: "A sufficient number of members not attending, by reason of the incursions of the savages, to form a Presbytery, those who did meet agreed to appoint a meeting at Dunlap's Creek the third Tuesday of October."[56] The summer was a horrible nightmare for the frontier inhabitants. The Indians attacked in large numbers with murderous frequency.

It was the year that the newly established county seat town of Hannastown was completely burned by Guyasuta and his relentless warriors on July 13.[57] Cabins were reduced to ashes. Cattle and crops were destroyed. Hardly a family existed that did not witness loved ones dying in agony. James Power was preaching at nearby Unity but escaped, while his family was in anguished torment as the hours passed and only news of the massacre was received.[58] Similar raids brought sorrow throughout all the frontier parishes and endangered the lives of all the pioneer pastors.

"What ear has not heard, what heart has not trembled and bled at hearing, of the many instances of cruelty? Has not the kind and indulgent husband and tender father often fallen into the hands of those bloodthirsty hounds? Has not the loving wife and affectionate mother been torn away from her husband and children and become the prey of savage cruelty? And have not many had their dearest children inhumanly butchered before their eyes? Such mournful scenes have not been few."[59] Not until Anthony Wayne penetrated far into the Indian country and won the decisive Battle of Fallen Timbers in 1794 were the settlers freed from recurring dangers of Indian raids.[60]

Reinforcements Strengthen the Presbytery

After two postponements, the third attempt to hold a second meeting of Redstone Presbytery proved successful. The Presbytery convened at Dunlap's Creek. Reverend Joseph Smith was present and officially enrolled as a member. He was accompanied by his elder, James Edgar, who later became an associate judge in Washington County. Smith was the oldest of the four Founding Fathers and the first to pass to his heavenly reward after a comparatively brief pastorate of twelve years at Buffalo and Cross Creek in Washington County. At this second meeting, a fifth minister presented his credentials and a letter of transfer from the New Castle Presbytery and was enrolled as a member.[61] He was the Reverend James Dunlap and was serving as pastor of Dunlap's Creek and Laurel Hill. These two churches in Fayette County had previously been served by Dr. Power in his original five-point field. Later Dunlap accepted the presidency of Jefferson College for a period of eight years.[62]

Dunlap was the center of a prolonged discussion at his first meeting with his brethren as a fellow presbyter. It was the first of a long series of disciplinary actions by which the new Presbytery sought to uphold high standards of morality among church members.[63] The Founding Fathers were determined that those who came to the Lord's Table would be worthy of the name Presbyterian. Their character must be different from nonchurch members.

In this particular case, Mr. Dunlap had refused to ordain a Mr. John Matson who had been elected a ruling elder and whom Mr. Dunlap accused of unchristian conduct. Mr. Dunlap was sustained in his action and Mr. Matson was rebuked by the moderator. Thus Presbytery, in its first action as a court of appeal, established the precedent of insisting that office bearers in the church set an example which others may safely follow. Ministers must have the courage of their convictions and must enforce the accepted rules of the church.

Within a year, two other ministers were also welcomed into the Presbytery at subsequent meetings, Reverend John Clark and Reverend James Finley. The former was serving "Western and Eastern Divisions of Peters Creek" which had been organized by Dr. McMillan in the year 1776.[64] Later these churches were to be known as Bethel and Lebanon. They are two of the thriving churches in Pittsburgh Presbytery which have a long unbroken record of service. Mr. Clark was a comparatively old but vigorous man of sixty-four years. Wearing a long white beard, he was affectionately known as Father Clark. At the honored age of seventy-nine, his body was laid to rest in the cemetery adjoining the church at Bethel, where now lie buried all the deceased pastors of that historic church.

The other welcomed addition to the Presbytery was Reverend James Finley. He accepted calls from "the two societies in the Forks of Youghiogheny," which still remain parts of the Redstone Presbytery but under their present names of Round Hill and Rehoboth. He had finally settled in the community which he had visited many times previously, beginning, perhaps, as early as 1771.[65] The membership of the Redstone Presbytery had now grown to seven ministers. So few they were and yet so resourceful and energetic! They were "the honored seven," all graduates of Princeton College, who throughout the next four or five years carried the burden of a vast developing field and laid successfully the firm foundations of Presbyterianism in what they rejoiced to call their "Western Zion."

Another important item of business which called for action at the second and subsequent meetings of the Presbytery was the assignment of missionary duties to the different ministers. Groups of Presbyterians at Tyrone and Muddy Creek, who had no minister, were asking for preaching and other ministerial services.

Throughout the next few years these calls grew in number and seemed increasingly imperative. The area of service was steadily widening as more settlers spread over the receding frontier. The seven members of Presbytery were all very busy as they attempted to serve adequately their widely scattered congregations. Still they were required to visit neighboring communities in response to formal requests for preaching. Definite assignments were made by the Redstone Presbytery to its ministers at every meeting to preach at specified points on a specified number of Sabbaths in answer to every appeal for preaching which was presented to Presbytery. To fail to meet these assignments was a breach of ethics and required an explanation which would prove satisfactory to the other brethren in Presbytery. During the first seven years, nearly fifty different places asked and received assigned dates for preaching services.[66] Those were stern days when the voice of duty must be heeded if the frontier was to be won for Christ.

Though these seven consecrated ministers needed help to meet these calls for preaching, they were extremely cautious in admitting new ministers into their membership. All credentials were examined carefully. Alexander Addison, a candidate from the Presbytery of Aberlowe in Scotland, asked to be taken under care of Redstone Presbytery at the December meeting in 1785. He produced credentials that he had been licensed to preach before leaving Scotland. Presbytery examined him carefully but was not satisfied with his replies. He was given permission to preach in Washington for a limited time, pending further examination. Delays lengthened while the advice of Synod was sought.[67] All were saved from embarrassment when Addison decided to study law instead of theology. The Presbyterian church lost a brilliant preacher, but the court of four Western Pennsylvania counties secured an outstanding judge who became a faithful elder in the First Presbyterian Church of Washington. With similar care Hugh Morrison, Jr., was examined. His request was declined.[68] No emergency seemed sufficient to induce the Presbytery to relax its caution in examining prospective members. Reverend Samuel Barr, after lengthy delays, was reluctantly received as a member and empowered to serve as pastor of the First Presbyterian Church of Pittsburgh.[69]

Presbytery Educates Its Own Candidates

But a new source of assistance was now becoming available to these seven struggling servants of Christ. If help could not come to them from the outside, they could train and develop capable ministers from within their own congregations. The first seven members of the Presbytery were graduates of Princeton College. They placed a high valuation upon the educational training of ministers. Yet they were practical enough to make necessary adjustments. They did not insist that young men cross the mountains to drink at the same educational fountains in the East. Instead, they diligently trained promising young men of their churches in the fundamentals of the arts, languages, and theology.

Much time was devoted at the meetings of Presbytery to the careful examination of these young men as they appeared before Presbytery for systematic trials and testings in preparation for licensure and ordination. No small part of that training was practice in preaching and sermon preparation. To pass an examination in experimental religion before seven fervent evangelists and to preach before seven learned Princeton graduates were severe tests for the young men whose only academic preparation was in the schools which these preachers were themselves conducting. These examinations were supplemented by assigned preaching responsibilities in the various places which had no minister. The requests for preaching were always greater than the ordained men could answer. Thus the young candidates for the ministry were kept busy, while at the same time they received invaluable training in the school of experience.

During the first five years of the organizational life of the Redstone Presbytery, no young men presented themselves as candidates for licensure. A long educational period was deemed necessary before they were ready. But during the Summer of 1786, John Brice and James Hughes appeared before Presbytery and asked to be given the necessary trials preliminary to being licensed to preach the gospel.[70] Later came James McGready and Joseph Patterson. Then Robert Marshall, John McPherrin, and Samuel Porter appeared at subsequent meetings. They were followed by George Hill, William Swan, Thomas Marquis, David Smith, and Boyd Mercer.[71] In all, twelve young men came forward during the last five years that Redstone remained an undivided Presbytery. It was a glorious harvest, the spiritual fruitage of the labor of seven men who realized that the future of the Presbyterian church lay in the dedicated lives of young men of conviction and consecration.

None of these twelve men had a Princeton education. They had, as its equivalent, an education imparted from the mind and soul of devoted pastors who knew what was the essential equipment for a successful ministry on the frontier. James McGready and Robert Marshall soon left the Presbytery to serve with flaming zeal in Kentucky. Under James McGready began that mighty revival in Kentucky which spread throughout Tennessee and North Carolina and upward into Western Pennsylvania and across the river into Ohio.[72] Truly the seven ministers of the Presbytery built even better than they dared dream when they imparted a religious fervor to the recruits they had enlisted for Christ and His Church.

How thrilling to turn the pages of the *Minutes of Redstone Presbytery* and to note the care with which these choice young men were trained and examined. "Presbytery examined them on the Latin and Greek languages and metaphysics, logic and moral philosophy, mathematics and natural philosophy—all sustained." "Presbytery assigned to Mr. Patterson an exegesis, 'Whether Miracles Are an Evidence of Divine Mission and What Miracles Do Prove Such Mission.'" "Mr. Brice had appointed to him a presbyterial exercise on Hebrews 11th chapter, the 27th verse." "Patterson and McGready examined on systematic theology." "Presbytery opened by a sermon on Philippians 2:12 by Mr. John Brice."

Thus the records go on as each candidate was carefully examined in a wide range of subjects. Each was assigned difficult Biblical passages to explain or to use as a text for a sermon before Presbytery. Each was given definite preaching assignments before ordination was conferred. That careful training paid rich spiritual dividends as some of these young men became outstanding religious leaders. Presbytery was growing by the process of developing its own ministers. New recruits were being prepared to serve as pastors in the new churches which were being organized throughout an ever-broadening Presbytery. The Presbytery, which was organized with four members, had grown to twelve members in 1793 when it was subdivided to form the Presbytery of Ohio.

Presbytery of Ohio Organized

This inevitable division could not longer be delayed. The new congregations were too widely separated for effective supervision by one Presbytery. Too much time was consumed in travel to the Presbytery's meetings. The genius of the Presbyterian system has lain in its flexible type of organization which fitted it for the needs of an expanding frontier. When the territory of any presbytery became too expansive for effective supervision, all that was needed was a vote by Synod setting off a group of ministers who resided in the more-distant section and constituting them a new presbytery. Thus Redstone had been formed out of Donegal Presbytery. Redstone sought permission to subdivide. Synod granted the request of five members of Redstone to organize themselves into the new Presbytery of Ohio.[73]

The dividing line between the two presbyteries was the Monongahela River and the Ohio River and northward on to Erie. Pittsburgh, the Gateway to the West, remained in the Redstone Presbytery, but the rapidly developing West was the responsibility of the Ohio Presbytery. This vast area of presbyterial supervision was subdivided in 1802 by the organization of the Presbytery of

Erie, to include the territory north of the Ohio River, and again in 1808 by the creation of the Presbytery of Lancaster in Ohio on its western boundary.

The Founding Fathers of Ohio Presbytery

The Upper Buffalo Church in Washington County, Pennsylvania, was the scene of the first meeting of the Ohio Presbytery on October 23, 1793.[74] The following five former members of Redstone formed the roll of the new Presbytery—the Reverend Messrs. John McMillan, John Clark, Joseph Patterson, James Hughes, and John Brice.

Of these, only John McMillan had been a member of the Redstone Presbytery from its initial meeting in 1781. He was continuing to serve the Chartiers Church (now the Hill Church) near Canonsburg and the Pigeon Creek congregation in Washington County near Eighty Four. He remained in this pastorate until 1793 when he resigned at Pigeon Creek to give his full time to the church at Chartiers and to his school at Canonsburg. There he died November 16, 1833, at the ripe old age of eighty-one, after almost sixty years of creative labor throughout Western Pennsylvania as pastor, preacher, educator, and moulder of public opinion in the realm of morals and politics.[75]

He had the unique distinction of being the only minister to serve as a founding member of both the Redstone and the Ohio presbyteries and was chosen on both occasions to preside as the first moderator. He was also honored by being elected the second moderator of the Synod of Pittsburgh in 1803. Endowed with tireless energy, resolute determination, and unconquerable will power, he used his remarkable gifts of body, mind, and soul for the glory of God and the advancement of Presbyterianism. From whatever angle the early development of Western Pennsylvania is viewed, the achievements of this pioneer Presbyterian leader are notable and decisive. Thank God for Dr. McMillan!

Reverend John Clark was seventy-five years of age when he

transferred his membership from the Redstone Presbytery to help organize and develop the Ohio Presbytery. To better conserve his strength, he closed his work at Lebanon and devoted his full time for six years longer to Bethel. But ebbing strength and advancing years were soon to deprive the Ohio Presbytery of his services. He was called from earthly activity July 13, 1797, less than four years after the new Presbytery had been organized.[76]

The other three founding members of the Ohio Presbytery had all been members of Western Pennsylvania churches when they first heard the call to the ministry and sought the educational training essential to preaching the gospel as Presbyterian ministers. John Brice and James Hughes were students together under Reverend Joseph Smith at Upper Buffalo. They were licensed to preach at the same meeting of the Redstone Presbytery on April 15, 1788.[77]

Reverend James Hughes, at the time he was licensed, was a scholarly young man of twenty-three years of age. Five churches eagerly sought his services as pastor. He accepted calls from the Lower Buffalo Church in Washington County and the Short Creek Church (now West Liberty, West Virginia). In this dual field of pastoral service, he was installed on April 17, 1790.[78] There he served for twenty-four years, until he bade farewell to his brethren in the Ohio Presbytery to join the Presbytery of Miami in Ohio. Four years later he became principal of the Academy which has since grown into Miami University. In that capacity he continued until death abruptly ended his career as preacher and educator at the early age of fifty-five years.[79]

Reverend John Brice's field of ministerial service, at the time of the organization of Ohio Presbytery, was also a dual charge. He had been installed as pastor of the congregation of Three Ridges (now West Alexander, Pennsylvania) and the Forks of Wheeling, West Virginia, April 23, 1790. Ill health necessitated his resignation seventeen years later. He continued, however, to preach within the bounds of the Ohio Presbytery for a few years longer. He also entered early into his eternal reward after a life span of only fifty-one years. He had been a man of nervous temperament, with occasional periods of great despondency of mind, but distinguished at all times by deep piety.[80]

Reverend Joseph Patterson, the fifth founding father of Ohio Presbytery, was privileged to reach the ripe old age of eighty years. He was one of the first three students for whose education Reverend Joseph Smith had begun the first school for ministers in Western Pennsylvania. In his journal he thus records his call to the ministry: "In the fall of the year 1785, being thirty-three years old, it was thought best, with the advice of the Presbytery of Redstone, that I should endeavor to prepare for the gospel ministry. There being no places of public education in the western country, I, with a few others, engaged in preparatory studies with the Reverend Joseph Smith of Buffalo congregation, Washington County."[81]

Upon completion of this presbytery-directed course of training, he was installed over the united congregations of Raccoon and Montour's Run. After a ministry of twelve years in these two churches, he resigned the latter church to devote his full energy to the Raccoon congregation. Declining strength closed his work at Raccoon in 1816 after twenty-seven years and six months of service.[82] His remaining years were spent in personal evangelism and in the sale and distribution of religious literature in Pittsburgh. His biographer wrote this tribute to his fidelity during those closing years: "At some seasons of the year, almost every day of the week would find him passing along the shores of our rivers, entering hundreds of boats containing families of emigrants from various parts of the world, kindly inquiring after the temporal and spiritual welfare of these often destitute and afflicted strangers, giving them such advice as to their secular concerns as they needed, and making sure that they were supplied with a copy of the Bible."[83]

Mr. Patterson was a man of great piety and a profound believer in the potency of prayer. He and Reverend Thomas Marquis were the first missionaries to be sent into Ohio by the Synod of Pittsburgh to preach to the Indians on the branches of the Maumee

River in the Summer of 1802. His journal is replete with surprising incidents, illustrative of the perils and privations these two pioneer missionaries faced and the zeal and faith with which they conquered discouragements.

Upon their return, Dr. McMillan greeted them with the friendly question, "How did you get on, Patterson?" "Well," he replied, "we started with no provisions but cornmeal and bear's grease. My stomach soon revolted at this fare. I must either return or get sick. So, as I believe in special prayer, we knelt down. I told the Lord I was willing to serve Him but He must give me something which I could eat or I would die." "Did He answer your prayer?" "Yes." "What did He give you?" "Nothing better to eat." "Then how?" "Why, you see, I laid down in His forest, slept safely under His care, and when I awoke, He had given me an appetite so voracious that cornmeal and bear's grease tasted good, which was as much an answer to prayer as though He had sent me beef and pudding."[84]

Presbytery Launches Constructive Program

These five ministers and twelve elders, representing different churches within the territorial boundaries of the Ohio Presbytery, formed the roll at the first meeting on October 23, 1793. Though their numbers were small, their faith and determination were adequate to the task of moulding the religious outlook of the rapidly developing rural area to the north and west of Pittsburgh. The minutes of the first meeting reveal that the policy of this second Presbytery in Western Pennsylvania was merely a continuation of the fourfold program which these same ministers had been carrying forward, while members of the mother Presbytery of Redstone, and which was to be characteristic of Ohio Presbytery's plan of procedure throughout the twenty-nine years it remained a predominantly rural Presbytery.

The central emphasis in that fourfold plan was an unwavering reliance on the power of prayer. Life on the frontier was rugged. Long hours of labor formed the daily routine of the pioneer ministers and elders. Yet when they gathered in their first meeting as a Presbytery, one of their first decisions was to give serious consideration to their "great need of Divine aid in order to due discharge of the important trust committed to them."[85] Together they spent a whole day in prayer "to supplicate Almighty God that He would take this infant Presbytery into His special care, that He would preside in all their meetings and enable them to act faithfully for God and be zealous for the promotion of Christ's kingdom in the world and that He would pour out His spirit upon the congregations under their care and raise up and qualify many for the important work of the gospel ministry."[86]

At the same opening meeting, the minutes record that "Synod having appointed the second Thursday of November next to be observed as a day of fasting and prayer to supplicate Almighty God that He would pour out His spirit upon the churches and accompany the means of grace with Almighty power for the conviction and conversion of sinners and the edification of His own people; and also to deprecate divine wrath manifested in the desolating calamities which are now abroad in the earth, the Presbytery heartily concurred therewith and enjoined it upon the congregations under their charge carefully to observe it."[87] Again and again, at subsequent meetings of the expanding Presbytery, the minutes record similar calls to prolonged seasons of prayer and fasting as epidemics of cholera, the ravages of war, and periods of religious decline and moral lethargy presented physical or spiritual perils. The members of the Ohio Presbytery determined to conquer for Christ, not in their own wisdom and might, but in the power of the Triumphant God.

But these early fathers also believed that prayer is most effective when energized by their own consecrated labors. As the second element in their fourfold program, they continued to set before each other an individual evangelistic duty which would carry them beyond the bounds of their own parishes and result in the rapid development of new churches. They assigned to each minister definite preaching responsibilities in communities where requests for ministerial services were presented to the Presbytery.[88] In all subsequent meetings similar requests in increasing numbers were welcomed and accepted. This evangelistic and missionary passion was a determining factor in making western Pennsylvania and eastern Ohio and northern West Virginia Presbyterian strongholds.

The third continuing policy was a zealous concern for the morals of the community. At this initial meeting, the members of Presbytery sat as a court of the church and heard charges of immorality against a member of the Mill Creek congregation and rendered the judicial verdict of "guilty."[89] The fidelity of Presbyterian sessions and presbyteries in pronouncing judgment on erring members was a controlling force in restraining immorality and in upholding and enforcing moral standards in frontier communities where civil courts were not easily available. At the stated meetings of the Ohio Presbytery, much time was spent in sifting evidence against infractions of a Christian code of ethics and morality. Immorality, slander, and dishonesty were the most frequent offences.

Nor were these ecclesiastical judges tolerant of any laxity among their own membership. Reverend Boyd Mercer was rebuked for profaning the Sabbath day by accepting a salary payment on the Lord's Day and using the Sunday preaching service for personal recriminations against those who were critical of his conduct. He was also censured for laziness in repeating his sermons instead of preparing new discourses.[90] Out of this concern for the moral integrity of individuals, in subsequent meetings of the Ohio Presbytery grew vigorous pronouncements and zealous crusades against organized evils which sought for financial gain to debauch the community.

The fourth phase of the Presbytery's program was a practical zeal for the education of future ministers. Only as capable young men were recruited and adequately trained could the Presbytery hope to minister successfully to new churches within its vast territory. The Ohio Presbytery willingly ratified the suggestion of the

Synod of Virginia that this new Presbytery join with the mother Presbytery of Redstone to superintend the seminary of learning at Canonsburg with Reverend John McMillan in charge.[91] This action initiated by Synod and ratified by Presbytery was only giving ecclesiastical support to the school which John McMillan had established previously in his Log College adjoining his home in the Chartiers congregation. He was largely instrumental in establishing this school at Canonsburg where he occupied the chair of theology. From this first training school was kindled the enthusiasm for adequate theological education which the Ohio Presbytery so vigorously manifested and which was later to motivate the organization of the Western Theological Seminary in Pittsburgh.

Young Ministers Ordained by Presbytery

The fruitage of this educational policy of the infant Ohio Presbytery was soon to be apparent in the presbytery-trained young men whose names were being added to the roll of that Presbytery. Reverend Thomas Marquis was the first addition to the five founders of the Ohio Presbytery. He had previously been licensed by the Redstone Presbytery and so was ready for ordination within a year after the new Presbytery was organized. His first charge was Cross Creek where he continued to serve until his health failed. A year later on September 29, 1827, death erased his name from the roll of Presbytery. He was famed as an attractive preacher. His sweet musical voice earned for him the title, the "silver-tongued" Marquis.[92]

Perhaps the most outstanding of the first group of young men who were trained by the Ohio Presbytery was Reverend Elisha Macurdy. One year after the Presbytery was organized, he heard the call to the Christian ministry. He enrolled in Dr. McMillan's academy at Canonsburg to begin the academic and theological training which would fit him to be ordained and installed as the lifelong pastor of the Presbyterian churches at Cross Roads (now Florence) and Three Springs along the road toward Steubenville.

Two years later his zealous evangelistic fervor prompted Dr. Anderson to invite him to assist at Upper Buffalo, November 14, 1802, in a prolonged Communion season which brought together members of various churches. Under the providence of God, his was the human voice through which the Holy Spirit set in motion the beginnings of the great revival of 1802, which altered to a marked degree the religious life of Western Pennsylvania.

Presbytery of Erie

The Ohio Presbytery grew rapidly. An increasing number of young men were being trained and ordained to serve in the newly organized churches throughout the Presbytery. Five of these young men settled among the people who were establishing homes in the expanding frontier north of Pittsburgh. Anthony Wayne's victory-dictated treaty of peace at Greenville, Ohio, in 1795 forced the Indians westward beyond Ohio and resulted in the surrender of the British forts along the frontier.[93] A vast area was now opened to settlement. The tide of immigration rolled westward from eastern Pennsylvania and New England and northward to Lake Erie. It was a challenging field for evangelism and the organization of new churches.

Youth, as always, responded to the call to difficult living along the frontier. The five young men who traveled on horseback had all been educated in the West and had caught something of the pioneering courage of Dr. McMillan, their teacher at Canonsburg. Some, like Reverend Thomas Hughes, came in response to a request from a group of Presbyterian families at Mt. Pleasant that Dr. McMillan send one of his young theological graduates to settle among them as their pastor.[94] Hughes was the first Presbyterian minister to locate in the territory north and northwest of the Ohio and Allegheny rivers. Others, like Reverend Samuel Tait, were sent out by the Presbytery "to preach where he could find hearers." He found a few who offered to help erect a log church at Cool Spring, about five miles from the present town of Mercer.[95] Like his teacher, Dr. McMillan, he was a man of great physical strength and thoroughly equipped for frontier life. On the other hand, Reverend William Wick, who accepted a call to the Neshannock and Hopewell churches in 1800, hesitated to enter the ministry because of his physical frailty. His fear was well grounded since he died after a brief ministry of less than fifteen years. Those years were distinguished by extensive missionary tours with Reverend Joseph Badger throughout the Western Reserve.[96]

Reverend Joseph Stockton was less than twenty-one years of age when he was licensed to preach. Accompanied by Reverend Elisha Macurdy, he journeyed on horseback among the settlers north of Pittsburgh and preached wherever a group could be gathered for an evangelistic service. The Presbyterians at Meadville invited him to return the next year to preach to them regularly and also at Little Sugar Creek. He was a scholar by nature rather than a preacher. For nine years he served as principal of the Meadville Academy. He then moved to Pittsburgh to become principal of the Pittsburgh Academy which later developed into the present University of Pittsburgh. His textbooks were used extensively throughout Western Pennsylvania.[97]

The fifth licentiate from the Ohio Presbytery to seek a field of frontier service north of Pittsburgh was Reverend Robert Lee. He was twenty-nine years of age when he accepted calls to serve as the pastor both at Amity and Rocky Spring in Mercer County. It was a discouraging field, covering a wide area where financial resources were inadequate for a minister's support. Yet he struggled in faith and courage for six years before moving to other fields of service in the Presbytery.[98]

These five men, all products of Ohio Presbytery, were attempting to shepherd the settlers north of Pittsburgh. They were comparatively close together, yet far removed from the more central meeting places of the Presbytery. The inevitable separation was authorized by the Synod of Virginia. A new presbytery, to be known as the Presbytery of Erie, was formed with these five pioneer preachers as the Founding Fathers. Five ministers! The same number who had been authorized to constitute the Presbytery of Ohio nine years earlier.

The first meeting of this third Presbytery was held on Tuesday, April 13, 1802, at Mt. Pleasant (Darlington), located in what is now Beaver County. The host pastor, Reverend Thomas Hughes, was given the honor of election as the first moderator. He had the privilege of welcoming two additional ministers from the Ohio Presbytery who had recently accepted calls to serve within the bounds of the new Presbytery. These reinforcements were Reverend James Satterfield, who was located at Moorfield and Neshannock churches in Lawrence County, and Reverend William Wylie, whose triple field of service at Fairfield and Upper and Lower Sandy extended into the adjoining counties of Mercer and Venango.[99]

Humbly these seven ministers and three elders approached their task upon their knees in reliance upon the God who had called them to be His representatives in a vast area of needy service. "Presbytery, taking into consideration their infant state and the growing prospects of the new settlement under their care and the necessity of Divine influence to aid and direct them in their arduous work, do resolve to spend part of tomorrow in supplication and prayer."[100] They were following the example of the founders of the Ohio Presbytery. They would move forward in the same fourfold policy in which they were trained—the program of prayer, evangelism, education, and moral integrity.

The Synod of Pittsburgh is Organized

With the formation of this third Presbytery, Western Pennsylvania Presbyterians were now ready for the culminating phase of the development of their early ecclesiastical organization. By action of the General Assembly at its meeting in Philadelphia in 1802, the Presbyteries of Ohio, Redstone, and Erie were constituted a Synod to be known as the Synod of Pittsburgh. Difficulties of travel, the need of closer synodical supervision, and a similarity of interests which brought the three presbyteries into a working unity, were the three motivating reasons for the separation from the somewhat distant Synod of Virginia.

The time and place for the first meeting was Pittsburgh on the last Wednesday in September, 1802. Twenty-one years had now passed since the organization of the Redstone Presbytery. Great progress had been witnessed throughout those years. When the Redstone Presbytery was organized, it had a membership of only four ministers. The Pittsburgh Synod reported thirty-six ministers on the constituting roll. All of these served at least one church. The majority were serving two or three churches. Moreover, it was reported at Synod that there were thirty-nine additional churches which were seeking pastors.

The meeting place was set at Pittsburgh, not because Pittsburgh was at that time the strong center of Presbyterianism which it was later to become. The site was chosen because Pittsburgh was conveniently located as an accessible point to which the ministers and elders could journey from the surrounding area. Dr. McMillan, who had served as the first moderator of the Redstone Presbytery, was privileged to preach the sermon at this opening meeting of the Synod. The following year he was selected as the moderator, a fitting tribute to the man whose pioneering zeal had been a mighty factor in the rapid development of Presbyterianism in his beloved "Western Zion."

For six consecutive years, Synod met annually in Pittsburgh where the strong men in the rural churches could be heard and where their influence could be felt in quickening the dormant religious life of Pittsburgh. Pittsburgh, in the opening years of the nineteenth century, was a sort of spiritual "no man's land" lying within the territory of Redstone and adjacent to the Ohio Presbytery. Two weak Presbyterian churches were struggling for life in that community. They remained unstirred by the revivals which were strengthening many of the neighboring churches. Perhaps

God needed a great personality like McMillan or Macurdy through whom to manifest His redemptive power. But no one seemed available in Pittsburgh. The cause of vital religion lagged until Reverend Francis Herron was called to the pulpit of the First Presbyterian Church April 3, 1811.

FROM PAINTING BY RALPH REICHOLD

DUNLAP'S CREEK CHURCH, MERRITTSTOWN, PA.
Oldest organized Presbyterian church in Western Pennsylvania.

REPRODUCED FROM "ANNALS OF OLD WILKINSBURG AND VICINITY"

BEULAH CHURCH AND GRAVEYARD
Brick building erected 1837. First Pastor, Reverend Samuel Barr, who at the same time was Pastor of the First Presbyterian Church of Pittsburgh, 1784–1789.

EARLY ARCHITECTURE OF WESTERN PENNSYLVANIA

JOHN McMILLAN'S LOG CABIN SCHOOL
Oldest building extant. Now situated at Canonsburg, Pa.

OLD STONE MANSE
Scene of first gunfire of Whiskey Rebellion, South Park, Allegheny County.

PHOTOGRAPH BY
REVEREND JAMES YOLTON

CHAPTER II Early Educational Development

THE first meeting of the Presbytery of Redstone adjourned on Thursday, September 20, 1781. A few months later, Reverend Thaddeus Dod completed the erection of a log cabin school where the first sessions were held in the Spring of 1782.[1] What connection, if any, there was between these two events of historic importance in the religious and cultural life of Western Pennsylvania is only a conjecture.

It seems logical, however, to conclude that the laying of educational foundations throughout the newly formed Presbytery must have been one of the important problems which the pioneer preachers discussed at the organizational meeting of the first Presbytery west of the Allegheny Mountains. Two days were spent in conference as the three ministers and three elders shared their hopes and aspirations for the vast area upon which they sought God's blessing and to which they had dedicated their all in service and sacrifice. The minutes of those two days of prayer and planning are tantalizingly brief and formal.

Demas Lindley, an elder in the Ten Mile Church, accompanied his pastor to the meeting of Presbytery in the Pigeon Creek Church. On their homeward journey, they reviewed together the high lights of the two-day meeting. They discussed practical plans for furthering the evangelistic and educational development of the vast area surrounding the two churches which Mr. Dod was serving as pastor. Shortly after the fall harvest had been gathered, Mr. Dod called together his neighbors to assist him in building a log cabin adjoining his home in what is now Amity in Washington County. The new schoolhouse was larger than any of the other cabins which served as the homes of the pioneer settlers.

Dod Opens His School

Throughout the winter months, the pastor canvassed his congregation. He sought promising youths whose interest he might enlist and whom he felt he could train as the future leaders in the religious and cultural life of the community. A number promised to attend in the spring. Mr. Dod was happy as he greeted his first students on the opening day of school. The roll was called and the customary "present" rang out lustily from such young men as "Messrs. James Hughes, John Brice, Daniel Lindley, Robert Marshall and Francis Dunlavy."[2]

Probably the Latin class was the first to receive his attention as the preacher-schoolmaster proceeded to instruct his students in the rudiments of grammar, vocabulary, and skill in reading. Latin was one of the chief courses of study in a classical school and, more especially, for those who had the ministry in view. Some of those present had little or no background in Latin, while others may have had some knowledge of the language. There were classes in other subjects that day. It was soon apparent to all that their work was cut out for them. These men were eager for an education and no assignment was too disturbing. They were privileged to have in Thaddeus Dod a master teacher who was able to inspire all who sat under him to greater accomplishments. Helen Coleman has written of him, "Dod had the scholar's touch. His students seem to have had remarkable careers."[3]

The opening of Dod's school on that spring day followed a precedent first practiced in America by Reverend William Tennent. This precedent characterized the spread of education in America for a hundred and fifty years. The idea may have come to him when he was a student at the University of Edinburgh, Scotland, while serving as a priest in the Episcopal Church in the north of Ireland, or after he became a Presbyterian pastor in America. The fact was that he organized a log cabin school on the Neshaminy in Bucks County, Pennsylvania, which became the pattern used by the westward moving church for several generations to come. Reverend Samuel Blair went out from Tennent's tutelage and established a similar school at Fagg's Manor. Reverend Robert Smith took the idea from Fagg's Manor to Pequea. The mother school on the Neshaminy and later at Princeton, New Jersey, along with all the other schools engaged in the training of prospective ministers, followed the policy of instructing pupils to set up schools in whatever locality they were called upon to serve.

Robert Smith, at Pequea, believing that some of his pupils would go out to the western country, emphasized especially that they should "look out for some pious young men and educate them for the ministry; for," said he, "though some men of piety and talent may go to a new country at first, yet if they are not careful to raise up others, the country will not be well supplied."[4] The impression was written deep upon Reverend John McMillan's mind for, in later years, he had occasion to recall Smith's words. "Accordingly," said McMillan in his manuscript, "I collected a few who gave evidence of piety, and instructed them in the knowledge of the Latin and the Greek languages."[5]

McMillan's Log Cabin School

Whether McMillan or Dod was the first to organize a parish school is a little difficult to determine from the meager data available. They were never rivals for the honor of priority; only collaborators in the great enterprise of laying the educational foundations in the backwoods of Pennsylvania. Probably McMillan may have started his school a little earlier.

Reverend Joseph Smith, in his "History of Jefferson College," has said that "It seems almost certain to us that he (McMillan) made the first movement in the cause of education" in Western Pennsylvania.[6] This effort was begun in 1779 or 1780 in a log cabin near the McMillan home. Smith has urged that this was an English school. So it may have been in part, but references to James Ross, who taught Latin, shows that it also had the characteristics of a Latin school.[7] McMillan lists the names of James Hughes, John Brice, James McGready, William Swan, Samuel Porter, and Thomas Marquis among the first students to take instruction from him.[8]

It may have been shortly after the McMillan school that Thaddeus Dod started his school as previously described. This school lasted for three years. It is believed that McMillan, pressed by his church and home duties, urged many of his pupils to avail themselves of the excellent classical instruction offered by Mr. Dod who was a brilliant teacher. In addition to the classical languages, Dod offered mathematical courses that prepared students to take up surveying. Since he was an exceptional mathematician, it was only natural that young men preparing to be surveyors, rather than to enter the ministry, should also come to him for training.[9]

A glance at the curriculum offered at the College of New Jersey by President Witherspoon gives us some insight into the probable courses of instruction at the Ten Mile school . . . "In the first year, they read Latin and Greek, with the Roman and Grecian antiquities and rhetoric. In the second, continuing the study of the languages, they learn a complete system of geography . . . , the first principles of philosophy, and the elements of mathematical knowledge. The third . . . is chiefly employed in mathematics and natural philosophy. And the senior year is employed in reading the higher classics, proceeding in natural philosophy and in mathematics, and going through a course of moral philosophy."[10] We thus see an emphasis upon three fields of study: the classical languages, philosophy, and mathematics. Dod became proficient in all three fields. It is assumed that he followed, as much as possible, the pattern of the College of New Jersey.

Smith Teaches Theology in His Kitchen

Just as McMillan appears to have sent his pupils to the Dod school when it opened on Ten Mile Creek, so Dod took advantage of the opening of Joseph Smith's school at Upper Buffalo (or arranged for Smith to open a school) and sent his pupils to enroll there. Among the students who enrolled at once were McGready, Porter, and Patterson. Soon Hughes and Brice joined them.[11] Smith had no suitable place of instruction aside from a newly erected addition to his home that served as a kitchen and supply room. His wife was gracious enough to turn this space over to him as a classroom. Thus the school got under way. The course of instruction, as in the other schools, undoubtedly emphasized the classical languages, the natural sciences, and the two types of philosophy—natural and moral.

In his work, "Old Redstone," Smith's grandson said that this school had the support of five congregations, namely, Buffalo, Cross Creek, Chartiers, Bethel, and Ten Mile; that the ladies of the congregations made summer and winter clothing for the students (the summer clothing being made of linen that had been dyed from the chemicals of new-mown hay). In all probability, certain of the students were housed by the Smiths and in nearby homes. Ministers and lay people frequently were willing to donate lodging and food in order that students might prepare themselves for the ministry.[12] Smith comments further on his grandfather's efforts by suggesting that this school, in all probability, was the first to open with a special view to the training of young men for the sacred office.[13]

Little more has been written about this "school of the prophets." This may be due in part to the assumption that these schools were all somewhat alike and that it had become an accepted fact that the pastors were making the necessary arrangements about keeping at least one school open for theological students. In closing his comments about Smith's school, his grandson said, "This school for the languages and sciences was continued for some time, and then, by some mutual arrangement, was transferred and reorganized near Canonsburgh, under the care of Dr. McMillan."[14]

The number of ministerial students in the area of Chartiers, Ten Mile, and Upper Buffalo was not sufficient to justify the operation of three classical schools at one time by ministers already burdened with the duties of their office. Students who began with McMillan were privileged to continue with Dod and then with Smith. Later the school was transferred back to McMillan before the academies assumed some of the responsibility for this training. Later generations have done a great disservice by suggesting that these men were rivals. There is not a shred of evidence in any of the records to support this opinion. Nothing could be further from the truth. "The Rev. Messrs. McMillan, Dod and Smith were not rivals nor antagonists; they co-operated harmoniously in the cause of education and religion."[15] It appears that each of these men had an abounding respect for the others. The Presbytery records show them assisting one another at such times as the Communion Sacrament was being observed. The listing of the Chartiers and Ten Mile churches, as giving assistance to the Smith school, and similar references reveal their eagerness to co-operate with one another. It was unfortunate that Dod and Smith passed from the scene of their labors before their educational efforts had little more than begun.

Presbyterians Promote Academy in Pittsburgh

These three log cabin efforts to lay educational foundations in Washington County soon aroused the interest of Presbyterians in Pittsburgh. Located there were educated men like the Reverend Samuel Barr, graduate of Glasgow University and pastor of the First Presbyterian Church; James Ross, a former Latin instructor in the McMillan school at Chartiers; Hugh Brackenridge, a College of New Jersey graduate, lawyer, legislator, and newspaper writer; as well as other prominent men. They were keenly aware of the community's lack of secondary education facilities and set out to do something about it in the face of discouraging conditions.

Pittsburgh in 1787 was only a squalid frontier trading town at the Forks of the Ohio. A cultured German physician, who had visited this frontier community four years previously, described it as a village of "perhaps sixty wooden houses and cabins in which live something more than a hundred families."[16] "The people," he commented, "were poor, lazy, ravenously greedy and unwilling to work for reasonable wages. They preferred to live by extorting exorbitant prices from travelers and strangers." The census of 1786 showed only one stone, one frame, and thirty-six log houses and six small stores. Two years later the population did not exceed five hundred people.[17]

The leading personality in fostering an academy amid these unpromising circumstances was Hugh Brackenridge. He was now a lawyer and a politician who had graduated from the College of New Jersey with the expectation of becoming a Presbyterian minister. After studying theology for a time, he was licensed to preach and in 1777 served as a chaplain in the Continental Army. But he never sought ordination. Instead, he entered the legal profession. In 1781 he established an office in Pittsburgh and soon distinguished himself as a community leader.[18] His position as a member of the Pennsylvania Legislature and founder of the *Pittsburgh Gazette* put him in a position where he could work from both ends at the same time. In 1786 he ran a series of articles in his paper advocating the establishment of a secondary school.[19] Later in the same year, after he took his seat as a member of the General Assembly of the Commonwealth, he introduced a bill requesting a charter for "Pittsburgh Academy." The charter was issued on February 28, 1787.

Along with the charter was "a grant from the heirs of William Penn of a piece of land at the corner of Third Avenue and Cherry Alley, as a site for the school, and a grant of five thousand acres of wild land in the northwestern part of the state to be used as an endowment."[20] Due to political rivalry with his colleague, William Findley, this generous provision was stricken out by the Pennsylvania Legislature and the nascent academy deprived of a sustaining endowment.[21] It has been said that Brackenridge tried to get the land opposite "the Point," and commonly referred to as the North Side, but again was unsuccessful.

The names of the original incorporators, as they appear on this first educational charter in Western Pennsylvania, present convincing testimony to the dominant part that Presbyterians played both in the inception and in the early development of what was to become the University of Pittsburgh. Mr. Brackenridge, who made the selection, chose twenty-one trustees, whom he stated, were among the most eminent and best qualified men in the western part of Pennsylvania.

Six were clergymen, of whom all but one were Presbyterians, and that lone exception was Reverend Matthew Henderson, an Associate Seceder (now United Presbyterian). Reverend Samuel Barr headed the list. He was followed by Reverend Messrs. James Finley, John McMillan, Joseph Smith, and James Power, four famous preachers who contributed mightily to the aspirations and ideals of the developing frontier. Of the fifteen laymen, the majority were aggressive leaders in Presbyterian churches, four serving also as the original trustees of the First Presbyterian Church of Pittsburgh.[22]

Presbyterian Leadership of the Academy

These twenty-one incorporators of the Academy formed themselves into a Board of Trustees and elected as the first secretary Robert Galbraith, a Presbyterian elder. They also chose as the first principal George Welch, whose background and religious interests have faded from the available records of the past.[23]

He was soon succeeded by James Mountain and the Reverend John Taylor, who shared equally the responsibilities of the principal. The former was a Presbyterian who had served previously in a similar capacity at Canonsburg Academy. The latter was an erstwhile Presbyterian clergyman who had transferred his clerical affiliation to the Protestant Episcopal Church and was struggling to develop in Pittsburgh a church of that denomination.

Toward the close of the century, these two men had resigned their joint responsibility and another Presbyterian clergyman was asked to serve as principal. The new schoolmaster was Reverend Robert Steele, who had arrived in Pittsburgh in 1799 to become the second pastor of the First Presbyterian Church. His willingness to combine the duties of preacher and teacher was the occasion of a happy announcement in the *Pittsburgh Gazette* of January 16, 1801. "The Trustees anxiously disposed to promote the growth, prosperity, and usefulness of the Academy have engaged two masters (one of them a respectable clergyman) of education, character, skill and experience, who teach the Greek and Latin languages, mathematics, reading and writing."

To facilitate his classroom work and private tutoring, this Presbyterian pastor moved into the small building which then housed the academy at Cherry Alley and Third Avenue.[24] But teaching school and, at the same time, struggling to raise money for the poverty-stricken Pittsburgh Academy absorbed too much of Reverend Robert Steele's time and energy. After two years of fruitful service, he felt compelled to resign in order to devote himself to the developing work of his church and the task of building a larger and more pretentious house of worship.

As his successor, the trustees selected Benjamin B. Hopkins, a graduate of the College of New Jersey, who during the three previous years had served as an instructor at that famous educational center of Presbyterianism. Financial difficulties and uncertain enrollment disheartened the youthful pedagogue. After four years of unrewarded effort, he resigned in 1807 to seek a more productive field of service. Pittsburgh was still only a frontier town, rejoicing in a building and trade boom, but absorbed in materialism and indulgence. The community now numbered four hundred homes but, religiously and educationally, progress was discouragingly slow. The First Presbyterian Church was a weak, struggling organization and included less than forty-five members.

Reverend Robert Patterson Heads Pittsburgh Academy

The harassed trustees, in seeking a principal for the Academy, again turned to the Presbyterian ministry, hoping, perhaps, that a clergyman could supplement the meager salary by Sabbath Day preaching. Reverend Robert Patterson was chosen to this important task of stimulating the educational interests of youthful Pittsburghers. He was particularly well qualified, both in native endowment and training. He brought to his new position the supplementary abilities of a scholar, teacher, preacher, and businessman. Born in a Presbyterian manse, educated at Canonsburg Academy and the University of Pennsylvania, trained by five years' experience in teaching at the latter institution, he felt called to the ministry and served four years and six months as pastor of Upper and Lower Greenfield in Erie County. He resigned in April, 1807, to assume the leadership of the Pittsburgh Academy.[25]

Throughout the three years of his successful administration, he assisted in the training of an unusually capable group of students who afterwards filled prominent public positions and who often spoke in grateful terms of his care and faithfulness as an instructor. He resigned to carry forward what proved to be his lifework, the printing and distribution of helpful literature. During those years, he also held an extended pastorate in the Hiland Church where his memory as a scholar and a noble Christian gentleman has long been cherished.

The Golden Age of the Academy

Reverend Joseph Stockton, another Presbyterian clergyman, was selected as his successor in 1809. He was called to the principalship of the Academy from a nine-year pastorate in Meadville and from four years' service as the first principal of Meadville Academy, now Allegheny College.[26] His induction into office ushered in the golden age in the early history of the Pittsburgh Academy and culminated in its expansion into the Western University of Pennsylvania, a name which it retained until the present designation, "University of Pittsburgh," was adopted in 1908. Enrollment increased rapidly, the direct result both of the prosperity and growth of the city and the distinctive ability of the new principal.

His fame, however, rests chiefly on the very popular textbooks he developed. His *Western Calculator* and *Western Spelling Book* were the first schoolbooks published west of the Allegheny Mountains and were used extensively for many years in homes, schools, and academies. He also was one of the founders and later a professor of Western Theological Seminary.

Incorporation of Washington Academy

But this enlarging academy at Pittsburgh was not the only log cabin school to grow into an academy through the zeal of Presbyterians for education. A simultaneous development took place also in the schools founded in Washington County by the three famed pioneer pastors: Dod, McMillan, and Smith. The establishment of their log cabin schools, as previously noted, had proceeded by several years the incorporation of the Pittsburgh Academy. Yet the academy in Pittsburgh was the first school west of the Allegheny Mountains to gain the legal status of an academy.

Hugh Brackenridge probably felt the thrill of triumphant achievement when he succeeded in having his petition for an academy approved by the Pennsylvania Legislature before any similar appeal had been made by his clerical friends from Washington County. He was a lawyer and so had an advantage over the preacher-educators in knowledge of legal procedures. Previously, they seemed not to have thought of the practical value of incorporating their schools as academies.

However, they were quick to follow Brackenridge's legal precedent. Almost immediately, John McMillan, with the assistance of Judges James Allison and John McDowell, petitioned the Legislature for an academy charter and a land grant that might be of some material assistance to the school. Associated with them were such ministers as Joseph Smith, Thaddeus Dod, and John Clark of the Presbyterian church, Reverend Matthew Henderson of the Associate Seceder Church of Canonsburg and Reverend John Corbly of the Muddy Creek Baptist Church.[27] Others named as members of the Board of Trustees were James Marshall, James Edgar, Alexander Wright, Thomas Scott, David Bradford, James Ross, David Redick, Thomas Crooks, James Flannegan, James Brice, John Hoge, Alexander Addison, and Alexander Baird. The charter was granted on September 24, 1787, just seven months after the granting of a similar charter to the Pittsburgh Academy.

The petitioners envisioned only one academy in their midst. They suggested the county seat town of Washington as the logical place for the Academy. A grant of some five thousand acres of land, located north of the Ohio River in what is now Beaver County, was forthcoming also at the time of the issuance of the charter. But this grant proved merely to be a disappointing delusion and a football of politics. It was too far away to be of practical use to the college and was sold about fifty years later.[28] Three of the trustees, while in Philadelphia, succeeded in enlisting the interest of Benjamin Franklin who contributed fifty pounds for the purchase of books. He also may have recommended a teacher for the school who did not meet the qualifications which the Board of Trustees deemed necessary.[29]

Dr. Dod Serves as Principal

Several unsuccessful attempts were made to find a principal. Finally, McMillan and others prevailed upon Thaddeus Dod to accept the position for a one-year term. This was more than the incorporators had anticipated or even hoped for. Dod was highly respected by his colleagues and considered the outstanding scholar.

Dr. Brownson wrote of Dod: "He was the finest classical and mathematical scholar of these eminent fathers."[30] Dod had given up his teaching efforts in 1785 because of his pastoral burden and limited physical capacities. It was evident that his motivating desire in accepting the appointment was simply an eagerness to get the institution started. The Board minutes for January 20, 1789, read in part: "Thaddeus Dod was appointed for the year to commence from the first day of March next with a salary of eighty pounds to be paid quarterly."[31]

Nearly two years after the charter was granted, Washington Academy was ready to open its doors. Though rich in land, it had no money for building purposes and was forced to use such accommodations as were available. As a temporary expedient, the second floor of the Courthouse was rented and divided into classrooms. Dod served not only as principal but as an instructor in certain higher branches of learning. David Johnston, who had come out to the western country following his graduation from the University of Pennsylvania, took over the teaching of English and was to receive a salary of fifty pounds. Cephas Dodd, in writing upon the life of his father, said that the first student body numbered from twenty to thirty students.[32] The early minutes of the Academy record that Dod brought to the attention of the Board the necessity for a set of rules to govern the student body. The matter was referred back to Dod to make such regulations as seemed necessary. Great stress, apparently, was being put upon cleanliness and social factors. Perhaps the little mention of curriculum was due to the fact that such matters were an established part of the educational process.

At the end of the specified year, Dod reminded the trustees of his expressed wish to retire. However, he was persuaded to remain an additional three months so that David Johnston, his assistant, might be altogether free to accept the principalship.[33] Scarcely had Dod stepped out of the Academy and returned to his farm in the Ten Mile Valley in July than a disastrous fire occurred. The Courthouse burned in the Winter of 1790–1791. Since there was no other available place, the educational activities of the Academy came to a temporary standstill. John McMillan and Matthew Henderson approached John Hoge, a wealthy man and trustee of the Academy, in an effort to secure a building lot on his land which had recently become the town of Washington. He opposed their plan and, with others, seemed to be content to allow the Academy to remain closed. The trustees were discouraged. Some resigned. Whether Hoge opposed the Academy because of McMillan and Henderson is not known.

McMillan later wrote, "So indifferent were the inhabitants of that town to the interests of literature in general and to the demand of the church in particular that, notwithstanding the State's donation, an academy could not be supported."[34] Jacob Lindley had a similar statement to offer: "The inhabitants of Washington at that time had but little piety, science, or liberality to build a house or sustain a literary institution, and none to sustain a preacher."[35] It is generally believed that, barring the unfortunate incident of the fire, the career of the Washington Academy would have continued unbroken. Joseph Smith in "Old Redstone" has expressed this opinion and added the reflection that the academy at Canonsburg would probably never have come into existence if the temporary suspension of the Washington school had not occurred.[36]

Canonsburg Academy Established

Just as the educational enthusiasts in Washington County were stirred to action as the result of the incorporation of the Pittsburgh Academy, so it is believed that some public-spirited gentlemen in the Canonsburg area were inspired by the early efforts to get the Washington Academy started and gave some thought to a school in their midst.[37] When the fire caused the suspension of Washington Academy and Mr. Hoge, who owned all of the vacant lots in Washington, had refused a donation of land for the Academy, the Canonsburg group considered it a real opportunity to do something in their area. McMillan was not unaware of the thinking of such men as Colonel Canon, Judges Allison and McDowell, Alexander Cook, Esq., James Foster, Thomas Brecker, Robert Ralston, and others. Following the refusal of Mr. Hoge, he, with Matthew Henderson, approached Colonel Canon on whose property Canonsburg had been laid out.[38]

The situation was ripe for a decision and considerable enthusiasm developed. At a meeting in July, 1791, six months after the suspension of the Washington Academy effort, the need of establishing a Latin school or academy was carefully discussed. This meeting was on the Monday following the sacrament of the Lord's Supper at the Chartiers Church. "With free expression of opinion and views, it was promptly and unanimously decided that the exigencies of the western country, including the interests of the church, required the establishment of a Literary Institution somewhere in the West."[39]

Some consideration was given to a location near the McMillan log cabin school. However, since Colonel Canon had promised not only to give the land but also to advance money for an adequate building, it was decided to locate the academy in Canonsburg. No time was lost. Opening exercises were scheduled for the next morning at ten o'clock in a small English schoolhouse near Canon's Mills. Instead of meeting indoors as planned, the rays of a July sun made an outdoor meeting more advisable "under the shade of some sassafras bushes, beside a worm fence" near the old schoolhouse.[40] David Johnston, now a principal without a school, resigned at Washington and became principal of the new Academy. The first students were Robert Patterson and William Riddle. Patterson, being the senior, was asked to recite first. The opening words from his chosen selection were "Quid agis."[41]

Just as McMillan had taken the leadership in getting the Washington Academy under way and in striving to perpetuate it, so now he became the leader of the Canonsburg effort and took the most prominent part in the opening proceedings. In addressing the assembled group, McMillan said, "This is an important day in our history, affecting deeply the interests of the church, and of the country of the West; affecting our own interests and welfare in time and eternity, and the interests, it may be, of thousands and thousands yet unborn."[42] Henderson offered the Invocation in which "everything proper to the occasion appeared to be remembered in prayer."[43] Joseph Smith closed the services also with prayer. Judges John McDowell and James Allison, both of whom were elders in McMillan's church, were present along with Craig Ritchie, Esq. Through the influence of the community leaders, an English school nearby was converted into a recitation hall until the new stone building, sponsored by Colonel Canon, could be occupied. Within a few weeks, the following students were in attendance: Abraham Scott, Robert Patterson, William Wylie, Thomas Swearengen, James Snodgrass, Ebenezer Henderson, James Duncan, James Allison, Joseph Doddridge, Dorsey Pentecost, James Dunlavy, Daniel McLean, William Kerr, Philip Doddridge, and Alexander Campbell.[44]

Stone Building Erected

Soon an impressive two-story stone building rose to completion to house the enlarging group of students. The enthusiastic Colonel Canon had loaned sufficient money to erect the building and generously permitted the trustees to repay him at their convenience. The good news that the Academy was now equipped to welcome additional students in its new building was properly advertised. A notice in the *Pittsburgh Gazette* of November 2, 1792, proclaimed the broad-range curriculum of the school and some of its special advantages:

"The building for the Academy at Canonsburg is now finished, and the institution under good relations. The grammar school is taught by Mr. Johnston; and the English, Euclid's Elements of Geometry; Trigonometry, Plane and Spherical, with the later application to Astronomy; Navigation, Surveying Mensuration, Gauging, Dialing Conic Sections, Algebra, and Bookkeeping by Mr. Miller; both well known for their attention and abilities. Boarding in the neighborhood to be had at good houses, at the low price of ten pounds, payable principally in produce. The situation is healthy, near the center of Washington County; the funds raised by the Presbytery are to be applied for the support of a certain number of scholars, annually, as directed by the Synod of the district to be appropriated to this Academy. It is hoped the public will regard, with a favorable eye this institution, and give it all the encouragement that it may deserve."

The new school received also the approval of the Redstone Presbytery as an embryo theological seminary for ministerial students in Western Pennsylvania. The Synod of Virginia, at its meeting in September of 1791, had already designated Washington County as the location of one of its two centers of learning, stating that this school should be "under the care of the Rev'd. John McMillan."[45] Acting upon this authorization of Synod, the Presbytery of Redstone within a month alerted its members to secure contributions and have them put into the hands of McMillan as treasurer. The following year the Presbytery unanimously agreed that "Canonsburg should be the seat of that institution of learning which they are appointed by Synod to superintend; and that all the young men taken upon the fund for the support of poor and pious youths shall be educated there."[46]

However, when a year later, in 1793, it became evident that the Washington Academy would reopen its doors, there was some Presbytery support for a motion to reconsider the advisability of naming Canonsburg as the representative school in Redstone Presbytery. The motion was lost. The previous action respecting Canonsburg Academy was confirmed, with the amendment that "if at a future date, another seminary of like nature should be erected in our bounds, we will not oppose a division of the funds."[47] Presbytery and Synod were broadminded enough to support both Jefferson and Washington academies as two equally worthy educational agencies of the Presbyterian Church in Western Pennsylvania.

The charter for "the Academy and Library Company of Canonsburg" was granted by the Pennsylvania Legislature on March 11, 1794. Contributions were solicited vigorously from the congregations of the Presbyterians and the Seceders throughout the western country. The purpose of the contributions was to repay Colonel Canon for the building costs, to pay teachers' salaries, and to assist young men in their preparation for the ministry. Some light is thrown on these financial procedures by a subscription paper passed in the congregation of Dr. Joseph Patterson. The paper reads: "James Ewing, 5 bushels of wheat, at 2 shillings; William Flannegan, 1 bushel of wheat, at 2 shillings; . . . James Laird, 4 bushels of wheat, at 2 shillings; . . . John McMillan, cash $1; . . . Mrs. Vallandingham, 6 yards of linen; . . . Hugh McCoy, 4 bushels of rye; . . . George Vallandingham, cash 7s6d."[48] The members of this and other congregations were supporting the academies within the Presbytery in the best way they could and with whatever substance they had to give. Their generous efforts were successful. The debt on Canonsburg Academy was quickly liquidated. Colonel Canon was completely repaid in 1796, only two years after the incorporation of the Academy, due largely to the zealous efforts of McMillan and Henderson.[49] Two years later, the Academy recognized the eminent service of John McMillan by electing him its honorary president.

Canonsburg Academy Becomes Jefferson College

About 1800 a movement was launched to convert the Academy into a college. McMillan, Allison, Cook, and Ritchie were named a committee to draft a petition to the Legislature praying for a "College at Canonsburg." Rapid progress had been made during the years of the Academy. In support of their petition, the following summary was given:

"In the course of a few years past, twenty-one young men, who are now employed in the professions of Divinity, Law, and Medicine, received the rudiments of their Education in this School, nine others have also completed their classical education, and are pursuing the Studies requisite to qualify them for one or other of the learned Professions. Thirty-two are at present employed in learning the Languages and acquiring the Knowledge of the Mathematics and Natural Philosophy, one Master and an Assistant are employed in Teaching the Learned Languages and another Teacher the other branches, each of the Masters have had a regular and extensive education and are men of fair character."[50]

The fact that the school was flourishing had much to do with the Legislature's decision to grant a charter as of January 15, 1802. The name was changed from the Academy and Library Company of Canonsburg to Jefferson College.[51] Inasmuch as Thomas Jefferson had been inducted into office of the President of the United States in March of the preceding year, it was thought a well-deserved compliment to Mr. Jefferson to name the College for him.[52] Though both Pittsburgh and Washington academies had been incorporated in 1787, the log cabin school at Canonsburg was the first educational institution in Western Pennsylvania to attain the distinguished status of a college.

The first Board of Trustees of Jefferson College was composed of twenty-one men, some of whom had been active in the affairs of the Academy. The majority met in April of 1802, when they took both an oath of allegiance to the country and a pledge to serve the College. Dr. McMillan was honored as the first President of the Board and Mr. Ritchie was named clerk. A principal was to be chosen, as was a professor of divinity and a professor of mathematics and natural philosophy. The Board elected the Reverend John Watson to serve as principal and professor of moral philosophy. Dr. McMillan was named professor of divinity, which he chose to accept in preference to the position as President of the Board. Mr. Samuel Miller was named as professor of mathematics, natural philosophy, and geography. Judge James Edgar was elected President of the Board.

Among the early students were John Johnston and James Hoge who had completed their work in the Academy and who later became prominent ministers. Students who had almost completed their work at the Academy were graduated at the Fall Commencement of 1802. This first class of graduates included Reed Bracken, Johnston Eaton, William McMillan, Israel Pickens, and John Rhea. All except Pickens became ministers of the Gospel.[53] Enthusiasm was running high for the college.

Suddenly, only three or four months after he began his work as principal and professor, John Watson became ill and died. He had been considered the most brilliant and promising young man of Western Pennsylvania in that day. He was a man of unusual endowments. One of his students said of him: "He possessed a mind pure, vigorous, and enlightened. He could unfold his ideas to others in language simple, clear, and forcible and not unfrequently eloquent. He was amiable in his disposition, conciliating in his manners—of unblemished morals and real unaffected piety."[54] His death was a severe blow. But in the Spring of 1803, the Board elected the Reverend James Dunlap to take Watson's place and the college resumed its stride toward success and popular favor.

Washington Academy Reopens

The incorporation of the Pittsburgh Academy in 1787, as noted previously, had stimulated the pastor-educators in Washington County to secure a similar charter for Washington Academy seven months later. Now the success of the academy at Jefferson stirred the citizens of Washington to aggressive efforts to restore the Academy they had permitted to languish into inactivity. The disastrous fire in the Winter of 1790-1791 had destroyed the Courthouse in Washington which had housed the Academy. Since no other building seemed available, the Academy had been compelled to discontinue for five years its work in laying the educational foundations of Western Pennsylvania.

The rebuilding of the Courthouse had absorbed money which might otherwise be used for education. The Whiskey Rebellion held the center of community interest and placed the Academy trustees on opposing sides. Educational problems had to await calmer moments.

Yet Washington was only nine miles from Canonsburg. The two communities were natural rivals. The spontaneous efforts of the Canonsburg group, in not only deciding upon an academy but also in the building of a suitable structure for it, wounded severely the community pride of some of the Washington group. John Hoge, who may have had his reasons for refusing McMillan and Henderson when they approached him concerning a donation of land, now, late in 1792, was ready to lend a helping hand.[55] He donated four lots on the corner of what are now Lincoln and Wheeling streets.

The announcement of Hoge's land grant brought a revival of interest in Washington. On July 20, 1793, the Washington Academy trustees took steps toward the erection of a permanent building which was to be brick, stone, or frame and about thirty-five feet in dimension. The proposed building was to be paid for by subscriptions.[56] The two-story stone structure proceeded slowly with walls twenty-three inches thick. In 1796 a bill was introduced into the Legislature that made available a sum of three thousand dollars to complete the present structure and add "additional buildings."[57] The grant, made in March, 1797, carried a condition to the effect that as many as ten students should be taught reading, writing, and arithmetic without any charge for tuition and that the limit for each student scholarship should be two years.[58] The edifice thus erected has been referred to as "the old stone building" and stands until this day.

In order that classes might get under way as quickly as possible, a temporary structure was raised on land now occupied by the

First Presbyterian Church of that city. The Washington Academy effort was revived and carried on from 1796 to 1806. Some of those listed as principals and teachers were David Johnston, James Dobbins, Benjamin Mills, and Matthew Brown. Dr. Brownson, in commenting on this revival of interest at the Academy, said, "during which period many youth from the town and vicinity, as well as some from abroad, received education here, in the best style of the Western country at that time."[59] The coming to Washington of Reverend Matthew Brown in 1805, to serve both as pastor of the First Presbyterian Church and as principal of the Academy, was the beginning of a new era in the educational life of the little county seat town which was to grow into a borough in 1810.

Washington Academy Becomes a College

Shortly after Reverend Matthew Brown became principal of the academy at Washington, an effort was made to have the institution transformed into a college. The Legislature, however, did not grant the request until March 28, 1806. The difference in time between the incorporation of Jefferson College and Washington College is explained by the action of the Legislature. When Absalom Baird, one of the trustees, petitioned the Legislature in 1801 for a grant of money, it was learned that a charter was in the process of being granted to Jefferson College. Naturally, the Washington group also petitioned for a charter at the earliest possible moment. The Legislature felt it unwise to issue charters within a short interval of time to two colleges so closely situated. Hence, it was determined that in five years after Baird's petition and four years after the Jefferson request was granted that a charter for Washington College would be forthcoming from the Legislature.[60] The real growth of Washington College can be dated from Matthew Brown's acceptance of the presidency on December 13, 1806.

Dr. Brown was a worthy successor to McMillan, Dod, and Smith who, beginning in 1781, had laid broad educational foundations in the western country. Upon these foundations, two academies, one at Washington and the other at Canonsburg, were erected in the face of pioneer hardships. The era under review closed with these two academies being granted all the power and privileges of colleges. Washington and Jefferson were thus launched successfully on their distinguished careers of service to the Presbyterian church and to education in Western Pennsylvania. They stood for a time as rivals, less than ten miles apart, later to be merged into the present Washington and Jefferson College at Washington, Pennsylvania.

CHAPTER III Extension Through Evangelism

NOVEMBER 14, 1802, was a new Day of Pentecost in the evangelistic history of the Presbyterian church throughout the entire Upper Ohio Valley. Late in the afternoon, the Reverend Elisha Macurdy climbed into the bed of a wagon to preach to part of the throng which had gathered for the communion service. It was a joint communion season in the open area surrounding the Upper Buffalo Church in Washington County. The pastors of several neighboring Presbyterian churches had accepted an invitation to bring their congregations and join in a prolonged season of prayer in preparation for the Holy Communion Sacrament. Some ten thousand people welcomed the invitations. Several ministers had already spoken when Dr. McMillan urged his former pupil to continue to exhort the eager communicants.

Macurdy had not expected to preach. He had no sermon prepared for the unexpected occasion. He did not even know his text. Trusting in the Holy Spirit for guidance and with the wagon bed as a pulpit, he opened the Bible at random to read from the Second Psalm. With the recent Whiskey Rebellion as the local background, he preached on the text: "Kiss the Son, lest He be angry." With tremendous fervor and inspired conviction, he pleaded for repentance. The conscience of sinner after sinner was quickened. Men fell to their knees prostrate in repentance and pleaded to God for forgiveness. Hundreds were stirred into emotional scenes of surrender. "The scene," said the Reverend Thomas Hunt, who was in the wagon with Macurdy, "appeared to me like the close of a battle in which every tenth person has been fatally wounded."

The services continued two days longer. The flames of The Great Revival, which previously had smouldered in several churches, including Macurdy's own congregation at Three Springs, West Virginia, now burst into a spiritual conflagration. Evangelistic services were held in other Presbyterian congregations of Western Pennsylvania and the Virginia Panhandle during the ensuing months. The revival soon spread rapidly as a conviction of sin brought many to their knees in repentance. Excitement was generated by a strange emotionalism that gave rise to conflicting rumors and divergent opinions.

Badger Journeys to Investigate

The garbled reports of the revival traveled far and wide. They reached the ear of the Reverend Joseph Badger who was traveling as a missionary among the isolated settlers in the Western Reserve. An eager desire to know the truth of the matter at firsthand motivated him to start on a wearisome horseback journey from Austinburg, Ohio, into Washington County, Pennsylvania. The nearer he came, at New Bedford, at Neshannock, and at Greersburg, he heard more startling stories as he interviewed the men and women who themselves had a part in the strange experiences of what had already come to be called the Falling-Work Revival.

Badger stopped to visit his new friend Elisha Macurdy at Briceland's Cross Roads, now Florence. Almost a year had now passed since the revival had broken out under Macurdy's preaching. In answer to Badger's eager and searching questions, Macurdy replied, "Ride over to Cross Creek with me tomorrow, and see for yourself." And so he did.

What he saw and heard and shared at Cross Creek and Pigeon Creek, Badger has carefully recorded in his autobiography. It is a trustworthy report. Joseph Badger was a man of mature years and sober judgment, a veteran of Bunker Hill and of the ill-fated winter expedition against Quebec. He was accustomed to dealing with all manner of men and forming his own opinions. Also, he was familiar with what had happened in his native New England under the preaching of Jonathan Edwards and George Whitefield two generations earlier, during The Great Awakening. He was an equally valiant soldier of the cross, whose public attacks on sin had made evildoers tremble.

Badger's Observations

Let us hear from his own lips some account of that skeptic's pilgrimage:

"Saturday morning, September 25, 1803—Rode from Cross Roads to Cross Creek, six miles. Here the people were assembling for a sacramental season. I preached in the afternoon to about three thousand people, the largest worshiping assembly I ever saw collected. They were conveniently seated in a grove, with a stand for the speakers raised about four feet above the people. In time of preaching there were many that cried out, and fell in a perfectly helpless condition. There remained a slight respiration, the only symptom of remaining life. In this situation many lay from two to six hours, without strength to move or speak; others were taken with trembling and loss of strength, and yet could talk freely. I could not learn from any with whom I conversed that their views of sin and of their danger and criminality were anywise different from what was common in New England, with which I had been conversant. But the effects on the system, so different and alarming, were totally inexplicable by any. The exercises of singing, exhortation and prayer were continued until about midnight, when the ministers retired; but the great body of the assembly continued on the ground through the night."[1]

The next day was Sunday when the communion sacrament was to be administered to all who had manifested evidence of repentance of sin and whose spiritual life was deemed worthy of acceptance at the communion table. Badger describes the sacred scene:

"Lord's Day, 26th.—Between the hours of eight and nine in the morning, prayer was attended by this great assembly. Rev. Mr. Scott led in the exercise. At about ten the public services began. Mr. J. Hughes preached. Mr. Patterson fenced, as it is called, the tables, in which he drew the line between those who were proper characters to partake of the sacramental supper, and those who were not. He then administered to the first table. I was requested to administer to the next. While a psalm was singing, the communicants rose from the tables, and others filled their seats. The tables were filled six times, with between eight and nine hundred communicants. Tokens of admission were taken by the elders after they were seated."

Badger continued in his volunteered ministry as he journeyed to Pigeon Creek where further evidences of spiritual regeneration strengthened his faith in the revival in which he was now sharing. He reports:

"The first Sabbath in this month the sacrament was attended at Pigeon Creek, at which time there was a very large assembly. There was present a medical gentleman who was an unbeliever in the Christian religion, but wished to gratify his curiosity. He took his seat in a pretty conspicuous place, and was well known to most of the people. Soon after the preaching commenced, Dr. H- began to feel himself in some danger of falling with others; he immediately started to go away; got about half-way through an opening, and fell to the ground, and cried out, 'Carry me away!' Three or four men took him up and carried him to a suitable distance, and sat down with him on the ground. He was all in a tremor, unable to support himself, and shook surprisingly, yet appeared to possess his mind fully. He said to the men, 'What does this mean? I have cut off limbs, and taken up arteries, with as steady a hand as a man ever had; and now I cannot hold these hands still if I might have a world. Oh, it must be the power of God! Carry me back where I can hear.'"

When the account was published years later, Mr. Badger added the comment: "He became hopefully pious, was elected an elder in that church, and lived and died a hopeful Christian." *Badger's Autobiography* is an important source document in the pioneer church history of the Upper Ohio Valley. His comments on the pioneering use of hymns are interesting:

"Watts's Psalms and Hymns had not until the year 1801 been sung in any church this side of the mountains, excepting one. The old Scotch version was everywhere used, with a strong prejudice in its favor. Being called to preach a sacramental preparation, in attending a prayer-meeting afterward I read the Hartford hymns; they made no disturbance. On the Sabbath I used them again; no objections. I ventured yet further, and used them in the great congregation mentioned above. Notwithstanding hundreds fell and cried out, yet order and decency were preserved in a remarkable manner. Some who came only to see were taken hold of powerfully, and made to feel they were sinners."

Much more might be quoted, from Badger and from others. But these vivid pictures drawn by an eyewitness convinced against his will, may suffice.

This then was the great Falling-Work Revival of 1802, still bearing abundant fruit a year later. In some respects it was a repetition of what had been occurring during the awakening in Kentucky, begun two years before, under the powerful preaching of James McGready, when camp meetings, mistakenly supposed to be an invention of the frontier Methodists, came into being. The camp meeting was not of any man's devising. It was born of sheer necessity. Crowds gathered, too great for any building. They had to be gathered in the open air. They came from too far away to return home at night. They therefore came prepared to sleep in the woods. The first camp meeting we know of in this area was at the Upper Buffalo Great Sacrament.

Preaching for a Verdict

This revival was undoubtedly kindled at Upper Buffalo and

Canonsburg in the strongly evangelistic training Joseph Smith and John McMillan gave their students of theology. Almost without exception these men, who went out as missionaries and pastors in the tristate area and far to the west, preached an awakening Gospel and brought many from the world into the church. Those coals from Canonsburg, as previously noted, first burst into flame at Three Springs under the preaching of Elisha Macurdy, who had been ordained just two years before, and installed over an eager and heart-hungry people. Even before his settlement, while preaching at Cross Roads and Three Springs as a licentiate, a considerable number of hitherto godless men and youth had been converted. Besides the elders, some forty young people had signed a petition to him to become their pastor. Immediately after his ordination Macurdy and one of his elders, Philip Jackson, made a covenant of prayer for the outpouring of the Holy Spirit in quickening power. Each had a prayer spot in the woods, where he spent much time alone. This then was not an evangelistic campaign planned and promoted by preachers. Like the awakening in Tidewater area of Virginia in the early eighteenth century, it was essentially a lay movement, a spontaneous revival awakened in answer to prayer.

While there were some regrettable excesses of emotion, some things for abnormal psychology to seize upon and exploit, the Falling-Work Revival was abundantly vindicated by its permanent results. Until then, a large majority of the frontier settlers were more pagan than Christian. French deism was rampant among the more intelligent, while very many of the people were unschooled, unchurched, and openly immoral and lawless. The towns were centers of drunkenness, carousing and Sabbath-breaking. What churches there were, with very few exceptions, were to be found in the open country. These were few, their congregations widely scattered, and their pastors and missionaries overworked.

In all the Upper Ohio Valley, from the Laurel Ridge westward, the Presbyterians, though the strongest communion, had only one hundred and five organized congregations in the Autumn of 1801, and of these, fifty-eight were pastorless.[2] The physically able ministers were almost living in the saddle, and ranging far and wide as missionaries among a half-heathen population. Badger, whom we have already quoted, reports after every journey over the Western Reserve, the godlessness and indifference he had encountered.

Permanent Results of Revival

During this revival, a very considerable proportion of the converts were mature men, many of whom were completely transformed in character and behavior. From among them came the church leaders during the years that followed—ministers, elders, and teachers. Little congregations that had been too weak to call a pastor grew strong in numbers and devotion.

It is unfortunate that statistical reports in those days were very meager, or wholly missing from the record. Such as are available show a strong and healthy growth in the number of communicants, and in the forming of new congregations and new presbyteries in the two decades following this movement of 1802. While this growth was partly due to the settling of the country by new migrants from the east and from the British Isles, it was also and more largely due to a continuing new life in the churches, and evangelistic zeal in all their ministry. The growth was just as great in counties already well populated, like Westmoreland, Fayette, Allegheny, and Washington, as in the newer regions beyond the Allegheny and the Ohio.[3]

Prayer for a New Awakening

In general, the effects of this awakening were clearly traceable through the first two decades of the nineteenth century. Then the emergence of a great moral issue, slavery, and of a bitter theological controversy, between the hyper-Calvinism that stemmed from Canonsburg and the New England theology that began to seep in by way of the Western Reserve, diverted the synods of

Pittsburgh, Ohio, and Western Reserve from the primary mission of the church. Decline in evangelistic zeal became increasingly apparent, so much so that in 1829 we find the Synod of Ohio taking this significant action:

"On account of the spiritual deadness and apathy generally prevalent in our churches, there is call for some special means warranted by the word of God, in order to awaken them from their lukewarmness and turn their attention to increased effort for the conversion of sinners and the advancement of the Redeemer's Kingdom. For this purpose it is recommended:

"1. that the first Thursday of December be observed throughout our churches as a day of fasting, humiliation and prayer for the outpouring of the Spirit of God upon them; and that the second Thursday of the same month be observed in like manner if there are two congregations under the care of one minister, so that both may have his labors on this occasion.

"2. that each member of this Synod spend one week in each congregation under his care, in connection with a brother in the ministry where it is practicable, in Preaching, Prayer, Exhortation and personal Conversation, for the purpose of exciting the attention of both Ministers and people, to the need of a revival of religion.

"3. that it be renewedly enjoined on all our churches to pray more frequently for their pastors severally; and that the evening previous to the Day of Fasting hereby appointed be especially set apart for this purpose.

"4. that every minister seriously reflect on his own efforts in the cause of God, compared with what that cause demands of him; that he may see how far he has come short of his duty, and be stirred up to greater faithfulness and zeal in the service of his Divine Masters."[4]

It may not be wholly without significance that the committee appointed to draw up this plan were all soon after to be found on the New School side.

Thus it becomes evident that while the Methodists and Baptists were the great revivalists on the frontier, the Presbyterians were the pioneers in revival. As Dr. W. W. Sweet, a Methodist, has pointed out, Presbyterians were the first to use the camp meeting as a method of winning the unchurched to Christ.[5] Indeed, camp meetings were not a plan drawn up in any office or worked out by any committee. They sprang up spontaneously, because the crowds that came to hear the evangelistic preaching of James McGready in Logan County, Kentucky, were too great to be accommodated in any building. They came from such distances that it was necessary for them to camp on the spot, and be there to hear more the next day, and the next. In some cases they did indeed contribute to wild excesses of emotion, and even to immorality; but they revealed the desperate heart-hunger of a lonely frontier folk, "scattered abroad as sheep not having a shepherd."

Revivals Previous to 1802

We have begun at its climax this story of evangelistic efforts to win Presbyterian converts throughout the expanding "Western Zion." However, the beginnings of that revival movement lie farther back. The little congregations scattered among the Pennsylvania hills had seen times of refreshing long before 1802.

When the Reverend Thaddeus Dod of Mendham, New Jersey, followed his old friends and neighbors who had established themselves on Ten Mile Creek in southern Washington County, Pennsylvania, he preached one of his first sermons to a little group of frightened men, women, and children huddled in a crude fort because of an Indian raid. There the presence of God was so manifest that a number of hitherto indifferent people were converted. Among them was Thomas Marquis, recently come from Opequon, Virginia, who later was known throughout the whole church as the Reverend Thomas Marquis, the "silver-tongued" Marquis, himself a most effective evangelist. The Reverend John McMillan, another of the "Four Horsemen of Old Redstone," had had several times of refreshing at Chartiers and Pigeon Creek, with considerable ingatherings of converts.

But chief among these ministers, who from the beginning each did the work of an evangelist, was the Reverend Joseph Smith of Upper Buffalo and Cross Creek.[6] All his preaching seems to have been aimed primarily at the conversion of sinners. It was solidly biblical, yet he did not hesitate to appeal to the emotions of men, as well as to their intelligence and their moral sense. Few men have equaled him in presenting the terrors of Divine judgment and the imminence of eternity. But he also opened the gates heavenward and poured the balm of Gilead into wounded hearts. Rough men rode weary miles to hear him, while children and youth loved him and sought his companionship.

It is true that the memorable "Great Sacrament" under the oaks at Upper Buffalo in November, 1802, when an estimated ten thousand people were gathered for three days, and when nine hundred, after careful examination by the session, sat at the Lord's table, was an event in the pastorate of his worthy successor, the Reverend John Anderson. Yet it is, in large part, to be accounted for by the flaming evangelistic ministry of Joseph Smith, who had laid down his armor ten years before, his physical strength burned out at the age of fifty-six.

There had also been awakenings and ingatherings during the preceding quarter century in many other congregations of Redstone and Ohio presbyteries—at Bethel and Mingo, at Dunlap's Creek and Laurel Hill, at Rehoboth, Mt. Pleasant, Salem, Congruity, Long Run, Beulah, and doubtless other places of which we find no written record. The "sound of a going in the tops of the mulberry trees" had long heralded the breaking of this storm in showers of blessing. Almost without exception, the earliest Presbyterian ministers west of the Alleghenies were lovers and seekers of the souls of men.

A Heritage of Revival

And that leads us still farther back. We must ask: how and where was the fire first kindled in the souls of these earliest frontier missionaries in Western Pennsylvania? The answer is this: in every case these frontier missionaries in the Upper Ohio Valley were spiritual sons or grandsons of Reverend George Whitefield and Reverend Gilbert Tennent, who had followed Jonathan Edwards as leaders of The Great Awakening in the middle colonies and in New England. Both Tennent and Whitefield had more than once preached to immense crowds near Joseph Smith's boyhood home at East Nottingham. It is likely that Smith as a half-grown boy heard them both.

John McMillan was born at Fagg's Manor shortly after Whitefield had made his second visit there. In Whitefield's *Journals,* as in the oldest Fagg's Manor records, the place is called New Londonderry. McMillan's parents, who shortly before Whitefield's first visit had come from Ulster to settle on the farm just west of the meetinghouse, must have heard him several times, and must have been brought under the power of his message. Perhaps Whitefield's preaching explains why John at his birth was dedicated by his parents to the gospel ministry. They had come into the Fagg's Manor Church under the ministry of Reverend Samuel Blair, a graduate of Tennent's Log College on the Neshaminy, and an intimate friend of Gilbert Tennent, who was a companion of Whitefield for weeks at a time on his preaching tours.

James Power was a younger contemporary of Joseph Smith as a boy at East Nottingham. His parents and those of Mrs. Power lived under strong revival influences during the pastorate of the Reverend James Finley in that community before he also came out to the Monongahela country.

Thaddeus Dod in his boyhood was almost a neighbor of the Dutch Reformed pastor and evangelist, Reverend Theodore Freylinghuysen, whose warmhearted ministry did much for evangelical Christianity in northern New Jersey, and who worked with both Whitefield and Tennent while the latter was pastor at nearby New Brunswick. Both Bound Brook and New Brunswick were only about twenty miles from Dod's home at Mendham. Also, Jonathan Dickinson and Jacob Green were well-known New Side leaders in that part of New Jersey during Dod's boyhood.

Jacob Jennings of Dunlap's Creek had come from Sumerville, from the Low Dutch Church, and from Freylinghuysen's tutelage. John Clark, "Father Clark" of Bethel and Lebanon, came over the mountains as an old man, his course almost run. His mind and spirit had also been fed from Whitefield's ministry. He had served churches in New Jersey and Maryland in which the tides of New Side zeal ran strong.

Reared Amidst Revival

James Finley, the first pastor at Rehoboth and Round Hill in the "Forks of the Yough," settled there after a notable ministry at East Nottingham, and after many missionary journeys through the wilderness, west and south. He, too, was an older man, past sixty. The others, the first four named above, were much younger, McMillan being only twenty-three when he accepted the call to Chartiers and Pigeon Creek. But Finley had retained much of the dew of his youth, and something of the fiery zeal of his older brother Samuel, who after a fruitful ministry at West Nottingham, over the line in Maryland, had been called to the presidency of Princeton while some of these "four horsemen" were students there. Some of them also had been influenced by his predecessor at Princeton, Reverend Samuel Davies, a spiritual son of Samuel Blair, and a disciple of Whitefield in his evangelistic ministry. Davies is still rated among the best preachers America has yet produced. These then were James Finley's spiritual roots, and James Power and Joseph Smith were his sons in the faith.

Reverend James Dunlap, pastor at Dunlap's Creek before Jennings, was another of the seven pioneer Western Pennsylvania preachers with a similar background. A native of Chester County, and a student of theology under James Finley at Nottingham, he crowned his ministry with eight years of service as the first president of Jefferson College.

One more man, who after initial reluctance became a leader of the revival, is Joseph Badger whom we have already quoted at length. Unlike the others, he was a New Englander. His forebears were not Scotch-Irish, but of the English dissenting stock. Their first home in America was at Newburyport, where afterward the influence of Whitefield was so marked, and where, under the pulpit of the old Presbyterian meetinghouse, Whitefield's body lies to this day. In his boyhood home in Connecticut, Badger was everywhere surrounded with influences and currents of thought that stemmed from Edwards and from Whitefield.

Indeed, of all our first-generation ministers west of the mountains who became revival leaders, Samuel Ralston at Mingo was the only one with a markedly different origin and training. He was Ulster-born and Glasgow-bred. He, too, came to the West as a licentiate of Newcastle Presbytery. Therefore, it is safe to assume that his heart had been well warmed in such an atmosphere. His ministry at Mingo and Horseshoe Bottom, now Monongahela, give proof of that.

We cannot speak from definite information concerning most of the elders and other lay leaders, of whom there were many. We do know, however, that some of them, like James Edgar, James Allison, John McDowell, and Patrick Scott had grown up under the same influences as their pastors, had come out of the same or nearby churches on the seaboard. Further, we are told that James Finley, while still at Nottingham, had sent into this western wilderness no less than thirty-four young heads of families, most of whom within a few years became elders in the frontier churches. All of these had felt something of the impact of the Whitefield revival.

In these men, and in these influences which had awakened them, lies the human explanation of the Falling-Work Revival of 1802.

Similarity to Great Awakening

Turn back again to take a second look at the revival movement in the middle colonies in the middle decades of the eighteenth century. Can one say as Peter did at Pentecost, "This is that?" It is obvious that there is much similarity in the type of leadership; also that some of the same phenomena accompanied the faithful preaching of judgment and repentance. In both revivals the leaders were very staunch Calvinists. They preached both from Sinai and from Calvary, appealing to men's fear of the righteous judgments of God, and then to their sense of gratitude for the love of God revealed in Christ's atoning death. They insisted on reformed lives as a proof of salvation, not as a way to win it.

A comparison of the sermons of Whitefield, Edwards, Tennent, and Samuel Davies, with the sermons of McMillan, Macurdy, John Anderson, and Thomas Marquis, reveals a remarkable similarity in both matter and method. In cold print they do not seem calculated to produce the amazing results of which we have evidence so abundant. But all these men concerned in both revivals spoke and lived with a passionate earnestness and sincerity that battered down men's resistance, and brought men trembling and crying, like the jailer at Philippi, "What must I do to be saved?" The zeal of God's house ate these men up. Davies, Blair, John Rowland, and William Robinson all died young—Davies at thirty-seven and Blair at thirty-nine. Jonathan Edwards reached fifty-five, Whitefield fifty-six, and Gilbert Tennent sixty-one. Our men in the West averaged a somewhat longer life span, for they were hardened by physical toil in the open. Only a few of them reached the promised threescore and ten. Like Henry Martyn, these all burned themselves out for God.

Letter of Samuel Blair

The strange physical effects manifested in those who came under conviction of sin were more pronounced and extreme on the frontier than in the East. Yet they were not lacking under the preaching of Edwards or Whitefield or Blair. Evidence of this appears in a letter written by Reverend Samuel Blair in 1744 to the Reverend Thomas Prince, pastor of the Old South Church of Boston.[7] The latter had requested from Samuel Blair a report of what had been happening at Fagg's Manor.

The letter is an interesting historical document and reads in part:

"Dear Sir: That it may the more clearly appear that the Lord has indeed carried on a work of true religion among us of late years, I conceive it will be useful to give a brief general view of the state of religion in these parts before this remarkable season. I doubt not then but there were some sincerely religious people up and down; and there were, I believe, a considerable number in the several congregations pretty exact, according to their education, in the observance of the external forms of religion, not only as to attendance upon public ordinances on the Sabbaths, but also as to the practice of family worship, and perhaps secret prayer too; but with these things the most part seemed, to all appearances, to rest contented, and to satisfy their consciences just with a dead formality in religion. If they performed these duties pretty punctually in their seasons, and as they thought with a good meaning, out of conscience, not just to obtain a name for religion among men, then they were ready to conclude that they were truly and sincerely religious. A very lamentable ignorance of the main essentials of true practical religion, and the doctrines nextly relating thereunto, very generally prevailed. The nature and necessity of the new birth, was but little known or thought of. . . .

"Thus religion lay as it were adying, and ready to expire its last breath of life in this part of the visible church. It was in the Spring in the year 1740, when the God of salvation was pleased to visit us with the blessed effusions of His Holy Spirit in an eminent manner. The first very open and public appearance of this gracious visitation in these parts, was in the congregation which God has committed to my charge. This congregation has not been erected above fourteen or fifteen years from this time; the place is a new settlement, generally settled with people from Ireland, (as all our congregations in Pennsylvania except two or three, chiefly are made up of people from that kingdom). I am the first minister they have ever had settled in the place; having been regularly liberated from my former charge in East Jersey. At the earnest invitation of the people here, I came to them at the beginning of November, 1739, accepted a call from them that winter, and was formally installed and settled among them as their minister the April following. There were some hopefully pious people here at my first coming, which was a great encouragement and comfort to me.

"I had some view and sense of the deplorable condition of the land in general, and accordingly the scope of my preaching that first winter was mainly calculated for persons in a natural unregenerate state. . . . I had knowledge of four or five brought under deep conviction that winter. In the beginning of March I took a journey into East Jersey, and was abroad for two or three Sabbaths. A neighboring minister, who seemed to be earnest for the awakening and conversion of secure sinners, preached to them on the dangerous and awful case of such as continue unregenerate and unfruitful under the means of grace. . . . Under that sermon there was a visible appearance of much soul concern among the hearers, so that some burst out with an audible noise into bitter crying (a thing unknown in these parts before). After I had come home there came a young man to me under deep trouble about the state of his soul, whom I had looked upon as a pretty light, merry sort of a youth. . . .

"The news of this very public appearance of deep soul concern among my people met me an hundred miles from home. I was very joyful to hear of it, in hopes that God was about to carry on an extensive work of converting grace amongst them, and the first sermon I preached after my return to them was from Matthew VI, 33. . . . In the improvement, I came to press the injunction in the text upon the unconverted and ungodly, and offered this as one reason among others, why they should henceforth first of all seek the kingdom and righteousness of God, viz., that they had neglected too long to do so already. This consideration seemed to come and cut like a sword upon several in the congregation, so that while I was speaking upon it they could not longer contain, but burst out into the most bitter mourning.

"I desired them as much as possible to retrain themselves from making any noise that would hinder themselves or others from hearing what was spoken, and often afterward I had occasion to repeat the same counsel. I still advised the people to moderate and bound their passions, but not so as to resist or stifle their convictions. The number of awakened increased very fast; frequently under sermons there were some newly convicted, and brought into deep distress of soul about their perishing state.

"Our Sabbath assemblies soon became vastly large, many people from almost all parts around inclining very much to come where there was such appearance of the divine power and presence. I think there was scarcely a lecture or sermon preached here through that whole summer, but there were manifest evidences of impressions upon the hearers, and many times the impressions were very great and general; several would be overcome and fainting, others deeply sobbing, hardly able to contain, many others more silently weeping, and a solemn concern appearing on the countenances of many others. And sometimes the soul-exercises of some (though comparatively very few), would so far affect their bodies as to occasion some strange, unusual bodily motions. . . .

"They saw that they had been contenting themselves with the form, without the life and power of godliness; and that they had been taking peace to their consciences from, and depending upon their own righteousness, and not the righteousness of Jesus Christ. . . . There were likewise many up and down the land brought under deep distressing convictions that summer, who had lived very loose lives, regardless of the very externals of religion. In this congregation I believe there were very few who were not stirred up to some solemn thoughtfulness and concern more than usual about their souls. The general carriage and behavior of people was soon very visibly altered. Those awakened were much given to reading in the Holy Scriptures and other good books. . . .

"Thus, Sir, I have endeavored to give a brief account of the revival of religion among us in these parts, in which I have endeavored all along to be conscientiously exact, in relating things according to the naked truth; knowing that I must not speak wickedly even for God, nor talk deceitfully for Him. And upon the whole I must say, it is beyond all dispute with me, and I think 'tis beyond all reasonable contradiction, that God has carried on a great and glorious work of His grace among us.

Samuel Blair."

This letter is the more noteworthy and weighty, because there is appended to it the following endorsement and attestation of six of the seven elders serving at that date in Fagg's Manor Church. The seventh elder was absent at the time.

"New Londonderry, August 7, 1744—We, the undersubscribers, ruling elders in the congregation of New Londonderry, do give our testimony and attestation to the above account of the revival of religion in this congregation, and other parts of this country, as far as the said account relates to things that were open to public observation, and such things as we have had opportunity of being acquainted with. Particularly, we testify that there has been a great and very general awakening among people, whereby they have been stirred up to an earnest, uncommon concern and diligence about their external salvation, according to the above account of it; and that many give very comfortable evidence by their knowledge, declaration of experience, and conscientious practice, of their being savingly changed and turned to God.

Signed: James Cochran, John Ramsey
John Love, John Smith
John Simson, William Boyd."

Descendants of some of these men are still, more than two centuries later, active in the Fagg's Manor congregation.

Revival Checked but Results Continue

The eighteenth century revival was quenched by the turmoil involved in the War of Independence, and by the flood of immorality and French infidelity which followed it, bringing sore need of a new awakening. But as we have seen, this when it came was nothing wholly new. It was in every essential particular the same kind of awakening, followed by the same beneficent results.

One permanent by-product of Whitefield's and Tennent's ministry was the unifying of the colonies in resistance to tyranny, and the impulse to build a new and independent nation. Among the results of the awakening west of the Alleghenies was the capturing of the new West for God and the Church. Another was the cooperation of many Christian bodies in that high endeavor. Some individuals and a few churches did indeed oppose the whole movement. For example, there was published in 1804 in Washington, Pennsylvania, a pamphlet signed by five Seceder ministers arguing at length against it and warning their people to have nothing to do with it. On the other hand, in some of these great open-air meetings, Presbyterian ministers gladly accepted the help of Methodists, Baptists, and Congregationalists. Nowhere in the Upper Ohio Valley did they go as far as in Virginia. A letter, written in 1802 by the Reverend Drury Lacy, Presbyterian, of Prince Edward County, gives an account of an agreement of Presbyterians, Methodists, and Baptists in that state to have church communion among themselves.

As the earlier movement had been stopped by war, so this in the West was halted, and men's attention diverted from the primary concern of all Christians, by a theological controversy, which temporarily split the Presbyterian church in the thirties and by the bitter struggle over a great moral and social issue of slavery, which split the church even more grievously again in the sixties of the nineteenth century, a separation which still persists. But the fire has never died. Finney rekindled it on the Western Reserve. Then came Moody. After him, Sunday, Chapman, Torrey, Biederwolf, and others, who held some of their most fruitful campaigns within our area. With these men were associated gospel singers of great awakening power. At least three of these singers came out of the churches of the Upper Ohio Valley—P. P. Bliss from Penfield in Clarion Presbytery, Ira Sankey from New Castle and Edinburg, and James McGranahan from Kinsman, Ohio, and Jamestown, Pennsylvania.

Now we have our New Life Movement, which continues to bear fruit. Yes, ours is a New Life Communion, committed by our history as well as by our Lord's command to the evangelization of our nation and the world.

CHAPTER IV Upholding Moral Standards

"William Frazer, you have admitted you are guilty of using unguarded expressions at different times and so bringing offense to the Church; thus the Session had decided that if you profess sorrow and promise to be on your guard for the time to come, we will admit you to the privilege of Baptism for your Child."[1] On August 10, 1789, William Frazer accepted this judgment of the Session of Dunlap's Creek Church in satisfactory repentance. He was readmitted to the distinguishing privileges of the Church, but only after the stern elders had read the record of his trial before the whole congregation.

The helpful influence of the rebuke was not as lasting as the elders hoped it might be since, in May of 1794, Mr. Frazer's character was again examined by the same Session. The occasion was the approaching celebration of the Sacrament of the Lord's Supper. In accord with the sacredness of the Holy Communion, unworthy persons were not permitted to partake of the sacrament. A diary of that period reports:

"Presbyterians of all descriptions did not approach the communion table without searching their souls to determine their fitness to partake of the sacrament. If there was anything of notable misconduct in their lives since the last communion, in all probability it would be inquired into by the elders of the Church session who constituted themselves a judicial body to try wayward members for violation of church discipline. If conviction followed, the Session would deny the offender the privilege of participating in the communion service . . . To the sincere Calvinist this was tantamount to a manifestation of his removal from the company of the elect."[2]

Especially at the communion season, the elders of the church inquired most diligently into the moral conduct of the lives of the members of the congregation. The rights of the accused were carefully safeguarded. Witnesses had to appear before the Session to sustain the charges lest innocent members be unjustly accused and so denied their rightful place at the Lord's table. Members who brought unfounded complaints were themselves subject to possible censure. Since no witnesses presented testimony when Mr. Frazer was being tried for his second offense, two elders of the Dunlap's Creek Church Session, Mr. Little and Mr. Beard, were appointed to inquire further and report back to the Session as soon as possible.

The necessary inquiry required considerable time since further discussion of Frazer's offense of slander was delayed until May 19, 1795. On that date the Session "after prayer proceeded to an affair that concerned William Frazer's character which before had been put off until inquiry could be made of Doctor Simon for which might be before the Session any day previous to the next sacramental occasion."[3] On June 10, 1795, William Frazer expressed his sorrow "for any ground or foundation that he may have given for offense and desires the same to be made public in the congregation."[4] We may assume it was a penitent William Frazer who received the communion the next day.

The Session Sits as a Court

For a number of years these local church sessions were the primary moral courts of the sparsely settled western frontier. Civil courts were set up as communities grew, but the traditional Calvinistic practice of controlling the life of its church members was not discontinued. The practice was grounded in Scripture and in the hearts of these Presbyterians who believed that discipline of its members was the prerogative of the Church of Jesus Christ, who Himself "had entrusted to the church officers the keys of the kingdom of heaven to retain and remit sins and reclaim offending brethren in the company of the elect."[5] Only the most obstinate offenders would go to the civil authorities. Even then they would be under the censure of the brethren for such action.

Everywhere on the frontier Presbyterian church sessions sought to establish and uphold moral standards. It was regarded as the solemn obligation of these church courts to purge any leaven that might infect the whole lump; to vindicate the honor of Christ, and thus to prevent the wrath of God from falling upon the church if the church became profaned by notorious and obstinate offenders. Church members must themselves be moral and ethical if moral standards were to be upheld throughout the community. They must set the example if others were to be inspired to follow.

As a result, these frontier sessions sat in judgment upon judicial cases which involved a wide range of offenses including adultery, Sabbath breaking, slander, stealing, unfair dealing, covetousness, disrespect of elders or parents, family quarrels, drunkenness, trespassing, and varied forms of indiscreet conduct. Hasty judgments were avoided. The regeneration, not the punishment, of the offender was the purpose of all disciplinary action. Forgiveness and a second chance were always available to the penitent who put his trust in the mercy and compassion of his Saviour. The peace, purity, and progress of the church were at all times the essential goals of those who sat on the Session as the first court of the Presbyterian church. In some cases the sentence was merely a stern rebuke to the offender by the minister. More severe offenses called for satisfactory evidences of repentance and a public confession of guilt before the entire congregation which sometimes had to be repeated on several subsequent Sabbaths.[6]

Appeals Taken to Presbytery

But the Session, then as now, was not the final arbiter. An appeal could always be taken to the Presbytery and, if necessary, to the Synod and General Assembly. The minutes of the pioneer Presbyteries of Redstone and Ohio are typical illustrations. Page after page in the recorded minutes of these Presbyteries quote testimony taken or refuted as various offenders were ordered to appear before Presbytery, or as the offending parties appealed to the Presbytery against conviction in the sessional courts of the local churches. The effectiveness of the Presbyterian church in upholding moral standards and insisting on righteousness and justice among its ministers and members is shown repeatedly in the many judicial cases which occupied much time at almost every meeting of presbyteries. A few illustrative instances will reveal the Presbytery functioning as a necessary court of appeals.

The Redstone Presbytery, while meeting at Pigeon Creek Church on October 16, 1792, considered a reference from the Session of Congruity congregation respecting "a certain James Christy and Rebecca Gordon." After hearing all the minutes of the Session relating to that affair, and duly deliberating thereon, Presbytery was of the opinion that "no credit ought to be given to the oath of Rebecca Gordon, and that there is no sufficient evidence to criminate said Christy as being the father of said Gordon's child—yet, as there appeared to have been unbecoming conduct between the above mentioned parties, Presbytery judged that neither of them ought to be received to distinguishing privileges, until Providence shall shed further light upon the matter."[7]

On another occasion the same Presbytery found that the Session of Bethel Church had acted unwisely in judging one David Tidball guilty of incestuous conduct. They saw the apparent prejudice of the witnesses, insufficient testimony and concurring circumstances, and declared that the Session's judgment should be set aside. At this same meeting at Long Run Church on October 15, 1793, there was a reference from the Session of Unity Church:

"Respecting a charge exhibited before the Session by Charles McRight holding forth that a certain Hugh Bean had acted contrary to an oath taken by him, to abide by the verdict of men in a case referred to them by said Bean and McRight, and also that Hugh Bean had said that Charles McRight had acknowledged himself to be the father of Hugh Bean's daughter's child, which acknowledgment Charles McRight denies. And having attended to the testimony produced, and taken all the light they could obtain, are of the opinion that Hugh Bean cannot be admitted to the distinguishing privileges in our church, until he acknowledge his wrong in swearing to abide by the judgment of arbitrators, not knowing but that judgment might involve him in sin, and for his not using every means in his power to fulfill the obligations of said oath. The Presbytery is also of the opinion that the testimony produced by Hugh Bean has exculpated him so far as the fact alleged against him in the latter charge, that they do not think him liable to any censure upon the account thereof."[8]

All of this was ordered to be read publicly in the congregation. To this meeting James Christy came to complain that he was aggrieved by the judgment of Presbytery the previous year. In the spirit of Christian patience, the Presbytery decided to reconsider its action at the next meeting.

Some appeals, however, due to insufficient or conflicting testimony, were too baffling for the Presbytery or even the Synod to decide. In such cases they wisely decided to leave the matter in the hands of God as, they did, for example, regarding a reference from the Session of Lebanon Church concerning one John Barnet:

"The Presbytery proceeded to the consideration of the reference respecting John Barnet, and after mature deliberation, came to the following determination, viz.: That although the oath of Jane Miller appears to lay a ground of much suspicion of immodest conduct and language in John Barnet—yet, as there are no circumstances to corroborate her evidence, and something in the acquittance she gave, that seems, in some measure, to weaken the force thereof—we are not clear peremptorily to judge him guilty, but must refer the matter to the judgment of the great day."[9]

The Redstone Presbytery, as a church court which sought to express the mind of God, felt fully justified in criticizing civil magistrates when they appeared not to be acting in accord with the laws of God. At its meeting in Pigeon Creek, March 11, 1783, Presbytery passed the following resolution "that magistrates belonging to our community, marrying any person in a way contrary to the prescriptions of the law respecting marriages, and all persons belonging to us, obtaining marriage either by magistrates or ministers contrary to the law, shall be esteemed censurable by the church."[10]

Even Ministers Subject to Censure

Nor were the ministers themselves immune from censure by their brethren in Presbytery. Ministers in the public administration of the duties of their office and in their private lives were expected to be above reproach, but not above criticism. Church members at any time could present complaints to the Presbytery. At certain meetings the churches were requested to state whether or not they were satisfied with the services and diligent care of their pastors or the preachers appointed over them by Presbytery.

Redstone Presbytery was only in its second meeting when a John Matson complained that his pastor, Reverend James Dunlap, had denied him ordination as a ruling elder. He charged also that Mr. Dunlap came to his house to wrangle with him. After listening to witnesses, Presbytery supported Mr. Dunlap and ordered Matson to submit to rebuke and admonition by the moderator of Presbytery.[11] At the following meeting Robert Hall complained that Reverend James Power had been too stringent in church discipline and had denied him the "common privileges of a regular church member."[12] Presbytery restored him to church privileges.

Reverend Samuel Barr, the first pastor of the Presbyterian church in Pittsburgh, was rebuked for "having omitted the Confession of Faith in Baptism and baptizing privately when it might have been done publicly and baptizing four persons, without proper inquiry into their moral character."[13] This rebuking action was only the first of a long series of complaints which were to mar the pastorate of Mr. Barr and which hastened his resignation.

Pittsburgh at that time was a crude frontier trading community. Religion was not taken seriously. John Wilkins, one of the church elders, admitted that "the majority were more inclined to interest themselves in horse racing rather than to contribute to the building of a church."[14] It was natural then to hear Barr complaining that "he has not been able to exercise church discipline; having too few to support him in that branch of duty." "Robert Galbraith and John Wilkins, elders of the church, have not supported characters becoming to their office but have indulged themselves in drinking and card playing."[15] He also charged Mr. Wilkins with "being idle with women, Mr. Dunning as not paying strict attention to his word and betraying a covetous disposition, and George Wallace with circulating false reports and preventing the congregation and himself from worshiping God in a peaceable manner."[16] The Session made its counter charges in this case to the effect that Mr. Barr had not carried out his duties as a clergyman with the necessary diligence.

Redstone Presbytery, after hearing the conflicting testimony, determined that Mr. Barr should have used more discipline than he did and should not have ordained such men as elders, knowing their practices. Presbytery also felt that he should have done much more in private to admonish and reprove the misconduct of the members.[17] The elders were rebuked sternly by the Presbytery and warned that if they continued such practices as Mr. Barr charged they would be further dealt with.

However, some of the congregation's charges against Barr were upheld by his fellow ministers in Presbytery. They concluded "that his conduct has been very injurious to the cause of religion and virtue; and that, without an alteration, it will continue to be so. Therefore, although we feel tenderly for him, we cannot see how we can justify ourselves before God, the world, and our own consciences, without declaring this as our judgment, viz.: that he ought not to exercise any part of his ministerial office until the mind of Synod is known thereon . . ."[18] An appeal was taken to the Synod of Virginia on October 22, 1789. Barr introduced new witnesses and new evidence. He was vindicated by Synod which concluded "that the charges exhibited by the Session and Trustees of the Pittsburg congregation, against Mr. Barr, are wholly unsupported; and he be considered in full and regular standing in the church."[19]

Particularly troublesome also and long continued were the efforts of the Ohio Presbytery, under the leadership of Dr. John McMillan, to prove charges of visible drunkenness against Reverend Thomas Ladlie Birch, who had come from Belfast, Ireland, and had been preaching within the bounds of Presbytery, especially in Washington. The trial and conviction, covering many pages in the minutes, were appealed unsuccessfully to the General Assembly and carried by Mr. Birch to the civil courts. Mr. Birch was convicted and all churches within the Presbytery were forbidden to accept his ministerial services in any way under the threatened penalty of ecclesiastical censure.[20]

Dr. McMillan, by this action, was vindicated; yet not without censure for his too violent use of language in condemning Mr. Birch. The Presbytery felt that Dr. McMillan should not have referred to Mr. Birch as a "child of the devil." In spite of the greatness and prestige of Dr. McMillan, he was required to accept a specific rebuke from his brethren in Presbytery. Justice, in their minds, must be impartially administered. Even the most outstanding minister must be Christian and judicial in his public use of language. A true minister must be above reproach.

The Whiskey Rebellion

Shortly after the Ohio Presbytery was organized, the members of that Presbytery had to face the most severe test of the ability of the Presbyterian church to uphold moral standards on the frontier. Resentment against the governmentally imposed excise tax on whiskey and the harsh methods of its enforcement was developing with increased intensity. "Liberty and No Excise" became the battle cry of pioneer settlers who had fought the War of the Revolution to be free from unjust burdens of taxation. Now for the youthful democracy to impose a hated excise tax upon a commodity which was proving profitable to farmers in certain sections of Western Pennsylvania seemed almost an insulting challenge to their patriotism and prosperity. Whiskey at that time was an established part of the social life of the community and also formed the basis of much of the community's economic resources.

Money Was Scarce

The Federal mint had only been set up in 1792. A good farmer rarely saw more than twenty pounds cash in a year's time. By barter, a high-proof whiskey could be exchanged for dry goods, groceries, hardware, or whatever was needed. The tax, however, had to be paid in hard money, oftentimes even before the whiskey was sold. Whiskey must be transported over the mountains before it could be sold at a profit to get the needed money to pay the required tax. One horse could carry only four bushels of grain over the mountains, but that same horse could carry twenty-four bushels when distilled into the highly salable whiskey. There were more than six hundred private stills in the West. Many of these were located in the farmer's home or in an outbuilding close by. It was unpleasant indeed to have collectors barging in, often ignoring the farmer's rights, while determining the capacity of the still and its production for the collection of the excise. Naturally no reputable men wanted the task of exciseman. When General

John Neville, who had opposed excise, was appointed chief inspector, he at once forfeited the good will of his neighbors.

A Heritage of Rebellion

The Ulster-Scotch had brought with them to America a hatred of the excise system in the British Isles. To resist taxes was a hereditary prerogative. In Scotland or Ireland it was said that to kill an exciseman was reckoned as an ample expiation for a multitude of sins. Robert Burns conceived a popular song:

"The deil cam fiddling through the town,
And danced awa' wi' the Exciseman;
And ilka wife cries, "Auld Mahoon,
I wish you the luck of the prize, man!"[21]

They might not have opposed paying a tax to the Federal government if the tax were based upon an equitable evaluation of their land and collected in a reasonable way. The obnoxious tax collectors everywhere aroused resentment which expressed itself in tarring and feathering some of the more irritating collectors. Soon the gathering bitterness threatened widespread violence and revolt which was called the Whiskey Rebellion. The flames of revolt were spreading throughout the four counties of Allegheny, Westmoreland, Washington, and Fayette.

Organized Opposition to Tax

On August 21, 1792, a meeting was held in Pittsburgh which brought together prominent leaders from the four counties. John Canon of Canonsburg was made chairman and Albert Gallatin, from New Geneva, was appointed secretary. Other prominent Presbyterian laymen were David Bradford, James Marshall, Edward Cook, Benjamin Parkinson, John Hamilton, John Smilie, and John McClelland. A remonstrance to Congress, praying for repeal of the tax, was ordered drawn up. The following very strong resolution against excise officers was adopted:

"And whereas, some men may be found amongst us so far lost

to every sense of virtue and feeling for the distress of this country as to accept offices for the collection of the duty: Resolved therefore that in the future we will consider such persons as unworthy of our friendship, have no intercourse or dealings with them, withdraw from every assistance and withhold all the comforts of life which depend upon these duties that as men and fellow-citizens we owe to each other, and upon all occasions treat them with that contempt they deserve, and that it be and is hereby most earnestly recommended to the people at large to follow the same line of conduct towards them."[22]

This point of view is hardly a message of Christian love to our fellowmen, but it was looked upon as needed discipline of wayward members of the community.

Presbyterian ministers sympathized with their parishioners in resenting the unpopular tax and urged moderation in enforcement or outright repeal of the tax law. When, however, reasonable opposition to the tax took the form of violence and physical injury to the government agents and possible military measures against the American army, the pastors in the Ohio Presbytery rallied and spoke out vigorously in favor of reasonable law enforcement. They denounced as unchristian all violent forms of opposition to the government's policy of taxation.

Hugh Henry Brackenridge, a Princeton-bred lawyer, in his *Incidents of the Western Insurrection,* characterized the popular resentment in vivid though exaggerated terms:

"A breath in favour of the law, was sufficient to ruin a man. It was considered a badge of toryism. A clergyman was not thought orthodox in the pulpit unless against the law; a physician not capable of administering medicine unless his principles were right in this respect; a lawyer could have no practice, without at least concealing his sentiments, if for the law; a merchant at a country store could not get custom. On the contrary, to talk against the law was the way to office and emolument . . . it was the shibboleth of safety and the ladder of ambition."[23]

Some few concessions were made as a result of these protests but they did not relieve the burden nor gain praise. President George Washington warned the settlers to "desist from all unlawful combinations whatsoever, having for object or tending to obstruct the operation of the laws."

Only a spark was needed to kindle hot resentment into a flame. The spark came when Major Lenox, assisted by Neville, had served warrants in the Peter's Creek area almost as a solicitation to violence when tempers were inflamed. A meeting was held at the Mingo Creek Presbyterian Church. Those who gathered were, for the most part, sober citizens, the backbone of the country, who were unwilling to act without first talking things over and considering the facts. After much discussion they decided to move upon General Neville's home, at Bower Hill, the next day and there plead with the General to desist in his efforts at enforcement and to urge him to unite with them in joint efforts toward the peace and protection of their country from tyrannous and oppressive measures. They decided to go armed in order to execute their purpose in case the General would refuse to agree. They were to meet the next morning at Couch's Fort with Major James McFarlane of Mingo Church as their commander.

Violence Erupts

The die was cast. The citizens advanced with grave and thoughtful faces and troubled hearts. The news of their coming leaked out. General Neville left his home garrisoned with a token force led by Major Kirkpatrick. Five hundred armed men on foot and on horseback set out the next day down the Washington-Pittsburgh Road toward Bower Hill. At Bethel, Reverend John Clark, the Presbyterian pastor of the Bethel and Lebanon Presbyterian churches, boldly stood in the path of the advancing army under the command of Major McFarlane, which had gathered on July 17, 1794, at Couch's Fort, about one-quarter of a mile west of Bethel Church. In an impassioned speech, the old man counseled against bloodshed and violence. He was convinced that their action could come to no good, but would only create a greater wrong. But his plea was in vain. The hot blood of passion was now aroused and must express itself in some form of destruction before reason and better judgment could ponder a more effective solution of what was undoubtedly a real grievance.[24]

Down the valley the angry protesters marched to Bower Hill. They marshaled their forces in front of the home of General Neville, which was situated about halfway up the hill. It overlooked the wooded valley and the open plain, beyond Pressley Neville's house at Woodville, where John Kane Hospital stands today. Peaceable methods were first tried. David Hamilton went out with a flag of truce to present their request. He was informed that Neville was not there nor would he give up his commission. Hamilton then asked for permission to search for papers. Kirkpatrick agreed to permit a search, but the crowd now demanded the soldiers' surrender.

After a few shots had been fired, a white flag was flown from the house. It proved to be only a trap. As Major McFarlane went forward to receive the surrender, he was at once cut down and killed. Passions now were fully aroused. The crowd was determined on revenge. Since it was only a matter of time until the house would be burned, Kirkpatrick surrendered. The house was plundered and the whiskey from the cellar brought out and distributed. Only the slaves' smokehouse was saved from destruction since it contained their food. The militia of justice had become a mob filled with drink. Many among those opposed to the excise were appalled at the results of that fateful summer day.

Another meeting at the Mingo Church was soon called to consider further action. The leaders of the Bower Hill march were there. Also in attendance were David Bradford, a Washington lawyer and son of an elder of Hill Church near Washington, who was becoming a leader of the radicals; John Canon of Canonsburg; and Edward Cook, a respected elder from Fayette County. These rather conservative citizens had come because they feared the people were out of hand. Lawyer Hugh Brackenridge presented a reconciling position: "What had been done, might be morally right, but it was legally wrong. In the construction of law it was high treason. It was a case within the power of the President to call out the militia." He suggested that they seek a general amnesty and avoid further violence. Many realized the predicament they were now in and they left the Mingo Church gravely. Certain radicals, however, decided to rob the mails, the Philadelphia-Pittsburgh Post, to see what action the government was about to take concerning the disturbance.

City of Pittsburgh Threatened

Another instance of resistance was a muster of approximately five thousand men at Braddock's Field, not far from Pittsburgh, under the direction of David Bradford. Their object seemed to be to march on Pittsburgh by force and obtain submission of the excise officials. Some of the more radical agitators wanted to burn Pittsburgh to the ground, looking upon it as a second "Sodom" where "the savages were contaminated by loitering with the inhabitants."[25] The city was worried. Leading citizens, including some of the elders or trustees of the First Presbyterian Church, sought a basis of reconciliation.

Eventually the more level-headed citizens were able to prevent the holocaust that might have been loosed from Braddock's Field. The unwise muster ended in the "army" marching through the main streets of Pittsburgh and having their thirst quenched by barrels of whiskey which Brackenridge had provided. The only fire that was kindled was the burning of one of Kirkpatrick's barns across the river in retaliation for the murder of McFarlane at Bower Hill. The resistance was to end a few short weeks after the rebellion had come to a head.

A meeting of delegates from the entire area was held at Parkinson's Ferry on August 14, 1794, to decide what answer might be given to the three United States commissioners whom President

Washington had appointed. David Bradford still held out for resistance. Brackenridge and Gallatin counseled acceptance of the Federal laws, while still presenting their grievances. A committee of sixty was appointed to confer with the commissioners at Pittsburgh August 20 to 23. Following the conference the delegates voted to submit to the laws and to accept an amnesty to which certain conditions were attached. This plan was accepted—though not without protest—at a meeting held in Brownsville August 28 and 29.

Presbyterian Pastors Advocate Obedience to Law

Before this decision could become valid, a concurring vote of the regular taxable inhabitants, plus all citizens over eighteen, was necessary throughout the four counties of the West. All recorded evidence indicates that the official position of the Presbyterian church was a decisive factor in the peaceful outcome of the insurrection and in obtaining a favorable vote to approve submission to law and order. Presbyterian pastors had consistently sought through preaching and counseling to check angry passions and deeds of violence. Prior to the voting on September 11, Reverend John McMillan, Reverend John Clark of Bethel, Reverend Samuel Porter of Congruity, Reverend James Finley of Rehoboth, and most of the other Presbyterian ministers took aggressive action to persuade their people to vote aye. This vote itself was a submission to the Federal laws and acceptance of an amnesty. In addition, each voter had to sign a promise: "1. To submit to the laws of the United States; 2. not to oppose the carrying out of excise laws; and 3. to support, as far as the law requires, the civil authorities in affording protection due to all officers and other citizens."[26] The signers promised they would "be careful and watchful to perform by Christian rules . . . as Providence shall give opportunity, and prudence direct." The signing continued over five years.

The fortnight before the vote was taken was one of tension and uproar, especially in Washington County. Dr. John McMillan's self-imposed task was to see that the Mingo Creek and Pigeon Creek congregations submitted, since many members of these churches had been deeply involved in revolt and violence. He received effective support from Judge James Edgar, a Presbyterian elder and Judge in Washington County, and already an active and persuasive reconciler from the Brownsville meeting. The seat of rebellion had been chiefly on Peter's and Pigeon creeks.

McMillan called a meeting of many who needed amnesty. They came in force but not with an eye to submission. The Judge made an able and conciliatory address, but, in turn, he and other speakers were pelted with mud and stones. A table on which the papers, which were to be signed, were lying was carried away and broken up in the general uproar. The reconcilers were disheartened but not defeated.[27] On an occasion previous to this, Judge Edgar had addressed a sacramental meeting on the subject of the insurrection with such a tenderness of Christian eloquence that few in that neighborhood participated in the rioting. Now it was necessary to use another means of reconciliation where talk had failed to produce all the desired results.

Lord's Supper Delayed

Dr. McMillan refused even to administer the sacrament of the Lord's Supper to the members of his congregations until they would submit to the plan of amnesty and promise obedience to law.[28] He had planned the celebration of the Lord's Supper for an early day in September. He postponed it until after September 11, purposing to refuse the Sacrament to those who had not signed the amnesty agreement and promise. He hoped that they would so value this means of grace that their signatures would be secured and the right relationship with their church be maintained.[29] Any who would be left out would feel a heavy sense of guilt as they would be under the discipline of the church. The right relationship with God was, after all, far more important in the last analysis than any hardships imposed by civil law.

McMillan called his congregations together early in September. A large attendance resulted. He "prayed and exhorted them." Then Reverend Samuel Porter preached on the text, Romans 13:1-7. The point stood out clearly in the words, "They that resist shall receive to themselves damnation." As he came to the application, he noticed frowning faces. Some arose to leave. He related a challenging anecdote and changed the tone of his sermon so that at its end almost all agreed to submit.[30]

McMillan and Porter, James Dunlap, John Clark, James Finley, Thomas Marquis, James Power, Joseph Patterson, and the other ministers, each in his own parishes, worked strenuously to control their people. Many of the elders, such as Judges Edgar and McDowell, supported them. These ministers dared to speak out against the fury of the times. They were tactful enough not to condemn too violently, since they recognized the injustices of the excise law. But they felt they were under the divine obligation of using the voice of the church and its courts to maintain order and uphold morality. Their sermons may not have been heeded by all, but those who did heed submitted to the law. The records of Synod indicate that the members in these congregations were well satisfied with the care and diligence of their pastors.[31]

Church Courts Take Action

In September of 1794, the Synod of Virginia passed a resolution to make the second day of November (after the congressional election) "to be observed as a day of fasting and prayer to confess our own sins and the sins of the land; to mourn over them before God, and to deprecate the Divine wrath manifested in many judgments which hang over our land in general and which more especially threaten this country because of the late very sinful and unconstitutional opposition which has taken place to some of the laws of the United States."[32] The Ohio Presbytery, which at that time was under the ecclesiastical supervision of the Synod of Virginia heartily concurred in this request. When the Presbytery met at Pigeon Creek on April 20, 1795, it was found "upon inquiry, that the day appointed for fasting and prayer by the Synod last fall was observed by all the members."

On April 29, the Ohio Presbytery also passed the following resolution:

"The Presbytery, on motion replied, that if any of those persons, who during the late disturbances, had an active part in burning property, robbing the mail, and destroying official papers of the officers of Government, shall apply for distinguishing privileges in our church, they shall not be admitted, until they give satisfactory evidence of their repentance. The Presbytery also did, and hereby do declare their hearty disapprobation of all vicious, illegal, and unconstitutional combinations against the Government, the laws, of officers of Government and do in the most earnest and importunate manner recommend and enjoin it upon the people under their care to be subject to all magistrates in lawful authority."[33]

Presbytery ordered "that the above minutes be read in the several congregations under the care of this Presbytery."

Thus the Presbyterian ministers and elders of the region stated the official position of the church and its resistance to incidents of the rebellion. The moral influence of these church courts was not taken lightly. Prayer and fasting were effective in upholding law. The admonitions were necessary, but not harsh. Satisfactory repentance was recognized as sufficient atonement for unlawful actions. Consideration and forgiveness were evident.

Conciliation and Calmness

The people's awareness of the guilt and sin their actions caused or might cause helped to break the backbone of the insurrection. Even David Bradford, a Presbyterian, whose activities had placed him foremost on the list of the rebels, when the government militia arrived on the scene late in October, was really quite prudent in restraining his supporters. It is recorded in Washington, D. C., that he signed the amnesty before the deadline. He was, however, forced to flee for fear of assassination and settled in Spanish West Florida. There he became a prominent and prosperous planter and lawyer.

Another meeting was held at Parkinson's Ferry on October 2, 1794, where the delegates resolved that the temper of the country was in favor of submission. The voting on the solemn promise had been successful and active resistance was over, but the country was still disturbed and dissatisfied. Many had been aroused to rashness who were not evil and depraved at heart. Commissioners were sent from this meeting and another on October 24 to convince George Washington and Alexander Hamilton that the army would be unnecessary, but still it was sent. Edgar and Gallatin could do nothing more than reassert that civil authority had been re-established.

Nonetheless the army arrived. Arrests were made and stills seized. Fortunately, the army did not stay long. It began its return November 19, leaving General Charles Lee behind with a small force to finish the task. On November 29, a general pardon was issued which saved all those entangled in legal processes and who had fled for fear of prosecution. The excise collection was set up again, but the law was finally repealed in 1803.

The church had proved itself to be the one stable factor in the uprising and in the years to follow. Without its resistance, both on the part of the clergy and laity, there might have been a far different outcome in this young America. The new government was tested and men awakened to the balance between their liberties and the laws under God. President Washington, on New Year's Day, 1795, issued a proclamation setting February 19 aside as a day of Thanksgiving for "the seasonable control which has been given to a spirit of disorder in the suppression of the late insurrection." The real crisis of the Whiskey Rebellion had been met, not by the overwhelming power of the government, though this may have been a part of Providence, but by the power of the spirit which continues to act in all hours of crisis.

CHAPTER V Competition For Converts

Our own Presbyterian missionary activity in the Upper Ohio Valley did not begin until 1766 when Reverend Charles Beatty and Reverend George Duffield arrived in Pittsburgh for a Sabbath day's preaching on September 7. They had been commissioned by the Synod of New York and Philadelphia to investigate the possibilities of successful missionary work among the Indians along the Muskingum River some one hundred thirty miles west of Pittsburgh and to make a survey of the religious needs of the frontier so that the Synod could plan an intelligent missionary and evangelistic program for this general area.

One of the worshipers in his *Diary* records that eventful Sunday: "Mr. Beatty preached this morning in the fort and Mr. Duffield in the town. Dined with them at the mess. After noon went to hear Mr. Duffield in the town." Two days later, "Mr. Duffield preached a very judicious and alarming discourse."[1] Refreshed in soul by these opportunities to preach in what was to become the city of Pittsburgh, Beatty and Duffield started westward on the assigned missionary campaign among the Indians living in the valley of the Muskingum. They returned after a two-month tour without leaving behind them any established work.[2]

These two pioneer Presbyterian missionaries, however, were not the first ambassadors of Christ to cut "a highway for our God" in the western wilderness. Nor were the subsequent years to witness an absence of similar efforts by other denominations to win the settlers for Christ and their particular denominational emphasis in worship and theology. Both competition and co-operation were to mark the progress of evangelism and the harvesting of souls. The closest interdenominational rivalry was destined to appear within the zealous advocates of the followers of John Calvin.

To the Moravians must go the honor of being the first Protestant group to develop religious work in the Upper Ohio Valley.[3] Their pioneer preachers included Reverend David Zeisberger, Reverend John Roth, and Reverend John Heckenwelder. Zeisberger built his first village of Christian Indians west of the Alleghenies at Goschgoschuenk (now Tionesta) on the Upper Allegheny in 1767. Nor did the Moravians stop on the eastern bank of the Allegheny. Two years later they had two mission stations on the Big Beaver River at Friedenstadt and Kuskuskoong. Within a year Zeisberger pushed sixty miles farther west, into the Tuscarawas Valley. There he built the largest Christian village of them all at Schoenbrun, in what was to become Tuscarawas County, Ohio. From there he branched out to Salem and Gnadenhuetten, and for a time had a station also in what is now Coshocton County, which he called Lichtenau.

In most, if not all, of these places, the Indians were living in substantial cabins, were provided with church and school, and were learning to produce and store food. In fact, these were probably the most effective missions to the Indians anywhere in that generation. McClure visited Friedenstadt and was amazed and delighted with what he saw there. He was kindly welcomed by Roth and permitted to observe some of his methods.[4] Each of these Moravian missionaries had his wife and children with him, and was setting the example of a Christian home. This was five years before Reverend James Power brought his family over the mountains.

In a real sense this was foreign missions. Indeed, work among the American Indians continued to be called foreign missions for a long time. It must be confessed that the Presbyterians did not succeed well with the Indians, though they tried hard in their

COURTESY OF ALDERMAN LIBRARY,
UNIVERSITY OF VIRGINIA

WILLIAM HOLMES McGUFFEY
Author of *McGuffey Readers.*

REVEREND JOSEPH STOCKTON
Principal, Pittsburgh Academy (now University of Pittsburgh), 1809–1822. Acting pastor, First Presbyterian Church of Alleghenytown, Pa., 1812–1831.

COURTESY OF
UNIVERSITY OF PITTSBURGH

Log Cabin Meeting House | A Meeting House of Second Class

A Meeting House of Third Class | First Presbyterian Church, Pittsburgh, Pa.

EVOLUTION OF WESTERN PENNSYLVANIA CHURCH BUILDINGS
Throughout Period, 1774–1869.

stations on the Sandusky and Maumee rivers.[5] But in serving the new white settlers on the Ohio and its tributaries, they were among the first and most fruitful. The immigrants who preferred their ministrations were easily the majority of the new population. Yet we must never forget that the Moravians preceded them, and did succeed in winning the Red Men to Christ and to the ways of peace. At the formation of Redstone Presbytery in 1781, when the Presbyterians had few church buildings, and these only tiny log huts, the Moravian Church at Schoenbrun could accommodate nearly five hundred worshipers, yet was scarcely large enough for the worshiping congregations.[6] All the details of this work, even to the plan of the village and the dimensions of the church, are in the Moravian archives at Bethlehem, Pennsylvania.

Other missionaries besides Presbyterians were also on this field from the first—Baptists, Lutherans, German Reformed, Anglican, and before the turn of the century, even the Methodists, though they were comparatively new to America. John Sutton and John Corbly are the best-known Baptist pioneers. Sutton, after several months of heroic work, founded the Great Bethel Baptist Church of Uniontown, Pennsylvania, in 1770. This is probably the oldest church with continuous existence now in Western Pennsylvania.[7] Corbly seems to have been at work in the wilds of what were to be Washington and Greene counties when McMillan first arrived. Almost his entire family were wiped out in an Indian raid, but that did not deter him from his ministry. In all that country his memory abides in honor.

The Lutherans had missionaries among the German immigrants in Westmoreland, Somerset, and Fayette. Their oldest surviving church apparently is Herold's, some miles southwest of Greensburg, fully organized as early as 1773. Its extant records, beautifully kept by the schoolmaster, are almost as old. The Episcopalians scarcely enter this picture of rivalries. Throughout the frontier they were few and feeble. The Scotch-Irish looked upon them with fear and disfavor, as leaning religiously toward Rome and politically toward autocracy. Memories of persecution in Scotland and Ulster still rankled in their hearts. St. Luke's at Woodville, one of their earliest parishes, was largely a family enterprise of the Nevilles, which did not increase its popularity in the neighborhood. The Lutherans, and soon after them the German Reformed missionaries, sought out only those of German origin; and the language barrier kept them well aloof for a long while.

Therefore, when competition appeared, it was somewhat in evidence between the Presbyterians and Baptists, and some also between Presbyterians and Methodists. But rivalry was chiefly among members of the Calvinistic family stemming from Scotland —Presbyterian, Seceder, Covenanter, and Associate Reformed. Staunch adherents of all these bodies crossed the Alleghenies very early. Speers Spring, now Chartiers of Canonsburg, was a Seceder group organized in 1775, the same year as Chartiers Presbyterian, only a mile away. It was not till 1781, however, that Reverend Matthew Henderson came from Oxford, Pennsylvania, to be its first settled pastor. Associate Reformed congregations were gathered in the 1780's at Bethesda in the "Forks of the Yough" (a Seceder group also functioned in the same neighborhood); at Brush Creek, later Bethel, in Westmoreland County; and at Dunlap's Creek in Fayette County. The Associate Reformed Church came into existence in 1782. All three of the Scottish Separatists were worshiping in separate groups on the frontier at the beginning and tended more and more to draw apart.

There were also a few who designated themselves by the Scottish terms, Burger and Anti-Burger; some also who were known as Reformed Dissenting Presbyterians. All these sought to maintain their identity and perpetuate their differences in the Upper Ohio Valley. Exact statistics for the pioneer period are not available, but it seems evident that no one of them, and probably not all of them together, equaled the Presbyterians in numbers.

The following facts will help to complete the picture. The first Covenanter or Reformed Presbyterian Church in Western Pennsylvania was established near Elizabeth in 1794 and bore the name Monongahela. The oldest in Ohio was at Massie's Creek, dating from 1810. Congregations appeared at Poland and at Utica about 1814. By 1812 they had a church on Brush Creek in Adams County, and by 1816 one in Cincinnati. In 1821 we find them as far west as Sparta in Southern Illinois. Yet Glasgow lists for them only forty congregations in Pennsylvania, of which twenty-eight were west of the Laurel Ridge, one in West Virginia, and twenty-six in Ohio. Eleven of these were within the Upper Ohio Valley.[8] Of the thirty-eight within the territory under consideration, more than half have long since disappeared. As for the others, Scouller lists in the Upper Ohio Valley one hundred eighty-nine Associate churches organized, and one hundred ninety-six Associate Reformed.[9] A few of these were received from the Reformed Presbyterians, or from the Reformed Dissenting Presbytery. At one time there were two that belonged to the Associate Reformed Synod of the South. During the same period and in the same area, the Presbyterians organized four hundred twenty-three congregations, counting only the ones which have survived to this day.

Church Buildings Erected as Rivals

Now begins the story of rivalry, which of course seldom found expression in official records. It became evident in many other ways, but most of all in the organizing of congregations and the locating of meetinghouses. A comparative study of the lists of congregations established west of the mountains by the four Presbyterian bodies yields such facts as these. During the pioneer period, when in most localities the population was very sparse, instead of always seeking out the destitute and unchurched neighborhoods, they were treading on each other's heels. Appendix B lists one hundred forty-one places where Presbyterian and Associate, Associate Reformed, or Covenanter congregations were formed within five years of each other, and at no greater distance apart than three or four miles, often indeed, almost side by side.

Sometimes the Presbyterians were on the ground first, and almost as often they were not. Thus the rivalry is evident on both sides.

Many communities might be cited, in which three or even four varieties of Presbyterians were struggling to gain a foothold in the same small village. A good example is the village of Savannah in the Presbytery of Wooster, Ohio, where the writer spent his childhood. At one time, shortly before the Civil War, there were in that hamlet of about three hundred souls a Presbyterian, an Associate Reformed, a Seceder, and a Free Presbyterian Church, besides a Methodist and a Baptist. The Seceders were first on the ground, the Methodists next. The Presbyterians and the Associate Reformed began about the same time, in 1833. Worshipers were drawn to each of these from all parts of the township, and beyond it. Most of the families of the Associate and Associate Reformed congregations had come directly from Ulster or Scotland.

Savannah is perhaps an extreme case. Yet conditions very similar obtained at Mansfield, at Cadiz, at Utica, at New Concord, and elsewhere in Ohio; also at Mercer, Merrittstown, Laurel Hill, "Forks of the Yough," New Alexandria, Buffalo, and Canonsburg. Running down a dated list, here are a few illustrations. In the same year that John McMillan organized Chartiers, 1775, the Seceders were also organizing at Speers Spring, only a mile and a half away. To this new church Matthew Henderson, McMillan's old Chester County neighbor, was called to serve as its first pastor in 1781.

When Upper Buffalo congregation was about to build in 1779, it set its house of worship less than two miles from Henderson's other charge at North Buffalo. In Cadiz, the Associate Reformed began in 1813, and the Associate, the following year. The Presbyterians organized a church in 1817, though they already had strong churches only a few miles away, at Beech Spring on the one side, and at Crab Apple on the other.

The Mt. Pleasant Presbyterian Church of Darlington was formed in 1797. Soon the Seceder church was entrenched on the same spot, with a Reformed Presbyterian church not far away. For thirteen years a Free Presbyterian Church also flourished in Darlington. To this day Presbyterians, United Presbyterians, and Reformed Presbyterians all hold forth in that village, almost within hailing distance of one another. In New Alexandria for many years, the same three branches of Scottish Calvinists occupied three corners of the same street intersection.

So the story might go on and on. The fact is encountered too often to be ignored. If one leafs through the pages of Scouller or Glasgow, one discovers at least thirty-five places in the Upper Ohio Valley where both Seceders and Associate Reformed had churches. In twelve of these places, there was also a Covenanter church. In a considerable number of other communities, the Presbyterians had Covenanters and also either Seceders or Associate Reformed for neighbors. This was true in Utica, Ohio, where for years the Covenanter church was the strongest of the three.

In all this, there seldom was any open hostility. Yet there persisted for a long time the conviction on the part of each group that it was its sacred obligation to seek out, minister to, and hold in line all those whose religious inheritance lay within their particular tradition, whether the bequest be from Knox directly, or through Richard Cameron or Ebenezer Erskine. Driven by this conviction, John Cuthbertson made his many wearisome journeys from his home on Octorara, now into New England, now far down into the Carolinas, now out into Western Pennsylvania.[10] Some early missionaries of all these communions, including the Presbyterian, seemed convinced that they were sent only to the scattered sheep of their own household. They felt little obligation to the multitude of white pagans on the frontier who, after all, were evidently the majority. He who saved a psalm singer from those who had strayed away to Watts was reckoned to have covered a multitude of sins of omission.

This of course was not true of them all. There were in all these various churches of the Presbyterian family men like Joseph Patterson, Elisha Macurdy, and Joseph Badger, who were zealous seekers of lost men; like Robert McGarraugh, of whom Eaton reports that in one year he visited every family in Clarion County.[11] But it was sufficiently true to account for the taking over by the Methodists and Baptists of leadership in the winning of the West for Christ. They were not seeking out Methodists and Baptists, to gather them into Methodist and Baptist churches. Few such were to be found. They were seeking sinners, to win them for their Lord. In the beginning these Presbyterians of every shade of blue had greater prospects of growth than any other body, for the very great majority of such new settlers as brought a vital faith with them over the mountains were of their persuasion. This meant a trained skeleton army, ready to be mobilized for the winning of the pagans about them. But, alas, too much of the leaders' energies was spent in controversy and theological hairsplitting. Thus the initial advantage was soon lost.

Our founding fathers apparently did not take very seriously the efforts of these frontier circuit riders whose schooling was so much less complete than their own. Even David McClure writes in his *Journal* in a tone that is near to contempt: "A few illiterate preachers of the Baptist persuasion have preached about, zealous to make proselytes."[12] Yet Jones, Corbly, and the Suttons were far from being illiterate men.

Energy Expended in Controversy

The pioneer preachers of Presbyterian stock did take each other seriously, for they were all well-disciplined in theology. Therefore, each group was eager to defend its own peculiar tenets and practices, and to disparage those of its neighbors. This sometimes led to bitter debates, and to polemic pamphleteering. Samuel Ralston of Mingo several times broke into print concerning the mode of baptism and concerning Psalmody. So did John Rea of Beech Spring, and others. On the Seceder side, John Walker of Harrison County, Ohio, the moving spirit in the founding of Franklin College, wielded a well-sharpened quill, as did John Black, Sr., for the

Covenanters. Most scathing attacks were made in print by all of these and several more, against Alexander Campbell and his innovations in doctrine and practice; perhaps the more bitter because he had been raised in the Calvinistic tradition, and because the Associate Presbytery had refused to receive him as a licentiate.

Equally virulent were the thunderbolts hurled at uninspired hymns, or Evangelical Psalmody as it was variously called, by such men as Robert Reid, Associate Reformed pastor at Erie, principal of an academy there, and chaplain of Perry's fleet on the lake. The following is a sample chosen from his pamphlet, *The Seven Last Plagues,* issued in 1828. He asserts that "The Christian world is at this moment a mass of corruption," especially those of the "larger and popular sects." He goes on to declare that one, perhaps two, of the vials of the wrath of God are poured out on those who have introduced "human inventions in the worship of God." He charges that those who bring Watts' Gospel Psalms and Paraphrases into public worship are guilty of blasphemy. There is much more in a similar vein.[13]

In a pamphlet he published in reply to Dr. John Pressly's review of his earlier work on prophecy, Ralston thus refers to Reid with evident distaste: "Mr. Reid is also of opinion that the witnesses mean men pious and intelligent, but generally ministers of the Gospel who testified during the reign of the 'man of sin,' not only against the errors in doctrine and worship of the Church of Rome, but of the Protestant churches, many of whom he considers as bad if not worse than popery itself; that it is a moral and not literal slaying of the witnesses that is meant; that they have been slain by the multiplicity of human inventions in the worship of God."[14] Ralston mentions the fact that works had been published by John Anderson of Service, by John Walker of Harrison County, by Alexander Gordon (quoted in the *Christian Monitor*) and by John McMaster, in favor of the exclusive use of the Psalms of David in worship; and by Black, Latta, Freeman, Ruffner, and Baird in defense of Evangelical Psalmody.

Pressly in his review had complained that Ralston "has endeavored by sarcasm and wit to exhibit me to the public eye in a ridiculous point of light," and that his language was "not consistent with a Christian spirit." Ralston replies that "when a man offers as argument what is absurd and ridiculous, I know of no other way of answering it than by showing that it is ridiculous and absurd."[15] He concludes: "Notwithstanding he assails me when in a very feeble state of health, and has protracted the discussion beyond all reasonable bounds; and notwithstanding he has in the discussion endeavored to fix upon unsoundness in the faith, without a shadow of proof, and to exhibit us to the public eye as destitute of moral rectitude, we freely forgive him, and wish him well."

Perhaps enough has been quoted to convey some impression of the spirit in which these theological controversies of the early nineteenth century were conducted in this region. It seems to have lacked somewhat both in sweetness and light.

In 1820 John Anderson of Service published a book in dialogue form, entitled *Alexander and Rufus: Dialogues on Church Communion,* in which Rufus is evidently a Seceder and Alexander his Presbyterian neighbor. In this, too, there is much biting sarcasm, and not a little sophistry. Yet it is a very revealing picture of the points at issue between the two communions. Then, too, there is the famous Seceder Manifesto of 1802, signed by five of their ministers and printed in Washington, Pennsylvania, in which they denounced the great Falling-Work Revival as a work of the devil, and warned their people not to attend the meetings nor have anything to do with it.

On occasion even a presbytery felt impelled to action to protect its members from false accusations by members of other Presbyterian denominations. The following resolution was passed by the Presbytery of Ohio on April 20, 1808:

"The Presbytery being informed that Mr. Kerr, a member of the Associate Reformed Synod, did, when assisting Mr. Calderhead in the administration of the Sacrament of the Supper last fall, declare that some of the Presbyterian ministers were Arminians and Socinians, and exhort his hearers not to attend their ministrations; also that Mr. Kerr had been written to respecting the matter, and requested to name the persons who held such tenets, but that no answer had been received. The Presbytery thought it their duty to appoint Messrs. Patterson, Gwinn and McLain a committee to wait on Mr. Kerr, and request him to name the persons who were guilty of propagating such doctrines, that they may be called to account and censured agreeably to their desert. Said committee to report at the next meeting of Presbytery."[16]

This Mr. Kerr was the Reverend Joseph Kerr, at that time pastor of Mifflin and St. Clair Associate Reformed churches, and later a professor in the Allegheny Theological Seminary. Mr. Calderhead, in whose church he made the statements quoted, was the Reverend Alexander Calderhead, pastor of the Associate Reformed Church of Short Creek, Ohio. The Ohio Presbytery's committee had a fruitless task. Mr. Kerr repeatedly refused to tell against whom he made the charges. Finally he said he had heard two young men make these assertions against the Reverend John McMillan, whom they had heard preach. One of the two young men denied having said it. The Associate Reformed Presbytery refused to deal with the matter. After much mutual recrimination, Ohio Presbytery dropped the case. This is one of several instances in which one Calvinist tried to discredit another of a rival body.

The invasion of Western Pennsylvania and southeastern Ohio by the Cumberland Presbyterians in the two decades, 1830–1850, rallied all other kinds of Presbyterians to unite in opposition to the intruders. When the Reverend Jacob Lindley, a son of Upper Ten Mile Church and a former student under McMillan, and the first head of what was to become Ohio University, went over to the Cumberland fold, all our ministers were deeply shocked. Many things were said and done against him and against Cumberland Presbyterianism which are not easy to justify.

But when Alexander Campbell, professing to overcome all sectarian divisions of Protestantism, succeeded only in adding another—the first new denomination to arise in the Upper Ohio Valley, all four kinds of Presbyterians were for once united with Methodists, Baptists, and others in resisting his encroachments upon the flocks of them all, which in some localities were serious. Indeed, it would seem that their common opposition to the Campbellites, later to be known as the Disciples of Christ, was what first taught the other Christian bodies of this area to speak and act in harmony. Even then they did not learn it perfectly.

Presbyterian Denominations Differ Over Slavery

There is one other issue to be noted in which Covenanters, Seceders, and Associate Reformed presbyteries bore a united testimony on one side, while the Presbyterians, alas, were arrayed on the other, and that concerned slavery. The Covenanter witness against the buying, selling, and exploiting of human beings was very positive from the beginning; that of the Seceders almost equally so. After the separation of their southern Synod, members of which were deeply involved, the Associate Reformed Church moved up to the same level. The issue had come before the Reformed Presbytery (Covenanter) first in 1798, when their ministers in South Carolina had given a warning to slaveholding members. Two years later the Reverend Alexander McLeod refused a call to Coldenham, New York, because some of its members owned slaves. The Presbytery supported him and enacted, "without a dissenting voice" that no slaveholder should be allowed the Communion of the church.

A committee, consisting of the Reverend James McKinney and the Reverend Samuel B. Wylie, was appointed to journey to South Carolina with the message of this court that the Covenanters there must either emancipate their slaves or be refused the Communion of the church. The committee was no less surprised than delighted to find with what alacrity those concerned came forward and complied with the decree of Presbytery. In one day, in the small community of Covenanters at Rocky Creek, not less than three thousand guineas were sacrificed upon the altar of principle. The Reformed Presbyterian Church then and forever cleansed her hands of the guilt of human slavery.

In the Presbyterian church, however, the trend was in the opposite direction. In 1787 the Synod of New York and Philadelphia had spoken out against the evils of slavery. Again in 1793 the General Assembly had uttered protests against it. In 1818, under the leadership of Ashbel Green, the General Assembly had declared: "We consider the voluntary enslaving of one part of the human race by another, as a gross violation of the most precious and sacred rights of human nature, as utterly inconsistent with the law of God, which requires us to love our neighbor as ourselves, and totally irreconcilable with the spirit and principles of the Gospel of Christ." After that, there remained only the logical next step of barring slaveholders and slavery-defenders from the communion table. But that step was never taken, though the vote on that pronouncement of 1818 had been almost unanimous, even commissioners from the South being generally for it. Certainly there was not a dissenting voice raised by any commissioner from the Upper Ohio Valley.

But in the 1820's the economic and political power of the slaveholding interests began to be felt. Cotton was coming to its throne as king. All the missionary and benevolent causes of the church leaned heavily upon the South for support. Under such pressures the Presbyterian church began a moral retreat until finally, in 1845, the General Assembly flatly declared that slaveholding was no bar to Christian communion. The votes of protest against that action came largely from this area, and from other Ohio and Indiana presbyteries.

Two years later, men who had declined the jurisdiction of the General Assembly on account of this backward step formed themselves into the Free Presbyterian Church, which took exactly the same ground on slavery as that long held by the Covenanters and the others. Its presbyteries of Mahoning and central Ohio, both largely in the Upper Ohio Valley, included in the late 1850's more congregations than the Covenanters had in the same area. The Covenanter congregations numbered eighteen, while the Free Church had twenty-nine congregations. It is interesting to note that Associate, Associate Reformed, and Covenanter ministers sat in almost every Free Church presbytery meeting, as corresponding members.

However, the slavery issue drove much deeper the cleavage between the Presbyterians, both Old School and New, and their sister churches of Scottish origin. When Reverend Thomas Finney asked for a letter of dismission to the Free Presbytery of Mahoning, his Presbyterian Presbytery of Coshocton granted him only a certificate of "former good standing," but not "a letter of dismission to a Free Presbytery."[17] The answer to a similar request was: "We know of no such body as a part of the church of Christ." It is not surprising that when the Free Church was disbanded at the close of the Civil War, a considerable number of its ministers and congregations became United Presbyterians.

Co-operation in Community Causes

All we have so far lifted out of the ecclesiastical records shows only the dark side of a picture in which, as in Rembrandt's paintings, there are many high lights as well as many deep shadows. It is encouraging to note that, in what might be called their extracurricular relationships, these men of various shades of Presbyterian faith usually got along well together, and in some cases were warm friends. Matthew Henderson, the Seceder, and John McMillan, the Presbyterian, were neighbors both in Chester and in Washington counties. They worked together in many enterprises for the welfare of the frontier settlers. So close were they that McMillan is said to have composed the epitaph on Henderson's tombstone in the Oak Spring Cemetery at Canonsburg.

When the first Board of Trustees for Washington Academy was

chosen, John Corbly, the Baptist, and Matthew Henderson were among the number. On one of his earliest missionary journeys to the West, McMillan records in his *Journal* that he preached in a Baptist meetinghouse. Co-operation in other educational enterprises soon followed the pattern set by the Washington Academy. It is evident in the founding of Canonsburg Academy, Pittsburgh Academy, Allegheny College, and notably of Franklin and Muskingum colleges. Generally one denomination took the lead and invited others to join with them. We find no record of a refusal. In the case of the founding of Bethany College by Alexander Campbell, we have not been able to consult the records.

In the matter of granting the use of meetinghouses for services by another denomination, there seems to have been a more liberal attitude than one would expect. But this does not mean that a pastor would encourage his people to attend these services. "Occasional hearing," as it was called, was long under the ban. Many cases of discipline and church censure for it are found in the records. Presbyterians were repeatedly admonished not to go to Methodist camp meetings, though the Presbyterians had themselves initiated this form of evangelistic effort.

The earlier records contain scarcely any names of men, outside their own communion, who had been invited to sit as corresponding members of a presbytery or council or conference. The earliest we find is the name of Joseph Badger, Congregationalist, who was so invited by Ohio Presbytery in 1800. Less than three years later, he became a Presbyterian and a member of Erie Presbytery. Other Congregationalists from Marietta and Granville sat in Ohio and Lancaster presbyteries soon after. Not until 1845 do we find a minister of another Presbyterian communion so welcomed. The man then so trusted and honored was Dr. James R. Wilson, Covenanter.[18]

The first Methodist corresponding member was seated by Ohio Presbytery in 1860, though two years earlier the Methodists had invited Presbyterians to preach in their pulpits in Canonsburg during a meeting of Presbytery. Some other presbyteries may have shown a somewhat more fraternal spirit. In the first volume of the Steubenville records, there is only one reference to a corresponding member, and he was a Presbyterian. Reverend James Miller, an Associate Reformed Pastor, was invited to sit with Zanesville in 1847.[19] In 1850 that Presbytery showed the same courtesy to a Lutheran.[20] Richland Presbytery, as early as 1826, invited Henry Lonsdecker, a German Reformed missionary; and in 1838, Reverend James Johnston and others of the Associate Reformed communion sat with them.[21] After 1850 the practice seems to have become increasingly common in all our presbyteries. But it was nearly fifteen years after the division of 1837 before a New School man was found sitting in an Old School presbytery. The middle walls of partition did not fall quickly or easily. Perhaps an epoch in brotherhood was marked in 1847 when St. Clairsville Presbytery at one meeting invited ministers of the Associate Reformed, Methodist, and Baptist churches to sit side by side as corresponding members.[22]

There was considerable competition and rivalry while our Presbyterian fathers were laying the foundations of our church throughout the Upper Ohio Valley, just as there had been similar rivalry in Britain and on our eastern seaboard. The oneness of the body of Christ was to our fathers far less evident and important than rigid loyalty to an ironclad creed and covenant. The word "ecumenical" had not yet been coined. These rivalries undoubtedly set brakes upon the wheels of progress for the winning of the West. They consumed energies needed for the seeking of the unsaved. The fact that rivalry was so keenly felt and so ardently pursued among all these five branches of Presbyterians left others, notably the Methodists and the Baptists, ofttimes alone in a task too great even for forces enthusiastically allied. It is then not surprising that throughout the Middle West these two great communions far outrank in strength all the Presbyterian bodies that are so belatedly learning to love and trust each other.

CHAPTER VI Emphases in Worship

What really significant contributions to the general worship of the Presbyterian church may one expect to find in the religious development of the Upper Ohio Valley? Will not changes found be typical of those occurring generally throughout the young church in America?

Doubtless some similarity to practices elsewhere will be noted. Yet, as no worth-while painting can be completed until all parts of the canvas are carefully filled in proper perspective, so no satisfactory over-all view of the developing Church is possible without proper attention being given to so significant a component part as this. It should be remembered that the Upper Ohio Valley was the principal avenue of church expansion westward from the Atlantic seaboard with its Old World traditions and customs. What occurred here prefigured, rather than followed, the changes that occurred wherever the primitive frontier became literate and sophisticated.

Professor Frederick J. Turner, in his classic interpretation of the development of America in terms of the expanding frontier, said of this area—"from the beginning the Ohio Valley seems to have been a highway for migration, and the home of a culture of its own . . . there can be no more important region than the Ohio Valley . . . her place will depend upon the contribution which her people and her leaders make to the cause of an enlightened, a cultivated, a God-fearing, and a free democracy."[1]

Professor Turner further credits the leaders of the area with these special accomplishments of national significance: (1) breaking the attenuated line of French forts and control points in the New World; (2) developing the pattern of an individualistic and democratic approach to the problems of government, responsive to religious emotion; (3) the germ of the Monroe Doctrine; (4) the theory that men going into vacant lands have the right to shape their own political institutions there; (5) "preemption" laws and homestead agitation, leading to Henry Clay's "American System"; (6) the promotion of the free exercise of the franchise; and (7) the accomplishment of having held apart for a considerable time, as a stabilizing force, sectional conflicts.[2] Surely the reactions of a group with such positive beliefs and ingrained prejudices as these nineteenth century Scots, Irish, Reformed, and Huguenot colonists cannot be without some significance both in their adjustments in worship and also in meeting all their other problems throughout the expanding years from 1802 to 1870.

I. THE BEGINNING THEORY AND CUSTOM OF WORSHIP

The "Foundation Years" (before 1802) saw individuals and denominations in this area maintaining, with but little change, the customs of worship brought with them from Europe.[3] In the lonely wilderness there was an understandable nostalgia for the worship and familiar ordinances of the homeland. The relatively few individuals and homes that had not lost their religious faith on the frontier—Latourette has estimated that in 1800 only 6.9 per cent of the population had any church affiliation at all[4]—usually had a really deep regard for the religious traditions of their "mother" churches. So long as the home presbyteries in Britain and on the Continent ordained and sent out a considerable share of the area's ministers and teachers, and a considerable part of its sustaining funds, it was inevitable that the general patterns of worship here would be influenced, if not controlled, by the homelands. This was true especially among the creedal groups with fixed patterns of worship and historic directories like the "Westminster Standards" of the Presbyterians.

However, allowing for minor sectarian differences, and the influence of strong personalities like Luther, Calvin, Knox, and Erskine, most of the Protestant groups had a common characteristic—negative, if you will—which expressed itself in some form of strong reaction against the rigidity and the patronizing intolerance of the Medieval Church in all matters of worship and sacramental observances. Basically, Lutherans, Calvinists, Anglicans, and the Sects had a dislike for what their study of New Testament and post-Apostolic sources clearly indicated was an unwarranted departure from the original simplicity in worship of New Testament times.

They knew Pliny (111 A.D.) had mentioned "reading of the scripture, expounding of its text, open discussion, prayer, and singing," in private homes or places of meeting, as characteristic of the early Church's worship.[5] They were aware, too, of Justin Martyr's description of corporate worship (153 A.D.): "on Sundays there was a gathering of the local church, and the memoirs of the Apostles or writings of the Prophets were read, the admonition or exhortation to copy the noble lessons, the sending up of common prayers, the saluting of each other with a kiss, and the offering of the president of the group 'as best he can' prayers and thanksgivings for the privilege of communion and distribution to each of the elements."[6] They found no scriptural warrant for medieval monasticism, the Hierarchy, the canonical hours, the strictly prescribed forms for baptisms, weddings, churchings, funerals, and especially the rigid pattern of the Mass.

Even if these children of the Reformation in the wilderness of the New World had not already noted or had explained to them the shift of emphasis from the ancient Gallican, Syrian, Egyptian, and Old Roman Liturgies to the prevailing Mass form, they instinctively rebelled at the unwarranted limitations placed upon Paul's doctrine of Individual Liberty in all things including worship. Across lines of denomination they denounced the ecclesiasticism that regarded the commemoration of Jesus' death in the Lord's Supper as an "unbloody sacrifice" offered by priests who in its administration claimed to be "making God." Pronouncements like that of Urban II, that "the hands which have the supreme honor of creating the Creator should not be subject to temporal authority" were blasphemous to them and, they were convinced, opened the way for many of the abuses of Establishment from which they were escaping by coming to the New World.

The Presbyterians in general condemned lighted candles in the churches, crucifixes, stations of the cross, highly contrapuntal music, and services in a language not understood by the worshiper. They felt, as Wyclif, a Roman cleric himself at Oxford, expressed it centuries before, "would that so many ceremonies and symbols in our church were not multiplied . . . in a carnal sensuousness which with their human traditions have more weight than the things they signify."[7] So, in villages and countrysides, the colonists of all Protestant groups in the Upper Ohio area found rising above their differences the common bond of opposition to medieval formalism and hierarchical ritualism.

Dignified but Unadorned Forms of Worship

Professor Vernon Bartlet used to tell his students in Mansfield College that religious worship is the expression of the sense of "worth or honor" which is done the divine Nature, and that it will vary with whatever notion of God and man actually prevails. Judged by this standard the turn of the nineteenth century clearly marks a transition in the experience of the Presbyterians of the Upper Ohio. The relative plainness of their forms of worship and the comparative absence of emotion would suggest theirs was an unornate, if not an unattractive, form of worship, with but slight appeal to the aesthetic instincts. That this is true is evident from the fact that very seldom are the actual forms of services of worship even referred to in contemporary records.[8]

To be sure, the primitive local conditions prevailing put severe limits on the possible varieties of worship experience. Rude houses of worship with equally primitive furniture and equipment, scarcity of suitable songbooks, lack of lighting facilities, and suitable heating in the rigorous winters of the area created difficulties. Long distances to be traveled to reach places of worship, and the large proportion of members, even in the case of villages and small-town centers, who lived at considerable distance from the church accentuated a sense of depressing separateness not conducive to friendly freedom and relaxation in worship.

Moreover, the major emphasis of a Presbyterian service then was scarcely conducive to popular appeal.[9] The prominence of formal theology in sermons frequently controversial and disputatious; the length and dogmatic nature of the sermons; the long formal prayers; the rigid insistence in most instances upon the measured meters of Psalmody to the exclusion of the more responsive hymns of Watts; the rigid exercise of discipline in the service of public worship in which offenders were publicly rebuked and required to "give satisfaction": it is certainly conceivable that such worship services would seem grim and forbidding to people generally. Those who remembered, or had been told of, the dignified quietly appointed churches and vaulted cathedrals of Scotland, England, Ireland, and the Continent, of the homogenous communities, of the accessibility of the houses of worship to all the parishes, must have been led, like captive Judah of old, "to mourn when they remembered Zion."

It should not be assumed, however, that either pastors or congregations were unappreciative of propriety and beauty in worship. That all should be done "decently and in order" had been embodied in their standards since the Westminster Assembly. From the Highlands and St. Giles, from Lutterworth and Westminster, from the Palatinate and Geneva, elements of propriety and good taste had been united in the background and personal experience of these frontier folk. Many of their forebears were familiar with

Knox's "Book of Common Order." It had become possible for many of them to accept the provisions of the Westminster "Directory for Worship." The psalms in metrical version, paraphrases, doxologies and a few hymns had attained some usage, and, indeed, the Psalter had already been published on the Atlantic seaboard.

Presbyterians Most Numerous in This Area

Significantly, therefore, it must be noted that by the turn of the century, the Presbyterians had established themselves much more generally than any other denomination in the Upper Ohio area. According to a survey conducted by Schermerhorn, an agent of the Missionary Society of Connecticut (1814), there were approximately one hundred fifty Presbyterian congregations and societies in Western Pennsylvania alone.[10] Many of these were small, the largest seldom exceeding two hundred fifty members, and about one-third of them were without pastors. Schermerhorn includes Congregationalists, Associated Reform, Associate Synod, and Covenanters among these, commenting that "those minor considerations concerning the externals of religion which now separated them and which originated in causes generally not existing in this country do not appear of significant consequence in a missionary point of view to merit separate notice."

It has been estimated that, on an average of 150 members to a church, there were about 22,500 Presbyterians in Western Pennsylvania alone.[11] Schermerhorn estimates the Methodist to number 3,787, the Baptist about 2,000, the Roman Catholic about 1,000, the Quakers 600, and an undetermined number of Lutherans in Somerset, Fayette, and Westmoreland counties. Evidently the Presbyterian worship and discipline were not entirely forbidding to the frontier families.

It ought to be remembered that a relatively large percentage of pagans in a frontier civilization is not unique. Wherever there have been a marked shift of population and altered living conditions, prompted by the possibility of gain, as in the Southwest, California, Alaska, or presently areas of the South Pacific, thither come many adventurers, fugitives, antisocials, and congenital rebels. Moral and religious conditions are difficult. The Kingdom of God usually is of slow growth, from seed sown in patience and faith, not through arbitrary fiat of a government or religious group.

The quelling of the Whiskey Rebellion in this area was accomplished not by force of arms, but by the influence of Christian leadership and consciences. The creation of the strong antislavery atmosphere here was due not to political pressure from without or economic advantages within the group, but to the sensitive consciences of the people who comprised the area, the official boards, and the congregations of these earnest folk. If they quarreled among themselves and with other sects about seeming trivia, it is apparent from their recorded statements and common procedures that their many fearless and unified actions came only from well-informed consciences.

That the settlers hesitated to characterize their first primitive places of worship as "churches" is evident from allusions to them as, for example, "a meeting house on 'Longs Run,' 'Forks Meeting House,' 'Laurel Hill Meeting House,'" "preached at Hall's Meeting House to a crowded audience," etc.[12] These buildings were sometimes used for secular purposes but continued to be regarded as places of worship.

As the character of the church buildings was improved, the nature of the service was also modified. McMillan's first church at Chartiers (1778c) was made of logs. It was unheated and had no organ. In winter worshipers kept warm only by wearing additional clothing and using blankets. But the next church building (1800c) was erected from stone and had stoves for heating. The third building, erected in 1832c, was still more capacious and convenient in arrangement, and much more comfortable. The Pigeon Creek church buildings followed in general the same pattern. The first building was of logs, with clapboard roof and door. It was replaced by a stone building and later, in 1829, by a brick structure. Often the families supplied their own pews.[13] These two churches are probably typical of the development generally experienced in the Upper Ohio area.

Difficult as it is to obtain examples of a considerable number of customs of worship in the area during this period, those uncovered are probably sufficient to an understanding of them in the same sense that available instances of church architecture, or of the types of schools, academies, and colleges, or of the typical instances of social customs and industrial expansion have made it possible to re-create rather completely the pattern of development of other situations such as worship in the same areas.

Patterns of Worship Are Quite Similar

Obviously, in a geographic territory extending from the Allegheny and Monongahela rivers to the state of Indiana, there will appear simultaneously, even if in unrelated patterns, forms of worship that were typical in general, but that differed according to the size, physical location, and general accessibility of the individual parish. Indeed, it might be expected there would be found considerable variations in customs of worship even between congregations that might stand in the relationship of a group about a "mother" church. The original churches, of course, gave substance and leadership to new congregations in more remote areas, at the same time that they contributed items of equipment for administrative and sacramental use.

But, what is even more important, they gave their blessing to families and individuals who lived near to the new church and elected to attend it, but who nevertheless carried with them to it their familiarity with, and preference for, the mother church's customs and forms of worship. It has been noted, as a prevailing pattern of development, that there usually went along with the supply pastor one or more elders from a sponsoring church, who assisted in the organization of the new church and aided in administering the sacraments, effecting a stable organization of the new body, giving help in planning and erecting churches, determining the pattern to be followed in equipping the new sanctuaries for worship.

It seems that the spread of the church followed to a marked degree the familiar process of growth by cell division. There were the common characteristics of spirit, form, and idea, the similar spiritual food of which they partook, the psychological "genes" that determine congregational individuality and habit, and the energizing power of the Holy Spirit to carry the surge of expansion outward and westward. Yet, in almost every instance, the parent body remained itself growing and making adjustments to changing conditions, and continued for decades and indeed generations to be vital sources of strength for their own families, and encouragement for further expansion.

In a few instances, inspiration for the new congregations seems to have sprung from discordant and dissatisfied families within an older or central church, and occasionally from resentments and hostilities which stimulated the appearance of new peripheral groups. But it seems evident that in matters of congregational organization, evangelistic zeal, and customs of worship the newer congregations evidenced and embodied the same customs as the parent group.

It should not be assumed, however, that in all cases the appearance of additional churches in a town or area was because of factional disputes in older bodies. Minutes of sessions and presbyteries indicate on the contrary a strong desire to have services more convenient to new settlements, or indeed, new sections of a town, or extended communities. Just as presbyteries and synods recognized the needless limitation to effective work imposed by distance and inaccessibility of presbyters, so in the organizing of new churches, the same rules seemed to have obtained. As a result of this internal and external expansion, a confusion in patterns of worship is sometimes observed.

II. PREACHING

In this area at least, and among its rugged Calvinists, the sermon was regarded as the most important part of public worship. Upon the preachers rested the grave responsibility for both the moral tone of their communities and the arousing and inspiring of their individual membership. This required both authority and compassion. Standards of public and private morals had to be established and defended. Doctrine had to be expounded so as to persuade and satisfy the sternly conscientious, if not technically educated listeners, not only of those things relating to future rewards and punishments, but of those revealing Christ's atoning sacrifice for, and personal love of, folk struggling with the tremendous discouragements of the lonely frontier. Atheistic speakers and heretical books had to be dealt with publicly—no mean task at the beginning of the nineteenth century. All this demanded and produced great preachers.

Joseph Smith, a Typical Pioneer Preacher

As a striking example of the personalization of many of these qualities, consider one, perhaps not the greatest among a strong group of preachers and spiritual leaders—Dr. Joseph Smith. His name is associated, during his tragically brief ministry, with Upper Buffalo Church. There his mortal remains still rest in the churchyard under a stone which bears, as an inscription, the tribute uttered by another great preacher, Thaddeus Dod: "Zion trembled when this Pillar fell."[14]

Judge Edgar, one of his church elders, in a letter dated October 22, 1802, described Smith's effective preaching, and probably expressed as well the characteristic appreciation of his people, thus: "Many were under deep conviction of sin and danger . . . about fifty in each congregation were added to the church. The work increased for three years. At the sacrament in Cross Creek the power of God appeared bowing many. The people did not get away from the meeting house green until long after night, and came back on Tuesday. This was the most solemn day I had ever seen in the house of God. Yet there were not more than two or three instances of crying out loud."[15]

Joseph Smith was not a man of robust health. In person he was tall and slender, of fair complexion, with a slight cast of one eye. It is abundantly testified that there was a piercing brilliancy about his eyes when he became animated. His dress was always unusually neat. His voice was remarkable for a quality that was described as both "terrific" and "prophetic." "I never heard a man," said the Reverend Samuel Porter, "who could so completely unbar the gates of hell and make me look so far into the dark bottomless abyss; or like him could so throw open the gates of heaven and let me glance at the unsufferable brightness of the Great White Throne."[16]

Smith's Favorite Sermon Themes

His favorite subjects were the importance and necessity of regeneration, and the immediate necessity of faith in Jesus Christ. His manner of speaking was rather that of animated conversation. His sermons were usually written out and read, and yet he would often rise to an almost supernatural grandeur, seeming to extinguish in his hearers all consciousness of time and place.

Two persons of good minds and critical judgment who had often heard him, describe their experiences thus: "It (Smith's eloquence) was altogether different from Dr. McMillan's manner. McMillan was sometimes awfully solemn and impressive. But Mr. Smith's manner had a stronger power about it totally indescribable." Another wrote:

"Even if his sermons had been correctly taken down as they fell from his lips, they could not afterward be appreciated . . . because neither the stenographer or printer has any types by which to express his tones, his emphasis, his holy unction, the holy vitality of his soul . . . when he commenced, if his flight was upwards, he was immediately out of sight of the growling critic. Or when arrayed with divine and awful majesty he uncovered the bottomless and wide-extending pit of woe whose billows of fire are ever lashed into fury by the almighty breath of an incensed and slighted Saviour . . . the sinner lost his coat of mail and retreated in terror or fell prostrate."[17]

He is said never to have elaborated his sermons by logical syllogistic formulas. Every truth he presented had the force of an axiom, and proper conclusions were drawn by every listener.

His last sermon, preached when he was weak and worn out, is preserved. It was preached in the Cross Creek Church, on the text, "Though we, or an angel from heaven preach any other gospel than that which we have preached, let him be accursed." Gal.1:8 Evidently he had a premonition of the approaching end, for he took occasion from this text to give the congregation a summary sketch of his preaching among them. It was said he seemed to them as though he was about to go to the judgment seat of Christ. When the sermon was concluded, he had to be helped from the pulpit to his horse, and it was necessary for him to remain nearby for a day or two and finally to be conveyed home in a sled. His disease was what was then known as "inflammation of the brain" and his sufferings, though brief, were excruciating. So long as he could speak, it is said, it was in accents of triumph.

Joseph Smith was a preacher of the terrors of the law, and on this account he was often given the title, "hell-fire" Smith. The story is preserved that on one occasion, while on his way to a meeting of the General Assembly in the East, he stopped over the Sabbath in a congregation where vital religion was at a low ebb. The minister, having heard of Smith's style of preaching, intimated to him that he would be glad if he would give his people one of his more moderate sermons, as it would better suit their taste. Smith, after giving out an impressive hymn and offering an unusually fervent prayer, arose and began his sermon by shouting, "Fire! Fire! Fire!" "If the very mention of the word so startles you," he continued, "what will it be to encounter the reality?" "Who can dwell with everlasting burnings?" "This is my text." We are told he thereupon delivered one of his most stirring discourses, as a consequence of which there was a complete change in the spiritual views and ministerial labors of the pastor, and the beginning of a revival of religion in the community.[18]

On another occasion, while administering the Lord's Supper to a large congregation, in summertime in a grove adjoining the meetinghouse, he rose to deliver a closing address. A considerable number of the group, having many miles to travel to reach their homes and do their evening chores, began to leave the service, some walking, some untying their horses, others mounting and about to ride away. Smith raised his clear piercing voice and began —"One word to those who are retiring. We are told that when the Supper was celebrated for the first time, none retired from the place until it was all over but Judas. If there be any Judases here, let them go! But also let them remember that what they have heard and seen here will follow them to their homes and to hell, if they go there!" The effect, it is said, was like an electric shock. All with scarcely an exception returned to their seats and hung upon his words with fixed attention until the benediction was pronounced.

That Smith was a master as well of pastoral theology will be apparent from a charge intended to be given on the occasion of the ordination of a candidate, but which due to Smith's illness he sent to be read by another. Note only these sentences describing the responsibility of a preacher: "Such is the awfully important consequence of every sermon, of every sentence he delivers in the name of the eternal God that every man must . . . cry out with the Apostle Paul 'who is sufficient for these things': . . . what application of mind, what skill, what prudence, what tenderness, what care, what fortitude and courage does such a one need . . . we must be crying out, 'O that we could get free from the stupifying influence of sin and sloth, and keep our spirits deeply impressed with the dread importance of eternal things.' "

Mid-Nineteenth Century Preaching

But as one passes to preachers of the middle decades of the century, a change in emphasis is apparent. No longer is their first concern the "importance of eternal things," with what this accent meant to pioneers and isolated folk facing the rigors and discouragements of the frontier. Now a new note is evident. Men must be saved from their sins, but at the same time challenged to serve Christ in the affairs of everyday living. Now they have more time on their hands, more social contacts, more books and newspapers, more knowledge of the larger world with its social and moral problems, and more temptation to pursue the technicalities of controversy. Consequently differences, many of them grievously deep, appear and the tendency to fall into cliques, rivalries, and general attitudes of intolerance becomes apparent. Preachers tend to become known, not as evangelists or soul winners, but as protagonists of some individual or eccentric view or emphasis.

It is, of course, inevitable that preaching, if it is to be timely, should be cognizant of the current conditions under which the hearer lives and the special problems he faces. Even strict scriptural exposition must be addressed to man's needs. Therefore, there came to be an era of controversy in which it seemed necessary to justify views held or enlist hearers in crusades. The so-called "ad hominem" principle appears with a vengeance, and the listener may be assumed to be asking, like Hamlet, "The concernancy, sir?"[19]

Among the controversies or new interests of the period, these are emphasized: the New School–Old School theological controversy, with its tragically divisive consequences in so many communities and presbyteries; deep-seated differences as to the educational requirements for ordination to the ministry, erupting in the detachment of the Cumberland Synod; the ominous division over slavery soon to split the church politically and geographically; heated arguments between members of the Presbyterian family, usually about worship procedures; running and vitriolic controversies with local Roman Catholics; the moral issues involved in voting or of holding office in a government that refused to be identified as "Christian"; the evils of gambling, betting, horse racing; support of immorality by attendance at the theater; public and promiscuous dancing; increasing nonobservance of the Lord's Day; the sale and use of alcoholic liquor. And, among the new extra-parish interests, appear emphasis upon the need for better educational facilities resulting in a veritable rash of academies, institutes, small colleges, and of additional theological seminaries, all with their demands on individuals and parishes for financial support and moral sanction. Finally, there developed at the pulpit and parish level an interest in *foreign* missions.

Obviously it is impossible to select one among the protagonists of so many views or challenging interests who would excel all the others in all of them. Few communities were without a distinguished leader in at least one of these fields, and some of them achieved fame not only Presbytery- or Synod-wise, but also by the General Assembly, and by the press and political opinion of the nation. But for our present purposes let us consider Dr. Elisha Pope Swift, of honored memory.

Elisha Swift's Pulpit Power

Dr. Swift is generally regarded as one of the really great men of the middle decades in this entire Upper Ohio area, both because of his remarkable abilities and because of the special causes he espoused and to which he gave his talents. He was, to be sure, the recognized founder of the Church's great Board of Foreign Missions. He was a leader in the entire life of this western area and a greatly loved pastor and parish administrator. In a rather remarkable way he possessed the qualifications of a great preacher as well.

Space does not allow an extended review of his birth, early life, and his work prior to the time he came to this area.[20] His immediate familiarity with the problems of the church as a son of the manse is apparent. His early efforts to support himself by teaching, as a clerk, and as a printer's employee all contributed to his poise, his well-rounded personality, and his good judgment. It is worth noting that it was during his student days at Williams College that he felt the call to the ministry and identified himself there with religious activities on and off the campus. Later, while attending Princeton Seminary, he became interested in the newly opening field of Foreign Missions, an interest he was never to lose.

It became his good fortune to know Adoniram Judson, Morrison, and others who were becoming world figures. He caught their enthusiasm which enabled him, like them, to disarm criticisms and to answer the arguments of those who urged that this area was in itself a proper exercise in missionary effort. He set his heart on going himself to the foreign field, but resources at the disposal of the Commission (Board) did not permit it. The serious and extended illness of his wife's mother complicated matters. But the Commission was quick to sense his great enthusiasm and unusual talents, and they retained him to labor as an itinerant representative, during which he visited Pennsylvania, Ohio, Kentucky, and Virginia.

In this capacity he came first to Pittsburgh where the congregation of the Second Church immediately began overtures to secure him as their pastor. In acquiescence to what he believed to be the leading of God's spirit, he accepted. In 1818 he began a ministry that in various forms was to continue until his death, April 3, 1865, just as the Civil War was ending.

That he was a really great preacher we cannot attempt at great length to establish. During his first pastorate, he carried on a schedule of activities that covered almost every night of every week. He allowed himself only five hours sleep daily, spending most of the remaining hours in study. It was said he preached more sermons and delivered more addresses for special causes than any other minister who ever lived in Pittsburgh. Though he was an excellent extemporaneous speaker and delivered many of his most effective addresses without the opportunity of previous preparation, he faithfully prepared his sermons, writing them out, his son states, in full. He preached without any notes or even an outline of his sermon, fixing the entire message in his mind verbatim by memorization. It has been said that his power as a preacher lay first, in the earnestness and sincerity with which he spoke, springing from his complete belief in and dedication to his task; second, in the positiveness and vigor of his presentation; third, in his finished style and literary excellence; and fourth, that he seems to have been one of those men, like Dr. James H. Snowden and Dr. Augustus H. Strong, who seemed to have all literature and history at his finger tips.

Dr. S. J. Wilson, who delivered his funeral address, said, "He was Websterian in the massiveness of his thoughts, in the sublimity of his conceptions, and in the grandeur of his diction." He was straight, tall, and slender with a large head and broad forehead, and his eyes, strangely like Joseph Smith's, seemed to seize and hold the attention of his hearers. It was commonly said he was the outstanding preacher of the area.

Reverend Richard Lea preserves for us the conversation of a group of actors who, over the week end in Pittsburgh, had gone to hear him preach. One said, "I would give a thousand dollars if I could move upon the stage as he walks up that aisle." "That voice," said the second, "would persuade me to be a Christian if I heard it long." And the third remarked, "I saw nothing but his eyes. He is all eye."

Assuming that it has been established Dr. Swift was a great preacher in his own right, let us close this regrettably brief résumé of one who was so great, and about whom there is so great an abundance of material one cannot even choose wisely, by noting that, unlike the preachers of the first decades of our period, Dr. Swift's versatility lay in dealing effectively with a number of subjects. The extent to which he drew his materials and developed his interest from things that were happening about him, appears to be characteristic of the era. In this respect he seems to differ from his immediate contemporaries chiefly in the extent and variety of that interest. He was the excellent prototype of all the others.

To be a preacher of the everlasting Gospel, but to interpret it in terms of a great enthusiasm for Foreign Missions; to follow in the steps of the Great Teacher, and also be a founder and loved teacher of the Western Theological Seminary for young preachers; to preach to the inspiring of young people to obtain a better education for the enrichment and usefulness of their lives, and at the same time be himself one of five teachers who comprised the first faculty of what is now the University of Pittsburgh; to return after an interlude of two and one-half years as Secretary of the Board of Foreign Missions, for which service he had resigned his pastorate at the Second Church, to again become a pastor in the same area in the First Presbyterian Church of Allegheny, and to serve for thirty years in that pulpit and there to end his ministry and his life: these must be marks of a great preacher, and of the change in preaching from the chiefly evangelistic emphasis, to the many-sided challenge of an age of controversy and new approach.

Later Preaching Emphases

As the previous period ended with the years immediately following the Civil War, culminating in the happy reunion of the Old and New School groups which significantly occurred in the heart of the Upper Ohio region, there began to appear evidences of yet another emphasis in preaching, one seemingly more characteristic of the entire church and not chiefly representative of the vigorous Calvinism of this area.

It found its expression not especially in evangelistic preaching, though preachers seem not to have avoided evangelism. Indeed, this age produced great preachers and evangelists who had all the fervor of Smith, McMillan, Power, and Dod. Nor was the emphasis of preaching conditioned so frequently as in the mid-century decades by expanding concepts, innovations, and multiform controversies, although these preachers by no means proclaimed a limited Gospel or evaded the challenge of moral and social evils.

The preachers of the later years in our period came to think and preach in terms of a general pastoral approach. Men and women at the local church level were organized and given responsibilities. Sectarian controversy was replaced by an apparent desire to live and let live—or at least to respect each other's opinions, if not to co-operate freely. Despite the tragic political consequences of the Civil War, there was accomplished the technical liberation of the slaves and the organization of numerous schools and colleges for colored people. The perennial challenge of vice, corruption, and questionable amusements, against which the preacher formerly had to lift his voice almost alone, became now the concern of the Church as a whole, and of entire communities and congregations.

Numerous good books, magazines, publications, tracts, and biblical materials became available to, and were read by, families. Preachers became less regarded as the only educated persons in a community or as lone paragons of social and cultural graces. Unless he chose to do so, the preacher no longer found it necessary to address his message to any special group or class of people in his community. Exercising good judgment and taste, and with sufficient evidences of diligence, modesty, and sincerity, the preachers of this period seem to have become increasingly free to preach as the Holy Spirit constrained them and the expanding work challenged them.

III. PSALMODY

For those who incline to view this period superficially, the mere mention of Psalmody suggests petty rivalries, bitter controversies at the congregational level, and dogmatism about most of the details of church worship, particularly its music. Nothing could be further from the truth. These pioneers and the founding fathers of our local churches took everything about religion seriously, and attached to each part of the service a significance largely lost to us.

On the frontiers the passive broadmindedness and convenient rationalizations that undermine zeal and breed polite cynicism had not vitiated either the individual faith or the ideals of a worship service.

If the pioneer pastors and congregations differed vigorously—or even violently—among themselves about the use of music in worship, it was because the question involved the text, and inferentially the authority, of the Bible, or the venerated traditions of the homelands, or the inviolate principles laid down by the Reformation. What they sang was an expression not of their aesthetic appreciation, but of their Faith. One may disagree with them or criticize their methods, but not patronizingly laugh at them.

Using the term Psalmody here to include both the general use of music in church worship, and also the more specific use of the Psalms in various versions as the actual body of music used, it is found that the many aspects of this broad subject would be a fascinating study in themselves, but of course impossible within the limits of this chapter.

Do not assume their services of worship were monotonous because of a lack of music in quantity such as is now common. From all sources extant we learn these people loved to sing. Dour though they might be in some respects, they were not so when they lifted their hearts and voices in worship. Under the open skies, the singing at the "tent" services seemed to have impressed even cynical observers. When these outdoor services gave place to small meetinghouses and more pretentious churches, these Scots and Scotch-Irish still were known as impressive singers.

Three aspects of this part of worship were both its strength and weakness:

(1) the prolonged controversy over the sole use of Psalms and which version to use;

(2) the prevailing spirit of reaction against innovation in methods of public worship;

(3) the emergence of an unsurpassed hymnbook for the musical service of worship.

Rous's or Watts's Version of Psalms

A scarcity of psalters, hymnals, and songbooks in many congregations was further aggravated by the question as to what books to buy. Fortunately, as we shall see later, this deficiency proved to be not an unmixed evil, due to the unique contribution the precentors made through the method of singing used. But for a long while there was neither an approved nor recommended book. Each congregation found it necessary literally to fight out within itself the final choice. For instance, the Synod of New York and Philadelphia, in 1763, side-stepped a request for a recommendation by stating that as a great number of the members of the Synod "had never particularly considered Dr. Watts's imitation, they are not prepared to give a full answer to the question . . . and the Synod have no objection to the use of said imitation by such ministers and congregations as inclined to use it."[21]

The next year the Synod declared itself still "not prepared to give a final answer thereto." Two years later it declared, "they look on the inspired Psalms in Scripture to be the proper matter to be sung in divine worship . . . yet will not forbid those to use the imitation of them whose judgment and inclination lead them to do so."[22] Eight years later they still did not express a judgment but instead appointed a committee. Twelve years later (1785) another committee was appointed. Two years later "the Synod did allow, and do hereby allow, that Dr. Watts's imitation of David's psalms, as revised by Mr. Barlow, be sung in the churches and families under their care."

But *Rous's Version* was most preferred and most generally used. Sometimes *Rous's Version* was used on the Sabbath days and Watts's psalms and hymns at prayer meetings (possibly giving rise to the custom even today of using the Hymnal for the Sabbath church service and a collection of gospel songs for the midweek service). There is a tradition that at a service of Mr. Dod's on Ten Mile, a Mr. Porter, hearing the group sing "Let Those Refuse to Sing Who Never Knew Our God," joined with them and afterwards was heard to remark, "If my conscience won't let me sing, I'll wring its neck."[23]

The fact remained, however, that books were hard to obtain. On occasion an affluent member of the congregation would for the sake of uniformity purchase enough books for the church.[24] But families ordinarily secured them wherever available and carried them, as did the children their schoolbooks, to the services. And, of course, whatever the edition or version, both the words and the tunes in most instances of the most desirable songs would somewhere be included. A harmonious solution of the difficulty usually depended on the absence of personal prejudices of the minister, the attitude of the Session, or the personality and guidance of the precentor.

While Luther's hymns were, for the most part, subjective and quasi-mystical, these psalms and paraphases were strictly objective. Their casting into metrical and rhyming patterns led in many instances to awkward grammatical construction and frequent ambiguity. But to the worshipers who used them, they were the text of the Holy Bible and less prone to human error than subjective hymns.

Numerous Versions

Julian in his *Dictionary of Hymnology* states there have been three hundred and twenty-six publications of the complete Psalter, beginning with Clement Marot's collection (in French) of thirty-nine psalms, which was published in 1537 at the court of Francis I, and running through translations into other languages and in publications like Coverdale's collection of thirteen (1538), George Buchanan's (1548), Sternhold's of thirty-seven (1549), the Hopkins edition of Sternhold's known as the John Day book (1563) which contained all the psalms, other metrical arrangements, the Creed, the Ten Commandments, and other ancient hymns.

But these colonists knew best the *Rous Version* translated by Francis Rous, a Presbyterian layman and lawyer. In 1643 his version was published with the approval of the Westminster Assembly. The Scots revised it and finally published it in 1650. It was the standard Psalter for two hundred years. Later, however, was the Tate and Brady version (1696) which was adopted by the Church of England and later by the Protestant Episcopal Church in the United States.

The first book printed on the American continent was a psalmbook known as the *Bay Psalmist*, and later on as the *New England Version*. Also there had been published an arrangement in Holland by the English refugees (1614) known as the *Ainsworth Version*, brought to the New World by the Pilgrims. Also, omitting a few others that might be mentioned, Dr. Timothy Dwight's *Version of Watts*.

When the controversies of the early period in this area about what music to sing are referred to, they are therefore between the *Rous Version* and the Watts's or Watts's-Dwight version.[25] The later arguments were between the sole use of Psalms and the additional use of Hymns by Watts, Doddridge, Wesley, Toplady, etc. This remained—and still remains—a basic ground of difference between the Presbyterians of our area and the Reformed Presbyterian and Covenanting Brethren. In 1756 disaffected persons in the Synod of New York, angry because the Synod refused to condemn the use of Watts, withdrew and organized a "Scotch Church" which was taken under the care of the Associate Presbytery. Between our General Assembly and other Presbyterian bodies, except the Cumberland Presbyterians, the breach was made complete. The use of uninspired hymns was made a ground for refusing communion to worshipers. Until 1831 Dr. Dwight's *Psalms and Hymns* remained the only book the churches of the General Assembly were permitted to substitute for the Scottish Psalter.

How acute was the problem of which version to use is apparent in a typical illustration. The Spruce Creek Church, while the Reverend J. White was pastor (1845–1847), was arguing rather bitterly as to whether to use the General Assembly's Book of *Psalms and Hymns* or the *Rous Version.* All but two of the Session of eight were in favor of *Rous's Version.* Fifty-eight members petitioned the Session to bring the matter before the congregation. The resulting vote was forty-seven to thirty-seven in favor of the Assembly Book. The Session thereupon requested the Presbytery to send a commission to inquire into the matter. The Presbytery, after considerable discussion, deemed it expedient to divide the congregation, declaring the majority to be the original or First Church of Spruce Creek, and the minority to become the Second Church. A subsequent effort to reconcile the churches by using both books only re-opened the controversy. The Second Church was finally disbanded and its members, forty in number, came back into the First Church by certificate.

Congregational Singing Led by Precentor

Any innovation in the manner of conducting the musical service also aroused reactionary resentment in many churches. Until organs and choirs became available, the musical worship was led by either one or two precentors whose responsibility it was to read the lines of the psalm or hymn, give the proper pitch for the beginning of the melody, and lead the singing of each line while sustaining the pitch and tempo. For this he had a pitch pipe or tuning fork. One gathers from many references that he was usually successful in giving his pitch, though occasionally the tune appears to have been pitched too high to the embarrassment of many and the amusement of the less serious.

In most cases the precentor was the most experienced and best-trained leader available, sometimes possessing musical qualities while lacking others ordinarily considered requisite. The First Church of Pittsburgh secured, about 1804, as its precentor a tavern keeper named Reed who seems to have been both efficient and held in popular respect. However, he also appears to have been an individualist or innovator, for he began a practice of "lining out" two lines of a hymn instead of one at a time. This departure, and dissatisfaction with his business were, it seems, among the grounds for the withdrawal of some of its members to establish the Second Church.[26]

In many communities, the precentor, necessarily otherwise gainfully employed, would organize and conduct for a small enrollment fee "singing schools" which greatly assisted in familiarizing people with music, in teaching them to read music in its primitive notation and arrangement, and in providing, in addition, suitable social contacts often lacking in isolated communities and towns. How emotional and hauntingly sentimental the character of the music was is apparent on examining the books used, and on remembering the character of the pre-Civil War and postwar songs.

In the early decades of our period, services usually began, as did Dr. John McMillan's, by the minister reverently ascending the pulpit and calling the congregation to worship by an expression like "Let us worship God."[27] Thereupon the people would stand and sing "Old Hundredth." Then the Scriptures were read and Prayer (often very long) was offered. The record of the McClellandtown Church reveals that men and women occupied separate sides of the church, with obvious possibilities for antiphonal singing, whether or not they were used. In this church, also, "the clerk stood meekly in front of the pulpit ready to start the meter and line out the hymns. The minister read the first two lines and then handed the book over the pulpit and down to the clerk who then started the music and did the rest of the lining out"—another indication, incidentally, of the scarcity of books.

Musical Instruments Resented

Sometimes the reaction to innovations was violent. Occasionally even now a home will be found in which is preserved a piece of organ salvaged on a Sunday after having been hurled into the family pew during the smashing of the organ the preceding week by an irate objector to the use of an instrument in worship. This temptation to violence was in no way limited to small isolated churches.

During Dr. Francis Herron's pastorate at the First Church of Pittsburgh, a bass viol was surreptitiously introduced into the choir loft and played when the choir was singing. One of the objectors to "unholy" instruments in the worship of God appears through ignorance to have been quite contented until on a certain Sunday, when the viol player either essayed a passage alone or missed a cue and found himself a soloist. Instantly the belligerent worshiper leaped from his pew and headed for the choir loft. A more pacific neighbor grasped him as he passed and asked him where he was going. "To the gallery," he replied, "to smash that fiddle." "Sit down, Tom," his friend replied, "it has been playing there a month and has never hurt us."[28] The objector, we are told, subsided.

It was suggested above that there may have been definite benefits resulting from precentor-led congregational singing and the lack of hymnbooks. Old people, within the memory of some of us who are ourselves along in years, used to quote at great length from the metrical versions of the Psalms and from great hymns of the church. For personal comfort, for neighborly consolation, for spiritual exercises, and for experience in religious fellowship, these older folk seemed to have an almost limitless supply of great church music from which to draw. Obviously the phraseology of the metrical version could not be learned from the prose text of the Psalms, nor could the hymns be memorized from nonexistent hymnals. Moreover, many of those most expert in quoting could not have done so from study because they could not read well enough to permit it.

How came it then that they knew and quoted so freely? We believe that, just as almost every boy and girl mastered the Shorter Catechism not by reading it but by hearing it read to them and repeating it by rote, so the frequent repetition of the words of the metrical versions and of hymns by the precentor's "lining them out" and then singing them together, line by line, resulted in thousands of people, otherwise slow at reading and writing, being able to quote the words and sing the melodies of much of the church music. If the method seems tedious and repetitive to us, it at least lent itself to the psychology of memorization. The positive spirit and enthusiasm of the singing of these frontier people—which has been so frequently commented upon by contemporaries—was probably due to the fact that they did not have to bury their noses in books as they sang.

Preparation of the Hymnal

Out of these somewhat primitive and often eccentric congregational practices, there emerged, through the offices of the General Assembly, a Hymnal which most Presbyterians believe is unsurpassed, if indeed equaled, by that of any other denomination in this area and the church at large.

When a committee of the General Assembly reported in 1830 that "Psalmody in all ages has been considered a most important part of the worship of God," all Presbyterian bodies—Presbyterian, Covenanters, Associate, and Associate Reformed—used principally *Rous's Version,* although by this time some innovations had appeared. It is a matter of record, however, that in 1787, two years before the organization of the General Assembly, ministers and churches were "cautioned to be charitable toward those who also used Watts's *Imitation of David's Psalms.*" This Assembly also allowed the use of Dr. Timothy Dwight's revision of Watts's Psalms and a selection of hymns chosen by Dwight. As a result of the bitterness and controversy arising from these permissive actions, the Assembly of 1820 appointed a committee to "digest and prepare a uniform book of Psalmody."

From this study the Assembly of 1830 approved *The Book of Psalms and Hymns.* An immediate effect of this compromise action was to hasten the withdrawal of many Presbyterian churches throughout the entire Upper Ohio area, and their union in most cases with the Associated Reformed Presbytery. It became one of the occasions that fanned the flames of controversy with the New England Congregationalists, ending in the division of 1837. But in any case, after the separation of 1837, the Assembly of 1838 ordered another revision which excluded evidences of the New England heresy, either expressed or implied, in the hymns adopted. This revision, when finally approved by the Assembly of 1843, was generally regarded as a great improvement over previous books. But it had one other improvement that radically influenced congregational singing: It provided "that appropriate music be appended to such portion of the edition of the said Book of Psalmody as may appear expedient to the Board of Publication."

This is the official beginning of the printing of the words and music together. Local congregations for many years had exercised the right of combining hymns and tunes as they locally preferred by singing the words of a hymn or psalm to a tune printed in the book in connection with other words. This necessitated holding the book open at both places and referring back and forth between them to the accompaniment of considerable rustling and waving of pages. Subsequently there was published a book with divided pages, such as is still in use in some of the Scottish churches, in which words and tunes can be matched.

This book was revised by the Assembly of 1866, and appendices were added containing the Ten Commandments, the Apostles' Creed, the Lord's Prayer, the Shorter Catechism, and the Directory for Worship. It was called *The Hymnal* and immediately became the target of protracted criticism. The *Presbyterian Banner* of January 31, 1866, after approving the format and general appearance of the book, remarked, "But we might as well say at once that we are not satisfied with the name. The word 'Hymnal' seems to us unmeaning, inappropriate, and finical. It has nothing in its past history or association to recommend it as a title for such a book.

This name is peculiarly objectionable in this region, especially as it conveys the idea of the entire absence of what are commonly known as 'The Psalms.' Far better would it have been to have adopted the name of the tune book published by our Board some years ago, and to have called it 'The Presbyterian Psalmodist.'"[29] Truly these Presbyterians could be at times a cantankerous lot!

The revision of 1874, following the happy reunion of 1870 (which actually marks the limit of our present study), was an excellent book receiving general approval for its usability, excellent taste, and thorough scholarship. The hortatory and didactic Psalms were in the main excluded, except for those whose associations were so strong in many hearts that it would have seemed an act of violence to have excluded them.[30] The remainder of the selections were from generally acceptable Psalms, and from recent and favorably received hymns.

From the precentor-led tent services to the well-ordered congregational singing from adequate and very acceptable hymnbooks is indeed marked advance. It is a significant symbol, also, of far-reaching changes that have occurred in worship generally during this period in the Upper Ohio area.

The Communion Service

By 1802 the theological bases upon which the theory of the sacraments rests had been fairly well agreed upon by the Presbyterians of the Upper Ohio Valley. To be sure there were other tragic divisions in which theology played a part and which will be reviewed somewhat in detail in Chapter x. But, aside from the action the Campbellites (later The Disciples of Christ) took to limit baptism to those alone who made a personal confession of faith in Jesus Christ and publicly expressed repentance for their sins, and also this same group's observance of the Lord's Supper every Sunday, only one controversy was related closely to the sacraments.

This controversy, which for a time seemed to call into question as well the prevailing theory of what the Church is, had as its most capable and widely known protagonist, the Reverend Dr. John W. Nevin, an instructor for a decade at Western Theological Seminary. The movement became associated with Mercersburg Theological Seminary—whither Nevin had gone from Western—and did imply a change in sacramental theory that caused considerable uneasiness in both the New School and Old School groups.[31] It can now be seen that the movement in this area was chiefly a local reaction towards ritualism and high church ecclesiasticism that was appearing across the Atlantic in Anglicanism, Roman Catholicism, Lutheranism, and Eastern Orthodoxy. Nevin was personally influenced by Newman and Wilberforce. In turn, he sought to influence the teachers and church leaders of this area to adopt, or at least to sympathize with, the somewhat reactionary spirit that was becoming evident against accepted Protestant tradition.

Nevin, and other proponents of his views, took exception to the prevailing theory of the nature of the sacraments, especially the Lord's Supper. At that time the usual position held was that the Supper was a symbolical and spiritualized partaking of Christ's Body and Blood, what was an approach towards Zwingli's position, rather than Calvin's or Luther's original ground. Nevin's theory of a more literal presence of the Body and Blood in the sacramental elements necessitated a modification in the thinking of the Church about its own nature, its authority, and its prerogatives.

Nevin frankly admitted this, for he wrote, "Our view of the Lord's Supper must ever rule and condition in the end our view of Christ's person, and the conception we form of the Church."[32] His position was a reversion to the high church concept of both worship and the Church. It had but little influence upon the clergy and churches in the Upper Ohio area, and in general, passed soon from the center of attention.

Administering the Lord's Supper

Other than the implications of the Mercersburg Theology on worship, Presbyterian churches in the Upper Ohio area, during the first six decades of the nineteenth century, were more concerned with the administration, rather than the theory, of the sacraments.[33] After congregations moved indoors from the "tents" and groves, actual administration of the Lord's Supper appears to have followed this general pattern. Tables (with naturally a limited capacity) were used for seating the communicants. From somewhere snowy linen was provided. The congregation partook of both elements. The bread was either such as was used daily in the homes and baked by some favored housewife, or a sweetened cookie dough cut into strips or squares suitable for sacramental use. So far as can be ascertained, unleavened bread was seldom used, and almost never any form that would suggest the pattern of the Roman Service.

The fact that many churches from present-day Scotland use ordinary table bread, from which the communicant breaks a small portion of a slice before passing it to his neighbor, seems to suggest that possibly those congregations in which plain bread was used may have been of Scottish background. Perhaps additional light will be thrown on this by future research. On the strength of the preference of families from France, Germany, and Holland for cookies and kuchen of various sorts, it may have been that these worshipers preferred the sweetened form of element.

As regards the wine, most congregations seem to have used the fermented sort. In most instances it was port. Exceptions appear among the Covenanter, Reformed, and Associate groups who consistently maintained that an alcoholic beverage, which might prove a temptation or stumbling block to one fighting an appetite for intoxicants, ought not be used in a religious service. If the unfermented form was used, again a housewife provided it either out of her own larder of canned fruits and juices or from a supply which was specifically provided in jars for communion purposes. Older persons recall instances of both methods being used.

As regards the actual serving, it was sometimes the custom, when communicants no longer seated themselves at the tables but remained in the pews, to request those wishing to participate to occupy certain pews, or one side of a sanctuary. This facilitated the serving of the elements, and also provided an alternative place where those, for any reason not partaking, might remain indoors until the close of the service. However, it seems that during clement weather many left the sanctuary and waited outside.

It should perhaps also be remembered that the Lord's Supper was not frequently administered. In many cases it was but twice a year, and preferably in spring and autumn when the weather might be expected to be favorable. Also it is a fact that the service was usually long both because of the serving at tables and the customary use of a limited number of goblets, and because of the retaining in the order of worship of the usual sermon. Sometimes, also, there was a closing exhortation that was somewhat protracted, as in the case of Dr. Joseph Smith's service above.

Tokens and Fencing the Tables

Two specific customs remain to be mentioned, both of which have all but disappeared from the local area: "fencing the tables" and the use of "tokens." When congregations were widely scattered and members had to come from considerable distances, services were often held on preceding Thursdays, Fridays, and Saturdays, as well as on the Communion Sabbath. The homes of those residing nearby were then thrown open for entertainment of more distant friends. Only those persons necessary to do the "chores" remained at home, or "commuted" on foot or horseback. As towns and more densely populated areas developed, the hindrance of distance was not a considerable factor and these services could be held in the evenings. Time was therefore available, either at a previous service or in connection with the Supper, for special admonition or warning based upon the injunction, "Let a man examine himself . . . for he that eateth and drinketh unworthily, eateth and drinketh damnation to himself."

As a means of assisting in this self-analysis, the minister usually delivered an extended and often dramatic exposé of sins to be repented of, and for which forgiveness ought to be sought.[34] We are told that wise ministers always included themselves in the categories presented (as would be indeed meet!) when they led worshipers to the throne of Grace. It does not appear, however, that these meetings became "testimony" services abounding in personal experiences. But they were doubtless very effective in stirring people from complacency and smugness. This was the custom of "fencing the tables." Probably it is the antecedent of the present "Preparatory Service," still deemed desirable in many churches.

Historically, it should be remembered that during the Middle Ages there was propounded to catechumens a specific list of dangerous and common sins, as they were being received into the church, and that standing before the altar and in the presence of the people, they were required to state after each sin after it was named and commented upon, "I do renounce it." Our fathers evidently believed one could best appreciate the scope of God's forgiveness when he was reminded specifically of "the pit from which he had been drawn."

The other custom—still in use in some British churches—was the use of "tokens."[35] Primarily these were distributed to members of the congregation at a preparatory service for presentation at the Communion Service and were an evidence that the person was in good standing and qualified to participate in the sacrament. Indifferent or unworthy persons were thereby automatically excluded until they had given "satisfaction" to the Session that they were worthy to share in the sacrament.

In the case of visitors or strangers, the tokens were not given until they had identified themselves and given evidence of their standing and worthiness. If this custom seemed to emphasize exclusiveness and nonfraternity, and perhaps in some instances it could have been so exercised, it was an effective means of reminding members that belonging to and claiming the privileges of the church entailed definite standards of belief and conduct.

CHAPTER VII Westward Ho!

Ever westward journeyed the Presbyterian pioneer pastors as they determined to claim for Christ the rapidly moving western frontier. There were no clear boundaries on the west to limit the territorial responsibilities of the creators of our American civilization as Presbyterian migrants and refugees sought, on the shores of a new continent, freedom to worship God and to obtain economic gain. Boundaries of the early presbyteries on the westward side always reached as far as white men had staked claims and built cabins.

Newcastle in 1717 extended at least to the Susquehanna River. Then Donegal, first set up in 1732 and re-established in 1760, had the Alleghenies for its outward horizon. Redstone in 1781 reached out toward "the setting sun." When the Presbytery of Ohio was carved out of Redstone in 1793, there was the same indefiniteness. Valid land titles were not yet to be had west of the Ohio River. The following year the decisive victory of "Mad Anthony" at Fallen Timbers on the Maumee River pushed the boundary farther back. None knew how far. At any rate, settlement in most of the Northwest Territory was now a comparatively safe adventure.

Like milestones set along a national highway even while it is under construction, the erection of presbyteries and synods marks the progress of our church across the nation. However, there were times, also, like that of the disruption of 1741, or that of the Excision Act in 1837, when these milestones seemed to be more like monuments to mark a battlefield. This story of church courts divided, and of courts erected in virgin territory, is a tedious and complicated one, which this chapter attempts to relate somewhat in detail. In what is intended to be a book of reference, some of these detailed facts, and even some wearisome dates, must be made available to the student of the future.

Organized Presbyterianism in America began long before a few ministers were gathered in Philadelphia in 1706 to form a presbytery. It included more than twice as many ministers and congregations as were represented there.[1] Only a few groups of Ulster Scots, scattered from Philadelphia south to Accomac, Virginia, were included in the Presbytery at its inception. Apparently Francis Makemie did not know, though Jedediah Andrews, Massachusetts-born and Harvard-bred, should have been aware, that there were English Presbyterian congregations in East Jersey and on Long Island, more than a dozen of them, which had not been invited to send representatives to that meeting. There were also a few scattered congregations of Scottish refugees in South Carolina, struggling for existence against restrictive laws and oppressive governors.

At that first meeting, the Presbytery doubtless received some information about these others, at least about the congregation of refugee Scots in Monmouth County, New Jersey, for at their second meeting they ordained John Boyd to be pastor of this flock which had remained shepherdless in the wilderness for a dozen years. When the blue banner was once raised on the banks of the Delaware, other Jersey and Long Island congregations and pastors quickly rallied to it. Only eleven years later the Presbytery had grown large enough to be divided into three; and a fourth, that of Long Island, added. In 1717 these four united themselves into a Synod.

It was at this time that the trickle of immigration from the north of Ireland was swelling into a flood which was to keep flowing in full spate almost down to the outbreak of the War of Independence.

Largely because there was a line of ships sailing with some regularity from Londonderry to Newcastle, the little town on the Delaware became the principal port of Presbyterian entry. From it Presbyterians fanned out north and south, but especially west, wherever cheap land could be had. Thus it came about that Newcastle Presbytery, "than which there is none older," to quote one of its distinguished living members, was soon ready for subdivision. The ancestry of all our presbyteries west of the Alleghenies is to be traced back to it. And it is to be observed that nearly all the surviving churches of "The Presbytery of 1706 are now on the rolls of Newcastle."[2] From this point we shall follow only those developments in which our own origins in the Upper Ohio Valley are involved.

In 1732 the western part of Newcastle, for the most part covering Lancaster and Dauphin counties, was erected into the Presbytery of Donegal. Only two years later, its ministers pushed their ministry across the Susquehanna, which hitherto had been the western boundary of civilization and settlement.[3] Indeed, for many a year Donegal had no western limits. When McMillan, Smith, Power, and Dod settled in Westmoreland, Fayette, and Washington counties, they were working within the bounds and under the direction of the Presbytery of Donegal. During the Disruption, Donegal was divided into Old Side and New Side presbyteries, then temporarily extinguished, but soon revived. It abides in strength to this day, a grandmother of us all.

First Presbyteries West of the Mountains

Of the first four pioneer preachers in the West—Smith, Power, and McMillan were all sons of Newcastle and licensed by that body. Smith and Power were also ordained by it. Smith was a pastor in Newcastle and a missionary under Donegal before crossing the mountains. Only McMillan was ordained by Donegal. All four served as missionaries of Donegal until, at their own request, all of that Presbytery lying west of the Laurel Ridge was, by act of the

Synod of New York and Philadelphia in 1781, erected into the Presbytery of Redstone, which is the mother of all presbyteries of the Upper Ohio Valley. In preparation for the forming of the General Assembly in 1789, the Synod divided in 1788 into the four synods of New York and New Jersey, Philadelphia, Virginia, and the Carolinas. Redstone Presbytery, by that action, was attached to the Synod of Virginia. Therefore, the oldest Western Pennsylvania churches were successively under the jurisdiction of three presbyteries and three synods, and many in Ohio under four presbyteries and four synods, before the division of 1837 confused things still further.

Our Presbyterian pathfinders, from the very birth of the General Presbytery in 1706, had followed close on the heels of the boldest frontiersmen. The paths they found and used were of three kinds —Indian trails, military roads, but for the most part waterways. One who would understand just how their dream took form must needs study topographical maps of the whole western country, which to most Americans now is very much "down east." McClure and Frisbie in 1772 followed up the Susquehanna, the Juniata and its Raystown Branch, then over the ridges beyond its headwaters, and down into the Ligonier Valley.[4] Finley and McMillan on their first journeys were guided along the Potomac to its upper tributary streams, then over the watershed down to the Tygart or the Youghiogheny, and on to the Monongahela.[5] With only the stars by night, and the moss on the trees by day to give directions, the flowing waters were their God-given guides.

The same pattern holds in the planting of the early settlements and the early churches throughout this region. Up the Allegheny the pioneers pushed, then on up the Redbank, the Clarion, French Creek, Oil Creek, the Brokenstraw or the Conewango; or up the Beaver and Neshannock, or up the Muskingum into the Licking or the Tuscarawas. Some of them turned left where Coshocton now stands, into the Walhonding, then into the Mohican, thence by Muddy Fork or Clear Fork or Black Fork, to the lands they had searched out for their homes. These and a hundred other streams, large or small, became for our fathers highways to the promised land. All along these valley paths the spiritual shepherds of the wilderness were following hard after them, with rod and staff, with broadaxe and Bible.

Rapid growth of population demanded a division of Redstone after only twelve years. Everything west of the Monongahela and the Allegheny was handed over in 1793 to the new Presbytery of Ohio, which was destined to be for seventy-seven years remarkably effective in the propagation of our faith. With the readjustments that followed the reunion of 1870, Ohio Presbytery ceased to exist under that name. The creation of new presbyteries north, south, and west had greatly reduced its area, though little if any, its strength in congregations, communicants, and ministers. The Presbytery of Pittsburgh became its successor and heir. This Presbytery of Ohio, after nine fruitful years of sending missionaries down into backwoods Virginia, up toward Lake Erie, and out across the Ohio into the Northwest Territory, underwent its first vivisection.

In 1801, in session at Winchester, Virginia, the following action was taken:

"At the united request of all the members present from the presbyteries of Redstone and Ohio, the Synod (of Virginia) did, and do hereby, establish a presbytery to consist of the Rev'd Messrs. Thomas Hughs, William Wick, Samuel Tate, Joseph Stockton and Robert Lee, including in their bounds all the churches N. and N.W. of the Ohio and Allegheny rivers, to the place where the Ohio River crosses the western boundary of Pennsylvania, and to be known by the name of the Presbytery of Erie."[6]

This is a more precise definition of boundaries than most of those drawn earlier. Yet it ignored the fact that the upper reaches of the Allegheny are in New York State, and it left the western limits wholly open "to the setting sun." So after twenty-seven years there were three presbyteries west of the Laurel Ridge instead of one. A natural sequence was the action of the General Assembly of 1802, gathering these three—Redstone, Ohio, and Erie into a new Synod of Pittsburgh. Even before it was formed, Ohio Presbytery had at least five congregations established in what was about to become the new state of Ohio, and Erie Presbytery had two.[7] The Synod of Pittsburgh at its first meeting formed itself into the "Western Missionary Society," and set its face steadfastly westward.

It will clarify the picture if we pause at four separate dates before the end of the eighteenth century to survey the range and location of known groups of Presbyterians who were being supplied with the Gospel, or were clamoring for it.

David McClure and Levi Frisbie, young Dartmouth tutors, engaged by the Synod of New York and Philadelphia for a missionary exploration tour that was financed by Presbyterians in Scotland, spent the Winter of 1772-73 in and about Pittsburgh. Their *Journal* records repeated preaching journeys from that center northeastward into the Conemaugh Valley, eastward into the Ligonier Valley, and southeastward up the Youghiogheny, thus reaching out for fifty miles or more in three directions.[8] In 1774 James Finley, energetic and mission-minded pastor at East Nottingham in the far southeastern corner of Pennsylvania, came into the west on what was probably his third busman's holiday from his parish. He confined his ministrations to the large triangle between the Monongahela and the Youghiogheny rivers and preached for three months and more in a dozen places from Round Hill to the Virginia line. In 1781 the new-born Presbytery of Redstone, and its members individually, received supplications for supplies from as far south as the Tygart Valley, 125 miles, and as far west as Wheeling and Grave Creek, sixty miles.[9] Between the years 1793 and 1800, requests came from, and preachers were sent to, Erie and Northeast, 150 miles away on Lake Erie, Short Creek and Cross Roads, Fort Steuben, Island Creek and Youngstown, well over in the Northwest Territory, and down into Virginia at least as far as Fairmont.[10] The field was growing far faster than it could be planted, much less cultivated.

Even earlier, Presbyterian missionaries from Kentucky planted churches in the lower Ohio Valley, in and near Cincinnati; but that is another story. None of these men, except James Welsh, came into the Upper Valley. He remained less than two years and took back as his wife one of Joseph Smith's daughters. On the other hand, Ohio Presbytery sent to Kentucky James McGready and Samuel Donnell. The Associate Reformed Church did send some men from Kentucky to do mission work within our borders.[11] For example, the Crooked Creek Church in Muskingum County, Ohio, now the New Concord United Presbyterian Church, was organized in 1812 by Abraham Craig of the Kentucky Associate Reformed Presbytery.

Three Presbyteries and a Synod

With this preview we turn to a genealogical account of presbyteries and synods in this area, with some glances at their initial membership, and the churches under their care.

By act of the Synod of New York and Philadelphia, and on petition of four missionaries sent out by the presbyteries of Donegal and Newcastle, but shut off by mountain walls from their brethren in the East and feeling sore need of mutual counsel and united planning in the face of their appalling task, the Presbytery of Redstone was erected out of Donegal in 1781, and directed to hold its first meeting at Laurel Hill, in what was to be Fayette County, Pennsylvania.[12] Because of threatened Indian raids, the three men settled west of the Monongahela dared not venture so far from their families and congregations. Therefore, they met instead at Pigeon Creek on September 17, 1781. This danger of Indian invasion hung over them for many months. The year was the darkest year of a dark decade on the frontier. Two attempts to hold a second meeting of the new Presbytery failed. It was not until October 25, 1782, that Redstone held its second meeting. Even so, Smith of Upper Buffalo and Cross Creek was missing from the first meeting, and Dod of Ten Mile from the second. Their fields were farthest west, closest to the Ohio and nearest to danger.

In an address before the Pittsburgh Presbytery in 1932, the writer ventured to describe the four pioneer pastors, McMillan, Smith, Power, and Dod as "the four horsemen of Old Redstone," and the title has been rather widely adopted. They almost literally spent their days and years in the saddle, or faring far on foot, "in perils of the heathen and in perils of the wilderness."

Several of the churches they served, which were taken under the care of Redstone Presbytery at its organization, had been gathered before the Revolution broke out.[13] There is good documentary evidence that for several of the oldest 1772 is the birth date. Several others had their beginnings in 1775 and 1776.[14] Redstone was organized just a month before the surrender at Yorktown brought the Revolution to a close. Eight years were to pass before Washington's inauguration marked the formal launching of our national government. By so much is organized Presbyterianism, even west of the Alleghenies, older than organized Americanism.

No formal listing of congregations within their bounds was attempted at that initial meeting of Redstone. It could not in any case have been complete, for these men had not yet explored their whole field. With every journey abroad they were to discover new groups of Presbyterians, who had gathered for worship regularly in cabins or barns or in forest glades and were praying for a preacher. At that first meeting, mention is made of Pigeon Creek, Laurel Hill, Muddy Creek, South Fork of Ten Mile, and Mt. Pleasant. From other sources we know the following congregations were already functioning: Chartiers, Upper Buffalo, Cross Creek, Upper and Lower Ten Mile, Raccoon, Montours, Bethel, Lebanon, Beulah, Pittsburgh, Long Run, Round Hill, Rehoboth, Sewickley, Unity, Salem, Dunlap's Creek, Tyrone, George's Creek, and possibly half a dozen more. How completely any of these was organized we shall probably never know, for sessional and congregational records of that early day are almost wholly lacking. They were too busy making history; they took little time to record it.

What is the birth date of a Presbyterian church? When it calls its first pastor? Some of these congregations were represented in Synod and Assembly before that glad day came. Or when its first elders were elected and ordained? In some cases that was not done until the first pastor was on the field. Or when a group of people have united themselves sufficiently to send to a presbytery, near or far, an appeal for a pastor or for preaching supplies? We know a child has been born alive, not when it is named, or baptized, or weaned, but as soon as we hear its first cry. We choose to accept a cry for the milk of the Word as good evidence that a living congregation has come to birth. These pioneer congregations were none of them organized by a committee of Presbytery, as we do it now, and then formally enrolled. Some of them, as the one near Fort Ligonier, had a building of their own before they even sent out a plea for preachers.[15] Others struggled along for nearly a generation with no church house at all.

The next event that vitally affected Presbyterians on the frontier came in 1788, when the Synod of New York and Philadelphia was expanded into four synods, the General Assembly created, and American Presbyterianism was formally launched on a national career. The infant Presbytery of Redstone was then attached to the Synod of Virginia. For fourteen years the men of Redstone, and for nine years the ministers and elders of Ohio Presbytery also, were expected annually to make the wearisome trip on horseback over the mountains to Winchester or Lexington.[16] In those days synods were not delegated bodies.

From 1783 on, this region was being populated more and more rapidly with settlers from the eastern seaboard, or directly from Ulster or Scotland. Particularly was this true of the lands west of the Monongahela in what are now Washington, Greene, Allegheny counties, and the Northern Panhandle of Virginia. In 1793 the expanding business of organizing and supplying churches made advisable the division of Redstone Presbytery. On their petition, the Synod of Virginia set off all the territory west of the Monongahela and Allegheny rivers into what was to be called Ohio

Presbytery.[17] Soon this new Presbytery became stronger than the mother Presbytery in congregations, ministers, and missionary outreach. Indeed, it is fair to say that throughout its seventy-seven years Ohio ranked first in real strength and influence among all the presbyteries west of the Appalachians, holding the position which its successor, the Presbytery of Pittsburgh, has maintained down to the middle of the twentieth century.

The new Presbytery of Ohio was organized at Upper Buffalo October 22, 1793, with the following five charter members: John Clark, John McMillan, Joseph Patterson, James Hughes, and John Brice.[18] Of the original apostolic quartet, Joseph Smith and Thaddeus Dod had already fought their good fight and finished their course. The congregations under the care of the new Presbytery were Chartiers, Pigeon Creek, Bethel, Lebanon, Montours, Raccoon, Mill Creek, Flats, Upper Buffalo, Cross Creek, Lower Buffalo, Short Creek, West Alexander, Forks of Wheeling, South Fork of Ten Mile, Muddy Creek, Washington, King's Creek, White Oak Flats, Mingo, Horseshoe Bottom, Pike Run, Stone Coal Fork, and Campbell's Tent. Of these twenty-four, sixteen had, or formerly had, installed pastors. Before 1775 not one had been in existence—an amazing growth in eighteen years. The men left in Redstone after this division were James Power, James Finley, James Dunlap, John McPherrin, Samuel Porter, William Swan, George Hill, Robert Marshall, David Smith, and Boyd Mercer. These two rolls already include five men who had been recruited and wholly trained here in the West.

Other Presbyteries Formed from Redstone

Redstone now included only the territory between the Laurel Ridge and the two rivers which unite to form the Ohio, but stretched from the New York line far down into Virginia. It was again divided several times before it was reduced to its present size, which now includes Fayette County and parts of Westmoreland, Allegheny, and Greene.[19] In 1830, by a painful operation, Blairsville

Presbytery was carved out of it on the north. What was Blairsville in the beginning now includes Clarion, most of Kittanning, even a bit of Northumberland. For a considerable time there was also a Saltsburg Presbytery within that area. Kittanning is its legal successor, although the boundary lines have been shifted two or three times. Below the Mason and Dixon Line the Presbystery of Grafton ultimately emerged. It, too, is a daughter of Redstone.

Before following the march of the Synod of Pittsburgh into the Northwest Territory, we must turn back to review the other changes in presbyteries and their boundaries in Western Pennsylvania previous to the split of 1837. Chronologically, first was the creation of Washington Presbytery in 1819, out of the southern part of Ohio. It included most of Washington and Greene counties, the whole of the Panhandle, and reached far down into the "back hills of Virginia." Indeed, its entire area had once been claimed by the Old Dominion. We cannot discover that the southern boundaries of Redstone and Washington were ever clearly defined in the early days.

Meanwhile, as early as 1808, Erie having grown to number sixty-five churches and nineteen ministers, eight of the ministers and sixteen or more congregations were separated from it to form the Presbytery of Hartford.[20] This new Presbytery at first included all of the Western Reserve, with two or three congregations in Pennsylvania. It was reduced by the organization of Grand River Presbytery in 1814. Then to the west Portage Presbytery appeared in 1818 and, still farther west, Huron Presbytery in 1823. All these presbyteries were under the Synod of Pittsburgh until 1825. Since the church of Hartford and some other churches in that area had become Congregational, the name of this original Western Reserve Presbytery was in 1833 changed to Beaver. We have not been able to find any accurate description of the boundaries between these presbyteries. On the north, each reached to Lake Erie and, on the south, to the southern line of the Reserve, which is the forty-first parallel.

Back in Pennsylvania, the year 1820 saw a further reduction of Erie Presbytery by the setting up of Allegheny, which occupied much the same territory as the later Presbytery of Butler. The general theory behind these changes was, that as soon as there were enough ministers and congregations to make a presbytery feasible, the distances to be traveled must be reduced by division. In horseback days it was no small undertaking to travel from Erie or Northeast to Beaver or Bull Creek for a meeting of Presbytery. It meant from two to three days of hard riding in each direction.

Again, in our search for these monuments of an expanding church, we cross the Ohio farther down. The Synod of Pittsburgh, in 1808, on the same day and by the same act that brought Hartford into being, also authorized the formation of Lancaster Presbytery, far out in Central Ohio.[21] Its eastern limit was to be the line of the "Seven Ranges," which meant approximately the eastern lines of Guernsey and Tuscarawas counties. This left a strip roughly two counties wide, between the Seven Ranges and the Ohio River, remaining under jurisdiction of Ohio Presbytery. The northern border of this new Lancaster Presbytery was the line of the Western Reserve. That line is clear and exact. As for the rest, we quote from the minutes of the Synod of Pittsburgh: "on the west by the line of the Kentucky Synod; on the south by the Ohio River; on the east and north by the line of the Seven Ranges and of the Hartford Presbytery; including the Rev'd Messrs. Stephen Lindley, Jacob Lindley, John Wright, James Robinson, and James Scott."

Apparently the location of these men was a clearer definition of area than any lines drawn on a map they did not possess. Jacob Lindley was at Athens, and had been up the Muskingum at Waterford. Stephen Lindley was stationed at Marietta, and John Wright at Lancaster. James Robinson had settled at Mt. Pleasant or Kingston in Pickaway County, whither he had just moved from Crooked Creek, now New Concord. James Scott was serving at Mt. Vernon. Thus this Presbyterian outpost farthest west included nearly all of central and southeastern Ohio. But it did not include the churches near the river in Jefferson, Harrison, and Belmont counties. These remained under the care of the mother Presbytery of Ohio. Such ill-defined boundaries later gave rise to some heated disputes concerning the oversight of congregations growing up along these hazy borderlines.

These men, who were the charter members of Lancaster, were all graduates of Jefferson or Washington College in Arts or Theology, or both. The original membership of Hartford Presbytery was of mixed origin. Some, like Wick and Boyd, were Western Pennsylvanians. Some were New Englanders, sent out by the Connecticut Missionary Society. Best known of these was Joseph Badger, veteran of Bunker Hill and Quebec, who, more than any other, deserves to be called the apostle of the Western Reserve. He came out as a Congregationalist, but presently transferred his allegiance to the Presbyterian church. The Connecticut Society was unable to find enough missionaries in their own ranks. In several cases they paid the salaries of men furnished by the Board of Trust of the Synod of Pittsburgh.

Period of Rapid Expansion

The years from 1808 to 1819 were a period of rapid and healthy growth in congregations, in membership, and in settled ministers. In the latter year came another organizational change. Ohio Presbytery was divided again into three, and Washington and Steubenville presbyteries came into being. Both these new presbyteries were much larger in area than today. Steubenville Presbytery at that time covered Jefferson, Harrison, Belmont, and Monroe counties, and, apparently, parts of Columbiana and Carroll. Washington Presbytery included not only Washington and Greene counties, but all four counties of the Virginia Panhandle. The next change in this quarter was the division of Steubenville in 1839 to form St. Clairsville.[22] But strangely enough, for some years Crab Apple in Harrison County considered itself a part of Washington Presbytery, perhaps the only case of "elective affinity" in all the Upper Ohio Valley. In 1814 Lancaster Presbytery was separated from the Synod of Pittsburgh, and Washington and Miami presbyteries from the Synod of Kentucky.[23] These three presbyteries were then erected into the Synod of Ohio which did not, by any means, cover the entire state.

Meanwhile, to the north, Hartford Presbytery had grown so rapidly as to require division in 1815, when Grand River Presbytery was formed out of its western and northern portions. Then, Grand River dividing in 1818, Portage emerged, and in 1823 to the west of it, Huron. In 1825 the General Assembly authorized a new Synod, named Western Reserve, which comprised Grand River, Portage, and Huron presbyteries. There was something more important than mere convenience in the formation of this new Synod. In these three northern Ohio presbyteries, many of the ministers and most of the congregations were of New England origin. They generally espoused the New England theology. They were enthusiastic also for the 1801 Plan of Union and were zealous for moral reform. The majority of the men of Pittsburgh Synod disagreed with them on all three counts. Therefore, the Synod of the Western Reserve was born, not of geography, but of theology, conviction, and policy. It was a product of elective affinity on a larger scale. It was one of the early tremors and fissures that heralded the earthquake of 1837.[24]

Somewhat later two more presbyteries were added to the Synod of Western Reserve. They were Cleveland and Michigan, the former made up of parts of both Portage and Huron. Similarly, over to the east, Erie Presbytery was divided again in 1820, its southern half taking the name of Allegheny. Its first meeting was held in 1821 at Butler. The Butler Presbytery is its legal successor. In 1822 the Pittsburgh churches were set over from Redstone to Ohio Presbytery. Clarion was added to the Old School Synod of Pittsburgh in 1841, Saltsburg in 1850, and Allegheny City in 1853.

Thus far the western progress and the formation of new presbyteries had developed in the way one would expect, namely, by the setting up of preaching stations as fast as the growing population justified it, the organizing of these into churches as pastors or missionaries could be found to man them, and the erection of new presbyteries and synods as rapidly as enough churches were formed to make this advisable. The difficulties of travel and communication necessitated much smaller synodical units than now. But the congregations drew generally from a smaller area than in the beginning, and the presbyteries were generally larger in area than in more recent years.

We see developing in these formative years exactly what we aim at now in our world-mission enterprise, a self-supporting, self-governing, and self-propagating church. Surprisingly little mission money came into this region from the East. The Synods of Pittsburgh, Ohio, and Western Reserve were carrying their own responsibilities and acting on their own initiative. For example, they set up their own machinery for missions and church expansion in 1802, and the Synod of Pittsburgh organized its own Western Foreign Missionary Society in 1831. The real secret of their success in church extension lay in the fact that synods and presbyteries required every minister, unless excused for good reasons, to spend from two to six weeks every year in missionary itineration in destitute places, or in the regions beyond.

Changes Due to Strife and Schism

Having now traced the happy growth of churches and the multiplying of presbyteries and synods during the first half century, we turn now to review briefly a period of strife and schism which resulted in adding three other kinds of Presbyterian churches in this area during the first half of the nineteenth century. Only a few details will be sketched now. The full story of controversy will appear in Chapter x.

The first controversy was caused by the invasion of Ohio and Western Pennsylvania by the Cumberland Presbyterians. It was the Falling-Work Revival, which began in Kentucky in 1800, and extended to Pennsylvania, Ohio, and Virginia in 1802 that brought to birth the Cumberland Presbyterian Church. This new Presbyterian denomination had its origin in Kentucky in 1806 in the protests of certain leaders against the rigidity which demanded on the frontier the same high educational standards for Presbyterian ministers as elsewhere. Its first presbytery, organized in 1810, grew into a synod in 1813 and into a General Assembly in 1829.[25] It was an attempt to adjust the church's policies, methods, and doctrines to the conditions of frontier life and was thus, as Dr. Zahniser has shown, a sociological phenomenon. It was also a rebellion of desperately earnest and consecrated men against a church that was giving more attention to theological hairsplitting than to the winning of souls to Christ and was losing the fervor of its pioneers.[26] The first Cumberland Presbytery in Pennsylvania was set up in 1832. There it expanded into three presbyteries and a synod, all the outgrowth of the work of five missionaries from Kentucky and Tennessee, who came in response to the plea of a group of Western Pennsylvania Presbyterians.

Soon after, a presbytery and, presently, a synod were found in Ohio also. In some parts of Western Virginia, Cumberland churches gained considerable strength. They drew off a good many of the more evangelistically-minded regular Presbyterians in the Upper Ohio area, split a few congregations, and attracted to their ranks a few strong leaders from the older body. The most notable of these was Jacob Lindley, a son of Ohio Presbytery, a graduate of Princeton College, and one of the founders of Ohio University at Athens. It is only fair to record that the principal growth of the Cumberland Church in the Upper Ohio Valley came not by proselyting but by evangelizing. Its growth served as a rebuke and a spur to the older church, which in many places had markedly declined in evangelistic zeal. When reunion was finally brought about in 1906, it was a man of this area, President James D. Moffatt of Washington and Jefferson College, who led the movement for reunion in our Presbyterian Church in the U.S.A.[27]

The next division was a sadder one. It tore the church asunder into Old School and New School branches. It came a generation later, in 1837. This was in considerable degree an Upper Ohio Valley story. In Ohio the working of the Plan of Union had developed increasing tension during those thirty years since 1801. The differences between the old Calvinism and its modified form in the New England theology were more keenly felt here than in most other areas. Here, too, the slavery issue, which entered into it as a second cause of division, was being more and more hotly debated. However, in the General Assembly of 1837, where the break came, it was the theological differences that were emphasized. Conventions had been held, one of them in Pittsburgh, in which plans were proposed for a drastic purging of the church by bringing to account men who were believed to have departed radically from the faith of their fathers. It was in that mood that the four synods, in which most of these men were serving, were excluded.

The Synod of the Western Reserve, partly in the territory under survey, was one of the four synods "exscinded" by the General Assembly of 1837. During the period of division, the Old School Presbyterians had only a handful of churches on the Reserve. Indeed, in two counties of northeastern Ohio, Geauga, and Portage, not a single Presbyterian church exists today. On the other hand, New School churches were to be found scattered over this entire valley, though they were very much in the minority. In Western Pennsylvania three New School presbyteries emerged, Pittsburgh, Erie, and Meadville. In Ohio outside the Western Reserve, there were set up the presbyteries of Athens, Pataskala, Franklin, Scioto, and Tuscarawas, which constituted the New School Synod of Ohio.

None of these presbyteries, either in Pennsylvania or Ohio, had great strength. They did, however, include some strong churches,

COURTESY OF
FIRST PRESBYTERIAN CHURCH,
PITTSBURGH

REVEREND
FRANCIS HERRON, D.D.

First Presbyterian Church, Pittsburgh, Pa. Pastor, 1810–1850. Moderator of General Assembly, 1827.

REVEREND
ELISHA P. SWIFT, D.D.

Pastor, Second Presbyterian Church of Pittsburgh, 1819–1833, Professor at Western Seminary and Founder of Board of Foreign Missions.

COURTESY OF
SECOND PRESBYTERIAN CHURCH,
PITTSBURGH

COURTESY OF FIRST PRESBYTERIAN CHURCH, WHEELING

FIRST PRESBYTERIAN CHURCH
WHEELING, WEST VIRGINIA
Oldest church building in northern West Virginia.

REVEREND
JAMES HERVEY, D.D.
Pastor, Old Stone Presbyterian Church, Wheeling, West Virginia, 1812–1859.

COURTESY OF PRESIDENT DAVID ALLEN

DAVIS AND ELKINS COLLEGE, ELKINS, WEST VIRGINIA
Arts and Science Halls

as Pittsburgh Third, Erie Central, Titusville, Canton, Massillon, Granville, Putnam of Zanesville, and Newark Second. By and large, the Upper Ohio Valley remained Old School. Western Seminary and Ohio Presbytery furnished much of the Old School leadership through the thirty years of separation. Twice its Assembly came to Pittsburgh. Two of its moderators were chosen from this area. In November, 1869, both General Assemblies came to Pittsburgh to ratify reunion.

The third controversy was over human slavery. It plowed deep and painful furrows up and down our land and left its mark on the Presbyterianism of this region. The General Assembly in 1845, after it had repeatedly refused to let any resolutions against slavery even come to the floor, finally adopted an ambiguous resolution which practically nullified the famous action of 1818, and seemed to many to be an abject moral retreat.[28] As a result, nine members walked out of the Assembly, declining its jurisdiction. A score or more congregations quickly withdrew and became independent. Soon these entered into correspondence with each other and began to draw together. The result was the organization of the "Free Presbyterian Church," which grew to about seventy congregations, eight presbyteries, and a synod, usually called the Free Synod of Cincinnati.[29] Their churches were scattered all the way from Lancaster County, Pennsylvania, to eastern Iowa. However, their principal strength lay in the two presbyteries of Mahoning and Central Ohio, both in the Upper Ohio drainage basin.

Though their numbers were small, their convictions were deep and they made good use of printer's ink. Besides their hatred of slavery, they took strong ground in behalf of temperance and against secret, oath-bound societies and did much to quicken the conscience of American Protestantism. With the close of the War Between the States, their mission was accomplished. Their ministers and congregations returned to the Old School or New School or the United Presbyterian Church. In Pennsylvania and eastern Ohio almost all of them had come out of the Old School body. So it was also in Illinois and Iowa. In southern Ohio and Indiana they were nearly all from the New School. These Free Church people were bitterly reviled by the Old School leaders. They stood on exactly the same ground as the Seceders, the two synods of the Associate Reformed, the Wesleyan Methodists, the Quakers, and the Mennonites, in excluding from communion slaveholders and all defenders of the slave system.

These three splits—Cumberland, Old School-New School, and Free Presbyterian—deplorable as they were, added strength to the church in its moral standards, in its evangelistic zeal, and in its responsiveness to human need. God made the wrath of men to praise Him. "For ulterior ends or honestly, Christ was being proclaimed; and for that will we rejoice."

A Confusing Picture Emerges

All of these divisions made for a blurred picture and tangled lines of organizational structure. During the forties and fifties there were four bodies, each called the Synod of Ohio. There were two presbyteries and two synods of Cincinnati, and two presbyteries of Columbus. When one consults the newspapers and journals of the period, this confuson of names can easily lead to a serious misinterpretation of facts. After 1837 both New School and Old School styled themselves *The* Presbyterian Church in the U.S.A. When one opens a volume of Assembly minutes during all those thirty years, one finds absolutely nothing on the title page to show whether it is a New School or Old School record.

Further, the reader needs to watch dates carefully, because of identity of presbytery names. There were, for example, an old Presbytery of Athens throughout the years 1821 to 1837, a Cumberland Presbytery of Athens from about 1832 down to 1906, also a New School Presbytery of Athens from 1838 to 1870, and a new Presbytery of Athens extending from 1870 to 1906, and still another set of records under the same name after the Cumberland Presbytery was absorbed.[30] Add to this the endless overlapping of boundaries of presbyteries which occupied the same general area, and the frequent changes in these boundaries, and you have a tale exceedingly tangled. A diagram in the end of this volume attempts to assist the reader in the untangling.

After the reunion of 1870 there was a period of experimental realignment that stretched out to twelve years before a reasonable stability was attained. Pennsylvania was divided among the four synods of Philadelphia, Harrisburg, Pittsburgh, and Erie. Ohio was similarly divided among the four synods of Cleveland, Columbus, Cincinnati, and Toledo.

The Synod of Pittsburgh in 1872 comprised the presbyteries of Blairsville, Pittsburgh, Redstone, Washington, and West Virginia. In the Synod of Erie were the presbyteries of Allegheny, Butler, Clarion, Kittanning, and Shenango.

The Synod of Cleveland was organized with the four presbyteries of Cleveland, Mahoning, St. Clairsville, and Steubenville. The Synod of Columbus had ecclesiastical jurisdiction over the presbyteries of Athens, Columbus, Marion, Wooster, and Zanesville, while the Synod of Cincinnati included Chillicothe, Cincinnati, Dayton, and Portsmouth presbyteries. Bellefontaine, Huron, Lima, and Maumee were grouped to form the Synod of Toledo.

The old synod names that were omitted are Western Reserve, Ohio, and Wheeling. The new ones which appear are Erie, Cleveland, Columbus, and Toledo. Old presbytery names also were discarded in this period of consolidation. Even the ancient and fruitful mother Presbytery of Ohio disappeared. Of the old presbytery names on the Reserve, only Huron survived. Gone were Richland, Hocking, New Lisbon, Oxford, Sidney, and Hamilton. Many an ancient landmark had been moved out of its place.

Only a few of the changes of the last seventy-five years need be noted. In Pennsylvania these important changes were the forming of Shenango Presbytery, the expansion of Pittsburgh Presbytery to include Allegheny, and the forming of the new Beaver Presbytery in 1908. In Ohio the number of presbyteries was reduced from seventeen to fourteen, with the elimination of Huron, Bellefontaine, and, in 1935, even good old Chillicothe, which had long been a pioneer in moral and social advance, and especially in its valiant fight against slavery. As we write, the fourteen presbyteries seem about to become seven, each with its own office and executive. The Presbyterian U.S.A. Synod of West Virginia did not appear until 1904. Finally, in 1906 the Cumberland synods and presbyteries in this area were dissolved, and their churches and ministers integrated into the Presbyterian Church in the U.S.A. units in their several areas. The last accession came with the coming over of the three Welsh Calvinistic presbyteries in Ohio and the one in Western Pennsylvania.

So stands the record of the westward expansion of Presbyterianism in the Upper Ohio Valley. In Pennsylvania, west of Laurel Ridge, there are nine presbyteries, three in West Virginia, and seven in Ohio. How long shall that number continue? Change is in the air with the recent merger in 1958 of the Presbyterian and United Presbyterian General Assemblies.

This survey of growth indicates several historic facts which are reflected in the original judicatories of this area and in the many modifications of them as the Presbyterian church became established throughout the drainage basin of the Upper Ohio Valley. In Ohio three streams of migration brought the original settlers into the Northwest Territory. Into the Western Reserve came New Englanders, bringing their peculiar heritage and traditions. Into the central counties all the way from the Ohio River to the Indiana line came second generation Ulster Scots, most of them reared in Pennsylvania, with their love of the old paths, and their rigid Calvinism. Into the southern and southwestern counties there came from Kentucky men whose fathers had come from Virginia and the Carolinas through Cumberland Gap into that dark and bloody ground. The synods and presbyteries reveal this threefold origin. Later changes resulted in large part from controversies which can be traced in considerable part to these diverse origins—

controversies over the New England theology, the Plan of Union for missionary extension, and the slavery issue.

The recent changes, however, have emerged out of the spirit of reunion and fellowship which was generated in 1870, and out of the need for efficiency in administration and in church extension. Most of these later factors will continue to play their roles in future changes, and to shape the pattern of many things to come, changes now forming in the womb of time. A renewed emphasis is taking new form in three directions—the evangelization of new Americans from central and southern Europe, in which Pittsburgh Presbytery has largely set the patterns for the whole church; second, the development of a new conscience on social, economic, political, and racial issues; and third, a more general and effective participation in the winning of the whole world to Christ.

Brief Résumé of Westward Progress

Westward Ho! was ever the onward cry of the Presbyterian church as it took organizational form west of the Alleghenies, and then thrust down its roots and conquered its inheritance throughout the Upper Ohio Valley. As a result, this region has become, above all others, the stronghold of Presbyterianism in the United States. Certain facts which lie further in the background merit a concluding re-emphasis.

First, the Presbyterianism of this region stems from the New Side Presbyterianism of the middle eighteenth century. There is scarcely a trace of those ideas, attitudes, and tendencies which we associate with the Old Side.

Second, all the pioneers, clergy, and laity alike, had felt the impact of The Great Awakening under Jonathan Edwards, and the evangelistic work of George Whitefield and Gilbert Tennent in the middle colonies. There was in the pioneer preaching an urgency, a conviction of the utterly lost condition of every man without Christ, and of Christ's complete sufficiency. They preached both the law and the Gospel with a power born of deep personal experience. They fought back the tides of godlessness, immorality, and infidelity in the new settlements, as men who must give account for the souls of their fellowmen.

Third, they went about their task with a full persuasion of the need of men educated as well as consecrated, even on the rough frontiers. This proved a handicap to their expansion, as compared with the Methodists and Baptists, but it gave the church a deeper rootage and a more solid foundation.[31]

Fourth, they did their work with a sense of national destiny. Their devotion to republican institutions, their inheritance from Scotland of a hatred and fear of ecclesiastical tyranny, the sense of civic responsibility that had made their fathers moral leaders and patriotic exemplars before all other clergy in the Revolution—these still burned in them and held them with grim zeal to hard and too easily forgotten high and holy standards which they would never sacrifice and of which we should be the grateful and determined heirs.

CHAPTER VIII Into West Virginia

When the Presbytery of Redstone was organized in 1781, West Virginia was merely a broad expanse of unexplored mountainous hills and valleys, dotted with the occasional cabin of the venturesome pioneer in search of tillable farm land. The old dominion of Virginia extended its colonial claims over much of this poorly plotted area of the West. It was not until 1863 that West Virginia was admitted to separate statehood. Presbyterians in Virginia felt a natural responsibility to their brethren who were establishing homes in the western portion of the state. A similar sense of responsibility was manifested also by the pioneer preachers in the Redstone Presbytery whose undefined western border has been poetically described as "westward to the setting sun."[1]

As a result, there were two somewhat simultaneous missionary advances into what is now the state of West Virginia. One extended directly westward toward the Ohio River into the area known as the northern Panhandle and also southward along the Monongahela River to Morgantown and Fairmont. This was the missionary effort of ministers from the Pennsylvania presbyteries of Redstone and Ohio and later Washington Presbytery. The other advance was from the Virginia presbyteries of Hanover, Lexington, and Winchester. That also was a two-pronged movement. The northern prong extended westward from Virginia into the eastern Panhandle at Shepherdstown and on toward Cumberland. The other prong was much further south and extended westward from Lexington, Virginia, to Lewisburg and the Greenbrier Valley and on into the Charleston area. From these two major sources of Presbyterian missionary and evangelistic zeal have emerged the continuing fervor which throughout the subsequent years has given rise to most of the Presbyterian churches scattered throughout the West Virginia of today.

Unfortunately, the divisive forces of the War Between the States split the Presbyterian church into its continuing northern and southern branches which carry the separate denominational names of Presbyterian Church U.S.A. and Presbyterian Church U.S. This division extended into West Virginia. Those churches in the northern areas which had been organized by Redstone Presbytery and its later presbyteries remained in the Presbyterian Church U.S.A., while the major portion of the churches which owed their origin to the Virginia presbyteries joined the Presbyterian Church U.S. Today only about one-third of all West Virginia Presbyterians are enrolled in the northern branch.[2]

Of these, more than one-half are in the Presbytery of Wheeling which covers the northern Panhandle section of the state.[3] The story of the founding and growth of this minority group of the Presbyterian church which is enrolled in the Presbyterian Church U.S.A. comprises the scope of this chapter on West Virginia Presbyterianism.

I. MISSIONARY MOVEMENTS FROM VIRGINIA

The story begins by following the trail of Reverend John McCue, the first missionary from the Hanover Presbytery, as he journeyed into southern West Virginia. The visitor pauses reverently on the threshold of the oldest Presbyterian church building in the state. On an oval stone placed above the entrance to this church in Lewisburg, he reads this quaint inscription: "This building was erected in the year 1796 at the expense of a few of the First Inhabitants of this Land to commemorate their affection and esteem for the Gospel of Jesus Christ. Reader, if you are inclined to applaud their virtue, Give God the Glory."[4]

Imagination seeks to make vivid once more those personalities of faith and humility who built so well that their consecrated handiwork of native limestone still houses groups of Presbyterian worshipers. Tradition relates that the devoted women of the congregation carried sand in saddlebags from the Greenbrier River, four miles away, which the men then mixed into mortar.[5] Their missionary and pioneering pastor was Reverend John McCue. He served from 1782–1791.[6] He had been sent by the Hanover Presbytery to visit the Presbyterian families who were establishing homes in the Greenbrier Valley and to establish "the first church on the western waters."

In an old log building on Feaster's Farm, two miles from Lewisburg, they first gathered for worship in 1783. The erection of a more commodious stone church at Lewisburg was made possible by a gift of twenty-five hundred dollars from Mrs. John Stuart. For that purpose she gave the entire legacy she had received from her father, Thomas Lewis.[7] Upon sacrifice and consecrated labor of that type, the foundations of Presbyterianism were laid in what is now West Virginia.

How well those foundations were laid is revealed in the groups of churches which call Lewisburg their "mother" church and in the long and devoted pastorate of Dr. John McElhenny.[8] Throughout the fifty-one years of his fruitful ministry, he founded Lewisburg Academy and Greenbrier College. The historian yearns to linger in the sacred precincts of that old church where the membership grew so rapidly that the house of worship had to be enlarged in 1830. But the separations of war have placed it in the Southern Presbyterian Church and so it has only a sentimental place in this narrative of the U.S.A. Presbyterian history of West Virginia.

Nor do the churches established further north in the eastern Panhandle require more than passing mention in this narrative. They were the fruits of the earliest movement of Presbyterianism westward from Virginia. Of these, the church at Shepherdstown, with a history extending back to 1720, has the unquestioned claim to the honor of being the oldest Presbyterian congregation in West Virginia.[9] But the separations of war have also removed them from the Northern Presbyterians. There are no Presbyterian Churches U.S.A. in the entire eastern Panhandle of West Virginia.

From Lewisburg to Charleston

The traveler now follows the Virginia trail of Presbyterian settlers as, moving westward, they built their homes in Greenbrier Valley and along the banks of the Kanawha River. At the junction of the Elk and Kanawha rivers, a group of twelve settlers had erected a fort in 1787 for protection from the Cherokee Indians. They called their place of refuge Fort Lee.[10] Rev. Mr. Crawford was sent by the Presbytery of Hanover to visit these settlers along the Kanawha River. No report or fruitage of his pioneering zeal is available, however. In 1789 a town was laid out. Fort Lee was then renamed Charleston. Seven years later, when the Courthouse was built, the total population numbered only one hundred.

Previously, in 1785, Hanover Presbytery had been divided and all of Virginia west of the Blue Ridge Mountains was placed in the newly formed Presbytery of Lexington.[11] One of its first missionary acts was to send Reverend William Graham to visit the outlying settlements. While journeying on his assigned mission, he was fatally stricken and died within a few days. His place as an itinerant evangelist was taken for a time by Reverend Robert G. Wilson, affectionately called Little Bobbie Wilson or Long Stocking Wilson. But he soon turned aside into Kentucky where he continued a ministry of twenty-five years.[12]

Other itinerant preachers visited the area, but it was not until the coming of the Ruffner family that a Presbyterian church was formed. In more ways than one, this famous Presbyterian family proved to be the "salt" of the community.[13] Joseph Ruffner had moved to Kanawha County in 1796. His business interests found expression in the development of the salt industry, but his spiritual interests were manifested in quickening the religious and educational life of the community. In his home an earnest group gathered for worship until a church could be erected upon the land which he donated to the "Society of Presbyterians" in 1816.

Meanwhile, his son, David Ruffner, had given sufficient land and some money for the establishment of Mercer Academy at Charleston.[14] In a room in that Academy, the Presbyterian church was organized by the Lexington Presbytery on March 14, 1819. The congregation chose as their official name the Kanawha Presbyterian Church.[15] Since part of the membership resided in nearby Salines (now Malden), a separate Presbyterian place of worship was built there by David Ruffner. It was called the Colonel Ruffner Meeting House. The two churches united in welcoming as their first resident pastor, Reverend Calvin Chadock, who served from 1820 to 1838. Of the first three new members to be welcomed by the Session, one was a colored man, appropriately named Adam, who joined on confession of faith.[16] The oldest of the Presbyterian churches in the southern portion of West Virginia thus began somewhat as an interracial church.

The subsequent years found the courage of the membership severely tested by fire which destroyed the brick building during the Winter of 1845–1846 and by the fires of controversy over the slavery question which split the congregation into two separate organizations. With the growth and enrichment of Charleston as the capital city of the new state of West Virginia, the historic Kanawha church has developed into one of the many influential churches within the Presbyterian family in that city.

Church Organized at Parkersburg

Like a three-pronged fork, early Presbyterianism extended from Charleston in three directions to the banks of the Ohio River. It moved westward to Huntington, northwest to Point Pleasant, and northward to Parkersburg. The churches established on the routes both to Huntington and Point Pleasant are now affiliated with the Southern Presbyterians, while the Parkersburg group of churches, including a small missionary offshoot of the Point Pleasant church at Ravenswood, alone remained with the Presbyterian Church U.S.A.

North from Charleston, where the Little Kanawha River flows into the Ohio River, a group of Presbyterians had settled. Here a town was incorporated in 1820 named Parkersburg in honor of William Parker. Lacking a Presbyterian minister, a few Presbyterians worshiped in the Baptist church where the Reverend James McAvoy was the community pastor. This experiment in united worship seems to have paid dividends for the Presbyterian element at least. After a time, Mr. McAvoy left the Baptist denomination and became a Presbyterian minister. A series of revival services, under his ministry in the Courthouse, resulted in a desire to organize a Presbyterian church. The Presbytery of Lexington approved the request. Reverend Nathaniel Calhoun, pastor of the Kanawha Presbyterian Church, and his elder, Judge Frey, were authorized to proceed to organize the First Presbyterian Church of Parkersburg on February 24, 1833.[17]

Again it was an experiment in racial integration. Of the twenty-seven charter members, twenty-one were white people and six were colored. The little group met for worship, first in the Courthouse and later at the schoolhouse. Subsequent growth in membership made possible the erection of a brick sanctuary at a cost of four thousand dollars in 1839. Reverend Festus Hanks was their first pastor and their leader in this venture of faith. He served during the foundation years from 1833 to 1842.

Like so many other Presbyterian pioneer pastors, Mr. Hanks was both a preacher and an educator. Early in his ministry at Parkersburg, he established the first coeducational academy in that area. The joint purpose was to prepare young men for college and to equip young ladies with a sound educational training in a well-conducted boarding school. Several prominent citizens of

Parkersburg, who later completed their education at Princeton and other institutions, and many women prominent in the social life of West Virginia obtained their preparatory education at the Hanks school. The Presbyterian church continued to grow with the development of Parkersburg. It is now one of the strongest and most influential Presbyterian Churches U.S.A. in the entire state.

The Hughes River Church

But Parkersburg was not Mr. Hanks's only field of creative labor. In 1834 he accepted an invitation from a few Scotch families to visit their settlement in Cairo and to preach to them. They had established their homes in the hill country some thirty miles from Parkersburg along the Hughes River. Just why this little group of pioneers had chosen that rugged terrain for their homes, when by journeying a little farther westward they could have obtained unoccupied and comparatively level farm land along the Ohio River, is a mystery locked up in human nature. Perhaps the hills of Scotland were in their memory as the controlling factor. Or they may have been lured by the variegated seasonal beauty of forest-topped hills and the sloping valleys of that particular region.

Mr. Hanks was touched by their spiritual earnestness and their lack of spiritual leadership. Regularly on the fourth Sunday of each month, he traveled the thirty miles of rough mountain roads to lead these isolated settlers in worship.[17a] With the possible maximum of one Sunday's preaching a month, he organized the little congregation into a church on April 12, 1835, under the authority of the Presbytery of Lexington. It was named the Hughes River Presbyterian Church. Not until 1870 was this Hughes River Presbyterian Church strong enough to erect a plain frame building for worship. The simple structure was of rural schoolhouse design with balcony and stained glass windows.[18] During the subsequent oil development at Cairo, this Hughes River church became a flourishing organization. But with the exhaustion of the oil supply, the church lost much of its strength in numbers and in finances. It is another of many illustrations of the effect of changing economic life on the prosperity and growth of churches.

Ravenswood Presbyterian Church

Ravenswood is the only other Presbyterian Church U.S.A. in West Virginia which traces its founding to Greenbrier Presbytery. It is situated on the Ohio River about thirty-five miles south of Parkersburg in a town with the trading advantages of a railroad junction and river traffic. To a small group of Presbyterian pioneer settlers in that community, Reverend Francis Dutton came in 1836. Mr. Dutton was a Princeton graduate and a former principal of Lewisburg Academy who had been licensed two years earlier by the Presbytery of Greenbrier. He began at once to serve as pastor of the Point Pleasant Presbyterian Church which he organized in 1836 and where he remained until his death in 1850. He devoted part of his time to organizing and developing a church at Ravenswood.

The formal organization took place in 1847 under the direction of the Greenbrier Presbytery which had been formed out of the Presbytery of Lexington. The small congregation worshiped in the homes of the members for ten years before a church building could be erected in 1857. It was a plain square structure, adorned with Gothic windows and with a typical slave gallery at one end of the building. The slave gallery has since been removed and other improvements made to the edifice which is still used and is in excellent repair.

This small Presbyterian church at Ravenswood, along with Kanawha, Parkersburg, and Hughes River, are the only four churches now enrolled in the Synod of West Virginia U.S.A. which owe their direct origin to the missionary zeal of Virginia presbyteries. These four churches, together with the subsequent growth of Presbyterianism in that part of West Virginia, now form the Presbytery of Parkersburg which was reorganized into its present boundaries in 1904. It is the smallest of the three West Virginia

U.S.A. presbyteries. In 1956 it reported a membership of twenty-five ministers and thirty-two churches with the total number of communicants only thirty-six hundred and thirty-one.

II. MISSIONARY MOVEMENTS FROM PENNSYLVANIA

The story of the expansion of Presbyterianism into West Virginia now focuses the reader's attention to the north upon the missionary zeal of the presbyteries of Redstone, Ohio, and Washington. From these three Pennsylvania presbyteries came the pioneering leadership which organized the oldest churches in what are now the West Virginia presbyteries of Wheeling and Grafton.

Old Redstone as "the mother presbytery of the West" felt an inescapable sense of responsibility to the Presbyterian settlers who were establishing their homes in an ever-widening frontier. These settlers were following one of two rather clearly defined trails of migration. Some were moving southwestward into what is now the northern Panhandle of West Virginia as they journeyed toward the Ohio River and along its banks to Wheeling. Others were seeking homes southward as they followed the Monongahela River and its tributaries on to Morgantown and Fairmont. Wherever Presbyterians settled, a missionary-minded Presbytery followed them with the gospel and the sacraments of the church. Requests for preaching were answered as quickly and as frequently as human energy and consecration could respond. The minutes of Redstone abound with the record of the appointments of ministers and licentiates to preach on assigned Sabbaths at widely separated points of appeal.

The Northern Panhandle Churches

The historian has no easy task in any attempt to fix the birthday of a pioneer church or to assign definite honors of priority. Just when is a church born? When a congregation makes its formal application to a presbytery for occasional preaching? Or is it when the congregation is formally organized under Presbytery's authority?

Or is a church born when it calls its first pastor? All three may be regarded as logical dates of origin or proof of existence. Some church congregations use one date in seeking the prestige of early origin; others use another starting point. As yet there is no agreement in dating the beginning of historic churches with the resulting differences in claims for such honor as priority in origin may impart. The present writer would not be so bold as to rush onto the field of decision when previous angels have been treading softly in uncertainty. The reader can make his own selection after evaluating the logic of historical facts.

Perhaps the West Liberty church can present the best historical claim to be the earliest preaching point in northern West Virginia. The name appears on the records first as the Ohio Courthouse; then as Short Creek, and, finally, the present name of West Liberty.[19] The second meeting of the Redstone Presbytery had been delayed until October 15, 1782, due to the severity of recurring Indian raids. Only five ministers constituted the little presbytery at that early date. Resources to meet calls for preaching were limited in the face of great need. Yet John McMillan was asked to preach on the third Sabbath of November of that year at the Ohio Courthouse.[20] His *Journal* indicates that he kept the appointment. This is the earliest record of any assigned preaching in northern West Virginia.

The scene may have been Black's Cabin on Short Creek where, on January 16, 1777, was held the first civil court in the entire Valley of the Mississippi. Or it may have been the Courthouse itself which was erected with an accompanying jail in April of that same year. Civil and divine justice were thus being upheld in their West Virginia beginnings at the same location, a coincidence which typifies Presbyterian continued emphasis on "the law and the gospel." This is the only reference to the Ohio Court in the original minutes. The name disappears but the preaching point remained a responsibility of the Presbytery. It is referred to only as Short Creek.

The next year, and frequently thereafter, Joseph Smith and Thaddeus Dod were asked to preach on specified Sabbaths at Short Creek. How many gathered for worship and why these Founding Fathers did not formally organize the worshipers at Short Creek into a Presbyterian church are the unanswered questions upon which hinge the decision of priority. Tradition, however, states that Joseph Smith did organize the church in 1788, one year later than the claimed date, for the organization of the congregation at the Forks of Wheeling.

Toward this congregation at Short Creek, the Redstone Presbytery felt a continuing responsibility. It asked John Brice and James Hughes, the first two young men whom it licensed to preach, to conduct worship services on specified Sabbaths at Short Creek. One of these young men, John Brice, became the first pastor at the Forks of Wheeling Church. The other, John Hughes, accepted a similar call to the Short Creek and Lower Buffalo (Pennsylvania) churches. He was ordained on April 21, 1790, by the Redstone Presbytery in the customary phrasing of the minutes, "did by fasting and prayer, and with the imposition of hands of the presbytery set him apart to the holy office of the gospel ministry."[21]

In that dual field, Hughes labored for twenty-four years. He found time also to preach to weaker churches in the surrounding area and to engage in missionary work among the Indians and settlers across the Ohio. His contemporaries regarded him as a "faithful and unpretending preacher" and as a zealous pastor under whose ministry a number of revivals were evident. For a time he served on the first Board of Trustees of Canonsburg Academy and as a trustee of Jefferson College. He resigned in order to devote himself more fully to evangelistic work in the Presbytery of Miami, Ohio.[22] Since 1922 the Presbyterians at West Liberty have joined with their Methodist brethren in a federated church with the Presbyterians furnishing the sanctuary of worship and the Methodists the preaching.

Though West Liberty is probably the earliest preaching point in the Panhandle, the Forks of Wheeling Church at Elm Grove may have been the first congregation to be organized into a Presbyterian church. Well-founded tradition places the date as the Fall of 1787. This small group of Presbyterian settlers along the Wheeling Creek made their first appeal to Redstone Presbytery on October 19, 1784, just three years after the Presbytery was organized. The minutes fail to record any action upon their request for preaching. The plea was renewed the following year with favorable results. Though Reverend Thaddeus Dod was busy shepherding his two congregations at Ten Mile in Washington County, Pennsylvania, and in teaching the school he had organized three years earlier, Presbytery commissioned him to preach on the second Sabbath of April to those who might worship together at the Forks of Wheeling.[23] Dod was asked to return three months later to preach on the second Sabbath of June, 1786.[24] As they listened to Dr. Dod's sermon, they were alert to the danger of Indian attacks and were ready to grasp their rifles in defense. No church edifice housed that little group of devout worshipers. They were gathered together in worship beneath an oak tree on the hilltop where the church cemetery stands.[25] The church they organized is still called the Forks of Wheeling or the Old Stone Church, as it is more familiarly known to local residents.

Calls for preaching were coming in from many other places throughout the vast territory included in Redstone Presbytery. No ministers may have been available to send to the Forks of Wheeling the next year, nor the following year. But Presbytery did the next best thing. It sent on a missionary tour during the Fall of 1788, the first three young men whom it was educating for the ministry. All three of these young men were instructed to include Wheeling in their missionary tour and to preach there at least once.[26]

Of these, John Brice may have preached the most effective sermons. As a result, four months later he received a call to serve that church in a dual pastorate with Three Ridges (West Alexander, Pennsylvania). The call was accepted. John Brice began his ministry in these churches as the first pastor of a church in northern West Virginia, although he was not ready for ordination until the fourth Thursday of April, 1790.[27] Mr. Brice continued as pastor until 1808 when ill health necessitated his resignation.

Throughout most of his ministry, the congregation worshiped in a three-sided shed called a tent. There the minister conducted the worship while the congregation were seated on log benches or stood in the open air, undisturbed by varying types of weather. But in 1807 the historic Old Stone Church was erected which remained as the distinguishing place of worship until it was replaced by a more modern structure in 1860.[28] The church was richly blessed by the lifelong pastorate of Reverend James Hervey. His ministry at the Forks of Wheeling extended from his ordination by the Presbytery of Ohio in 1812 to his death in 1859.

Mr. Hervey's missionary zeal throughout his long ministry resulted in the organization of three other Presbyterian churches. He nurtured into life the First Presbyterian Church of Wheeling where he preached until it was strong enough to call a pastor in 1831. For several years he gathered together for worship a group of Presbyterian families at Wolf Run, about four miles northwest of Cameron. Patiently he labored with the ten or twelve people who attended his preaching services at Dallas and saw the congregation grow large enough to form the West Union Presbyterian Church on September 23, 1831. To his new church he gave one-half of his time for nine years, receiving as compensation an annual salary of one hundred and sixty dollars.

Dr. Hervey was a strong character who made an indelible impression on the religious life of the entire area especially as a leader in the temperance movement. His forty-seven years of consecrated service laid the broad foundations upon which have been built one of the leading churches of West Virginia. This Forks of Wheeling Church at Elm Grove is often referred to as the "mother" church of all the Presbyterian churches in the city of Wheeling.

Three Springs Presbyterian Church

As the traveler drives along Route 22 through Weirton Heights, his attention is attracted by a historical marker. As he reads that bronze tribute to a historic past, he notes that it marks the spot where stood another of the pioneer Presbyterian churches in the West Virginia Panhandle. Here James Campbell in 1790, with the assistance of a group of neighbors, built a large church on his own farm.[29] In the records of the Redstone Presbytery, it is called Three Springs Church. It is now relocated and rebuilt in the heart of industrial Weirton and renamed the Cove Presbyterian Church. As soon as their church was built, this group of Presbyterian neighbors petitioned Redstone Presbytery to send them a visiting preacher. Presbytery responded by sending Reverend John Brice to lead them in worship on the third Sabbath of November.[30] In July of the following year, Mr. Brice returned for another Sabbath Day's services. Later, in November of that same year, Reverend James Hughes, another neighboring Presbyterian minister, spent an entire day in spiritual leadership through worship and instruction. West Virginia Presbyterians in those pioneer days of small beginnings had to be grateful for meager spiritual favors with the blessing of a sermon only at infrequent intervals. As additional men were licensed to preach by the Presbytery, preaching became more frequent but never more than four times a year. Preachers were scarce. They had to divide their time in order to preach among numerous congregations who were seeking the comforts and warnings of the Gospel.

Better days were soon to dawn. Growth in the number of ministers made advisable the division of Redstone into two presbyteries in 1793. The Panhandle churches were placed in the new Presbytery of Ohio. Preaching at the Three Springs was still very sporadic for several years. But on October 17, 1798, a consecrated churchman of thirty-nine years of age presented himself to the

Presbytery of Ohio as a candidate for the ministry. He was none other than Elisha Macurdy.

After completing the necessary course of education, Macurdy accepted a call to Three Springs and Cross Roads (now Florence, Pennsylvania).[31] Soon the influence of this tremendous personality was felt throughout the entire church in Western Pennsylvania and the Panhandle area of West Virginia. His name is linked particularly with the great Revival of 1802 which first began to be manifested in Macurdy's congregation at Three Springs where a small group of devout women met for prolonged prayer. Soon it spread far and wide, influencing the social and religious outlook of the entire Upper Ohio Valley. In the wake of this historic revival came the "Sunday School, the Prayer Meeting, the Missionary Movement, the crusade against strong drink and the crusade against slavery."[32] Macurdy continued in his dual field of service until 1824 when he resigned from the Three Springs Church to devote his full time to the church at Florence.

Presbyterians in Wheeling Town

The First Presbyterian Church of Wheeling is another of the strong churches in the northern Panhandle area which traces its uncertain beginnings to the missionary zeal of the Redstone and Ohio presbyteries. Though the Presbyterians in that city must yield to the churches already named the prestige of age, yet they can defend an authentic claim to the honor of now worshiping in the oldest church building in that section of West Virginia.

Just when Presbyterian preaching began south of old Fort Henry, along the Ohio River in the growing village of Wheeling, is shrouded in uncertainty. Confusion of names with the Forks of Wheeling in the early records of Presbytery is difficult to avoid. As early as 1791 there is the record of an appointment of Reverend John Brice to preach at Big Wheeling on the second Sabbath of March.[33] Mr. Brice at that time was serving as pastor of the Forks of Wheeling Church in neighboring Elm Grove, only five miles distant. It is natural to assume that he would be interested also in the spiritual welfare of Presbyterians who were included among the pioneer settlers. In 1802 Presbytery received a "supplication for supplies" from the congregation of Wheeling Town. Reverend James Hughes, another neighboring pastor in the Panhandle, was appointed to preach on the third Sabbath of November.

With such occasional preaching as Presbytery could provide, supplemented by the volunteered service of Mr. Brice and later his successor, Joseph Stevenson, the little group of Presbyterians in Wheeling were held together in an informal fellowship of worship. Population was only about two hundred when Reverend James Hervey became pastor of the Forks of Wheeling Church in 1812. Hervey was a zealous missionary pastor, an aggressive advocate of righteousness, and a preacher of power and persuasion. He was one of the great personalities of Presbyterianism, a man of cherished memory and permanent influence throughout a wide area.[34]

Soon he was preaching with some regularity at Wheeling and his Session was accepting responsibility for the spiritual oversight of the unorganized congregation. For his services he received some compensation, probably a specified amount. The minutes of Ohio Presbytery on April 22, 1818, contain this interesting evidence of contrasting promptness in payment: "Mr. Hervey reported ye Forks of Wheeling clear until the first of November last and Wheeling Town in arrears about $400."[35]

Wheeling was now growing rapidly. It was the county seat. Brick houses were replacing log cabins. The old Cumberland Trail, along which the settlers had slowly wended their way to establish homes in the receding frontier, had become the Cumberland Pike. Conestoga wagons were rolling over its improved highway. In August, 1818, the first mail stage began regular service to Wheeling. Growth throughout the community was inevitable. Two years before, Noah Zane had given land "to the mayor and commonality of Wheeling, Virginia" for the purpose of erecting thereon a Presbyterian church.[36] Since the congregation was as yet unorganized, title to the property was placed in the hands of the borough officials to hold in trust until the congregation could be organized and trustees elected.

The congregation still looked to the Session of the Forks of Wheeling Church for the sacraments and spiritual direction. The two congregations in 1819 could only report a joint membership of one hundred and thirteen, including seven new members who had been added that year. It was not until May 26, 1826, that Wheeling was organized with forty-four charter members as a separate church by Elisha Macurdy. He was acting under the authority of what had then become the Presbytery of Washington, in whose territorial bounds Wheeling had been placed.[37]

However, construction of the church edifice had already begun, perhaps two years earlier, when on September 4, 1823, seven trustees were chosen on a temporary basis for the definite purpose of erecting the planned sanctuary and securing the necessary funds. Work progressed slowly so that the fifty-four-foot-square building was not ready for use until 1825. When the town of Wheeling celebrated the fiftieth anniversary of the Declaration of Independence on July 4, 1826, the meeting was held in the newly constructed Presbyterian church.[38] It was an imposing structure of Grecian architectural design, the finest church building in the community, surpassing those which the Methodists and Episcopalians had previously built.

So well did those Presbyterians build that the original edifice still stands. It proudly claims to be the oldest building in downtown Wheeling. Repaired on several occasions to protect it from the ravages of time, and enlarged to provide additional facilities for greater efficiency in service, this historic sanctuary has been retained in its original simplicity and beauty. There the large congregation of the First Presbyterian Church of Wheeling still worships to the glory of God and with such pride in the past as comes from the authentic claim that they are worshiping in the oldest

Presbyterian Church U.S.A. building in the entire state of West Virginia. But even more worthy of pride is the fact that twenty-seven sons and daughters of this First Presbyterian Church of Wheeling have been ministers or missionaries to foreign lands.[39]

Other Presbyterian churches were organized later within the expanding city limits as Wheeling developed into a prosperous industrial center and became the largest city in West Virginia. For sixteen years Wheeling had the honored distinction of being the capital of the state. The Second Presbyterian Church was organized in 1848 largely as a colony of the First Church. It was followed one year later by the organization of a Third Presbyterian Church.

Among the distinguished pastors of the Second Presbyterian Church have been the Rev. Dr. Samuel J. Wilson, who resigned after a short pastorate to serve for twenty-seven years on the faculty of Western Theological Seminary and the Rev. Dr. James D. Moffatt, who closed a ten-year ministry to become president of Washington and Jefferson College. As moderator of the General Assembly in 1905, he led the successful movement to unite the Presbyterian and Cumberland denominations. He was reared in the Second Church of Wheeling. As a young man directly from Princeton Seminary, he succeeded his father, Reverend John Moffatt, in the pulpit. Like Elliott Swift in the First Church of Allegheny, he was another exception to the Biblical observation that "a prophet is not without honor save in his own community."

As the city expanded into the suburbs, other Presbyterian churches were developing. In the suburban area of Warwood, now a part of Wheeling, a Presbyterian church was organized in 1905, composed of twenty-two charter members. In 1956 this thriving congregation of four hundred and fifty-six members climaxed a fiftieth anniversary celebration with the dedication of a new edifice for worship and religious education.

In another favorable suburban area, the Vance Memorial began in 1893 as a mission Sunday School in the Leatherwood School House with fifty pupils and teachers. Four years later, on the site where many years before had stood the pioneer cabin in which James Vance was born, was erected a beautiful church building of Romanesque design. The church was the gift of Mr. J. N. Vance, a prominent Wheeling industrialist, in memory of his parents, James and Mary Vance. Additions and improvements have since been made to the building to adapt it to meet more effectively the growing needs of a prosperous residential area and to enable it to house the broader and more diversified program of a modern church. The Vance Memorial Church in 1957 reported the largest membership of any Presbyterian Church U.S.A. in West Virginia.

Expansion Along the Monongahela River

The mother Presbytery of Redstone did not limit its missionary activities to the development of these new churches in the upper Panhandle area of what is now Wheeling Presbytery. Simultaneously it was assigning different members to travel southward toward the headwaters of the Monongahela River and to visit places like Morgantown, Fairmont, and Clarksburg throughout the present Presbytery of Grafton. Wherever settlers were establishing homes and whenever supplications for preaching were received, this missionary-minded Presbytery was eager to carry the gospel through Presbyterian messengers of faith and consecration.

The story of the beginning of Presbyterianism in the upper Monongahela Valley is quite similar to the missionary ventures into the Panhandle. At the same meetings of Redstone Presbytery, requests for preaching were received from both areas. The same ministers were sent into both areas on assigned Sabbaths as the pioneer ministers traveled extensively to Presbyterian settlers. First, pastors like James Dunlap and Thaddeus Dod were appointed in the Spring of 1786 to preach on specified Sabbaths to the settlements along the Cheat River.[40] Then new recruits for the ministry, such as John Brice, Joseph Patterson, John McPherrin, and Samuel Porter were commissioned to visit Morgantown and Monongalia County during each of the following years and to supplement the visits of the older pastors.[41] The minutes reveal a faithful eagerness to respond to additional requests for preaching as frequently as other duties would permit.

In the Vicinity of Morgantown

Morgantown is first mentioned by name on October 21, 1788, when John Brice was asked to preach there on the third Sabbath of March. Joseph Patterson was assigned to follow him two weeks later. This rather exceptional arrangement indicated that a considerable number of Presbyterians had traveled along the old Catawba Trail and were finding homes along the banks of the Monongahela River. Among these was Colonel William McCleary who was the pioneer leader both in church and civic projects.[42] The settlement had been incorporated as a borough in 1785 and was gaining some importance as the seat of government of Monongalia County and as a trading and industrial community.

Just when a Presbyterian church was first organized is not known with certainty. An oft-quoted community tradition credits the organization to Reverend Joseph Patterson on November, 1788. However, there is no supporting testimony in the minutes of Redstone Presbytery that Patterson preached at Morgantown earlier than March of the following year. He was not ordained until November 11, 1789.[43]

The first pastor was Reverend Ashbel G. Fairchild whom Presbytery ordained as an evangelist on July 1, 1818. He was in the employ of the Western Missionary Society and appointed to serve in the Morgantown Missionary Circuit.[44] His responsibility was not only to preach to the Morgantown congregation on a part-time basis, but also to itinerate among the other Presbyterian settlements in the Upper Monongahela Valley. During the week he taught in the newly established Monongalia Academy, which later developed into the present University of West Virginia.[45]

An act of the General Assembly of Virginia had previously set apart a half-acre lot as the Sepulchre Lot. Since both the Presbyterians and Methodists had secured burial grounds elsewhere, the Sepulchre Lot became available as the site of a church. The leadership of Presbyterians in Morgantown at that early date is revealed in the fact that, of the nine trustees of community property, seven were Presbyterians and the remaining two were Episcopalians. These trustees voted to give the property to the first church group who would build upon it. In a spirit of true Christian unity, the Presbyterians and Episcopalians agreed to erect a stone and brick building which "shall be the property of the Presbyterian and Protestant Episcopal Societies jointly and their successors forever."[46] The building, begun in 1819, was not ready for worship until 1822.

The dedication of the church was visible evidence that the Presbyterian congregation was gathering new strength. Mr. Fairchild was asked to discontinue serving as a traveling evangelist and teacher and to become the installed pastor of the church, but only for one-third of his time. During the remaining portion of his time, he was to serve as pastor of the George's Creek and Greensburg churches. Presbytery approved this threefold pastorate and installed Mr. Fairchild in his triple parish on July 2, 1822.[47] In this broad range type of ministry, he continued until 1827 when he resigned at Morgantown to continue in the other two fields.

With the installation of Mr. Fairchild as their pastor, the Presbyterians began to develop a sense of ownership of the building they were occupying with the Episcopalians. Presbyterians at Morgantown grew in number and prestige. This was true especially under the pastorate of Reverend James Davis, Mr. Fairchild's successor, who served throughout a fruitful ministry of eighteen years. On the other hand, their Episcopalian brethren were few in number and feeble in zeal. They had no formal or separate organization until 1868. At that time they presented a belated claim to one-half of the original lot and the repaired building. The claim was tested in court. The common-sense ruling was that the Presbyterians had exercised their claim for fifty years whereas the Episcopalians had forfeited their legal right through inactivity. Title was legally given to the Presbyterian congregation which had used and maintained the property. A new and enlarged sanctuary was then erected on the original lot.[48]

Farther Up to Fairmont

The Redstone Presbytery, after licensing Robert Marshall in April, 1790, to preach the gospel, sent him on an extended missionary tour which included a visit to the Presbyterian settlers along the upper Monongahela River in the vicinity of Middletown (now Fairmont[49]). Their letters of greeting could well have been the words of the Apostle Paul: "To the church in thine house." Mr. Marshall may have gone directly to the homes of two brothers, Thomas and Nathan Hall, who with their families had settled in 1785. Without the benefit of clergy, these brothers had started religious services in their home and had invited their neighbors. Here they formed a Bible-study class on the Sabbath Day. The Fleming and the Barnes families soon joined them as a nucleus for family worship and study. As the months and years passed, Thomas Marquis and David Smith and others from the Presbytery also responded to their pleas for preaching. The services alternated between the Halls and the Flemings.

Reverend Thomas Cooley, a wandering preacher from a distant presbytery, was given permission to preach over an extended period at Middletown and Clarksburg during the Summer of 1792. Any hope of having him as a pastor was dashed by the brethren of Redstone Presbytery. After carefully examining Mr. Cooley, they decided that his ministerial credentials were forged.[50] Seven years later revived hope of securing a pastor again rose and fell into discouragement when Middletown and Morgantown joined in calling Andrew Gwin, a young licentiate of Redstone. But he declined their call and accepted instead the pastorate at Pigeon Creek, Pennsylvania.[51]

Discouragement and some fading enthusiasm may have followed

their long and futile search for a pastor. It was not until 1815 that the congregation was formally organized into a church. Six years longer elasped before the faithful members of the little congregation left their private homes of worship to dedicate their first sanctuary. Still it was only a one-story unpainted, frame building erected out of roughhewn lumber. It stood directly across from the site of the present Courthouse. Instead of a central entrance, the worshipers entered by one of two widely separted doors on the front, the men using the one and the women the other. Perhaps this was a matter of convenience since the men and women sat on opposite sides of the building. If any one of the worshipers felt a little sleepy during a long sermon, he availed himself of the privilege of standing in a determined effort to keep wide enough awake to hear the message of the preachers who were visiting at infrequent intervals. Tradition reports that at times there were more people standing than sitting. The sermons were long and the benches were hard.

Such persistent determination at last won a just reward. In 1831 the church welcomed Reverend Cyrus B. Bristol as the first resident pastor. Middletown became Fairmont. Growth and prosperity followed. The large Fairmont Presbyterian congregation now worships in a commodious and beautiful sanctuary erected in 1916. From its membership five missionaries have gone forth in distant service for the universal Saviour of mankind. These honored five include Mrs. A. R. McFarland, who gave forty years of her life as a pioneer missionary with Shelton Jackson in Alaska, Miss Hildra Hellstrom, who served twenty-one years as a missionary nurse in Korea, Miss Clara Lloyd, who retired in 1950 after having been in India since 1914, Reverend Lorentz Emery, who has been serving since 1946 in Colombia, South America, and his brother, James H. Emery, who has been stationed at Guatemala, Central America, since 1952. The Fairmont Church has carried a share of the financial support of some of these representatives of a missionary-minded congregation.

Throughout the long years that Middletown had been seeking a pastor, other Presbyterian settlers in northern West Virginia were similarly petitioning both the Redstone and Ohio presbyteries for ministers. These included Clarksburg, Sandy Creek, Tygart's Valley, Prickett's Settlement, Good Hope, Stewardstown, and French Creek. Both presbyteries responded with the usual assignment of ministers to preach at specific points on a specified number of Sabbaths. Thus French Creek emerged into an organized Presbyterian church in 1819, Buckhannon in 1820, Clarksburg in 1829, Sugar Grove and Laurel Point in 1835.

Assistance from Missionary Societies

Of these new churches French Creek and Buckhannon had been the most fortunate in their early search for a pastor. A group of Presbyterians and Congregationalists from New England had settled in Upshur County along the French Creek.[52] Reverend Moses Allen from Redstone and Reverend Thomas Hunt from the Ohio Presbytery had visited them and preached occasionally. But these pious settlers yearned for something more frequent than an occasional sermon. They were determined to help themselves. They experimented with the novel idea of gathering together for worship each Sunday and of having one of their number read a sermon written by some prominent minister. This novel idea, begun in 1812, developed into a custom of long standing. Even after a pastor was installed among them, the custom of having a layman read a sermon was continued as a traditional part of the communion service.

These pioneering worshipers also decided to assist themselves by writing letters to their friends in New England. They explained their spiritual needs and their yearning for someone to bring to them the consolation of the sacraments. The Lord apparently does help those who help themselves. The Central Association of Hampshire County, Massachusetts, responded in 1816. This New England group commissioned a traveling missionary, Reverend Asa Brooks of Hatfield, Massachusetts, to visit the towns and settlements in the vicinity of Buckhannon and French Creek. He was authorized "to perform the work of an evangelist by dispensing to the people, to whom you are sent, the pure doctrines...... to extend the blessings of gospel grace in the recovery of sinners to God and in the establishment and consolation of His saints.... Be a good steward of the mysteries of God. Faithfully keep the trust which we commit to you as becometh that servant who expects to give an account of his stewardship at the Great Day."[53]

Mr. Brooks remained as a missionary an entire year. He journeyed back to New England. But his heart was in Upshur County. He felt impelled to return. He was given credentials of transfer to the Presbytery of Redstone. On April 20, 1819, after careful examination, he was enrolled as a member. Both the French Creek and Buckhannon congregations called him as their pastor. He accepted and formally organized Presbyterian churches in both communities.[54] The first entry in the minute book of the French Creek Church records the official merging of Presbyterians and Congregationalists into a united church. "There being in this settlement a number both male and female, having letters of recommendation from different Congregational churches in Massachusetts with which they were united previous to their emigrating to this place, and wishing again to be favored with church privileges, a time was publicly appointed for the election of ruling elders."[55] This is the first instance of the effective working of the Plan of Union in West Virginia.

To that distinction another first might be added to the credit of this venturesome French Creek Church. Here was organized in 1828 the first Temperance Society in West Virginia. So effectively did it carry forward its war against the use and sale of intoxicating liquors that Upshur County never had a licensed saloon.[56] Those New England settlers at French Creek were truly a pioneering and precedent-setting group with consecrated zeal.

In 1829 Mr. Brooks and the elders from French Creek organized a Presbyterian church in Clarksburg forty miles away. Soon he resigned his pastorate at French Creek and moved with his eight children to Clarksburg. There he continued to serve until his death on December 23, 1834. There he lies buried under the present church. A tablet and an impressive stained glass window help to keep fresh the memory of a noble leader who laid broad foundations of Presbyterianism in northern West Virginia.

Missionary Established Sugar Grove Church

But the Congregational Association of Massachusetts was not the only missionary-minded group which sought to reinforce the expansion program of Redstone Presbytery in what is now Grafton Presbytery. The General Assembly's Board of Domestic Missions sent at least one man into the field. The Sugar Grove Presbyterian Church is the continued result of his missionary labors. In addition, he served as the first pastor of the Fairmont Church.

The minutes of the Session of the Sugar Grove Church record that "Rev. Cyrus Beecher Bristol, a missionary from the Assembly's Board, commenced preaching at Stewart's Run December, 1831."[57] Three years later a church was organized with eighteen members. Services were held in the home of William Stewart until a church could be erected. This pioneer building was destroyed by fire in 1845.

The little congregation then moved to a more convenient location on Dent's Run where the present Sugar Grove Church now stands. Membership has never been large. The church was affiliated for necessary support first with the Fairmont Church. Mr. Bristol served both congregations as pastor for four years. Later Sugar Grove was yoked with Morgantown which was much closer. Through the years this Sugar Grove Church has been cherished as one of the notable rural landmarks of the historic past.[58] Annual reunions have joined former members and interested friends in appreciative recognition of the part played by rural churches in quickening the spiritual energy which has manifested itself in the lives of individuals who are scattered far and wide in Christian service.

Another missionary sent into somewhat the same area was Reverend Loyal Young. He was the first young man to enter the ministry from the congregation of the French Creek Presbyterian Church in Upshur County. He was only a lad of five years of age when his father, Robert Young, moved the family from Charlemont, Massachusetts, to establish a pioneer home in 1818 along the bank of French Creek in West Virginia. Robert Young was one of those New England Congregationalists whose letter had resulted in the coming of Reverend Asa Brooks as a visiting missionary. He was a charter member and the first elder elected when the Presbyterian church was organized in French Creek. Under the kindly ministration of a devout father and a noble pastor, who was his first teacher, Loyal Young's thoughts turned naturally to the ministry.[59]

After graduating from Western Theological Seminary in 1832, he was chosen as an agent of the Western Missionary Society. His first appointment was to visit Virginia and North Carolina. He traveled in the cold of winter on horseback to Morgantown and Beverly, up the valley of the Tygart and across the Cheat Mountain. He stopped at numerous places enroute, preaching wherever he found an opportunity. One of these places was Hot Springs. The audience was in a careless, hilarious mood and uninterested in a serious spiritual service. After several failures to catch the attention of the group, Mr. Young repeated this story, told previously by Dr. Plumer in a neighboring community:

"A Dutchman and his son were driving through a strange area. They came to a place where a spring was bubbling up out of the ground. They stopped to get a drink of water. The father started to drink. No sooner had the very warm water crossed his lips than he spit it out and shouted to his son: 'Hans, drive on quickly. This water is hot. Hell is not very far from this place.' "[60]

Attention was caught. The application was apparent. Young proceeded to drive home his message and its warning, but with what result the traveler-preacher did not record. After completing his assigned journey, he accepted a thirty-five-year pastorate at Butler, Pennsylvania.

Dr. Young returned to West Virginia at the age of sixty years to spend his remaining ministry of twenty-three years at French Creek, Buckhannon, Parkersburg and other neighboring churches. His eight children all grew to Christian adulthood and took a deep interest in church work. Three of his sons were ordained as elders in the Presbyterian church. One was a teacher among the Choctaw Indians. Two were ordained to the Presbyterian ministry. Of these, one was the Reverend S. Hall Young, the heroic missionary to Alaska.[61] "How far yon candle throws its beams," observed Shakespeare. The ever-widening influence for good of that little church on the banks of French Creek is unmeasurable.

Years of Growth and Harmony

From this wide diversity of sources, streams of Presbyterianism were thus flowing into various parts of western Virginia which now forms the state of West Virginia. Watered by these different streams, Presbyterian churches in increasing numbers were organized and grew in spiritual strength. The churches in the Panhandle area were under the jurisdiction of Washington Presbytery as part of the former Synod of Wheeling. Those at the headwaters of the Monongahela River were included in the Redstone Presbytery under the Synod of Pittsburgh. Churches in the central and southern regions had ecclesiastical ties with Greenbrier Presbytery and with the Synod of Virginia. Three presbyteries and three synods, looking in three different directions for presbyterial and synodical planning and supervision, yet all united under one nationwide General Assembly. The three presbyteries worked together in close co-operation. They assisted one another in establishing new churches and in upholding moral standards. The New and Old School Schism was not a disturbing factor, with ecclesiastical loyalty to the Old School branch.

The Effects of War

But a storm was already gathering on the horizon. Controversy over slavery was crystalizing into sharp differences of opinion in the civil and religious councils of church and nation. The resulting bitterness could not be restrained within the bonds of brotherhood. Division was inevitable. The strife of war split the church and nation in twain as brother lifted sword against brother. The War Between the States banished slavery. But it left a trail of entrenched bitterness that only time is slowly healing. The western counties of Virginia could not support their mother state. In 1863 West Virginia was recognized as an independent state and made a member of the Union. West Virginia itself was split by differences of opinion and conflicting loyalties. She gave thirty-six thousand of her sons to the Federal Army and about ten thousand to the Confederate forces.

Parts of the newly formed state of West Virginia were overrun by both Confederate and Federal armies. Guerilla warfare was carried on in many sections with the resulting destruction of church property. At Point Pleasant the Presbyterian church was taken over by the Union soldiers and used both as barracks and as a hospital. A complete renovation was necessary before it again was a fit sanctuary for worship. At Buckhannon the church building was completely destroyed. Bricks being used to construct an Institute for the church at Baxter were appropriated by the encamped soldiers who used them for ovens and chimneys. The loss was such a blow to the little congregation that the school had to be abandoned. At Reedsville soldiers used the church building as a place of assembling and loitering on their way to Newburg. At Sistersville the church was closed for five years. The French Creek Church was carelessly burned to the ground while being used as an encampment. Confederate soldiers swept bare the entire Upshur Valley of everything that could be used for food, carrying away cattle valued at over thirty thousand dollars.[62]

But the greatest tragedy of the war, from the viewpoint of the Presbyterian church, was the division into a Northern and a Southern Presbyterian church. This division still remains although time has concealed most of the other scars of the conflict. The separation was particularly tragic in West Virginia where Presbyterianism has always needed the strength which comes from unity in organization as well as in mission.

An unmarked line, extending in an easterly direction from Point Pleasant, on the Ohio River, to the eastern border of the state where it touches the most southern point of Western Maryland, became a new "Mason and Dixon Line" of West Virginia Presbyterianism. Almost all churches north of that line remained with the Presbyterian Church U.S.A. South of that line, almost all the churches were enrolled in the Southern or U.S. Presbyterian Church.[63] Only one additional letter in the official names, yet what an insurmountable barrier to unity! In extent of territory and in the number of churches, the majority strength of West Virginia Presbyterianism ceded to the South where it still remains.

There was, however, one exception in the South—the Kanawha Presbyterian Church of Charleston. This oldest of Presbyterian churches in that area seemed about equally divided in sentiment. For ten years the Kanawha church persistently tried the compromising position of neutrality. During that decade of uncertainty, the church functioned independently of Presbyterian control. It refused to join either of the separated branches of Presbyterianism. A decision had to be made eventually with the inevitable result. The church itself split. A number of prominent families withdrew. They formed themselves into the First Presbyterian Church of Charleston and joined the Greenbrier Presbytery as part of the southern denomination. The little continuing group of twenty-five retained the name and joined the West Virginia Presbytery of the Presbyterian Church U.S.A. Charleston is still a divided Presbyterian stronghold. The original Kanawha Church has grown into a large aggressive organization and has helped to develop two other Presbyterian Churches U.S.A. In the meantime, however, the southern branch has expanded into fifteen churches throughout the city of Charleston.[64]

New Boundaries of Presbyteries

With the division of the denomination came new presbyterial boundaries. The General Assembly in 1863 authorized the formation of a new presbytery to be known as the Presbytery of West Virginia to include all the churches below the southern boundary of Pennsylvania. That action made a new and extensive presbytery which covered all the Presbyterian Churches U.S.A. in West Virginia. Distances of travel seemed too great to some churches. They flatly refused to join the statewide presbytery. They preferred to remain in Washington or Redstone Presbytery.

Only four ministers and their elders responded to the organizational meeting of the West Virginia Presbytery on the first Tuesday of October, 1863.[65] They faced with courage and consecration the gigantic task of developing the Presbyterian Church U.S.A. in West Virginia. Throughout the entire presbytery, there were only eight organized churches with a total membership of six hundred and forty-three. Many of the church buildings had been damaged by the war. Congregations were discouraged. The minutes of the Presbytery throughout those years of struggle and reorganization have been lost for the period from 1863 to 1874.

The story of the heroism of their faith cannot be told in detail. Only occasional reports are available. Glimpses of the pathetic needs throughout that struggling presbytery are given in the desperate plea of Dr. Loyal Young to the entire denomination for aid from the Five Million Dollar Memorial Fund which General Assembly had raised in celebration of the reunion of the New and Old School branches. Dr. Loyal Young had returned to his boyhood scenes in West Virginia. Since 1868 he was serving as pastor of that enterprising little church along the French Creek in Parkersburg Presbytery where he had first heard the call of the ministry under the leadership of Asa Brooks. He was devoting the mature years of his life to rekindling spiritual enthusiasm throughout the Presbytery torn by the strife of civil war. Thus

Dr. Young records his tour of observation in the early Fall of 1870:

"Yes, here I find a few Presbyterian churches. Twenty miles westward is Weston where we have fifteen members organized into a church, with not a shelter to screen them from the heat of summer or the chill blasts of winter when they meet for worship, unless some other denomination opens their doors. Twenty miles further, after passing through several gorges, I reach Glenville, on the Little Kanawha, where there are eight church members and no house of worship, their house having been destroyed during the war. Twelve miles distant northwest is Lebanon with a few members and no house of worship. Ten miles north is a church to which I sent a minister, statedly, Buckhannon. But they have no house of worship of their own, their church having been destroyed during the war."[66]

After thus picturing the wreckage of war in Presbyterian churches, he specified very modest sums of money which could be used wisely in the above needy fields:

"We need $1,500 from others to assist the church in Weston in building a house of worship. If we had a house of worship, there is a prospect of a flourishing congregation soon. We need $1,000 to assist the people of Buckhannon in rebuilding their church destroyed in the war. We need $800 to assist Lebanon church to build a house of worship. We need $1,000 to assist Glenville. We need $500 to assist the people of French Creek to complete their academy. There is now no school in the state under the Presbyterian influence. There is no college or academy nearer to us than sixty miles."[67]

Some help did come from the Board of Domestic Missions to supplement the greater help from the people themselves. These churches did gather strength. Progress was slow. The churches were widely separated. Attendance at Presbytery involved long journeys on horseback. Loyal Young related that he had to travel on horseback a distance of two hundred and thirty miles on the round trip from French Creek to Ravenswood to be present at the spring meeting of Presbytery. Enroute, however, he preached ten times to small groups of worshipers.[68] All opportunities to extend the cause of Christ must be utilized.

When the roll of the Presbytery of West Virginia was called in 1874, sixteen ministers were present. Still that was only a small number when the territorial bounds of the Presbytery included all Presbyterian Churches U.S.A. in the state of West Virginia except those in the Northern Panhandle area which remained in Washington Presbytery. In 1892 the Synod of Pennsylvania approved the request of West Virginia Presbytery that it be permitted to change its name to Parkersburg Presbytery as more expressive of the actual working territory of the Presbytery.

The final changes in name and territorial boundaries were made eleven years later when the Synod of West Virginia was constituted to include all Presbyterian Churches U.S.A. in the state. The three presbyteries necessary to form this Synod were secured by dividing Parkersburg into two presbyteries. The western part retained the name Parkersburg. The eastern half was known as the Grafton Presbytery. Also the churches in the Panhandle were withdrawn from the Washington Presbytery and organized into a separate presbytery which bore the local name Wheeling Presbytery. The new Synod of West Viriginia was thus composed of the presbyteries of Wheeling, Grafton, and Parkersburg. Synod met for organization October 18, 1904. Reverend J. H. Flanagan, pastor of the Grafton Church, was elected the first moderator.[69]

The bounds of this Synod of West Virginia became the boundaries of the state. A sense of solidarity was imparted. Enthusiasm and interest were concentrated on a more common task. The Presbyterian Church U.S.A. had at last achieved statewide unity; a forecast perhaps of that greater unity when all Presbyterians throughout the state will become one in organization and resources as well as in spiritual purpose. As it is now, a certain amount of overlapping of presbyterial boundaries and responsibilities and some rivalry between churches are inevitable, if not harmful.

Presbyterian Contribution to Education

An encouraging step toward this forthcoming unity was taken in 1908 when West Virginia Presbyterians, both U.S. and U.S.A., merged their educational interests in the united support and control of Davis and Elkins College at Elkins, West Virginia. It is the only Presbyterian college in the entire state of West Virginia. Though Presbyterian ministers had organized and taught in many local academies, none of these academies reached the status of a continuing Presbyterian college. Nor did any of these secondary schools or academies continue in service beyond the achievement of their immediate objectives. Presbyterians have never been eager to develop or maintain a competitive system of education through their parochial schools. With the development of public schools, they have unselfishly withdrawn the support of their own private and secondary schools. They have always concentrated their energies and resources upon the more Christian task of initiating and fostering schools in neglected areas when tax-supported institutions were not yet available or were still ineffective.

Even the famous Pattie Stockdale School in the mountain area at Colcord, in Raleigh County, was permitted to close when adequate public schools became available.[70] Throughout three decades, this famous boarding school for girls had been imparting moral and cultural ideals which changed the attitudes of many homes in the surrounding communities. Its curriculum had provided the usual eighth-grade education but, in addition, had given training in religion, cooking, sewing, gardening, agriculture, and homemaking.[71]

The full story of the contribution of Presbyterians to the development of the educational agencies in West Virginia would be a thrilling report of sacrificial zeal and patient determination on the part of heroic Presbyterian pastors. The Mountaineer State owes a tremendous debt of gratitude to these zealous Presbyterian pioneers of a new day who sowed the seeds of education and who cultivated rural institutions of learning along the entire frontier development. Only occasional references have been made to these educational forebears as the preceding narrative has been unfolded. The institutions these Presbyterian leaders initiated have either yielded to tax-supported schools or have been absorbed in nondenominational Teachers colleges, as at West Liberty, or in a state University, as at Morgantown.

Davis and Elkins College was fathered by the Southern Presbyterian Church. It was born amid a developing conviction in the minds of leaders in the Lexington Presbytery that the church should establish a college in West Virginia.[72] The new school opened its doors on February 1, 1898, to welcome a student body of six boys and four girls with seven additional students who attended evening classes and were working throughout the day. At first only a preparatory school curriculum was available. The new institution was appropriately named "The Elkins College Academy" since it was the definite plan to establish a "high grade classical school at Elkins to be nurtured into a college."

An initial financial campaign for thirty thousand dollars was authorized throughout Lexington and Winchester presbyteries.[73] Two state senators, H. G. Davis and S. B. Elkins, gave the developing college necessary acreage from a farm near Elkins and generous financial support. Thus located and supported, Davis and Elkins College was officially launched as a Presbyterian college on September 21, 1904, with fifty students, of whom forty-two were in the "prep" school.[74] Each year the college enrollment increased. At first the students were limited of necessity to residents from Elkins and other nearby areas. But, with the laying of paved roads connecting Elkins with the outside world, the service range of the college was widened.

Convincing evidence that the college was now well launched in the collegiate world appeared in the publicized success of its football teams—a popular criterion of true academic status. The coach of the team was none other than Dr. Marshall A. Allaben, the president of the college himself. The vigorous president had added to his administrative duties and teaching tasks the coaching of a football team as an important part of a well-rounded curriculum. After three previous years of experience, the year 1909 was acclaimed as "a glorious season." Full credit was given to the president-coach. The development of the team continued beyond his resignation in 1910. That year, under a student coach, the Davis and Elkins goal line was not crossed all season. The only blots on a perfect record were the two field goals scored by Marshall College.[75] So steadily did the college continue to expand its enrollment that in 1926 the administration felt that it was expedient to abolish the preparatory department.

The college, which had first been launched as a venture of faith among Southern Presbyterians, had expanded in 1908 into a vision of a college for all Presbyterians in West Virginia. The Presbyterian Church U.S.A. was invited to share jointly with the Presbyterian Church U.S. in the control and support of the school.[76] This evidence of Presbyterian unity in education has continued as the harmonious and well-established policy in the developing life of the college.

The year 1923 was a memorable and transitional year for the college. Mrs. Hallie Elkins, the daughter of the late Senator Davis, presented to the college, as a dormitory for women, her palatial home known as Halliehurst. The gift included a large tract of land of sixty-two acres which became the new site of the college. Growth was accelerated. On June 4, 1926, a new Science Hall and a new Liberal Arts Hall, with a central heating plant, were dedicated amid impressive ceremonies in which a large group of state educators participated. The faculty had expanded to nineteen. The student body had reached an enrollment of six hundred. Only two hundred and thirty-seven of these, however, were full-time students in either the college or preparatory school. The Kelly Observatory had been completed to house a Newtonian reflecting telescope, the only one of its kind in the state.[77] All this evidenced the pre-World War II progress of an all-too-inadequately financed college.

Further growth has seen the college expanding to include the present campus of one hundred and thirty-two acres and the erection of Graceland, a dormitory for men, and other additional buildings. The total property evaluation is now approximately two million dollars. The student body, formerly drawn only from the surrounding communities, includes representatives from many states and several overseas countries. In 1957, enrollment included five hundred and forty-six full-time students. Each year the college is the host for the meetings of the Synod of West Virginia, U.S.A., and for conferences of youth groups of the Synod and Synodical of the Presbyterian Church U.S.A. Likewise, the women of the Presbyterian Church U.S. hold their annual training school at Davis and Elkins during June.

Better things and still larger service lie before the college under the leadership of its gifted and consecrated president, the Rev. Dr. David K. Allen, who has been serving in that capacity since 1954. The "Dawn of a New Day" began in 1957 when a campaign for one million dollars was oversubscribed in memorials and gifts from churches, organizations, and individuals.[78] Presbyterians in West Virginia are united in the support of their only college and are determined to broaden its effective service to the church. May there be an equally strong determination to unite the Synods of the two denominations in all phases of statewide service for the advancement of the Kingdom of God through the co-ordinated work of the Presbyterian church in all of its branches.

CHAPTER IX Academies and Female Seminaries

I. ACADEMIES

THE OUTSTANDING contribution of Presbyterians to early education throughout the Upper Ohio Valley was the development of an extensive network of academies as the first educational institutions west of the Allegheny Mountains. The second chapter of this book has traced the early growth of the three famous pioneer academies of Pittsburgh, Jefferson, and Washington and their subsequent development into great institutions of higher learning which continue to serve with ever-widening effectiveness.

The period 1802–1870 witnessed the multiplication of similar academies, as Presbyterian ministers and laymen sought to provide a basic cultural education throughout the growing settlements on the expanding frontier. A few of these Presbyterian-established academies developed into colleges. The great majority, however, sought merely to serve their own communities on the secondary level and to train students for college. These Presbyterian academies were organized to meet a real need for education; not to advance the glory of Presbyterianism or even to propagate the faith, except as they prepared young men for the Presbyterian ministry.

With the growth of public high schools and other educational institutions, these Presbyterian academies were permitted to fade into history with only the memory of their service to remain as an interesting monument to a transitional epoch that is gone. Yet they live on in the ideals of the communities they served so nobly.

Every presbytery throughout the Upper Ohio Valley has within its bounds at least one proudly recalled academy whose religious and educational contribution is a challenging memory. A review of some of the more influential of these academies reveals the great contribution the Presbyterian church made to the developing educational life of the Upper Ohio Valley.

Greersburg Academy

In Beaver County at Greersburg, now Darlington, still stands the "old stone pile," as the Old Stone Academy was fondly dubbed. It has a long list of distinguished alumni, but its chief claim to immortal fame is that here William Holmes McGuffey, America's most influential educator, received his early education. The Academy was established by the Reverend Thomas E. Hughes perhaps as early as 1803. The records of Erie Presbytery do not take cognizance of the educational activity at Greersburg until 1806. At that time the Presbytery urged the churches to "give their aid to erect an academy at Greersburg," and "the legislature of the State appropriated six hundred dollars towards it when the charter was granted."[1] Mr. Hughes was the school's first principal and worked tirelessly to promote education in this place. He visited the New England states in his zeal to get new ideas for his new school. For more than thirty years, Dr. Hughes served the Presbyterian church and the little academy in Darlington.

One evening, while riding alone in a wooded area not far from Youngstown, Ohio, Mr. Hughes heard a woman praying aloud in a garden near her house. She was pleading in prayer for her little boys and dedicating them to God. Mr. Hughes was so impressed that he made an inquiry about the family and the result was that special arrangements were made to have one of the boys come to his Academy.[2]

That lad later became famous as the Rev. Dr. William H. McGuffey, an educator and writer of *Eclectic Readers.* These "Readers," together with his *Eclectic Spelling Book,* reached the phenomenal sale of twenty-two million copies and exerted a dominant influence in the cultural and moral development of that period. Greersburg prepared him for Washington College, from which institution he received his A.B. with honors in 1826. The Presbytery of Oxford, at a meeting on October 8, 1830, ordained him to the ministry. In addition to his teaching, he preached on Sunday with some regularity. Teaching, however, was his true love and field of unique service.

Mr. Hughes, in setting up his school at Greersburg, was carrying into action the injunction of Reverend John McMillan, his theological instructor at Canonsburg, who urged his students not only to preach the gospel, but also to establish schools where ambitions could be stirred and characters moulded throughout the week. Money to carry forward a school was scarce. Luxuries were few and frills avoided. A hint of this necessary austerity appears in the minutes of the Board of Trustees of the Academy in the early years where the menu for the students was prescribed as follows: "Resolved, that breakfast shall consist of bread with butter, or meat, and coffee. Dinner of bread and meat, with sauce. Supper of bread and milk."[3]

It is assumed that with increased prosperity both the physical and the intellectual menus were broadened throughout the thirty years Dr. Hughes served as principal of the Academy. He was assisted in his work by devoted preacher-teachers like James Rowland, Robert Dilworth, and J. R. Cunningham. Young men were fitted to continue their work at Jefferson or Washington colleges. Many entered the Presbyterian ministry.

Meadville and Bassenheim and Cross Creek Academies

Meadville Academy, later to become Allegheny College, was the next Presbyterian educational effort to get under way. Joseph Stockton also had studied theology under Dr. McMillan during the same years, in part, when Thomas Hughes was at Canonsburg.

He also had received from Dr. McMillan the injunction to establish an academy in the community where he had been serving as pastor since 1801. Four years of pastoral service was necessary before Stockton could organize an academy as part of his ministerial service to the community. Four years later, in 1809, he moved to Pittsburgh to accept the principalship of the Pittsburgh Academy. He also was a writer of textbooks and the most influential educator in the years of Pittsburgh's early development. After ten years' service as an academy, the school at Meadville developed into Allegheny College under Presbyterian leadership until it became a Methodist school.

Little is known of an academy which Presbyterians organized in Zelienople called The Bassenheim Academy. Even exact dates are not available. A beginning was made around 1825-1827, in the baronial castle built by Baron von Basse, the founder of Zelienople. A Mr. Saunders and the Reverend Aaron A. Williams, D.D., were among the teachers or principals at this Academy. Mr. Williams was a Jefferson College man of the Class of 1826, who taught and preached in Zelienople during the year 1832–1833. No information is available on Mr. Saunders. Some scanty details of the work of this Academy are given in *The Life and Letters of Dr. William A. Passavant.*[4] The building in which the Academy met was destroyed by fire in 1842. The date of its closing is uncertain. It is generally believed that some famous men attended the old Academy, although the names are not recorded.

The educational activities of Presbyterians were in evidence also at Cross Creek in Washington County. In the early days of the Reverend Thomas Marquis, that "silver-tongued" orator, it was thought unwise to start another academy so close to the Canonsburg and Washington institutions. With the arrival of the Reverend John Stockton, who began a fifty-year pastorate in 1827, a new appraisal was made. Within a year the Cross Creek Academy was opened. It was not to be considered as in competition with the colleges nearby, but was both a presbytery and a secondary school.

In addition to Mr. Stockton, a graduate of Washington College, others who taught in the school were Samuel George Marshall, Robert McMillan, and Thomas M. C. Stockton, the pastor's son. Thirty young men who attended this Academy are known to have entered the ministry.[5]

About the same time that the Reverend John Stockton was opening his academy at Cross Creek, the Reverend John McCluskey, a Jefferson graduate, was organizing an academy at West Alexander.[6] Though his pastoral duties were exacting, Mr. McCluskey was able to direct the school for several years with limited assistance. A steady increase of students resulted in the selection of a Board of Trust. The selection of this Board played a part in the granting of a charter by the state (1840) and in the decision of Washington Presbytery to receive the Academy in 1849 as both a parochial and a presbyterial school. When the founder of the Academy, now "Dr." McCluskey, turned the work over to his successor, the Reverend William H. Lester, in 1853, forty-four young men had prepared themselves for the ministry, thirty-two of whom were Presbyterian. The good work continued and young students were able to secure a preparatory education at a minimum expense. Most of those who were interested in advanced study entered Jefferson or Washington College.

Elders Ridge Academy

The best known of all these Presbyterian academies in Pennsylvania and the most widely influential over an extended period of service, was the famous academy at Elders Ridge near Saltsburg. One year after the Reverend Alexander Donaldson began his lifelong pastorate in this small rural community, he opened a Log Cabin school for boys who were interested in an education. This was in June of 1839. Within a year he had thirty-one students. Mr. Donaldson, a graduate of Jefferson College, was a man of striking personal appearance and an able scholar. He had found a fertile field in which to labor. After fifteen years the yearly enrollment of his Academy had grown to one hundred and thirteen. The Reverend John Barnett gave him some assistance in the early years.

Some who taught at the Academy were J. A. McKnight, John M. McElroy, John C. Thorn, James E. Caruthers, S. S. Gilson, W. W. McLane, and others. In 1848, Blairsville Presbytery, as was the custom in other presbyteries, took this Academy under its supervision. The school was to be known hereafter as the Blairsville Presbyterial Academy, but with the rise of similar schools in the Presbytery, the original name of Elders Ridge persisted.

Much helpful information is available regarding this famous Academy, since Professor T. B. Elder, a long-time associate and assistant to Dr. Donaldson, has written a lengthy account of the school. He described the early years when little thought was given to academic organization and related how the Academy was formally opened on April 16, 1847. Though the school was then located in Blairsville Presbytery, it soon began to receive students from other counties.

Because of Dr. Donaldson's relationship with Jefferson College, an arrangement was made to transfer students in the lower classes of the College to this Academy for the beginning work of their college course. This brought representatives to Elders Ridge from surrounding states and gave the school something of a national reputation. Many families, within an area of two miles, accommodated the students with board at one dollar a week. This was increased, over a period of time, to as much as three dollars and fifty cents a week. Because of what seemed to them the high cost of boarding, it became customary for students to rent rooms and board themselves for as little as one dollar a week. This in turn was succeeded by the boarding club idea which averaged two dollars a week.

From a log cabin school, the Academy grew to a two thousand dollar, two-story brick building, 48x32 feet, which provided recitation rooms, literary society rooms, a main hall (assembly) and student rooms.[7] It should be noted that the building program was financed by Mr. Donaldson who borrowed money and paid six per cent on it for over twenty-two years.

The curriculum in the early years was classical in nature with teaching in Greek and Latin and perhaps Hebrew. The catalogue for 1890 shows courses in Arithmetic, Physiology, Latin, Algebra, English, History, Geometry, Greek, and Surveying. Though the Academy gave way in time to a four-year high school, it is believed that the course of instruction at the Academy was similar to that of the present-day college. Professor Elder wrote:

"The whole number of students who have enjoyed the benefits of the institution thus far is somewhat over 2,500, or including the females who, for over ten years, were taught by a different teacher, over 2,600. Of these, over 150 have become ministers of the gospel, one at a youthful age sitting as moderator of the General Assembly . . . nine are foreign missionaries . . . eighty became physicians . . . ninety have been admitted to the bar . . . six have honored the bench. In educational work . . . one as a college president."[8]

One of the most prominent graduates of Elders Ridge was Sir James C. R. Ewing, who served the Presbyterian church in India and was knighted in 1915 by King George V of England.

Dunlap's Creek Academy

Organized a decade later than the Elders Ridge Academy was the very popular Dunlap's Creek Academy. It had its origin in the Dunlap's Creek Presbyterian Church located at what is now Merrittstown, Pennsylvania. There on May 22, 1848, a meeting was held to gather subscriptions, contributions, and elect trustees to the proposed Academy. Action followed rapidly during that summer. The Reverend Samuel Wilson, pastor of the Dunlap's Creek Church, was designated the founder, made president of the Board of Trustees, and later principal of the school. He was the great grandson of Dr. James Power, the first pioneer pastor who had the courage to locate his family in a parish west of the Allegheny Mountains and who had settled at Dunlap's Creek.

A petition was sent to Redstone Presbytery, asking that the new Academy be placed under its jurisdiction. In April of 1849, the Presbytery accepted the responsibility. "Sound religious instructions with secular learning," became a part of classroom procedure.[9] The constitution provided that no one should serve as principal who was not a member of the Presbyterian church and that all principals should sign a statement of conformity. The successive principals were Samuel Wilson, James Black, James C. Power, S. B. Mercer, S. J. Craighead, T. Davis Ewing, D. Harvey Sloan, J. D. Patterson, and O. W. David. Thirty-eight students enrolled for the second session beginning in April of 1850. Two years later the students numbered fifty. During the subsequent years enrollment fluctuated widely. In 1858 there were only seventeen students; forty-eight in 1864; fifteen in 1870; and forty-nine in 1895.

The minutes of March, 1853, record that the recitations in catechisms were good; that each student in the classical department would be assessed fifty cents; and each student in the common branches twenty-five cents a session as a contingent fee towards furniture and repairs. This report of 1853 is the first in which the names of girls appear as students. Political excitement in 1856, the war rumors, and finally the war itself caused the enrollment to fluctuate from session to session, but on the whole, the work at the Academy went on unabated.

The courses of study, as listed in the catalogue of 1863, included: Spelling and Defining, Reading (Osgood's Fifth); Penmanship, Geography (Mitchell's); Mental Arithmetic (Stoddard); Written Arithmetic (Ray's); English Grammar (Greene); History of the United States, Trigonometry and Surveying, Latin Grammar (Bullion); Latin Reader (Bullion); Caesar, Virgil, Livy, Cicero, Natural Philosophy (Parker); Familiar Science (Peterson); Physiology (Cutter); Rhetoric (Coffee); Algebra (Davis and Loomis); Geometry (Loomis); Conic Sections (Loomis); Greek Grammar (Bullion); Greek Reader (Bullion); Xenophon's Anabasis, Herodotus, and Elocution. In addition to these academic subjects, such "ornamental" subjects as piano music, guitar music, vocal music, painting, drawing, and French (Volve's Ollendorff) were taught as the need arose.[10]

The academic year was divided into two sessions of five months each with April and October as vacation periods. The tuition fees for a term were ten dollars for languages and higher mathematics, eight dollars for the natural sciences, six dollars for the English branches, ten dollars for piano, sixteen dollars for guitar, ten dollars for painting, eight dollars for French, and six dollars for drawing. Tuition was paid in advance and excellent board could be obtained for from two dollars to two dollars and fifty cents a week.

When the school was discontinued in 1896, the last reported enrollment was forty-nine pupils. It had prepared thirty-three men for the ministry.

Witherspoon Institute and Glade Run Academy

The Witherspoon Institute at Butler is another pioneer academy, with a long record of distinguished service to the church and community, which was born in the vision and aggressive leadership of a Presbyterian minister. Reverend Loyal Young, D.D., who served the First Presbyterian Church of Butler from 1833 to 1868, opened the school in the basement of his church on May 13, 1850. Three years previously, the Presbytery of Allegheny had approved the plan for a school with the decision that the "Presbytery as soon as practicable establish an academy under its care for the education of our candidates for the ministry."[11] Out of this movement the Witherspoon Institute emerged. The charter was granted in 1849. Although Clarion Presbytery had been invited to co-operate, Witherspoon became an Allegheny Presbytery endeavor with Mr. Young and the Butler church providing the leadership and most of the finances.

Within a year Dr. Young had enlisted sufficient interest in the small school to erect an adequate building on North Main and East Clay streets. He was aided in the financing by a grant of twenty-five hundred dollars from the Commonwealth of Pennsylvania. Subsequent growth resulted in the sale of the property to the English Lutherans for six thousand dollars, and the erection of an enlarged structure on Institute Hill. Besides carrying the ministerial and pastoral duties of the Butler church, Dr. Young served the Academy as its first principal for three years.[12] To his fidelity and loyalty, until his removal to West Virginia, the Institute owed much of its success.[13] Associated with the Dr. Loyal Young was Mr. David Hall who later became a prominent Presbyterian minister.[14]

But Dr. Young's vision and enthusiasm had exceeded his good judgment. The heavy indebtedness discouraged the Presbytery. The costly institution with its attractive building was sold to a group of businessmen who then continued it as a nonsectarian academy. At the height of its popularity in 1882, it had an enrollment of one hundred and seventy-two students and a corps of seven teachers. The student body had totaled eleven hundred. Of these, twenty-five young men went forth into the ministry and many others were trained for the professions of teaching, medicine, and the law. The Rev. Dr. S. Hall Young of Alaskan fame, and Dr. Walter Reed, in whose honor the great hospital in Washington, D. C., was named, were Witherspoon men. Through the years the principals were the Reverend Martyn Ryerson, Mr. J. R. Coulter, the Reverend John Smalley, Mr. James S. Boyd, the Reverend W. I. Brugh, and the Reverend J. W. Hamilton. The school served Butler and the Presbyterians for a quarter of a century until lack of financial and personal support forced its closing. Though the Institute building long ago passed into commercial hands, the district continues to be known as "Institute Hill."

In the neighboring Presbytery of Kittanning, and opening just one year later than the Witherspoon Institute, was the Glade Run Classical and Normal Academy located at Dayton, Pennsylvania. It also was principally an enterprise of the local Presbyterian church. The Rev. Mr. J. M. Jones, an 1851 graduate of Washington

College, had come to Glade Run Church and begun his work with enthusiasm. The Academy opened on October 27, 1851, with Mr. Jones as the principal. The session of the church agreed to pay the principal's salary for the first year. The Academy was classified as "a select parochial school" but the public gave it the title of Glade Run Academy. For the first two years, classes met in the church. A substantial frame building, 28x30 feet, with twelve-foot ceiling and adorned with a belfry and bell, was then erected. Increased enrollment necessitated an additional fifteen feet for classroom purposes in 1863. An interesting feature was a "Female Department" to the Academy, with a boardinghouse for the young ladies. The trustees also encouraged disabled veterans to attend the Academy. In 1865 a spacious residence was built for them where they could live, rent free. This may have been the first Church Veterans' Aid Plan.[15]

Academies in Ohio

Now we leave for a few minutes our tour of Presbyterian academies in Pennsylvania to view a few typical schools of Presbyterian influence or origin across the state line in Ohio. First we pause for a brief visit at the Savannah Academy where Dr. E. B. Welsh, who has written four chapters in this book, received his secondary education.

Savannah Academy came sufficiently late in the educational effort to be listed as co-educational from its inception in 1856. The Reverend Alexander Scott, a Martinsburg Academy and Jefferson College product, organized this school in 1856. The fact that the four churches in Savannah helped to govern it shows its non-denominational aspect. Yet, for sixty years, its governing board was predominantly Presbyterian and its principals, with one exception, were Presbyterian. The student body never exceeded one hundred and fifty in number and the faculty never more than five. The curriculum was overweighted on the classical side. One of the first women to graduate there was also one of our first Presbyterian missionaries to Japan, Mary Park (Mrs. David Thompson). Other prominent alumnae of Savannah, who responded to the call from the foreign field, were Dr. Richards who went to South Africa and Addie Houston (Mrs. Robert Lennington) who spent her life in Brazil. Among the better-known classmates of our own Dr. Welsh at Savannah are John Fackler, an attorney of Cleveland; Harry Simon, a businessman of Toledo; Lewis F. Smead, a world-renowned surgeon of Toledo; and Lloyd Paxton, a railway auditor. Savannah boasted four buildings but, like most of the academies, gave way to a township high school in 1916.[16]

Another Presbyterian academy in Ohio of particular interest is the Vermilion Institute of which the Rev. Dr. Sheldon Jackson, the famous pioneer missionary to Alaska and an honored former moderator of the General Assembly, is a distinguished graduate. The school was founded by interested citizens of Haysville in 1846. Through the influence of Reverend William A. Colmery, pastor of the Presbyterian church in Haysville, his fellow townspeople donated the school to the Presbytery of Richland four years later. Mr. Colmery had graduated from Washington College in the Class of 1840 and moved to Haysville following his ordination.

To secure more adequate financial support, the presbyteries of Coshocton and Wooster were asked to assist the Institute, and so control for a time was given to Wooster Presbytery. However, in 1875 the school was returned to interested educators of Haysville because of mounting financial and supervisory difficulties. After Mr. Colmery left Haysville in 1855, the work was taken over by the Reverend S. Diefendorf, who later relinquished it to Dr. A. F. Ross. The school appears to have done excellent work. At one time (1860), as many as two hundred and twenty-five students were enrolled. References have been made to a continual revival of religion that took place. During Dr. Diefendorf's administration, the institution reached its peak.[17] He was able to stimulate the thinking of the students and managed to keep the costs at an attractive level. About one hundred of its alumni studied for the gospel ministry.

Miller Academy, which began operation in Washington, Ohio, in 1851, was the educational child of the Zanesville Presbytery. The Reverend James Anderson of the Class of 1826, Washington College, became the first principal in conjunction with his pastorate of the local Presbyterian church. He was succeeded in 1854 by the Reverend J. E. Alexander, a Jefferson College graduate of the Class of 1839. The school had considerable success before Mr. Alexander moved to New Jersey in 1863. The historian, writing in 1858, said "Miller Academy has already rendered a vast service to the cause of education and religion. Its works praise it."[18] However, the Academy was not able to survive the disturbances of the Civil War period.

Among the many other efforts for education that were being made throughout Ohio, was an academy at Martinsburg, Ohio. This school, or academy, was founded by the Reverend Henry Hervey. Hervey took his theological work under McMillan at Jefferson, and upon graduation, stayed on at the college and taught for five years. In 1830 he was ordained and became pastor of the Martinsburg Church. All of the young ministers of that day were urged to launch, if possible, an educational effort. Hence Hervey began at once to organize an academy as a part of his pastoral work. It was a very fine school for a generation or more, but was unable to survive the Civil War crisis. At least two pastors of the Martinsburg Free Presbyterian Church served as instructors there. It was a school that prepared young men for college or supplied them with the achievements of a classical education. Presbyterian names, such as Simeon and Moses Brown, Dwight and Henry Hervey, Alexander Scott, and others, are associated with this Academy.[19] The closing of Martinsburg in the early sixties meant more students for Savannah and Vermilion, which were not too far removed.

Sometime after the Reverend Richard Brown, a graduate of Jefferson College in the Class of 1822, became pastor of the New Hagerstown Church in 1836, he founded the New Hagerstown

Academy and was its first principal. The date claimed for the founding of this school in southeastern Ohio is 1840. In later years the principalship of the school fell to the Reverend Alexander Swaney who was also pastor of the local Presbyterian church and a Jefferson graduate of 1839. A son of the first principal, John Howard Brown, taught at the Academy from 1869–1871 and became the principal in 1875. Female students are listed as having attended, but it is not known when they were first accepted. About fifty of the male students entered the Gospel ministry.

Other Academies in Western Pennsylvania

We return from this brief visit to some of the Presbyterian-sponsored academies in Ohio and take a quick survey of other typical Presbyterian academies that stimulated zeal for education throughout Western Pennsylvania. Our curiosity is aroused at once by the familiar name, Jefferson Academy. No, it is not the original Jefferson Academy established by John McMillan, but a restored Jefferson Academy. As a result of the consolidation of Washington and Jefferson colleges, a new Canonsburg Academy came into being in 1869. There was a stipulation in the preunion plans that an academy should be established at the community which lost the college and that the college property in that community should be placed, as much as possible, at the disposal of the new academy. When it was determined that the college would be located in Washington, a Board of Trustees was chosen to organize the academy at Canonsburg. The Reverend William Ewing, a Washington College graduate of 1842, was chosen as the first principal. The Academy was divided into two departments: a classical department to prepare young men for college, and a normal school designed for the special education of teachers. The student body of this new institution increased to well over a hundred in the first five years and its success was a pleasant surprise to all its well-wishers.[20]

Leaving Washington Presbytery, we turn toward Kittanning

Presbytery for a second visit and a brief survey of four other academies within its territorial bounds. We observe that the Saltsburg Academy, or Memorial Institute, had its inception in the Winter of 1851 when a select school was opened in the basement of the Presbyterian church. The Reverend W. Woodend, a Jefferson graduate of 1839 and pastor of the church, became the first principal and professor. J. W. Winters was the assistant teacher. Classes began in the Spring of 1852. Miss Amanda Christy, a graduate of Washington Female Seminary, was employed to supervise the girls. After her marriage to the Reverend J. A. Brown, she and her husband accepted the management of the Academy. The name, "Memorial Institute," came about in 1869 when the Presbyterian congregation of Saltsburg purchased the Academy property and changed the name in commemoration of the reunion of the Old School and New School branches of the Presbyterian denomination which had taken place that year. Dr. Woodend, who had begun the work in 1851, rejoined the Institute in 1871 as its directing head.[21]

Kittanning Presbytery's school was the Leechburg Institute. It was opened for both sexes in 1853. Mr. A. S. Thorn, a Presbyterian student at the Western Theological Seminary, served as the first principal. It began as a co-operative effort between the Presbyterians and the Lutherans. Soon the work passed into the Presbyterians' hands and the school became known as a Presbyterian Academy. About 1870 financial difficulties and the weak support of the Presbyterian constituency forced the school to close.[22]

The Indiana Classical School was another Presbyterian institution to open its doors in November of 1855. The Reverend Andrew McElwain, a graduate of Washington College in the Class of 1844, who served as the Presbyterian pastor in Indiana from 1852 to 1872, became the school's first principal. Elias M. Clark, W. P. Moore, and James A. Ewing assisted as teachers in the short life of the school. The beginning of the Indiana County Normal School removed the need of any other educational institution in that community and the Presbyterians graciously closed their school to avoid unprofitable competition.

Covode Academy was another Presbyterian school that came into service during the 1860's in Kittanning Presbytery. This school was organized by the Mount Pleasant Church at a meeting of the session in the Spring of 1862. The educational effort was launched to meet the needs of the growing community. The name chosen was in honor of the Honorable John Covode, a Westmoreland County Representative in Congress. The session and trustees looked after the Academy until 1870 when the Methodist Episcopal Church of Covode was granted an equal share in the control of the school. The average number of students a year was thirty-five. The instructors were competent, but generally stayed for only a short time.[23]

The fourth of these lesser-known academies in Kittanning Presbytery was the Slate Lick Classical Institute, organized in 1865. Its aim was to present the languages and higher branches of learning to all who might be interested. Mr. David S. Tappan, a student from the Western Seminary in Pittsburgh, was invited to be the teacher. During his term of service at the school, it was referred to as "Tappan Institute." The Reverend D. H. Sloan, a Washington College graduate of the Class of 1859 and an instructor at the Dunlap's Creek Academy, was invited to succeed him as the principal. The Institute used as its classrooms the facilities of the old Presbyterian church for nearly five years and later, the basement of the new church. At no time was there a permanent or suitable building. Yet the school continued for nearly a quarter of a century, during which time it trained a thousand students for vocations, professions, and other walks of life.[24]

Two schools in the Blairsville Presbytery should also be visited before we close this appreciative survey of the Presbyterian academies that served successfully in an age that is gone and which live only in the quickened lives of their graduates and in the memory of a grateful church.

The first is Laird Institute, located at Murrysville and formerly known as the Turtle Creek Valley Academy. It was the creative labor of the Presbyterian pastor, the Reverend Francis Laird, who was assisted by students from the Western Theological Seminary. It reached, however, its greatest success under the Reverend George M. Spargrove, a Washington College graduate of 1855, who was the Presbyterian pastor and principal after 1866.[25] It was he who had the name changed to Laird Institute. This school was largely attended, ably led, and well respected until the need for its service was met by the high school movement about 1890.

The last of the secondary schools, which Presbyterians organized before the era of high schools removed the need, was the Poke Run Academy, established in 1890. This Academy grew out of a summer school in the vicinity of Mamont that was taught by Stewart Shaw and the Reverend Henry Baine, pastor of the Poke Run Presbyterian Church. This school, and later the Academy, had the support of the church and it prepared young people for teaching in the public schools. The average attendance was about fifty students a term but, like other academies of its kind, it finally gave way to the high school movement. It was said of it, as could be said with equal appropriateness of all these academies: "The Academy filled a great need. In a measure it took the place of the high school; it prepared teachers when normal schools seemed afar off; it prepared young men and women for college."[26] Like all the Presbyterian academies of that fruitful era, it dispensed secular learning with a Christian spirit, thereby strengthening both mind and soul.

II. PAROCHIAL SCHOOLS

Closely resembling these Presbyterian academies, but with a more definite religious objective, were the Presbyterian Parochial Schools. Here again Ohio Valley Presbyterians were pioneers in a phase of educational policy which has since been adopted very largely by another branch of the Christian church. It was during the period from 1840 to 1870 when public schools were only beginning to attain their present standard of efficiency and when they were often referred to as "godless." Educational opportunities in the smaller communities were largely on a privately supported basis. Our Presbyterian fathers always believed that education was essential in a democracy and that it was the duty of the church to take the lead in developing educational opportunities throughout the community.

It is not surprising then that Presbyterian leaders in the Upper Ohio Valley would join with the parent denomination in a policy of establishing parochial schools. A resolution was adopted by the General Assembly in 1844 which officially committed the Presbyterian church to the promotion of a parochial school in every congregation.[27] The growing fear that the "godless" public schools were not properly training the youth of the land gave impetus to the movement. As a result, the popularity of the parochial schools grew for the first eight years. The total number of schools organized, so far as can be learned from existing records, was two hundred and sixty-four, distributed through twenty-nine states, the largest number being in Pennsylvania, New York, and New Jersey.[28]

These schools were motivated by a desire to promote a knowledge of the Bible.[29] The Presbyterian church, not being an established church, had no parishes in the old world sense. Parochial schools were "under the care of the session." It was a time of threatened secularization in education throughout the land and the church leaders hoped that this would encourage the growth of parochial schools. However, just the opposite happened. People became reluctant to speak out in defense of any religious program which would be in competition to the public schools which were increasing in popularity.

Parochial schools existed on the primary, secondary, and even the college level. For the most part they were primary and secondary schools. Classes were held in various places; the residence of the minister, a log cabin, in the church "session room" or "lecture room." Some churches went to considerable expense in the erection of suitable buildings. The equipment ranged from the most mediocre to average or a little above. Some had libraries, but a common plea was for books. Scientific apparatus was sometimes available as were maps and globes. The seats were generally pine slabs and only a few schools had seats with writing tables or lids attached. The students and teachers were largely responsible for the janitor work. Circumstances regulated the time of the school terms and the tuition.

The school year was divided into two, three, or four terms.[30] Pupils who were within walking distance lived at home. Some schools boarded students in neighborhood homes or dormitories at the rate of one dollar to one dollar and fifty cents a week. Teachers were employed either at a fixed rate or dependent upon tuition received. The more prosperous churches erected pretentious buildings. The smaller ones paid rent for the use of a building or erected a small schoolroom near the church. Scarcely any two schools had quite the same custom as to the way tuition was reckoned. In some cases it was a flat rate; for example, two dollars or two dollars and fifty cents for each pupil a semester or term. . . . Other schools had higher flat rates; as much as fifty dollars a year.[31] The Board of Education aided schools conforming to their rules. Scholarships, stock shares, and endowment added to the financial welfare of the effort.

On January 3, 1857, the *Presbyterian Banner and Advocate* published an article concerning the flourishing work of the parochial schools. A "benevolent and judicious friend" had again, as he had done for several years, given to the Board of Education his annual donation of five thousand dollars for the support of these schools. An excerpt from his letter reads: "I believe that God has a great work for us to do in this country; and much depends upon Him, on the Presbyterian Church; . . . especially by training the rising generation in the truth."[32] Church sessions could obtain from twenty-five to a hundred dollars, if needed, for their schools from the Board. Frequently the pastor of the church was the teacher or principal. Other teachers were appointed by the session.

In these parochial schools, the usual branches were taught. The special feature was the addition of daily religious instruction from the Bible and from the catechisms.[33] The duty of planning the curriculum rested with those responsible for the school, most often the minister and the session. Typical of the "general subjects" taught is this list as given by Sherrill—reading, writing, spelling, arithmetic, grammar, algebra, geography, Latin, Bible, catechism, and hymn singing.[34] The idea of discipline was prevalent and a subject was calculated to "train the mind." Girls were permitted "ornamental" subjects, such as music, vocal and instrumental, drawing and painting, and courses in "artificial flowers and hairwork."[35]

Generally, the main text was the Bible and the Shorter Catechism. Additional textbooks carried much Biblical material. Sometimes shown as an oddity would be an old *Hornbook,* which was a sort of paddle covered with transparent material, containing the alphabet, the Lord's Prayer, the Ten Commandments, and the Apostles' Creed. Teaching material included the *New England Primer,* a small vest-pocket book with the alphabet in Scripture verses, the Lord's Prayer, questions on the Bible, the Shorter Catechism, and others. "*The American* (Blue-back) *Spelling Book* prepared by Noah Webster . . . had on thirty-six of the one hundred sixty-six pages, statements on religion, Bible facts, Bible characters and Christian doctrines."[36]

In schools that had secondary or academy status, the course of study was quite similar to that which existed at the Glade Run Academy in Blairsville (Kittanning) Presbytery. The records show that the following books were used: "Henderson's Test words; Osgood's American Fifth Reader; Brooks' New Normal, Mental and Raub's Arithmetic; Geography, Grammar, Clark and Reed, and Kellogg, other authors used for reference; Methods of Teaching, Raub; Physiology and Hygiene, Steele; Algebra, Ray's part

1st, and Loomis' Treatise; Geometry, Trigonometry and Surveying, Loomis; Natural Philosophy, Steele; Latin Grammar, First Latin Book, and First Greek Book, Harkness; Caesar, Virgil, Horace, Cicero's Orations, Chase and Stuart, or Harkness; Greek Grammar, Hadley or Goodwin; Xenophon's Anabasis, Boise (three books); Homer, and Arnold's Greek and Latin Prose Composition."[37] Although the emphasis here may appear to be strictly academic, the institution was nevertheless owned and operated by the church and all teaching had a Christian emphasis.

In the Upper Ohio Valley region, there were ten of these parochial schools during this period at the following churches: Bethel Church, Upper St. Clair, 1837-1872, in Ohio Presbytery; Connellsville, 1849-1853, Laurel Hill Church, Woodvale, 1853-1862, and Rehobeth Church, Belle Vernon, 1855-1859, all in Redstone Presbytery; Donegal, 1851, Ebensburg, 1853-1855, and Glade Run, 1851-1870, all in Blairsville Presbytery; New Brighton, 1849-1851, and North Sewickley, 1847-1873, both in Beaver Presbytery; and the West Manchester German, Allegheny City, 1868-1870, of Allegheny City Presbytery.[38]

Many problems confronted the Presbyterian leaders in the maintenance of these parochial schools. The unrest of the Civil War years hastened a reconsideration by the General Assembly. A solid block of southern Presbyterians supported state in preference to church-governed education. The difficulty of diverting tax money was recognized when only a few places received tax funds and then only for a short time. More important was a dread of the inevitable confusion which would result if "all the religious groups in the country were to create their own schools and insist upon government support."[39] Presbyterians did not want a plural system of schools based on competing religious emphases. The local church members were unwilling to assume the financial burden. Teachers' salaries were often woefully inadequate.

Dr. James McCosh, president of Princeton, declared that he was in favor of public education and claimed that the church was not

ELDERS RIDGE ACADEMY, ELDERS RIDGE, PA.
Founded by Dr. Alexander Donaldson, 1839.
Above building erected in 1850. Burned, February 19, 1936.

COURTESY OF DR. DWIGHT R. GUTHRIE

WITHERSPOON INSTITUTE, BUTLER, PA.
Established by Dr. Loyal Young, 1850. Closed, 1875.

CENTENARY MEMORIAL

FEMALE SEMINARY, STEUBENVILLE, OHIO
Founded by Dr. and Mrs. C. C. Beatty, 1829. Closed, 1898.

COURTESY OF DR. WILLIAM RUSCH

WASHINGTON FEMALE SEMINARY, WASHINGTON, PA.
Founded, 1836. Disbanded, 1946.

fitted to run the schools. The prime purpose of the church school was to encourage young men to enter the service of the church and after twenty years, this aim had not been realized.[40] The public schools had proved that they were not "godless institutions." Students trained in them had become respected leaders.

Moreover, the Sunday School movement "organized" in America in 1824 was growing and was filling at least part of the need. All of these factors hastened the closing of the remaining Presbyterian parochial schools in the 1870's. Add to these the fact that Presbyterians did not wish to separate themselves from the people of their communities and that they did not enjoy being a divisive influence and our evidence is complete as concerns the wisdom of abandonment of the parochial school effort. The Synod of New York's special committee reported that it was "'unthinkable' that the public schools should be abandoned" and that if "'godly parents' did not send their children to the public schools, these schools would be much more likely to become godless."[41] The opportunity for education was to be broad and to include all children and not just children of any one class or denomination. Public education must be a unifying factor in a democracy, not a fragmentizing or divisive agency. Presbyterians, reaffirmed by the action of their General Assembly in 1957, believe in and continue to support a unifying public system of universal education.

III. FEMALE SEMINARIES

Masculine chivalry has taken pride in giving first place to the ladies in the realms of courtesy and personal consideration. But no such claim can be put forth for the ladies in the field of education. The early leaders of the Upper Ohio Valley were eager to establish schools for the sons of the community, as shown in the development of academies and colleges. The girls had to wait patiently in their homes for the better day of equal educational opportunity.

To Mrs. Mary Olver belongs the credit for establishing the first academic boarding school for girls in the Upper Ohio Valley. Her school was opened in Pittsburgh in 1825, but soon transferred to more adequate facilities at Braddock's Field. Though she was the pioneer in Pittsburgh, Mrs. Olver was not the initiator in female education. As early as 1649, an unnamed schoolmaster in New Hampshire had been engaged to teach both male and female children. Later in that century the Society of Friends designated that their public school, the forerunner of the famous William Penn charter school, was to open its classes to both sexes. By the middle of the eighteenth century, the Moravians had organized a school for girls, and in 1789 a private school for girls, or an academy was opened at Medford, Massachusetts. In 1821, Miss Emma Willard's Female Seminary was established at Troy, New York.

Thus Mrs. Olver's precedents were few and her effort a courageous venture of faith when she launched her school in 1825. Ten years later she moved her school a second time and relocated along the Ohio River near the town of Sewickley where it became prominent as the Edgeworth Ladies' Seminary. After Mrs. Olver's death in 1842, her daughter, Mrs. M. J. Flower, became the head mistress. A year later the school closed for a period of three years. The school reopened in 1846 under the supervision of the Reverend Daniel E. Nevin and his wife. They had influential contacts among the Presbyterians and Episcopalians in Pittsburgh, so the Seminary began to prosper. It was chiefly a boarding school during these years and was noted for its high standards of education and its excellent religious spirit.

This Seminary was the first institution of its kind west of the mountains and therefore became an inspiration for the establishment of similar institutions in the area. During the administration of the Reverend Aaron Williams, a disastrous fire, February 11, 1865, reduced its assets to a point beyond recovery and the Seminary closed its doors.[42]

Steubenville Female Seminary

Encouraged by the success of Mrs. Olver's Seminary in Pittsburgh,

Miss Hetty Davis, who married the Reverend Charles C. Beatty in 1827, realized a childhood dream of establishing a school of her own. The Beattys made a trip to the eastern schools to discover the best type of curriculum and administration for young ladies. Thus equipped, Mrs. Beatty, assisted by her husband, opened the Steubenville Female Seminary at Steubenville, Ohio, on April 13, 1829, four years after Mrs. Olver's pioneer venture. It was the first school of its kind in what was known as the Northwest Territory.

The Seminary classes began in the Beatty home on High Street with seven pupils. A preparatory department for small children was the next project. This naturally became a feeder to the Seminary. While the Seminary was in operation, the Rev. Mr. Beatty was pastor of the First Presbyterian Church and later, the Second Presbyterian Church. He was a genius in the field of finance. He not only kept the Seminary in a prosperous condition, but was responsible for many acts of philanthropy during his lifetime. It was the prosperity of the Seminary, coupled with his methods of tithing and investment, that made him a tremendous financial success.[43] Doyle, in his *Twentieth Century History of Steubenville and Jefferson County*, says: "Without detracting an iota from Beatty's part in the enterprise, we think the main credit for its inception, as well as for much of its subsequent success, was due to Mrs. Beatty."

The first six graduates received their diplomas at the commencement exercises in 1833. These were the first of more than five thouand young women who were educated as Christian housewives, missionaries, or teachers. The Beattys relinquished their holdings in the Seminary to Dr. and Mrs. A. M. Reid in 1866 for the sum of twenty-five thousand dollars. The new leaders continued to develop the work and brought the institution to its highest degree of culture and refinement in the next twenty years. They were followed by such persons as the Rev. Dr. Davis, Miss Northrup, Miss Sheldon, and Miss Mary Stewart. Miss Stewart was in charge of the school in 1898 when it was deemed wise to close because of increasing competition from the high school movement which was getting under way at this time and which lessened the need of the Seminary.

Washington Female Seminary

The third Presbyterian female seminary to be opened in the West was at Washington, Pennsylvania, then a community with a population of about two thousand. This new Seminary, located on East Maiden and Lincoln streets, was destined to outlive both of its predecessors. It had its beginning sometime in 1834 when a group of citizens, led by Rev. Dr. David Elliott, met in the parlor of the Honorable T. M. T. McKennon.[44] Many such meetings were held but finally land was purchased from Alexander Reed. Shares of stock were sold and Mrs. Francis Biddle of Philadelphia was employed as principal. Classes began in 1836. In another two years a suitable building for the purpose of boarding pupils was opened. The leadership of the Seminary was very shortly turned over to Miss Sarah Foster, a graduate of Miss Emma Willard's Seminary at Troy, New York. Her marriage to the Reverend Thomas Hanna brought no interruption in her labors.

Under Mrs. Hanna the school came to maturity with courses in Primary subjects, grammar, arithmetic, geography, history, geology, natural philosophy, Latin, algebra, geometry, chemistry, botany, logic, orthography, and similar subjects. For these subjects, there were eleven teachers and one lecturer—a man.

Mrs. Hanna's biographer has described her as "tall, thin, energetic, having masculine courage, religious fervor and a motherly nature." She was thoroughly progressive and frequently had to win her way, over the rather cautious trustees, with the determined plea, "Well, just let me try it." When advancing age closed her distinguished service to the Seminary, a summary revealed that "her graduation list had reached five hundred and forty-seven names. Of these, ten or twelve became devoted missionaries, more than one hundred have been successful teachers, and a fair proportion have gladdened ministers' homes as wives and mothers."[45]

Mrs. Hanna was succeeded as principal by Miss Nancy Sherrard, an alumna and vice-principal of Steubenville Seminary. She has been described as of "commanding appearance, with a face that was sweet in repose." A very strict disciplinarian, she had a tendency to inspire wholesome fear in her students. She gave her young ladies weekly lectures on good manners, conduct, and etiquette. Just before vacations, she would warn them while on the train to "beware of the well-dressed villain."[46]

She forbade dancing and visits from the neighboring college boys. Both of these "crimes" she dealt with severely. During her twenty-three years' service as principal, the Seminary expanded and prospered. Modern Languages, Art, and Music enriched the curriculum. A preparatory department was added.

The Seminary continued a strong institution well into the twentieth century. But changing times and the growth of other schools lessened the enrollment with the inevitable result that the Seminary was discontinued in 1948. Among its distinguished graduates who have served on the foreign field may be mentioned Miss Lucinda Crouch Leamon (China), Mrs. Jennie Sherrard Ewing, Mrs. Fanny Corbett Hays (China), Mrs. Ellen McIlvaine Mechlin (Persia), Mrs. Clara Linton Hamilton (China), and Mrs. Margaret Woods Hamilton (China).[47]

Olome Institute

The long-time rivalry between Washington and Canonsburg as educational centers was a motivating factor in launching a female seminary at Canonsburg in 1844. The influence of the Edgeworth, the Steubenville, and the recently established Washington Female Seminary stirred the citizens of Canonsburg to action. Mrs. O. J. French announced that she would become the principal of a Select School for Young Ladies. The attendance of young women in separate schools was well-established by this time and a number availed themselves of this opportunity. The accommodations were soon insufficient and by 1847 more adequate buildings were purchased.

It was then that Olome Institute, as it was titled, assumed the more distinct features of a boarding school. In the following year, other classrooms were erected and a third story was added to the already commodious boardinghouse. With the additions that were made, the school was, by the middle of the century, able to accommodate one hundred girls.[48] The Institute was now equal to those in other localities.

All of the subjects and accomplishments that formed a part of female education were offered. Such subjects included Reading, Orthography, Writing, Arithmetic, Geography, English Grammar, and lessons in History, Botany, Physiology, and Philosophy. In the advanced classes the students were permitted to study Astronomy, Geometry, Algebra, Rhetoric, Moral Philosophy, Evidences of Christianity, and Analogy of Natural and Revealed Religion. There were also classes in Music, Drawing, Painting, and French. The admission fees were similar to those in other schools, with a cost of fifty dollars a term for board, washing, and light, plus tuition of six dollars a session for first-year students, which was increased to fourteen dollars a session for seniors. There were extra charges for Music, French, Painting, fire in sleeping rooms, pew rental, and other so-called incidentals.

The Institute continued until 1866. This was the best organized effort for female education in Canonsburg, but it is to be recognized that there were similar schools there. It is believed that Matthew Brown carried out such a project in his early years at Canonsburg. Later, in 1861, Professor William Smith of Jefferson College began such a work. These all flourished for a time and finally gave way to the co-educational effort on the part of the Canonsburg Academy which followed the union of Washington and Jefferson colleges.[49]

Blairsville Female Academy

A similar school for young women was founded at Blairsville, Pennsylvania, in 1851 by the Reverend George Hill, pastor of the Presbyterian church in that community. He succeeded in persuading several wealthy men to finance a building program. For the first year and a half, he served as principal. The mantle of leadership then fell upon the Reverend Samuel Shepley and his wife. The catalogue for 1887 shows a faculty of ten and a student body numbering sixty-four. The work was carried on in a large three-story building, heated throughout by steam.

For a time this Seminary was referred to as Blairsville College and was on the list of accredited institutions of the Presbyterian church in Pennsylvania. However, because of the lack of proper endowment and equipment, it was in no position to compete with similar schools and so closed its doors in 1913. The record names a number of principals who served at Blairsville. There were several hundred graduates.

Pennsylvania Female College

Presbyterians in this area ventured forth also into the field of higher education for women and initiated the organization of Pennsylvania College for Women, now named Chatham College. It had its origin in Pittsburgh in 1869, when the Reverend W. T. Beatty, pastor of the Shadyside Presbyterian Church, suggested the project to several farsighted friends. These gentlemen raised a sum of twenty thousand dollars for this purpose, which made possible the establishment of the Pennsylvania Female College in the East End of Pittsburgh. The charter was dated December 11, 1869. The constitution adopted contained various stipulations, namely, the institution must be high in educational facilities, of sound and thorough religious influence, and the president and a majority of the trustees must be of some branch of the Presbyterian church.

The *Presbyterian Banner* of July 20, 1870, joyfully related that "the Trustees of our Presbyterian Female College have purchased the fine residence of Mr. George A. Berry and ten acres of land for the use of the institution. The location is a very beautiful one, on high ground between Shadyside and East Liberty, in this city." A month later we read that "Reverend James Black, D.D., has accepted the presidency of this institution . . . This institution will be open for the reception of Boarders and Day Scholars on September 28." Nearly a year later there was mention of an "able corps of instructors—twenty-two in number—a larger Faculty than any other institution in the State."[50] In other places "the beautiful buildings," the "easily accessible location," and the "home-like discipline" are emphasized.

The original investment mushroomed in a few years into an investment of one hundred and forty thousand dollars. The first president, the Reverend James Black, D.D., who was elected July 22, 1870, had already attained an excellent reputation as a professor at his Alma Mater, Washington College, as vice-president of Washington and Jefferson College, and as president of Iowa State University. He was a man of scholarly ability and untiring energy. After five years of service, when much was accomplished with the assistance of able teachers, he resigned to accept the chair of Greek at Wooster University.

In June, 1875, the Reverend Thomas C. Strong, D.D., a former principal of Wells's Female College at Aurora, New York, was chosen as his successor. The institution continued to prosper. The early years of the college were auspicious and the classes were well attended. Yet, in spite of liberal backing by interested laymen, the institution had the usual financial troubles that plagued other schools. It was fortunate to have founders who were broad-minded, reverent men and women who were liberal in their religious views.

This educational period from 1800 to 1870 was most successful and prosperous for the Presbyterians of the Upper Ohio Valley. They founded a number of academies, parochial schools, and female seminaries. No other religious group has matched their efforts in this area of service.

CHAPTER X Changes Through Controversy

As the nineteenth century opened, the Presbyterian church was in a strategic position for advancement in numbers and service, not only in the rapidly settling Upper Ohio Valley, but also throughout the entire nation. The denomination had completed its nationwide organization and new presbyteries were being formed rapidly. Three weeks after George Washington had been inaugurated the first President of the United States, the General Assembly of the Presbyterian church was organized with a nationwide program of missionary expansion. Dr. John Witherspoon, the only clergyman who had signed the Declaration of Independence, was chosen to preside over the opening session on May 12, 1789.

Presbyterian ministers and laymen in all the colonies had taken a leading part throughout the successful struggle for the independence of the thirteen original colonies. The Presbyterian church had almost unitedly supported the cause of freedom. Its ministers were well-educated leaders and graduates of recognized educational institutions. Two-thirds of the entire population had a Presbyterian or at least a Calvinistic background. The Scotch-Irish settlers, who were migrating westward, were establishing themselves throughout the vast areas of expansion beyond the mountains of the Laurel Ridge.

The Synod of Pittsburgh had been organized in 1802 with three constituent presbyteries of Redstone, Ohio, and Erie. Dr. John

McMillan, the great pioneer preacher in Western Pennsylvania, was then a mature leader of fifty years of age as he arose to preach the sermon on the opening of Synod in the First Presbyterian Church of Pittsburgh, September 30, 1802. With the enthusiasm of achievement, he could survey the past three decades of advancement as strong Presbyterian churches dotted the hillsides of western Pennsylvania and eastern Ohio, and as thirty-six Presbyterian pastors responded to the initial roll call.

McMillan, with three other pioneering associates, had organized the Presbytery of Redstone in 1781 at a time when the region was still ravished by recurrent Indian raids. But the victory of General Anthony Wayne, at the Battle of Fallen Timbers in 1794, had now resulted in peace and the subsequent tide of westward settlement. Dr. McMillan gazed prophetically into a future that seemed to promise great expansion for the church he loved and for which he had labored so courageously and devotedly. As he spoke, great revivals were springing up along the westwardly moving frontier. In 1800, the entire membership of the Presbyterian church throughout the United States was only 20,000. By 1837 the membership rolls had multiplied to include 220,000. Thus within 37 years the membership of the Presbyterian church increased elevenfold. The harvest truly was white with ripened opportunity, but the laborers in the spiritual vineyard were all too few.

This rapid growth presented new problems in expansion. Inevitable adjustments had to be made both in the thinking and in the programing of the denomination. Differences of opinion soon appeared as divergent plans and contrasted emphases struggled for leadership. The Presbyterian church has always been a democratic institution, giving to its members and leaders an opportunity for the expression of diversity of opinion. It seems to be the habit of the Presbyterian church to unify its diversity of opinion upon the anvil of controversy, with the sparks of argument and thought flying widely, as new programs and policies are hammered into practical and progressive form. But, where agreements cannot be reached tolerantly and harmoniously, temporary schisms are prone to emerge so that contrasted policies can be worked out separately while passions cool and time tests the new creations of controversy. The New Side and the Old Side Schism of 1741–1758 was one of these testing periods of separation and subsequent reunion in the bonds of denominational brotherhood.

The rapidly expanding Presbyterian church was now to pass through four successive schisms of separation as controversy gave rise to the Cumberland Presbyterian Church, the New and Old School Division, the Free Presbyterian Church, and the Northern and Southern Branches. All four of these schisms were to affect the future growth of Presbyterianism throughout the rapidly settling Upper Ohio Valley. Two of these schisms had their origin in unsolved problems of polity and theology arising from evangelistic fervor. The other two arose from conflicting views of social and economic problems, particularly the question of human slavery. Three of these schisms were subsequently healed in the fellowship of reunion. The fourth schism still awaits a growing realization of brotherhood. The story of these four schisms within the brief span of six decades is the scope of this chapter.

THE GREAT REVIVAL

November 14, 1802, will ever remain a memorable date in the history of the expanding Presbyterian church throughout the entire Upper Ohio Valley. As previously described in a preceding chapter, on that day, the flames of the great Revival of 1802 were kindled at a camp meeting in connection with the open-air communion service at Upper Buffalo in Washington County. Similar evangelistic services were soon held in many other churches over a widened area in Pennsylvania and Ohio. New converts were welcomed into church membership. New enthusiasm was manifested in all phases of religious activity and morality. Classes for instruction were formed as education replaced emotionalism.

New life soon appeared in the increased calls for preaching in all three presbyteries. The members of these presbyteries accepted many assignments to preach on specified Sabbaths even though in their own churches they were busy cultivating the spiritual harvests of these years of reviving zeal. New churches and new presbyteries were organized. In 1808 the Presbytery of Ohio was subdivided by the formation of the Presbytery of Lancaster in Ohio. In the same year Hartford Presbytery was formed out of the Erie Presbytery and included a portion of northwestern Pennsylvania and the Western Reserve area of Ohio. Six years later the Presbytery of Hartford was similarly divided to form the Presbytery of Grand River. That same year, 1814, the Synod of Ohio was formed as Presbyterian churches grew in number and size.

While the redemptive effects of the Revival of 1802 continued to multiply and strengthen the churches in the great rural areas of western Pennsylvania and eastern Ohio, Pittsburgh seemed strangely untouched and unconcerned. Population was increasing in this Gateway to the West. By 1810 it had reached 4,786. The things of religion, however, seemed to be of slight interest. Materialism and pleasure, with its evils of indulgence, were deemed more important. The two small Presbyterian churches in Pittsburgh, with a membership respectively of only 65 and 30, struggled in vain against apathy and worldliness.

The situation changed soon after the arrival of the Reverend Francis Herron in the First Church and the Reverend Elisha Swift at the Second Church. Herron was installed April, 1811, and Swift on the first Wednesday of November, 1819. These two men formed a perfect team, with powers that supplemented but never rivaled each other. Both were gifted with unusual powers of leadership, personality, and conviction. Both were used mightily in transforming the spiritual outlook of Pittsburgh and in developing Presbyterian power and prestige in the city. Both won nationwide recognition—Dr. Herron as moderator of the General Assembly and Dr. Swift as the founder of the Board of Foreign Missions. The Western

Theological Seminary in Pittsburgh was largely the creation of their joint efforts.

I. CUMBERLAND PRESBYTERIAN CHURCH

As the continuing effects of the great Revival of 1802 were extending throughout Western Pennsylvania and Ohio, a similar flame, which had been kindled some years earlier, was burning in Kentucky and Tennessee. Out of this revival, and following a long series of misunderstandings, came the first of four schisms and the organization of the Cumberland Presbyterian Church in 1810. The name Cumberland was given the area by the Scotch-Irish immigrants in honor of the Duke of Cumberland. He was the hero of the Battle of Culloden, in Scotland, 1746, which protected Scotland from a return to the tyranny represented by the House of Stuart and Roman Catholic dominance. News of the victory reached the Scotch-Irish settlers as they migrated westward throughout what they then called the Cumberland Trail, the Cumberland Valley, the Cumberland Gap, the Cumberland Country, the Cumberland Mountains, The Cumberland Presbytery, and The Cumberland Presbyterian Church.[1]

The human agent in this independent but concurrent revival was the Reverend James McGready. He was reared in North Carolina where he developed into a young man of high moral ideals and religious habits and with a desire to be a minister.[2] An uncle brought him to Pennsylvania to be educated at McMillan's school. While attending a preparatory service previous to the Communion Sacrament he listened to the soul-stirring sermon of "hell-fire" Smith. He saw himself, not as a self-righteous student for the ministry, but as a sinner needing forgiveness and regeneration. His whole life was changed. The fires of evangelism burned in his heart. He continued his study under the direction of McMillan and Smith. On August 12, 1788, he, with Joseph Patterson, was licensed by the Presbytery of Redstone to preach the Gospel.[3]

Shortly afterward McGready journeyed southward to begin his ministry in his boyhood state. Immediately he attacked the sins of formality and indifference among the church members. Fervently he preached, prayed, and pleaded for a revival of vital and soul-redeeming religion. Everywhere he went he kindled the fires of evangelism. In Logan County, Kentucky, where he was pastor of three churches, he drew up a "Preamble and Covenant" which he and his congregation signed. They pledged themselves to observe the third Saturday of each month, for a year, as a day of fasting and prayer for the conversion of sinners. They covenanted also to spend a half hour every Saturday evening and Sunday morning in pleading with God to revive His work.[4] Within a year a revival broke out in one of his churches which extended to the other two churches during the next two years.

From this small beginning, McGready was used of God to start a revival movement that soon spread throughout the southern portion of the state and into Tennessee where indifference to religion and low moral standards were prevalent. Others joined him in house-to-house testimony and exhortation. At great camp meetings McGready and a small group of like-minded preachers stirred thousands, amid excesses of emotionalism that aroused the antagonism of their more sedate brethren in the Presbytery and Synod. These men, in opposing the revival, complained of what they called the evils of bodily exercises, disorders in public worship, women exhorting, too free communication of the sexes, doctrinal errors, spiritual pride, and censoriousness.[5] The revivalists defended their movement and methods in acrimonious replies. The inevitable misunderstanding grew in bitterness as good men differed in methods of advancing the Kingdom of God. Yet the revival went forward with increasing zeal. Dr. Samuel Ralston, a Western Pennsylvania minister who assisted with the revival, thus testified to its genuineness:

"It has reclaimed the wicked and the profligate and transformed the lion into a lamb. It has brought professed deists to become professed Christians and turned their cursings into blessings and their blasphemies into praises. Many, very many, give evidence by their life and conversation that they are born of God."[6]

The Reverend David Rice, in preaching the opening sermon at the Synod of Kentucky in 1803, reviewed the revival in these words:

"The songs of the drunkard are exchanged for the songs of Zion; fervent prayer succeeds in the place of the profane oaths and curses; the lying tongue has learned to speak the truth in the fear of God, and the contentious firebrand is converted into a lover of peace."[7]

The entire outlook of the Cumberland area was transformed. New churches were organized. Hundreds of converts were seeking in vain for pastors. Again the harvest was great, but the laborers were all too few.[8]

Good earnest men of deep conviction came forward as volunteers. Many of them lacked the education which the Presbyterian church has always insisted was a prerequisite for intelligent preaching. They did not have the means to leave their families to continue a classical and theological education. They were impatient of delays. The Presbytery did the natural, but ecclesiastically irregular, thing in hastily training and licensing a few men whom the churches were demanding as itinerant evangelists. The question was not about the great importance of a classical education upon which all were agreed. "It was whether, after we had done our utmost in educating men for the ministry, we may supplement the supply by licensing judicious men of piety and promise to work among the perishing, even when these men have not a collegiate education."[9]

The majority in the Synod of Kentucky said "no." They refused to lower Presbyterian standards even in a quick effort to save souls. The rules of the church, they believed, were a wise protection and should not be ignored even for a temporary gain that later might result in greater difficulties. Exceptions soon become established precedents, they argued. The Presbyterian standard of an educated ministry must not be imperiled. These church leaders who lived east of the mountains had such a dread of the possible consequences to the church of lay-evangelistic preaching that they seemed unable to appreciate and understand the pressing problems of the western frontier which were basically economic in origin.

Added to these differences of opinion regarding methods of evangelism and the wisdom of using untrained men in seasons of rapid expansion, there was a third area of disagreement—namely, the sanctity of doctrine. Some of the young men ordained by the Cumberland Presbytery confessed to certain mental reservations while accepting the Confession of Faith.[10] Their difficulty lay in the oft-debated questions of man's complete freedom to accept the offer of salvation and God's sovereign decrees and His limited plan of election. The niceties of debate and the importance of theological minutia did not appeal to these rugged revivalists. They were pleading in emotional earnestness to the sinner to change his ways and show some visible evidence of his repentance and his personal experience of conversion. They were concerned chiefly with results. They preferred the pragmatic test of changed lives. They claimed the freedom of action. They chafed under the delays of debate.

Presbytery of Cumberland Organized

With both sides spurning a possible compromise on these three phases of disagreement, the result was inevitable. A small group of the leaders in revivalism withdrew in February, 1810, to organize the independent Presbytery of Cumberland.[11]. The Reverend James McGready, the outstanding leader of the whole revival movement in that Cumberland area, could not see his way clear to join his friends in a schismatic movement. Loyalty to the Presbyterian church controlled his decision. He made his peace with the Synod of Kentucky to continue in the fellowship of his denominational brethren.[12] But the new branch of the Presbyterian church bore the stamp of McGready's convictions and consecration which Dr. McMillan and Dr. Smith had breathed into his soul during the days of his tutelage in Western Pennsylvania.

Only four ministers responded to the call to organize, as an act of protest, an independent Cumberland Presbytery. These four men did not expect to form a new Presbyterian denomination. They still hoped that their persistent difficulties with the Kentucky Synod could be solved in peace and unity. Their hopes proved futile. The rupture widened. The Cumberland Schism, as it was first called, became a new Presbyterian denomination. The General Assembly regarded these secessionists as a separate and independent denomination, to be treated as any other distinct branch of the Christian church.

The membership of the new Presbytery increased as zeal in revivalism won converts rapidly along the crude frontier. The small schismatic group of four conscientious missionaries steadily added to their membership through the hasty education and ordination of candidates for the ministry. What courage and consecration motivated these new pioneering preachers who were deadly in earnest and aflame with zeal for Christ! As McDonnold so dramatically records:

"There were no pastorates, no salaries, no possibility of earthly honors. To travel unpaid on horseback across wild wastes to the homes of pioneers in the new settlements; to swim rivers and sleep on bare ground; to go hungry and half clad; to belong to a struggling little church whose doctrines and practices were diligently ridiculed; to preach in floorless log cabins, or gather the rough frontiersmen in camps around some spring, and there labor day and night for a week that poor lost sinners might be saved, and that the new territories might not all be given over to infidelity; and after all this to die in poverty at last, was the prospect before that generation of preachers."[13]

Such zeal and consecration could not fail to produce a spiritual harvest. Within three years the Cumberland Presbytery subdivided itself into the three presbyteries of Logan, Cumberland, and Elk. Together they constituted the Cumberland Synod on April 9, 1813.[14] Sixteen years later the organization of the new denomination was completed in the constituting of the General Assembly, May 19, 1829, with eleven presbyteries.[15] It continued its separate existence until it added its strength and zeal to the parent denomination by the reunion of 1906, although a small group of the unconvinced remained as a separate denomination under the old name, "The Cumberland Presbyterian Church."

The Cumberland Church Enters Western Pennsylvania

The new denomination found its greatest field of service in the South where amid frontier conditions its evangelistic emphasis proved most helpful. There it developed its largest membership and exerted its most fruitful influence. As the frontier moved south and westward, the extension of the Cumberland Church followed. Throughout its entire history, its chief mission was to the frontier.

Not until after 1830 did the Cumberland Church move northward into the region of the Upper Ohio Valley where it was destined to exert an influence that was greater than its comparatively small membership might indicate. This movement northward to Pennsylvania and Ohio was the result of an invitation from Presbyterian brethren. It was not the act of an intruding or competing denomination.

The fires of revivalism in Western Pennsylvania had burned low. Spirituality had declined. A lack of fervor was evident. The more evangelistic preaching of the Cumberland missionaries might be the answer, thought some of the Presbyterian ministers and elders in Washington County, Pennsylvania. Two agents of Cumberland College had previously entered eastern Ohio and western Pennsylvania in search of funds to support that college.[16] Their visit created an interest in the work of the Cumberland preachers.

The result was an invitation from some of the elders of a vacant church in Washington County to send a Cumberland missionary to preach to them. In response, the Cumberland General Assembly in 1831 appointed five young ministers to visit Western Pennsylvania and to respond to any invitations for evangelistic preaching.[17] Two of these men, the Reverend A. M. Bryan and the Reverend John Morgan, came to Washington, Pennsylvania, on July 14, 1831. They remained to continue their entire ministry in Western Pennsylvania. Soon they were joined by a third missionary, the Reverend Alexander Chapman, and some months later by the Reverend Robert Donnell and the Reverend Reuben Burrow, the other commissioned missionaries.

They were cordially welcomed by the Reverend Jacob Lindley, pastor of Upper Ten Mile Presbyterian Church and by the Reverend Cephas Dodd, pastor of the Lower Ten Mile Church, who opened their churches to them for evangelistic preaching. At the close of the first service in Mr. Lindley's church, seventy-five people responded to the call for converts. During a Sunday service shortly thereafter, over one hundred joined the church. The attendance exceeded the capacity of the church building.

Stirring revivals followed. Hundreds "from the most intelligent and moral down to the most ignorant and profligate came forward, deeply affected with a sense of their lost condition."[18] The revival movement spread. Camp meetings, lasting from four to seven days, were marked by some three hundred additions to Mr. Lindley's and neighboring churches. Western Pennsylvania, which had fired the soul of the Reverend James McGready before he had journeyed southward, now was again aflame in revivalism, rekindled by the preaching of these products of his Kentucky revival.

Opposition Results in Organization of Churches

Throughout all this successful revival, no effort was made by these visiting evangelists to organize Cumberland churches. Their purpose was to further the revival and then return southward. The organization of Cumberland churches was largely the result of Presbyterian opposition to the rather emotional type of revival which the Cumberland preachers seemed to generate. When after two years Mr. Lindley's own Presbytery took action, ordering his church to "exclude the Cumberland preachers from the pulpit of the Upper Ten Mile congregation," both he and a majority of the congregation withdrew from the Presbyterian Church U.S.A. and reorganized themselves into the Bethel Cumberland Presbyterian Church.[19] Similar experiences followed elsewhere as the revival spread into adjacent areas. Waynesburg, Uniontown, and the region around Brownsville sought the services of Cumberland ministers who seemed more enthusiastic for evangelism than were the Presbyterian pastors. Further opposition to the Cumberland type of revival resulted in the organization of new churches to minister to the continued spiritual needs of hundreds of new converts. Thus the Cumberland Presbyterian Church became established in Western Pennsylvania and neighboring eastern Ohio.

This promising field of missionary expansion was organized into the Presbytery of Washington. At its initial meeting in May, 1832, four ministers constituted the Presbytery.[20] At a subsequent meeting seventeen months later, the Presbytery had grown to include twelve ordained ministers, three licensed preachers, and seven candidates. They represented seventeen congregations with a total membership of twenty-eight hundred, a striking proof of the effectiveness of the revival.[21]

Prominent Cumberland Pastors

Perhaps the most successful of the first generation of Cumberland ministers in Western Pennsylvania were the Reverend John Morgan and the Reverend A. M. Bryan, two of the original missionaries sent to light the fires of evangelism in Washington and Greene counties. Morgan found his effective field of service in Uniontown. Here he organized a church which soon developed into the largest Cumberland Presbyterian church in Pennsylvania and which is now known as the Third Presbyterian Church of that city. Here was reestablished the previously abandoned Madison College. Throughout the next eight years, this college was largely promoted and sustained by Cumberland Presbyterians, though not directly under church control.[22]

Mr. Morgan took a very aggressive interest in this revitalized college and served for a time as professor of Moral Science. The college expanded into an enrollment of one hundred and fifty students.[23] After hampering denominational friction among the Board of Trustees, it was discontinued when Cumberland educational interests became centered in Waynesburg. Unfortunately, Mr. Morgan's physical strength was not sufficient to sustain his zealous efforts and passionate yearning to save souls. He died at the comparatively early age of thirty-six years and was laid to rest in the cemetery at Uniontown.

His successor in that thriving church was the Reverend Milton Bird, one of the four original members of the Cumberland Presbytery of Washington. Bird continued as pastor until his death thirty-one years later. Throughout much of that time, he was the Stated Clerk of the General Assembly of the Cumberland Church and published the official denominational paper, *The Cumberland Presbyterian.* Largely because of his prestige and skilled leadership, the Cumberland Presbyterian denomination did not split during the Civil War as did several other denominations.

From the Uniontown area came many of the earlier active ministers of the Cumberland communion. Honored names include the Reverend Samuel Bowman, the Reverend Joseph Bowman, and the Reverend J. M. Gallagher, D.D., who founded nearly a dozen Cumberland churches in areas farther northward.

The other outstanding original missionary was the Reverend Alfred McGready Bryan. He was a born preacher, with unique gifts for the pulpit, but with comparatively little formal education or subsequent scholarship. While a candidate for the ministry, he was asked to prepare the usual discourses and to write a trial sermon. He protested that he had no sermon and could not write one. The Presbytery was about to reject him when young Bryan's mother, who was attending Presbytery, pleaded with one of the preachers: "I tell you the boy can preach, if he can't write. Appoint a time and let him try." The Presbytery was touched by the mother's earnest entreaty. They did set an appointed time. The youthful orator preached with "such fervor and sincerity of conviction as to make all the reverend ecclesiastics weep." From that day until his death, A. M. Bryan manifested a rare power to move the hearts of his hearers, young and old.[24]

After conducting several successful revivals in Washington, young Bryan, unlike the other Cumberland missionaries, was attracted to Pittsburgh where he sought in vain for a church of any denomination which would open its doors to permit him to preach. Nothing daunted, he preached on the streets and in open lots. His unusual gifts as a preacher attracted great crowds who were eager to hear his evangelistic preaching as he stressed the universal salvation of all who would respond to the gospel invitation. "Christ died for all," he dramatically shouted. Results followed. Hundreds of converts joined various churches in the city as the fruitage of his preaching, which resembled Whitefield's both in his emphasis and power. On a missionary journey to Meadville, he met similar opposition from the clergy who refused to admit him to their pulpits and even canvassed the community on a house-to-house basis in a futile effort to persuade the people not to hear the heretic. Bravely he faced the opposition of his ministerial brethren as he preached on the street and in private homes. From among the many converts, he organized a Cumberland Church with an initial membership of ninety-three.[25]

Pittsburgh was the scene of Bryan's true life's work. In 1833 he organized the First Cumberland Presbyterian Church of Pittsburgh. A sanctuary was erected on Smithfield Street between what is now Forbes Street and Fourth Avenue. But a disastrous fire destroyed the entire building and the adjacent residence of Dr. Bryan. A larger structure was then erected in 1842 on Sixth Avenue, the present site of the Duquesne Club which is directly opposite the First Presbyterian Church. Here he continued to preach until his death in 1861.

The early rapid increase in the number of Cumberland Presbyterian churches made necessary within ten years the organization of a second presbytery in Pennsylvania. The new presbytery assembled for its first meeting, April 14, 1837, in Uniontown and received the name Union Presbytery. Very appropriately, the Reverend John Morgan, pastor in that city, was selected as the first moderator. In Ohio, the Presbytery of Athens was formed with a few churches, following a series of revival meetings. At one of these meetings in Athens, Ohio, of the forty-six who professed conversion, fifteen afterward entered the Christian ministry.[26] However, Cumberland churches never thrived in Ohio as they did in Western Pennsylvania. The rolls of the three Ohio presbyteries, as late as 1886, could number only seventeen ministers and one ministerial candidate. Among the stronger churches were Athens, Covington, Lebanon, and Waterford.

The Presbytery of Athens was joined with the two Pennsylvania presbyteries to form the Pennsylvania Synod of the Cumberland Church October 11, 1838. The reports of the presbyteries the following year revealed an enrollment in the Synod of twenty-two ministers, eight licentiates and eleven candidates with a total of thirty-five congregations and thirty-two hundred and fifty-seven communicants. Such was the visible fruitage of ten years' missionary labor of the Cumberland Presbyterians in Pennsylvania and Ohio.[27]

Waynesburg College

Perhaps the most important action taken by the Pennsylvania Synod in 1840 was the decision to organize a college within the bounds of the Synod and to raise a fund of thirty thousand dollars for the endowment of a synodical college.[28] After an attempt to establish a college at Beverly, Ohio, had failed, the Synod in 1849 accepted the invitation of a group of citizens to assist in developing a synodical college at Waynesburg, Pennsylvania. Classes began that year in the Cumberland Presbyterian Church and in a rented hall. Early in November of 1851, Waynesburg College was formally opened in a new three-story brick structure, 70 by 50 feet, named Hanna Hall, which had been erected at a cost of six thousand dollars.[29]

Among the four graduates at the first Commencement a year later was Alfred Brashear Miller. He was destined to serve the college as professor and president throughout a memorable career of forty years. In an autobiographical sketch, Dr. Miller thus summarized his tribulations as president in a manner reminiscent of the Apostle Paul:

"I have been compelled to preach in order to live, sometimes supplying points twenty miles distant; I have been compelled to deny myself books greatly needed; to stay home when I should have traveled; to walk many miles because I could not afford to pay hack fare; to be harassed with debts that have eaten up the mind as cancers eat the flesh; in short, to do a great many things, which doing and not doing hindered my usefulness as a public servant of the church. At one time I edited *The Cumberland Presbyterian,* did all the necessary correspondence of the office, and kept the books, at the same time teaching six hours at the college, exercising general oversight of its financial affairs and often preaching twice on the Sabbath."[30]

Sustained by such sacrificial devotion in the presidency, and in spite of various vicissitudes of finance, the college persevered toward academic achievement and in broadening areas of service to church and nation. The college was part of the heritage bequeathed to the Presbyterian Church U.S.A. in the merger with the Cumberland Church in 1906. The Synod of Pennsylvania is happy to claim Waynesburg as one of its denominational colleges with a long list of distinguished alumni and alumnae. The first five foreign missionaries sent out by the Cumberland Church were graduates of Waynesburg College.[31] Of these, the Reverend J. B. Hail and his brother, the Reverend A. D. Hail, labored long and devotedly in Japan. Waynesburg was the only Cumberland Presbyterian college to be located within the territory of the Upper Ohio Valley.

Though continued missionary expansion broadened the scope and increased the number of its churches in Pennsylvania and Ohio, the Cumberland Presbyterian denomination never developed great strength in this area. It continued to be a missionary and evangelistic denomination and found its most rewarding opportunities of service and growth on the frontier as it expanded into North Carolina, Georgia, Kansas, Missouri, Alabama, Arkansas, and Texas. At the time of the reunion in 1906, only about 5 per cent of the total membership of the Cumberland churches was located in the general region of the Upper Ohio Valley. Some sixty churches were in Pennsylvania and a smaller number in Ohio with some strength also in certain parts of West Virginia. Many of these churches were rural or situated in small towns, particularly in mining communities.

Included, however, were some churches of considerable size which still remain as strong Presbyterian churches. Among these are the Third Presbyterian Church of Uniontown, Central Church of Brownsville, the Shady Avenue and Lemington churches in Pittsburgh, the Central Church of Washington, McKeesport, and Tarentum, the Presbyterian Church of Waynesburg, California, Charleroi, Clairton, Bentleyville, and Punxsutawney. The strength of Presbyterianism, particularly in Western Pennsylvania, was definitely increased both in numbers and evangelistic zeal by the reunion of 1906.

II. THE OLD SCHOOL AND NEW SCHOOL SCHISMS

The Reverend David Elliott, D. D., professor of theology in Western Theological Seminary, was serving as moderator of the General Assembly in the crisis year of 1837 when that supreme judicatory of the Presbyterian church took the historic act which resulted in the separation into the Old School and New School branches—a separation which continued until the reunion at Pittsburgh in 1869. It was a meeting for which Dr. Elliott and his fellow leaders of the more conservative wing of the church had made careful preparation to secure the necessary majority vote. The vote for moderator had been close, 137 votes for Elliott against 106 votes for Dr. Baxter Dickinson, the opposing candidate.[32] Having won the moderatorship, the leaders of the conservative group believed that they had sufficient strength to execute their plans for what they felt was the reform of the Presbyterian church. Motions were presented and passed exscinding from the church four entire synods and one additional presbytery. This drastic action was taken because the majority in the General Assembly believed that the majority of ministers and elders in these synods were guilty of laxity in emphasizing Presbyterian polity and doctrine.

Three of these four condemned synods were in northern New York and one in the Western Reserve area of northern Ohio.[33] It was a major ecclesiastical operation. It resulted eventually in the loss to the denomination of five hundred and thirty-three churches and over one hundred thousand communicants.[34] But major operations are sometimes necessary for the life and health of the patient. For a similar therapeutic gain, this ecclesiastical operation was deemed necessary by the Presbyterian doctors of divinity. The unity and sanctity of the Presbyterian church must be preserved even at the cost of suffering in numbers and friendships. Unity, Dr. Elliott felt, was more precious than size.

The following year, commissioners from these excised synods appeared at the annual meeting of the General Assembly in Philadelphia. Dr. Elliott was serving as the retiring moderator. He refused to recognize the validity of their credentials for enrollment as members. He ruled out of order all efforts to argue on behalf of the four synods. Thwarted in every parliamentary procedure, the members of the four synods and their sympathetic friends withdrew from the Assembly.[35] Under a moderator of their own choosing, they reassembled in another Presbyterian church and organized themselves into what they claimed was the legal General Assembly of the Presbyterian Church. The separation was complete. The denomination was split into two assemblies. The New and Old School Schism was now an unfortunate reality.

The New School group was joined by other synods and presbyteries in addition to those which had been exscinded. Eventually the New School included about four-ninths of all the ministers and membership of the church. The Old School had about 120,000 members whereas the New School had an enrolled membership of 100,000. Of these, only 10,000 were in the South. The separation was largely along sectional and racial lines, with the New School strength lying chiefly in New England, New York, and northern Ohio. It coincided in the main with the racial demarcation between the Scotch and Scotch-Irish, who had moved westward from New Jersey and Pennsylvania to Ohio, and the New Englanders who had settled or migrated through northern New York into the Western Reserve in Ohio. Perhaps the incompatibility of their diverse temperaments and general attitudes toward slavery had as much to do with the resulting separation as did the publicized doctrinal and polity differences each upheld so vigorously.[36]

The Plan of Union of 1801

The separation thus officially constituted was the unhappy result of previous years of strife over unsolved problems of doctrine and program arising on the rapidly expanding northwest frontier. For years, Presbyterians and Congregationalists had worked together in peace and harmony according to a Plan of Union adopted in 1801.[37] The Plan was largely inspired by the needs of the rapidly expanding frontier in western New York and northern Ohio. By this Plan the two churches agreed not to compete with each other but to permit the use by both denominations of each other's ministers in organizing new churches, which then would be free to make their own choice of a denominational membership.

Many New Englanders, who had moved into New York and

eastern Ohio, thus became Presbyterian since the Presbyterians had been the more aggressive in establishing churches in those areas.

Under this Plan the Presbytery of Ohio had begun a vigorous missionary expansion into the Western Reserve area through the Western Missionary Society which had been organized in 1802. Ten years later, practically all the missionaries on the Reserve were Presbyterians.[38] The salaries of many of these itinerating preachers were paid by the Connecticut Missionary Society. "Furnish us with suitable men, and we will pay them as we pay our missionaries from this quarter—$6.00 a week."[39] The Presbyterians profited greatly by this Plan. Membership of the Presbyterian church grew rapidly from 28,901 in 1810 to 173,329 in 1830, a sevenfold increase in 20 years.[40] Gradually the Congregational Church was almost completely absorbed as new presbyteries and synods were formed from the growing membership. As one Congregational leader expressed it: "The milk from their Congregational cows was being churned into Presbyterian butter."[41] Or to quote from another Congregational source: "When the lion and the lamb lie down together, the lion has little to fear."[42] The result was the development of many Presbyterian churches containing strong Congregational elements.[43] The Plan of Union seemed to be a welcomed success from the viewpoint of the expansion of the Presbyterian church.

Not so, however, in the judgment of the more conservative Scotch-Irish Presbyterians. They viewed with alarm these transplanted New Englanders who retained Congregational sympathies and who interpreted "to suit their taste" some phases of the Confession of Faith. The early missionaries, sent into this region by the Western Missionary Society, were graduates of Canonsburg Academy and had received their theological training under Dr. John McMillan. There could be no question of their theological convictions nor of their devotion to Presbyterian polity. Through their zealous efforts, the Western Reserve was won to the Presbyterian rather than to the Congregational Church as they worked cooperatively under the Plan of Union.

But many of the newer missionaries had not received this Presbyterian indoctrination before being ordained by the new presbyteries formed in the Western Reserve. They were products of churches in which strong Congregational leanings were still manifested. As a result, they were under suspicion by their more orthodox brethren in the General Assembly. They were sneeringly referred to as "Presbygationalists." The fear was expressed that the church was being "Yankeeyed" by this influx of ministers who had leanings toward Congregationalism or had come out of a less orthodox New England background.

As their numbers increased, the conviction grew in the minds of the conservative group that the Plan of Union was not a good thing for the Presbyterian church. It was a contaminating influence which must be checked by discontinuing the Plan. It was for that reason that General Assembly in 1835 voted by a small majority to abrogate the Plan of Union which had been in operation since 1801. Had the Assembly merely voted to discontinue their acceptance of the Plan, the unity of the denomination might not have been seriously imperiled.

But the conservative group took extreme measures. They declared that the Plan itself was unconstitutional since it had never been submitted to the presbyteries for the necessary ratifying vote. Hence, since it was originally unconstitutional, all churches and ministers which had been brought into the Presbyterian church through its functioning since 1801 could not legally be regarded as parts of the Presbyterian church and so were declared cut off from its membership. Included were the Synod of Western Reserve and the three New York Synods of Utica, Geneva, and Genesee, which similarly had been organized under the "unconstitutional" Plan of Union. These four synods were thus declared not to be a part of the Presbyterian church in the United States and hence not entitled to membership or vote in the General Assembly.

Nearly one-fifth of the entire membership of the General Assembly was thus cut off.[44]

Controversy Over Foreign Missions

A second cause of friction, which also had its roots in Western Pennsylvania, was the question of control of the church's missionary program. Should the Presbyterian church direct its own missionary work, or should it be carried forward under an interdenominational Board? The Pittsburgh Synod said the Presbyterian church should have the direct planning and sustaining of its missionary activities. Accordingly, in 1802, the Synod organized itself into the Western Missionary Society, with the definite objective "to diffuse the knowledge of the gospel among the inhabitants of the new settlements, the Indian tribes, and, if need be, among the interior inhabitants where they were not able to support the gospel."[45]

For twenty-seven years the Synod conducted its own home missionary task. In 1829 the Synod transferred all its assets to the Board of Missions of the General Assembly which had been organized one year earlier.[46] The Foreign Missionary program was still under the direction of an interdenominational organization called the American Board of Commissioners for Foreign Missions which had been organized in 1810 by the Congregationalists.[47] To this Board many Presbyterians voluntarily gave financial support.

Dr. Swift, the pastor of the Second Presbyterian Church in Pittsburgh, felt that this form of voluntary support was not sufficient. He believed that a foreign missionary program was an inherent and inescapable duty of the church. He so argued before the General Assembly in 1831. The majority did not share his viewpoint and preferred establishing closer affiliation with the American Board for Foreign Missions. He then turned to present his plea to the Synod of Pittsburgh where he met with greater success. His resolution was adopted. Synod resolved "that it is expedient forthwith to establish a Society or Board of Foreign Missions on such a plan as will admit of the co-operation of such parts of the Presbyterian Church as may think proper to unite in this great and important concern."[48] The Western Foreign Missionary Society was organized as the official agency of that Synod. Dr. Swift was elected its recording secretary. The society grew rapidly. It sent its first missionaries to India and Africa. Two years later Swift resigned his pastorate to accept the full-time leadership of the society he had created.

When the General Assembly, for the first time in its history, met in Pittsburgh, it seemed to Dr. Swift and his fellow leaders in the Synod of Pittsburgh that the time had come to transfer from the Synod to the General Assembly the responsibility for the foreign missionary program which the Synod was carrying forward so successfully. A resolution to that effect was presented and approved. It authorized the appointment of a committee to work out the necessary details of transfer and to report at the meeting next year.[49] When the report was presented in 1836, the supporters of independent or interdenominational missionary societies were in the majority. They rejected the plan to place the missionary enterprise under denominational control. Instead, they reaffirmed their desire to continue to function on a voluntary basis through the interdenominational American Board for Foreign Missions.[50]

This action irritated the advocates of denominational missions. Carefully they laid their plans for the next year. Success crowned their efforts. They were in the majority as the General Assembly reconvened in 1837. They elected Dr. Elliott as the moderator. They carried their resolution approving plans for transferring Foreign Mission work from the Synod of Pittsburgh to the General Assembly. They organized a Board of Foreign Missions on a strictly denominational basis and severed their former connection with the American Board.[51] Foreign Missions thus became and still continues to be the responsibility of the Presbyterian church as a whole. The General Assembly of 1837 which declared illegal the

Plan of Union, and thus ruled out of the church the four synods which had been organized under that Plan, also dissolved further connections with the American Board.

Both actions were in defiance of the New School party. Separation was now inevitable. Two separate denominations under two distinct General Assemblies were to direct the destinies of Presbyterianism until 1869. After a long and bitter legal battle, the Supreme Court of Pennsylvania officially declared the Old School Assembly to be the continuing legal Presbyterian Church, with the right to retain the denominational name and the invested funds of the denomination and to hold the property of Princeton and Western Theological Seminaries. It was a bitter blow to the New School group who then called themselves The American Presbyterian Church.[52]

In the inevitable process of organizing and regrouping of presbyteries, the Synod of Pittsburgh with all its presbyteries voted to remain a part of the Old School Assembly. Its members were basically conservative Scotch-Irish Presbyterians. They felt a similarity of conviction with the Old School. Very few ministers and churches throughout Western Pennsylvania cast their lot with the New School Assembly. Of those who did withdraw, the most prominent was Dr. David H. Riddle, pastor of the Third Presbyterian Church of Pittsburgh. He and his church enrolled in the newly formed Presbytery of Pittsburgh. He was joined in the organizing of this New School presbytery by the Reverend Samuel M. Sparks of the Minersville Presbyterian Church and by only two other churches, one at Greensburg and the other at Unity. As might be expected, Dr. Riddle was chosen the first moderator.[53]

This Presbytery covered a wide range of territory but included only a few churches. Financial conditions at that time were not favorable to missionary expansion. Western Pennsylvania lay prostrate in the wreckage of the panic of 1837 which had leveled all economic values and spread confusion and despair in finance and business.[54] Yet the struggling Presbytery did succeed in estab-

COLLECTION OF GEORGE SWETNAM

THIRD PRESBYTERIAN CHURCH OF PITTSBURGH

Sixth Avenue and Cherry Way. (Site of Penn-Sheraton Hotel) Scene of Reunion of New School and Old School branches of the Presbyterian church, November 10, 1869. General Assembly met in this church in 1895 to celebrate twenty-fifth anniversary of Reunion.

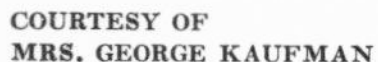

COURTESY OF
MRS. GEORGE KAUFMAN

REVEREND
WILLIAM L.
McEWAN, D.D.

Pastor of Third Presbyterian Church of Pittsburgh, 1894–1931. Under his leadership the church moved to present location, Fifth and Negley avenues, and present church was erected, November 1, 1903.

REVEREND
HUGH THOMSON
KERR, D.D.

Pastor of Shadyside Presbyterian Church, 1913–1945. Moderator, General Assembly, 1930. President, Board of Christian Education, Presbyterian Church U.S.A.

COURTESY OF
THE PITTSBURGH PRESS

lishing the Fifth Presbyterian Church in downtown Pittsburgh and in reorganizing the defunct Presbyterian Church of Birmingham (South Side). In 1840 the Presbytery could report only seven ministers. Yet this feeble Presbytery was signally honored in 1850 when one of its members, Dr. David Riddle, was elected to serve as moderator of the General Assembly of the New School. He was the only minister from the Upper Ohio Valley area to be selected for that highest office in the New School Assembly.[55]

In the region north of Pittsburgh, where the presbyteries of Erie and Meadville had been organized, the growth of churches was more numerous but many were small and without pastors. The statistics of 1849 record eight ministers and fourteen churches in Erie Presbytery; six ministers and thirteen churches in Meadville Presbytery; while Pittsburgh Presbytery could claim nine ministers but only eight churches.[56] The New School branch was never very thriving nor popular throughout Western Pennsylvania. This section remained a bulwark of Old School Presbyterianism.

Results of the Old School and New School Schism

Even though this New and Old School Schism was the unhappy product of years of controversy, it was not without some blessing to the Presbyterian church. The sad consequences of division were somewhat offset by three definite gains to the church. When equally consecrated and capable leaders cannot agree within a denominational bond, it is better sometimes to work separately in harmonious groups rather than to expend energy and engender strife in struggles for sincere convictions.

In the first place the separation demonstrated that unity is essential to growth. Throughout the four years immediately preceding the separation, the General Assembly reports indicate that the growth of the church not only was stunted but that the membership actually decreased for a net loss of 15,031 members.[57] Apparently, religion lagged when the energies of its chosen leaders were expended in careful preparation for the platform of controversy and in the struggle of faction against faction to control the policy of the General Assembly. There may have been other contributing causes, such as a reaction from the enthusiasm of the preceding revival period, or even the widespread spirit of speculation which resulted in the disastrous panic of 1837. Nevertheless the embittering zeal in controversy must carry a large portion of responsibility for this four-year decline in membership.

However, after the separation, the results in membership changed abruptly. The presbyteries and ministers with Congregational leanings and more liberal interpretations in theology withdrew to form the New School Assembly. That left the Old School Assembly in almost unprecedented doctrinal homogeneity. Differences of theological opinion in the Old School Assembly were comparatively trifling and never troublesome. Leaders throughout the entire denomination were united in faith and polity and in a crusading zeal to preserve the faith once delivered to the saints and authoritatively formulated and applied in Princeton theology.[58] The numerical results of this unity were evident in a remarkably rapid and sustained growth in membership. Throughout the decades of 1840–1860, the total population of the United States expanded about 82 per cent. Yet during that same period, the Old School church grew in membership 131 per cent.[59]

Nor were the New School brethren far behind after they achieved a working unity. When the New School men met as an Assembly in 1838, they found themselves a rather conglomerate mass of conflicting plans and hopes. Their chief bond of union was the conviction that the four exscinded synods had suffered a great injustice and that they must maintain their identity as Presbyterians. On questions of polity, program, and doctrine they were widely separated. They needed the merging influence of time and discussion to bring unity to faith and action.

As a result, the first two decades witnessed only a comparatively slow growth. Some of the churches, which were Congregational in polity, left the Presbyterian fold to be enrolled as members of the

Congregationalist denomination. Others, who were Presbyterian in sympathy and whose resentment soon cooled, reunited with the Old School Assembly. Many of the New School leaders were younger men whose enthusiasm and ambition needed the restraining wisdom of experience.[60] To achieve co-operative unity and to develop the ecclesiastical machinery essential to a smooth-working organization were no easy tasks. The New School of necessity grew slowly. In twenty years it could report a net increase in membership of only 30,000.[61] Unity was finally achieved. The New School, like the Old School Assembly, became a close-knit and unified body. As a result, the last ten years of the New School were the most fruitful. The membership at the time of the Reunion reached the total of 173,000, a net increase for the entire three decades of division of about 70 per cent.[62]

Denominational Boards Are Vindicated

The three decades of division also demonstrated the value of denominational Boards and Agencies. The two Assemblies were great laboratories in which contrasted forms of church programs could be worked out separately, each within the comparative harmony of a denominational fellowship. One of the great causes of friction, as previously noted, was the question of denominational versus interdenominational control of foreign missions and education. The Old School, under the leadership of Dr. Swift and his associates, had organized the Presbyterian Board of Foreign Missions after previous years of success under the direction of the Synod of Pittsburgh. The New School group had fought the plan in 1837 and voted to continue with The American Home Missionary Society and The American Board of Commissioners for Foreign Missions. When the two groups split into separate Assemblies, each continued the policy of its choice. Each welcomed the opportunity to test out the value of its cherished plan. The Old School functioned through Presbyterian Boards of Missions and Education. The New School turned its financial support to The American

Home Missionary Society and the Board for Foreign Missions.[63]

What was the result of these contrasted experiments? After two decades of unsatisfactory experimentation, the New School terminated its allegiance to interdenominational agencies and organized its own denominational Boards.[64] Experience proved the value of committing these great causes to denominational Boards which are under the direct control of the General Assembly. The problem was solved successfully by separate experimentation in two great ecclesiastical laboratories. The wisdom of the Pittsburgh plan was vindicated, to become the established policy of the reunited denominations.

The Wisdom of Centralization

A third gain by the period of division was a demonstration of the value of centralized control under the authority of a General Assembly. The question of the relative powers of Presbytery, Synod, and General Assembly had long been a contentious problem in the developing history of the Presbyterian church. The powers of the Synod was one of the grave points at issue giving rise both to the New Side and Old Side Schism in 1741 and later the Cumberland Schism in 1810. It was in evidence also in the strife which gave momentum to the New and Old School Schism. The Old School body believed in the value of a Presbyterian polity that gave full authority to the General Assembly as the final administrative and judicial court of the denomination. The New School group, on the other hand, would limit the power and prestige of the General Assembly so that never again could it abuse its power, as they thought it had done, by cutting off from the denomination four synods and their constituent presbyteries. So again the problem found its answer in the two contrasted schools of experiment during the period of separation.

The New School body in 1840 changed its Form of Government to make the synods and not the General Assembly the ultimate court of appeal. It also provided that the General Assembly should meet only once in three years and not annually.[65] Other changes were also experimented with in an effort to demonstrate the relative importance of synods and the General Assembly. The result was quite disappointing. After a decade of discouraging experimentation, the New School leaders discovered they lacked central authority and a strong bond of union. They returned to the former policy of annual meetings of the Assembly.[66] They learned the wisdom of a central administrative body and a final court of appeal. They abandoned their experiment in decentralization of the denomination. When the time of reunion drew nigh in 1869, they were ready to accept again the authority of an Assembly, which at times may make mistakes, but which is essential to denominational strength.

With these and similar problems worked out to mutual agreement in the denominational laboratories of contrasted experiment and with time healing the wounds of friction and with death calling to her heavenly reward the more embattled leaders in controversial oratory, the two denominations found themselves cherishing a mutual desire for reconciliation and reunion. In working out an acceptable basis for this desired unity, Presbyterians throughout the Upper Ohio Valley made distinct contributions. Dr. Charles C. Beatty, pastor of the First Presbyterian Church of Steubenville, Ohio, had been elected moderator of the Old School Assembly in 1862. At his suggestion the Assembly adopted a resolution proposing an annual friendly interchange of commissioners between the two General Assemblies. Four years later he was appointed chairman of the Committee on Reunion of the Presbyterian church. In that capacity he labored with great ardor until reunion was achieved.

Serving with him on the committee of fifteen were Dr. William D. Howard, pastor of the Second Presbyterian Church of Pittsburgh, and Mr. Robert McKnight, a Pittsburgh lawyer who was serving as a ruling elder in the Central Presbyterian Church of Allegheny. Another Pittsburgh lawyer, Henry W. Williams, an elder in the Third Presbyterian Church and Judge of the Supreme Court of Pennsylvania, was a member of the similar Committee on Reunion of the New School Assembly.[67]

Through the efforts of these two committees, a mutually agreeable basis for organic unity was achieved after careful discussion and diplomatic compromise. The plan for Reunion was presented to the separate Assemblies in 1868. Both Assemblies approved it. In 1869 both Assemblies voted to meet later that year in adjourned session.

Very appropriately the place selected was Pittsburgh, the city whose leaders had played an important part in the events leading up to the schism. Dr. David Elliott, of Western Theological Seminary, had been the moderator whose stern and perhaps injudicious decisions had precipitated the schism. Now another Western Seminary professor, Dr. Melancthon W. Jacobus, was the Old School moderator. November 12, 1869, was a memorable day in the history of Pittsburgh Presbyterianism. The Old School Assembly met in the First Church and the New School in the nearby Third Church. Both Assemblies adjourned simultaneously. Each group, headed by its moderator and other officers, advanced to meet each other in cordial greeting of Christian brotherhood. Marching two by two, the Assemblies proceeded, Old School and New School, down Wood Street and up Fifth Avenue and along Smithfield Street to Sixth Street to the Third Church for the Reunion Convention. Hundreds lined the streets and cheered as the marching procession sang in triumph, "The Year Of Jubilee Has Come."[68] The schism had faded into history. After three decades of separation, the two great branches of the Presbyterian church were fused into a permanent unity. In May of the following year, the united church met as the 82nd General Assembly of the Presbyterian Church of the United States of America. Enthusiasm for greater achievement was contagious. Joyfully, and with a faith born of conviction, the Assembly voted to raise a fund of five million dollars to propagate and strengthen the reunited church.[69]

III. SLAVERY SPLITS THE CHURCH

Doubtless to those who had prayed and worked for this harmonious reunion of the Old and New School Assemblies, it did seem that The Year of Jubilee had come. But it was only a partial coming. Already, differences of opinion on the morality of slavery had split both branches of the church and caused two additional schisms.

The New School Assembly had been the first to experience the disruptive effects of contrasted opinions on a moral issue which became clothed in the rather sacrosanct garment of economic gain. Slavery was not economically profitable in the North, where voluntary immigration furnished an adequate labor supply throughout an area of small individually owned farms and rapidly developing industrial towns and cities. In the South, where immigration was comparatively slight and where vast plantations were operated by a comparatively small group of planters, slave labor seemed both necessary and profitable. Under such circumstances where church members, especially the more prosperous contributors, were obtaining their revenue from contrasted sources, it is quite difficult even for consecrated ministers and elders to think clearly and without bias on any moral problem of the church. A person's thinking is often conditioned by his environment and inherited convictions. Hence what seems clearly right in one state or one section of the country may appear to equally sincere men to be wrong in other areas. Thus it has always been. Illustrations are numerous and convincing but need not be quoted.

It is no surprise then, while reading through the minutes of both the New and Old School Assemblies, to find the question of slavery reappearing frequently and to note that men from the South were searching their Bibles for possible texts to justify that which seemed to be an essential part of the financial structure of their church and community. Nor to discover, on the other hand, that men in the North were thinking more clearly on a moral problem which brought no financial gain to their communities and which, on the contrary, aroused their righteous indignation. So, as a rule, the northern clergymen and elders were somewhat eager to have the higher church courts of their denomination denounce slavery, while the southern church leaders were resentful at any intrusion upon their economic life and vigorously opposed any pronouncement against slavery. In between were the harmonizers who believed that the peace and unity of the church were more paramount than purity of morals. They tried to keep such explosive issues as slavery buried in committees or expressed in innocuous resolutions that could offend none of the brethren.[70]

Free Presbyterian Church Organized

The overwhelming strength of the New School Church, as previously noted, lay in the North where slavery was economically unsound. It was in that Assembly that efforts to place the church on record against slavery were most frequent and persistent. So persistent were the antislavery group that within less than a decade the New School experienced two distinct schisms, but for two contrasted reasons. One group split because the New School Assembly was too cowardly in its pronouncements against slavery.[71] The other withdrew because the New School Assembly was too positive in its declarations.

The first group to withdraw was led by John Rankin, Dyer Burgess, and eight or ten others of like conviction. In 1847 they organized themselves into the Free Presbytery of Ripley, Ohio, with some eight or nine churches.[72] Men of like conviction joined them. The movement spread. Two other presbyteries were organized. In 1848 the three presbyteries were united into the Free Presbyterian Synod of Cincinnati, to be later renamed and expanded into the Free Church Synod of the United States.[73] E. B. Welsh, in a carefully documented study published in Slosser's *They Seek A Country,* reports that this new branch of the Presbyterian church listed seven presbyteries with at least sixty-five congregations, spreading from Lancaster County in eastern Pennsylvania to central Iowa. Most of the strength of this small and little-known denomination lay in the area of the Upper Ohio Valley. Its leaders were men of sound doctrine who were willing to sacrifice everything for a cause which found expression in this distinctive slogan: "No Christian fellowship with slaveholders, whose gross sin is compounded of theft, murder, and adultery."[74] The Free Presbyterian Church never grew large. It was born to propagate a cause. It lived to enlighten the North and to sensitize the popular conscience. It died in the knowledge that its purpose had been achieved. The slave was freed after a bloody and costly war. The Synod met for the last time in 1863. Its small membership was absorbed in neighboring churches of the Presbyterian family.

IV. SOUTHERN PRESBYTERIAN CHURCH FORMED

The other group to withdraw from the New School was the southern element which resented what it felt were too stern strictures against slavery. It was a schism which did not lie within the area of the Upper Ohio Valley and so needs a mere mention.[75] The disruptive occasion was the adopting by the New School Assembly in 1857 of a series of drastic resolutions condemning slavery.[76] In resentment the southern members withdrew and organized themselves into a separate New School Church in the South. It took as its official name, "The United Synod of the Presbyterian Church."[77]

The Old School Assembly was more successful in straddling the slavery issue and so succeeded in maintaining its sectional unity four years longer. Previously, however, in 1845 a few men of deep conviction in some presbyteries in Western Pennsylvania and Ohio had withdrawn in protest. They helped organize the Free Presbytery of Ripley. Most of the members of the Free Presbyterian churches scattered throughout Pennsylvania and eastern Ohio had formerly been enrolled in Old School churches.

Memories of the Schism of 1837 were haunting the Old School leaders. They dreaded another schism. Frantically they strove to preserve unity and even stretched their consciences in statements they regretted later.[78] As old Cyrus McCormick, of harvester fame and a Virginia-born Presbyterian, said: "The two great hoops holding the Union together are the Democratic Party and the Old School Presbyterian Church."[79] But the irrepressible conflict was deeper than surface unity. It was in reality more even than a moral crisis. The question at issue was a struggle between two great economic systems—an agrarian system based on slave labor and an industrial system based on a man's right to choose his place of employment.

The Old School Church could no longer straddle so fundamental an issue in the life of the nation. The church must take a stand. It did so. It passed the famous Spring Resolutions in 1861.[80] That act was the signal for the Southern Presbyterians to withdraw. They formed the Presbyterian Church in the Confederate States which in a few months joined with The United Synod of the Presbyterian Church. Thus the two southern parts of the New and Old School Assemblies united to form The Presbyterian Church of the South.[81]

The natural and inevitable decision to merge also the northern branches of the New and Old School Assemblies followed nine years later. The two Assemblies agreed to form a reunited Northern Presbyterian Church. Minor controversies were thus forgotten as sectional unions were forged by changing economic conditions. Only one schism now remains to be healed. The reunion of the Northern and Southern branches of the nationwide Presbyterian church awaits the melting power of brotherly love.

CHAPTER XI The Growing Edge of Conscience

I. TEMPERANCE

IN the western part of the Upper Ohio Valley at Hillsboro, Ohio, was inaugurated in 1873 what has been described as "the most remarkable movement against intemperance in the history of the world. Unique in its methods, widespread in its results; and, although a failure as regards its direct purpose, nevertheless it accomplished much good, and advanced public sentiment toward the reformation of the great evils of the vice of intemperance."[1]

The day was December 24, 1873. The place was the Presbyterian church in the village of Hillsboro, in southeastern Ohio. The occasion was the aftermath of an address by Dr. Dio Lewis, that singular combination of homeopath, physical culturist, and reformer. On the evening before, he had spoken at the town's music hall, describing the evils of intemperance, and how the women of Port Byron, New York, his boyhood home, had met in the village church and pledged themselves to persevere until a victory had been won. Their plan, which proved a success, was to go in a body to the liquor dealers, appeal to their better nature, and ask them to cease the traffic.

At Hillsboro the women listened to talks by pastors of the village churches and several local officials, and signed this compact: "With God's help, we will stand by each other in this work, and persevere therein until it is accomplished; and see to it, as far as our influence goes, that the liquor traffic shall never be revived." A committee of fifty leading citizens of the town was formed to aid the women with moral and financial support, pledging more than twelve thousand dollars to the cause. They called their movement "The Crusade."

On Christmas morning, the women met again at the same church and, at nine o'clock, one hundred and fifteen of them filed out, formed a procession, and marched to the four drugstores. Two of these agreed at once to cease dealing in hard liquor, a third pledged himself to sell only where he, as a doctor, felt it was needed as medicine; but the fourth, W. H. H. Dunn, refused even to discuss the matter.

On Friday, December 26, the women met again at the church and visited the eleven saloons of the village. These all proved as defiant as had Mr. Dunn. He, in the meantime, had sent the Crusaders a letter which read:

"Ladies: In compliance with my agreement I give you this promise: that I will carry on my business in the future as I have in the past; that is to say that in the sale of intoxicating liquors I will comply with the law; nor will I sell to any person whose father, mother, wife or daughter sends me a written request not to make such sale."

The women continued to hold prayer meetings in Mr. Dunn's store for about a week until he locked them out, after which they kept up their meetings on the street in front of his place, despite the fact that the weather was very cold. By January 30, five saloons had been closed and strong pressure was continued on the others. A Cincinnati paper published the inside view of one of these saloon visits, as reported by a young man who was there:

"He and a half dozen others, who had been out of town and did not know what was going on, had ranged themselves in the familiar semicircle before the bar, and had their drinks ready and cigars prepared for the match, when the rustle of women's wear attracted their attention, and looking up they saw what they thought a crowd of a thousand women entering. One youth saw among them his mother and sister; another had two cousins in the invading host, and a third, still more unfortunate, recognized his intended mother-in-law. Had the invisible prince of the pantomime touched them with his magic wand, converting all to statues, the tableau could not have been more impressive. For a full one minute they stood as if turned to stone; then a slight motion was evident and lager beer and brandy smash descended slowly to the counter, while segars dropped unlighted from nerveless fingers. Happily, at this juncture the ladies struck up: 'Oh Do Not Be Discouraged, For Jesus Is Your Friend.' It made a diversion and the party escaped to the street, scared out of a year's growth."

At the end of January, Mr. Dunn formally threatened suit against the women if they continued their pressure, but they built a tabernacle of "canvas and plank" directly in front of his store, and continued to hold their meetings there. After a long-drawn-out lawsuit, Mr. Dunn at last won a verdict of five dollars, which was appealed, and the case finally settled out of court. The women had become disheartened by this time and gave up their efforts.

Their example, however, had attracted wide attention, being reported through the press of the entire nation. Several of them had also become active temperance speakers, and during the years that were to come their "crusade" was to have a far wider effect than the five saloons and three drugstores which submitted in Hillsboro —indeed a far wider effect than the most sanguine of their number could ever have dreamed.

Widespread Use of Whiskey

The work at Hillsboro was not by any means the first blow for the cause of temperance which had been struck in Presbyterian churches of the Upper Ohio Valley. Nor, when one sees the background of the effort, is it surprising that the work proved difficult. From the earliest settlement of the area—yes, and even before that time—whiskey had been the lifeblood of its trade and of its society. The first white men who penetrated the area from eastern Pennsylvania were fur traders, much of whose business was accomplished by selling rum and other spirits to the Indians. The Reverend Charles Beatty, Presbyterian chaplain in General John Forbes's advance against Fort Duquesne, discovered his best way of getting the men to religious service was to issue their daily ration of grog at that time.

As settlement advanced, whiskey was almost the only commodity which could be sold at a profit despite the necessity of a packhorse trip of almost two hundred miles across the mountains. In an area almost bare of money, it was virtually legal tender. Almost every farmer either ran a still or had whiskey made for him by his neighbors, as the reader will recall in Chapter IV with its discussion of the Whiskey Rebellion. Liquor was partaken of by all members of the family, and when visitors arrived it was considered only polite to offer a couple of ounces of liquor, which was seldom if ever refused. Speaking of this bad custom prevailing, an old writer remarks: "A man could not be born, christened, married, nor buried without liquor, and it met him at every intermediate step from birth to death. But it is due to the ladies of that period to state that they were habitually abstemious, seldom more than tasted it, and some few not even that."[2]

When little Thomas Mellon, later to found Pittsburgh's greatest fortune, made his first trip into Pittsburgh on foot as a boy of nine, the lunch provided by a family friend for his return journey of more than twenty miles was not an unusual one for a small boy of that day—a chunk of bread and a half pint of whiskey.[3]

Temperance societies and "teetotal pledges" were then unknown; and though intoxication was considered both disgraceful and sinful, moderate drinking was thought to be neither. That it was hurtful and dangerous to drink at all, seemed to occur to none. That spirits should not be made, excepting in very small quantities, nor kept, sold, nor given away by any but regular druggists, under all the wholesome restrictions guarding other poisons, had not been thought of by the wise or the foolish, by saint or sinner.

Anti-liquor Agitation Begins

Although sentiment against the unrestricted use of liquor was slow to appear in the Upper Ohio Valley, the Presbyterian church was in the forefront of the contest when it was at last drawn in the late 1820's. An early instance of temperance action, of uncertain date but certainly one of the first, occurred at Dunlap's Creek, the "Old Stone" church in the Monongahela Valley, which is perhaps the oldest Presbyterian congregation still active west of the Allegheny Mountains. Ebenezer Finley, Jr., the son of an elder and later himself an elder in the congregation, had recently married and was planning to build a barn by the then common method of having a "barn raising." He went to his father and the pastor, the Reverend William Johnston, and confided that he was not going to provide any whiskey.

"Ebenezer," they said, "You can't do it. The men won't work without it."

"Well, I'm going to try it," he replied.

The day came, and his neighbors were invited, and came to the raising. Ebenezer, who could talk faster than a machine gun, mounted a timber, and addressed them:

"My friends and neighbors, I have invited you here today to help me raise a barn, and I am not going to furnish any whiskey. I have plenty of cider and apples to which you are perfectly welcome, but if any of you are dissatisfied you needn't lend a helping hand, and there will be no hard feelings on my part."

There was a little grumbling by some of the men, but finally all lent a helping hand, and the barn went up without a single accident—something unusual on such occasions. It was the first temperance wedge in the Monongahela Valley—perhaps west of the mountains.[4]

Once a stand was taken, sentiment crystallized rapidly and Dr. Francis Herron, of the First Presbyterian Church of Pittsburgh, presided at a general meeting of friends of temperance held on

March 26, 1830.[5] At least one society had been formed before this, but its numbers were greatly increased at this meeting. Speakers pointed out that 129 tavern licenses had been issued in 1829 in Pittsburgh and 162 in other parts of the county, making one licensed house for every 123 men, women, and children. In the same year, more than a thousand residents of Pittsburgh had presented a petition to the grand jury asking that the number of saloon licenses be decreased, but the reduction in 1830 was only to 123. At first these societies were strictly confined to favoring temperance, but in July of 1833 a total abstinence society was formed in one of the Presbyterian churches at Pittsburgh.[6]

Among the notable early advocates of total abstinence was Eliza Graham, daughter of the Reverend James Graham, pastor of old Beulah Presbyterian Church, a few miles east of Pittsburgh. A family tradition reports that when a sewing society of the church was meeting at the pastor's home, his wife told Eliza to bring in refreshments, which in that day included whiskey. Eliza left the room, but did not come back, and later said it was the only time that she ever disobeyed her stepmother.[7] Members of the church were so much impressed by her quiet action that they founded a temperance society. The date is uncertain but prior to 1833, since it was on November 5, 1832, that she married the Reverend Adam Torrance and went with him as a missionary to the wilds of Ohio.[8]

Eliza had been violently opposed to the use of strong drink from the time that she was a young girl, perhaps as early as about 1820. Finally she urged her father to call a meeting at the church in the interest of temperance. Her friends were horrified and thought that it would only cause trouble, but the meeting aroused great interest and was the beginning of a temperance crusade in the community. Her father gave up serving liquor in his home or to men who were working for him on his farm.[9] Some of Eliza's numerous young men admirers were far from enthusiastic on the subject of temperance, and one of them was bold enough to tell her: "Why, Miss Eliza, you'll never get a husband if you talk like this." Eliza replied: "I don't want a husband who does not talk like this."[10]

Reformers Meet Opposition

Not all was smooth sailing for the temperance cause, however, even in the churches. In a letter to *The Pittsburgh Advocate,* Mr. Graham relates an experience:

"Sir: Some weeks since I attended a temperance meeting at Bethel Associate Reformed [later United Presbyterian] Church in Plumb Township. When I arrived at the place I found the house full to overflowing and four clergymen—one Covenanter [Reformed Presbyterian], one Antiburger [Associate Presbyterian], one Union Seceder [Associate Reformed Presbyterian], and one Presbyterian. The pastor of the church, the Reverend William Galbraith, was delivering the most intemperate address I ever heard. He said he had proved to demonstration that Christ drank wine and we take him for our example. He said the Scripture was a permission to drink wine and consequently not to drink it as a common beverage was sin . . . He said that the Temperance Reform was a humbug and Satan transformed into an Angel of light . . . In conclusion he read some extracts from a periodical of the improper conduct of a temperance speaker who addressed the people at the door of the church while the pastor was preaching in the house, evidently with the design to induce his hearers to believe we were all fanatics, fools and madmen.

"When he—the Reverend Pastor—concluded he politely invited any minister present to express his views on the subject. Brother McC—rose and replied to him in a speech of near two hours and with considerable severity answered the pastor's arguments . . . and boldly charged him and the Brethren on his side with being afraid to preach Temperance lest they would have to address empty pews. I succeeded Mr. McC—and spent an hour in examining the Rev. Galbraith's phillipic with unusual mildness and good nature and concluded by offering the apology I could devise for his want of courtesy for abusing us in his own church after inviting us to attend . . . that he was so in the habit of abusing other denominations that he did it without intending it or knowing it.

"Mr. C—then addressed the audience. He said . . . that he had once signed a Temperance Pledge . . . but since he had examined the Bible more carefully he doubted the propriety of such Associations, but if a man was fully persuaded in his own mind he would not say he did wrong in signing a pledge.

"The Rev. G—was the last speaker. He declared himself practically on our side for 10 years past but . . . he could not sign a pledge because Catholics and Infidels were temperance men."[11] The two laymen who are referred to in the letter are impossible to identify with certainty and "Mr. C—" can hardy have been Charles Carothers, an elder of Beulah Church.

Early during the first temperance activity, Mr. Carothers had bought a new still but had not erected it when he went into the village of Wilkinsburg where his son, Charles Jr., had a store. Since all stores at the time sold whiskey, the father told his son of the purchase and promised him a supply of whiskey on his next visit. But the son said, "Do not bring any, father, I have decided that it is wrong to drink whiskey and I shall never sell it again."

The father thought over his son's action on his drive home to the farm. He added to his son's "if it is wrong to drink whiskey, then it is wrong to sell it," the codicil "and wrong to make it." After it was learned he did not plan to operate the new still, he had many offers to buy it, but refused to sell. "No," he said, "since it is wrong to drink, then it is wrong to sell, then it is wrong to make it, then it is wrong for me to sell you the means of making it." The still remained unused until at last it was corroded and worthless.[12]

Another letter which Mr. Graham wrote to *The Advocate* tells of a meeting in a Washington County church, where several drunken men were forbidden to enter the church, within which the pastor was attacking the temperance movement. One, however, did get in, and when the speaker uttered a particularly bitter criticism of the reform cause, the drunk would wave his hat and cry out "Hallelujah! Hallelujah! You're the preacher for me."[13]

Opposition to the temperance movement sometimes became very strong, as in the attack on Frank Johnston and his celebrated Negro brass band when they played for a temperance rally in Old Allegheny on May 16, 1843.[14]

Two years earlier the "Washingtonian" temperance movement, which had been launched at Baltimore, had become so strong at Pittsburgh that a temperance hall was built in Allegheny, commonly dubbed by scoffers the "Temperance Ark." While the celebrated Negro musical group was in Pittsburgh, they were invited by some of the principal temperance advocates to give a series of benefit concerts at the Ark, which they generously agreed to do.

At the time of the first concert, a large crowd of men and boys gathered about the structure and attempted to break up the concert with jeers, catcalls, and other noise. At the close of the entertainment, the band members were set upon by the mob with sticks, stones, and rotten eggs. Johnston, who was considered one of the best cornet players in America and had recently taken his band on a tour of Europe, was slightly wounded. Three or four members of his group were so seriously hurt that they were confined to their rooms for several days. Two arrests were made and both of these were acquitted since no one could testify to anything except their having been present at the time of the outbreak. However, another concert was scheduled on the evening of May 20, and everything went off quietly enough.

Aggressive Temperance

Among the outstanding advocates of temperance at Pittsburgh in this period was John Hannen, builder and first warden of the old Western Penitentiary, of whom the Reverend E. P. Swift once remarked: "For years he stood among the eldership of these cities, and I may say of this synod, as pre-eminent for the depth and vigor of his pieties, the consistency of his Christian life, and the abundance of his evangelical effort to do good."[15]

Dr. Swift, for thirty years pastor of the First Presbyterian Church of Old Allegheny and outstanding supporter of Home Missions, was himself a strong advocate, not only of temperance, but of prohibition. *The Presbyterian Advocate* reported a "very large and cheering meeting" had been held by the women of Allegheny city on February 24, 1852, in Dr. Swift's church to organize for petitioning the legislature in behalf of a proposed prohibition law. Dr. Swift occupied the chair and the Reverend John Taylor Pressly, pastor of the Allegheny Associate Reformed Church, contributed between five and six hundred names, signatures by women within the bounds of his congregation. About three hundred and fifty more signed at the meeting and arrangments were made to carry the petition to every house in the city.

Five years earlier a local option vote had gone heavily for the drys of Pittsburgh and Allegheny, but the Supreme Court ruled the referendum law unconstitutional. Although great numbers of petitions for a state prohibition law were sent to the Legislature in 1852, they did not secure its passage. An act passed three years later restrained the traffic by requiring special licenses and the closing of all saloons at midnight on Saturday, a requirement which was bitterly fought by most of the tavern keepers.[16]

To this "new license plan" we may trace a Pittsburgh folk song which was widely sung during the last third of the nineteenth century:

SOHO ON SATURDAY NIGHT

They tell us in Soho on Saturday night,
Most every person you meet, they are tight;
The men with their bottles, their wives with a can,
And young girls go prowling around like a man.
One woman I met, I'll never forget,

She fell in a sewer and she got wringin' wet,
The crowd gathered 'round her all thinkin' her dead,
But then she got up, and quickly she said:

Chorus:

Oh, isn't it queer how some women drink beer?
They drink and they drink and get tight.
And the new license plan, it ain't worth a damn,
In Soho on Saturday night.[17]

Despite such jests there is evidence that at least for awhile an honest effort was made to enforce the law. *The Presbyterian Advocate* contains the note, "We are much gratified to see that Mayor [Ferdinand E.] Volz has issued his proclamation warning all the shopkeepers against the sale of intoxicating drinks on the Sabbath. The mayor appears determined to execute the laws. Let all good and orderly citizens lend him their cordial cooperation."[18]

But if an honest attempt to encourage temperance and enforce the law had been made at the beginning, it evidently did not continue long. Two years later, *The Presbyterian Banner and Advocate* lamented:

"Grog-shops stare us in the face. Drunkards stagger along the streets, making night hideous with their yells . . . Brawls are frequent, and murders are by no means few. Widows and orphans mourn over the graves of husbands and fathers slain by intemperance. And strange as it may seem, 'the drinking customs of society' threaten a return. Young men meet together to converse, to smoke, and to sip wine. At the annual meetings of the stockholders of banks and insurance offices, the wine, it is said, sometimes flows freely. And again, at some of our large parties and weddings, if reports are true, liquors in abundance are provided, and old and young partake. Even women, blooming maidens pure and lovely, will put the wine-cup to their lips and drink to the health of, and in company with, young men."[19]

And on July 14, 1860, *The Presbyterian Banner* said: "That intemperance is on the increase among us cannot be doubted by any one who keeps his eyes open. The large increase of drinking houses is proof of this. It is high time for the friends of temperance to awaken to duty if they are not willing to see the enemy altogether victorious."

The beginning of the War Between the States evidently served only to make the situation worse, as on December 7, 1861, *The Presbyterian Banner* said: "Can nothing be done to check this terrible vice? Drinking houses line the streets of our cities and villages. In many places the drinking habits once banished from the family table and the social party are being restored. Drunkenness infests the halls of legislation, the quarters of the officers, and the barracks and tents of our soldiers. Drunken men reel at the corners, polluting the pure air of heaven with their breath. Thousands of homes, which might and should be abodes of bliss, are impoverished and made wretched by drunkenness."

Prohibition Advocated

Nevertheless the temperance advocates continued their work and we find *The Presbyterian Banner* hammering away, now and then reporting renewed interest, or jeering at Jay Cooke's advocacy of a plan to finance the war debt with revenue from liquor.[20] By 1869 sentiment had advanced so far that on July 7 that same periodical once again openly waved the flag of prohibition:

"The ravages of intemperance are again awakening public attention. The need of something effective in the way of restricting or removing the evil altogether, is freely acknowledged by all who have a proper regard for the best interests of mankind. The subject is entitled to the gravest consideration. Christians and philanthropists cannot shut their eyes so as not to see the terrible effects of liquor-drinking. Nor dare they refuse to give their influence and active co-operation, in proper and well-directed efforts, to deliver the captives and destroy temptation.

"In this matter of 'Prohibition' two things are of vital importance. (1) Before any such law can be enacted, a public sentiment must be awakened which will demand it. The people must be aroused before legislators can be reached. (2) Where the law has been adopted there must be public sentiment demanding its enforcement and that will sustain the proper authorities in doing so. Without this the best law on the statute books becomes ineffective. Hence, we would urge the discussion of the great subject of temperance or total abstinence in the pulpit, on the platform, through the press, and in the social circle."[21]

W. C. T. U. Is Organized

Such was the situation when word of the crusade at Hillsboro set the reform spirit aflame at Pittsburgh. Weak or moribund organizations in many churches and communities suddenly sprang into life. In many Upper Ohio Valley counties, the history of the Woman's Christian Temperance Union begins with the phrase, "The first meeting was held in the Presbyterian Church . . ."

At Pittsburgh the first meeting on record was held February 24, 1874, with about one hundred women and half as many men at the Temperance Alliance Rooms.[22] This group was thickly sprinkled with Presbyterians of almost every order. On March 2, after considerable discussion, a permanent organization of county temperance units was arrived at. A constitution was adopted the next day at a meeting in the Second United Presbyterian Church. Meeting almost daily, the women increased in number. On March 16 they boldly faced the fact that the license and Sabbath laws were continually violated by taverns and saloons. That afternoon some two hundred and fifty fell in line for a march to the mayor's offices of both Pittsburgh and Allegheny, where they were assured that any suggestions they had to offer would be given due attention. They made suggestions which were blandly disregarded and, after a day of fasting and prayer, determined to launch their crusade on April 8.

Since this was a signal for action, only those who were desperately earnest dared to turn out for the occasion. The number included twenty-two women and one man, attorney A. W. Black, Jr., who always accompanied his aging mother during the entire progress of the crusade. News spread like wildfire that the crusaders were coming and as they advanced toward the Courthouse district, first the sidewalks and then the entire streets were jammed with a mass of pushing, crowding, elbowing people.

Yells and cheers—but principally laughter—filled the air as the women proceeded, until they came to a halt in front of the Scotch Hill House operated by John McFadden, across the street from the Courthouse. Mrs. Samuel J. Collins asked the proprietor if he would permit a prayer meeting in the saloon. He politely refused, but agreed to leave the doors open while services were held on the sidewalk. After some twenty minutes, the temperance forces moved on again to the nearby wholesale liquor store of Stevenson and Dillinger. After a further period of singing and prayer, the women circulated among the crowd and got a number of persons to sign the pledge of total abstinence.

Next day the women were at their crusade again. This time they were ordered by police to move on; and when they refused, a warrant for their arrest was issued. About forty women were taken to the office of the mayor, who lectured them like a Dutch uncle and then released them, threatening jail if they continued their tactics. On the third day, the march was continued and a police lieutenant arrested three of the leaders. All the rest of the women followed his lead and were surprised to find themselves conducted not to the mayor's office, but to the central police station. After half an hour's wait, Attorney Black was fined fifty dollars and costs and two women twenty-five dollars each, which were paid under protest in order to take an appeal.

Two days later, on Saturday, May 23, more than forty women turned out early in the afternoon and this time they all were arrested. As they marched two by two into the lockup, they sang,

"Am I A Soldier Of The Cross." Instead of being placed in the courtroom as before, they were taken into the "bullpen," where there were cells on both sides, and locked up there to await the regular police court at 4 P.M. In the meantime, they marched up and down the corridor singing and conducting prayers. But such a crowd had gathered before the hour of the hearing, that it was decided to accept a ten-dollar deposit from each one for later appearance. At about four o'clock the door was opened and the women marched out arm in arm, singing the Doxology. The hearing was set for 4 P.M. Monday; but in the meantime, attorneys for the group had appealed the case to a higher court. On May 27 the Courthouse was so packed for the hearing that it was almost impossible for the defendants to appear. After consultation, the judges delivered their opinion as follows: "Singing and praying on the streets is not disorderly conduct. The decision of the acting mayor should be set aside; restitution awarded; fines and costs returned; the city to pay the cost."

From this time on the crusade was carried out with no opposition by the law in Pittsburgh, where it was observed in late summer by a young Illinois feminist named Frances E. Willard, who had formerly taught at a girls' college in the city.[23] She was so much impressed by the work that she turned immediately from her effort to secure votes for women and became a leader in the temperance movement. Years later she wrote of her experience:

"The Crusade had lingered in this dim-colored city well-nigh a year and when I visited some old friends I spoke of it with enthusiasm and of the women who were, as I judged, from the morning paper, still engaged in it here. My friends looked at me with astonishment when I proposed to seek out these women and go with them to the saloons. But, too polite to disappoint me, they had me escorted to the headquarters of the Crusade, where I was warmly welcomed and soon found myself walking down street with a young teacher.

"We paused in front of Schiffner's Saloon, on Market Street. The ladies arranged themselves along the curbstone. At a signal from our grey-haired leader, a sweet-voiced young girl began to sing, 'Jesus the Water of Life Will Give.'

"At a signal we moved on, and the next saloon keeper permitted us to enter. I had no idea of the inward appearance of a saloon. The tall stately lady who led us placed her Bible on the bar and read a Psalm. Then we sang, 'Rock of Ages.' One of the other women then whispered to me that the leader wished to know if I would pray—it was strange perhaps, but I felt not the least reluctance as I knelt on the sawdust floor with a group of earnest hearts around me and behind them filling every corner and extending out into the street, a crowd of unwashed, unkempt, hard-looking men. This was my Crusade baptism."[24]

The next day Miss Willard left Pittsburgh by train for Chicago, where a group of women were holding a temperance rally. Within a week she had been made president of the group which eventually spread over the entire nation. Impressed by the action in Pittsburgh, she suggested the name which had never been used previously except by the Pittsburgh organization. It was: Woman's Christian Temperance Union.

II. SLAVERY

Except that sentiment moved much more quickly and to a more definite end, the case with slavery was much the same as that with regard to the misuse of alcoholic beverages. During the period of early settlement in the Upper Ohio Valley and of Pennsylvania in general, there was little sentiment against human slavery, even in the most enlightened nations. Slaves had been held in eastern Pennsylvania before the arrival of William Penn. Penn himself and many other Quakers were slaveholders.[25] A large percentage of the settlers of the Upper Ohio Valley had come from Virginia, a colony where slaveholding was firmly entrenched.

Nevertheless, sentiment against human slavery did grow rapidly in the Commonwealth. In 1780, even before the end of the Revolutionary War, a statute was adopted to end such bondage forever in the confines of Pennsylvania.[26] This law of 1780 did not affect those who had been born in servitude prior to its being enacted. It merely provided that children of slaves born after that date should be free, although remaining as servants to their masters until twenty-eight years of age. This was not considered unfair, particularly since most orphan children and many others were indentured to masters for their food and clothing, and sometimes to learn a trade, until reaching their majority. Many free families voluntarily indentured themselves for a term of years in order to secure the money for their passage to the New World. The first Federal census, in 1790, showed that there were six hundred and seventy-five slaves held in the counties comprising the southwestern part of Pennsylvania, or one slave to every twenty-four white persons.[27]

Presbyterians naturally held slaves just as did anyone else. In the *Pittsburgh Gazette,* in 1787, appeared the advertisement: "To be sold to any person residing in the country: a Negro wench—she is an excellent cook and can do any kind of work in or out of doors. She has been registered in Westmoreland County. Produce will be taken, or cattle of any kind. Enquire of Col. John Gibson, Fort Pitt."[28] Colonel Gibson was one of the founders and an original trustee of the First Presbyterian Church, Pittsburgh.[29] On May 5, 1804, another Presbyterian, James Robinson, advertised: "I will sell a likely Negro man. He is about twenty-seven years of age and a slave for life, and has been brought up a farmer. For terms, apply to the subscriber, living on the bank of the Allegheny River opposite Pittsburgh."[30]

The Reverend James Power, first of the "Four Horsemen" to arrive within the bounds of what they later organized as Redstone Presbytery, owned a slave.[31] Another early Presbyterian, the Reverend James Finley, registered eight slaves under the Pennsylvania law of March 1, 1780.[32]

Yet even in these early years, there was a sentiment for freedom.

In 1793 Hugh Henry Brackenridge, who had planned to be a Presbyterian minister but had turned to the law, took up the case of a free colored woman who had been captured in Pittsburgh and returned to slavery in Kentucky. He won the case and had her brought back to Pittsburgh and released a free woman.[33] Regardless of church affiliations, however, in this period there was little sentiment against slavery even in the northern part of what is now West Virginia, or eastern Kentucky, although most of the early population of Ohio was against human bondage from the earliest settlement.

The act of 1780 should have virtually done away with slavery in Pennsylvania by 1820. Around Pittsburgh there were scarcely more than ten or twelve slaves held at that time.[34] But in nearby Washington County, which bordered on (West) Virginia, some residents claimed the right to hold grandchildren of slaves under the act of 1780 until the practice was stopped by Supreme Court decision in 1826.[35] Even as late as 1833, an investigating committee of the State Senate found that in nearly all the border counties of southwestern Pennsylvania a practice had grown up of importing slaves from Virginia on condition they would be emancipated after serving a few years, usually seven.[36]

The Missouri Compromise of 1820, which virtually outlawed slavery north of the Mason and Dixon Line and the Ohio River, gave a strong impetus to movements for African colonization, although sentiment for abolition in the South was yet more than a decade away.

Antislavery Agitation Begins

Although in Washington County the practice of slaveholding held on longest, it was there that opposition to slavery developed soonest. The first abolition society of southwestern Pennsylvania was organized in Washington County on January 26, 1824.[37] The meeting had been announced in a newspaper advertisement a month earlier, calling upon citizens of the county and vicinity who were "favorable to the formation of a society for the abolition of slavery, and for endeavoring to ameliorate the condition of the African race," to meet at the Courthouse. Nearly fifty persons joined the group, which was named the Western Abolition Society.

The principal address was made by the Reverend Andrew Wylie, brilliant young Presbyterian minister and president of Washington College. He announced that the basic principles of the society were: (1) to ameliorate the lot of the free Negroes of Pennsylvania; (2) to prevent them from being kidnapped and sold in slave states; and (3) to carry into effect proper plans for opposing slavery in general. Many other antislavery societies were organized, although most of them still sought the proper solution through African colonization, as did the one organized in 1826 in the First Presbyterian Church of Pittsburgh. Nearly half the officers of the society were Presbyterian ministers or elders.

With the arrival of the mid-1830's, abolition was freely talked and the immediate emancipation of all slaves diligently urged. A Pittsburgh antislavery society, strongly supported by Presbyterians as well as others, was formed on October 4, 1833, even before the founding of the American Anti-Slavery Society in Philadelphia. It urged the abolition of slavery, though not by violence. Its constitution stated its purpose as follows:

"Whereas, we believe that no man can hold another as property without violating the plain principles of justice and humanity, as expressed by natural conscience and declared in the Word of God. And whereas, there are in these United States more than two millions of human beings, constituting one-sixth part of our population, held as property liable to be bought and sold like beasts of burden and exposed to the caprice of their respective masters; and, whereas, there are nearly half a million of persons in these United States who, though nominally free, are by public sentiment excluded from equal rights on account of their color; and, whereas, we believe that sound policy as well as justice requires that the government of equitable law should be immediately substituted for that of despotic will, and that all men without respect to any physical distinctions should be admitted to the rights, privileges and immunities of free citizens, according to the same equitable rule of qualifications; therefore we do agree to form ourselves into a society to be governed by the following constitution."[38]

Argument waxed hot, even among those who had no love for slavery, and some of those most strongly for abolition sometimes took hasty action. Young Dr. Francis Julius LeMoyne, destined to become a national figure in the antislavery movement, broke with the First Presbyterian Church of Washington, Pennsylvania, because its pastor was opposed to forceful abolition.[39] In Indiana County, Dr. Robert Mitchell, another Presbyterian, took similar action and for the same reason.[40] The churches, as institutions, still took little interest in the question of slavery, and the presbyterial records of Redstone and Washington make no mention of the "peculiar institution" of the South.[41]

But the leaven was working. More and more, antislavery and even abolition societies were being formed, including a student group at Washington College, doubtless due to the influence of President Wylie.[42] By the Fall of 1838, there were twenty colonization societies in Western Pennsylvania and in October of that year a convention of antislavery societies was held in Pittsburgh.[43] When Pennsylvania's constitution of 1838 limited the right of suffrage to white men, Presbyterian leaders from Pittsburgh sharply opposed the move.[44] Despite the conservatism of the church courts in general, Presbyterian ministers were among the leaders in the antislavery movement in all its phases in southwestern Pennsylvania and often in Ohio, and occasionally even in (West) Virginia and Kentucky.

Fugitive Slave Law Arouses Furor

Although public sentiment may at times move slowly in a democracy, there are moments when it crystallizes at high speed. Such a moment came in 1850 with the passage of the Fugitive Slave

Law, permitting agents in free states to capture Negroes who had fled from their masters and to return them to bondage in slave states. In Pittsburgh the news of the law precipitated a mass meeting in the market house square, which although it adopted reasonable and temperate resolutions, nevertheless towards the end lacked little of becoming a mob scene.[45]

When Robert M. Riddle, editor of the *Commercial Journal* at Pittsburgh, and his brother, Dr. David H. Riddle, pastor of the Third Presbyterian Church, recommended moderation, they were bitterly denounced. Despite the fact that both of them had expressed their opposition to the Fugitive Slave Law and were only urging obedience until it could be repealed, Mrs. Jane Gray Swisshelm, the abolition leader and bitter anti-Calvinist, wrote in her *Saturday Visiter:* "Any of our southern friends, who want business done in their lines in our dirty city, should direct their communications to our good friend Robert M. Riddle, or Judge Baird, with a special request for prayers for their success from the Reverend Dr. Riddle."[46] Judge Baird was castigated because he had argued that slavery was a question each state must decide for itself.

Ever since 1820 a stream of escaped slaves had been pouring through Pennsylvania and Ohio by various routes of the "Underground Railway." Despite the fact that the fugitive slave law made it a crime for a citizen of a free state to conceal an escaped Negro, the number of such escapes and of those who helped them continued to swell in volume. William Stewart, a prominent Pittsburgh businessman, vividly recalled a typical experience. "The bridge at Niagara Falls is the haven to which we send all hunted slaves. On a Sunday morning I was just starting for church when a well known knock touched my door. I knew at once that church for me was in another direction. I opened my door, leisurely went out and turned to the right towards the East. About a block away there was a little covered carriage that was very much in use in Pittsburg at that time. They were called dearborns. When I left my own house there was a gentleman walking between the carriage and me. We did not speak to each other, but he turned down the first street. The curtains of the dearborn were all rolled up and no person but the driver could be seen. I was in charge of the dearborn. It was made with a double bottom and the slave was lying flat between the upper and lower bottoms. The driver kept going on very leisurely.

"There was a ferry about where the Fortieth Street bridge is. We both got on the same ferry, but the driver never changed words with us. He was one of our wealthiest citizens and was wearing a fine pair of false whiskers. After we crossed the river the driver drove on the tow path of the canal. Finally the dearborn and the man in sight turned on a road running across Pine Creek below Sharpsburg. There another man came out of a house. The new man took his place, while the first took another direction, no one having spoken a word since we started. The dearborn was then driven into a lonely place in the woods, where there was a 'station' provided with all manner of disguises. Provided with these the slave was started on his way to Niagara. After leaving Pittsburg they were scarcely ever captured."[47]

Dr. Plumer Refused to Pray for Victory

Against Southerners, or those suspected of Southern sympathies, feeling often flared high, despite the known high character of the persons believed to favor or tolerate slavery, particularly after the passage of the Kansas-Nebraska Bill in 1854.

One outstanding victim of such feeling was the Reverend William S. Plumer, D.D., a native of Greersburg (now Darlington), Beaver County. After graduating at Washington and Lee University and Princeton Theological Seminary, Plumer had preached in Virginia and Maryland until 1854 and had married a Southern girl before coming to Pittsburgh as a professor at Western Theological Seminary. He had helped to organize and was pastor of the Central Presbyterian Church of Allegheny, and was a man of the greatest ability and spirituality, but following the outbreak

PITTSBURGH AFTER THE GREAT FIRE OF 1845

COLLECTION OF GEORGE SWETNAM

POLICE STATION, DIAMOND ALLEY, PITTSBURGH
Where the Temperance Crusaders were imprisoned, May 23, 1874.

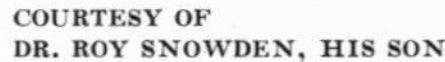
COURTESY OF
DR. ROY SNOWDEN, HIS SON

REVEREND
JAMES H.
SNOWDEN, D.D.

Pastor, Second Presbyterian Church, Washington, Pa., 1886–1911. Editor of the *Presbyterian Banner,* 1898–1917; 1926–1936. Professor at Western Theological Seminary, 1911–1924.

REVEREND
DAVID McKINNEY, D.D.
1795–1879

Founder of the *Presbyterian Banner* in 1852. Editor, 1852–1864.

COURTESY OF
THE PRESBYTERIAN BOOK STORE

of the War Between the States, he came strongly under attack by a minority of his own congregation.

In spite of repeated requests from members of his congregation, Dr. Plumer had refused "to lead the congregation in prayer to God for His blessing upon the government in efforts to put down the Rebellion and in thanksgiving when God gave victory to our arms." Because of his continued refusal, the congregation appealed to Allegheny Presbytery. With only Dr. Plumer refusing to vote, Presbytery by unanimous action "resolved that it is the duty of all ministers in conducting the devotions of the sanctuary to pray earnestly to God for His help in this time of trial that He would sustain our Government; that He would give success to our armies . . . and restore to us unity and peace as a people." Still Plumer refused to comply. His reasons, as stated in a lengthy defense, did not satisfy his congregation nor the editor of *The Banner* who described them as "labored and evidently evasive."[48]

At a later meeting, Presbytery felt that Plumer was wrong in his persistent refusal and ordered that "he cease from the exercise of his pastoral office in the Central Church until his fame is cleared of the reproach herein alluded to." Presbytery also expressed belief that "the interests of the Western Theological Seminary require that the Directors of the Seminary to suspend the labors of the Rev. Dr. Plumer in that institution until the next meeting of the General Assembly."[49]

Sentiment in the Central Church was divided. Dr. Plumer was held in high esteem as a preacher and pastor. But the agitators were aggressive and bitter. At a showdown in the Summer of 1862, as many as 174 members of the church stuck by him, while only 91 were in opposition. But, as was often the custom in that day, voting was not by the number of communicants but by the prestige of the protesting members and the amount of money subscribed by them. A check showed that the 174 who were for Dr. Plumer were listed for total subscriptions of only $3,465, while the 91 who opposed him had contributed $4,927. Plumer felt impelled to resign both from the Central Church and the Seminary. So bitter was popular sentiment against him that when he removed to the South to accept a church at Pottsville, Virginia, he had to leave at night taking his goods out in a wheelbarrow because no one would haul them for him.

Dr. Plumer spent the rest of his life in the South. He became a professor in Columbia Theological Seminary in 1866, where he continued until his death fourteen years later. Central Presbyterian Church never recovered from the blow. Seventy-seven of the ninety-one rebellious members left the congregation to form the North Presbyterian Church. As the waterfront area of Pittsburgh's North Side gradually deteriorated, Central Church died a slow and painful death. Perhaps Dr. Plumer would have had less difficulty in any other area of Pittsburgh, or almost any other area in the Upper Ohio Valley. In Greene County, next to the (West) Virginia line on two sides, there was so little feeling against slavery that apparently nothing was thought of the fact that the last registered slave, in 1845, was the property of the Reverend James A. D. Henderson, a Cumberland Presbyterian minister.[50]

Supported War to Free Slaves

While there was any chance of preserving peace and union, the *Presbyterian Banner* held to a policy of moderation. Its editor, Dr. David McKinney, was not hesitant to make clear his exact position —which was largely one with that of most of the church:

"Slavery is the subject now, in the political world, and it is likewise very much so in the moral and Christian world, so far as the United States is concerned. Utter silence, then, on the part of journalists, would seem to be indifference or a dereliction of duty; while speaking amid so much excitement, must, almost necessarily subject to misrepresentation and enmity. We have not been silent. We have spoken not nearly as much as we thought and felt, but enough to bring upon us many reproofs. And we mean still to continue to speak; but always the words of truth and soberness, and always for edification. We have no idea of leaving a subject so vastly important, entirely in the hands of infidels and fanatics as to religion and of extremists and the lovers of gain, in political and social life.

"The question is not directly a practical one with us, as slavery does not exist where we live and have our principal circulation; but, indirectly, we are deeply concerned in it. We have church fellowship, in communion, in the promulgation of doctrine, in the inculcating of duty, and in the exercise of discipline with those who are masters and those who are servants; and we have state interests, many and great, in and under a popular government, which recognizes and controls the institution."[51]

The editor quotes in supporting approval this succinct judgment of Dr. Nathan Rice: "Slavery is a human, not a divine institution; controlled by human law, yet recognized, though not sanctioned by the Scriptures; and regulated also by Divine law."

He then gives his sentiments in the following propositions:

1. I hold to the unity of the human race—that "God hath made of one blood all nations of men for to dwell on all the face of the earth."
2. Consequently I hold, that the command—"Thou shalt love thy neighbor as thyself" applies, in its full force to every human being.[52]

Within a week after the attack on Fort Sumter, Presbyterian ministers of the Pittsburgh area met to discuss the crisis. The Reverend E. P. Swift was called to the Chair, and after a full and free discussion, the following resolutions were adopted:

"RESOLVED, that as ministers of Jesus Christ, Prince of Peace, we look with horror, and as citizens of the beneficent Government, with inexpressible grief upon the madness of those who are leading this rebellion, and threatening to plunge our beloved country into all the horrors of internecine war.

"RESOLVED, that as men and as Christians we love and cherish the government of our country and avow to it our unalterable attachment and unconditional allegiance.

"RESOLVED, that we regard the attempt now being made by what is called the Confederate States of America to subvert the constitution and the government of the land as treasonable and the very last degree iniquitous.

"RESOLVED, that we regard those who in any way afford them aid, comfort, or countenance, as enemies of our country.

"RESOLVED, that being called in the Providence of God to conduct the public devotions of the people, we will pray specially on public occasions for the Divine blessing upon the President of the United States and all associated with him in the Government, for the army now assembling for the defense of our liberties, that if they must come in conflict with rebels, God will give them the victory; that He will defeat the armies and bring to confusion the counsels of the enemies of the Government."[53]

Two and a half years later, Ohio Presbytery, meeting in Canonsburg, Pennsylvania, resolved:

"That whilst we repudiate everything like party politics and party strife, we regard the maintenance of the Government in its purity and oneness, as essential, not only to the liberties, civil and religious, of our own land, but also of the highest importance, if not essential, to the liberties of all lands; and that we earnestly urge that the prayers and labors of all Christians be directed to this end."[54]

This was much the position of Presbyterians in general, not only in Pennsylvania and Ohio, but in what is now northern and western West Virginia, who took up arms in defense of the Union, but equally in the cause of freedom for all men.

Also they did more, for they remembered their principles long after much of the nation had forgotten the cause in the orgies which followed the conclusion of the War Between the States. The Assembly of 1865 had united Indianapolis and Philadelphia committees as the General Assembly's Committee on Freedmen, which in 1882 became the Board of Missions for Freedmen. But after the end of the war, it was hard to get churchmen in many areas to take it seriously.

Not so in the Upper Ohio Valley. The Board's 1888 report stated: "Among those consulted it was found that only ministers and elders from Pittsburgh and its vicinity would agree to undertake the work. At the beginning and for no inconsiderable time afterwards, the churches of Pittsburgh, Allegheny and the surrounding country were the only ones freely opened in behalf of the Freedmen."

III. OTHER MORAL MOVEMENTS

Not even during the heat of the excitement over abolition or temperance did the Presbyterian churches of the Upper Ohio Valley forget or neglect the many other moral questions which constantly arose. Although the records of Redstone and Washington presbyteries make not one mention of slavery, resolutions may frequently be found in opposition to horse racing, Sabbath desecration, and "non-Christian amusements such as balls, dances . . . theatrical exhibitions."[55]

For many years Presbyterians at Pittsburgh fought a running battle against the theater and the circus, a battle not completely dropped until after the opening of the twentieth century.[56] Gambling apparently was not frowned upon in the early period, and an unsuccessful lottery was even resorted to to help raise funds for the first building of the First Presbyterian Church of Pittsburgh.[57] But by the 1850's the conscience of most church people had been aroused against it.[58]

The question of Sabbath observance was a continuing one, with only a very late and gradual loosening of former strict observance. Even during the heat of civil war, Presbyterian ministers of Pittsburgh passed the following resolution: "We deplore the vast amount of Sabbath desecration which has attended the excitement consequent upon the outbreaking of civil strife; . . we will urge upon our fellow citizens to refrain from all unnecessary demonstrations on that sacred day, and remember that as we look to God for His blessing upon the land, we must, as a people, keep His commandments."[59]

Divorce was another moral problem that stirred the conscience of the Presbyterian church. Over a period of months, concluding with the issue of August 14, 1850, the Reverend Nathaniel West printed in the *Presbyterian Advocate* a scholarly and comprehensive series of discussions of the laws of divorce and the attitude of the Presbyterian church in regard to them. The articles reveal both the high ability of the author, and the deep interest felt in such matters by the church of that day.

The need of a hospital in Pittsburgh was felt keenly by civic-minded Presbyterians. In 1846 the editor of *The Presbyterian Advocate* sounded the challenge:

"Hear what people say of us—'The city of Pittsburgh, in Pennsylvania, has seven sectarian newspapers and one hundred and ten churches, but no hospital for the sick, or asylum for the poor insane.'

"How long will it be before this cause of reproach against our city is removed? Members of churches, professing to be followers of Him who came to 'heal the sick, to cast out devils, and to preach the gospel to the poor,' is not your Christian character tarnished by this wrong?[60]"

The following December the same editor was glad to report that the hospital, which later became West Penn Hospital and Dixmont Insane Hospital, were on the way, although he admitted with some chagrin that a Catholic group had hurried matters and made their institution, Mercy Hospital, the city's first.[61]

On March 22, 1854, *The Presbyterian Advocate* asked editorially: "Ought there not to be a 'Young Men's Christian Association' in Pittsburgh?" One was quickly organized largely through the efforts of Western Theological Seminary students.[62] By 1856 Dr. M. W. Jacobus of the Seminary was teaching a Bible class in the Association Hall, with more than sixty members.[63]

In March of 1861, an article in the *Presbyterian Banner* viewed with alarm the rise of immoral conditions in Pittsburgh, including the great increase in liquor shops, billiard rooms, and gambling, and the introduction of free concerts in drinking houses, "which is but one degree above the great iniquity of the 'dance houses' that have been such a pest to New York and Philadelphia."[64]

Nor were Presbyterians absent from the organizing of such institutions as the Home for the Friendless, Society for the Improvement of the Poor, and other similar institutions. Contrary to the oft-repeated canard as to the harshness of Presbyterian morality, those of the Upper Ohio Valley could never forget their duty to care for the suffering, nor the words of Him who said, "Whosoever receiveth one such little child in My name, receiveth Me."

CHAPTER XII The Church's Fourth Estate

THE UPPER OHIO VALLEY was the cradle of Presbyterian religious journalism. Here were initiated pioneer ventures of faith and vision that not only contributed effectively to the moulding of religious convictions throughout the expanding western frontier, but which have left a continuing heritage in the present-day periodicals of the Presbyterian church. The Founding Fathers in this area believed that an informed church member is an asset essential to the successful advance of the Kingdom of God.

This conviction found initial expression at the very first meeting of the newly constituted Synod of Pittsburgh. The vast territory of the Presbytery of Redstone had been subdivided by the formation of the additional presbyteries of Ohio and Erie. The members of these three presbyteries were meeting in Pittsburgh on September 29, 1802, to organize themselves into the first Synod west of the Allegheny Mountains. To Dr. John McMillan, the "Apostle of Presbyterianism in the West"[1] had been given the honor of preaching the sermon at the opening of this historic five-day meeting of the Synod. Much necessary business crowded the docket during those organizational days as the infant Synod formulated its committees and planned the scope of its expanding tasks. Yet time was taken to discuss something new and audacious.

A motion was presented "that Synod endeavor to promote the publication of a magazine and that twelve members be chosen to be editors thereof."[2] The novel idea had almost no guiding precedents even in the more settled eastern coastal areas. Resources for such a venture of sacrificial labor were extremely limited. During the discussion, it was stated that similar magazines were being circulated both in England and America and that "a few copies had appeared in this remote part of our sinful world." With the courage and consecration that had always distinguished the pioneer preachers of Presbyterianism in Western Pennsylvania, Synod was ready to accept the challenge of a new opportunity to serve. The motion was passed.

The following twelve ministers were named to serve as the editors and promoters of the magazine: John McMillan, Thomas Moor, John Anderson, James Hughes, Samuel Ralston, and George Scott from the Presbytery of Ohio; John McPherrin, David Smith, and Samuel Porter from the Presbytery of Redstone; William Wick and William Wylie from the Erie Presbytery. The twelfth member chosen was Joseph Badger, a missionary who was itinerating throughout the Western Reserve in Ohio under the direction of the Missionary Society of Connecticut and who later joined the Erie Presbytery.

A subcommittee of three was entrusted with the more direct responsibility of preparing the monthly magazine.[3] The three were comparatively close neighbors in Washington County. Dr. John McMillan, the chairman, was pastor at Chartiers, Thomas Moor at Ten Mile, and John Anderson at Upper Buffalo. All were busy pastors, especially John McMillan who seemed tireless in energy and a genius for hard work. In addition to his duties as pastor and professor of divinity at Jefferson College, he was willing to head up this new venture in religious education.

The Western Missionary Magazine

But the difficulties of publication were greater than the inexperienced editors had anticipated. The first issue did not appear until February of the following year. The delay in publication was modestly explained in this sentence of apology and determination on the first page: "Many obstacles and difficulties have prevented engaging sooner in this work, but if we wait for their total removal, it can never be undertaken."[4] The new publication of forty pages was printed in Washington, Pennsylvania. It bore the title, *The Western Missionary Magazine and Repository of Religious Intelligence.* As the name indicated, the proceedings of the Western Missionary Society, which was none other than the Synod of Pittsburgh itself, claimed the first attention of the preacher-editors. Missionary objectives in those early days were "to diffuse the knowledge of the gospel among the inhabitants of the new settlements, the Indian tribes, and if need be, among the interior inhabitants, where they were not able to support the gospel."[5] The purpose of the editors was "a sincere desire to transmit to posterity faithful records of the work of sovereign grace in the hearts of men."[6]

But the scope of this pioneer venture in religious journalism was much broader than a mere reporting of missionary progress. The editors aimed to make their monthly magazine a journal of broad-range interest and information. The introduction thus outlines their wide purpose: "To contain—Original pieces, Extracts from religious subjects, Biographical sketches of persons who have been useful and eminent in the church, Ecclesiastical history, Information respecting missions, Narratives of revivals of religion, Remarks on the fulfillment of prophecies as they respect the present day, Expositions of difficult passages of Scripture, Accounts of remarkable dispensations of providence, Evangelical hymns—together with whatever else may advance genuine piety and pure morality."[7]

It was truly an ambitious undertaking; an almost impossible venture of faith in view of the difficulties of travel and of gathering information. One's soul is stirred as he turns the pages of that pioneer magazine, browned with age, yet printed on paper of a high quality which has withstood the stress of more than a century and a half. The great Revival of 1802 had been sweeping over western Pennsylvania, eastern Ohio, and Kentucky. Thrilling records of spiritual advance fill the pages as James McCready relates the "Narrative of the Revival of Religion in Logan County," as Thomas Marquis records redemptive revivals in the Cross Creek Presbyterian Church, and as the editor traces through several consecutive issues the "Revival of Religion in the Western Country, especially in the bounds of the Presbytery of Ohio." The first poem was a hymn of thanksgiving, "Rejoicing In a Revival of Religion."[8] An editorial defended these revivals from the sneers of skeptics who had charged that the great Revival of 1802 was only "the manifestation of a spirit of fanaticism and delusion." As further defense of the spiritual validity of a revival movement, the editors reprinted in serial form a long sermon by Jonathan Edwards, printed in Boston in 1741, entitled, "The Mark of a Work of the True Spirit."[9] The Reverend Thomas Hughes described his missionary journey with James Satterfield among the Indians in the Detroit area and George Scott reported on his "Missionary Trip to Indians on Sandusky River." The spirit of God was moving. The magazine sought to relay it to the hearts and minds of the reading public.

Enthusiasm in the souls of the preachers was also demanded. "An Essay on Enthusiasm, especially in Preaching," was a pointed rebuke "at any lukewarm, temporizing method of treating religious subjects. Even though it may be popular, it is still beneath the dignity of the Christian religion and will not bear the test of that tribunal to which we all are hastening."[10] Other typical editorials discussed "The Importance of Early Piety," "Distinguishing Truth from Error," "Thoughts on the Perseverance of Saints," and "God Is Glorious in Visiting the Iniquities of the Fathers upon Their Children."

The editors were much encouraged as they reported to the Synod in 1803. The members of the Synod shared their optimistic forecast of the experimental efforts to edit and promote *The Western Missionary Magazine* under the patronage and direction of the Synod. Commendation took the form of a motion that "Messers. McMillan, Moor and Anderson, the managing editors of the magazine, be rewarded for their services in this business."[11] But the sacrificial editors insisted on serving without salary and refused to accept any financial compensation. It was to continue as a labor of love, not of personal profit. All profits were to be "deposited in a fund for the support of missions to the heathen and to such settlements as yet are not in circumstances to support the gospel."[12]

But this cherished promotion of missions was not to receive much financial support from the magazine. When its editors presented their second report to Synod in 1804, they had not found the past year very encouraging. Subscribers were all too few. Though the magazine was being sold to subscribers for 12½ cents a copy and 14 cents for single issues to nonsubscribers, that low price for a magazine of 40 pages was either beyond the financial reach of impoverished Presbyterians or its contents did not have sufficient appeal to hard-working parishioners whose energies were absorbed in the exhausting struggle for a livelihood. Synod debated the advisability of discontinuing its unrewarding venture in religious journalism.

Reluctance to abandon its pioneer efforts found expression in Synod's action to continue the magazine another year "provided the editors find the number of subscribers sufficient to encourage them, otherwise not."[13] The necessary sustaining list of subscribers could not be enlisted. Another year of effort was not rewarding. The Presbyterian church was not yet ready to support a monthly periodical. The magazine suspended publication, but with some evidence that it was not entirely a financial failure. "When the editors presented their final report to Synod, they stated that profits arising from the sale of the magazine which had been collected by them amounted to $334.32, which sum has been paid into the missionary fund."[14] Those early Presbyterians at least did not set a precedent of closing a novel experiment in the red.

The Weekly Recorder

The scene now shifts to Chillicothe, Ohio, where we witness the second Presbyterian experiment in religious journalism. Here in

1814 was established *The Weekly Recorder.* Under numerous changes of size, location, and name this oldest of the Presbyterian weekly periodicals continued to serve the Presbyterian church throughout the Upper Ohio Valley over a period of a hundred and twenty-three years. It was best known by its last name, *The Presbyterian Banner,* which continued publication as a privately sustained periodical until 1937.[15]

The guiding genius in this second venture in the field of religious journalism was the Reverend John Andrews. Because of the influence of the precedents he set and the broad-range contents of the weekly religious newspaper he established, he may well be called the father of Presbyterian journalism. Born on Piney Creek, Maryland, September 16, 1768, he entered the ministry in Mecklinburg County, North Carolina, and itinerated in evangelistic work in Kentucky.[16] In 1807 he moved to Chillicothe, Ohio. For a few years he had charge of the academy in that community and taught Latin and Greek.

He found time to serve as a contributing editor to the *Evangelical Record* which had commenced publication in Lexington, Kentucky, in January, 1812. Why not establish a weekly periodical in Chillicothe, he pondered. Chillicothe had been for a time the seat of government of the whole northwest territory and so was a community of some prestige. Here in 1798 the Reverend William Speer, from the Presbytery of Redstone, had organized a Presbyterian church. Here also the Synod of Ohio was constituted in 1814. A religious newspaper, he felt, was needed to bind the settlers together and to strengthen their convictions. On July 5, 1814, while the American Army was winning the Battle of Chippewa on Canadian soil, this pioneer Presbyterian editor printed as an experiment the first issue of what he named *The Weekly Recorder.* The annual subscription price was $2.00. It contained eight pages of three columns each, on paper 9½ x 11½ inches.

The prospectus, which Mr. Andrews had printed three months earlier in announcing his venture of faith, forecasted its broad-range scope. "The paper," he wrote, "will be conducted on a plan different from that of any other publication in the United States. It will embrace a variety of subjects under the three general heads of Theology, Literature and National Affairs. It is presumed that every friend of genuine religion, good morals and intellectual improvement will see at once the propriety and necessity of promoting its publication."[17]

An Outline of Editorial Policy

Advertisements, of course, would be welcomed as essential in sustaining the new periodical. But the pious Presbyterian editor reserved the right to choose his advertisers on a high plane of morality. He would stoop to no compromising of conviction for commercial gain. He stated definitely in his prospectus: "Advertisements of all such as contain notices of horse races, puppet shows, theatrical exhibitions and other similar practices and amusements" will be rejected. The newspaper columns would also bar "all wrathful invectives and personal abuse. Partial inflammatory political discussions will be invariably excluded . . . Theological controversy will never be introduced without imperious necessity" but "if the doctrines of the Reformation shall be wantonly assailed, the evidences by which they are supported will be clearly stated . . . Also any respectable denomination of Christians will be vindicated from unjust and slanderous imputations."[18] Presbyterians may well be proud of the high ideals and broad-minded vision of its pioneer editor in the field of religious journalism. He established standards that have become long-cherished precedents in the field of religious journalism.

With high hopes of success and with the enthusiasm of sincere conviction, John Andrews launched his precedent-setting newspaper as a weekly periodical. At that time *The Weekly Recorder* had almost the entire Presbyterian church as a possible source of subscriptions. *The Religious Remembrancer,* which had begun publication in Philadelphia about six months earlier, was its only possible competitor. *The Boston Recorder* appeared a little later and was planned to serve only the New England churches. Soon *The New York Observer* was also published, seeking to serve the church at large. Only occasional copies of these eastern publications crossed the mountains.

Though *The Weekly Recorder* did have for its field of service the entire area west of the Allegheny Mountains, most of the territory was an undeveloped frontier, spotted with scattered farms and crude villages. The need of a religious periodical was not generally apparent. Andrews' paper covered chiefly local news of Chillicothe and surrounding Ohio territory. It contained but few references to Pittsburgh or Western Pennsylvania and featured general news of a secular nature. It appealed chiefly to a rather limited Ohio constituency. For seven long, discouraging years, Andrews struggled to achieve his goal. Financial resources were dwindling. The brave editor was confronted with two alternatives. Either he must fail in Chillicothe or move to a more settled area where a supporting clientele might be more easily developed.

Andrews chose the latter alternative. He communicated with his Presbyterian brethren in Pittsburgh. They invited him to attend the next meeting of the Synod of Pittsburgh. He discontinued his paper in Chillicothe with the issue of October 6, 1821. A few days later he attended the meeting of Synod as a corresponding member from Ohio. He was delighted when Synod, at the suggestion of Dr. Elisha Swift, appointed a committee "to inquire into the expediency of establishing a periodical publication of religious intelligence under the sanction and patronage of this Synod designed to disseminate religious instruction to the churches under our care."[19] The committee, later in the meeting, presented a favorable report. Considerable opposition developed. The report was referred back to the committee where it was amended and modified. Synod adopted the resolution to authorize a "weekly paper principally devoted to the great interests of evangelical truth and piety," but stipulated that "the Reverend John Andrews be appointed the editor of said publication and that on his own responsibility he undertake the establishment, support and direction of the same." The Synod of Pittsburgh thus voted to recommend a second venture into the field of religious journalism, nineteen years after it had unsuccessfully launched *The Western Missionary Magazine.*

The Pittsburgh Recorder

John Andrews now transferred to Pittsburgh both his paper and his residence. *The Weekly Recorder* was renamed *The Pittsburgh Recorder.* It was printed on Fourth Street, a few doors below Market Street. The first issue appeared January 25, 1822, with a subscription price of $2.00 a year.[20] It was comparatively small in size, 5½ x 8½ inches, and sixteen pages of two columns. Two years later it was enlarged to 19½ x 13 inches, but only four pages.

The scope and purpose, as outlined by the editor for the new periodical, were largely the same broad-range objectives he had sought to achieve in *The Western Recorder.* "It is intended for the diffusion, not only of religious, but every other kind of useful information." A committee of seven ministers was appointed to assist Mr. Andrews by furnishing material for the periodical.[21]

Andrews had now an official sponsor and a new location in the largest city west of the Allegheny Mountains. But he was confronted with the same old problems of finance and lethargy. He was both the editor and the publisher who must carry the full responsibility for the financial success of the paper. Pittsburgh was a growing industrial city with a population of 7,258. It proudly welcomed that same year the Western University of Pittsburgh. But "in 1821 the city experienced the greatest business depression this community was ever called upon to endure."[22] Debts and bankruptcy were widespread. The little money available was either hoarded in terror or demanded by Eastern creditors.

The two-dollar subscription price of the new paper seemed high with money so scarce. Dr. Swift loyally urged greater support for the paper. Better days soon dawned financially for Pittsburgh.

Sufficient subscriptions were secured to enable Andrews to continue his paper throughout a seven-year period of alternating success and discouragement. But it was a constant struggle, straining both the faith and the financial resources of the editor.

The Spectator

Thinking perhaps that a new name and an altered format might attract more subscribers, Andrews, in January of 1828, changed the name of his weekly periodical to *The Spectator*.[23] All in vain. Andrews resigned to the Synod of Pittsburgh in October of that year and asked for the appointment of a new editor. When he closed his work in December, the paper had only four hundred and forty-seven paid subscriptions, the visible fruitage of seven years' unrequited labor of sacrifice and love.[24]

If Andrews had done nothing more than to record the story of religious activity in Western Pennsylvania throughout the seven years of his service as an editor in Pittsburgh, he would have placed posterity in permanent debt to him. The story of the growth and enrichment of Presbyterian churches, biographical sketches of leading personalities, sermons, editorials reflecting the religious thinking of that period, and news of secular and religious activities filled its pages and made the past stand forth in the vivid portrayal of eyewitnesses. How perennial many problems seem to be! How persistently men of faith must struggle to uphold ideals! A traveler reported that in 1825 East Liberty was a small village of twenty houses, one store, but three taverns; that Wilkinsburg was only a village of twenty-five wooden houses, yet it had five taverns. He philosophizes in words that might be heard today: "Taverns are excessively multiplied in many parts of our country and prove a temptation to multitudes who are forming habits of intemperance in the use of ardent spirits."[25]

Ministers troubled by the late arrival of worshipers might find some personal comfort in reflecting on unchanged habits of humanity in that regard. A clergyman, whose congregation had given him much vexation by tardiness in worship, began his discourse one Sabbath morning with these words: "When I came here to begin worship last Sabbath morning, I believe there were not twenty people in the chapel. At the weekly lecture, it was the same and again this morning. My heart is pained. What can you mean by this conduct? Do you mean to worship God? Then I must tell you plainly, and with the authority of a Christian minister, that this is no worship. God will not accept it at your hands." The editor remarked dryly that the next Sabbath almost every person had assembled by the time the pastor had ascended the pulpit.[26] Dare we be that frank today?

Nor would this Presbyterian editor countenance any frivolity or humor in the pulpit. A correspondent had reported that "a certain clergyman is in the habit of preaching the most solemn truth in such a way that some of his audience are frequently observed smiling and laughing; in fact, it is said the minister himself is sometimes seen to laugh at his own wit." Then follows this rebuking query: "Can much good be done when the preacher intermingles the sacred truths of the Bible with that low wit which drives from the mind all seriousness, and is so far below the dignity of the subject, the office and the occasion?"[27] The tone of the question carried its own negative answer to the reader. Seeking to save souls was a serious and solemn search in the service of the Saviour.

No Compromising of Convictions

Those preachers who are still troubled in soul by widespread Sabbath desecration may be encouraged to recall that the editor spoke out in wrathful denunciation of a Sunday Water Party. An advertisement in the *Pittsburgh Gazette* announced that "the Steamboat Pennsylvania will leave the Market Street wharf for Economy (now Ambridge) on Sunday morning, July 2, at 7 o'clock in the morning and return to Pittsburgh at 7 o'clock same day. Passage one dollar." Editor Andrews expressed his righteous indignation against "so unhallowed and presumptious a project as an excursion for pleasure on the Lord's Day to the town of Economy in contempt of the religious part of the community and of the supreme authority of Heaven."[28] What might he say about present-day professional baseball and football on Sunday!

Nor were plans for erecting a theatre viewed with any complacent equanimity. Rather, the editor speaks in pungent criticism. "The proposal for erecting a threatre in Pittsburgh is equally a subject of regret and an evidence of increasing depravity. Every reflecting mind, who values the evidence of education and the improving of the mind above the demoralizing influence of theatrical exhibitions, will not hesitate to discountenance the project. This city has not, as yet, obtained a reputation for classical taste or critical scholarship. We want more education. As for the morals of our youth, they are already sufficiently lax, without theatrical inducements."[29]

Despite the opposition of the editor and probably also of his Presbyterian brethren, the theatre was built to the possible detriment of the "morals of our youth." But this source of evil was not long to remain a menace. Within two years it was no more. In grateful relief the editor wrote: "The theatre in our city, which has been an annoyance to the citizens resident in this vicinity and a source of corruption to our youth, we are happy to say is now demolished. This must be a subject of gratulation to the friends of good morals. It is sincerely hoped that none of our citizens is so lost to a sense of moral obligation and regard to the good of society, as to encourage, in the future, the contaminating amusements of the drama."[30] In the editor's virtuous judgment, black was black and white was white. There were no overtones of gray in his understanding of right and wrong. A contemporary of the editor in a later reflective evaluation wrote: "Mr. Andrews had the piety and intelligence for his work as editor but was wanting in audacity and was too poor to go into great expenditures."[31]

The Christian Herald

The Synod of Pittsburgh experienced difficulty in finding someone to purchase *The Spectator* and to succeed Mr. Andrews as editor. All seemed to shrink from so thankless and so unrenumerative a task. After much persuasion, the Reverend Samuel C. Jennings, a brilliant young preacher who had graduated recently from Princeton Seminary, agreed to accept the difficult undertaking. "You can take it," he was urged, "and if you do break up, you can still preach."[32] With that utter absence of illusion about financial success, Jennings began his unsolicited duties of service with the first week of January, 1829.

The new owner and editor changed the name of his religious newspaper to *The Christian Herald.* His purpose was to signify that the distinctive aim of the paper was to aid in proclaiming the Gospel.[33] He entered upon his duties with the crusading enthusiasm of youth and with the consciousness that great movements were beginning to stir in the Presbyterian church. Western Theological Seminary was entering its third year with a student body of fifteen and a faculty of two full-time professors. The Synod of Pittsburgh was zealously promoting Home and Foreign Missions. Controversy was stirring within the Presbyterian church over theology and the social questions which soon were to erupt into the New and Old School Schism. The temperance movement was gathering momentum. Revivals of religion were appearing in many areas of western Pennsylvania and eastern Ohio. The paper was enlarged to provide additional space for news and controversial discussion.

Separate parts of the paper were set aside for the special interests of ministers, laymen, parents, and children. A religious newspaper, the new editor believed, was needed "for the benefit of families. A family is a little community, the several members of which need instruction in their several places, both by precept and example."[34] Through a weekly periodical, he felt, they could learn much from biographies recording the experience of other people.

The Christian Herald, at that time, was the only religious paper of any denomination within an area of one hundred miles of Pittsburgh. Religious newspapers were being well supported in other sections of the nation. The only paper in this area should be similarly well supported, he reasoned. For those who paid in advance, the subscription price was still only \$2.00; but from those who paid at the end of the year, \$3.00 were required.[35] The new editor apparently believed Presbyterians in those days had financial resources since a special feature was a monthly listing of bank notes at National Holmes Exchange and also general commodity prices.

Jennings was especially zealous in supporting the stand which the Synod of Pittsburgh had taken in 1828 against intoxicating liquor and in recommendation of total abstinence from all ardent spirits. He was determined to arouse the dormant conscience of the church to an aggressive war against liquor. His agitation was contrary to the convictions and habits of many of his readers. Some discontinued their subscriptions in protest.[36] Yet he would not compromise. At times he devoted as much as half of the paper to news and propaganda on behalf of temperance and total abstinence. Throughout four years of slowly enlarging success, he continued his efforts to sensitize Presbyterian consciences to the need of moral and civic righteousness.

Jennings felt that he was not receiving sufficient support to justify further financial sacrifices on his part. The paper was merely meeting expenses. "Pastors and other friends sustained us so that we lived but made nothing above expenses," he confessed.[37] Jennings had to supplement his income by serving as pastor at Sharon, a small rural church a few miles north of Pittsburgh. He welcomed the opportunity to transfer both his unprofitable investment and his editorial duties to the Reverend Thomas Dickson Baird, an older man and one better fitted in temperament for the theological conflict which was beginning to arouse the Presbyterian church.[38] Jennings was a firm supporter of the Reformed faith but he had no desire "to spend precious time to fight as those who beat the air."[39] Moreover, his health had been undermined by work and worry. He preferred to devote more of his energies to the Lord in the pastorate.

The Presbyterian Preacher

Shortly before Jennings surrendered his position with *The Christian Herald* in July, 1832, he had announced his plan to edit a new monthly publication of a somewhat different type. The first issue appeared in June, 1832, under the title, *The Presbyterian Preacher.* It was the first experiment by Presbyterians in the use of color as an attractive cover.

This new publication continued to serve Western Pennsylvania churches until 1838.[40] Its purpose, as expressed in the subtitle, was to print each month "original sermons by living ministers in the Presbyterian Church." It took the form of a 16-page monthly and sold for $1.00 annually in advance. The opening sermon was by the Rev. Dr. Miller of Princeton, New Jersey, on "The Importance of Gospel Truth." Each issue contained only one sermon, printed in full covering the 16 pages—a much longer sermon than would be heard in modern pulpits or read in present-day periodicals. The second number featured Elisha Swift's sermon on "The Character of God." Many of the preachers were on the faculties of theological seminaries or were college presidents.

The sermons were generally doctrinal in emphasis. Nonessential differences, existing among Presbyterians or between them and other denominations, were rarely discussed. The emphasis in these sermons was on the more fundamental truths of Sacred Scripture as stated in the Westminster Confession. They were phrased so as "to persuade and not to irritate."[41] They were written in a comparatively popular style to afford "common readers" an understanding of the reasons for believing and maintaining fundamental truths which have a "great influence on the practices of men." Jennings was never a doctrinal controversialist at heart. He cherished his new monthly as a happier expression of his editorial talents.

The Pittsburgh Christian Herald

But the Reverend T. D. Baird who succeeded Jennings as editor of *The Christian Herald,* now renamed *The Pittsburgh Christian Herald,* seemed emotionally constituted to enjoy the thrill of controversy. He entered his new work in 1832 with the prestige of having been elected that year the moderator of the Synod of Pittsburgh.[42] He was an active participant in the planning of the foreign missionary work of the Synod and a leader in the uncompromising decisions which led to the division of the church into the Old and New School branches. "To contend earnestly for that faith which was once delivered unto the saints," he believed was the imperative duty of all Christian ministers, especially Christian editors.[43]

The pages of his paper reveal him as a consistent contender for his distinctive Presbyterian convictions and as a doughty warrior who believed he was fighting the Lord's battle when he hurled his theological darts against his Christian brethren of other creeds. His long and well-planned debate with the Roman Catholics absorbed much space over a period of many months.[44] The cholera epidemic was raging in Western Pennsylvania that same summer with deadly sorrow in many families. Reports on its progress were given weekly. A united day of prayer was held beseeching God's healing mercy and was followed some weeks later with a community day of thanksgiving for the passing of the late pestilential disease.[45] But even an epidemic merited less space than a religious controversy.

The New and Old School conflict was another arena where editor Baird fought vigorously for the orthodox faith. His logically reasoned editorials and his ringing challenges were effective in holding the Synod of Pittsburgh to an almost united support of the parental denomination. New subscriptions cheered the heart of the pugnacious editor as he reported that "between four and five hundred new subscribers had been received since the first of the year."[46] But the dual responsibility of serving both as editor and publisher was proving too great a strain upon his weakened vitality. Broken in health after six years of this exhausting toil and with less than three months to live, he persuaded a fellow minister, the Reverend William Annan, to purchase and edit the paper. Baird had doubled the number of readers of his paper. He had fought a good fight for causes he believed to be truly Presbyterian. He had won the esteem of friend and foe and was admired for his candor, his honesty, and his devotion to his convictions. His last issue was dated September 27, 1838.

The Presbyterian Advocate

Another editor and publisher and another name for the same periodical! Such was the oft-repeated experience of this pioneer Presbyterian paper which continued to be published in Pittsburgh. The city and its immediately surrounding towns could boast of a total population of over 46,000. With upwards of 40 clergymen, a university, two theological seminaries and numerous factories, metropolitan Pittsburgh was a rapidly growing community of widening prestige and influence.

The new Presbyterian editor was the Reverend William Annan. He preferred to call his religious newspaper *The Presbyterian Advocate and Herald of the West.* Two years later, in 1840, it was shortened to *The Presbyterian Advocate.* The general format of the paper, which had grown into full newspaper size, was continued. The same editorial policy and scope were also maintained except that the paper was less controversial in spirit and more literary in its contents.

Annan felt that the opportunity to purchase and edit a religious newspaper was a providential call to serve the church. A persistent throat ailment had made preaching an impossibility for over a year. He was compelled to relinquish public speaking and so welcomed the opportunity to express his thoughts through the printed page."[47] "To preach with the pen and the press is the only substitute for the proclamation of the voice." He was devoted to his task, genial in spirit, and tolerant with those who disagreed with him. The fine Christian spirit which the ministers of the Old and New School branches manifested toward one another in the Pittsburgh district was a source of joy to him. He excluded from his paper anything which might impair that fellowship and opened its pages to encouraging news from both branches of a divided church. He labored sacrificially to preach to a steadily widening circle of readers "the unsearchable riches of Christ."

His faith and resources were severely strained in the Spring of 1845. That was the year of the great fire which destroyed a large part of the city of Pittsburgh and rendered hundreds homeless. Included in a vast area of destruction and loss were the printing plant and presses of *The Presbyterian Advocate*. Publication had to be suspended on April 9. But on May 14 the paper was reappearing, saved by proper insurance and the venturesome courage of the editor.[48] When in 1848 one thousand new subscriptions were received, he at once purchased new type and enlarged his paper. "This makes it the largest strictly Presbyterian journal in the United States," he confided to his readers.[49] For seventeen years he continued in his cherished responsibility.

Throughout all those years, the pages of *The Presbyterian Advocate* reflect approvingly the spirit of harmony between the pastors of the New School and Old School churches and the premature efforts in Pittsburgh to heal the schism. News of the growth of the churches was glowingly recorded. Sincere sympathy was expressed when the buildings of both the Second and Fifth Presbyterian churches and the Western Theological Seminary were destroyed by fire. Efforts of Presbyterians to build hospitals, develop a Y.M.C.A., and to support temperance hotels are mentioned with approval as illustrative of the leadership of Presbyterians in community enterprises.

Recurring controversies between Protestants and Catholics also find expression frequently, but only in editorial rebuttal to unreasonable claims made by Catholics and to attacks on Protestants as previously printed in *Pittsburgh Catholic*.[50] But in spite of any proneness to argue, Presbyterians still remained tolerant and generous toward their Catholic brethren. When the new St. Paul's Roman Catholic Cathedral was erected, the leaders of that church openly boasted that large sums of money had been contributed by Presbyterians. In recording their boasting, the editor could not avoid asking if any Pittsburgh Presbyterian church could similarly boast of financial assistance from Catholics. Inter-religious generosity seemed to be only a one-way street.

Editorial Play on Names

The editor had his humorous as well as his broad-minded characteristics. In his idle playful moments, when he was not absorbed in financial or editorial worries, he found time to study the recently published statistics of the General Assembly recording the rather odd names of Presbyterian ministers. Perhaps to his own surprise and the amusement of his readers, he discovered that among the clergy there were the following most interesting combinations of occupations, moods, and creatures based on the ministers' names.

"The mechanical trades seem to be well represented. There are 2 Carpenters, 3 Coopers, 3 Masons, 16 Millers, with but 2 Mills, 9 Taylors, and one Mann. There are also a Barber, a Chandler, and a Painter. But the most favorite trade is that of Smith, of which there are no less than thirty-three.

"There is a variety of secular employments—3 are Gardners and 3 are Potters, with a supply of Potts. There are also a Hunter, a Fisher, a Shepherd, a Sailor, and a Waggoner.

"In the provision line there is nothing extra, though there is some good Bacon, with an expert Carver, plenty of Rice, with 1 Cook and 7 Bakers.

"There is no great variety of liquors, though there are Beer and

Perry and Porter, and fine Wines. The supply cannot be great as there are but 2 Hogsheads, with a considerable Leake, not yet stopped.

"Of colors there is some variety. Full 26 are Brown, 8 are Gray, 4 are Black, and only 9 White.

"In regard to temper, 1 is Bland, another is Cross; one is Blythe, another is Moody; one is Wiley, another is Greedy; 2 are Sharp, 3 are Swift, and 1 is Slack. Among them all there is but one Wiseman; one Goodman, and one Christian.

"There is moreover but one Virtue, one Comfort, one Hope and one Life, adorning and animating the whole clerical corps.

"The quadrupeds are not a few. There are a Buck, a Lamb, a Bullock and a Colt, with 4 Harts, and a single Fox, followed by no less than 7 Lyons.

"Of feathered fowl, there are Crows and Cranes, Robins, Swans, and Martins—of which last there are full 11.

"There is 1 Town with a single Street, and 2 Churches, with 6 Bells, all well toned. There is but 1 House, with 3 substantial Walls, and 1 upright Post. Yet there are 10 convenient Halls and also 7 Wells, and 1 copious Spring, for the refreshment of weary pilgrims.

"In the distance there are visible 2 Forrests, 2 Hills, and 2 Glens. In another direction are a Marsh, with many Reeds, 2 Parks, with several Lanes, and 4 Fields, with but a single Weed.

"Death's doings are also visible, for there are no fewer than 7 Graves."[51]

A General Assembly Paper Advocated

But editor Annan could not view with his habitual tolerance and equanimity a new experiment in Presbyterian religious journalism which was being advocated prematurely, but which was destined many years later to be the established policy of the Presbyterian Church U.S.A. The new plan was suggested by the Reverend David McKinney, pastor of the Hollidaysburg Presbyterian Church in neighboring Huntington Presbytery. His experience in soliciting subscriptions for church papers convinced him that these periodicals were too expensive for the average church member to purchase.

He conceived the idea that the Presbyterian church itself, under the direction of its General Assembly, should establish a religious newspaper and publish it at a price so low that every family in the entire denomination could and would subscribe. His novel plan included the suggestion that each church subscribe for its members at the rate of $1.00 per family. "One man might give $5.00, another $3.00, another $2.00. Many would give their $1.00; some fifty cents and some even twenty-five cents. The dollars would be made equal to the families in number."[52]

The Presbytery of Huntington approved his plan and recommended it to the General Assembly for consideration.[53] A committee was appointed, with Dr. McKinney as the chairman, to study the proposition for a year and to report back to the Assembly in 1851. Action was again postponed until the following year. At that time there were being published nine Presbyterian weeklies with a total subscription of only 25,000 or about one-fifth of all Presbyterian families.[54] The largest, *The New York Observer,* had 5,000 subscribers. These periodicals were usually sold on an annual subscription base of $2.50.

The privately published church papers vigorously opposed the idea and ridiculed its author. Annan printed a number of articles designed to reveal the folly of the novel suggestion. "It is the most hazardous project ever suggested to the church. Free Presbyterians must have a free press and they will contend to the death before they will submit. The proposal puts unlimited power in the hands of an individual, the appointee of the General Assembly who, for a year at least, shall be the pope of the church to issue his bulls."[55]

The General Assembly which met in Charleston, South Carolina, was highlighted by a vigorous and prolonged debate. Upon the floor of the Assembly in 1852, David McKinney advocated zealously the plan of a denominationally supported weekly at a price within the range of every family. He pleaded in vain. His thinking was too far in advance of the majority of his contemporaries. His plan was rejected. The Assembly preferred to leave in private hands the printing of church periodicals. What seemed impractical in 1852 became a reality in 1945 when General Assembly authorized the establishment of *Presbyterian Life* on a somewhat similar plan. Dr. McKinney's dream of an every-family church paper has now reached practical fulfillment in the every-family plan of *Presbyterian Life* which is reaching over a million subscribers.

The Presbyterian Banner in Philadelphia

What David McKinney failed to persuade General Assembly to do, he now attempted on his own resources. He resigned his church at Hollidaysburg and moved to Philadelphia. Here he invested some $10,000 of his own money in purchasing necessary equipment.[56] Though in Philadelphia he was in direct competition with *The Presbyterian,* published at $2.50, he believed that a sufficiently large number of subscribers could be secured to operate profitably at $1.00 each. He took as his guiding text these words from the 20th Psalm: "In the name of our God, we will set up our banners." Hence the chosen name for his paper was *The Presbyterian Banner.*

With no previous editorial experience and with no supporting group of friends, but with only an all-absorbing conviction to motivate him, he launched his enterprise. The first issue appeared September 18 at an experimental price of $1.25 annually. This issue contained a long article advocating that preachers' salaries be increased to an amount adequate to meet their needs. The earnest appeal may have added to the paper's early popularity. Eight months later Dr. McKinney reported to the General Assembly a total of 10,000 subscribers, "which is greater than any other weekly bearing our denominational distinction."[57] Of these, "3,000 had never previously received any religious paper."

Secular as well as religious news was inserted weekly. The editor sought to include in each issue something to interest all ages in the family. A special feature was a brief sermon to help people who do not go to church. Beginning with the third year, the price of the paper was reduced to $1.00 as Dr. McKinney had originally hoped he could do when he projected his campaign for an inexpensive paper based on a large subscription list.[58] The highest peak he reached was 15,000 subscribers.

The Presbyterian Banner and Advocate Merge in Pittsburgh

The natural result followed. *The Presbyterian Advocate* in Pittsburgh was unable to meet the competition of Dr. McKinney's cheap paper in Philadelphia. The annual subscription price was reduced to $1.75, later to $1.50. Some new subscriptions were received, but the financial resources were weakening. Mr. Annan, the editor, was convinced that the number of Presbyterian journals was too numerous to maintain the highest efficiency. So he suggested to Dr. McKinney that *The Advocate* and *The Banner* be merged. His suggestion met with a hearty response. Dr. McKinney agreed to purchase the resources of *The Advocate* and merge the two papers in Pittsburgh under the joint name *Presbyterian Banner and Advocate.*[59] Five years later, the word "Advocate" was dropped and the familiar name resumed. The last of the numerous changes in name had now been completed. For more than three-fourths of a century, the name, *The Presbyterian Banner,* was to become a household word in Presbyterian homes and the recognized voice of independent Presbyterian thought throughout the entire Upper Ohio Valley.

With the sale of the assets of *The Presbyterian Advocate,* the Reverend William Annan retired as an editor. He had served well the Presbyterian church in that editorial capacity since 1838. In a kindly spirit of Christian love and tolerance, he had revealed unswerving loyalty to the Old School branch of the denomination. But his paper had a comparatively small subscription list. Allowing for those who were already subscribers of both papers, the merged periodical began with a subscription list of approximately fourteen thousand.

The Presbyterian Banner in Pittsburgh

David McKinney, the editor and proprietor, was an aggressive journalist who was never content in the mere enjoyment of the status quo. He was motivated by the conviction that, "next to the pulpit, for good in enlightening and directing the mind of the church, the religious press possesses an influence that should not be neglected. Readers not only are more intelligent than those who do not have the paper but they are more attached to their church and are more liberal in supporting benevolent causes of the church."[60]

In the opening issue of November 17, 1855, he announced a broadened and expanding policy in a bigger newspaper which he offered for $1.50 per year. Later his paper boasted a "European correspondence that is unrivalled in any other American journal in breadth of view, reliability and general usefulness. It gives a complete view of business, opinion, religious concern and things in general in New England, New York and Philadelphia, a feature to be found in no other religious newspaper. The compendium of Domestic and Foreign news is prepared with much care and labor and gives by far the most reliable news for the public. Nor are the claims of the garden and the farm forgotten." All that and more for $1.50!—the more being the regular features of sermons, editorials, church affairs, and "selections from books, magazines and other newspapers to interest the parent, the Christian, the man of literature and learning and the children."[61] In size and scope "The Banner" of that period resembled a daily newspaper rather than a modern religious journal. To write, edit, and print a paper of that size was a terrific and time-consuming burden.

Turning the pages of those recorded years of labor and enthusiasm, the reader notes such typical, but not theological, editorials as "The Absence of Spiritual Warmth in Our Congregations"

(Presbyterian, of course), "Our Extravagance," "Inadequate Pastor's Salaries," "What Is to be the Future of Our Sabbath" and "Prayer for Our Country?"[62] How applicable and timeless certain themes remain even in a changing social culture!

The eye of the reader is also attracted by the editor's love and devotion to the Presbyterian church as expressed in another editorial: "Presbyterianism I hold to be the true religion. It is the religion of the Bible in its best and purest form. It is to be maintained and propagated. Charity I would cherish. Other Christians I recognize and love, but I am bound on principle, in feeling and by covenant to uphold and diffuse Presbyterianism, honestly believing it to be the most excellent."[63]

Perennial problems keep reappearing. An article complains that preachers are careless in the preparation of their sermons, bringing "incoherent stuff," not "beaten oil into the sanctuary." A correspondent bemoans that "men over 45 years who may need to leave a charge find it very difficult to obtain a new settlement, and sometimes people even try to shove off a pastor who is advancing in life." What can preachers do about it? The editor offers this sage advice: "Root yourself so deeply in the affections of the people that they will not be tempted to seek other loves, and strengthen your mind by fresh study, so that the congregation will not need to yearn for a new teacher." The editor also has a bit of advice to the congregations whom he believes must consent to give up the "cruel tyranny of compelling clergymen to preach two sermons every Sabbath, besides a lecture in the week. There is no profession in the country worked as hard and paid as poorly as the clergy." One sermon a week is all that a busy pastor can prepare and deliver to the edification and enjoyment of the congregation.[64]

"The Banner" spoke with no uncertain voice on the troublesome question of slavery. Its editor had long been conscious of the inherent immorality of slaveholding and sought to arouse a Christian conscience against it. To him, slavery was a sin against God.

Throughout the war, the pages of "The Banner" resounded with

COURTESY OF WOOSTER COLLEGE

WOOSTER COLLEGE, WOOSTER, OHIO
Kauke Hall, main recitation building.

COURTESY OF DR. WILLIAM RUSCH

WASHINGTON AND JEFFERSON COLLEGE, WASHINGTON, PA.
Administration Building, erected 1793. First used by Washington Academy, later by Washington College. A fine example of early architecture in Western Pennsylvania.

GROVE CITY COLLEGE, GROVE CITY, PA.
Harbison Memorial Chapel
Presented in memory of Samuel P. Harbison, 1931.

COURTESY OF PRESIDENT STEWART

WAYNESBURG COLLEGE, WAYNESBURG, PA.
A. B. Miller Building, oldest edifice on campus.

calls to patriotism and full support of the government. It was the first of the religious papers to propose and advocate the loyal and decided stand for the government taken by the General Assembly in 1861. In a letter to his son in the service, Dr. McKinney wrote, "The Banner's influence is acknowledged in the guiding and steadying of public sentiment. It is my lot to write, as well as to speak, so plainly that men cannot pass by in indifference."[65]

New Editors for Presbyterian Banner

"The Banner" now rested on a firm financial foundation. It could boast of the largest circulation among Presbyterian weeklies. Its influence was felt over a wide area. Dr. McKinney had been its editor for nearly twelve years. Rising prices of materials had compelled him to raise the subscription price on two occasions, reaching $2.00 per annual subscription.[66] As the editor had reached his seventieth birthday, he felt that younger leadership might promote increased effectiveness. He sold his profitable venture to the Reverend James Allison and Professor Robert Patterson. The new editors and proprietors entered upon their joint labors with the issue of February 10, 1864. They continued together until death terminated their partnership in 1889.

Mr. Allison came to his editorial duties from a very successful pastorate of fifteen years in the First Presbyterian Church of Sewickley, Pennsylvania. He was no stranger to religious journalism, having served on "The Banner" staff as news correspondent, book reviewer, and weekly commentor throughout almost the entire period of Dr. McKinney's editorship.[67] He was a forceful personality, a vigorous writer, and a man of great influence throughout the entire denomination. It was his wise leadership which, more than any other single factor, brought the New and Old School branches of the church into a happy reunion in 1869 on the basis of the Westminster Standards.

He was ably assisted by Professor Robert Patterson, a son of the Reverend Robert Patterson, one of the first principals of the Pittsburgh Academy (now the University of Pittsburgh). Like his distinguished father, he was an educator, first as professor of mathematics in Jefferson College and later in a similar capacity at Centre College in Danville, Kentucky.[68] He brought to "The Banner" the splendid resources of a scholarly mind, a brilliant writer, and a Christian spirit. The distinctive and harmonious abilities of these two gifted personalities, lifted "The Banner" into the heyday of its glory and made it a creative force in the thinking of the entire church and in the convictions of its enamoured readers.

The Family Treasure

Dr. McKinney's service to Western Pennsylvania religious journalism did not cease with his withdrawal from "The Banner." On April 2, 1864, with the assistance of his invalid son, the Reverend Isaac N. McKinney, he issued the first number of a new monthly magazine called *The Family Treasure*.[69] It was an attractively illustrated and well-printed publication of 64 pages to be sold at an annual price of $2.00. The wide range of its reading matter included much that could be classified as theological, historical, literary, social, and practical household information. Its aim was both religious and literary and sought by its varied contents to interest all ages throughout the family. Numerous contributors enlivened its pages with interesting stories, poems, timely articles and biographical sketches of preachers. The editors themselves commented on a wide variety of religious and secular news and featured devotional meditations.

Following the sudden death of Isaac, his brother, the Reverend William W. McKinney, became the assistant editor. Together father and son issued their joint publication with increasing success for several years and with over three thousand subscribers. In 1867 the Reverend W. T. Findley of Zenia, Ohio, purchased the magazine and reissued it from Cincinnati under the changed name, *Our Family*.[70] This enabled David McKinney to serve on a full-time basis as Librarian of the Presbyterian Book Store and as Superintendent of Missions in the Presbytery.

Dr. Snowden Edits "The Banner"

After the death of Professor Patterson in 1889, Dr. Allison, with the help of a group of Pittsburgh ministers, carried for ten years longer the full responsibility of editing and publishing *The Presbyterian Banner*. His failing health demanded that younger shoulders assume the burdens he had borne so triumphantly. That younger man was the beloved and brilliant James H. Snowden.[71] His coming ushered in the modern era with continued reduction of the format to magazine size and with increased emphasis on religious news and specialized departments of study.

In the early years of his editorship, he was assisted by Dr. James D. Moffatt and Dr. John A. Marquis, two outstanding leaders whom the Presbyterian church called to serve as moderator of the General Assembly. His venerable career as a journalist culminated in his death on Saturday morning, December 19, 1936. So deeply did Dr. Snowden engrave himself in the admiration and affection of the church throughout the Upper Ohio Valley, that many of his readers still live to cherish the memory of his long and noble service. To them Snowden and "The Banner" continue to be almost synonymous.

Dr. Snowden came to the editor's chair under most favorable circumstances. The influence of "The Banner" had been broadened by a merger with *The Presbyterian Messenger*, another Pittsburgh Presbyterian weekly which had been established five years earlier, with the Reverend Joseph T. Gibson as its editor. The two Pittsburgh papers had covered somewhat the same journalistic field, with "The Banner" as the recognized exponent of the conservative element in the Presbyterian church and "The Messenger" as the spokesman for the more liberal forces.

Under Dr. Snowden's broad catholicity and balanced judgment, the two viewpoints were fused into Christian unity and "The Banner" became liberal in spirit and conservative in conviction, a critical yet commendatory advocate of enlarging knowledge and revealed truth. Dr. Snowden was too broad minded to be concerned with petty quarrels and too well grounded in the fundamentals of his faith to be alarmed by passing winds of doctrine and egotism. "To his task of interpreting church and world affairs, he put the wealth of his scholarship and the wisdom of his disciplined mind. Trained in the old school, he mediated to the new. With the grace of open-mindedness, he held fellowship with the clergy of all churches and with interpreters in the field of science and literature."[72]

Dr. Snowden revealed himself as a man whose resources of thought and energy were amazing. Not only did he determine the contents of the paper and write the notable editorials which made it so outstanding, but each week he presented a survey of world news and for years wrote the Sunday-school lessons and prayer meeting topics and book reviews. Never less than five pages a week were his personal contributions to "The Banner" throughout the first nineteen years of his editorial career. At the same time he was serving either as pastor of the Second Presbyterian Church of Washington, Pennsylvania, or as professor of theology in the Western Theological Seminary and writing numerous books on a wide range of topics. "Those who knew him best marveled at his industry. He was never idle. He did easily what other men would not attempt to do."[73] During his so-called spare time, he wrote twenty-four books, in addition to sixteen annual volumes of Sunday-school lessons.

The Closing Decade of "The Banner"

Dr. Snowden's long service with "The Banner" was interrupted for a nine-year interval from 1917 to 1926, when he was persuaded to accept other journalistic opportunities, notably as editor of the

Presbyterian Magazine. His place with "The Banner" was filled by the joint service of Dr. Joseph T. Gibson, the former editor of *The Presbyterian Messenger*, and by Dr. William A. Kinter, who had resigned as pastor of the First Presbyterian Church of Ambridge, Pennsylvania. It was a beautiful and most fruitful partnership, uniting into co-operative activity two capable and devoted servants of the church.

But the death of Dr. Gibson in 1922 brought to an abrupt close the united service of these two devoted friends of "The Banner." Dr. Kinter's health did not permit him to assume the full editorial burden. Plans for a merger with another Presbyterian periodical were discussed and tentatively agreed upon.

However, Dr. Kinter felt that the critical issues which were then disturbing the church required the strengthening, not the discontinuing of any of our church papers. Pittsburgh was asked to rally to the financial support of this historic paper. Dr. Ogden M. Edwards, Jr., a member of the Shadyside Presbyterian Church, willingly accepted the challenge. Generously he gave of his means to broaden and enlarge the scope and constituency of "The Banner." Throughout a period of fifteen years, he underwrote the expenses of an expanded budget, which advances have totaled approximately one hundred thousand dollars. In all of these unselfish and unannounced gifts of love, he was encouraged and advised by his pastor, Dr. Hugh Thomson Kerr, who contributed with equal generosity of his time and wisdom throughout that entire period. His weekly radio sermons and his numerous articles and editorial comments were most inspiring and deeply appreciated features of "The Banner."

Dr. George McPherson Hunter served as editor for a period of two years. He was succeeded in 1926 by Dr. Snowden who for ten years again gave to "The Banner" readers the ripened fruitage of his venerable ministry. He was assisted for several years, beginning in 1931, by the Reverend Paul Patton Faris, who served in the capacity of managing editor. Readers were indebted to Dr. Faris for the attractive format and legible type in which "The Banner" appeared during the concluding half-dozen years.

During the months that elapsed after the death of Dr. Snowden, the editorial responsibility was carried by Dr. Arthur Burd McCormick. In this later period the prestige of "The Banner" was greatly influenced by the editorial contributions of such notable ministers as William Henry Boddy, William E. Brooks, Ralph Cooper Hutchison, Hugh Thomson Kerr, John A. Mackay, Donald Mackenzie, and Joseph R. Sizoo, who composed its staff of contributing editors.

Departmental Writers and Correspondents

No record of these closing years in the life of "The Banner" would be complete without a brief appreciative mention of the continued helpfulness of those who had carried the responsibility in the specialized departments of "The Banner." In the earlier period in the development of the paper, the editor wrote the material for a number of these regular features. But then later the editors availed themselves of the help of a number of departmental writers.

Dr. Robert MacGowan furnished homiletic and poetic inspiration in his highly prized column, "The Quiet Hour." Dr. Arthur B. McCormick broadened the vision of his readers in his comprehensive editorial summary of "The World As I See It." Dr. Gaius Slosser, Dr. Hugh T. Kerr, Jr., and others evaluated the "Best In Recent Books."

Dr. W. A. Kinter, Walter A. Squires, Dr. George W. Brown, and Dr. William W. McKinney prepared the discussions of the "Sunday School Lesson." Miss Natalie H. Snyder, Dr. Kinley McMillan, William S. Wise, C. J. Patterson, Dr. John O. Nelson, and the Reverend Roy C. Blair applied the "Christian Endeavor Topics" to the changing interests of youth and gave practical guidance in Christian activity. They laid among young people the broad foundations of church loyalty upon which the Westminster Fellowships were soon to be built throughout most of these Presbyterian churches. In the opinion of many readers, these departmental helps were among the most useful features of "The Banner's" diverse program of service.

Pageant and Presbyterian Life

With the issue of December 16, 1937, *The Presbyterian Banner* closed its long service to the Presbyterian churches throughout the Upper Ohio Valley. The oldest of the Presbyterian weeklies at last was absorbed in *Pageant,* a monthly publication published by the Board of Christian Education in Philadelphia. That official magazine, though short-lived, was one of the experimental ventures which have resulted in the highly successful *Presbyterian Life,* the official semimonthly periodical of the Presbyterian church and now the United Presbyterian Church in the U.S.A. New times have demanded new measures and new publications. Regional Presbyterian periodicals had served well their day and generation. They were no longer needed in this area and so ceased to exist except in the memory of a grateful church.

CHAPTER XIII Higher Education

ALL SEVEN OF THE Presbyterian preachers who came to Western Pennsylvania during the pioneer period of Redstone Presbytery were graduates of the College of New Jersey (now Princeton). They brought to this frontier country an appreciation of the importance of education and a determination to establish, as soon as possible, Presbyterian schools and colleges which could provide the educational advantages they themselves had received in the East.

Their immediate objective was the education of young men for the ministry throughout the ever-expanding frontier. Their broader purpose, however, was to build an educational system which would meet the needs of the community for general and specialized education in all aspects of life. The first fruits of this continued zeal for education in the hearts and minds of Presbyterian leaders appeared in a long list of academies and, later, female seminaries, as previously reviewed. Some of these secondary institutions of learning served for an extended period and then gave place to a tax-supported educational system. Others have developed into colleges which have compiled an inspiring record of service under changing conditions and which continue to serve the church as cherished institutions of higher education. The story of the expansion in service of these Presbyterian-supported colleges is a thrilling tale of vision, consecration, enthusiasm, sacrifice, and undaunted determination.

WASHINGTON AND JEFFERSON COLLEGE

The two academies of Canonsburg and Washington had become the colleges of Jefferson in 1802 and of Washington in 1806. Located less than ten miles apart, they were rivals in educational leadership and prestige. In 1865, the governing Boards of both colleges agreed that these two neighboring Presbyterian colleges could serve more effectively as a single institution with combined resources and united appeal for increased support.

As separate institutions they had carried the early burden of Presbyterian education in the Upper Ohio Valley. The pages of the history of this area are replete with the names of their graduates who moulded the culture and fashioned the ideals of the broadening area of activity in the expanding settlements and amid an increasing population. Dr. Matthew Brown Riddle, the famous professor at Western Theological Seminary and himself a graduate of Jefferson College in 1852, paid a glowing tribute to the transforming influence of these two colleges. In an address celebrating the 25th anniversary of the merger of Washington and Jefferson colleges, he testified: "These two colleges have been a greater power for good in the region west of the Allegheny Mountains and the eastern part of the great Mississippi Valley—a greater power than any other of which we know. Now I do not except the Christian Church, for the reason that the power and influence of the Christian Church have been largely exerted through these colleges."[1] The pattern did not change with the merger of the two colleges.

Circumstances, more than desire, brought about the jointure of Jefferson and Washington colleges. The precarious financial condition which had plagued these schools became aggravated by the national crises of the War Between the States. Salaries had been cut as low as seven hundred dollars per year. Faculties were not up to full strength. Debts were increasing at both institutions. Unsettled conditions brought about not only a decrease in student enrollment, but also a state of restlessness evidenced by a resentment against church restrictions. Sensible and progressive alumni and friends knew that one college could easily and more effectively meet the demands for higher education in the area.

At this crucial time, the Rev. Dr. C. C. Beatty, Steubenville pastor and "female" educator, came forward with an offer of fifty thousand dollars on condition that the two colleges would merge.[2] Dr. Beatty had been concerned for the welfare of both colleges because of his greater interest in the Western Theological Seminary. The alumni of the two colleges met jointly in Pittsburgh at an early date since the offer expired at the end of one year. They submitted the following plan to the two Boards: that the united college be called Washington and Jefferson College; that the Senior, Junior, and Sophomore classes meet in the Jefferson building at Canonsburg and the Freshman classes in the Washington buildings; and that the College some day be located at one of the sites and a preparatory school be established at the other. The Legislature granted the charter as of March 4, 1865.[3]

The Board of Trustees at once sought to secure a President of national stature in the hope that wounds might be more easily healed and the College might prosper. The Rev. Dr. Robert J. Breckenridge, a former president of Jefferson who had gained national recognition through his support of Lincoln and the Union cause, was approached but he declined the honor. The Board then selected the Rev. Dr. Jonathan Edwards, a Hanover College graduate and a Philadelphia clergyman, who not only possessed a famous name, but who had distinguished himself in many ways. Special "circulars" were sent to alumni and friends announcing his inauguration and enlisting support for the "two-in-one" college.[4]

College Located at Washington

The next four years were comparatively uneventful until, on April 20, 1869, President Edwards submitted his resignation. Of equal or greater importance was the fact that the Board, on the eighth ballot voted, by the necessary two-thirds, to locate the entire College at Washington, Pennsylvania. Previously Uniontown, Pennsylvania, Steubenville, and Wooster in Ohio had made overtures of one kind or another to the new united college.[5] When it was rumored that a vote was to be taken, offers were received also from the University of Kittanning (Pennsylvania), and the Western University of Pennsylvania (Pittsburgh) to join with them in their respective communities. Canonsburg citizens offered a sixteen thousand dollar endowment to keep the college in their community, but Washington outbid them with an offer of fifty thousand dollars.[6] The glorious heritage was at Canonsburg, but the hopes of the future were at Washington which was not only the county seat but was located on the National Highway.

The inauguration of the next President, the Reverend George P. Hays, D.D., took place in September of 1870. He was a Jefferson graduate of the Class of 1857 who had served pastorates in Baltimore and Allegheny (Pittsburgh). He served the College for ten years. This period called for "peculiar tact and ability on the part of its presiding officer."[7] The outlook was very discouraging. Three cases concerning the College had been appealed to the Supreme Court of the United States. These were later resolved in favor of the College. There were also the problems of dissatisfied alumni, of reduced attendance, and of diverted patronage. Gifts to the College, for example that of Dr. LeMoyne, were being withheld or given with conditions attached. Dr. Hays, born and reared in Canonsburg, was fully aware of the sensitive as well as the critical situation. He threw the weight of his youth, his pleasing personality, and his tremendous energies against the threatening impasse. Gradually the tide of sentiment turned in favor of the College. The Board was persuaded to engage money-raising agencies to secure one hundred and fifty thousand dollars for building purposes and set a goal of five hundred thousand dollars over a five-year period.

Results fell short of the goal, but the publicity proved a great asset. The immediate result was the remodeling and the enlargement of "Old Main" at a cost of seventy-three thousand dollars.[8] Dr. Hays strengthened the financial structure of the College considerably. A gift of twenty thousand dollars from Dr. F. J. LeMoyne, an alumnus of Washington and a practicing physician in that town for fifty years, was offered in 1871 and received one year later. This gift was to endow a chair of agriculture and correlative branches of the science. In 1874, Dr. Beatty gave another twenty-five thousand dollars to endow "the Steubenville chair of Greek." Dr. LeMoyne gave an additional twenty-one thousand dollars to endow and equip the chair of applied mathematics.

There were other matters than finance occupying the attention of the early leaders, as revealed by the catalogues of the period. The college year included three terms and three vacations.[9] The courses of study by departments were: "Logic and Evidences of Christianity," "Intellectual and Moral Science," "English Language," "Mathematics," "The Greek Language," "Modern Languages," and "Agriculture and Correlative Branches."[10] The 1879 minutes of the Board read, "No professor's son will pay tuition if attending college."[11] The strain of office had become too much for Dr. Hays. In June of 1881 he resigned to accept the pastorate of the Central Presbyterian Church of Denver, Colorado.

Growth of the College

Under the leadership of the next President, the Rev. Dr. James D. Moffatt, the College experienced its first real growth. His long tenure of office extended from 1881 to 1914. Dr. Moffatt was an alumnus in the Class of 1869 (the early days of the union) and had spent one year of his college life at Washington and three years at Canonsburg. He built well upon the foundations laid by Dr. Hays. In 1884 the Board purchased the "Old Fair Ground" for seven thousand and twenty-five dollars for a student athletic field. This occasioned "Pandora," the college yearbook, to comment: "The most popular and beneficial improvement that has been made about the College for years was the purchase of the old Washington Fair Grounds."[12] A stone gymnasium, one hundred ten feet by sixty-five feet, with two stories and a gallery, was completed in 1893. By 1890, enrollment had increased from one hundred and eighty-six to two hundred and sixty-three and the endowment was reported as passing two hundred and fifty thousand dollars. The College was gathering momentum.

The forward movement was further evidenced in 1893 when the Board ordered an electric lighting system installed throughout the campus. Property, formerly occupied by the Union School, was purchased in 1889. It became known as North Hall and was used for recitations and biology over a period of years. Two years later the James H. Hopkins property at Beau and College streets was purchased as a dormitory for the Academy students. In 1912 it became the site of a college dormitory and is now known as Hays Hall. Mr. J. V. Thompson endowed the President's chair in 1901 with a gift of one hundred thousand dollars which was the total estate left him by his father and mother.[13] The following year the Centennial Memorial Fund drive brought a total of four hundred twenty-three thousand, four hundred and eighty-three dollars.

The interest awakened by this effort resulted in the Memorial Library building, aided largely by substantial gifts from Mr. and Mrs. William R. Thompson in memory of his mother. The will of George M. Laughlin in 1909 stipulated that one hundred thousand dollars was to be given to the College to endow a professorship in honor of the donor and his wife, Elizabeth McKennon Laughlin. The last major improvement to the physical plant under Dr. Moffatt's regime came in 1912 with the construction of Thistle Physics Building given by Dr. Joseph L. Thistle. The annual catalogue (1950–1951) paid high tribute to Dr. Moffatt and remarked: "The thirty-three years of his administration of the college were years of unbroken progress."[14] He retired April 15, 1914.

His successors in the presidency included Dr. Frederick D. Hinnitt (1914-1918); Dr. Samuel C. Black (1919-1921); Dr. Simon S. Baker (1922–1931); Dr. Ralph C. Hutchinson (1931-1945); and Dr. James H. Case, Jr. (1946–1949). The present President, Dr. Boyd Crumrine Patterson, began his administration in 1950.

The past quarter of a century has witnessed the second period of the growth of the College. More property and additional buildings, including the Judge John McIlvaine Memorial Hall, the Davis Memorial Hall, the Jesse W. Lazear Chemistry Hall, the Mellon Dormitory for Freshman Men, the Upper Class Dormitory, the Lockhart-Langley House, and the College Chapel, have been added to the campus. In 1957 a Student Activity Building, costing three hundred and twenty-five thousand dollars, was opened and about two hundred thousand dollars was spent on the Athletic Field and Stadium. The present drive for funds is scheduled to continue for ten years and has for its objective additional facilities to include a large auditorium, a new gymnasium, and a building to house a larger library. There are now ten national fraternities on campus: Phi Kappa Psi, Phi Gamma Delta, Beta Theta Pi, Phi Kappa Sigma, Delta Tau Delta, Phi Delta Theta, Kappa Sigma, Alpha Tau Omega, Lambda Chi Alpha, and Pi Lambda Phi. Several of these have their own houses, with an average of thirty men in each house.

Distinguished Alumni of W & J

The roster of outstanding men who had attended or were graduated from either Jefferson or Washington colleges before or after the union is impressive. Space permits the naming of only a few of the many prominent alumni since the union into Washington and Jefferson. The Rev. Dr. James C. R. Ewing of the Class of 1876 did outstanding work at Forman Christian College in India. Adolphus C. Good of the Class of 1879 distinguished himself as a Presbyterian missionary to the French Congo and the Bulu country in the German territory to the north. He prepared a Bulu primer and translated the New Testament into the native language. Being something of a naturalist, he collected hundreds of species previously unknown.[15] Jesse W. Lazear of the Class of 1888, a physician, sacrificed his life in the work of the United States Army Yellow Fever Commission in Cuba. A Chemistry Hall, constructed by alumni and friends on Washington and Jefferson campus in 1940, was dedicated as a memorial to him. Samuel B. McCormick, of the Class of 1880, became a Presbyterian minister and served both as a clergyman and educator. His crowning achievement was his service as Chancellor of the Western University of Pennsylvania from 1904 to 1920. In this period the name was changed to the University of Pittsburgh and a firm foundation laid for the great institution into which it has grown.

Another Presbyterian minister and educator was the Reverend John L. Marquis of the Class of 1885. After three pastorates and ten years as associate editor of *The Presbyterian Banner,* he became President of Coe College at Cedar Rapids, Iowa. In 1916 he was chosen moderator of the Presbyterian Church U.S.A. General Assembly. Josiah V. Thompson of the Class of 1871 won fame and fortune as a coal operator and banker in Uniontown, Pennsylvania. In addition to the endowing of the President's chair at the College, he served as a trustee from 1889 until his death in 1933. Dr. James A. Kelso of the Class of 1892 was long the President of the Western Theological Seminary.

Another prominent alumnus is Boyd Crumrine Patterson, who has been President of the College since 1950. After his graduation in 1923, he took both a Master's degree and a Doctor of Philosophy degree at Johns Hopkins University. His interest in mathematics led him to a professorship at Hamilton College where he remained for twenty-three years. In his several years at Washington and Jefferson, he has been instrumental in the progressive development of the educational life of the College and in the extension and enlargement of the physical properties. He is an able leader for the institution. Scores of other alumni living today have distinguished themselves.

Many are curious about the status of Washington and Jefferson College in the Presbyterian picture of this day. The College is now "free from any ecclesiastical control" but it is affirmed that "the College retains its traditional association with the Presbyterian Church."[16] In retrospect it may be said that the College, through her alumni, has contributed more to the history of the Presbyterian church than any other college west of the Allegheny Mountains. All Presbyterians who have a knowledge of this school rise up in admiration and say, "Thank you, W & J."

PIONEER COLLEGES FORMERLY SPONSORED BY PRESBYTERIANS

Allegheny College is another of the higher educational institutions founded by Presbyterians in the early nineteenth century. It is the fruitage of the labors of the Reverend Joseph Stockton, a Presbyterian pastor and educator in Meadville, Pennsylvania. The College was projected at a meeting held in the Courthouse on June 20, 1815. Two years later a charter was granted with the Reverend Timothy Alden as President. After eighteen years of struggle, the disheartened trustees turned the institution over to the Pittsburgh Annual Conference of the Methodist Episcopal Church.[17] Presbyterians at that time had organized more colleges than they could adequately support.

The education-minded Upper Ohio Valley Presbyterians launched a school at Oxford, Ohio, which is now Miami University. It was chartered in 1818 and had Presbyterian ministers for presidents for sixty years after its founding.[18] The Reverend James Hughes, who had labored long at Lower Buffalo, served Miami as its "first teacher." James H. Brown, in his study of Ohio Presbyterianism, calls attention to the strong Presbyterian emphasis in the leadership of this institution.[19]

The Western University of Pennsylvania, previously discussed in the second chapter, was the next Presbyterian-supported college to be chartered. It has been served by many Presbyterian presidents and board members.

Franklin College chartered in 1825 was the first college with a definite religious objective to be opened in Ohio. Prominent clergymen, such as William McMillan, Joseph Smith, and Edwin H. Neven, served this school in their day. After a time, this work at New Athens, Ohio, was abandoned and the school became absorbed by Muskingum College. Franklin's alumni catalogue of 1908 shows that three hundred and fifty-six ministers, ten foreign missionaries, two United States Senators, ninety-one lawyers, nineteen judges, and seventy-one physicians were among its graduates.[20]

Western Reserve College, another Presbyterian-sponsored institution, came into existence in 1826. At that time the Congregationalists of the Western Reserve of Connecticut were co-sponsors, but the school soon became predominately Presbyterian in its influence. About one-fourth of the graduates during the first fifty years became Presbyterian ministers or missionaries.[21]

Marietta College at Marietta, Ohio, traces its origin back to 1800. But it was not until 1832 that it was incorporated as "The Marietta Collegiate Institute" and still later that it was to be called Marietta College. The founder and early leader was the Reverend Luther G. Bingham, a Congregational minister. It has been said of Bingham that he was "Presbyterian in spirit" and "was installed as the Congregational minister by the Athens Presbytery."[22] There was a strong Presbyterian constituency in that part of the Ohio Valley. Up until 1885, the College was more Presbyterian than Congregational. Lane Seminary of Cincinnati drew a large number of its ministerial-minded graduates. It was after 1885 that the College's Congregational affiliation became more pronounced.

These former Presbyterian colleges either have burned themselves out, like bright stars of other years, or are continuing in a still greater service to education under other sponsorship. Their influence has been felt throughout the headwaters of the Ohio and has advanced the cause of education in the Presbyterian church.

WAYNESBURG COLLEGE

Waynesburg was the second to be organized among the four early Presbyterian colleges of the Upper Ohio Valley that still continue in expanding service to the church and community. Its roots go back to Greene Academy of Carmichaels, Pennsylvania, founded in 1810.[23] This Academy, like similar schools of that period, provided secondary education for students of limited means, especially those looking forward to the Christian ministry. Although it remained nondenominational, it was liberally supported by the Cumberland Presbyterians. To it they sent their pre-theological students. The rejuvenated Madison College at Uniontown served for a short interval, 1838–1846, as a background factor in the history of Waynesburg College. Its collapse came, however, shortly after the failure of the church college at Beverly, Ohio. Cumberland Presbyterians were thus left without a college in the Upper Ohio Valley.

The gap was filled in 1849 when the Cumberland Presbytery of Pennsylvania accepted the offer of a group of citizens in Waynesburg who had "subscribed about five thousand dollars for a three-story brick building on a town lot, fifty by seventy feet, on College Street."[24] Plans were soon under way to establish a college at Waynesburg. At the same time the Reverend Joshua Laughran, principal of Greene Academy, decided to close his work at Carmichaels and to open an academy in Waynesburg. This provided a welcome opportunity to invite Mr. Laughran to merge his academy plans with the new college and to become the first President of Waynesburg College.

Classes began in September of 1849. The Charter was issued on March 25, 1850, stipulating that the College would be under the control of the Cumberland Presbyterian Church.[25] In the Autumn of that same year, "the Female Seminary" division of the College was organized under the direction of Mrs. Margaret Kerr Bell. Early in November of 1851, classes were transferred from their temporary location in the churches to Hanna Hall, a three-story brick structure given to the college by the citizens of Waynesburg.

The Presidents of Waynesburg

With the inauguration in 1859 of Reverend Alfred Brashear Miller as President, the College was launched on an expanding career of service.[26] He had been a member of the first class to graduate in 1853 and continued with the college as President and Professor for forty years. Among his achievements was the erecting of an administration building which is now a memorial to his name.

Following the long tenure of Dr. Miller, changes in the presidency were frequent. Dr. J. W. McKay of the Class of 1883 served only one year as President, but was instrumental in the launching of a campaign to liquidate a thirty thousand dollar debt. The next President was Dr. Archelaeus Ewing Turner who served for four years during the time political and theological discussions were taking place regarding the union of the Cumberland and the Presbyterian Churches U.S.A. "This brought about some rapid changes, including the administration of Dr. Alvin Fayette Lewis of one year, 1904–1905."[27] Dr. F. J. Bucher served as acting President from 1905 to 1908. He was followed by Dr. William M. Hudson, Class of 1892, who served until 1911. The leadership for the next three years was in the hands of Dr. Ezra F. Baker who was in turn succeeded by Dr. H. P. Houghton. When Dr. Houghton was called to the presidency of Carroll College in 1918, Dr. McKay was urged to take over the reins of the College once again. He began his work with vigor but before long a serious accident forced his retirement.

When the Presbyterian Church U.S.A. was merged with the Cumberland Presbyterian Church in 1906, Waynesburg was welcomed as one of the colleges in Western Pennsylvania under the control of our denomination. It reported to the Pennsylvania Synod and the Board of Christian Education. No close affiliation was established until 1949 when "an agreement was entered into between Waynesburg College and the Synod of Pennsylvania by which the College came directly under the control of the Presbyterian church. Its trustees and its President are henceforth to be approved by the Presbyterian Synod of Pennsylvania."[28]

This closer relationship to the Synod was one of the many achievements of the long presidency of Dr. Paul R. Stewart, the present President. He is an alumnus of Waynesburg College in the Class of 1909. He was chosen acting President of his Alma Mater during the early Summer of 1921 and assumed full control of the College a year and a half later. His long and successful service has marked the second era in the expansion and development of Waynesburg. Under his leadership, student enrollment has increased, a consecrated and capable faculty enlisted, and financial resources greatly enlarged. "Waynesburg College," remarked Senator Martin, "has been fortunate in having church leaders as its Presidents and as members of its faculty."[29]

Location and Buildings

The buildings and campus of the College are on the high ground that overlooks the downtown section of the community.[30] The first building, Hanna Hall, is now used for offices and classrooms, with the third floor utilized as a men's dormitory. Miller Hall, which was built as an administration building, is sufficiently large that it houses such facilities as the administration offices, classrooms, and a large auditorium. Walton Hall and the Day Corridors form a unit of construction which provides dormitory space for women, dining room accommodations, and recreational facilities. Sayers Manor, made possible through the gifts of Judge and Mrs. A. H. Sayers, has been set apart as a residence for upper-class women. Madison Hall contains classrooms, an auditorium, and a workshop for those interested in the field of drama. The Board has taken the original structure and, with the use of government funds, has remodeled it so that it now takes care of the departments of English and Drama.

The Old Mill, situated opposite to the gymnasium, was originally a flour mill built during the days of the Civil War. It now houses the Chemistry Department. A fine mansion, named Ivyhurst, was bequeathed to the College by the late Mrs. Robinson F. Downey of the Class of 1879 and is utilized by the departments of Music and Art. In 1955, the old Library in Miller Hall gave way to the pleasing new Library-Museum. The student-faculty joint effort, in transferring the books from the old to the new library, received publicity throughout the area. Another new endeavor is that of the Community Gymnasium which is a combined enterprise of the borough and the College. It is a center where both men and women may receive instruction in physical education. This building has been so arranged that it provides dormitory space for about one hundred men students. Recently the residence of Judge and Mrs. Challen W. Waychoff was purchased by the College and serves as a needed dormitory for women.

"Thirty-four properties have been added to our campus," reports Dr. Stewart, "including a number of buildings now being used as temporary residence halls. A few of these will have some permanency. Two dormitories have been completed. Another dormitory to accommodate one hundred and twenty-eight men is now rapidly rising. Ground will be broken for still another dining hall and a dormitory in a few days. Other buildings which we hope to see realized in the future are a science hall, a classroom building, and finally, above all and in the most commanding position overlooking the town, a chapel."[31]

Distinguished Graduates

When Waynesburg College observed its centennial in 1949–1950, a survey revealed a number of alumni who had attained distinction as measured by *Who's Who in America*.[32] Among those listed in the *Centennial Bulletin* are: "Stephen Leslie Mestrezat, 1869, who rose to a position on the bench of the Supreme Court of Pennsylvania; William Henry Black, 1876, who became President of Missouri Valley College, and in 1888 was Moderator of the Cumberland

Presbyterian Church; Albert Baird Cummins, LL.D., 1903, who served as Governor of Iowa and then as a United States Senator; William M. Hudson, 1892, who became President of the College and later President of Blackburn Junior College in Illinois; Thomas H. Hudson, 1894, a brother of the former, who was President Judge of Fayette County for many years."

One of the most prominent graduates of the College is Edward Martin of the Class of 1901. After a long and distinguished military career with the rank of major general, he rose to leadership in the affairs of state. He has served as Governor of the Commonwealth of Pennsylvania and is completing his second term as one of Pennsylvania's two United States Senators.

Since the Centennial Brochure was published, other names have been added from *Who's Who,* including Admiral Vane Morgan Hoge, 1925, since 1947 chief of the Medical Services Bureau in the United States; Thomas E. Morgan, 1930, physician and congressman; Sol Levine, 1938, head of the electronic and control department of the Glenn Martin Company; Dr. James Lewis, 1939, first assistant to Dr. Jonas Salk; and Roy E. Furman, 1922, the present Lieutenant Governor of Pennsylvania.[33]

Under the guidance of the Inter-Board Commission of the Board of Christian Education and the Board of National Missions of the Presbyterian Church U.S.A., Waynesburg has conducted a Student Service Project which serves the community through its churches and Sunday schools. This program not only assists in the training of Directors of Christian Education and pre-theological students, but also supplies a student ministry to Presbyterian churches as well as churches of other denominations in the area. Students engaging in this "circuit-riding" are eligible for special tuition rates.

Waynesburg College has long had the dream that it might become "the well spring of Christian leadership."[34] Its past and present contributions bid fair to the realization of this goal. "Dr. Miller and others closely related to the College believed that religious training should take precedence over any other cultural activity."[35] Dr. Stewart's thirty-seven years give added meaning to those words of testimony of Judge Knox. They strengthen the cherished hope that Waynesburg "is destined to be one of the foremost collegiate institutions under the Presbyterian banner."[36]

THE COLLEGE OF WOOSTER

Early in the nineteenth century, Presbyterian leaders of Ohio began thinking in terms of a college distinctly their own. Many of them had been trained at Princeton, Jefferson, or Washington colleges and were anxious to advance the Presbyterian tradition of education in their state. At this time, Ohio consisted of three synods: Ohio, covering the eastern and central part; Sandusky, the north and west; and Cincinnati, the south and western portions of the state. As early as the 1840's, the Reverend James Hoge of Columbus urged the three synods to collaborate in a Synod College.[37] From 1850 to 1865, locations such as Bellefontaine, Cleveland, Chillicothe, West Liberty, Hillsboro, Springfield, and others were considered. But the outbreak of the War Between the States and the failure of any community to raise the hundred thousand dollars suggested by the synods postponed the selection of a final site.

With the close of the war, the Reverend James A. Reed began a concentrated effort to have the College established at Wooster. He had been vividly impressed by an oak-crowned hilltop overlooking the town and in his mind's eye he saw the Wooster of tomorrow situated at this spot. Mr. Ephraim Quinbee, town banker and staunch Presbyterian, was easily persuaded to donate the whole tract of twenty acres if the college could be located there.[38] The synods showed interest. Soon the Rev. Mr. Reed was busily engaged in an endeavor to raise one hundred thousand dollars in the Wooster area. Encouraged by the prosperity that had come to Ann Arbor, Michigan, and Oberlin, Ohio, as a result of a college in their midst, Wooster reached its objective.

On December 18, 1866, the state certified the incorporation of the institution as the University of Wooster.[39] A year later all Presbyterian churches of Ohio joined in an effort to raise two hundred and fifty thousand dollars for an endowment fund. The Board of Trustees decided, on February 23, 1869, "to admit female students to the university upon entire equality with males."[40] On May 10, 1870, the University, as was the custom in that day, attached to itself the Charity Hospital Medical College of Cleveland as its Medical Department. It was some time later before a preparatory school could be added. While all of this was taking place, a main six-story structure was completed in preparation for the opening day. It was of such proportions that *The Presbyterian Banner* said of it, "This is the finest college building in the United States."[41] On the seventh of September, 1870, the trustees and the assembled dignitaries held the inaugural ceremonies for the first President, the Rev. Dr. Willis Lord.

The next day classes began with a faculty of five and a student body of thirty men and four women.[42] The faculty consisted of Professor Orange N. Stoddard, natural sciences; the Reverend W. H. Jeffers, Greek and Latin; Professor Samuel J. Kirkwood, mathematics and astronomy; the Reverend A. T. Fullerton, English language and literature; and Professor Robert C. Dalzell, modern languages.[43] Dr. Lord, with his commanding personality, gave the College its needed prestige from the beginning. After three years, he stepped aside because of ill health and was succeeded by the Rev. Dr. A. A. E. Taylor of Cincinnati.[44]

Dr. Taylor was something of a promoter and went throughout the synods securing both students and financial aid. The College under his ten-year regime made considerable progress. An observatory and a gymnasium were constructed, enrollment increased, new departments were organized, faculty was replaced in part and enlarged, and the endowment fund was strengthened. During this administration the College had its full share of student pranks which brought discipline and an occasional expulsion.

Progress Under Different Presidents

The next President was the Rev. Dr. Sylvester F. Scovel who came from the pastorate of the First Presbyterian Church of Pittsburgh in 1883.[45] His tenure of office, which covered sixteen years, began in a very quiet way but progressed to new heights. The faculty and the student body increased, new courses were added to the curriculum, more endowment was raised, and the wings to the main building were constructed. A substantial gift was received from Mr. Frederick Hoover of Sandusky, Ohio, for the erection of a residence for young women. Soon "Hoover Cottage" became the center of the expanded social life of the College. When Dr. Scovel's administration came to a close, it was said of him that "he had made his own right contribution to Wooster's life . . . he had widened Wooster's horizons. Most of all, he had given to the College in himself, a rare personality, vigorous, cultivated, reserved, sincere, and deeply spiritual."[46]

The Rev. Dr. Louis E. Holden was elected to the presidency in July of 1899.[47] With him came a new age for Wooster. He was a man of tremendous energy and vitality who was determined above all else to raise the standards of Wooster. The burning of Old Main in the early morning of December 11, 1901, seemed a great tragedy. Out of the ashes came a remarkable enthusiasm and determination to lift the College to new heights.

Dr. Holden had the temerity to approach such prominent men as Andrew Carnegie of New York, Louis H. Severance of Cleveland, and Henry Clay Frick of Pittsburgh. Substantial gifts were received from each of these men, but Carnegie's gift of one hundred thousand dollars was contingent upon the raising of a similar amount within sixty days. Once again the loyal supporters of Wooster rose to the challenge. Within a period of one year, five buildings were begun to replace the one which had been destroyed. The new Wooster was assured through the inspired leadership and devoted support of its President and Christian friends.[48]

During the years of the First World War, the College was led by Dr. John Campbell White, of the Class of 1890, who had been both a missionary and world Y.M.C.A. leader. He was succeeded by the Rev. Dr. Charles F. Wishart who served the College for a quarter of a century. Under his administration the College progressed through years of changing prosperity, depression, and war. The physical plant, the endowment, the faculty, the student body, and the place of the College in the Church and society were strengthened. Dr. Howard F. Lowry has been President since 1944. He carries on the traditions of advancement and progress at Wooster.

Leaders in All Walks of Life

The University of Wooster graduated its first class in 1871 and, from that time to the present, many of her alumni have attained distinction. *Who's Who* (1955–1956) lists eighty-nine alumni and former students, twenty-nine honorary alumni, five faculty members (non-alumni), and one graduate department alumnus.[49] Only a few of the many noteworthy alumni can be listed herein: W. Rush Taggart, 1871, vice-president and general counsel of Western Union; S. Hall Young, 1875, prominent Alaskan missionary; James H. Hyslop, 1877, famous psychologist and professor at New York University; Mrs. Ella Alexander Boole, 1878, long-time president of the National and World W.C.T.U.; Dr. Johnson Fleming, 1898, missionary and professor of missions at Union Theological Seminary.

Other famous alumni include Harry M. Gage, 1900, president of both Huron and Coe colleges; Robert C. Caldwell, 1904, former ambassador to Portugal and Department of State adviser; Albert I. Good, 1906, veteran missionary to Africa and ornithologist; Herbert Rice, 1906, president of Forman Christian College, India; Robert D. Workman, 1913, chief of Navy Chaplains and Rear Admiral; Keith C. Seele, 1922, Egyptologist and professor at the University of Chicago; and TzeTong Teng, 1924, Major General of the Chinese

Army on Formosa. Four graduates have been chosen as moderators of the General Assembly of the Presbyterian church: Samuel S. Palmer, Jesse H. Baird, Hugh Ivan Evans, and Paul Wright.

A closer look at the careers of a few alumni will serve to give a clearer conception of Wooster's accomplishments. Prominent in the list of early graduates was Jonas O. Notestein of the Class of 1873. He gave his entire life to the College as professor of Latin language and literature. He edited the *Wooster Quarterly* for more than thirty years. His daughter Lucy wrote the book, *Wooster of the Middle West,* using her father's notes as a nucleus for background material.

One could not attempt to write the story of Wooster, however brief, without some reference to the Compton family. Elias Compton finished his undergraduate work at Wooster in 1881 and his divinity work at Western Theological Seminary in 1883. He returned to his Alma Mater immediately and for forty-five years taught such courses as English, Latin, and Philosophy. Throughout the greater part of that period, he was Dean of the College and in 1919 served as acting President.[50]

His four children all have distinguished themselves in one field or another. Dr. Arthur Compton, 1913, winner of the Nobel prize in 1927, has long been a distinguished physicist and educator. He made notable contributions in the field of atomic research during the war years and then became Chancellor of Washington University in St. Louis.[51] Wilson M. Compton, of the Class of 1911, prepared for a career in economics and industry. He has published several books on economics, and has served as a professor and as a former president of Washington State College. Until recently he was chairman of the Council for the Advancement of Small Colleges.[52]

Karl T. Compton, of the Class of 1908, distinguished himself in the field of physics and administration. He was called in 1930 to be President of the Massachusetts Institute of Technology where he served until his recent death.[53] Mary, who became the wife of

Dr. C. Herbert Rice, served as a missionary in India and worked with her husband in providing leadership for the Forman Christian College. She now lives with her husband in retirement at Wooster.

Carl V. Weygandt, 1912, is another noted graduate. Since 1933 he has been a Chief Justice of the State Supreme Court of Ohio. Robert E. Wilson, 1914, went from Wooster, where he received Magna Cum Laude honors, to M.I.T. where he studied chemical engineering. In 1922 he became associated with Standard Oil of Indiana and has been chief executive officer since 1945. He is now chairman of the Board of Trustees at Wooster and Weygandt is vice-chairman.[54]

No survey of Wooster's alumni would be complete without reference to Howard F. Lowry, President since 1944. He finished his undergraduate work in 1923 and received his Ph.D. degree from Yale in 1931. He served the College as instructor and professor from 1923 to 1925 and from 1929 to 1940. He then became professor of English at Princeton University, which position he held until he was recalled to his Alma Mater, this time as President.[55] Wooster has flourished under his exceptional leadership and his progressive educational policies.

A New Approach to Education

Wooster has prided herself for a dozen years upon her new approach to the program of education. Yet in no way has she altered her basic principle of maintaining a Christian emphasis in the teaching of liberal arts and sciences. The *Adventure in Education* is a part of an organic growth within the college's heritage.

Under this plan the Wooster student is asked to know "something (1) of the achievements in the arts which we call the humanities and the workings of his own mind, and (2) of the eternal values studied in philosophy and religion; these are combined in Group I of our new curriculum. The student at Wooster is asked to know something also (3) of the world of nature and scientific method (Group II) and (4) of the society in which he lives, works, and has a part to play (Group III). The pattern seeks finally some over-all meaning and integration."[56]

This pattern necessarily involves pursuance of general and special courses. The plan is termed "bifocal" in that it gives the student an opportunity to change from "a near view to a far view and back again." The first two years follow somewhat the usual liberal education policy of a Christian college. The Junior and Senior years show a distinct change in method with two-fifths of the student hours given to the major and closely related fields; two-fifths to courses outside the major field; and one-fifth to an independent study in the major field under the direction of a faculty adviser and with departmental supervision.

"This implies that a student in his Junior year will begin an investigation of some special topic. He shows evidence of his progress through the writing of several papers or the carrying out of a significant investigation. Near the end of this year he takes an examination in his major. In the Senior year, he is prepared to write a more comprehensive paper or solve a more intricate problem. He is required to pass a comprehensive examination 'over the general field of his major study.'"

A Synodical College

Wooster passed into the ownership and control of the consolidated new Synod of Ohio in 1882 making it a "Synod College." Since 1914 it has been called The College of Wooster. The Women's Advisory Board, which was established in 1892, concerns itself with the problems and interests of women students and the support of women's church groups of the Synod.

In recent years there has been a phenomenal growth in the physical plant. The latest buildings which were added to the campus are: Matthew Andrews Hall (1954), a dormitory for men; Otelia Compton Hall (1955), a residence for women; and Wagner Hall (1957), another dormitory for women.[57] The pre-Centennial development brochure lists a total of ten new buildings that the College hopes to build out of the twenty million dollar development program goal.[58] Wooster has clung tenaciously over the years to an ideal stated in the articles of incorporation, namely, the "Promotion of sound learning and education under religious influence."[59] Herein lies part of the secret that has made Wooster great and placed her in the upper bracket of educational institutions.

Today, of the several Presbyterian colleges of the Upper Ohio Valley, there is none more closely allied to the Church than Wooster, nor more outstanding in the list of American colleges.

GROVE CITY COLLEGE

Grove City College was the last of our Presbyterian higher educational institutions to be organized and to continue in expanding service throughout the Upper Ohio Valley. It is located in a community of eight thousand people, about sixty miles north of Pittsburgh. Like most of our other colleges, it began as an academy.

Mr. Richard M. Thompson, who later entered the ministry, organized a select school there in the Summer of 1858.[60] He continued his school until 1864 when the Reverend William F. Dickson, the new pastor of the Presbyterian congregation, and his wife accepted responsibility for continuing the school.[61] They were gifted educators and gave the school considerable prestige throughout the area. The early catalogues of the Academy gave much credit to these early founders of the select school of Pine Grove, as the town was then known.[62]

When the Dicksons moved from Pine Grove to Coultersville (West Sunbury), Pennsylvania, a good leader was needed to carry on their work. The future of the Academy seemed uncertain, but a young man, Isaac Conrad Ketler, indicated his willingness to assume the leadership. He had done well in the school of the Scrub Grass community near Emlenton before he decided to take up the work at Pine Grove. In April of 1876, he reopened the community's select school, or Academy, with only thirteen students enrolled.

The first term was so great a success that when the fall term began, eighty students were in attendance. Mr. Samuel R. McClelland, one of the original pupils, was employed as an assistant. Soon two more instructors were added, Miss Emma McConnell and Mr. S. L. Black, both in the field of music. The first Board of Trustees consisted of five local men.

The Pine Grove Normal Academy received its charter in 1879 and sold capital stock to take care of its expenses.[63] The original four acres of the campus had been a part of the farm of Mr. J. G. Cunningham and was in the middle of his orchard.[64] Soon the Academy building was erected and as many as five hundred and thirty-eight students were enrolled. A dormitory for ladies and a twelve-room music hall were in use by the Fall term of 1883.[65]

From an Academy to a College

In these early days, the trustees had planned a curriculum which included business, music, teacher training, and college preparatory work. But the idea of having a college was foremost in their thinking. The Court of Common Pleas of Mercer County authorized this necessary change in the charter as of November 21, 1884. The Academy became Grove City College. The full-fledged College enlarged its curriculum to include scientific and advanced classical courses of study. To its physical plant the trustees, through the sale of more stock, were able to add in 1888 an administration building. This was a large brick structure of four stories which was very much needed.[66] In the years immediately before 1900, Dr. Ketler had a strong faculty with men, such as James B. McClelland, John A. Courtney, Frank W. Hays, Samuel Dodds, Hermann Poehlman, Alva J. Calderwood, and others.[67]

It was evident to Dr. Ketler that the College could not progress far under its system as a stock corporation. Assured of the support of such men as Joseph N. Pew, W. L. Pierce, Samuel P. Harbison, A. P. Burchfield, Edward O'Neil, the Reverend J. T. Gibson, and others of the Pittsburgh area, Dr. Ketler went to his Board of fifteen trustees with a daring plan. There were more than two hundred and fifty persons who held stock, ranging from one share, worth ten dollars, to two hundred shares, worth two thousand dollars. These stockholders were asked in a meeting, November 3, 1894, to surrender their stock. Dr. Ketler assured all that the College would remain solidly Christian and with only limited denominational control. The votes of the stockholders were cast and "it must ever be to the honor of the community that the desired change was made without one dissenting vote."[68] This was definitely a tribute to Dr. Ketler's leadership and was a vote of confidence from the townspeople.

The amended charter of December 10, 1894, made it possible for the Board of Trustees to be increased to thirty. In the following January, the Board was reorganized with fifteen new members. The new men included five ministers, a substantial group of Pittsburgh businessmen, and others from the nearby scene. The stockholding feature was eliminated and the College then took its place "in the class of eleemosynary or charitable institutions."[69] Mr. Joseph N. Pew was elected President of the Board and served in this capacity until his death in 1912. Under his leadership the College enlarged its physical plant and academic program. The faculty was further increased; the new emphasis on science resulted in the construction of an addition to the Administration Building; a new Library was secured as a gift from Andrew Carnegie; the building of a gymnasium; and plans for a dormitory for men—all were among the accomplishments of this era.

Shortly after the College began, a six-weeks' Summer School term was instituted. By 1892 this was lengthened to a ten-weeks' term. Some eighteen years later, Dr. Ketler wrote in the College catalogue, "As yet Grove City is the only institution (of Pennsylvania) offering a Summer term of full college value."[70]

A Popular Summer Bible School

The next forward step was the establishing of a Summer Bible

School in 1897. A School of Philosophy was also established for those who wished to do graduate study during a summer session and follow-up work throughout the year.[71] Throughout this summer session, the mornings were given over to lectures, the afternoons to personal conferences and fellowship, and the evenings to popular meetings. Some of the world's outstanding clergymen and professors were brought to the campus. The expected annual deficit was divided between Mr. Joseph N. Pew and Mr. Samuel P. Harbison. It was not uncommon to have as many as four hundred enrolled.[72] The summer faculty included at times Dr. Borden P. Bowne of Boston University, Dean A. T. Ormond of Princeton University, Sir William Ramsay of Aberdeen, Scotland, Professor Robert Dick Wilson of Princeton Seminary, and nearly a dozen other leaders. Little wonder a large enrollment was attracted.[73]

Dr. Ketler and Mr. Pew in Partnership

The years of 1912 and 1913 saw the loss, through death, of the President of the Board of Trustees and the President of the College. Mr. Pew and Dr. Ketler had worked as a team through the years. The story has been told of Mr. Pew's request to Isaac Ketler to go into the petroleum industry with him at Parker City. At that time Mr. Pew had said: "Why don't you give up teaching and go into the oil business with me?" Later Dr. Ketler visited Mr. Pew in Pittsburgh and said, "Years ago you asked me to go into business with you. Now I have come to ask you to go into business with me."[74] Mr. Samuel P. Harbison and other business and religious leaders approved the work at the College and Mr. Pew indicated his willingness to invest in the program of educating young people.[75] What a wonderful investment this was and how well he upheld the hands of Dr. Ketler!

In the last Board meeting before Mr. Pew's death, it was recommended that consideration be given Mr. Pew's son, J. Howard Pew, a 1900 graduate of the College, and to his nephew, Mr. John G. Pew, as possible members of the Board. The names were submitted and approved that day. "The action seemed almost prophetic, because in the following October, Mr. Pew died unexpectedly at his desk from a heart attack."[76] Dr. Ketler had lost a lifetime friend and the College a loyal supporter.

Dr. Isaac Ketler was a real son of the Upper Ohio Valley. Although not born in the area, he had grown up at Blacktown near Pine Grove. He received his education at the Edinboro Normal School in Edinboro, Pennsylvania; the National University at Lebanon, Ohio; and at Wooster University. In 1888 he graduated from Western Theological Seminary in Pittsburgh and was ordained to the Presbyterian ministry.[77]

When Sir William Ramsay stepped to the railway platform in Grove City in the Summer of 1913, he learned of the sudden death of Dr. Ketler. Two years later he wrote an estimate of Dr. Ketler's educational work in which he said, "It was in the nobility and boldness of his educational idea that Ketler's supreme merit lay . . . He was a creative president for he made a college out of nothing . . . Dr. Ketler was a man of strong religious feeling . . . It was his courage that carried him through every difficulty. He was a strong man, absolutely devoid of fear, and winning the respect ultimately of almost every opponent."[78] Today, forty-five years later, to the older residents of Grove City, Dr. Isaac Ketler remains the vivid, forceful, dynamic character that he was during the formative years of the College. In his funeral sermon, Dr. William J. McConkey compared Dr. Ketler to Moses—so great was the stature of the man.[79]

Weir Ketler Chosen President

The presidency of the Board of Trustees was entrusted to Mr. Frederick R. Babcock and the mantle of the College presidency fell upon Dr. Alexander T. Ormond, professor of Philosophy at Princeton University. Less than two years later, Mr. Babcock revealed to Dr. Ormond, when the two were discussing the young Mr. Weir Ketler, that the youth was being groomed to succeed someday to the presidency. Little did Mr. Babcock know that before the year would pass, Dr. Ormond was to suffer a heart attack and die. On December 20, 1915, Weir C. Ketler was made acting President and the following June, President.[80]

The young Dr. Ketler, a graduate of Grove City in the Class of 1908, had done postgraduate work at Yale. He began his work with the same consecrated and devoted zeal that had characterized his father. In the first year, the endowment was increased by more than one hundred thousand dollars. The business course was reorganized by him so that it included two years of regular college subjects and two years of business subjects. Mr. J. Howard Pew and Dr. Isaac Ketler had decided, shortly before the latter's death, that the site for the men's dormitory, in memory of Joseph N. Pew, should be on the high elevation across Wolf Creek from the College campus.

New Buildings on the Upper Campus

It became the privilege of the young Dr. Ketler to develop the idea of an Upper Campus adjoining the Memorial dormitory. In this he was ably assisted by Mr. J. Howard Pew, who became to him what the elder Pew had been to the elder Ketler. In 1922 a large tract of land east of Wolf Creek was purchased from the McMillan family, and in 1930 the Washabaugh property of forty acres lying east of the McMillan property was added. The building program on the Upper Campus began in 1929. Mr. W. L. Clause of Pittsburgh was then the President of the Board. Before long he was succeeded by Mr. J. Howard Pew. Mr. Pew, aided by the other members of the Board, and the President of the College have shown brilliant and devoted leadership throughout the ensuing years in the execution of the Master Plan.

Harbison Chapel and the Hall of Science were the first units to be constructed. These were dedicated in 1931. A year later the Isaac C. Ketler men's dormitory was completed. In another few years a very large dormitory for girls was built by the Pew families in memory of Mary Anderson Pew, wife of Joseph N. Pew. Then followed a magnificent administration building as the result primarily of the gift of Harry J. Crawford, long a trustee. Shortly afterward Lincoln Hall, a dormitory for men; West Hall, an addition to Mary Anderson Pew Dormitory; and South Hall, a residence for men, were added. Since 1950, a new Recreational and Alumni building, as well as the Henry Buhl Library building, have been constructed. All of these buildings are magnificently equipped and represent an investment of several million dollars. In addition to these physical improvements, the faculty was enlarged, salaries were increased, and the enrollment reached its highest peak in the history of the College.

All this steady progress took place during the years under Dr. Weir C. Ketler, in spite of two World Wars, the Korean War, and the depression years of the late twenties and the thirties. He is well known, admired, and respected throughout the land in educational circles and many honors have been heaped upon him. He retired July 1, 1956, after forty years of devoted service as President. Even as the older people of the community honor and revere the memory of Dr. Isaac Ketler, so they, and those of lesser years who have known his son, realize what a lasting monument a consecrated father and son have built to the cause of education and Christianity, not only in the Upper Ohio Valley, but throughout the world where their influence has been felt.

Stanley Harker Succeeds Weir Ketler

Since July of 1956, Dr. J. Stanley Harker of the Class of 1925, a Presbyterian clergyman and a 1950 Ph.D. graduate of the University of Pittsburgh, has been President of the College. After four pastorates, he became President of Alma College, Alma, Michigan, in 1951. Through tireless efforts he raised the financial and scholastic standards of that Synod College. In his short term of office at Grove City, there has been a determined effort to continue the growth of the College through the enlargement of the faculty, the raising of salaries, and other progressive measures. The old Carnegie Library building has been converted into a Music Hall and other buildings on the Lower Campus have undergone remodeling. A commodious new home for the President has been constructed at the entrance to the Upper Campus. A new classroom building is now under construction in a quadrangle near the Buhl Library and the recreational buildings. These continued improvements and developments have been the result largely of Mr. J. Howard Pew's inspiring leadership. Greater things still lie ahead for Grove City College which has come forward rapidly since 1884.

Some Distinguished Alumni

Grove City has its list of graduates who have made notable contributions to human welfare. In addition to those previously mentioned, the College points with pride to the Rev. Dr. Frank E. Simcox and his wife, May Gilson Simcox, both of the Class of 1890, who were missionaries in China until martyred in the tragedy of Paotingfu during the Boxer Rebellion; Richard D. Laird, 1894, Judge of Westmoreland County Court for many years; Alva J. Calderwood, 1896, professor of Latin for fifty years and dean of the College; the Reverend Harry A. Rhoades, 1904, long associated with the Chosen Christian College and Mission, Seoul, Korea; Harold W. Dodds, 1909, former President of Princeton University; F. Paul McConkey, 1909, prominent Presbyterian clergyman; Walter E. Page, 1911, Eastman Company research scientist; Creig S. Hoyt, 1913, chemist of renown and recent Dean of the College; George C. Southworth, 1914, engineer in physics for A.T.&T. and Bell laboratories; Frank D. McClelland, 1921, former President of Pikeville College and now Dean of Maryville College; John F. Bohlender, surgeon and Major General in the Military; Clifford M. Bowden, 1925, prominent New York lawyer; Alexander M. Slavcoff, 1927, nationally known urologist; Frank J. Soday, 1929, research chemist and vice-president of Chemstrand; R. Heath Larry, 1934, Pittsburgh lawyer and administrative vice-president of United States Steel Corporation. These and many others show the diversified contribution which the College has made to the life of the nation and the world.

During the founding days of the College, J. N. Pew wrote to Isaac Ketler, "Make the College healthful, for that is essential. Make it beautiful, for that is an education."[81] That bit of wisdom has been the dynamic conviction which has guided the institution through the years. Since its founding, the College has endorsed a liberal arts and science program. It is affiliated with the Presbyterian Church U.S.A. and operates under the Presbyterian Standards for Colleges.[82]

CHAPTER XIV The Mount of Sacred Science

"Wherever Presbyterians went, they carried a demand for education. Piety and learning were never separated; and the crowning glory of all education was the study of theology."[1] Those words, taken from a recent catalogue of Western Theological Seminary, might well be a summary of the motivation and determination of the Founding Fathers of the Presbyterian church throughout the Upper Ohio Valley.

In spite of the pressure of essential tasks in organizing and administering to expanding congregations and the need of missionary journeys throughout an ever-widening frontier, these pioneer pastors set before themselves the task of training young men to preach and serve as pastors in newly settled areas. Though Western Seminary was not established by the General Assembly until 1825, many capable ministers had been educated, trained, and ordained by Redstone and Ohio presbyteries in the years of difficult beginnings through the consecrated zeal of that notable trio of pastor-teachers: John McMillan, Joseph Smith, and Thaddeus Dod. The organization of Western Theological Seminary in Alleghenytown was the culmination of continued interest in theological education which had an untiring advocate in the personality and leadership of Dr. McMillan.

If Western Seminary were disposed to press reasonable claims to priority and the prestige of age, it could date its beginning from the year 1785. The scene is the kitchen of the Reverend Joseph

Smith's log cabin in Upper Buffalo in Washington County. Three earnest young men had accepted his invitation to study for the Presbyterian ministry. All three—James McGready, Samuel Porter, and Joseph Patterson—proved themselves to be diligent students, and later famous preachers.[2] Joseph Smith's training school for ministers was not the earliest venture in education since both John McMillan and Thaddeus Dod had begun teaching academic subjects as early as 1782.[3] Soon the three original students were joined with two others, James Hughes and John Brice, from Dod's school. The curriculum included languages, the arts, and theology, as essentials to a well-educated ministry. Three years of study, using such books as were available, but depending chiefly on their pastor-teacher, were necessary before Redstone Presbytery deemed three of these young men sufficiently well trained to be licensed to preach.[4]

Because of declining health, in 1787 or 1788, Joseph Smith turned his pupils over to John McMillan for continued instruction in theology. McMillan's one-room log cabin college has since been removed to Canonsburg where it is still a revered shrine.

THE FIRST STAGE—VOLUNTEER LOG CABIN SCHOOLS

The pioneer efforts of Smith and McMillan to educate young men for a frontier ministry marks the first stage of theological education in Western Pennsylvania. It is the stage where one man on his own initiative and in his own home sought to meet a vital need of preparing young men for the mighty task of preaching the Gospel. The school which John Anderson, the pioneer minister of the Associate Church (now United Presbyterian), opened in a two-story log building adjoining his home at Service Creek in 1794, is a similar illustration of this first stage of theological training.[5]

In order to recreate the general atmosphere of life and thought in a Western Pennsylvania Presbyterian community of this period, let us read the words of the Reverend Richard Lea who, though living a few years later than the period under consideration, painted the following vivid picture:

"The West was just settling . . . traveling difficult, money scarce, everything tended to form an independent race, who 'trusted God and kept their powder dry'. . .The family altars burned brightly. The catechisms were taught to the children. The church was filled . . . Books were few . . . Pastors were expected to have the 'five points' of doctrine in their morning prayer, to extemporize two sermons, explain the psalm, avoid hymns and manuscripts, must visit the sick, preach funeral sermons, and were always welcomed at 'Log rollings,' made Captains at the 'husking frolic,' partook of the best bed, the best food, and the best whiskey their parishioners could afford . . . The preachers held to the literal interpretation of the Bible. Creation was God's Word, spoken about six thousand years ago. Man was not with these fathers ever a molecule, or a monkey. The fall was not a myth. Job's trials were real . . . and those terrible words 'weeping, wailing, gnashing of teeth, the worm which never dieth, the fire which shall never be quenched, the impassable gulf, and the vengeance of eternal fire' did not mean conscience only, or some punishment ending with more or less speed."[6]

The wilderness of the western country demanded a tough, fibrous resiliency in the men who were to confront it. The education and culture of the pioneer preachers had come from eastern colleges which, in turn, had received it from British and Scottish universities where Reformation and Renaissance had combined to produce the ideal of the learned and dedicated Christian gentlemen. The first settled pastors on the frontier sought to uphold the educational ideal which was firmly established by Roger Ascham and the Christian Humanists of Tudor and Puritan England. It was a combination of religious piety, respect for the reasoning intellect, and appreciation of the mellowing values and the moral grandeur of the best Greek and Latin literature. The Latin the boys were learning was a key to open not only the treasures of Virgil and Horace, but also the classic doctrines of Reformation theology.

THE SECOND STAGE—PRESBYTERY-SUSTAINED SCHOOLS OF THEOLOGY

The second stage was the fostering of a theological school by church judicatories. In 1791 the Synod of Virginia passed a resolution which was to have historic significance in furthering theological education. The resolution in part reads: "That the Synod of Virginia undertake the patronage of a seminary of learning for the purpose of educating young men for the Gospel ministry. The Synod recommends that there be two general institutions for learning conducted under the patronage of this body; one to be established in Rockbridge County, Virginia, under the care of the Reverend William Graham as the president, and the other in Washington County, Pennsylvania, under the care of the Reverend John McMillan . . . The Presbytery of Redstone shall superintend the Seminary in Washington County."[7]

Further, it was the desire of Synod that, where necessary, presbyteries subsidize the education of capable young men at these approved theological schools. Listen to this forward-looking resolution: "As there are a number of pious youth in our country, who might be very serviceable in preaching the gospel, but through want of sufficient ability are unable to obtain an education, it is the intention and desire of Synod that the ministers in their respective presbyteries shall seek out such, and that they, being examined and approved by the Presbytery, shall be placed in the respective seminaries, at the expense of the Presbytery who shall approve them."[8] Churches were instructed to raise funds for this laudable purpose. The money was to be regarded as a loan, not a gift. "These youths, upon obtaining their education, at the expiration of one year after being settled, shall begin to refund to the treasury the expenses of their education in such time and manner as the Presbytery shall direct."

On October 18, 1792, the Presbytery of Redstone "unanimously agreed to appoint Canonsburg to be the site of that institution which they are appointed by Synod to superintend." In subsequent minutes of Presbytery, there are evidences of the fidelity with which the Redstone Presbytery accepted its responsibility, a responsibility which the Presbytery of Ohio shared following its organization in 1793. The minimum time to be spent by young men in the study of divinity before they could be taken on trials for the ministry was lengthened to three years at the suggestion of General Assembly.[9] Committees of the two presbyteries were appointed to attend and to review the work of the Canonsburg Academy, to examine the students, and to raise contributions for the support of the Academy. The idea of an educated ministry, which is part of the Calvinistic tradition, must be upheld even amid the difficulties of pioneer life when demands for clergymen exceeded the meager supply.

When Canonsburg Academy became Jefferson College in 1802, Dr. McMillan was given the formal title of Professor of Divinity.[10] "His mode of teaching was by written lectures, containing a complete system of theology. This system the students transcribed, and were expected to recite literally. It contained a concise discussion of all the principal doctrines, with copious notes and quotations from Scripture. It was concise, condensed, lucid, and forcible."[11] So highly was this theological department of Jefferson College regarded that, in 1814, the college appointed a committee "to prepare and present to the Synod of Pittsburgh at its next meeting, praying that measures may be taken for erecting and maintaining a Divinity Hall to be connected with the college."[12]

No action on this request of the college was taken by the Synod. Perhaps meager financial resources made the plan seem impractical at that time. However, in 1821, Synod felt the need of strengthening Dr. McMillan's department of theology by improving its library facilities:

"Whereas, it appears to this Synod that a number of promising young men who are setting their faces toward the Gospel ministry, are not in circumstances to attend the Theological Seminary at Princeton; therefore, Resolved that this Synod take measures for procuring a library for the benefit of such, to be under the control and direction of this Synod. That it be recommended to every member to solicit books or moneys for this important purpose, and that this library be located at present in the edifice of Jefferson College at Canonsburg and placed under the care of the Reverend John McMillan, D.D., Professor of Theology in that Seminary."[13]

But Dr. McMillan was getting old. The end of his teaching at Jefferson College was drawing nigh. The torch of theological education must pass to younger hands. A new era in the training of Presbyterian ministers was already beginning. General Assembly, not the Presbytery nor the Synod, was to carry forward a task so nobly begun on the western frontier. It has been estimated by Dr. Matthew Brown, the first President of Washington College, that at least a hundred ministers had received their theological education under Dr. McMillan.[14] Some authorities put the number as high as two hundred. Of the first twenty-eight on the roll of Erie Presbytery, embracing a period of twenty years of its history, twenty-two pursued their theological studies in the West and no less than eighteen at Dr. McMillan's Log Cabin.[15] McMillan, both in his Log Cabin and at Jefferson College, had carried forward with enriching success the theological training which Joseph Smith had initiated in his wife's kitchen in 1785.

THE THIRD STAGE—THE GENERAL ASSEMBLY SPONSORED SEMINARY

The rapid growth of the church and the demand for more and more ministers soon made inadequate both the isolated, one-teacher household school and such theological training as was available at Jefferson College and similar institutions. A general philosophy of post-college theological training was forming within the church. Certain tensions were contributory factors. The faith needed new and freshly trained defenders against eighteenth-century rationalism, which was coming across the Atlantic from England and the Continent. The piety of pentecostal excitement or of introspective quiescence was in tension with the Reformed faith, resting as it did upon creed and demonstrable logic. The independence of pioneer Presbyterians and the isolation of the students in training for the ministry were endangering the unity of thought and opinion of the various church courts. The call to carry the Gospel to the American Indian and, later, to the heathen in distant countries was increasingly urgent.

Out of consideration of these and other problems there emerged the idea of a school separated from the college for the exclusive training of ministers. The Plan of Princeton Theological Seminary is the literary monument of this movement. It was written almost unaided by Ashbel Green and resulted in the establishment of that Seminary by the General Assembly in 1812.[16] This became, in turn, the plan of Western Theological Seminary, which was established in Alleghenytown, Pennsylvania, in 1825, as the result of much agitation by the Synod of Pittsburgh for a second theological seminary to be developed in the West.

The site selected was not Canonsburg, though that seemed to be the logical location and the Synod of Pittsburgh had previously expressed a preference for the scene of Dr. McMillan's pioneer school.[17] Thirteen communities bid for the privilege of having a seminary in their midst. Alleghenytown offered what seemed to General Assembly to be the most favorable bid and the most advantageous location. Alleghenytown became the permanent home of General Assembly's second venture into the realm of theological education.[18]

Other denominations in the Reformed tradition, such as the Dutch Reformed, the Associate Presbyterian, and the Associate Reformed, had already founded schools for the training of ministers at New Brunswick, New Jersey, Service, Pennsylvania, and New York City. In the same year in which Western Seminary was established by the Presbyterian church, the Associate Reformed Synod of the West opened its school in Pittsburgh.[19] The actual holding of classes of Western Theological Seminary in the session room of the First Presbyterian Church of Pittsburgh in 1827, with four students and two instructors, was merely the final step in an unbroken line of theological education that began with Joseph Smith and his household school and expanded under the teaching of John McMillan at the Canonsburg Academy and Jefferson College.[20]

The one seminary at Princeton, New Jersey, was inadequate. The entire sweep of territory from the Alleghenies to the Mississippi was being rapidly populated. Ohio, Indiana, and to a certain extent, Kentucky, were the states to be served by the church, together with Western Pennsylvania and Western Virginia. The attractive offer of the citizens of Alleghenytown of a large section of the public commons, including the imposing hill opposite Mt. Washington, where one could watch the main water route West, the Ohio River, won over all other offers.

Western Theological Seminary

On October 16, 1828, there was a meeting of the Synod of Pittsburgh in the First Presbyterian Church of Pittsburgh called for the purpose of installing the Reverend Jacob J. Janeway as first professor in the new Western Theological Seminary. Classes had already been conducted for almost a year under the instruction of the Reverend Joseph Stockton and the Reverend Elisha P. Swift. The meeting was opened with prayer by Dr. John McMillan. Dr. Swift then entered the pulpit to deliver the sermon of installation. It was a notable address and an eloquent statement on the purpose of theological education. After speaking of the need of an educated ministry, Dr. Swift proceeded to consider the need of schools for this educated ministry:

"By theological seminaries, I intend, all such public institutions as make it their distinct and leading aim to superintend, direct, and facilitate the professional studies and sacred researches of young men, intended for the ministry, in their acquisition of Biblical, theological, and experimental literature. While this definition does not exclude such institutions as comprise only a few pupils, under the care of a single teacher, or those which form, as is the case with most of the established churches in Europe, but a separate department in a university; it applies especially to such distinct seminaries, whether at home or abroad, as are founded in charity and prayer, for the purposes of sacred literature alone, as have a competent endowment, a sufficient number of approved professors, and a valuable collection of choice and approved works."

At another point in the sermon Dr. Swift says:

"... How favorable must such fraternities of young men, all alike professedly devoted to the service of an eventful ministry; comprising many whom pious charity has searched out and brought forward and put in the track of so sublime and glorious a destiny: dwelling in edifices, and amidst repositories of learning, all consecrated solely to the service and honor of Jesus Christ; furnished with earthly incentive to the cultivation of piety and Biblical knowledge; where kindred hearts mutually warm and quicken each other; where a sort of standard of attainment, of piety, and talent is formed, and no useful means of devolving human powers of moral excellencies are overlooked; where intellect coming into collision with intellect, in all the intimacies of daily companionship are stimulated and sharpened for a generous and sacred contest for excellence; in fine, where asperities and defects of character and habit are likely to be corrected; where those prejudices which obscure religion, and those fears and conceptions which becloud it are likely to be removed, while brotherly love and lasting friendships are cemented, and the heart, under every variety of instruction, and every form of intercourse is moved to the earnest pursuit of personal holiness."[21]

Such was the high and noble vision of theological education in the Upper Ohio Valley one hundred and thirty years ago. As we reflect on this sermon, we see that the prime concern is the formation of character in the theological student. The task confronting the church was simple. The western development of the country needed churches and ministers; the ministers must be strong, able, culturally self-sufficient and dedicated. Dr. Swift himself was from New England, educated at Williams College and Princeton Seminary, and at one time hopeful of serving on the foreign mission field. His life and work, however, centered in Pittsburgh. His hand was in education, both secular and theological, in missions, and in the pastorate. There was no phase of the church life of his day with which he was not familiar. He spoke on the subject of theological education with the authority of wide experience.

The First Edifice

Not only was there a high and noble vision of education enunciated by the very able speaker; there was also a high and noble edifice in the process of construction on the hill overlooking the confluence of the Monongahela and Allegheny rivers and the rise of the Ohio. Dr. Swift in his sermon (probably with a directing gesture) spoke of "yonder hill, already designated as the mount of sacred science." A committee had been appointed by the Board of Directors of the Seminary to draw up plans for a building. The tersely worded instructions speak only of an "edifice not exceeding in dimensions the Theological Seminary at Princeton, three stories high." The hill itself was to have beautiful drives and walks, terraces, arbors, and fountains.

Even though the completed structure and its setting never fulfilled the lofty dreams of the Board, yet it was an impressive accomplishment. The building consisted of a central edifice, sixty feet in length by fifty in breadth, of four stories having at each front a portico adorned with Corinthian columns, and a cupola in the center; also, two wings, of three stories each, fifty feet by twenty-five. It contained a chapel with a gallery for the library; suites of rooms for professors, rooms for the steward, and about eighty dormitory accommodations for students.

There was a conscious attempt to express in structure and setting

WESTERN THEOLOGICAL SEMINARY, ALLEGHENYTOWN, PA.
First Building. Erected, 1831. Destroyed by fire, 1854.

COURTESY OF WESTERN THEOLOGICAL SEMINARY

HERRON HALL
Central building of the Quadrangle. Erected, 1915.
Used for classrooms and administration.

PROFESSORS AT WESTERN THEOLOGICAL SEMINARY

REVEREND
DAVID ELLIOTT, D.D.
Professor of Theology, 1836–1871. Moderator of General Assembly, 1837.

REVEREND
JOHN WILLIAMSON NEVIN, D.D.
Professor of Church History, 1829–1839.

PROFESSORS AT WESTERN THEOLOGICAL SEMINARY

REVEREND
MATTHEW BROWN
RIDDLE, D.D.
Professor of New Testament Literature, 1887–1916.

REVEREND
JAMES ANDERSON
KELSO, D.D.
Professor of Hebrew and Old Testament Literature, 1897–1943. President, 1908–1943.

COURTESY OF GEORGE SWETNAM

MRS. CHARLES BEATTY
Founder with her husband of Steubenville Female Academy and generous contributor to other educational institutions.

MRS. MARY COPLEY THAW
Generous contributor to Presbyterian causes. Member, Third Presbyterian Church, Pittsburgh, Pa.

COURTESY OF SHARPSBURG PRESBYTERIAN CHURCH, SHARPSBURG, PA.

MISS MARTHA E. KELLY
Missionary to Japan, 1894–1901. Due to ill health returned to Sharpsburg, 1902–1929. Large bequest to begin Presbyterian Home for the Aged.

the values of the Seminary for the church and the community. It stood at the Gateway to the West, watching over the endless procession of humanity moving toward the setting sun. Pittsburgh was only a town; Allegheny was but a village. There were four students, an uncertain teaching staff. The students had to help with the construction; funds were low. Yet Western Theological Seminary rose majestically on the mount of sacred science as a force for Christian virtues, for decency and good order, for the hope of an eternal life amid the confusion and change of a new world in the making.

The Library

Another phrase of Dr. Swift's sermon demands our attention. He speaks of "a valuable collection of choice and appropriate works," that is, a library. About five months after the sermon was delivered, the work of construction on the hill was delayed for lack of money, and Dr. Janeway, the newly installed professor, resigned and returned to the East. The Reverend Allan Ditchfield Campbell, a member of the Board, offered to collect a theological library in the British Isles. The detailed narrative of this journey can be read in Dr. Campbell's own records, "The Founding and Early History of the Western Theological Seminary."[22]

It is interesting to read of his experiences with representatives of the various divisions of Non-Conformity in England and Scotland. He met with no serious denominational barriers. The needs of a school in the western wilderness of America to serve the religious life of the vast territory of the Ohio and Mississippi valleys aroused sympathy, and there were contributions of both books and money. Edward Irving, who in 1832 was to found the Holy Catholic Apostolic Church, and Thomas Chalmers, who in 1843 was to lead the Disruption in Scotland, gave books for the new library.

Dr. Campbell was a close friend and admirer of President Andrew Jackson and had obtained from the latter letters of introduction to various circles of British life. When he was not talking about

Western Seminary, he was talking about Andrew Jackson, explaining his character to the puzzled British and telling them of his Christian loyalty and churchmanship. Dr. Campbell returned to the Seminary with a library of about two thousand volumes to be shelved in the circular gallery of the new building and to be called the "English and Scottish Library." To this was added the library from the estate of the Reverend Charlton Henry of Charleston, South Carolina, by the good offices of Dr. Francis Herron, the pastor of the First Presbyterian Church of Pittsburgh.

The Students

Let us turn our attention next to the kind of student who came to Western Theological Seminary to receive professional training for the Christian ministry. In general, we see him as a young gentleman disciplined in the Greek and Latin classics at Jefferson, or Washington College, or at the Western University of Pennsylvania. He was expected to have some ability with his hands either as a farmer or as an artisan. In the basement of the new Seminary building was a woodworking shop for the students' use. He knew the rudiments of physics, chemistry, and mathematics. He was trained in logic and had some experience in public speaking in the literary clubs of his college.

Luther Halsey wrote of the students at the close of the second academic year as follows:

"The students have been respectful in their deportment to the instructors and industrious in the prosecution of their studies. Their intercourse with one another affectionate, and their conduct 'toward them that are without' discrete. They have employed themselves as far as compatible with their engagements with the Institution, in promoting intelligence and piety in the city and vicinity, being all connected with some of the Sabbath schools, and most of them auxiliaries in the distribution of tracts, Bibles, etc. In a word, we cannot but believe they have been 'growing in grace and knowledge of Our Lord Jesus Christ.' "[23]

The curriculum was divided into three classes: Biblical (first year), Theological (second year), Ecclesiastical (third year). The Reverend John Williamson Nevin assumed instruction of the first group and of this course he wrote: "... A thorough foundation (is) to be laid in the study and interpretation of the Holy Scripture, which is the basis of all sound theological knowledge. It is our wish that every student who finishes an entire course in the Seminary shall have critically read the whole of the New Testament in Greek and most of the Hebrew Scriptures, besides being well grounded in Jewish and Christian antiquities and the canons of criticism."[24]

The homes of the majority of the students were in the rural counties and villages of Western Pennsylvania where Scotch-Irish parents lived frugally and raised their families in moral strictness. Many of these families had been touched by The Great Awakening in the first years of the nineteenth century and thereafter maintained habits of personal and household piety. An essential part of this piety was a consciousness of the condition and destiny of those outside the Faith. The American Indian, the Hindu in India, the Chinese, the African became the concern of all convinced Christians. When the young men from these Christian families came to Western Seminary to train for the ministry, many of them set their faces toward "them that are without," as a life mission. The students formed their own missionary society within the school for the purpose of study and discussion.

Life in Western during these early years is difficult to picture owing to a scarcity of firsthand accounts. There were student disciplinary problems which the small faculty dealt with. There was a constant financial crisis which Dr. David Elliott for the most part dealt with. The litigation concerning the grounds of the Seminary was a continual harassment. In 1852, the building on the hill was described as follows:

"... its appointments and accommodations ... were not such as to encourage luxurious habits, or to unfit young men for the practice of self-denial in the ministry. The ascent from the street was laborious, the furniture meagre, the walls bare, the descent in either direction dangerous for those not accustomed to stand in slippery places, the outlook from the windows less exhilarating than might have been expected, in view of the cloud of smoke which made it difficult at times even to trace the outline of the hills, or to discern the meeting of the rivers."[25]

On the night of January 23, 1854, the Seminary burned to the ground, with no loss of life, but with some damage to the library and complete loss of the students' effects. The fire must have been spectacular, especially to the citizens of Pittsburgh living at the Point. The word circulated throughout the city that "the preacher factory was on fire." The growing industrialism of the community can be seen even in this humorous epithet, "the preacher factory."[26] On the day after the destructive fire, plans were drawn up at once for a new building.

The Professors

The teachers of the Seminary are, in any estimate, the most important part of its educational function. The impact of their personalities, the wisdom of their counsel, the refinements of their culture, the energy and warmth of their Christian commitment are values, the most important, as they are the most illusive, to record. Elisha P. Swift, Luther Halsey, John Williamson Nevin, and David Elliott were the great men in the early years.

No less should be said of Francis Herron, who, though not a teacher, was the champion of the school in General Assembly, Synod, Presbytery, and the public in general, and was the guiding hand in the Board of Directors. Allan D. Campbell served the Seminary as a founder of the library, financial agent, and instructor on polity. Each one, in his own way, fought for and suffered for Western Seminary against repeated discouragements and catastrophies. The drive and stamina of pioneer Presbyterianism were in full exercise in the lives of these men.

Salaries of the professors were inadequate and almost constantly in arrears. An unpublished letter of John Williamson Nevin dated December 10, 1860, and addressed to the Reverend Allan D. Campbell gives an interesting account of Nevin's own situation.

". . . I have no record by me of my own connection with the Seminary, and my memory of dates and particulars is so uncertain that I find it hard to reduce things for the most part to precise historical narrative. I only know in general that I became connected with the Seminary in the beginning of December, 1829, in association with my friend Dr. Luther Halsey, and that I continued in connection with it 'till the Spring of 1840, when I felt it my duty to obey the call which took me to Mercersburg. My salary before my marriage A.D. 1835 was $800 per annum; after that, the usual rate of $1500 . . . My salary was never paid when due, and I got no interest on arrearages, but was glad to get the principal as I could by piecemeal when it suits the churches to replenish our lean treasury. At one time the arrearages had run up to nearly $2000. Still, all was paid in the course of time. When Dr. Halsey left I had to take the department of ecclesiastical history, along with my own . . . For such extra service I never asked or received any extra pay. I preached nearly every Sabbath all the time in different places—the last year by appointment of Presbytery as a stated supply for a congregation (Hilands) which paid a small salary for the service; but this salary went to the Seminary, not to myself—the last installment of it I received and paid over to the Seminary treasury after I came away."[27]

Many of the Presbyterian churches of Pittsburgh and adjacent communities were strengthened by the leadership and ministries of Seminary professors. As can be seen in the above-quoted letter, it was an economic necessity when Seminary salaries were low and uncertain. However, the services of Dr. Melancthon W. Jacobus to the Old Fifth (Central) Church, and of Dr. Samuel Jennings Wilson to the Sixth Church were richly rewarded in the life and work of these congregations. Dr. William S. Plumer, professor of Pastoral Theology, was minister of the Central Presbyterian

Church of Allegheny. Although his inflexible Old School Calvinism, and stern refusal to recognize the slavery problem as a proper theme for the pulpit were the causes of much hostility, yet "there can be no doubt about the fact that Dr. Plumer was a very unusual man and a successful preacher. His congregation at Central Church grew rapidly under his pastorate and he became famous from the day of his installation as Professor of Western Seminary."[28]

The North Presbyterian Church of Allegheny was formed in protest against the supposed pro-South loyalties of Dr. Plumer. Another Seminary professor, Dr. Archibald A. Hodge, served this congregation from 1866 to 1877 when he went to Princeton Seminary. During his tenure, "by his outstanding intellectual attainments and forceful preaching, he had attracted to the church many who could appreciate his abilities."[29] In later years Dr. Matthew Brown Riddle was to give much of himself from his duties at the Seminary to North Church.

The theological controversy which resulted in the division of the Presbyterian church into Old School and New School factions deeply affected Western Seminary. Dr. Elliott was moderator of the General Assembly in 1837 when the split occurred and Dr. Melancthon Jacobus, professor of New Testament from 1851 to 1876, was moderator at the time of the reunion in 1869. Through these years the faculty of the school was, in general, an adherent of the Old School, but did not engage in the sharp polemics which marked the scene in Philadelphia and other centers of Presbyterianism. The theology of the Princeton Seminary faculty and the long shadow of Ashbel Green were reflected in the conservatism of Western throughout this entire period. Elisha P. Swift and Francis Herron, both on the Board of Directors of the Seminary, and highly influential in the local presbyteries, were Old School and wielded their influence in Western Pennsylvania.

As Dr. John C. Hare has shown in his study of the Presbyterian church in Pittsburgh during this period, the division was costly.[30] The church did not grow and was quickly outdistanced by the

Roman Catholics and the Methodists. The financial struggle of Western Seminary was in large part the result of a lack of unity throughout the denomination. However, during these same years, the deep question of slavery was, in a sense, re-knitting the divided church in one area while it was separating it in another. The first wound was healed in 1869; the second is still with us.

Western Seminary reached its largest student enrollment in the years immediately preceding the outbreak of hostilities between the states. In 1856 a new building, "Seminary Hall," whose architecture showed considerably less imagination and nobility, was dedicated, not on the eminence overlooking the rivers, but on an acre lot on Ridge Avenue. In 1859 a second building was erected, four stories high with eighty-one single rooms. It was known as "Beatty Hall" in honor of Mrs. Hetty E. Beatty who, with her husband, the Reverend Charles C. Beatty, of Steubenville, was a generous benefactress of the school. This was to accommodate a student body of more than one hundred and fifty. In 1872 a library building was constructed, and in 1877 Beatty Hall was razed to make room for a new dormitory to be known as "Memorial Hall" to honor the reunion of the Old and New School divisions of the Presbyterian church.

As was said earlier, the theological position of the Seminary was conservative and in accord with the lines set down by the professors on the faculty of Princeton Theological Seminary. A natural result was the loss of several of Western's professors to Princeton. Dr. Archibald A. Hodge, a son of Charles Hodge, taught at Western from 1864 to 1877 when he joined the Princeton faculty. The writings of the Hodges, both father and son, sum up the conservative theology of the Presbyterian Church in classic form. Benjamin Breckenridge Warfield and Robert Dick Wilson, who taught New Testament and Old Testament, respectively, at Western, were called to Princeton in 1887 and 1900. They, too, were outspoken champions of a theology resistant to the counterclaims of the science and culture of the new century.

Professor Matthew Brown Riddle

There was, however, from 1887 to 1916, another influence on the faculty and student body of Western Seminary which radiated from the life and teaching of Matthew Brown Riddle. He was born in Pittsburgh in 1836, a son of the Reverend David Riddle, who was pastor of the Third Presbyterian Church. His father was one of the very few ministers in the area of Pittsburgh who, with his congregation, joined the New School ranks in 1837, and thus opposed the almost solid block of Old School sentiment in Western Pennsylvania. But the opposition was not bitter, owing chiefly to the honesty, sincerity, and charm of David Riddle. The son, through his mother, was a descendant of Dr. Matthew Brown, President of Jefferson College, from whom he inherited verve and emotional sensitivity. The result was a personality of sheer incandescence.

Matthew B. Riddle commanded national and international respect as a New Testament scholar. He served on the American Committee for the revision of the Bible. But it was as an exciting, fearless, and compassionate teacher that he influenced the Seminary and the community most. The meticulous concern for truth; the spontaneous, natural challenge of all hypocrisy and tyranny; the candid, simple trust in God brought into the life of the Seminary a new concept of the Christian life and a new understanding of authority. This was the period of growing uncertainties on Biblical matters. Darwinianism, textual criticism, German scholarship, geology and archaeology were apparently shifting the foundations. Matthew Brown (Bunky) Riddle did not necessarily have the answers to all current questions; but, in some mysterious way, he was the answer.

The faith and life of this man became a powerful element in the theological controversies of the 1920's, when fundamentalism and modernism were the issues. The students coming under his influence were able to meet the storm with courage, equanimity, and a salutary good humor. The faculty of Western Seminary, under the leadership of Dr. James Anderson Kelso, who had been among Dr. Riddle's early students, maintained the attitude and temper which he had so impressively created during his twenty-nine years of teaching. The professors, for the most part, had received post-graduate training at continental universities after Seminary; they possessed a broad and rich literary and social culture; they were frank and clear in defining their theological positions. The Seminary was free from the extremes of fundamentalism and liberalism.

No small element in the affect of the Seminary on the community and on the students at this time was the personality of Dr. James Snowden, professor of theology. As editor of *The Presbyterian Banner,* he reached a wide public; as a teacher of theology, he prepared the young men under him for the stress of doctrinal debate. In both spheres of activity, Dr. Snowden exhibited a salty common sense and balanced judgment. No Presbyterian church in Pittsburgh withdrew from the denomination in the nationwide strife. Western Seminary, in its faculty and students and alumni, calmly walked the middle road.

It is interesting to observe that whereas in the theological conflict of the mid-nineteenth century, Western Seminary supported the conservative position of the Old School, in the tensions of the early twentieth century, its faculty, especially in the fields of Biblical criticism and social ethics, opposed the extremists.

New Seminary Buildings

In the years immediately preceding the First World War, the Seminary was almost completely rebuilt. English collegiate architecture, with its connotation of Medieval and Renaissance scholarship and learning, was the style adopted for the three new buildings—Herron Hall, Swift Hall, and Memorial Hall. Herron and Swift halls formed the two sides of a proposed quadrangle; a chapel and a building of classrooms were to be built at a later time. In 1933 the former library was renovated into an apartment building of seven suites.

In 1947 one wing of Memorial Hall was converted into twelve small apartments for married students. Five years later the Seminary received as a gift from the Pennsylvania Transformer Company the large house on the corner of Brighton Road and Ridge Avenue which has accommodated Seminary offices, lecture rooms, and living quarters for a number of students.

It has not been the aim in this chapter to give merely a chronicle of events in connection with the establishment and subsequent life of Western Theological Seminary. We have been at some pains, although with considerable ineptness, to deal with the intangibles of purpose, tone, personality, and influence of this institution. The theological crisis of the 1920's and early 1930's in the Presbyterian church was the occasion for the Seminary to define with some clarity its position with regard to the issues of the controversy. There are, however, other areas where recognizable tendencies are to be found.

Western has been a regional school, drawing its students from Pennsylvania, West Virginia, and Ohio. The large majority of its graduates have taken their pastorates in these same three states. The establishment of seminaries at Chicago, Cincinnati, Omaha, Dubuque, and San Francisco relieved the Seminary in Pittsburgh of its initial task of providing ministers for the expanding West, thus making the name Western somewhat anachronistic. As a result, the pastorate in the towns and rural areas of the above-mentioned tristate region has been the common goal of Western graduates. Western Seminary has not been a large school. It attained its highest enrollment, as was previously stated, in the few years before the War Between the States, and after the Second World War. This has not been by conscious design of the directors or the faculty, but has been a situation resulting from many causes, some obscure, some obvious.

At the risk of the charge of pure subjectivity, the present writer feels impelled to define, however vaguely, the spirit of Western. It cannot be documented with facts or testimonials; and it may be rejected as inexact and imperfect. However, the following is an assay at catching the wind in a net. Owing, partly, to the traditional smallness of the institution and to the close relationship with the active life of the church in a strongly Presbyterian area, the prevailing tone of the school has encouraged the inner development of personality of students. The external marks of ministerial training have always been subordinated to the internal convictions of a divine vocation. The consciousness on the part of the student of the wide gap between the awesome magnitude of the task of the ministry and his own small abilities invariably produces in his personality a genuine humility, one aspect of which is a sense of humor and a sensitivity to the ridiculous and the pathetic.

There have been few specialists among the graduates; the vast majority are "general practitioners" with a general orientation of the total personality toward the multiple work of the parish ministry. The teachers of Western have put their teaching first, and the pastoral care of the students as an essential part of that teaching. All of these factors combine to send into the life and work of the church year after year a group of young men modest as to their own capacities, but alert to the human problems of everyday life, and dedicated to the person of Jesus Christ as the final and only answer.

With the union of the Presbyterian Church U.S.A. and the United Presbyterian Church of North America, theological education in the Upper Ohio Valley will undoubtedly reflect the life and spirit of the emergent denomination. Pittsburgh is at the center of a heavy concentration of Presbyterian congregations whose needs must be met by the educational program of the united church. From each side of the Union there is a goodly heritage which includes many strong churches, a generous and loyal membership, and the two Theological Seminaries—Western and Pittsburgh-Xenia. The services and facilities of both Seminaries are needed either as separate institutions or as an integrated Seminary.

CHAPTER XV The Distaff Side

PERHAPS WE Presbyterians in the Upper Ohio Valley have overplayed the apostolic injunction to "let the women keep silence in the churches." To judge by our history, we long required them to keep silence—almost everywhere.

With few exceptions our sectarian, as well as our religious histories, have been almost entirely concerned with the doings of the men of the Presbyterian church. The biographies inspired by the Presbyterian church have laid very much the same emphasis on masculine personality and leadership in service. Even when it was a woman who wrote, mention of her own sex was often limited to saying that some notable minister's wife was a helpmeet for him. Though silent, the women were not inactive. They left records of sacrificial service to the Presbyterian church which place us in their permanent debt. Their activities in church and community merit much greater emphasis than this single chapter of reflective review and appreciative tribute.

The great individualists among the women of the Ohio Valley, however, have not been Presbyterians as a rule. There was no Presbyterian church in which a woman has exercised a towering influence such as that of Gertrude Rapp in the pietistic Harmony Society, or the followers of Ann Lee among the Shakers. The annals of every Methodist district are full of the praises of some widow like Uniontown's Ann Murphy. But it has not been so with the Presbyterians. Research reveals no woman like Margaret Shoemaker, the Kiskiminetas Valley Baptist, whose defense of her children's inheritance made a nation laugh, but at least in the West taught it a lesson in equity.

Nor do we find many early newspaperwomen in our church history like Jane Swisshelm or Anne Royall, who both hated Presbyterians like poison and used their pens with trenchant effect alike against members and doctrines of Calvinistic groups. Nor Lotta Bengough, who was a first-rate newspaperwoman and a heroine of the War Between the States. Although Harriet Beecher Stowe was in a sense a daughter and wife of the Presbyterian manse, she was all her life at heart a Congregationalist, and it would be fudging the point to class her as an example of the achievements of Presbyterian women.

Nowhere among the Presbyterian annals is there an example of a woman such as Mad Ann Bailey, who took a terrible toll of vengeance among the Indians of West Virginia and Ohio for the slaying of her husband, or even (thank goodness) a Martha Grinder, that gentle, motherly little Pittsburgh woman who nursed the sick but poisoned heaven only knows how many of them.

Yet the case for Presbyterian women is neither so bad nor so colorless as this might indicate. There were many notable ones, often unsung, not because their virtues were the less but because virtue and heroism were so common among them. In their quiet approach to greatness, they are reminiscent of Mrs. Hannah Grant, who at the very hour when her son was being inaugurated as President was observed by a neighbor sweeping off the porch of her Ohio home. Among the Presbyterian women of the Upper Ohio Valley, such virtues and abilities as they did have were so common that in looking at individuals we often appear to be seeing types.

The Pioneer Woman—Massey Harbison

The first such type, in time and perhaps in importance as well, is the Pioneer Woman, of whom no more worthy or notable example need be sought than Massey Harbison. Mrs. Harbison, the original of whose first name has been guessed variously as being Massah, Mary, or Mercy, was not a Presbyterian by birth. Born into a Congregational family in New England about 1770, she was, before her marriage, Massey White; but let us not be chauvinistic. Whatever she may have been born, she lived and died in the Calvinistic faith and the membership of the Presbyterian church.

Traveling with her family towards the Ohio Country in the Fall of 1786, she was detained with them over the winter at the newly formed town of Brownsville, on the Monongahela River. There she met and married John Harbison, a youth not much older than herself. Two years later they were living in the wildest inhabited district of Pennsylvania, near the mouth of the Kiskiminetas River, in a log cabin with a dirt floor, largely the construction of their own four hands. In 1791 she fled from raiding Indians, taking with her two young children, and pregnant with a third, which was born in Reed's blockhouse while her husband was risking his life as a scout with General Arthur St. Clair, who suffered one of the most disastrous defeats of American arms on November 4, far over into Ohio. Such an experience might well have been enough to daunt any but the bravest heart. Yet, after being shot through the body and narrowly escaping capture in St. Clair's debacle, John continued to serve his pioneer neighbors as a scout, and Massey continued to live and bring up her children in the wilderness.

On May 22, 1792, within shouting distance of a fort, Indians broke down the door of her cabin, dragged her from bed by the feet, and carried her away captive. There were thirty Indians in the party with two renegade whites. But for her shouts to alarm the garrison, the slightly defended fort would itself have fallen prey to the raiders.

We pause as Mrs. Harbison herself later described the incident:

"The Indians, when they had flogged me away with them, took my oldest boy, a lad about five years of age, along with them, for he was still at the door by my side. My middle little boy, who was about three years of age, had by this time obtained a situation by the fire in the house, and was crying bitterly to me not to go, and making little complaints of the depredations of the savages.

"But these monsters were not willing to let the child remain behind them; they took him by the hand to drag him along with them, but he was so very unwilling to go, and made such a noise by crying, that they took him by his feet and dashed his brains out against the threshold of the door. Then they scalped and stabbed him, and left him for dead. When I witnessed this inhuman butchery of my own child, I gave a most indescribable and terrific scream, and felt a dimness come over my eyes, next to blindness, and my senses were nearly gone. The savages then gave me a blow across my head and face, and brought me to my sight and recollection again. During the whole of this agonizing scene, I kept my infant in my arms . . .

"We went from this place about forty rods, and they then caught my Uncle John Currie's horses, and two of them into whose custody I was put, started with me on the horses towards the mouth of the Kiskiminetas, and the rest of them went off towards Puckety. When they came to the bank that descended towards the Allegheny, the bank was so very steep, and there appeared so much danger in descending it on horseback, that I threw myself off the horse in opposition to the will and command of the savages. My horse descended without falling, but the one on which the Indian rode who had my little boy, in descending, fell and rolled over repeatedly; and my little boy fell back over the horse, but was not materially injured. He was taken up by one of the Indians, and we got to the bank of the river, where they had secreted some bark canoes under the rocks, opposite the island that lies between the Kiskiminetas and Buffaloe . . .

"Here I beheld another hard scene, for as soon as we landed, my little boy who was still mourning and lamenting about his little brother, and who complained that he was injured by the fall, in descending the bank, was murdered. One of the Indians ordered me along, probably that I should not see the horrid deed about to be perpetrated. The other, then, took his tomahawk from his side, and with this instrument of death killed and scalped him. When I beheld this second scene of inhuman butchery, I fell to the ground senseless with my infant in my arms, it being under and its little hands in the hair of my head. How long I remained in this state of insensibility, I know not . . .

"The first thing I remember after witnessing this spectacle of woe was the severe blows I was receiving from the hands of the savages, though at that time I was unconscious of the injury I was sustaining. After a severe castigation they assisted me in getting up and supported me when up. The scalp of my little boy was hid from my view, and in order to bring me to my senses again, they took me back to the river, and led me in knee-deep. This had its intended effect. But 'the tender mercies of the wicked are cruel.' "

The savages dragged their victim along towards the site of present-day Butler. Weary of life, she refused to carry the pack one Indian laid on her shoulders. She fully expected them to kill her as a result. Instead, the other savage, who had claimed her as his squaw, was delighted with her spirit and said she was right. After traveling all day without food, they reached an Indian encampment north of Butler a little before dark.

Mrs. Harbison continues her story: "That night they took me about three hundred yards from the camp, up a run, into a large dark bottom, where they cut the brush in a thicket, and placed a blanket on the ground, and permitted me to sit down with my child. They then pinioned my arms back, and left my hands only with a little liberty, so that it was with difficulty that I managed my child. Here in this dreary situation, without fire or refreshment, having an infant to take care of, and my arms bound behind me, and having a savage on each side of me, who had already killed two of my dear children that day, I had to pass the first night of my captivity . . .

"But the trials and tribulations of the day I had passed had so completely exhausted nature, that notwithstanding my unpleasant situation, and my determination to escape if possible, I insensibly fell asleep and repeatedly dreamed of my escape, and safe arrival in Pittsburgh, and several things relating to the town, of which I knew nothing at the time; but found to be true when I arrived there."

The savages watched all night, and when morning came, one went back along the trail to see if they were followed, while the other, who had murdered her older son, took out the scalp, prepared a hoop, and stretched it to dry.

"Those mothers who have not seen the like done by one of the scalps of their own children," Massey commented later, "will be able to form but faint ideas of the feelings which then harrowed up my soul." She tried to snatch his tomahawk to kill the savage, but he detected her plan and cursed her. After a difficult day she was again tied up overnight and again kept dreaming of escape.

"Early on the morning of the 24th, a flock of mocking birds and robins hovered over us as we lay in our uncomfortable bed. They sang, and said, at least to my imagination, that I was to get up and go off. As soon as the day broke, one of the Indians went off again to watch the trail, as on the preceding day, and he who was left to take care of me appeared to be sleeping. When I perceived this, I lay still and began to snore, and he fell asleep. Then I concluded it was my time to escape. I found it impossible to injure him with my child at the breast, as I could not effect anything without putting the child down, and then it would cry and give the alarm; so I contented myself with taking from the pillowcase of plunder taken from our house, a short gown, handkerchief, and a child's frock, and so made my escape, the sun being then about half an hour high."

Mrs. Harbison walked to Connoquenessing Creek, and down it for some distance, until in midafternoon she discovered it did not flow towards the Allegheny River and was taking her farther from home. Then waiting until dusk when she could take her direction from the stars, she marked her course and lay down to sleep. Just at dark of the second day, she was gathering leaves for a bed when the baby cried. After putting it to the breast to quiet it, she heard a man running after her in the direction she had followed. Crouching under a fallen tree, she heard an Indian come to the spot where the child had cried and stand there still as death for two hours before he gave up and rejoined his companions.

Through rain, cold, and the rough wilderness, she fled down to and along Pine Creek until she neared the Allegheny River. It was her sixth day, almost without any food and of the most horrid suffering.

"In this almost helpless condition . . . I came to an uninhabited cabin. Though I was in a river bottom, yet I knew not where I was, nor yet on what riverbank I had come. Here I was seized with the feelings of despair, and under those feelings I went to the uninhabited cabin, and concluded that I would enter and lie down and die, as death would have been to me an angel of mercy in such a situation and would have removed me from all my misery. Such were my feelings at this distressing moment. Had it not been for the recollections of those sufferings which my infant would endure, who would survive for some time after I was dead, I should have carried my determination into execution."

Just then, too, she heard a cowbell and followed the sound until she came opposite to the fort at the point of the island six miles above Pittsburgh. From Tuesday to Sunday she had wandered through the wilderness, still protecting her babe, but so haggard that a near neighbor had to ask her identity and could scarcely believe it when told. Women at the fort pulled one hundred and fifty large thorns out of her feet, some of which had stuck completely through, coming out above the instep.

Yet less than two years later, although the Indians were still on the warpath and her husband still serving as a scout, the Harbisons moved seven miles farther into the wilderness, where she was often alone for a month at a time and commented in later years that she commonly saw more wolves than human beings. There, as soon as neighbors began to settle the area around them, she and John Harbison helped to organize the Bull Creek Presbyterian Church, which has continued to serve the district for more than a century and a half. She continued to work hard and bear children—thirteen in all—of whom only three, including the two murdered by Indians, were dead before her own demise in 1837.[1]

The Devoted Wife—Lois Badger

Both during the pioneer period and later, in peacetime and in war, the Devoted Wife was a common but nonetheless magnificent type of Presbyterian woman. She who comes most readily to mind in such a role is Lois, the wife of the Reverend Joseph Badger, early missionary in the Presbytery of Erie. On February 23, 1802, at a most unseasonable period of the year, she began the journey of nearly five hundred miles with her husband and several children from her native New England to the northwestern Pennsylvania and northern Ohio district in which Mr. Badger was apostle to an area of thousands of square miles.

"The outfit was a four-horse wagon, in which were stowed his wife and six children, together with their household effects. Soon the missionary family encountered snow, that increased in depth until his wagon wheels became solid with snow and mud, and they were fain to construct a rude sled, on which the wheels were laid, having been taken from the axles, and upon these the wagon body was placed and the journey resumed. At Troy, New York, the snow failed, the sled was discarded, and the wagon restored to its original condition. But the mud was fearful. Onward the noble horses toiled, one accident after another happened, until finally the forward axletree broke, bringing them to an unwilling halt. There was no wagonmaker near, nor any other mechanic that was available. So remembering his war experience, Badger collected what tools were at hand, procured a piece of timber, and made a new axle with his own hands. His next accident was the breaking of his kingbolt, replaced at an expense of two dollars. He reached Austenburg, Ohio, at length, after a journey of two months."[2]

Living in a primitive cabin during her husband's long periods of missionary travel, Lois Badger suffered bereavement in the death of at least one child; and once the house with all its contents was burned in his absence. Yet if she ever complained or gave any evidence of regret, her husband's *Journal* fails to make any mention of the fact.[3]

Mary Power Was Both Courageous and Capable

But if Lois Badger was brave in going into a wilderness where she faced hardship and want, what shall we say of Mary Tanner Power, who faced not only these difficulties, but also the imminent danger of savages on the warpath when she crossed the mountains in the Autumn of 1776? Mary Power was no young, adventurous girl, but a woman of thirty-four years, with four young daughters, and expecting a fifth child. Rebecca Power, born a month after her parents reached the Dunlap's Creek congregation in the Monongahela Valley, was the first child born into the family of any Presbyterian minister west of the Allegheny Mountains.[4]

The Reverend James Power had crossed the mountains as a theological student in 1772, and again as a licentiate in 1774, the year he organized the Dunlap's Creek Church and perhaps three others.[5] Maybe it was irregular for a mere licentiate to take so much authority upon himself, but that was no day for standing on ceremony. Now he was bringing his family to the new land which had suddenly been plunged into the midst of a war. The Eastern Colonies had warned residents of Western Pennsylvania to return nearer the coast, because it would be impossible to protect them against the attacks of Indians. But the people of the West had chosen to stand their ground and even supplied men to fight the Redcoats as far away as Quebec, New England, and South Carolina.

After three years, the Reverend James Power moved from Dunlap's Creek, where Mary's parents lived, to present-day Westmoreland County, an even more dangerous area. He and Mary were living there in 1781 when he helped to organize Redstone Presbytery. She was alone with her daughter in the Summer of 1782 when a war party swooped down upon nearby Hannastown, killing and burning and carrying off captives. Her husband was at Unity Church, even nearer the scene, when the raid occurred. For several horrible hours she remained in suspense before he was able to let her know he had escaped the danger.[6] Yet Mary Power continued to carry on her work without complaint, although the work included caring for their eight small daughters (three of whom followed in her footsteps by marrying Presbyterian ministers) and operating a farm.

In a day when little attention was paid to women's labors, it was related that once when another member of Redstone Presbytery gave home tasks as a reason for nonattendance, Mr. Power was mildly critical. He had never stayed away from Presbytery for such reasons, he said, and hoped he never would. Whereupon an elder who knew the situation spoke up without rising from his seat: "No thanks to Brother Power for all his bragging about his punctuality. We all know what sort of a wife he has to manage for him, at home."[7]

The faith that upheld Mary Power on her dangerous journeys and in her constant labors was not misplaced. She lived to see the land at peace, to bring up all her daughters in the nurture and admonition of the Lord and see them married, and to become the grandmother of a numerous and distinguished progeny, dying in 1820, in her seventy-ninth year.

A Wife and Soldier—Elizabeth Berry

It would be scamping the subject of the Presbyterian Devoted Wife to omit mention of Elizabeth Gilmore Berry, the only Pennsylvania woman whose name was enrolled in a company of frontier scouts during the war for American independence. Born in 1754 in the British Isles, Elizabeth Gilmore and her sister Ann came to America in 1776 or 1777. In a shipboard romance Elizabeth gave her heart to John Berry, a young North-of-Ireland man who was on his way to help the Colonies in their fight against England. Their love could not stand in the way of the call of duty, so the two girls settled near Valley Forge while Berry enlisted in Washington's army.

A family tradition says that it was not Elizabeth Gilmore who first formed the idea of enlisting in the Cumberland Rangers, but that her sister Ann secretly married, dressed herself as a man and enlisted with her husband. Following his death, according to the story, she recovered his body and brought it back to their Lancaster County home for burial, while Elizabeth took her place in the Rangers.

We do not know when or how the masquerade was discovered, but the name of Elizabeth Gilmore appears in the record of the Cumberland Rangers as having served from 1778 to 1783. Some historians have tried to dismiss the record by suggesting that she may have served as a nurse—though anyone who would suppose this to be the case knows little of the Continental Army and far less of so dauntless an outfit as the Cumberland Rangers. Had she been a mere camp follower, she certainly would not have been included on the rolls any more than were the numerous women camp followers of other outfits. Although she married Berry in 1780, there seems little doubt that for five years she carried a rifle and took her turn as a scout with the Rangers, sharing danger and hardship with the rest of the outfit.

Yet Elizabeth Gilmore Berry never at any time boasted or made capital of her experiences as a soldier. In 1794 she and her husband bought two hundred and fifty-one acres in Washington County, Pennsylvania, from George Washington, where they lived quietly until her death on August 23, 1823. She is buried beside John Berry in the cemetery of Robinson Run Presbyterian Church. Her sister, Ann Gilmore Boyle, is buried only a few miles away in the cemetery of the Hill Church, beside her own husband—was he her second?

The Grand Dame—Lydia Boggs

Lest it should be supposed that excessive humility was always one of the failings of Presbyterian women of the Ohio Valley, let it go on record that another of the types of notable Calvinist women was the Grand Dame, than whom none could be more typical than Lydia Boggs. Apparently there is no record easily available to prove that Lydia Boggs was ever a member of or brought up in any Presbyterian church. But often there is no historical proof of matters of which we are virtually certain. Family names, district history, and other antiquities of the district around Wheeling, West Virginia, provide strong circumstantial evidence that she was a member of this church.

A daughter of Colonel William Boggs, who was in command at Fort Henry (Wheeling) during the siege of 1782, she came into historical view at that time as a girl of nearly seventeen. A few months later Lydia Boggs married Colonel Moses Shepherd, a wealthy neighbor, though no more wealthy or socially prominent than Colonel Boggs. They built a home at Elm Grove, a few miles east of Wheeling and for many years were extremely prominent in the civic affairs of the district. There they entertained many of the important men of America who passed Wheeling on the way between Pittsburgh, Philadelphia, Baltimore, or Washington and the West. Henry Clay was a frequent visitor at the home—so frequent that his visits occasioned gossip and, if they did not change the course of empire, at least changed the course of the great National Road, connecting the nation's capital with the West. Originally the plans had been for the road to run from Cumberland, Maryland, either to Pittsburgh or Steubenville, Ohio. Legend says that Clay was irked at having to drive his carriage through the mud each time he went to the Shepherd home. In any case he joined with politicians in Uniontown and Washington, Pennsylvania, and required the new road to be built from Cumberland to Wheeling through those two towns.[8]

Just after her death the editor of the Wheeling *Register* wrote: "The fine stone mansion at Elm Grove, the home of Moses Shepherd, is justly historic. No home in the West has entertained more sumptuously, and the hospitality dispensed was unsurpassed in the Mississippi Valley. The house is spacious, handsome, and substantial. It was furnished especially with a view to the large hospitality of which it was intended to become the center. The entire upper part was thrown into one spacious drawing room, which with the other apartments was furnished in the best style of the day. The tapestry was manufactured especially for the rooms . . .

"Mrs. Shepherd was a fashionable lady at the gay court of Washington. She had ample means and gratified her taste for dress to the fullest. During the lifetime of Colonel Shepherd, these visits to the National Capital were yearly continued; and after his death in 1833, she kept up her annual pilgrimage to the Federal metropolis. It was during one of these visits that she met General Daniel Crugar, a member of the House of Representatives from New York. They were married and he transferred his residence from the Empire State to the Old Dominion. General Crugar died in 1843. For some years after his death she continued her visits to Washington; and the writer, meeting her there in the Spring of 1850, escorted her to President Taylor's levee. She was then eighty-six years old (actually in her eighty-fifth year) and not one of the least observed on that brilliant occasion."[9]

Lydia Boggs Shepherd Crugar died in the Fall of 1867, aged one hundred and one. If there was anything to the gossip about herself and Henry Clay, she certainly felt that it was nothing to hide, for she erected a monument in honor of the famous politician, her two husbands, and herself.

But perhaps the most revealing thing about the character of Lydia Boggs is in her answer when she was asked shortly before her death about the controversy over whether it was really Betty Zane who had made the famous run with powder for the settlers' rifles during the siege of Fort Henry. Mrs. Crugar replied that she clearly recalled the incident and that it was not Betty Zane, who was in Philadelphia at the time of the siege, but a girl named Molly Scott. She added, however, that she could not see why anyone was so much concerned over whether it had been Betty Zane or Molly Scott. "Any of us would have been glad to do it," she said.

Typical Charitable Women

Once again, prominent in the Presbyterian church in the Ohio Valley, was the Charitable Woman—and her name was legion. Down through the years there have been so many in every large town and in many small towns and villages that it is difficult to choose any for special honor. Shall we name Elizabeth O'Hara Denny, always a leader in any good enterprise? "It will not be too much to say of Mrs. Denny that next to the name of Dr. Herron, hers will be found most intimately interwoven with the real life of the church as experienced during the last two generations. From the age of nineteen, when with her mother she professed her faith in Christ, her whole life was turned with singular sincerity and devotion to His service, and continued undiminished until her pilgrimage of more than fourscore years was ended.

"Full of love for the word of God, she taught many of the daughters of the church to prize and practice its holy precepts. While freely giving of her means to every good object, she found time, even when surrounded by pressing family cares, to give attention and counsel to many important benevolent societies, being president of one, the Allegheny Orphan Asylum, from its founding, during the remaining half century of her own life.

"Simple and unostentatious in matters of taste and expenditure, her example has made the occupants of the pews of what has often been called 'the aristocratic First Church,' conspicuous as least given to display. She was adorned with the ornament of a meek and quiet spirit, and clothed with humility. Who now is fitted to worthily wear her mantle?"[10]

Shall we speak of Mrs. Mary Wilkins or Mrs. (General) William

Robinson, whom the same writer places next to Mrs. Denny? Or Mrs. Luther Halsey, founder of the Protestant Orphans' Home, which still, after more than a century, does great service? Or even down to our own day Mrs. Harriet Duff Phillips, who as a girl watched her father found Pittsburgh's South Side Hospital and had been throughout her long life one of its mainstays? Perhaps we might name Mrs. Ellen Murdoch Watson, born in Pittsburgh in 1831, whose work under the United States Christian Commission in the War Between the States caused the 100th Pennsylvania Volunteer Regiment to give her the title, "The Soldiers' Friend." Married to William Watson of New Castle, Pennsylvania, she did not allow her work to cease after the end of the war, but continued with many charitable and reform movements, helped with the early organization of the Women's Christian Temperance Union and Anti-Saloon League, and was active almost until her death in 1913.

But perhaps none ever so clearly typified the goodness and the mistakes, the achievements and the failures of the Presbyterian Charitable Woman as Mrs. Mary Copley Thaw. The daughter of Josiah Copley, a newspaperman and religious writer, she came to Pittsburgh as a girl from the nearby town of Kittanning, shortly before the regrettable conditions in prisons, camps, and hospitals of the Civil War inspired the Pittsburgh Sanitary Fair to raise money for a relief fund. Her brother John had gone into service—and to his death. When an appeal for funds was made at a meeting in the First Presbyterian Church, Mary Copley contributed a ring which he had given her because she had nothing else to offer.

William Thaw, a rich widower who was passing the collection plate, saw the gift and asked permission to redeem the ring and return it personally to the giver. Within a short time they were married and for many years Mrs. Thaw was an outstanding wife, mother, and patron of charity. For a decade, Mrs. Thaw and one Presbyterian neighbor handled almost the entire personal charity of a growing industrial city from her back door. Later she helped found the Society for the Improvement of the Poor, the Young Woman's Christian Association, and many other noteworthy organizations.

Perhaps it was in her personal stature, however, that Mrs. Thaw stood highest, and in her reaction to trouble within her own family, especially in the life of her son Harry whose lurid trial was featured in the newspapers of that period. It was her hour of tragedy, but her head and her principles were held high.

Outstanding Missionary Women

Again, when we come to the question of the Missionary, Presbyterian womanhood is so rich in examples that it is difficult to choose. Shall we first think of the beautiful Cornelia Brackenridge? Charming, talented, and one of Pittsburgh's best families, she married the Reverend William Speer in August, 1846, and sailed with him almost immediately for China. She was never to reach her field. She died in Macao the following April, aged only twenty-four. Her last words were, "I am willing by God's grace to suffer, recover, or die."

Or shall we think of the tall, slender, gentle Nancy Henderson? Born in the Forks of Cheat in northern (West) Virginia in 1795, after teaching in a women's school in Pittsburgh until 1833, she went as a missionary to the Wea tribe of Indians in what was then the wildest-known West. There she survived great danger, and after returning, became the wife of Richard Forrest of Allegheny and a leader in public movements in her home district until her death in 1871.

Perhaps no other labored more fully than Evangeline Metheny, of Kittanning. The daughter of a medical missionary, she was taken when only a few months old to the field he had served before the furlough on which she was born. There she grew up with work in Turkey and Syria, laboring as a missionary until in 1917 her services were required by the American Red Cross in the war emergency. Knowing Turkish, Arabic, Greek, and Italian, and adding to it all a tender understanding of the people among whom she chose to work, she was the ideal person for such a task. During her Red Cross days, soldiers lovingly called her "Polyglot Metheny." Not until well into age did she retire, and then it was to her home in Beaver Falls, Pennsylvania, to write a book, *North and East of Musa Dagh,* which revealed the great heart which stopped beating before it was published in 1950.[11]

Career Women of Distinction

Only in later years, except in teaching and missionary endeavor, do we find that principal character of today's Presbyterian life—the Career Woman. The writer, the lawyer, the scientist, the administrator, or occupant of the many other fields were scarcely opened to women until a generation ago.

Whom shall we principally name? Mary Roberts Rinehart? No. Although she was born a Presbyterian and showed the good effects of her training, she was never enthusiastic about the church and later left it. Agnes Sligh Turnbull, author of historical novels? Louise Homer, the opera singer? Emma Guffey Miller of political fame? Sarah Soffel, the first woman to be named Judge of the Allegheny County Court in Pennsylvania? Elizabeth Moorhead Vermorcken, who was for seventeen years a teacher of English at Carnegie Institute of Technology and then wrote noteworthy books? All are worthy, but let us pass them by.

Perhaps Dr. Louise Lyle best represents Presbyterian women during this developing period of career activity. Hers was a threefold career—the wife of a Presbyterian minister, the acting pastor and rebuilder of a Presbyterian church in Wheeling, and the founder and first administrator of the Presbyterian Hospital in Pittsburgh. Her diverse career as a wife, preacher, and physician has enabled her to achieve unique distinction in three essential fields of service to Christ and His Church. We pause merely to pay tribute to her courage in adversity, her unwavering devotion, her pioneering zeal and her determined resourcefulness under varying circumstances. The details of her memorable career are related in the closing chapter of this book, as the story of the development of the Presbyterian Hospital makes vivid her faith and fortitude and as she triumphed over the discouragements of feeble finances and the skepticism of the clergy.[12] The Hospital is her monument in brick and stone. It is symbolic of a less visible monument in the grateful memory of thousands who rise up to call her blessed.

Women Organize for Service

Nor were the women of the early Presbyterian churches of this area at all backward about uniting themselves in joint efforts for the common good. Long before the general introduction of Sabbath schools or other church societies, they were busy with good works, laboring hand in hand.

As early as 1785 the women of Bethel Church, a still thriving and growing congregation a few miles south of Pittsburgh, began meeting to make clothing for the young men who were studying with the Reverend Joseph Smith of Buffalo, Washington County, Pennsylvania, and who later became the first young ministers licensed by Redstone Presbytery. Soon the women of four other congregations, Buffalo, Cross Creek, Chartiers, and Ten Mile, all in the same district, joined in the work. They dyed homespun linen with fresh hay to make summer suits for the students, and sent homespun woolen goods east of the mountains to be "pulled and dressed" and returned to be made into suits.[13]

Naturally, beginnings were small. We may tend to laugh at the early "Cent" or "Penny" societies which they organized at first. But, if we do, it will be because we fail to understand how primitive was their pioneer living and how scarce was real money in the area. In a day when the pastor of a large church might receive only three hundred dollars a year, partly in goods and services, a cent a day throughout the year was no small sacrifice, but a gift greater than the average today in many church societies.

Early in 1816 a Presbyterian women's society with a broad range of service was organized in Chillicothe, Ohio. "A constitution was adopted and subscribed to by over twenty women, and there is reason to hope that the number will be considerably augmented." Agreeably to the constitution, "the Society will consist of females only . . . , and they are to be such as sustain a religious or moral character. Those who become members are required to pay one dollar in advance, and one cent a day throughout the year, to be discharged quarterly.

"The funds are to be distributed in the following manner: one fourth is to be sent to the Theological Seminary at Princeton, and one fourth to the Theological Seminary at New York (Auburn) to be applied to the use of such students in this state as have been received as candidates for the ministry by some Presbytery, and are preparing to attend either one of the aforesaid seminaries, and for which they may require assistance. The remaining fourth *(sic)* is to be distributed in alms for the relief of the indigent, and in procuring books for poor children who may attend Sunday schools in this place."[14]

Even before this, more or less organized solicitation of benevolent funds had been carried on by the women of the churches for missions and other causes. In the minutes of the General Assembly of 1811 we read: "Benevolence is always attractive, but when dressed in a feminine form possesses peculiar charms. Hard indeed must be the heart which can resist the example or the solicitation of a mother, a wife, a sister, or a friend when that example and solicitation are for the promotion of the public good. We hope the spirit which has animated the worthy women of whom we speak will spread and animate other bosoms."[15]

Indeed, it is worth noting that almost the first avenues to be opened in the emancipation of women were through the churches, though even there the progress was slow, as is often the case with social change.

In 1815 a Female Cent Society had been organized in the First

Presbyterian Church of Pittsburgh, and made the first recorded gift by women for home missions, a generous sixty dollars.[16]

Three years later followed the Female Charitable Society of Poland, Ohio, and in 1819 the Female Mite Society of Scrubgrass, and the Female Charitable Society of Fairfield, both in Pennsylvania. The Bethel Missionary Society was organized in 1822 in the church which had first inaugurated sewing for the ministerial students. Forty-four of its one hundred six members were women.[17]

Women's Missionary Societies Organized

About 1828 some young girls of the First Presbyterian Church of Pittsburgh organized a "Mite Society," making penwipers to sell to their schoolmates at five cents each for the cause of missions. By 1833 they were able to raise thirty dollars for the cause.[18] In 1836 they reorganized as the Young Ladies' Missionary Society. The second annual report, published in the *Pittsburgh Christian Herald* for January 11, 1838, reveals that the first year's work had raised one hundred dollars, and the second had doubled that amount. Of this, nearly half had come from the work of a subsidiary Sewing Society. The group had sent one hundred and fifty dollars to the Presbyterian Foreign Missionary Society and still had fifty dollars on hand.

By 1840 they were so active that they contributed eight hundred dollars, which had been raised through their first "Annual Sale," the name "Fair" being disapproved by the Session. Members subscribed fifty cents a year and were fined if absent from the afternoon sewing sessions, which as the "Annual Sale" time approached were continued as late as 9 P.M. Except for their own gifts and those of two men of the congregation, the entire sum was raised by sewing, which they did by hand, and by selling food which they had prepared. They advertised the sale, held on December 24, with a rhyme:

> Friends and neighbors, "all hail,"
> Won't you come to our sale,

And examine the tasteful variety
Of things useful and gay,
Which we mean to display,
And all made by the Sewing Society?

Ladies come, one and all,
And give us a call;
We are sure you will not find us dear:
Our prices are low,
And our work, we well know,
Is as good as you find anywhere.

The rhyme, which ran to eight stanzas, was written by a member of the church choir.[19]

The Synod of Pittsburgh pledged fifteen hundred dollars in 1836 to the work of the Western Foreign Missionary Society, and suggested the formation of missionary associations. Women of the Allegheny Presbyterian Church almost immediately formed a Foreign Missionary Association, and within a little over a year had raised one hundred and eleven dollars for the cause.[20]

By 1832 we find a Female Missionary Society at Wheeling, West Virginia, and three years later another at nearby Washington, Pennsylvania. In 1837 there was a Female Cent Society at Middletown (now Fairmont, West Virginia), and by 1848 Female Missionary Societies at Plain Grove and Butler, Pennsylvania.[21]

The *Pittsburgh Recorder* for April 11, 1826, contained the report of a "Female Bible Society of Pittsburgh" which "has now reached the close of the fifth year of its existence." Its annual contribution of $27.36 made a total of over two hundred and eleven dollars, but marked "a gradual, though a very perceptible decline," the paper noted. It attributed this in part to a feeling in some quarters that the work of buying and distributing Bibles was "unsuitable to the female character."[22] Though there is nothing to indicate that the Society was sponsored by Presbyterians, there seems little doubt that Presbyterian women would have had a part in it. Presbyterian women were also active in the Ladies' Tract Society of Allegheny, in 1844, and the Home for Destitute Women, in 1868.[23]

Despite considerable agitation against the changing status of women in the Presbyterian church, as well as in other fields, the work continued to grow. During the nearly two decades following the outbreak of the War Between the States, many women's societies, principally for missions, were organized, locally and by presbyteries and synods.

As early as 1870 a Woman's Foreign Missionary Society had been organized in Philadelphia, and within the next half-dozen years many, if not most of the churches of Western Pennsylvania, had women's foreign mission groups which affiliated with it.

Early in 1878 Dr. Sheldon Jackson, the noted home missionary, sent out a church-wide call for a women's convention for home mission work to meet at Pittsburgh on May 24, simultaneously with the General Assembly.[24] After the meeting had been opened with singing, Bible reading, and prayer, Mrs. W. A. Herron of the First Presbyterian Church of Pittsburgh was called to the Chair, and Mrs. Wilson N. Paxton of Allegheny was made secretary. Letters indicating interest in the work had been received not merely from many Presbyterian groups which could not be represented, but from societies belonging to other churches.

There was much debate as to whether to work only for home missions, or to include the foreign field and unite with a group already active in New York, which supported both causes. Final action was delayed in order to work out an agreement. Mrs. Sylvester F. Scovel of Pittsburgh was named first on a committee of twelve to hold conversations which resulted in the formal organization of the Woman's Executive Committee of Home Missions, and she became its vice-president.[25]

Thus women's work was firmly launched in the churches of the Upper Ohio Valley; and, as the years have passed, it has been an increasingly important part of the work of the area.

CHAPTER XVI Peace Through Conflict

ZEALOTS ARE GOOD SOLDIERS. They give their means, even their lives, willingly for a cause in which they believe, and they accept enthusiastically and loyally the leadership of those who they believe have been rightly called to responsibility. They have not been limited to any one age or race, nor do they seem to have appeared in response to any single pattern of circumstances. Given a worthy challenge, they seldom weigh their own comfort or safety against duty. If their cause appears to be just, they have no hesitancy about standing alone, often for a cause that is already lost.

Therefore they accomplish the impossible! Gideon's ancient watchword, "The sword of the Lord and of Gideon," has reverberated through the corridors of history. In effect, it was the battle cry of David and Israel in the vale of Elah. Through three terrible years of unbelievable suffering, it beat back the investing legions of Titus from the battlements of Jerusalem. As a cross in the sky, it brought victory to the eagles of Constantine at the Mulvian Bridge. It enabled Charles Martel at Tours to hurl back the Moslem host about to engulf western Christianity. Fired by this spirit the wretched, emaciated Crusaders streamed from the gates of Antioch, and armed with cudgels, stones, and broken weapons followed the holy Lance—God's presence and protection, they believed—and stumbled through the smoke and dust of the hopeless battlefield to crush the elite cavalry of Kerbogha. "Deus Lo Vult" they whispered in their dying agony. Escovedo from the ruins of a broken, decimated Holland wrote to his master, Philip of Spain, about the stubborn Dutch, "They are determined to remain free, Sire, and to live as they believe."

It may well be that in the Scotch-Irish and Puritan stock of this Upper Ohio area there is in background and theology a similar conviction of a divine mission for themselves, and of faith in a God who loves justice and hates tyranny and oppression. They remembered the insistence of John Knox that Christians ought to resist tyranny and evil to the death. Their theology affirmed—as it still does in 1958—that one "may lawfully now under the New Testament wage war upon just and necessary occasions," and that one is forbidden to take life "except in case of public justice, lawful war, or necessary defense."

Upon coming to the New World these pioneers brought with them their deep convictions. They believed they were led by the Spirit of God to leave their homes and countrysides to face the rigors of a strange, inhospitable wilderness and there to establish an order in which men should be free to worship God as they chose. Bancroft comments, "The first voices publicly raised in America to dissolve all connection with Great Britain came from Scotch Presbyterians."

In any case, the General Synod of the Presbyterian church, in 1775, on the very eve of the American Revolution, addressed a pastoral letter to its constituency stating, among other things, "Be careful to maintain the union which at present subsists through all the colonies, adhere firmly to their resolutions, and let it be seen that they are able to bring out the whole strength of this vast country to carry them into execution."

As Colonists, They Fought for Freedom

Colonial Presbyterians out of bitter experience feared the power and vengeance of the British Church-State. They rebelled, not so much against the trifling taxes on documents and tea, as against the presumption of the Church and State in abridging their political and religious liberties. So the North Carolina rebellion gave rise to the Mecklenburg Declaration, and eventually to the Declaration of Independence for all the colonies, under the leadership of such staunch Calvinists as James Madison, Patrick Henry, Alexander Hamilton, and John Witherspoon.

It is not to be wondered, therefore, that George III branded the American colonists who resisted as Presbyterian "Rebels," or that Walpole in Parliament facetiously observed that "Cousin America has run off with a Presbyterian parson." It has been estimated that more than half the officers and soldiers of the American forces in the Revolutionary War were of Presbyterian extraction and the war was commonly spoken of in England as "The Presbyterian Rebellion."

All this is to say that this stock of the Upper Ohio, while not inclined to provoke or precipitate war, does not shrink from supporting such principles as they believe are just and necessary. The Presbyterian church does not require of its members that they participate in war. Rather it has zealously protected the right of exemption from military service of its members who can establish, both on grounds of conscience and legality, their claim to exemption. But they incline to believe the blessings of liberty of conscience, good government, and political freedom are not attained without sacrifice. In the Revolutionary War and all subsequent wars which they believed just and necessary, they have proved themselves loyal and have given their sons and husbands willingly at the call of duty.

Military Officers from Ohio

During the War Between the States the contribution of the Ohio part of our area in high-ranking officers is amazing. The Presbyterian church numbers among her distinguished sons, by birth or adoption, Generals U. S. Grant, W. T. Sherman, Philip Sheridan, D. C. Buell, George Crook, James B. McPherson, George A. Custer, Irvin McDowell, Alexander McCook, Godfrey Weitzel, W. B. Hagan,

George B. McClellan, James B. Steadman, Jacob D. Cox, James A. Gilmore, Benjamin Harrison, James A. Garfield, Rutherford B. Hayes, and Major William McKinley. Almost incredible that so many of the greatest leaders of that war should come from so small an area! These are not all Presbyterian. But they comprise to a remarkable degree the leadership of the Northern forces.

In connection with the last three just named, the following incident came to our attention during World War II, and so far as we know, it has not in the present form been published. An officer of the Regular Army, now retired, related it on the strength of his father's participation in the incident. His father was an orderly clerk of the 8th Ohio Regiment in 1861, and as such was a competent stenographer. He was with the Regiment and the larger component to which it belonged as they were passing through Washington early that summer on the way South.

The troops, he related, were allowed to fall out for a brief rest on the south lawn of the White House. Seeing the soldiers on the lawn, President Lincoln walked down to greet them informally. On being invited to speak to them, Mr. Lincoln, according to the clerk's record, spoke as follows: "I happen to temporarily occupy the big white house back there (pointing toward it) as President of these United States. It is in keeping that any of your sons may look to come here as President, just as my father's child has. In order that your children may have the same privilege in this battle for life that I have had, the war must go on, the Nation is worth saving."

Naturally the troops were thrilled by President Lincoln's presence and impressed by what he said. The most extraordinary part of the whole incident, however, was that of the men to whom President Lincoln spoke that day as they rested on the White House lawn, three of them later did occupy the White House—James A. Garfield, Rutherford B. Hayes, and William McKinley. At least two other instances are on record when the President spoke to Ohio troops under similar circumstances. The phraseology is somewhat similar, too. But, considering the conditions under which troops were moved through Washington, the friendliness and informality of Mr. Lincoln, and the likelihood that he would be prone to express the same general idea in probably somewhat the same language, this seems likely to be an authentic incident, and certainly the subsequent coincidence is remarkable.

FOUR TYPES OF MILITARY SERVICE

Since nationwide conscription has become the prevailing method of securing military personnel and young men are officially advised to wait until drafted, and since the individual is subject not only to call but to one or more subsequent resummonings once a name is in the hopper, there is no longer much opportunity for appeals to patriotism and national honor to be used effectively. It would not only be futile, but unjust to all concerned, to attempt to distinguish between enlistees and conscriptees, or to list totals by racial, religious, or geographic categories. Therefore, some other standard of evaluation must be sought.

It can probably be found through what might be called personality or morale factors necessitated by war. And these can be found well exemplified in four distinguished sons of this area: General Thomas J. (Stonewall) Jackson, General Benjamin Harrison, General Edward Martin, and General Richard K. Mellon.

This list by no means exhausts the roster of honored soldiers of our constituency. To attempt to name them all would be futile, and to omit anyone, regardless of rank, would be grossly unjust. These, however, may be typical and illustrative of the principles we conceive the Presbyterians who have come from the Upper Ohio (and certainly others as well) have objectified in war.

I. The Career Soldier: Thomas J. Jackson

First consider the contribution of the career member of the armed services. Whether from previous personal service or from observation, he believes that until reliable means are discovered and adopted of assuring peace, and the use of peaceful methods alone is adopted to preserve liberty and justice, it will be necessary to have well-trained personnel in the armed forces, adequate materials and supplies for their necessary support, and general and technical educational facilities which will enable all personnel to render their service with self-respect and good conscience. He believes it is criminal to impress people into a service where their lives depend on thorough training, upon the best and latest in equipment, and certainly upon the unquestioned advantage that comes from good morale, and then desert them to inefficient training, murderously inadequate weapons and equipment, and the feeling that, at least during the period of their military service, those so impressed into the regular service have become the objects of avoidance, if not contempt and scorn, by the citizenry generally. Even at the cost technically of continuous jeopardy to himself as a member of the regular forces, he is willing to contribute whatever he can to meet the grave needs of national defense.

An excellent illustration of a highly conscientious and deeply religious Christian soldier, and one of the outstanding religious personalities of this or any other area, is the regular army soldier, Thomas J. (Stonewall) Jackson. During his brief span of life (he died at the age of thirty-nine) he seems to have exemplified, as few in any vocation ever have, the religious principles good people covet.

He was born in Clarksburg, West Virginia, in the year 1824. Left an orphan and almost penniless by the death of his father, and deprived of opportunities for education by his poverty and the necessity of supporting his mother and the home, he obtained an appointment to West Point after overcoming almost hopeless difficulties in academic qualification. Despite the ridicule his social deficiencies and his general ineptitude provoked, he persisted and was seventeenth in his class when graduated and was highly honored both by his commission in the artillery and his service in the Mexican War.

For ten years following that war, he served as professor of Artillery Tactics and Natural Philosophy (an unusual combination!) and won the respect and love of his pupils—as demonstrated later on the battlefield and at the fireside—that made his regiment, his brigade, his corps, and his army all but invincible. It was in no sense a fraternizing or resort to expediency that obtained for him the love and personal loyalty of his men, but a recognition of his personal fidelity, his absolute insistence on fairness and discipline, and his deeply religious approach to every situation or crisis.

Superiors and subordinates knew "Old Jack" to be completely dedicated to his cause and willing to give his all for it, as indeed he so shortly did. They knew his promises could be relied upon, and that with the most scrupulous care of which he was capable he would deal with every situation. They also knew that his judgments on men and situations were slowly arrived at and but seldom reversed. If many of them did not know the details of his daily habits of prayer, Bible reading, solitary meditation where possible, and his intense loyalty to his home pastor and church in which he was a deacon and to his chaplains, they all knew that there was evident in him a fervor, an intensity, and a complete devotion to their common task that stirred them to seemingly impossible heights of endurance and sacrifice.

Every Christian citizen, especially one in the heritage of our church here in the Upper Ohio, should read the complete story of the life of this devout Christian. Space here does not permit references to the many instances of his deep modesty, his devotional life unhindered by the vicissitudes of war, his implicit faith in the presence and guidance of God, his unquestioned submission to God's will throughout all his life and amazingly in the days following his fatal injuries on the battlefield of Chancellorsville. None can read his story and remain unmoved by his deep sense of the presence of God and of the divine purpose being accomplished in men and nations, even if at times in mysterious ways.

Thomas Jonathan Jackson epitomizes in an almost ideal fashion the contribution many other Presbyterians of the Upper Ohio have striven also to make in the tragic circumstances of war. Without ostentation or recognition, they have elected to serve the nation as a life's work. They have implemented her necessities by their own sacrifices. They have seldom received, and even less sought, the thanks of their fellow citizens, especially in the years of peace. None can estimate, and certainly none deny, the value their influence, convictions, and skills have been, and inevitably must continue to be, to our nation in her hours of critical need.

II. A Conciliator: Benjamin Harrison

Victor Hugo, in his dramatic portrayal of the battlefield of Waterloo on the night following the conflict, describes the mounds of dead friends and foes intermingled, the hyena-like rapacity of the prowlers stripping dead and dying, and the moans and expiring agonies of the wounded. Through the twilight and then the moonlight, Blücher ferociously pursues the dazed fugitives, and Napoleon as in a trance is led from the scene of the debacle. Says Hugo, "There was not a cloud in the sky. Though the ground may be blood red, the moon remains white. *This is the indifference of nature.*"

This is another way of saying that the terrible excesses of even the most cruel war are at their worst transitory, and that love and justice will ultimately prevail through wills that are innately noble. For after the violence of war and unleashed passions are past, order must once again be restored and men are destined to return to the normal ways of peace.

The Upper Ohio Valley gave the nation, in the person of Benjamin Harrison, a worthy example of this redeeming fruitage of war in the quiet courage of one who performed dangerous duties in battle in a Christlike spirit; which, while hating the evil loves and forgives the evildoer and is the means of re-establishing the divine order of peace that even nature, as Hugo felt, seems to prefigure.

The desirability of peace is a hard, often unpopular, lesson to be learned, but, by faith and self-control Harrison learned and exemplified it. President Lincoln had been blocked in every move for peace and reconciliation with the South by the implacable "Irreconcilables" of his time. President Johnson likewise had been hounded and ultimately broken by the hatred of the same group. Rutherford Hayes and his supporters had been for their efforts at conciliation branded as "Half Breeds" by the now self-designated "Stalwarts" who sought to thwart every step towards reconstruction. But Harrison, a personal sharer in the victory in battle, won an even greater victory in peace.

He was born in 1833 at North Bend near Cincinnati. His great-grandfather was a signer of the Declaration of Independence. His grandfather, William Henry Harrison, was ninth President of the United States and fought with General Anthony Wayne at Fallen Timbers. His father was a member of Congress. He himself was graduated from Miami University and, in 1853, was admitted to the bar in Cincinnati, and shortly thereafter moved to Indianapolis where he soon became one of the leading lawyers of the area.

When the storm of war broke, he offered his services to the nation, for he was strongly opposed to the institution of slavery and was sympathetic to the unhappy lot of the negro people, as were many others in the Cincinnati area at that time. He was authorized to raise a regiment (a custom of the time) and was chosen as its colonel. Later he was breveted a brigadier general for "gallantry in command of a brigade." His regiment fought under his fellow Ohioan, General Don Carlos Buell, in Kentucky and Tennessee, marched with Sherman to Atlanta, was returned to Thomas for the defense of Nashville, and again was sent back to Sherman for his march north through the Carolinas. He won particular recognition in these campaigns at the battles of Kennesaw Mountain, Peach Tree Creek, and Nashville.

Back in civilian life, he felt strongly the need of conciliating the people of the Southern States, and, like Rutherford Hayes, regretted the corrupt, intolerable regime of the "Carpetbaggers." President Hayes had withdrawn the Federal troops which supported the Republican officeholders, but for some time there was naturally a division of political opinion on the question. Harrison threw his influence with Hayes and Garfield and, on Garfield's election to the presidency, was invited to join his cabinet. However, he preferred his seat in the United States Senate. He was chairman of the committee which promoted the admission of the states of North Dakota, South Dakota, Montana, Idaho, and Washington, with their persistent problems of adjustment with the resident Indian tribes. Later, during his own administration, he saw these states admitted. He was also active in the Committee on Indian Affairs and the Committee on Foreign Relations, and was a strong advocate of the reform of the civil service.

During his presidency, he was instrumental in arranging a meeting of the Pan American Congress at Washington, the outlawing of the Louisiana Lottery, the convening of an international monetary conference, the settlement of the conflict with Chile, the establishment of commercial reciprocity with a number of foreign countries, and the peaceful settlement of long-standing difficulties with both Great Britain and Germany. He was also successful during his administration in bringing about a reduction in the national debt while at the same time he modernized and increased the strength of the navy.

After returning to private life, he appeared before the International Tribunal of Arbitration in Paris in behalf of Venezuela in its boundary dispute with Great Britain. He was generally known as a pacificator, analyzing both in his addresses and writings the organization and functions of government. Though defeated for a second term of the presidency, largely by strikes and labor upsurgence during the weeks of the campaign, he received until the end of his life the respect of the nation and the appreciation by Christian people generally for his concern in seeking ways of peace and conciliation.

III. The Citizen-Soldier: Edward Martin

From this Upper Ohio Valley has come also a remarkable support for the belief that the citizen-soldier, when properly taught and adequately equipped, is more nearly the ideal of our nation and probably of our religiously responsible people than any method of self-defense available, because personnel are less likely to forget the ways and thought processes of peace when they live and are trained in the atmosphere and fellowship of their home communities. Even when they are required to be mobilized for extended foreign service, their hearts and minds are closely bound to their homes and peaceful interests. Consequently, they are also more quickly and satisfactorily demobilized as units of common previous experience and accomplishment.

George Washington, the Founder in a real sense of our country, died believing firmly that the citizen-soldier was the greatest material assurance of safety and guarantee of peace the new nation could have. Himself an officer of the militia, having found it necessary on a number of occasions to join in the military defense of the colonies, he believed and demonstrated to his own satisfaction that such emergency service was fully adequate to safeguard the country in time of war. In his farewell address, September 19, 1796, he advised the newly formed Union that by such measures, "They will avoid the necessity of those overgrown military establishments which, under any form of government, are inauspicious to liberty, and which are to be regarded as particularly hostile to Republican liberty." He was well aware from bitter personal experience that such soldiers must be thoroughly and continuously trained, that they must be completely armed and equipped and familiar with the use of their weapons and that they must be recognized and dealt with by those in authority not grudgingly and parsimoniously but as an integral part of the nation's defense. When so welcomed and administered, he believed the citizen-soldier most nearly satisfied the requirements of a peace-loving, nonmilitary people.

The Upper Ohio territory has been an effective "pilot" area in proving the effectiveness of the National Guard as an efficient method of solving the problems together of peace and war. The Twenty-eighth Infantry Division (Pennsylvania) was recognized in World War I as one of the three greatest divisions from all components of the army, and its record is a glorious one. In World War II it was reorganized three times as a consequence of frightful battle losses. Yet its units have returned after each mobilization and become absorbed quickly into the life of the communities from which they came. It is today prepared to make again, if necessary (which God forbid!), the transition from the duties of peace to those of war.

Our Upper Ohio Presbyterians share particularly in this fruitage through a large number of officers and enlisted men of the area who have had distinguished records in the Pennsylvania and Ohio Divisions, but in a special way in one who has been a distinguished figure in the Church, in the Army, and in National Politics.

Major General and United States Senator, Edward Martin was born in a Presbyterian home in the historic Ten Mile community of Greene County, Washington Presbytery. He was graduated from our Waynesburg College, and following his admission to the Bar has practiced law in Western Pennsylvania, participated actively in her religious life, held her highest elective offices, and commanded her Twenty-eighth Division. He has served as Auditor General, State Treasurer, Adjutant General, and as Governor of the Commonwealth, as well as her representative in the Senate of the United States for twelve years.

As a lad nineteen years of age, he participated in the Philippine Campaign of the Spanish-American War. Rising through the ranks, he was an officer in the Mexican Border Campaign in 1916, and was mobilized with the Division in 1917 for World War I, in which as a battalion and regimental commander he rendered outstanding service. He was awarded the Distinguished Service Cross with oak-leaf cluster for bravery in action, and the Purple Heart with oak-leaf cluster for wounds sustained. When the Division was mobilized in 1941 for its long, grueling service in World War II, he was its Commanding General and served faithfully until compelled by over age in grade to retire.

But his service to the church has been equally distinguished. In Washington Presbytery and the Synod of Pennsylvania, his services have been freely given. He has been Vice-President and a director of the Pennsylvania State Sabbath Association, and a member of the Department of Church Co-operation and Union of our Church. He has been for many years a member of the Board of Trustees of Waynesburg and Washington and Jefferson colleges. He has been also for many years an elder in the First Presbyterian Church of Washington, Pennsylvania.

No man in the Presbyterian Church U.S.A., and probably in any other denomination in the nation, can speak on religious matters from a wider or richer experience alike in war, in the church, and in politics. He has abundantly earned the right to be regarded as typical of the fruitage of the Upper Ohio area in confirming and validating the judgment held of the Christian worth of the citizen-soldier.

IV. The Co-ordinator: Richard K. Mellon

The canny teamster who declined to demonstrate his skill with his bull whip by flicking a roadside hornets' nest, "because," he said, "they're organized," had somewhere learned to respect the possibilities of co-operation.

Strangely enough, humans are reluctant to practice its advantages, particularly when jealousy and rivalry keep them separated and at cross purposes. Normally even the dangers of war are not sufficient to unite them, except for the briefest period of supreme peril when it may already be too late. Economies have collapsed and wars have been lost because no common denominator for efficient participation could be agreed upon.

The Upper Ohio area, guided in considerable part by its Presbyterian industrialists and businessmen (See list in Chapter xx on pages 521-525), has had some measure of success in bringing to its maturity the fruitage of war as expressed in co-operation. Service clubs and chambers of commerce have endlessly discussed its possibilities and diligently promoted its ideals; but it remains for the grim realities of possible defeat and annihilation because of poorly planned war efforts to force people to think realistically and in perspective. It could well be these principles of co-operation were initiated generations ago on the Clydeside and in the Midlands to preserve the vulnerable heart of the British Empire. But it has remained for Clairton, Duquesne, McKeesport, Pittsburgh, Ambridge, Wheeling, Youngstown, Warren, and scores of other similar industrial centers, to establish in the last two World Wars the absolute indispensability of intelligent concerted effort in production of the material sinews of war.

For one who has not personally witnessed it, it is impossible to conceive of or appreciate the magnitude and tempo of the war effort in this area. The hundreds of thousands of men and women at all hours of the day and night streaming to and from the mills; the prodigal expenditure of millions of tons of raw materials and the priority of their transportation; the infernal din and confusion of production: these present a pattern so abnormal and irreconcilable with normal life and business that even now they can scarcely be believed. Yet out of the apparent confusion appear rapidly and in seemingly limitless quantity guns, armor plate, fabricated products, structural steel, aluminum products, precision instruments, war heads, and an additional almost unbelievable list of vitally necessary high priority items. A check sheet of all the products required and produced, if it were not too highly classified to be made public, would be seen probably to rival the lists of signatures on an ambitious politician's nomination petition filed in a state capitol.

Of course, this miracle of production does not happen by chance, nor can its details be left completely to the unrelated individual efforts of the thousands of production organizations. A correlation of parts must be accomplished that will function as smoothly and efficiently as the administrative mechanics of a military army or corps or division. Teams must be trained, simultaneously equipped, and synchronized, so that each needed item or group shall be in its place just when needed. Logistic schedules must be carefully prepared and strict conformance required. The needs of the employed personnel must be anticipated and satisfied for health and sanitation, safety and medical requirements, recreation and entertainment. Distribution of needed personnel must be foreseen and provision made for their housing. And all the other thousands of specific demands must be promptly met.

At the summit of this vast effort in every community, and at the area nerve centers, must be adequate intelligence to finance and direct all these various tasks; to make tremendously increased payrolls available at the necessary moment and without fail; to act as a buffer between producers and the rigid, sometimes seemingly cantankerous inspection requirements of the government agencies. Responsible and experienced bankers, credit agents, and business representatives are vitally necessary.

Here we happily introduce one who in a sense is representative of hundreds of others who must be efficient and intelligent, but one who in himself, and in the heritage both of resources and experience, merits personal and grateful recognition for his own contribution and for representing what must in this respect be a vitally important fruitage of war—the organization and inspiring leadership of a tremendous production team, which has the grim responsibility for the proper administration of hundreds of billions of dollars and for the ultimate success or failure of a war effort.

We cite here specifically Major General Richard King Mellon,

GENERAL
BENJAMIN HARRISON
Brigadier-General in 1865.
United States Senator, 1880.
Twenty-third President of the United States, 1889–1893.

GENERAL
THOMAS J.
(STONEWALL)
JACKSON
Famous military leader of the Confederacy. Killed accidentally, May 10, 1863.

GENERAL
EDWARD MARTIN

Commanding General, 28th Infantry Division. Governor of Pennsylvania, 1943–1947. United States Senator, 1947–1959.

GENERAL
RICHARD K. MELLON

Pittsburgh industrialist. Assistant chief of staff of the International Division of War Department in Washington. Awarded Distinguished Service Medal.

one in a stable succession of those Scotch-Irish whose ability, patriotism, and integrity have given individuality and tremendous economic power to the area.

Born in Pittsburgh and educated there and at Princeton, General Mellon entered the business and banking tradition of his grandfather, Thomas Mellon, and his father, Richard B., and his uncle, Andrew W. Mellon. Of the financial strength and physical ramifications of the empire he helped to build and of which he is now the head, it is not necessary to speak here. It is perhaps pertinent to remark only that it does not rest upon one product or interest but is amazingly diversified so as to be in immediate contact with almost every business or industry of the entire Upper Ohio area.

General Mellon has not been insulated against the dangers and hard realities of life. Nor has he allowed his indispensability to the complex ramifications of his business to separate him from community and national concerns. As a young man nineteen years of age, he served with the Air Corps as a student pilot in the First World War. He was commissioned as a Major at the beginning of the Second World War and promoted rapidly to Lieutenant Colonel and Colonel. He served as the Director of Selective Service for the State of Pennsylvania, then as assistant chief of staff of the International Division of the War Department in Washington until the war's end. Subsequently, he was made Brigadier General and then Major General in the Army of the United States, and was awarded the Distinguished Service Medal by the United States government in recognition of his important service.

Since the war his personality and experience have been the motivating power and financial strength behind the vast improvements made in downtown Pittsburgh, in the University center, and in the integration of the transportation facilities of the entire area. Without his direction and support, the strutting and braying of officious politicos would have been just that.

General Mellon typifies in a remarkable way, therefore, the

fruitage of contribution in the war efforts that Presbyterians of the Upper Ohio have in the Providence of God made to the well-being and safety of the nation.

Resumé

Strangely enough, as we view them now in retrospect, each of the men we have considered as typical in his category—Stonewall Jackson, Benjamin Harrison, Edward Martin, and Richard Mellon—has been modest, quiet, and unostentatious. Each, so far as one may judge another, has been personally religious and actively concerned in the support and well-being of our church. Each has brought to life and society as a consequence, in part at least, of his military accomplishments and interests, some values we believe are most worthily reclaimed from the usual moral disintegration and destruction so common to war. Each receives at the hands not only of his fellow Presbyterians but of men everywhere a deserved measure of respect and gratitude.

These are a few instances, at least, in a limited number of fields of civil and national responsibility in which the Presbyterians of the Upper Ohio area have made an earnest contribution toward peace even during unwelcomed conflict.

CHAPTER XVII Changing With Conditions

THE UPPER OHIO VALLEY was already a Presbyterian stronghold when the historic reunion of the New School and Old School groups was consummated in Pittsburgh on November 12, 1869. The merger, however, released new spiritual energy and created new enthusiasms which began at once to be manifested in the enlarging service of the Presbyterian church throughout the entire Upper Ohio Valley during the subsequent decades of change and expansion.

The old Ohio Presbytery, which had zealously advocated policies which made the Schism of 1837 inevitable, was discontinued after seventy years of creative leadership. In the consolidation and reorganization, the Presbytery of Pittsburgh was formed which previously had been the name of the New School presbytery in this area.[1] Rapid growth and financial prosperity crowned the zeal of its lay and clerical leaders. Within four decades, this aggressive Presbytery could claim the largest church and Sunday-school membership of any presbytery in the entire denomination.[2] When the General Assembly convened again at Pittsburgh in 1931, the Pittsburgh Presbytery included 137 churches with 202 ministers on its roll. Communicant members numbered over 70,000 while over 50,000 were enrolled in the church school. That year $2,023,675 had been contributed for local church expenses and $833,046 to support the benevolent and missionary program of the denomination at home and abroad. Notable indeed was the yearly statistical fruitage sixty years after the Reunion.

That primal position was maintained until recently when, through presbyterial merger or population increase, both Philadelphia and Los Angeles forced Pittsburgh Presbytery into third place among Presbyterian presbyteries. The denominational merger in 1958 with the United Presbyterian church may have restored Pittsburgh to a position of leadership. The entire Upper Ohio Valley can boast today of a larger concentration of Presbyterian resources and membership than any other area in the United States.[3]

All Pittsburgh had been stirred by the dramatic pageantry of reunion and reconciliation as the two separated branches of the church again became one in a grand public confession of Christian unity in old Third Church, then located on Sixth Avenue. Strong men wept in the joy of restored fellowship. The "Year of Jubilee" seemed to have come. Under the inspiration of deep conviction, the united General Assembly suggested that a Thank Offering of a million dollars be raised. With the courage of faith, an amendment lifted the proposed goal to five million dollars.

The mover of the motion testified: "I am sure that when we look upon the church as it is today, its wealth, and what it is able to do with self-denial; this sum is small enough."[4] It did prove small enough. When the total amount raised was reported to the General Assembly two years later, the surprising sum was announced as $7,607,499.71. Of that amount, $3,236,475.61 was spent for the erection of new church buildings in an expanded program of church extension.[5]

New Churches in New Communities

More than a proportionate share of that total amount was raised and expended throughout the Upper Ohio Valley. This triumph of faith marked a turning point in the service of the Presbyterian church to the entire community. New goals in benevolence-giving made possible new standards of achievement. The reunion in Pittsburgh ushered in a new era of expanded vision and service as the apparently impossible became an achieved reality. In 1870 the Presbyterian churches throughout the Pittsburgh area numbered only thirty-six. Ten years later they increased to fifty-one churches. At the close of the next decade, Presbyterian churches totaled sixty-three. Five years later in 1895, the number had grown to seventy-four.[6]

This multiplication of Presbyterian churches was chiefly in the suburbs. It was a missionary effort to keep in step with the rapid growth of population. In 1870 Pittsburgh and Allegheny could claim a population of only 139,434. Twenty years later the census reported 314,710.[7] Presbyterians were attempting to bring the influence of the church into these newer communities and centers of population on a neighborhood basis. The immediate neighborhood was the area of each church's concern in Christian fellowship. The day of large urban churches had not yet dawned in the Pittsburgh district. Each church aimed to hold and to serve its own community. Preaching, pastoral service, and Sunday-school instruction were the threefold phases of service with music and fellowship as added joys throughout the church family.

The South Side church organized in 1851, Carnegie in 1853, Mt. Washington in 1857, Bellefield and Wilkinsburg in 1866, Shadyside and McClure Avenue in 1867, Bloomfield and Bellevue in 1871, and Knoxville in 1872 are illustrative of the carefully directed missionary outreach of the Presbyterian church in many newer communities during this period of community expansion. Some of these community churches have grown into prosperous and dynamic organizations and continue to serve aggressively the constantly changing community environment. Others have passed through a cycle of expanding opportunity and encouraging growth, and have declined in membership or have been merged or discontinued as Presbyterian churches. The life span of a church varies with its possible service radius and the denominational desires of a shifting membership.

Fellowship Amid Separation

The Synod of Pittsburgh, and particularly the Presbytery of Ohio, had contributed no small part to the movement which made the Schism of 1837 inevitable. Yet the resulting separation into the Old and New School branches did not result in personal bitterness or hampering strife throughout Western Pennsylvania. The dominant Scotch and Scotch-Irish elements in Western Pennsylvania remained almost solidly in the Old School Presbytery of Ohio. They exerted an influence in shaping theological convictions and moral ideals far beyond their numerical strength. Farther north, however, in the areas of Erie and Meadville and the Western Reserve portion of northern Ohio, a numerically strong and influential element had come from New York, Connecticut, and Massachusetts. Their more liberal New England traditions and philosophy imparted a natural sympathy with the New School branch.[8]

In Pittsburgh the few ministers who united with the New School Assembly worked in closest co-operation with their Old School Presbyterian brethren. When devastating fires destroyed the Second and later the Third Presbyterian Church buildings, the remaining sanctuaries were shared for worship and fellowship.[9] Throughout the period of separation, a series of missionary and evangelistic conventions rekindled religious enthusiasm and consecration. To these conventions came Presbyterian leaders from the neighboring synods of Ohio, Pittsburgh, and Wheeling. Pittsburgh was selected since it was "looked to, from all parts of the land, as the city whose central location, the spirit of the people, the tone of religion, and the influence in the regions related to it, as the most suitable for some of those great convocations whose transactions have formed eras in the great efforts to deepen and spread the efficiency of the Gospel of salvation."[10]

Of the four great conventions which met in 1842, 1857, 1861, and 1867, perhaps the most influential was the meeting in 1857. Men gathered from a radius of two hundred miles. The power of the

Holy Spirit seemed to surge within the vast assembly in the First Presbyterian Church. Strong men were almost speechless with emotion. A mighty revival followed in many of the surrounding presbyteries and in some of the Pittsburgh churches. Among the great addresses given on that memorable occasion was the stirring sermon of Professor Melancthon Jacobus of the Western Theological Seminary. The sermon was published and distributed far and wide. It produced a quickening influence even among Presbyterian missionaries in faraway India. They reported as "having been greatly refreshed by what we have heard of the Lord's dealings in America."

Inspired by this spiritual awakening in Pittsburgh, the following year the Presbytery of Lodiana issued a call for a world-wide Concert of Prayer during the first week of January.[11] The call won an immediate and continued response. The annual observance of the Week of Prayer is part of the spiritual fruitage of that Pittsburgh Convention. From Pittsburgh to Lodiana! From Lodiana to Pittsburgh came the continued call to prayer. Thus back and forth the spiritual forces call to one another across the continents and the years in a swelling antiphonal of prayer and praise.

DOWNTOWN CHURCHES EXPAND PROGRAM

With the passing of the years, inevitable changes took place in the downtown sections of Pittsburgh. The small community church, with its members located within easy traveling range, was soon hampered by a changing environment. Industry began pouring forth the smoke and dirt which caused Pittsburgh to be known for years as "The Smoky City." Throughout the decade of 1870–1880, Pittsburgh was described as the blackest, dirtiest, grimiest city in the United States. Visitors, driving through the city in cabs, reacted in amazement at the soot and cinders pattering against the windows like steadily falling rain. The warm summer air carried into open windows an annoying odor as it drifted from the seventy-five stables in the downtown section alone. "A month in

Pittsburgh," remarked Herbert Spencer, "would justify anyone in committing suicide."[12]

Little wonder then that the wealthier citizens sought relief and moved to the more attractive residential communities on the North Side, in Oakland, Shadyside, and as far away as East Liberty. Industrial workers occupied downtown homes. Business enterprises expanded with the increasing population and prosperity of the growing city. New and more impressive sanctuaries of worship were erected as old ones were outmoded or destroyed by fire.

Popular preachers, including Seminary professors, occupied the downtown pulpits. They were able to attract worshiping congregations in large numbers. Dr. Elliott Swift had proved to be a worthy successor to his famous father in the First Church of Allegheny. He had a brilliant neighbor in Dr. Archibald Hodge who was preaching to crowds in the rather recently organized North Church. Dr. William Paxton, perhaps the greatest preacher of his day, had succeeded Dr. Francis Herron in the pulpit of the First Church. Leading industrialists formed its membership and strengthened its resources of finance and prestige. Dr. William D. Howard, in the Second Church, similarly adorned that pulpit located in an impressive edifice on the corner of Penn Avenue and Seventh Street. The Third Church was experiencing difficulty in retaining for any extended pastorate a successor to Dr. David Riddle. Consolidation or removal seemed to be logical alternatives to the overcrowding of Presbyterian churches in the downtown area. The First and the Second Presbyterian churches chose to remain while the Third, Central, Fourth, and Sixth churches removed to more productive fields of community service.

The First Church, which had been blest with a loyal and influential membership and the strong preaching of Dr. Sylvester F. Scovel, as Dr. Paxton's successor, determined to meet the challenge of a changing community by an enlarging program of service. The church was still in its original location on ground deeded for church purposes by the Penn heirs. It was in the older and less attractive part of the city. Welcomed opportunities for service among unchurched young people were found in the nearby Young Men's Christian Association and the Young Women's Christian Association. A program of lay-evangelism was developed. The church staff was enlarged by the employment of the Reverend S. C. Faris as a city missionary. Miss Ellen McNutt also was employed for part-time service among girls and mothers in a program of visitation on behalf of the Sabbath school. A Board of Deacons was organized for the first time in the history of the church. An $18,000 manse for the minister was built and a Sabbath school erected at a cost of $24,000.[13] These achievements were all the more remarkable since the years 1873–1882 were a period of financial depression in the city and often referred to as "the big panic."

When the terrible labor riots during July of 1877 spread terror throughout the city, with the burning of the railroad cars, and even threatened civil war between the State Militia and the angry strikers, Dr. Scovel was asked to serve as a mediator. So definitely had he won the confidence of the community that he and Bishop Tuigg were appointed as clerical peacemakers to persuade the strikers to desist from further bloodshed. He urged them to rely on legal measures and the verbal presentation of the justice of their cause for a reasonable solution of the issues in the strike. It is the first record of a Pittsburgh Presbyterian clergyman called to serve as an arbiter in a labor dispute. The following Sabbath day, Dr. Scovel preached to his congregation on the supplementary theme, "The Supremacy of Law."[14]

Under Dr. Scovel's creative leadership, the church grew steadily. Membership increased from 451 to 712 throughout the decade 1870–1880. The First Church was the largest church in the Pittsburgh Presbytery. It was with great regret that the congregation bade farewell to its popular pastor when he resigned to accept the presidency of Wooster College, Ohio, where he served until his death in 1910.

Dr. George Purvis and Dr. David Breed, who followed Dr. Scovel in the pastorate, were brilliant, dynamic preachers who knew how to attract and interest large congregations at both the morning and evening services. But their pastorates were brief. Both resigned to teach young men at Presbyterian theological seminaries. Hundreds of Presbyterian preachers throughout the Upper Ohio Valley owe an inestimable debt of gratitude to Dr. Breed, the long-time professor of Homiletics at Western Seminary, for his practical guidance in preaching and pastoral evangelism.

Dr. Alexander's Transforming Leadership

But it was Dr. Maitland Alexander who altered the entire outlook of this downtown church and built for it that program of multiplied community service which made the First Presbyterian Church of Pittsburgh a mighty institution in the developing city. He came to the pastorate at a crucial but strategic time. When he was called to Pittsburgh in 1899, the church had a recorded membership of only 667, as contrasted with 770 a decade earlier.[15] Death and removal to residential areas had weakened the financial and leadership strength of the church. Instead of centering his gaze upon a church that was dwindling in membership and finances and threatened by the encroachment of business interests, Maitland Alexander dreamed of a great church centered in a great city and extending its varied services far and near and attracting to its work and worship multitudes who might come and go. In him, his biographer states, "was the rare combination of administrative genius, quick intellect, distinguished pulpit ability, and magnetic personality."[16] He was thus equipped to transform his vision into an organization and into a building.

The time was ripe for an aggressive change in outlook and program. Downtown Pittsburgh was beginning a renaissance with the emergence of the Golden Triangle. Steel was making possible new and higher buildings. Henry W. Oliver was entering upon those large transactions in real estate which were to give Pittsburgh a new business look. He offered the church a long-time lease for the privilege of erecting a large building on the corner of Wood Street and Sixth Avenue. This necessitated the removal of the old church on Wood Street and rebuilding on the present site on Sixth Avenue.[17] A profitable rental and a generous bonus were offered which the church officials accepted. Additional gifts made possible the completion in 1905 of an impressive cathedral-like sanctuary, with a church-school building equipped with facilities for recreation and institutional services to the community.

An enlarged staff was recruited for specialized activities to carry forward an expanded program on a seven-day basis. The employment of a church missionary, a church nurse, a dietitian, and a physical director, the organization of clubs for men, boys, and girls, clubs for underprivileged mothers and working girls, a sewing club, the purchase of a summer church camp on Indian Creek for both sexes and all ages, and a broadened preaching and educational program—all were phases of the practical fulfillment of Dr. Alexander's dream and drive. Amazing results followed. A receding church became a growing and a serving church, a beehive of activity.

In addition to other phases of civic and educational responsibility, Dr. Alexander found time to serve for over twenty years as President of the Board of Directors of the Allegheny General Hospital, an institution to which he gave much leadership and generous support. His unanimous election as moderator of the General Assembly of the Presbyterian Church U.S.A. in 1915 was a fitting recognition of his creative ministry in Pittsburgh. The membership rolls multiplied. When Dr. Alexander resigned, after a ministry to the city of twenty-nine years, the membership roll of the church numbered 2,955. The Sunday school had an enrollment of 1,525. Both totals were the largest in the entire Presbytery of Pittsburgh at that time.[18]

For over a quarter of a century, his successor, Dr. Clarence Edward Macartney, carried forward a similar program of wide-range civic ministry in this downtown church that had successfully adjusted its religious and institutional activities to a changing environment. Even the additional handicaps of an open Sunday and inadequate parking facilities did not restrict the large worshiping congregations that found spiritual stimulation in the multiplied preaching and pastoral services of a remarkably gifted preacher and able administrator.

Perhaps the most effective of the distinctive features of Dr. Macartney's service to the community was the development of a Tuesday noonday luncheon and fellowship meeting for businessmen. It had its origin in the expressed desire of a group of six well-known business leaders. One Tuesday they had met with Dr. Macartney for lunch and prayer. They were thrilled by an informal description of his recent visit to the Holy Land. Among them was Robert Gibson, an elder in the church and manager of The Presbyterian Book Store. The next Tuesday each man brought a friend. From that small beginning has developed a weekly gathering of men which frequently has numbered over one thousand. They met in the church to share together the inspiration of a hymn, a prayer, and a brief spiritual message from the heart and experience of a great preacher before returning to their offices to face anew the pressure of the day's problems and responsibilities. This noonday fellowship continues to be a popular feature of the church's program of service with no decline in attendance or enthusiasm.

This historic downtown church faces the future with vision and optimism under the guidance of Dr. Robert J. Lamont, the present pastor, who is ever alert to new opportunities of service. In 1955 an addition costing five hundred and forty thousand dollars increased greatly the church's educational and institutional equipment to serve further a changing environment. It is the fifth change in edifice upon the original site of worship in 1787.

Second Church Remains Downtown

The Second Presbyterian Church, like its neighbor, the First Church, also chose to remain a downtown institution and sought to serve a changing community. Founded in 1801 as an act of dissatisfaction with the pastor of the First Church, the little congregation struggled for life until the famed Dr. Elisha Swift gave it prestige and won a sustaining membership. Debts and a disastrous fire in 1850 hampered for a time the progress of the church. Subsequent rapid growth was due largely to the preaching popularity and leadership of a succession of capable ministers.

At the turn of the nineteenth century, its membership was larger than that of the First Church. The consecrated Dr. S. Edward Young was in the pulpit. Out in "the highways and hedges" he went, attempting to compel people to come into the Kingdom. He was not content to preach merely to those who would attend church. In the parks and theaters, he preached, seeking an audience.[19] Through this type of community service, the membership grew to more than a thousand in 1900. Thus he had gathered a congregation of ordinary folks who were united in a democratic fellowship. Enthusiastic Gospel singing and the absence of the restraints of ritual stirred the emotions of large worshiping congregations of people of moderate circumstances.

The inevitable financial problems of that type of downtown church seemed to make advisable the sale in 1904 of the valuable corner property on Penn and Seventh avenues for a half million dollars. The proceeds made possible the purchase of the synagogue owned by the Jewish congregation and still left a substantial balance as a sustaining endowment. The building was extensively remodeled for Christian worship. Parlors, dining rooms, and adequate Sunday-school rooms were added to broaden the scope of the church's service and to promote fellowship as a family group.[20]

In this new location on Eighth Street, the congregation of the Second Church faced optimistically the challenge of continued Christian service to a changing downtown community. Dr. George Shelton in the year 1910 was called from Nashville, Tennessee. His warm southern graciousness and evangelistic fervor drew large worshiping congregations. He preached not only during the regular morning and evening services in the sanctuary but also in the big Alvin Theatre throughout eight midwinter seasons of revival services. During the early period of his 25-year pastorate, the church attained its largest numerical strength. As the church celebrated its 125th anniversary in 1927, Dr. Shelton thus reviewed the fruitage of the years:

"This church has furnished distinguished leadership in every department of life: as a governor of Pennsylvania, an ambassador to Germany, a consul to Greece, a mayor of the city, judges in our high courts, business and professional leaders, educators, and men and women of letters. But above all, here a vast number of noble men and women of everyday walks of life have found inspiration and strength for performing the common tasks of life in a most uncommon way."[21]

In 1931 an unsuccessful effort was made, under the leadership of Dr. Shelton, to unite the Second Presbyterian Church with both the Central and the First Presbyterian churches of Allegheny in a threefold merger. The resources of the three churches were to be pooled, their buildings sold, and a new cathedral-like edifice erected at a central location on the North Side. The three churches were temporarily merged. Some property was optioned for purchase.

The plan, however, proved impracticable. Second Presbyterian Church was continued in its location on Eighth Street in Pittsburgh, while the two North Side churches were united as the First-Central Presbyterian Church. The sanctuary and equipment of the First Church of Allegheny continued to be more than adequate for the needs of the united congregation in that changing downtown area on the north side of the Allegheny River. The recent closing of the famous Boggs & Buhl store, after eighty-nine years of service, is a further indication of the decline of a formerly proud area where, it is stated, "at one time resided one-third of all the millionaires in the United States."

Removal Rejuvenates the Third Church

The Third, Fourth, Central, and Sixth Presbyterian churches felt the futility of further expenditure of Presbyterian resources in the downtown area of shifting population and business expansion. Each in turn moved to newer residential areas where more encouraging opportunities of service seemed available. Service to the downtown section of the city was left to the First and Second churches which were making the necessary adaptation in program and resources.

The members of the Third Presbyterian Church were still worshiping in their impressive edifice on Sixth Avenue and Cherry Alley where the Penn-Sheraton Hotel now stands. The vast sanctuary seating thirteen hundred people had been the scene of the Reunion of the New and Old School. In 1895, General Assembly met again in that same church to celebrate the twenty-fifth anniversary of a happy and fruitful reunion. Enthusiasm was quickened. Just one year previously, the beloved Dr. William L. McEwan had begun his memorable pastorate of almost thirty-eight years. The church had a membership at that time of more than six hundred.

Irrepressible changes, however, were in process that necessitated basic readjustments. An effort had been made previously, and approved by Presbytery, to merge with the Second Church.[22] But hampering discord in both churches resulted in rescinding the decision to unite. Removal to another location seemed the only solution. Dr. McEwan thus describes the Pittsburgh which greeted him upon his arrival in 1893.

"When I began my pastorate, there was not a high building in the city. There was not an apartment house anywhere. The streetcar lines had not been consolidated. Little cars drawn by mules or horses brought people to the heart of the city from the outlying districts. The cable line, part of the way to Wilkinsburg, was nearest to the rapid transit. There were no members of the church who lived nearer than a mile and most of them further from the church."[23]

The hope of the uncharted future lay in the Session whom Dr. McEwan described as "a remarkable body of men, commanding the respect of the community, devoted to the interest of their church and examples of what elders should be in their Christian lives." He lists them: "Judge Thomas Ewing, an upright judge and a great man; Dr. Cyrus B. King, a beloved physician; Colonel W. A. Herron, as widely known and as universally honored as any man in the city; Mr. C. L. Rose, wonderfully gifted in prayer; Mr. S. M. Willock, of rare faithfulness and unimpeachable integrity; and Professor Joseph F. Griggs, the saint and scholar."[24]

A congregational meeting voted unanimously to move to the East End even though many of the members were living on the North Side and their new church would be five miles or more from their homes. A merger was effected with the Church of the Covenant which added seventy-eight members.[25] The lot on the corner of Fifth and Negley was purchased. In 1897 Pittsburgh was experiencing another of its recurrent financial depressions. Yet by October 17 of that year, a handsome stone chapel had been built and was ready for use by the merged congregations. The present sanctuary itself was dedicated November 1, 1903. The surrounding community grew rapidly into the finest residential section of Pittsburgh. Prosperity and prestige marked the rapid development of the church as an attractive center of worship, with scholarly preaching and the best in music.

When Dr. McEwan resigned after reaching seventy years of age, the church membership numbered seventeen hundred and twenty.[26] The church was supporting generously its missionary program at home and abroad. Dr. S. Hall Young in Alaska and Dr. Albert I. Good in Africa were among the better-known missionaries who were supported by this church. They and many others have preached the Gospel in widely separated fields of consecrated labor as part of the fruitage of a church whose vision of service was not limited to its residential environment. Dr. McEwan could include as part of the fruitage of his transplanted pastorate the raising of some four and a half million dollars. Nearly two-thirds of that amount was given to benevolence in a variety of missionary and educational causes.

Even attractive residential communities undergo the changes of time. Apartment houses replace beautiful homes as hired help becomes an insuperable problem in days of high wages and high taxes. Large estates are broken up into sites for smaller homes. The Third Church felt the need of enlarging its program of facilities to serve better a changing community. An aggressive program of development was launched by the present pastor, Dr. Frederick B. Speakman. In September of 1951, a new educational and recreational building was dedicated at an approximate cost of $730,000. It has proved a popular meeting place for many civic, cultural, educational, and religious groups and organizations, in addition to housing a greatly expanded program.[27] A membership of approximately 1,700, guided by the services of three full-time ministers, has kept pace with the changes of the past decade and welcomes new opportunities of service.

EXPANSION AT EAST LIBERTY

The East Liberty Presbyterian Church is another interesting illustration of a changing church in a changing community, but with sufficient resources to enlarge successfully its facilities for service. Like the First Church, it has remained in its original location while the environment shifted from a residential to a business district. The church was organized in 1828 amid a rural setting of homes and farms. A small group of Presbyterians had chosen as their first pastor the Reverend William B. McIlvaine. He came to East Liberty a youthful licentiate from Princeton Seminary. He remained to serve a developing church throughout a pastorate of forty years until he was succeeded by his young associate, the Reverend John Gillespie.

The community and the church had begun to grow rapidly when the Pennsylvania Railroad was extended to Pittsburgh in 1853. In the generosity and loyalty of the Negley and Mellon families, the congregation found the necessary assistance to modernize and expand repeatedly the church facilities. Throughout the years, five buildings have been erected on approximately the same plot of ground as the congregation grew and as it constantly sought to be of expanding service to a developing community.

A novel feature of Dr. Gillespie's ministry, which began in 1865, was a pioneer children's church. It met on a Sabbath afternoon each month and was planned especially for the youth of the congregation. At this service Mr. Gillespie would portray very graphically Bible scenes and draw impressive lessons from Bible characters and incidents. In that manner, he made lasting impressions on youthful minds.[28]

Dr. John Gillespie continued to serve the church until 1882. He was a diligent pastor who called upon his growing congregation regularly and systematically twice a year, in the spring and the fall. He would announce from the pulpit each Sunday in which part of his parish he would call that week. He expected his people to be home, ready to receive his pastoral ministrations. He became irritated if any parishioner failed to respond to his knock on the door. One Sabbath morning, after making his usual announcement of the week's pastoral itinerary, he added: "I hope you will be at home and welcome your pastor." By way of explanation, he remarked in incriminating rebuke:

"One day last week, as I was tying my horse to a post, I glanced at the house and saw the lady just leaving an upstairs window. I walked up the walk to the door and rang the bell. I heard a servant girl come through the hall and heard the lady call softly, 'Jane, Jane.' 'Yes, Ma'am,' replied the girl. 'That is our pastor. Tell him I am not at home.' 'Yes, Ma'am.' 'Jane, Jane, be real nice to him.' 'Yes, Ma'am.' "

And then Dr. Gillespie continued with pointed frankness, "And that lady is within the sound of my voice this morning."[29]

The Reverend J. P. E. Kumler, who moved to the East Liberty Church from Cincinnati in 1884, led the church in a period of growth which resulted in the building of a beautiful new sanctuary which housed the congregation in worship until the present Gothic cathedral was erected. Dr. Kumler inherited an organization of 533 members. When he retired 17 years later, the membership had grown to 1,349. It was the largest congregation in Pittsburgh at the turn of the century.[30] Moreover, during those years, the pastor was unselfishly dismissing groups of his members to organize and carry forward other Presbyterian churches in the East Liberty area.

Dr. Kumler thought several smaller churches could serve the expanding community better than one large centrally located church. In 1887 he dismissed forty members to form the nucleus of the Point Breeze Church at the intersection of Fifth and Penn avenues. Five years later forty-eight members went forth as a colony to help start the present Highland Avenue Church. Still the membership grew, making imperative additional facilities to house the large Sunday school. The new unit, harmonizing with the stone sanctuary, was completed for use the year after Dr. Kumler had closed his pastorate. It was named "The Kumler Memorial Chapel" in honor of Dr. and Mrs. Kumler.[31]

But why Dr. and Mrs. Kumler? Thereby hangs an interesting tale. Mrs. Kumler was a remarkable woman. The Sunday before Dr. Kumler began his work in Pittsburgh, the pulpit of East Liberty Church was being supplied by the Reverend Richard H. Allen, a secretary of the Board of Freedmen. He spoke very highly of Dr. Kumler and then added, "He has a wife who is worth her weight in gold to any congregation." The remark brought a smile of indulgence as the congregation pictured a petite little helpmeet. But when Mrs. Kumler appeared the next Sunday, with an evident weight well over two hundred pounds, there was an amused consensus of opinion that Dr. Allen may have been too liberal in his high estimate of her value. Soon, however, the congregation concurred in Dr. Allen's evaluation.

Mrs. Kumler proved herself a most valuable wife for the new pastor.[32] Under her leadership the women of the church were organized into missionary bands and circles. The Obey Band, The Golden Rule, The Co-Workers, and The Nellie Cuthbert Band are typical names of these numerous bands, which resembled the present-day circles in the Women's Association. These bands engaged in friendly competition against one another in their zeal to broaden and strengthen the missionary enterprises of the church. Mrs. Kumler's influence continues to live in the life service of many whom she quickened in missionary zeal.[33]

Gothic Cathedral Erected

It was a great day in the history of the East Liberty Presbyterian Church when in 1930 Richard B. Mellon and his wife, Jennie King Mellon, offered to remove the old church and replace it with a Gothic cathedral which would cover an entire block. The offer was gratefully accepted. There it stands, a memorial to the faith of their parents and grandparents, one of the most imposing church edifices in the country. To his pastor, Dr. Stuart Nye Hutchison, Mr. Mellon confided, "We are building this church as an expression of our faith in the future of the Christian Church."[34]

The worshiper finds himself surrounded with masterpieces of grandeur and beauty which the finest craftsmanship in wood, stone, and stained glass have produced to symbolize and suggest the permanence and peace of the Christian faith. No expense has been spared. Nor has artistry been restrained in the magnificent fulfillment in material form of a vision of adequacy and completeness. Suggestions from the great Gothic cathedrals of past centuries have been merged to create something new and distinctive in a modern era that refuses merely to conform with the past. The towering spire, reaching from earth's shadows toward heaven's light, attracts the attention of the passer-by within a circumference of several miles and impresses him with the centrality of spiritual things even in a world of materialism and pleasure-seeking.[35]

Adjoining the church, and unified into the central edifice, is the church house. Spacious and carefully equipped, it provides abundant facilities to carry the religious impulse into many helpful phases of social, educational, recreational, and cultural life. Over one hundred rooms of varying sizes and designs provide facilities for a vast program of departmentalized church-school instruction, bowling, gymnasium activities, conferences, scouting, dining, reading, handwork, first aid, and so forth. Programs are planned for all ages and require the supervision and direction of a staff of employed leaders and volunteer assistants. The bowling alleys, with ten leagues operating every week, are perhaps the most popular recreational activity. As a tribute to his leadership in planning the building and his administrative skill in developing the broad-range program of service to the community, the pastor, Dr. Hutchison, was honored with the moderatorship of the General Assembly in 1942.

The present leadership of the church remains mindful of its responsibility both to the members of the church and to the community in a maximum use of the extensive facilities of this well-equipped church. Through careful scheduling, many groups, not directly connected with the church, are granted opportunities to center their own programs in assigned parts of the building. "Our church policy has always been prompted by a sense of responsibility to the community at large," explained Dr. Charles P. Robshaw, the present pastor.

A Red Cross unit, a chapter of Alcoholics Anonymous, a nursery school operated by the church but open to all children of the community, the East Liberty Kiwanis Club, the Nurses' Basketball Team from Shadyside Hospital, church teams from other congregations in a local Protestant Churches' League, the weekly meetings of the Peabody High School released time Religious Education program, the Commencement program of Western Theological Seminary, and numerous special activities of many religious organizations all find a welcome at the Presbyterian church which has become the vital religious center of East Liberty.[36]

The East Liberty Presbyterian Church has rejoiced also in its success as a colonizing church. Individual members have organized mission schools throughout the district. Some of these mission Sunday schools have developed into churches. Other groups of devoted workers left the parent church to organize new churches in the general area of East Liberty. Throughout the years these daughter churches have included the Mt. Olive Church in Squirrel Hill in 1861, the Shadyside Presbyterian Church in 1867, the Westminster Church in 1869, Latimer Avenue in 1894, the Park Avenue Church in 1881, the Point Breeze Church in 1887, the Highland Presbyterian Church in 1892, an Italian church, and the Valley View Presbyterian Church in 1914.[37] The Mt. Olive Church was merged with the Sixth Church when that congregation moved from downtown in 1903 to its present location on Forbes Street and Murray Avenue. The Westminster Church never did thrive and was disbanded after eleven unsuccessful years. The Park Avenue Church now houses the Bethesda congregation and is strategically located in the center of a large and growing negro population.

Shadyside Church Contributes to Education

The Shadyside Presbyterian Church has been the most successful of these numerous colonizing efforts of the East Liberty Church. Sunday afternoon, April 29, 1860, Mr. Thomas Aiken, an elder in the East Liberty Church, and his Presbyterian neighbor, Mr. William B. Negley, organized a Sunday school. At that time there were no other Presbyterian families in the small community of twenty families. These two Presbyterian pioneers and their wives formed the teaching corps for forty pupils.[38] The newer families moving into the community were chiefly Presbyterian. A prayer meeting was soon added to the program of the expanding school. This grew into a need for a church. A one and a half acre lot was purchased as a site for the church on the corner of Amberson and Westminster Streets. A charter was secured and plans laid for the erection of a church building. The Pennsylvania Railroad permitted the group to worship on Sunday evenings for the next ten months in the station house at Shadyside.

The guest preacher on two occasions was the Reverend William T. Beatty who was returning from General Assembly to his home in New Jersey. His sermons stirred the congregation. He accepted their call. July 8, 1867, was a memorable date. It marked the organization of the congregation into a church, the formal call of the pastor, and the dedication of the church sanctuary—a most unusual triple feature in the history of any Presbyterian church. Appropriately, Dr. Scovel of the First Church and Dr. Gillespie of the East Liberty Church organized the new church. The former had contributed fourteen from his membership and the latter eleven members to form the Shadyside Church which was then organized with twenty-nine members.[39] The remaining four were from United Presbyterian and Methodist churches.

Among these non-Presbyterian charter members was Robert Pitcairn who had been very active in the early development of the church and especially the Sunday school. He possessed a passionate love for children and the talent for constructive service. He was something of a musician and the church's first chorister. He taught the young people to sing with the fervor of a transplanted Methodist. Singing became a popular and attractive feature. This Methodist-tinted fervor in song may not have appealed to the more staid and prosperous Presbyterian families who were moving into Shadyside and joining the rapidly developing church. At least Robert Pitcairn (R. P. as he was fondly nicknamed) was no longer the chorister. Some felt the music had lost its appeal. In the pathos of nostalgic memory, a discouraged member wrote:

No! I ain't goin' to church no more;
Ther ain't no sort o' good in it.
Ther's preaching? Yes! and praying too,
But I can't find no food in it.
I only sits and thinks of days
Thet mem'ry's allus bringin'
Of days thet's now long past and gone
When R. P. led the singin'[40]

Music of a different type was soon to bring an unusual distinction to the Shadyside Church. One of the daughters born to Dr. and Mrs. Beatty, during their 17-year pastorate at Shadyside, was the renowned Madame Louise Homer. Her rich, melodious, contralto voice charmed the ears of music lovers in a world-wide ministry of music in the opera and on the concert stage. Though the personnel of the church choir changes, church music of a high quality is a constitutive part of Shadyside at worship. The new church organ installed in 1957 is one of the finest in America.[41]

The service of the Shadyside Church, in the realm of education, has been both distinctive and widespread. The original charter was for "religious and educational purposes."[42] Two months after the church was dedicated, a select day school was established in the church building. The principal was Mr. Henry J. Gourley, who later became mayor of Pittsburgh. The charter had specified that the church "provide rooms and suitable teachers to instruct the children of all those who have subscribed fifty dollars, or upwards, toward the purchase of the lot and the erection of buildings, and such other children only as said trustees may permit to enter, provided that a reasonable tuition fee shall be paid for every child so being taught."[43] This private school for the families of the church continued until 1876 when it was discontinued and the charter amended.

In 1869, two years after the Shadyside Church was organized, a second venture in the field of education was launched. The congregation felt that a college for women should be developed somewhere near the church. A sum of $20,000 was pledged toward the purchase of ground and the erection of suitable buildings. Other generous givers responded. Through the leadership of the pastor, Dr. Beatty, the Pennsylvania College for Women was launched that same year. Three years later an additional $10,000 was given by the church as a thanksgiving offering. The continued expansion and broadened service of the college have been made possible by the sustaining gifts of leading members of the Shadyside Church who have served also on its Board of Trustees. The present enlargement of that institution, now renamed Chatham College, is a source of deep gratitude to those whose vision and leadership have maintained the school and guided its development.

The Shady Side Academy is another honored institution which owes its origin to the educational vision of the Shadyside Church. At the close of a special prayer meeting for schools and colleges in the Spring of 1883, a group of the church officers gathered in the pastor's study to take definite steps in organizing an academy for boys in that growing community. Dr. William R. Crabbe, who had been conducting a similar school in Allegheny and who served for many years as an elder in the Shadyside Church, was employed as headmaster of the new academy. On the very site on Aiken Avenue where the first Sunday school was organized Dr. Crabbe in September of that year opened the Shady Side Academy.

Removed through the years to other locations, this Academy has continued as a high-grade preparatory school. It has a long list of alumni whom it has equipped for college and subsequent careers of usefulness to society.[44] Since 1954 the educational zeal of the Shadyside Church has found new opportunity in the development of a weekday Nursery School for children of preschool age. A staff of six conducts the school, with an enrollment of seventy-four pupils.

During the long and distinguished pastorate of Dr. Hugh Thomson Kerr, who served the Shadyside Church from 1913–1945, the church sought opportunities of service among the students on the nearby campuses of the University of Pittsburgh and Carnegie Tech. In the Fall of 1915, Dr. Kerr formed a supper club for Pitt students. With a purposeful effort to emulate the heroic faith of young Horace T. Pitkin, who had died a martyr's death in 1900, while serving as a missionary in China, the new organization called itself the "Pitkin Club." It was a student group for the frank discussion of varied religious and personal problems, as well as the application of Christianity to society, the business world, and international affairs.

Eleven students from Carnegie Tech invited Dr. Kerr to lead a similar group among them. The new club adopted the name Teknon. It was the first Christian organization at Carnegie Institute of Technology. The subsequent movement for a Y.M.C.A., a Y.W.C.A., a Baccalaureate sermon, and a chapel service on the campus are direct fruits of the influence of the Teknon Club. At the present time, both Pitkin and Teknon clubs, together with students from Chatham College, meet each Wednesday evening for dinner at five-thirty and a joint discussion. The average attendance is between eighty and a hundred.[45]

This pioneering program of the Shadyside Church among these three educational institutions has now been supplemented and strengthened by the establishment of a Westminster Foundation with headquarters in the Bellefield Presbyterian Church. The preliminary organizational work began the year Dr. Kerr closed his pastorate. The actual program of service to the students started to function two years later when the Reverend Charles Blaker was employed as the full-time director. His successor, the Reverend Vincent Stratton, has expanded the program with many activities which now include student counseling, dinner clubs, campus seminars, and practical work projects. A particularly pleasing feature of intercollegiate fellowship is the weekly Tuesday evening dinner conference in the Bellefield Presbyterian Church. These dinner meetings draw together in fellowship and inspiration students from the Medical Center, University of Pittsburgh, Carnegie Tech, and Chatham College. The program is distinct and separate but co-ordinates with a similar discussion group in the Shadyside Church in a dual effort to quicken religious zeal among Presbyterian students at these Pittsburgh schools.

Undoubtedly, the widest religious service of the Shadyside Church has been its radio ministry which was initiated in 1922 by Dr. Kerr and continues under Dr. Howard C. Scharfe, the present pastor. The broadcasting of the Sunday afternoon Vesper Service over KDKA was one of the pioneer efforts to use the radio for the widespread proclamation of the Gospel. Communications from appreciative listeners have reached the church from every continent. The first message ever received in the Arctic regions was sent by Dr. Kerr from the Shadyside Church. Likewise, the first radio message to be heard in the Antarctic was also broadcast by Dr. Kerr. A bronze tablet in the church commemorates the historic fact that from the Shadyside Church the universal Gospel of redemption was first proclaimed from pole to pole.[46] Since 1951 the Sunday morning service has been broadcast over station KQV with a re-broadcast over KDKA on Sunday night.

Dr. Kerr's other services in the field of education included, among others, membership on the Board of Trustees of the University of Pittsburgh, the presidency of the Board of Directors of Western Theological Seminary, and the presidency of the Board of Christian Education of the Presbyterian Church U.S.A. In recognition of his broad-range service to the church, Dr. Kerr was honored with the moderatorship of the Presbyterian General Assembly in 1930.

The church has attempted to keep pace with a changing community. The original frame building was replaced by a stone sanctuary in 1875 and again in 1890 by the present edifice. Extensive remodeling was completed in 1938. It is now "one of the finest and best examples of Romanesque architecture to be found anywhere in this country."[47] In 1952 the Sunday school was remodeled and expanded and the Parish Hall enlarged to provide additional space for dining, recreation, and dramatic activities.

From an original membership of twenty-nine, the church has grown to eighteen hundred and seventy-eight. The Sunday school, which began with forty students and four teachers, has an enrollment in 1958 of four hundred and thirty-one pupils and twenty-eight teachers. The enlarged church staff includes three ministers, a director of religious education, three secretaries, one kitchen manager and three sextons. Apartment houses are rapidly replacing mansions and large houses. As a result, the population of the community has increased over 60 per cent during the past twenty years. New demands and new opportunities continue to confront the church and to call forth the utmost of consecration and wisdom of its enlarged staff.

MISSIONARY WORK BROADENED AND INTENSIFIED

The continuing influence of Presbyterianism cannot be gauged by merely relating the achievements of these and other great churches which have adjusted their programs to meet the needs of changing communities. Of equal importance, perhaps, is the continued contribution of the numerous small neighborhood churches which labor in communities of contrasted environment with a discouraging lack of visible growth. Some of these churches, like McClure Avenue, Homewood, Knoxville, and First Church of Allegheny, were formerly large and prosperous organizations. The changed community has left them with reduced membership, but with an inescapable problem of community service.

Others like Troy Hill, Blackadore, Millvale, Etna, and Providence have felt the weakening influence of a changing clientele. They serve as Inner Mission churches, requiring some financial support from the Presbytery. The historic Central Church (Fifth), which flourished under the preaching of Professor Melancthon Jacobus and which moved from its downtown location on Sixth Avenue and Smithfield Street to the corner of Fifth Avenue and

Seneca Street, continues only as a mission-supported Neighborhood House in the Soho district. Likewise the North Church, while retaining its regular schedule of worship, has supplemented its service to a changed community by using its building as a Neighborhood House.

Typical of the broad-range activities of a Neighborhood House is the schedule of this North Church. It still occupies and keeps in splendid repair its beautiful building which is a much-admired and exceptionally fine example of Byzantine architecture. The congregation, two-thirds of whom live within walking distance of the church, welcome to all the church's activities their neighbors regardless of class, race, or religion. The seven-day program includes Sunday-school classes for men, women, and children, a bowling club on Monday evening, Youth Fellowship on Wednesday, Boys' Club on Tuesday, Girls' Club on Thursday, Children's Club on Wednesday afternoon, prayer and healing services on Wednesday, adult choir on Thursday, Dorcas Social Service Club for women on Tuesday, and a daily kindergarten program. The pastor, the Reverend Robert W. Young, is assisted by the full-time service of Mrs. Harry Davenport. Her salary is paid by the Presbytery of Pittsburgh. Thus the church through Jesus Christ offers to all in the community who will accept: "Friends you can trust, healing for your body, mind, and soul, faith in God's Word, peace in your heart and home, and hope for the future."[48]

GROWTH IN THE SUBURBS

The same changes in community environment, which have weakened formerly strong urban churches, have also imparted to famous old rural churches new and expanded opportunities. Some of the country churches, where preached the Founding Fathers in the pioneering days of Redstone and Ohio presbyteries and which had declined from their former glory, now find themselves in the midst of rapidly growing suburban areas. They have modernized their sanctuaries and have added educational and recreational buildings to serve more people than ever before. Historic Bethel Church, where "Father" Clark defied the leaders of the Whiskey Rebellion, has 1,400 members and requires the services of two pastors. Beulah Church has been rebuilt in a modern tentlike structure at a cost of $725,000. Pigeon Creek, where Redstone Presbytery was first organized, has been attractively renovated with a white New England interior. Long Run, one of the oldest churches in Western Pennsylvania, has a completely equipped educational unit. The typical list could be continued. Changing times have greatly altered ever-present opportunities to proclaim, with new appeal, the unchanging Gospel of a changeless Christ.

This shifting of population and the expansion of the suburbs has resulted also in the recent organization and development of many new churches as the Presbyterian church continually seeks to serve newer communities. Some of these new churches have grown rapidly and are equipped with splendid facilities to serve their communities in all phases of religious activity. For example, Mt. Lebanon was organized in 1925. The statistical reports for 1958 reveal that it has the largest church and church-school enrollment of any Presbyterian church in the Pittsburgh Presbytery. Its Sunday church school is exceeded in membership only by the Third Presbyterian Church at Uniontown which is entitled to the honor of being the largest Presbyterian church school throughout the entire Upper Ohio Valley.

Neighboring Dormont, organized in 1907, has had a similarly rapid growth. It now ranks fourth among the Pittsburgh area Presbyterian churches both in church and church-school membership. The five largest church schools are all in suburban communities surrounding Pittsburgh. These schools, in addition to Mt. Lebanon and Dormont, include Pleasant Hills (organized 1940), Bethel (1776), and Westminster (1947). Bower Hill (1951) is growing rapidly and may soon surpass the First Church of Pittsburgh which continues to house the largest church school in Pittsburgh. These large suburban church schools have adequate educational equipment. They are pioneering in various aspects of religious education especially among adults.

A comity arrangement with the Council of Churches of the Pittsburgh area seeks to avoid unnecessary duplication of churches in these newer suburban communities. Expanding opportunities of service, as far as practical, are alloted among the different denominations. Church extension is based upon a survey of the needs of the community and the expressed preferences of its citizens. Presbyterians have co-operated heartily in this wise effort to avoid the denominational competition of a former period. Community resources are thus concentrated in fewer and better-equipped churches as members who formerly held their individual membership in various denominations now experience the joy of co-operative activity in community churches.

The Pleasant Hills Presbyterian Church, for example, includes representatives from twenty-four denominations in its rapidly growing membership. The Edgewood Presbyterian Church is an outstanding illustration of the long-time effectiveness of a church's ability to serve an entire community on an interdenominational basis. Organized in 1891 it has remained the only church of any faith or denomination in the borough of Edgewood. It is Presbyterian in organization and polity, yet it has always sought to be ecumenical in spirit and fellowship. Frequently a majority of its officers had previously transferred their membership from other denominations. In contrast, the adjoining but larger borough of Wilkinsburg has thirty-two churches to serve a population of thirty-eight thousand. Their co-operative community efforts have defeated the persistent efforts of the liquor business to establish saloons within the corporate limits of what is often called "The Holy City," or "City of Churches." A two-mile radius, with the First Presbyterian Church of Wilkinsburg as the center, would include seventeen churches of the Presbyterian family.

Initial Efforts among Germans

The rapid industrialization of the Pittsburgh area attracted newcomers of various racial and language backgrounds. Toward these foreign-speaking people, the Presbyterian church, as the largest and most influential Protestant group, has felt a particular responsibility. The initial efforts began in October, 1854, when the Reverend J. J. Waldburger, a German minister, was received by the Presbytery of Ohio to work among the German-speaking people. No effort was made to organize a separate church. Services were held in the First Presbyterian Church of Pittsburgh and the Second Presbyterian Church of Allegheny, with the result that one hundred families were reached in worship and pastoral visitation.[49]

Five years later a German Presbyterian church, with twenty-five members, was organized in Manchester as a missionary enterprise of the Presbytery of Allegheny City.[50] Progress was slow and discouraging, causing the editor of "The Banner" to remark: "To make good, sound Presbyterians out of Germans is a difficult matter. Their early training, their social habits, their modes of thought are so widely different from ours, that it is not easy to bring them into acquiescence with Presbyterian doctrines and order."[51] Apparently only English-speaking groups, particularly the Scotch and Scotch-Irish, were destined by nature to wear successfully the purple robes of Presbyterianism.

The Presbyterian missionary urge struggled to surmount these barriers of race and nationality. Even the Germans' "low view of the Sabbath and their convivial and drinking habits" did not quench consecrated enthusiasm. Into the center of the Germans' social life, where angels might fear to tread, rushed the Presbyterians. They organized a Sabbath school in Allegheny over a lager beer saloon. There the school met regularly until growth required a larger room. The school then descended one flight of stairs and used the lager beer saloon itself. Attendance reached as high as three hundred in what was popularly called "The Lager Beer Sun-

COURTESY OF
FIRST PRESBYTERIAN CHURCH,
PITTSBURGH

REVEREND
MAITLAND
ALEXANDER, D.D.

Pastor, First Presbyterian Church, Pittsburgh, Pa., 1899–1927. Moderator, General Assembly, 1914.

REVEREND
CLARENCE EDWARD
MACARTNEY, D.D.

Pastor, First Presbyterian Church, Pittsburgh, Pa., 1927–1953. Moderator, General Assembly, 1924.

COURTESY OF
THE PITTSBURGH PRESS

WRECKAGE LEFT BY RIOTERS AT PENNSYLVANIA RAILROAD'S TWENTY-EIGHTH STREET ROUNDHOUSE, JULY 21, 1877.

COLLECTION OF GEORGE SWETNAM

BATTLE AT TWENTY-EIGHTH STREET, JULY 21, 1877
Philadelphia troops firing on mob during railroad labor riots. Sketch by John Donaghy at the time.

day School."[52] Fortunately, the sale of beer and of all other alcoholic beverages was forbidden on Sunday in Presbyterian Pittsburgh of that period.

Work among Negroes

With this successful breaching of racial barriers as an encouraging precedent, Presbyterian work was broadened to include other nationalities and races. The Presbytery of Ohio next felt the importance of organizing a church among the negro people who were rapidly increasing in number. They totaled eighteen hundred and two in the population census of 1870. A number of these Negroes had been reared under Presbyterian influence and desired to be connected with a church composed of their own people.

Pittsburgh Presbyterians had long manifested an interest in their brethren whose skin was of a darker hue. As early as 1817, members of the First Presbyterian Church had organized a Sunday school for one hundred negro children. Later this school was transferred to the former building of the Second Presbyterian Church on Diamond Alley. The school appears to have been a spiritual success. The report of the Directors five years later reviewed in rejoicing the progress of those years. "Before the school began, the colored people of the city spent the Holy Sabbath in idleness, dissipation, and wickedness; now in seeking God, in prayer, singing His praise and learning to read His Word."[53]

But the first Presbyterian church to be organized for Negroes was the Grace Church in 1868. Money for a twelve thousand dollar edifice on Arthur Street above Centre Avenue was raised by Dr. David McKinney. He took a special interest in this little congregation of sixty-seven communicants and guided them amid their difficulties in developing an organization under the leadership of the Reverend Charles Hedges, their first pastor.[54] Throughout the years of community service, the congregation has grown into a membership of eight hundred and forty-three. It is the largest Presbyterian church of negro people in Pittsburgh. The Reverend

Harold R. Tolliver has served the church with notable efficiency since his graduation from Western Theological Seminary in 1931.

From Grace Church have developed both the Bethesda and the Bidwell Street Presbyterian churches. Each of these three churches is self-supporting. They co-operate to serve the negro population of Presbyterian inclination. More recently, an integrated Presbyterian church has been organized on Robinson and Terrace Streets with a membership of approximately an equal number of white and negro people. Appropriately, it has been named the Friendship Community Church. Perhaps it forecasts the typical Presbyterian church of the future, the fruitage of additional years of emphasis on human brotherhood. Already a number of predominantly white Presbyterian churches are proud to claim some negro brethren in their church membership.

Many Nationality Groups

About the turn of the century, the Presbytery extended still further its service among various nationality groups. The Reverend Vaclav Losa was secured to work among the Bohemians and people of kindred tongues in the vicinity of McKees Rocks. Some of his converts became missionaries and colporteurs. Soon a school was organized to train religious workers who understood the various languages and the backgrounds of the people living in foreign-speaking communities. The school was opened October, 1904, with a carefully prepared curriculum and continued for twenty-three years.[55] Several times Dr. Losa went to Europe to enlist suitable students.

Churches were organized among the Italians, Bohemians, Slovaks, Ukrainians, Magyars, and French. Due to constantly shifting population and decline in immigration, none of these churches became large; yet they met a real community need. In 1930 a missionary staff of twenty-nine was at work among thirty different nationalities. Many of these centers of Christian influence were truly international in their service to a polyglot community. One worker reported eighteen nationalities in her mission. Several have had thirteen and seventeen.[56] With the progress in Americanization, many of these Sunday schools and missions have been merged into other Presbyterian churches in the community. At the present time, about thirteen workers are employed to carry to communities of diversified backgrounds the unifying Gospel of a universal Saviour. The Presbyterian church, like the Master Himself, "seeks not to be ministered unto but to minister." The goal of the Presbyterian church is changed lives, won for Christ by changing methods amidst changing environments.

CHAPTER XVIII All Ye That Labor

All up and down the Ohio Valley, but nowhere more than in Pittsburgh, the period from 1870 to 1950 was a time of social upheaval, of change that too often erupted into violence, or subsided only into a troubled peace of mutual distrust and fear. In the church as well as in the market place, the problems of capital and labor, of poverty and wealth, of human rights and property rights provoked severe conflict. The travail is seldom easy when great matters are being brought to birth.

Ever since large industries had begun to develop, and increasingly with the massive industrial expansion which accompanied and followed the War Between the States, the clouds of labor unrest had been gathering, ever more and more dark. The storm broke with crashing fury in mid-July of 1877, in an extensive railroad riot which for three days brought almost complete disorder in Pittsburgh, taking control of the city out of the hands of its proper officials for the first time since Bradford's raid during the Whiskey Insurrection.

RAILROAD STRIKE OF EIGHTEEN SEVENTY-SEVEN

Ever since the beginning of the Panic of 1873, railroads all over the country had been taking part in an orgy of cutthroat competition, often operating at far below cost, in an effort to grab from their rivals what little business was to be obtained. As in all such competition, employees of the lines were among the principal sufferers.

Wages had been reduced again and again, hours increased, and the work load piled as high as possible upon every man's back. Officials and workmen alike were tense with the strain and worry of the situation, when a 10 per cent wage cut and a more than comparable increase in the work load provided the match which set off the powder keg.[1]

Riots on a small scale had followed the announcement of wage cuts in several places on the Baltimore and Ohio Railroad. For a time it appeared that Pittsburgh might escape trouble. Men on the Pennsylvania Railroad grumbled at the wage cuts but continued to work until President Tom Scott issued an order that, beginning July 19, 1877, all trains were to run as double-headers. The order cut off many employees. Since the trains of that day used the old link-and-pin couplers and hand brakes, it placed an almost intolerable and highly dangerous burden on all train crews, especially the brakemen.

The crew of the first such train refused to work, and when railroad officials attempted to run the train, the mob blocked operation. Strikers and sympathizers completely took over the yards from Thursday through the following Tuesday, peacefully at first, but with violence rising to a crescendo on Saturday afternoon. Police sent by the mayor, when railroad officials complained, did very little and the mob only laughed at an order from the sheriff to disperse. He wired Harrisburg and three companies of Pittsburgh militia were assigned. They were mostly in sympathy with the strike and allowed things to take their course until the commander wired again for reinforcements.

By the time a division of Philadelphia soldiers reached Pittsburgh on Saturday afternoon, the strain was beginning to tell. Aboard the train for twelve hours, the soldiers were tired, hungry, and ill-tempered. The strikers were also out of patience, and the Saturday afternoon closing of steel mills and other factories had caused thousands of sympathizers to gather at the railroad yards and on the nearby hillsides. The soldiers resorted to their bayonets to disperse the crowd and were met with a shower of stones.

Then the shooting started. The first fire of the troops killed sixteen men and boys, mostly innocent bystanders, and wounded many others. The crowd drew back to the edge of the yards, but low rumblings of anger indicated there was trouble ahead. The troops held their ground until darkness began to fall, then fled in panic to the railroad roundhouse and barricaded themselves inside. The crowd followed with a rush and besieged the place, even blazing away at it with a small cannon taken from the Pittsburgh militia. Three soldiers were killed and several others wounded.

In the meantime the mob had gotten completely out of hand. Its members began breaking open and looting freight cars and setting fire to trains and even the terminal station. At dawn Sunday, the Philadelphia troops fled from the railroad yards, fighting a rear guard action until they were given shelter in the Allegheny County Workhouse ten miles away. The crowd, completely out of hand, burned sixteen buildings, carried away goods of all kinds, and even broke into stores in the city business district for guns and other valuables.

By dawn on Monday, the fury of the crowd had worn itself out and the town was virtually quiet. President Rutherford B. Hayes ordered Federal troops to the city. By the time they arrived on Tuesday, there was little to be done except serve as guards to permit the operation of the few trains which could be put on the road despite the damage.

Attitude of Church toward Strikers

Although a few weeks later the railroad riots were denounced as wholly the fault of the workers, public sentiment at first was almost equally divided. Several newspapers criticized the troops for opening fire and felt that real violence could have been averted had they been more levelheaded. The churches might have been expected to be at least as sympathetic with the workmen as was the public press, but this appears not to have been the case.

The Presbyterian Banner did express sympathy for the financial plight of the workers, but denied they had any right to use other than the mildest means to keep their places from being taken by those who wished to work. "The last reduction of wages by the Pennsylvania Railroad Company and its connections necessarily fell very severely upon the laborers and the freight train men. It was impossible that they should not deeply and sorely feel all these things coming upon them in quick succession, especially at a time when bread and meat, the indispensable necessities of a workingman's life, were sold at high rates. For them a deep sympathy was excited everywhere. They certainly had a right to quit work if they saw fit to do so; but they had no right to endeavor by intimidation or force to prevent others taking their places."[2]

Nowhere in the paper's coverage of the outbreak was there any suggestion that the troops had been even partially to blame, although it was suggested that "the higher railroad officials would have lost nothing by a conference with the men and the free interchange of views." The editor moralized that while the strikers did not intend to cause any damage, they had sowed the whirlwind, and added sagely: "Never yet has any permanent benefit been derived by laboring men from strikes."

Severe pressure may have been exercised on "The Banner" by leading Presbyterians, who included a large proportion of the wealthier men of the city. For in a later issue, the tone seemed to have completely changed. Not only did no suggestion of sympathy for the strikers remain, but the very matter of unionism itself was viewed somewhat with alarm in this editorial comment: "A nice distinction has been drawn between the strikers and the mob; but the strikers were themselves a far more dangerous mob than the miserable wretches who pillaged and burned the cars and depot, and must be regarded as furnishing far more occasion of alarm for the future."[3]

The following week, an editorial expressed concern over the problem of the unemployed in cities. But its best suggestion was that nothing could be done to alleviate such conditions except to discourage young men from leaving the farm.[4] The Reverend Thomas Johnston of Tally Cavey, pastor of a rural church in northern Allegheny County, contributed a long letter taking the laissez faire position that economic laws had to work and if the poor got stepped on, it was their bad luck.

A final blast at the riots was fired with the warning that: "The Trades Unions are injurious to both employers and employees; the sooner they can be broken up . . . the better it will be for all parties. They are generally in the hands of scheming revolutionists or idlers and constitute one of the worst forms of tyranny."[5] The issue also contained several touching stories of how employers had been wronged by their workers, and fictional pieces about strikers who got religion and were immediately delivered from all their troubles.

Seminary Professor Alarmed by False Issues

Nor was this the last, nor yet the most severe, blast of the Presbyterian church against those who were involved in the 1877 railroad riots. On the evening of November 20, another broadside was fired by Dr. S. H. Kellogg, in his inaugural address as professor of Didactic and Polemic Theology at Western Theological Seminary. Dr. Kellogg deplored the tendency of Americans "to look with a degree of contempt upon various usages current in other countries, regulating dress, position, and forms of speech, which usages are intended to express and confess difference in position, relations of authority, and subordination."[6]

Dr. Kellogg carefully pointed out that wealth, among other things, was ordained by God to give special prerogatives: "Has it not," he asked, "been forced upon our attention of late that multitudes around us, when they shout for 'liberty,' mean only emancipation from the restrictions of law and the conservative ordinances of society, and would, if possible, realize their conception of 'equality' by an indiscriminate leveling of all distinctions in station and power among men, and by refusing to admit those legitimate prerogatives, which in God's ordination are conferred by means of wealth, education, and moral eminence?

"If we wish to see this spirit of wild political individualism and materialistic lawlessness carried out to its extreme logical form, we unfortunately have it in that communism which in our country and in Europe is daily becoming a more and more important and significant element in the political situation. For the avowed object of the communist is the subversion of authority, the leveling and destruction of that divinely ordained order of society wherein individual men by various personal gifts are made by God superior to others, and invested with power over their fellows."[7]

Then, referring directly to the railroad riots, Dr. Kellogg said: "Since the startling and terrible events of last summer in our own midst and elsewhere, many have anxiously speculated as to the causes and occasions of such a revelation of destructive lawlessness. Many causes, with more or less reason, have been assigned; such as hard times, alleged injustice on the part of capitalists toward the laboring classes, an unsettled currency, excess of production over demand, all these and many other causes and occasions of the present attitude of our masses, have been assigned. But while it is doubtless difficult to estimate the actual potency of the several forces which are operating in our midst, to my mind all these theories alike fail, in that they do not go to the root of the matter.

"If I mistake not, the Christian historian of the twentieth century will rightly recognize in the destructive tendencies of our vaunted civilization, the working of that spirit of godless lawlessness, which has been generated by the materialistic and God-denying scientific philosophy which is so fashionable at present among the multitude of partly educated men and small philosophers. I believe that so far from being due to causes merely external and occasional, to be remedied by improved legislation and various apparatus of social and church reform, it has its radical cause deep in the prevailing speculative doubt and unbelief in the fundamental truths of theism. It is simply the natural result of a godless scientific philosophy."[8]

CLEAVAGE BETWEEN CAPITAL AND LABOR

How did such a situation come about in the individualistic, liberty-loving Presbyterian church? How can we explain such a complete disregard of human suffering, such scorn and neglect of the poor, such virtual deification of property rights and men of wealth? A century earlier, half a century, even more recently than that, the Presbyterian church had kept its doors and its heart open for the poor. Its ministers could preach without quibbling from the second chapter of James, and its wealthy men and church officials were good employers and open-handed citizens.

The answer must lie in the sudden, almost tumorous, growth of towns and industry in the Upper Ohio Valley, and especially Pittsburgh and its suburbs, which had grown far too fast to keep track of themselves. In 1830 Pittsburgh had only 12,542 people and Allegheny 2,801. After a decade they were still small enough that practically everyone in town knew everyone else, Pittsburgh having only a little over 21,000, Allegheny City 10,000. Even in 1860, Pittsburgh had only a little over 49,000 and Allegheny not much more than half as many. With a few exceptions, the captain of industry still lived beside his mill, or at least visited it frequently, and knew virtually all of his workmen by name and by sight. If the wage he paid was sometimes inadequate, at least he knew when his employees suffered sudden need or disaster and was quick to bring help. Such a paternalistic system of economy, while leaving much to be desired, at least had the virtues of kindness, friendliness, and mutual aid. There were few layoffs, little poverty except among the degraded, and comparatively little suffering even in the worst times. As in the early days of Rome, "the great man helped the poor, and the poor man loved the great."

But by 1870 Pittsburgh's population had jumped to more than 86,000 and that of Allegheny to 51,000. With a strong demand for labor, thousands of immigrants were being funneled into the district, principally from Europe, with promises of good wages and good working conditions, so that by 1880 Pittsburgh had increased to above 156,000 and Allegheny to nearly 77,000.[9]

No longer did the millowner live beside his mill, or his sons begin their own careers as workmen there. The tremendous profits of the wartime years and the expansion period which followed had sharply increased the caste system. The millowner, whose father had three hundred workmen and knew them all, might now have from one to five thousand, and know only a few in person. With no knowledge of their personal problems and unusual needs, he could not understand why the wages he and others had always been accustomed to pay were not sufficient. Usually, he blamed the employees as being greedy. In addition, with an increasing number of the employees newly arrived from Europe and speaking a strange tongue, it was easy to blame everything on "foreigners" or "anarchists."

Also, even from the first settlement of the area, the strong-willed individualists of the Pittsylvania Country had entertained little love for unions, and employees little interest in them. Before 1820, a shoemakers' strike had ended abruptly when a judge ruled that organizing a union was a crime because it "interfered with trade."

The increase in number of employees beyond personal and friendly acquaintance with the "boss" was most important, however. It is significant that the first real labor riot at Pittsburgh was in the cotton mills, affecting the first industry to reach a size where the employees would not be personally known by their employers. In that strike the workers, mostly women and children, had been working twelve hours a day, until a state law forbade more than ten hours for women and child workers, "except by special agreement." When the employees refused to consent to a continuance of the long hours, and resisted having their wages cut in accordance with the shorter day, the employers closed down the mills for the month of July. When they attempted to reopen one of the mills on July 31, a riot occurred, although it resulted in little damage.[10]

Although the writer could find no record of any church or presbytery uttering a protest or criticism either against the proceedings, or against the conditions which had brought on the riot, the Presbyterian church in the Upper Ohio Valley was not completely oblivious to the welfare of workers. In 1830 the Reverend Job F. Halsey, pastor of the First Presbyterian Church of Allegheny, preached a sermon which resulted in the formation of the Pittsburgh Bethel Union, a mission for the boatmen who ever since colonial times had been the roughest, toughest, and most neglected labor group in the district.[11]

Almost eight years later we find Dr. Francis H. Herron holding services for the boatmen at a room fitted up for them "at the corner of Wood and Water streets, upstairs." About one hundred persons attended.[12] Two decades later a full-time chaplain had been put to work among the ten thousand men and boys employed in the river trade, and the annual report presented the condition of the Bethel as "most hopeful."[13] There was also a Prison Reform Society, headed by the Reverend David H. Riddle, whose purpose was "the improvement of Public Prisons and their inmates; the alleviation of the sufferings of prisoners, so far as it may be done without defeating the ends of public justice; the support and encouragement of reformed convicts after their discharge, by affording them the means of obtaining an honest livelihood, and encouraging and sustaining them in their efforts at reform; and also the reformation of any other class of our fellow creatures, whom we may discover to be abandoned and degraded."[14] Presbyterian churches took part in other good causes too, especially supporting national and foreign missions.

Church Is Indifferent to Social Injustice

But somewhere in the excitement over freeing slave labor and the war which this involved, most of the desire to help the unfortunates at our own door appeared to have been lost. It was easy, too, to argue that good wages were hurtful rather than helpful to workmen: "But it cannot be denied that there are many things just now calculated to awaken apprehensions in the prudent, and deep solicitude in the pious. Many of the old paths have been deserted, and some of them with no great loss, but others with fearful risk. The people are excited. The whole public mind has become feverish. Regular labor has no attractions. Steady gains and advances are not enough. Fortune, distinction, and fame are not sought by constant and progressive steps, but by some sudden move.

"Money is abundant to a degree never before witnessed in modern times. The government is compelled to strew it almost broadcast; and there is something very like a general scramble to seize it. Vast wealth has been speedily acquired by many who a short time ago were poor. Expensive habits of life have been introduced. Notwithstanding the enormous prices at which all that gratifies the tastes of the people and ministers to luxury and display is held, never was the cost regarded so little as now."[15]

Even in the face of what had occurred in 1877, and less serious strikes in coal and other industries, Presbyterians of the Upper Ohio Valley, who talked so glibly about the wind planted by the men who formed unions, were unable to see the whirlwind which the churches were being forced to reap along with all the rest of the community. In 1881 when a small group of earnest men met in Pittsburgh and formed the American Federation of Labor, most churchmen shook their heads in sage disapproval and feared the worst. When Samuel Gompers described the conditions among the children of six to eight years employed in the tenement cigar shops, adding "Shame upon such crimes; shame upon us if we do not raise our voices against it," there appears to be no record of any churches having joined in his protest.

There were other strikes, too, with violence and bloodshed. At the Morewood Mine, forty miles from Pittsburgh, eleven strikers were shot dead in 1891 by fifty guards armed with Winchester rifles for nothing more than pulling down a board fence. About seventy-five others were wounded.

THE HOMESTEAD STEEL STRIKE

Yet the most famous of all strikes in the Upper Ohio Valley occurred in July of 1892 as the result of Henry Clay Frick's effort to break the union at Andrew Carnegie's Homestead steel plant. Although unions were not strong in the Valley, the Amalgamated Iron and Steel Workers held a well-entrenched position at several Pittsburgh district mills, at none more strongly than the Homestead plant. Its members were paid on tonnage rates, based on a steel price minimum of twenty-five dollars a ton. Frick moved to reduce their base pay and also to make the contract expire in January instead of July 1. The men were willing to compromise on pay but felt that a January contract date would put them in a very poor position for a strike.

On July 2, 1892, Frick closed the plant, announcing that any workers who wanted to retain their jobs would have to sign a nonunion agreement. Although they did not know it, he had contracted in late June for three hundred armed Pinkerton detective "guards" to be brought into Pittsburgh on July 5 so that he could open the mill in defiance of the union next day. Tempers were raw on both sides and the men hung Frick in effigy and posted pickets who prevented even officials from getting into the mill. Frick tried to slip his warriors into the mill in two covered barges pushed by the river boats, "Tide" and "Little Bill." But word had leaked out and the strikers were ready for them, also armed with rifles and shotguns.

The two sides fought a pitched battle for hours, with three Pinkertons and seven strikers killed and a number of others wounded. At last the invaders surrendered on a promise of protection, although several of them were seriously beaten by the crowd before they could reach a skating rink where they were later turned over to the sheriff for safekeeping. Governor Robert Pattison rushed the National Guard to Pittsburgh and the mill was reopened, non-union, under the protection of their bayonets.

To judge by *The Presbyterian Banner,* there was even less sympathy in the church for the embattled men of Homestead than for the rioters of 1877. The issue for July 13, 1892, contains a long statement given by Mr. Frick, but only a few brief, unsympathetic paragraphs on the position of the workmen. The editor believed it had been a mistake to bring the Pinkerton guards in "at that particular juncture," but added that it was "not easy to set aside the reasons given by Mr. Frick." He principally blamed Governor Pattison for not having sent troops to the mill before the trouble developed.

"Wage earners certainly have the right to combine for mutual assistance and protection, to refuse to work when they regard the pay as insufficient," said the editorial, "and also to endeavor to persuade others not to take their places. But not by violence," the editorial hastily added. The July 20 issue continued the same theme, with even less charity. It spoke of the "folly and wickedness" of the laborers and predicted and urged a return to work. Not one word of blame was expressed against Mr. Frick or the company. An editorial urged that the strike rioters be prosecuted, but declared that the Pinkerton men were justified in firing on the pickets.[16]

"The Banner's" position was not typical. Several newspapers and a great proportion of the public were strongly in sympathy with the steelworkers. Then on July 23 a young Russian anarchist named Alexander Berkman rushed into Frick's office at the lunch hour and tried to kill him. It was a senseless move. Although Berkman had no connection with the strike, it doomed all hopes of the strike's success, swinging a large segment of public opinion instantly behind the intended victim. "The Banner" agreed that the attack had not been incited by the strikers, but insisted that it was "a result of their actions," and demanded that they cease picketing. The next week's strike story was largely a blast against "anarchists" in the labor movement.[17]

Apparently there was still some public support for the strike as late as August 10 when "The Banner" said: "The talk in some of the newspapers and from some of the pulpits about bringing the soldiers here to shoot down innocent men, women, and children was simply nonsense." The editorial urged prosecution of the strikers, stating: "A large number of arrests have been made, and many yet will be held for court. This is the proper method of dealing with offenders."[18]

Church Is Unsympathetic with Attempts to Organize Labor

It is hard to see from this distance how a church whose Master had proclaimed: "Come unto Me all ye that labor and are heavy laden, and I will give you rest," could be so completely one-sided and so bitter. Perhaps the secret lay in the fact that almost three-fourths of Pittsburgh's industry was controlled by Presbyterian money. Perhaps the Master was right when He spoke of how hard it was for a rich man to enter into the Kingdom. A strong segment of the Presbyterian church in the Upper Ohio Valley fought blindly and bitterly against any effort of workers to organize and even, at last, against any effort to reach laboring men with the Gospel. The Reverend Charles Stelzle, who did such magnificent work in the Presbyterian Labor Temple in New York, reveals in his autobiography, *Son of the Bowery*, that a group of Presbyterians from Pittsburgh forced the Board of Home Missions to abolish his department for the evangelization of the laboring masses.

But what the organizational efforts and all the appeals of labor could not do to awaken the conscience of the Presbyterian church at Pittsburgh, labor's bitter defeat at Homestead did do at last. Not at once, for the utter rout of labor unions following Homestead appeared to most churchmen of Pittsburgh as a great victory for the forces of law, order, and religion. No blindness can equal that which sometimes affects the well-intentioned.

The defeat of unionism at Homestead was so complete that almost a decade later every effort to rally labor's forces was ending in complete defeat. The Amalgamated Association organization tried every mill in the Carnegie system. A singular run of bad luck followed them everywhere. Not a move could they make that was not instantly reported to the superintendent of the works. Every man in the employment of these establishments knew what would happen to him if he were discovered joining or aiding a labor organization. The system of that company for getting information was found to be so perfect that in some instances the managers seemed to know in advance what was contemplated.

The story of labor's defeat is similar to that of former attempts to organize the Homestead works after the great strike of 1892. An open attempt was made by the skilled workmen to organize in 1895. Meetings were held in the opera house at Homestead. The result was that the company broke up the lodge in short order and thirty-five of the most prominent members of the lodge were discharged.

Another attempt was made early in 1900. This time the men went about it secretly. They held their meetings in Pittsburgh. In a short time they had a good-sized organization. Then, like a bolt from the blue sky, the company let the new-made union men know that it was cognizant of every move that had been made. It was known just what men had attended the meeting once and names were given of workmen who had attended two and three times. "As a result of this attempt to organize, fourteen men were discharged, and that is what caused the Amalgamated Association to fail in the present crisis."[19]

The Plight of the Working Man

But the defeat did not affect the steel union alone. Steel has long been at Pittsburgh, and throughout America, a barometer for other business and industries, not only as to price and wages, but almost across the entire economic board. Year after year the laboring population of Pittsburgh, steelworkers, glassworkers, laborers, clerks, and servants sank deeper and deeper into the economic mire of inadequate wages, poverty, slum living, and the disease and depravity which inevitably accompany and follow such conditions. Pittsburgh churchmen liked to think that this was only true of "foreigners" and Negroes who somehow were a matter of no concern to the church. But a large section of the native-born and Presbyterian population was sucked down into the same quagmire with those who had newly come to the Upper Ohio Valley from Europe and from the mountains and plantations of the South.

With an amazing shortsightedness, Pittsburgh industry and business pushed their supposed advantage over their employees to its utmost, forcing steelworkers to labor twelve hours a day, seven days a week when the mills were running full, for a meager wage of one dollar and sixty-five cents a day. Clerks worked even longer hours, often sweeping out the stores before daylight and working until nine or ten o'clock in the evening, and longer on Saturday. Families unable to live on such small wages found it necessary to resort more and more to sending their children into the factories to labor long hours for paltry sums, merely in order to be able to have the necessities of life. Girl clerks, who found it impossible to live on a mere three dollars a week, were forced to submit to the attentions of their employers to get even slightly larger wages, or to resort to full-time or part-time prostitution in order to keep body and soul together. A sociologist who visited and surveyed the slums of Pittsburgh reported that only in Canton, China, and in the slums of Naples had he ever seen poverty and degradation to compare with conditions he found in Pittsburgh.[20]

Vice and crime bred extensively in such a situation, and soon made common cause with Power in political affairs. Economic power in such a degree can always permit the exercise of political power, for with the bread and butter of his family at stake, it is hard for a worker to stand as a heroic crusader for the right.

Repeatedly workmen were discharged at Duquesne for refusing to vote the way the company wished. One employee stated that he had been called into the office of his superintendent and remonstrated with for working against the company ticket, and an indirect threat of discharge was made. Other citizens of unimpeachable standing in Braddock, who were not steelworks employees, reported that in the Spring of 1908, preceding the May primaries, men were induced to vote for the candidates favored by the corporation by promises of a resumption in industry if the right men were nominated.[21]

Industrialists Dominate Politics

Most damaging testimony regarding the interference of the Steel Corporation in politics came from a source clearly authoritative. For obvious reasons the name of the informant could not be listed. "A short time before the primaries of May, 1908," he said, "orders came from the New York office of the United States Steel Corporation, to the general superintendent of the Edgar Thomson plant at Braddock, directing him to order the department superintendents to line up their employees for the Penrose candidates for the legislature. The general superintendent called a meeting of the department superintendents and delivered the orders. This created considerable dismay, for local option was an issue in the primaries and the Penrose candidates were opposed to local option. Some of the superintendents were already prominently identified with the local option party and had been assisting in organizing the campaign. How they could with honor or self-respect abandon the issue at this point was not clear to the officials. But the answer to the objections was clear and to the point. They were told that their first duties were to the corporation. They must, accordingly, break any or all promises and work for Penrose, because the United States Steel Corporation needed him in the Senate."[22]

So complete was the enslavement of Pittsburgh politics that a nationally known author declared that the self-perpetuating power of its political machine was the most complete that ever existed in America: "I know of nothing like it in any other city. Tammany in comparison is a plaything and in the management of a city, Croker was a child beside Chris Magee."[23] The better elements of the city from time to time became aroused, but found themselves virtually helpless, partly because so many church leaders were themselves members of the political ring. It was only when the Russell Sage Foundation took Pittsburgh for its first study and published the complete and horrible findings in a series of six volumes, that the churches of Pittsburgh discovered to what a depth their city had fallen.[24]

Lincoln Steffens' revelations in magazine and book form might be shrugged off as "muck-raking," but Pittsburgh church people could not ignore the unhappy revelations in *The Pittsburgh Survey.*[25]

PRESBYTERIANS ARE STIRRED INTO ACTION

However unwilling they were to recognize the true situation, Presbyterians could no longer shut their eyes to the futility of the program which had been theirs for half a century—the program of declaring pious platitudes while men and women were starving, of conducting cold backdoor or institutionalized charity, and of substituting deep concern over heathen in foreign lands for a recognition of problems at the door. Typical of some Presbyterian efforts for Pittsburgh's economically unstable residents was the organization of the Woods Run Settlement House by the McClure Avenue Presbyterian Church. Although for the past half century the settlement has had an outstanding record of achievement, in its early years it amounted to little more than an attempt to proselyte the poor of other faiths by charity which at times took the form of throwing loaves of bread out upstairs windows for the poor and starving to scramble over in the streets.[26]

Let it not be felt because these things are said here that the Presbyterians were sinners "above all the Galileans" at Pittsburgh in this respect. Few, if any, other denominations, except those which had almost their whole membership among the poverty-stricken workers, had shown more vision or made more effort at social outreach. The one outstanding exception was Calvary Episcopal Church, whose program for brotherhood, decency, and good government during the 1880's under the rectorship of the Reverend George Hodges was the real beginning of a movement whose effect is still one of the best influences in Pittsburgh. With these exceptions, it was and is true in the Upper Ohio Valley, as elsewhere, that "in dealing with social problems caused by industrialization, the Presbyterian church was in the forefront of American denominations."[27]

Even in the darkest days there had been bright spots in the picture of Pittsburgh Presbyterians seeking to understand and carry out the will of the Master. Before 1870 the Reverend John Launitz, polyglot pastor for fifty-three years of the First German Presbyterian Church, had labored in the "working districts." About the time of the Homestead trouble, as if to compensate for the blunder committed by so many Christians, he greatly widened his work and began to hold preaching services in French, then in Italian, in the First Presbyterian Church of Pittsburgh, East Liberty Presbyterian Church, and the church at Tarentum. He was a gifted linguist, preaching with great power in English, German, French, and Italian. Out of the beginning he made grew the oldest and largest Italian work in Pittsburgh, which is located at the corner of Larimer Avenue and Mayflower Street, and the French work at West Tarentum. He sowed the seeds for the United Presbyterian French Mission at McDonald, Pennsylvania.

Partly as a result of his labors, and even before the publication of either *The Shame of the Cities* or *The Pittsburgh Survey*, the Presbyteries of Pittsburgh and Allegheny, now the Presbytery of Pittsburgh, appointed a joint committee to begin serious investigation of possible service. The problems were great and perplexing— so much so that they hardly knew how or where to begin. In the providence of God they found a leader in the Fall of 1900, who for many years was at the head of all departments of Presbyterian work among various European nationalities of Pittsburgh. He was the Reverend Vaclav Losa, born in Moravia and brought up in the Reformed Church of Bohemia. He had graduated from college in Europe and studied at Union Theological Seminary in New York.

At the time of his call to Pittsburgh, Dr. Losa was pastor of a large and flourishing Presbyterian church in Nebraska. "It was only because his heart so yearned for his Slavonic people and kinsmen when he saw them in Pittsburgh that he could be persuaded to undertake a missionary work among them, a work so fraught with danger and so terribly neglected. The work was opened in the most densely populated and unpromising, though needy, section of the county at Schoenville, McKees Rocks, Pennsylvania. Since the opening of this work in 1900, there has been a steady growth in the missionary activities of the Presbytery of Pittsburgh among the foreigners."[28] Dr. Losa attracted hundreds by singing on the streets in Schoenville. He opened a night school for English study, a sewing school, a kindergarten to interest the children and to enable their mothers to get their work done, a tent meeting, and a lantern show. These things were always looked upon as elementary and not fundamental—as means to an end and not the end in itself.

The Presbytery of Pittsburgh also made large and effective use of colporteurs, keeping from one to six men in the field all the time, whose business it was to visit every community where congestion was thickest, to go into homes where they could, and sell or give away Bibles and parts of Bibles in all the tongues of the people. They distributed millions of pages of tracts and of scriptures, spoke many languages, preached on the streets, and prayed in homes, hospitals, and jails.

Much of the literature needed was secured from Reformed churches in Europe until the supply was cut off after 1914. When stocks on hand were exhausted, the Presbytery of Pittsburgh printed the literature and reproduced many thousands of copies of some of the best tracts, and at times supplied the American Tract Society, the Chicago Tract Society, and other agencies, with worth-while material.

The foreign editorial staff of the Presbytery of Pittsburgh also supervised the editing and publication of three of the weekly foreign language periodicals put out by the Board of Publication and Sabbath-school work. Two of these were weekly family papers with circulation covering the entire United States, Canada, and many parts of Europe. The third was a primary Sunday-school paper whose influence was great among the children and whose parents also often found it useful to allay their hunger for something to read in their own language.

Presbyterian School for Christian Social Workers

Recognizing that individual and community life was best reached through the home, Pittsburgh Presbytery sought to enlist workers who could speak the language of the immigrant peoples. To find American women willing to do the work was difficult; to find those competent for it was virtually impossible. Immigrant women with training for such work could seldom be found. The Presbytery in 1904 established a Presbyterian Missionary Training School at Coraopolis, in the Ohio Valley a short distance south of Pittsburgh. Its curriculum provided a three-year course in English, Bible studies, lectures on various topics of popular interest, and physical hygiene with three months of internship in various hospitals of the city, covering first aid to the injured, care of children, dietetics, and sanitation. During the last two years of the course, practical instruction was given each student in house-to-house visitation with some graduate worker in the field. Each student was also taught plain sewing, cooking, housekeeping, and kindergarten teaching.

Only foreign-speaking girls were accepted at the school. Besides being taught English, they were given special instruction in half a dozen other languages so that when students had completed their course, there was hardly a family in any community to whom they could not minister effectively and with whom they could not converse at least understandably. Following graduation they were placed in such centers of need as had the most settled foreign population and gave the best hope of results. In 1917 the Presbytery of Pittsburgh had eighteen such graduate Bible women in service.

In addition, the Presbytery employed thirteen ordained foreign-speaking ministers. Their work proved particularly rewarding. We quote an appreciative testimonial: "They are ministering every day in the week to the uplift and instruction of the people, and during the week, when occasion offers, and always on Sunday they are preaching and teaching in at least ten languages. The hospitals know them and welcome them; the county jail, the workhouse, and the Riverside Penitentiary find in them a spiritual illuminant, and their services are often sought. The human shark who would stuff his maw with the saved-up earnings of the poor, untaught foreigner knows these ministers and fights shy of them on every occasion. These are the men on whom the Presbytery depends in seeking to solve the problem of bringing the Gospel to the foreigner in our midst. They are ever ready and capable of rendering aid to businessmen as the employers of foreign labor, thus making it possible for them to do and to get good from their relationship as employers.

"Some of the great factories pay largely each month to the Presbytery's treasurer for the support of this work, recognizing that it brings to them large dividends in the efficiency and sobriety of their employees. At a Presbyterial communion service held recently in the First Presbyterian Church of Pittsburgh, the Scripture was read by an African minister, the opening prayer was made by a Bohemian minister, the sermon was preached by an American minister, the consecration of the elements of communion was made by a French minister and an Italian minister, and among the elders distributing the elements were a Ruthenian and a Slovak. Such a service was never held in Pittsburgh before."[29]

In spite of all this work, there were still some Presbyterians in Pittsburgh in 1910 whose creed was much the same as that expressed almost two decades later by Dr. Samuel B. McCormick,

Presbyterian minister and chancellor of the University of Pittsburgh: "The people of Pittsburgh are individualists. They hold themselves responsible to God and their own conscience and nothing else counts. They attend to their own affairs and are willing to let other people attend to theirs, and while this sometimes leads to unfortunate results in political affairs, it is rather a good principle of behavior."[30]

But with the publication of *The Pittsburgh Survey,* no honest Christian could keep his eyes closed for long to the results of such a policy. Suddenly the Presbyterians of Pittsburgh realized that the degradation of their city was twofold. The enormous concentration of wealth at the so-called "top" of society resulted in a degrading luxury which was often ruinous to home life. Such people often had no settled home, traveling so much that children were neglected or turned over to the care of servants.

At the other end of the social scale was a poverty which was at once a challenge and an appeal. It was a poverty such as that which aroused the righteous indignation of the United Presbyterian Brotherhood Convention in 1912: "The kind of poverty that makes a man go hungry and wear shabby clothes and rotten shoes; that compels him to raise his children in the slums; that makes life a blighted thing; that makes thieves and sycophants of men; that robs them of dignity, and tempts them to dishonor; that makes them discouraged, bitter, hopeless, blasphemous; that drives them to seek oblivion in drugs and drink; that tempts the poor, overstrained girl to sell her virtue; that gives children no better chance for vigorous life than sickly plants in some foul cellar; that puts a blight and a mildew and a slime on every holy, beautiful possibility of life; that exacts grinding, unremitting toil, and that gives in return not life, but bitterness, that consigns to a life as empty of dignity and gladness and hope, as pit or tomb; that makes the spirit sordid, harsh, mean, irreligious, vengeful, bitter, anarchistic, murderous. This sort of poverty Jesus never meant to have with us always; it is in His eyes monstrous and accursed and of the devil; and from it, and from the selfishness that permits it and makes it possible, He came to set us free."[31]

LABOR'S COMPLAINT AGAINST THE CHURCH

Many church people discovered with shocked surprise how the churches' timidity and emphasis on wealth had looked to the laboring man. A spokesman for the impoverished working man thus unburdened his soul: "In the industrial district surrounding Pittsburgh, a wonderful opportunity exists for organized Christian service. But the churches do not see this opportunity because their point of view is individual, not social. There are in the churches of Allegheny County ministers who are doing heroic service, but there are too many, preaching every Sunday to steelworkers' families, who never have stepped inside a steel mill and who do not know a Bessemer converter from a puddling furnace. It is because of this lack of knowledge of some of the real problems of life that the ministers sometimes deliver their heaviest blows against secondary evils while the prime wrongs, the ones that dry up the roots of the community life, may escape their wrath.

"To make my point clearer, I will refer to one of the biggest problems in the steel mills today—that of Sunday work. There is no doubt of the evil of the practice that makes men toil seven days in the week. Its results are bad physically, intellectually, and morally. The ministers have combatted Sunday work, but they have directed their energies more frequently against drugstores, confectionery and fruit stores, and amusements, than they have against the United States Steel Corporation with its thousands of employees working the 'long turn.' They have, it is true, requested the superintendents of the steel mills to eliminate Sunday work as much as possible. But there has been no determined effort to enforce the Sunday closing law against the steelworks, as there has been in the other quarters named. This is partly due to the fact that the ministers have not informed themselves properly as to the extent of Sunday work. Some of them are in possession of the essential facts, but many other ministers seem to be in almost complete ignorance or indifference.

"Another reason is the fact that the steel companies are considered too powerful for successful attack. If this be true, we are in a bad way. If the forces of righteousness in a community dare not attack corporate wrongdoing, but must devote their energies only to the small offender, the time will not be long deferred when the hands of those who would see justice done will be effectually tied . . . The fact, however, that the ministers do not generally understand the workingman's problem, and do not seek to understand, well enough to sympathize fully with the hardships of their lives, has tended to make the workers lose interest in the church. Even deeper has been the estrangement which has arisen because of the hesitancy of the clergy to speak as boldly against the large offender as against the small."[32]

It took either a very calloused or a very bigoted person not to feel his conscience burn within him when he read: "There are a good many churches in this borough supported generally by women. The preachers don't have any influence in securing better conditions for the men and they don't try to have. They never visit the mills, and they don't know anything about the conditions the men have to face. They think the men ought to go to church after working twelve hours Saturday night. They could accomplish a lot if they would try to use their influence in the right direction. Let them quit temperance reform until they get better conditions for the men. It is no time to preach to a man when he is hungry. Feed him first, then preach to him; so with the workingman. Get a decent working day with decent conditions for a man, then ask him to stop drinking. Let the preacher find out how the men work; go and see them in the heat and smoke and heavy toil; let them notice the crushed hands, broken arms and amputated limbs and find out what the workingman is up against, and then try to better his condition."[33]

An Awakened Social Conscience in Action

Who can be surprised if such words stung the pride of many of the Presbyterians in the Upper Ohio Valley? But it had the happy effect of awakening conscience to such an extent that no church in any area in the entire nation has since been more ardent in its work for the poor, the underprivileged, and the "stranger within our gates," than the Presbyterians of the Upper Ohio Valley. Since the days of Dr. McCormick's youth and the Battle of Homestead and the protest against Dr. Stelzle, not only have times changed, but the personnel of the Presbytery of Pittsburgh has also changed. A most significant part of the change is in the presence there of a score of younger ministers who cannot be ignored, alumni of the Presbyterian Institute of Industrial Relations, operating under the Board of National Missions.

After months of discussion and planning, largely sparked by Dr. William F. Orr, professor of theology in the Western Theological Seminary, the Council on Industrial and Interracial Relations was finally brought into being by action of the Presbytery of Pittsburgh on December 14, 1948, in adopting the report of a special committee headed by Dr. G. Mason Cochran. An excerpt states:

"Pittsburgh is the only place which is both a great industrial and a great Presbyterian center . . . In trying to face the responsibilities of this situation and of this hour, we believe that the general policy of our Board of National Missions in industrial and interracial relations is sound, namely, that it is the task of the local church to serve all the people in its area. We need to study and develop techniques for meeting the needs of the mixed and changing groups which are within the bounds of the local parish."[34]

Since 1950 special in-training courses have been held in Pittsburgh where young pastors-to-be have held jobs in mills and factories, supplemented by after-hour discussion groups, to give them an opportunity to understand problems of the so-called labor group, and the challenges of ministry among them. Thirty-two attended the summer seminar held in Pittsburgh in 1951.[35]

Pittsburgh Presbytery Pioneers in Human Relations

The *Manual* of the Presbytery of Pittsburgh (1952) provides: "The Council on Industrial and Interracial Relations shall consist of fourteen members, of whom three shall be members of the Board of Trustees of Presbytery; three shall be members of the Presbytery's Standing Committee on Social Education and Action; three shall be alumni of the Presbyterian Institute of Industrial Relations; one a member of a negro or interracial church in the Presbytery; and four, either ministers or laymen from the Presbytery at large."

The Council on Industrial and Interracial Relations has been most active during the past six years under the leadership of Dr. Willard C. Mellin, pastor of the First Presbyterian Church of Oakmont, in the Allegheny Valley, and the Council's chairman since 1952. On May 13, 1957, largely because of this work, the Presbytery of Pittsburgh received the $500 Award and a bronze plaque from the Levinson Foundation given each year to "that person or group making the greatest contribution to the field of brotherhood during the year." The Foundation cited the Presbytery's work in integrated housing, carried out by the Council. Special recognition was given by the Foundation to Dr. John K. Bibby, the executive of the Presbytery, and to Mrs. Margaret J. Hofer, director of the C.I.I.R.

In accepting the award, Dr. Mellin said, "The Council on Industrial and Interracial Relations is grateful for public recognition of this phase of the Presbytery's work. The success of the endeavors which led to this award is due to the dedication of each local church to the position of the Presbytery and to the church's desire to give reality to this ideal." At the same time Dr. Mellin announced that the C.I.I.R. had taken membership in the tristate chapter of the

Industrial Relations Research Association for the Reverend James Gillespie, its chairman of Industrial Relations, and for Mrs. Hofer. Many other Ohio Valley Presbyterian groups are interested in this association which promotes the free exchange of ideas among those who are interested in industrial relations and related subjects.

Surely this is a far cry from the days when between the lines of Presbyterian comment on the railroad riots of 1877, one might also read the inquiry: "Am I my brother's keeper?" Too long Presbyterians throughout this area hesitated and stammered. Finally an awakened social conscience has responded in a thunderous "Yes."

CHAPTER XIX Unto the Ends of the Earth

TIME WAS WHEN the Redstone country was itself on the far horizon of missionary vision for colonial America. Beatty and Duffield, McClure and Frisbie undertook adventures for Christ just as perilous as that of Paton to the South Seas or Livingstone into Africa in later generations. The planting of the Presbyterian church west of the Alleghenies was in considerable part a foreign mission enterprise, supported with money and men by our brethren in Scotland and England.[1]

So Redstone and Ohio presbyteries were baptized into the missionary spirit in their early infancy, and when they were come to years and strength, that missionary spirit moved them to reach out into regions beyond. Before they learned to walk, they were creeping toward new frontiers. In the very first meeting of Redstone Presbytery, at Pigeon Creek in 1781, much time was spent in prayer "for the Lord's sheep, scattered abroad without a shepherd." Supplications for occasional preaching were received, but appointments to meet these needs were deferred to the next meeting. An Indian raid made that meeting impossible. Another appointment failed for the same reason.

Finally at Dunlap's Creek an entire year later, four ministers, burdened with their own far-flung parishes, pledged themselves each to spend two or three Sabbaths preaching and visiting in unchurched settlements ten to thirty miles away. This initial action set a pattern for the following years, even for generations. Six men accepted such missionary preaching appointments at the Autumn meeting in 1783. Every one involved a wearisome journey afoot or on horseback. Again in the Fall of 1784, each of the six members of Presbytery accepted appointments, totaling seventeen, to seven widely scattered places. Ten years later some of these were counted among the strongest congregations in the West.

In June of 1785, Presbytery directed all their congregations to observe a special Day of Prayer for revival and for missionary zeal and sacrifice. The call was in these words: "The Presbytery taking into serious consideration the unspeakable goodness of God in planting His Church in this, not long since, a howling wilderness, the habitation of savages; in accompanying His ordinances with the almighty influences of His Holy Spirit; and considering also the great danger we are in of provoking God to withhold these gracious influences, and that multitudes are still careless and hardening under the means; do therefore think it their incumbent duty to appoint a day of fasting and prayer to be observed in their respective congregations to implore a more plentiful outpouring of divine influences upon the Church in general, and upon His infant church in this land in particular; and at the same time to acknowledge with gratitude the many mercies both special and common conferred upon us. We do therefore appoint the first Thursday of September next to be observed for the above purpose."[2]

This historic action may well be accounted the forerunner of the "monthly concert of prayer for missions," the annual "week of prayer," and the "world day of prayer," all of which have meant so much to the life of our churches of the Upper Ohio Valley in later years.

At the Presbytery meeting of August 16, 1786, there was rejoicing and acknowledgment of answered prayer, when two young men, James Hughes and John Brice, offered themselves as candidates for the ministry and, therefore, for missionary service. When later these two young men were licensed to preach in the Spring of 1788, and McGready and Patterson late that same year, the next action of Presbytery in each case was to hand to the licentiate a formidable list of missionary appointments.

Schools to Educate Pastor Missionaries

The seriousness with which this whole problem, of training men to evangelize the frontiers of our country, was met appears best in the recorded action of the Synod of Virginia in 1791 at Winchester, with John McMillan as moderator. An overture was brought in, urging the devising of a plan "calculated to educate persons designed for the Gospel ministry, in that way which may be most suitable to fit them for that office."[3] Seven men were chosen to that committee. They were Joseph Smith, William Graham, John B. Smith, John McMillan, Joseph Patterson, William Wilson, and Moses Hoge, three of them Redstone men, indicating the leadership of the Upper Ohio Valley in the far-reaching proposal made. A considerable part of the Synod's time that year was spent in hearing and debating their report.

Out of that discussion emerged a plan for the formation of two schools: Liberty Hall in Rockbridge County, Virginia, which trained scores of missionaries for Virginia, the Carolinas, Tennessee, and Kentucky, emerging finally as Washington and Lee University; and Canonsburg Academy in Washington County, Pennsylvania, out of which grew Jefferson College. Most of the mission work in Western Pennsylvania, Ohio, Western Virginia, Michigan, and Indiana, down to about 1840, some also in Kentucky, was done by the graduates of this pioneer school.

Among these graduates were some really heroic men who deserve a place in the church's missionary Hall of Fame: men like Robert McGarrah, patriarch of the region which later became Clarion Presbytery; James McGready, the fiery Kentucky evangelist; John Wright, earliest apostle of central Ohio; and Archibald Hanna, who in Wayne County, Ohio, endured hardships and privations almost beyond our believing; and also Jacob Lindley, son of Upper Ten Mile congregation, first pastor ordained and installed in southeastern Ohio in 1803, and soon called to found and lead the oldest of the Ohio colleges, Ohio University at Athens. The character and work of such men should be better known by the church today.

Smith's "kitchen school of theology" and McMillan's log college and John Anderson's Seceder Seminary at Service were all born of a missionary motive. Those Founding Fathers in the Synod of Virginia, and especially those of Redstone and Ohio presbyteries, were strongly convinced that Christian colleges and theological seminaries form the foundation structure of the mission enterprise. If the church of the mid-twentieth century could find its way back to their convictions, all our colleges and theological schools might receive more adequate support.

WESTERN MISSIONARY SOCIETY

In the memorable year of 1802, the Synod of Virginia was divided, and the Synods of Kentucky and Pittsburgh set up.[4] Among the very first actions taken at the first meeting of the Synod of Pittsburgh was to resolve the Synod itself into the Western Missionary Society as it resolutely set its face toward the setting sun. The purpose of the Synod in this precedent-setting action was thus phrased: ". . . to diffuse the knowledge of the gospel among the inhabitants of the new settlements; the Indian tribes, and if need be, among the interior inhabitants, where they were not able to support the Gospel."[5] "This," says Dr. Thomas C. Pears, Jr., "is the first clear acknowledgment that the church itself is a Missionary Society, a principle which was to be definitely acknowledged later on by the entire church, through the deliverances of the General Assembly of 1847 and 1867."[6]

The next step was the organization of a Board of Trust, to be an executive committee for the discharging of the missionary responsibility it had just assumed as its primary business.[7] This small body of men became in fact a Board of National and World Missions, though not at first incorporated, and not given any such ambitious name.

In that same year the General Assembly was setting up its Board of Domestic Missions, but the men of the Upper Ohio Valley had a great missionary task laid on their very doorstep. They knew more about what was to be done than men in New York or Philadelphia, and were sure they could do it better. And they were right. During its first quarter century, the Assembly's Board did not show any marked energy or initiative, while such men as Elisha Swift, James Hughes, Elisha Macurdy, and the others who wrought with them obeyed the injunction which became a motto of the modern missionary movement. They "expected great things of God and undertook great things for God."

All that had gone before was prelude. With the Western Missionary Society, the world-wide outreach of Presbyterianism in this area and in America began. The Society envisioned at first a home and a foreign field. Their home field was the expanding white settlements across Ohio and into Indiana, as well as struggling congregations nearer at hand. Their foreign field was at the beginning no farther than the Sandusky and Maumee river valleys, where considerable numbers of Indians of two or three tribes still had their villages. They were people of another color, a strange language, and a pagan religion. The Western Missionary Society sent its first missionaries to them. For the most part these were Western Pennsylvania pastors who were released from their congregations for several weeks or months for this service. These men could learn little of the Indian tongues and had to work through interpreters. It did not prove a very effective way. The business of missions was being learned by the trial and error method. The church has long since learned that no very fruitful evangelizing can be done until the language, the customs, and the faith of the people are learned.

Missionary Work Among Indians

Probably the first men to spend any considerable time among the Indians were Joseph Badger and Thomas E. Hughes, in the Autumn of 1801.[8] Among others who participated were Elisha Macurdy, James Hughes, Michael Law, and Alexander Cook. Mr. Cook was ordained by Ohio Presbytery for the specific purpose of equipping him for the Indian work, probably the first foreign missionary ordained west of the mountains. As late as 1815, the Board of Trust undertook to establish a mission among the Senecas at Cornplanter's town, where Oil City now stands, and called on the churches for increased contributions to maintain it.[9] But the project fell through.

New light has recently been thrown upon this Indian mission work by John Johnston, long-time U. S. Indian Agent, with headquarters at Piqua, Ohio. We quote from his personal narrative:

"About forty years ago this tribe (Wyandots) contained 2,200 souls. In March, 1842, when as commissioner of the United States I concluded with them a treaty of cession and emigration, they had become reduced to 800, of all ages and both sexes. Before the Revolutionary War, a large part of the Wyandots had embraced Christianity in the communion of the Roman Catholic church. In the early part of my agency the Presbyterians had a mission among them at Lower Sandusky, under the care of the Reverend Joseph Badger. The War of 1812 broke up his benevolent enterprise. When peace was restored, the Methodists became the spiritual instructors of these Indians, and continued in charge of them until their final removal westward of the Missouri two years ago. (Johnston wrote this in 1845.)"[10]

A much earlier report appears in a letter written by Johnston to his superiors in Washington, June 17, 1819:

"The Wyandots came from the country near Quebec, about 250 years since. In their migratory excursions they first settled in Detroit, then removed to the upper end of Lake Michigan and settled near

Mackinaw. They engaged in war with the Indians there, and separated into two companies, one of which went to the northward; and the other, which was the more numerous, returned to Detroit, and finally extended its settlement along the shore of Lake Erie, all the way to Sandusky Bay. Their language is entirely distinct from that of any other tribes in Ohio. Many words are pure Latin. All the time the French had dominion in Canada, the Roman Catholics maintained a mission among them. They were nearly all baptized by the missionaries, and nearly all the aged people still wear crucifixes in their bosoms under their shirts.

"Between the years 1803 and 1810, the Presbyterians supported a missionary and a farming establishment among them, on Sandusky River. A few converts were made by them, who were put to death by the Catholic Indians, on account of their religion. The British traders were all opposed to the mission, and had influence enough to get General Hull to unite with them against the missionary, Reverend Joseph Badger. Mr. Badger was recalled by the Synod, and was succeeded by the Reverend J. Hughes. The minds of the Indians having been agitated by the prospect of hostilities between England and the United States, which were commenced at Tippecanoe by the impostor called the Prophet, the mission was withdrawn. For three years past the Wyandots have had a Methodist preacher, a man of color, among them. His name is Stewart. His preaching has wrought a great change among them. About fifty persons in the nation publicly profess to belong to the Protestant Church. A school is about to be established for them at Upper Sandusky."[11]

Perhaps the most appealing project in Indian mission work was undertaken by Elisha Macurdy and his wife. They brought with them Indian boys from the Sandusky villages to live in their home at Florence, treated them like their own children, trained them in the Christian faith and in the English language, and sent them back to be evangelists among their own tribesmen. At least four were thus trained. The name of one of them, known as Barnett, is found on a bronze tablet on the old mission chapel of the Methodist Mission at Upper Sandusky. The Presbyterian work in northwestern Ohio was disrupted by the War of 1812, and a few years later the Methodists took over what was left of it. But it was not long until men of our Western Missionary Society were being sent to Indian tribes in Michigan, Illinois, and beyond the Mississippi.

Work Among Settlers in Northwest Territory

Meanwhile, they had pushed out to the new settlements in the Northwest Territory, made possible by Anthony Wayne's decisive victory at Fallen Timbers in 1794. So far as the record shows, James Hughes was the first man sent by Ohio Presbytery across the river.[12] This was in 1797, although he or others had probably preached there earlier on their own initiative. His assignment was in response to a "supplication" from Indian Short Creek, later to be known as Mt. Pleasant. Churches were organized there and at St. Clairsville and Crab Apple in 1798. In 1800 Joseph Anderson was installed pastor of the three congregations. He was the first pastor installed by Ohio Presbytery in the Northwest Territory.[13] In 1800 there were churches at Island Creek and Steubenville; in 1802 at Two Ridges; in 1803 at Waterford—these all within a few miles of the river. The year 1804 saw work begun at Crooked Creek in Muskingum County, and at Lancaster and West Rushville, as we know them now, in Fairfield County. The westward march under the Blue Banner of aggressive Presbyterianism was well begun.

Before 1831, men of Canonsburg and Washington, and others directed by the Board of Trust, were at work in Indiana and Illinois. Soon they would be crossing into Missouri and Iowa. A missionary purpose was written into the charter of Western Theological Seminary when it was established in 1825 at Alleghenytown (now Pittsburgh). Thus the basic importance of theological education to the missionary enterprise was emphasized even more than it had been in 1791, when the Synod of Virginia had taken its history-making forward step. From its beginnings, Western Seminary has played a noble part in furnishing the church with its missionary adventurers. Of that more will be mentioned later.

WESTERN FOREIGN MISSIONARY SOCIETY

The year 1831 witnessed another milestone of missionary advance. In that year the mission-minded Synod of Pittsburgh embarked on the most daring adventure of all. The leaders of that Synod had failed to persuade the General Assembly to organize a Presbyterian Board of Foreign Missions. Undaunted, they then established their own "Western Foreign Missionary Society."[14] That venturesome action and their persistence in developing the work of that Society was, in the judgment of Dr. Pears, "their crowning achievement and was by far the greatest single contribution that Western Pennsylvania has been privileged, under the Providence of God, to make to the cause of Christ and the extension of His Kingdom."[15]

Interest in carrying the Gospel to the non-Christian world overseas was only beginning to stir the church. During the first two generations of its existence west of the Laurel Ridge, the church had faced tasks so mountainous at its very doors that it could not see over them. The need overseas was largely beyond its horizons. The modern missionary movement in Britain began when William Carey went to India in 1793, though in Scotland, England, and especially in Germany and Denmark, there had been some attempts at mission work overseas even early in the eighteenth century.

These efforts had been felt in America in several ways. Francis Makemie had come to America as an emissary of the Ulster Presbyterian Church. Count Zinzendorf and his Herrenhuters came as missionaries to the New World and began work among the Indians at once. Whitefield and Wesley crossed the ocean with a like motive, and it is evident that Whitefield's mission tours did much to awaken the missionary impulse all along our seaboard. The mission tour of McClure and Frisbie to the Monongahela and Muskingum valleys in 1772–1773 was, to be sure, directed by the Synod of New York and Philadelphia, but it was financed by a Scottish missionary society. All this had its effect upon the missionary interest and outlook in the Ohio Valley, but slowly.

The more immediate events that led to the action of the Synod of 1831 were very much entangled with those which brought about the disruption of our church in 1837. Growing out of the famous haystack prayer meeting at Williams College in 1806, the American Board of Commissioners for Foreign Missions was organized as a voluntary society, self-perpetuating and accountable to no church courts. It was designed to be the agency through which American Protestants of whatever communion might channel their gifts for the carrying of the Gospel to the non-Christian world. The experience of twenty-one years of its work had engendered a deep dissatisfaction in many quarters of the Presbyterian church, and especially among the conservatives of Western Pennsylvania and Ohio. It was hard to maintain loyalty to an organization which owned no loyalty to them and their church.

The American Board had already made an excellent record of service to the Kingdom. But if, as the Synod of Pittsburgh had declared at its very inception, the church itself was a missionary society, that church should do its own mission work. It should choose the men through whom its missionary activity should be carried on. Most of our churches, perhaps all of them, had already contributed to the work of the American Board, but with growing reluctance. We have not been able to discover any names of missionaries sent out from Upper Ohio Valley churches under the American Board. There may have been a few. At any rate all these factors contributed to the eagerness with which the Synod of Pittsburgh accepted the proposal to establish a Board of its own.

Other impulses also lay back of their decision. Like comets from outer space, various nations afar had begun to swing into the range of their vision. The slave-trade tragedies compelled them to think of Africa, especially those sections of the West Coast which were the original home of the Negroes in America. The spectacular career of Warren Hastings, his impeachment, and the generally high-handed and cruel conduct of the British East India Company had occupied much space in American newspapers for years and had focused public attention on India and farther East. The earlier Turkish atrocities in Syria and Armenia, the struggle for independence in Greece, the famine and misery in many parts of Asia Minor had turned the sympathies of the entire western world to the Near East.

Aggressive papal policy in Latin America and elsewhere had alerted the Scotch-Irish, who inherited a hatred and fear of whatever might bring advantage and growth to Romanism. Captain Cook and other adventurers who followed him had brought home and spread abroad their fascinating tales of hitherto unknown peoples on the myriad islands of the South Pacific, all steeped in savagery and ignorance, all desperately needing the Gospel that lifts men up and makes them free. The Great Commission—"into all the world"—was taking on new meaning, and a tide of conviction was rising in Presbyterian hearts throughout this region. So abundant fuel was ready for the spark that Elisha Swift of the Pittsburgh Second Church struck in that Synod meeting of 1831.

The Leadership of Dr. Swift

If men are to be given any credit for a movement so manifestly born of God, that credit goes first to Elisha P. Swift. Other men upheld his hands—Elisha Macurdy, Francis Herron, A. D. Campbell, and David Elliott notable among them, together with such laymen as Harmar Denny, John Hannen, and Benjamin Williams of Mingo. One scarcely dares to single out any, for there were thirty-six good men and true on that first Board, but Swift was *facile princeps* among those mighty men. Not only did his zeal and eloquence bring the Society into being, but he was immediately chosen to serve as its executive secretary. This work he carried in addition to his pastoral duties for a year and a half. He then resigned from the Second Church of Pittsburgh to give to it his undivided attention through more than two years of appalling discouragements, by which he was never daunted.[16]

Swift came honestly by his missionary fervor. He was a direct descendant of John Eliot, the apostle to the Massachusetts Indians, the first American Bible translator, and perhaps to be counted the first foreign missionary produced by the church in the western world. He attended Williams College while it was still under the spell of the haystack prayer meeting and its aftermath. He became a volunteer for foreign mission service under the American Board but was providentially prevented from going out. In Pittsburgh he discovered God's will for his life and his niche in the world-wide building of the Christian church. "O death, how strong thou art, to still the beating of that heart whose pulsations were felt to the remotest limits of the world," exclaimed Dr. Wilson. "For is there a land on the earth, upon which blessings have not descended in answer to the prayers of Dr. Swift?"[17]

Robert E. Speer paid him even higher tribute. In his address at the Centennial Convocation of the Western Theological Seminary Dr. Speer declared: "Back of the organization of the Western Foreign Missionary Society lay a great principle and a great personality. The principle was that the work of Foreign Missions is not an optional interest by the church to individuals and voluntary associations. Our fathers here in Pittsburgh conceived instead that the missionary obligation is the obligation of the church in her essential character, and that every member of the church is committed to this obligation."[18]

Dr. Speer then quoted one of the first utterances of the new Society. "The Presbyterian Church owes it as a sacred duty to her glorified Head to yield a far more exemplary obedience, and that in her distinctive character as a Church, to the command which He gave at His Ascension—'Go ye into all the world, and preach the Gospel to every creature.' It is believed to be among the causes of the frowns of the great Head of the Church, which are now resting on our beloved Zion, in the declension of vital piety and the disorders and divisions that distract us, that we have done so little—comparatively nothing—in our distinctive character as a church of Christ, to send the Gospel to the heathen, the Jews, and the Mohammedans."[19]

Dr. Speer then quotes with deep appreciation these burning words of Elisha Swift himself as he pleaded before the Synod in 1831 for the organization of the Society: "On what appointment do pastors and elders sit in the house of God and hold the keys of the Kingdom of Heaven, but that which commissions them to go and disciple all nations? If, at the bar of such courts, by the very fact of their lawful existence, the perishing heathen have no right to sue out the payment of a Redeemer's mercy, then the most material object of their sitting is canceled: and that neglected, starving portion of mankind, who enter with a specific claim, are turned out to find relief by an appeal to the sympathy of particular disciples. Will the great Head of all principality and power stay in judicatories where the laws of His Kingdom are so expounded? Until something more is done for the conversion of the nations, what article on the docket of business shall be relevant at any meeting, if this is not? Shall a worthless, unsound delinquent be told that, according to the word of God and the constitution of the church he has a right to come and consume hours of time in trifling litigation; and shall a world of benighted men, who have received as yet no hearing, and no mercy, and no information that Christ has left a deposit for them also, be turned over to the slow and uncertain compassion of individuals?"[20]

"It was the principle embodied in these utterances," observed Dr. Speer, "that made the fathers in this old Synod of Pittsburgh restive under the idea that the Presbyterian churches should conduct their missionary work through the American Board. They had great respect and even greater reverence for the American Board, and wished it well, but they could not accept the principles on which they believed it rested, and they were unwilling to abide by a method of missionary work which did not commit the church as such, and all its courts and organizations and its fundamental constitution, to the missionary obligation. It was this divergence of view, as truly as any doctrinal division, which led to the separation into Old and New Schools. And the reunion of the two churches carried with it the acceptance by the reunited church of the principle which our fathers here held vital."[21] That last statement of Dr. Speer is a noteworthy historical judgment.

The General Assembly that precipitated the division also took over the Western Foreign Missionary Society, moved it to New York, and made it the General Assembly's Board of Foreign Missions. Under that name it continued for one hundred and twenty-six years, until in 1957 a change of name marked a significant new direction in policy and method. It is now the "Commission on Ecumenical Mission and Relations."

The Society Faced Courageously a Tremendous Task

The Synod of Pittsburgh in 1831 loaded upon the shoulders of the founders of this new Western Foreign Missionary Society a tremendous task for which they had no training, no precedents to guide them, no built-up clientele, and no funds. They must rouse the entire membership of all their congregations. They must study world needs and select the places for their initial undertakings. They must recruit men and give them special training. They must find money sufficient to launch their first endeavors. They must develop an art of Christian approach to non-Christian peoples. Their success in planning and developing their world task is one of the most remarkable chapters in Presbyterian history. They laid the deep and broad foundations on which rests our splendid structure of foreign missions which is supported by recent annual expenditures of over eight and a half million dollars. "They displayed permanent wisdom in selecting their fields of labor, their earliest efforts developing into the most successful Presbyterian missions. Surely they had the inspiration of a Divine leader, and the enthusiasm of an immortal faith."

To everyone's surprise, the finding of volunteers for foreign mission service proved the easiest of their undertakings. "Whom shall we send and who will go for us?" Almost at once two young graduates of Princeton Seminary presented themselves—John Pinney and Joseph Barr. Nearly always it has been found that the men were ready before the money. Eager young life has been laid on the Lord's altar more readily than the gold of their fathers with which to equip and sustain them. These first two were designated for Liberia, to which the ill-advised and conscience-salving African Colonization Society was just then turning the attention of the church. But Barr was called by death before they sailed. Pinney went alone early in 1833. After four months of exploring, he returned to seek more recruits.

November 6 of that same year he sailed again for the West African coast with three companions, John Cloud, a recent graduate of Western Seminary, and Mr. and Mrs. Matthew Laird. After only a few months, Cloud's life was claimed by the deadly African malaria. While nursing him both Mr. and Mrs. Laird contracted it and died within twenty-four hours of each other. Again Pinney was left alone. It was a crushing blow to the Board in Pittsburgh and especially to Dr. Swift, but they did not for a moment falter or think of giving up.[22]

Replacements Are Recruited

They had in the meanwhile enlisted John C. Lowrie and William Reed with their wives. Lowrie had graduated from Western and had spent a year of graduate study at Princeton in preparation for his lifework. These four sailed May 30, 1833, and, after a long and trying voyage, arrived in Calcutta five months later. Within a month Mrs. Lowrie was dead of tuberculosis. Soon Mr. Reed was stricken, started homeward with his wife, but died and was buried at sea.

Eight missionaries had been sent out, now six were gone. Pinney was left alone at Monrovia in Liberia, and Lowrie was alone at Lodiana, in the Punjab of far northern India. The Presbyterian Yearbook of Prayer still perpetuates the mistaken statement that Lodiana was the first city in the world to which missionaries of the Presbyterian church were sent.[23] Green's official history of the Western Foreign Missionary Society makes it clear that Pinney and his companions were in Monrovia earlier by several months.

It is further to be noted that in Calcutta, Lowrie and Reed took counsel with Carey, Duff, and Marshman, and chose their field of work carefully with amazing insight into the importance of the step they were taking. They found the Lodiana district unoccupied by any other mission, the altitude fairly high, the mountains accessible if there were need to recuperate, and the people there, especially the Sikhs, more vigorous, independent, and promising than the people of the lower river plains.

The death of three-fourths of its initial missionary force brought consternation to the Society at home, and to the church. But it brought also renewed consecration to the task. Dr. Swift's immediate appeal for more funds and more volunteers brought prompt response. In Western Seminary alone, five men offered themselves. Within a year, two of them, John Newton and James Wilson, were on their way to join Lowrie at his faraway outpost. There Newton was to serve for fifty-six remarkable years, dying at his post in 1891. Of the others, Robert Orr and Joseph Travelli became our pioneers in China and Edward Cope fulfilled his ministry in India, and later in Ceylon. Another, William McCormick, had offered himself also but died only a few weeks later, with his theological course not quite completed. Orr, besides his work in China, had a part in opening our Presbyterian work in Siam, now Thailand.[24] Has there ever been a more evident answer to the prayers of God's people of the Upper Ohio Valley?

Answers to prayer for missionary success were manifest also in the quickened spiritual life of the Pittsburgh area and in the development of a unifying interest in the cause of missions. Dr. James Matheson, who represented the Congregational Union of England and Wales, made a visit to Pittsburgh in 1834. His observations as an outsider are interesting. "In all my intercourse with the ministers of this town, the professors of the Theological Institution, and pious laymen connected with benevolent and religious societies, I find the most enlightened views of Christian policy. The religious interests of the world appear to receive much of their attention. Yesterday I met with the Board of Directors of the Western Foreign Missionary Society. The progress of this Society has been equal to that of our most favored institutions at home. Its income for the last year was seventeen thousand dollars, and it has been only two years in existence. It is only about fifty years since the first preacher passed over the Allegheny Mountains into the Valley of the Mississippi . . . In the Synod of Pittsburgh there are now twenty-three thousand communicants, and about a hundred thousand hearers of the Gospel, besides Christian churches of other denominations.

"But not only has this good been effected for the people themselves. In this infant town they have begun to feel for, and to assist the heathen. How surprising that from this distant region messengers of peace should be sent forth to Northern India, Western Africa, and even to Jerusalem itself. The two former countries already have devoted and well-trained missionaries from this Society; and arrangements are now making to establish missions in Palestine, Asia Minor, and China."[25] Apparently the early record of the Western Foreign Missionary Society was impressive in the eyes of a man familiar with the achievements of the Society for the Proclamation of the Gospel, the Congregational Missionary Society, and the Scottish societies.

To quicken interest in missions throughout the churches, these pioneers in the missionary movement launched a monthly magazine. They recognized the power of the printed page and were convinced that an informed church is likely to be an interested church and an interested church will become a sacrificial church. In the second year of its corporate existence, the Western Foreign Missionary Society issued *The Missionary Recorder*. It must have been a most effective medium, quickening missionary interest and giving. The present-day reader, as he turns the pages of the few precious copies that are available in the library of Western Seminary, feels his soul stirred by the record of "the triumphs and defeats, the sorrows and the rejoicings, the heroic achievements and victorious martyrdoms of those epic years." The reality of a dynamic faith stands forth with challenging clearness.

Each issue contained much current missionary news and was well edited. This "chronicle" was the precedent which the Board has continued to follow in a list of missionary periodicals which became *The Home and Foreign Record, The Church at Home and Abroad, The Assembly Herald,* and similar publications. Printer's ink is still being used lavishly and effectively to promote this primary business of the church. It is another reason to be grateful for the precedent-setting zeal of the missionary pioneers in the Upper Ohio Valley.

An Experiment in Africa

The death of his co-laborers had left Pinney alone in Africa. He was unable to endure the trying climate for more than three years, which is the same term our Board allows its workers to stay in the Cameroun now. When he returned to America, the field was for a year and more unoccupied. In 1837 the Society tried as an interesting experiment the sending out of negro missionaries who might be better able to endure the climate. They found a young colored licentiate, Ephraim Titler of Philadelphia Presbytery, who was willing to go. He sailed from Wilmington, North Carolina, in 1836, in a vessel chartered by the Colonization Society. The 1838 report continues: "It is the intention of the Committee, as fast as it can procure suitable and educated colored men, to strengthen and enlarge this mission. The employment of colored men for building up the Redeemer's Kingdom in Africa, the Committee now believes, has not been sufficiently attended to by the churches. Their own most painful experience in the loss of their first missionaries; the lamentable loss of lives among the missionaries of other societies, and particularly of that noble institution, the Church of England Missionary Society, have brought the subject of some other agency strongly before the Committee." This experiment was not a complete success. Our Board even now looks in vain for negro missionaries for its West Africa field.

For a short period the Society had taken over a work in Smyrna which had been started by another organization. The Society received the one missionary under its care and sent out a printer and his wife, who remained only a short while. Soon the work had to be suspended, though it was located in a place of appalling need. It was only after long years that work in Smyrna was begun again.

MERGER WITH BOARD OF FOREIGN MISSIONS

When in 1837 the General Assembly voted to organize the Board of Foreign Missions to "superintend and conduct by its own proper authority the work of Foreign Missions," the Western Foreign Missionary Society felt elated. Eagerly the resources and personnel of the Society were turned over "lock, stock, and barrel" to the Board in New York. The last report was made from Pittsburgh the following year. That closing report revealed that the Society was ready to launch a new mission in China, that two men, the Reverend Robert W. Orr and the Reverend John A. Mitchell, were under appointment and ready to sail. They had been trained in Western Seminary, recruited from churches in the Upper Ohio Valley and supported financially by churches in this area.

The same closing report made vivid missionary expansion in India. There the number of missionaries had grown to fourteen, and the number of stations to five, Allahabad having been opened in 1836, Sabbathu and Saharanpur in 1837, and Fatehgarh in 1838.

In 1842, five years after the creation of the New York Board, Dr. Lowrie was able to report three missions, five stations, seventeen ordained missionaries, one printer and one teacher, nearly all with wives on the field to help in the work, two print shops and book binderies, several elementary schools, and four organized churches. Medical work had not yet been undertaken.

Honorable Walter Lowrie

Second only to Elisha Swift, in the annals of the pioneers of Presbyterian foreign missionary activity, is the name of Honorable Walter Lowrie. In 1836 he succeeded Elisha Swift as secretary of the Western Foreign Missionary Society and continued in that capacity with the Board of Foreign Missions until 1868, when failing health caused him to lay aside the work which had been dearer to him than life itself.

The title "The Honorable" was not only an appropriate recognition of the unimpeachable integrity of his character, but it is also the customary respect due one who had served for seven years in the Senate of Pennsylvania and later as United States Senator from Pennsylvania for six years. He had been reared on his father's farm in Butler County. There he learned the meaning of hard labor in various forms as he struggled to receive an education under the tutelage of the Reverend John McPherrin who was a graduate of Dr. McMillan's school at Canonsburg and perhaps the most prominent clergyman in the area north and west of the Allegheny River. He had planned to enter the ministry, but a rather impetuous early marriage to a gifted girl and the subsequent rebuke by Presbytery turned his thoughts away from the ministry to teaching and politics.[26] In the latter field he rose to eminence. He had been serving for twelve years as secretary to the Senate of the United States when he accepted an invitation to succeed Dr. Swift as secretary of the Western Foreign Missionary Society at a sacrificial salary that was too meager to pay the living expenses of his family.

The cause of foreign missions had become the burning passion of his heart. He felt called of God to devote his prestige, the power of his intellect, and every ounce of his energy in extending the Kingdom of God throughout the heathen world and in arousing the Presbyterian church to aggressive support of an ever-expanding program and budget. "He was as simple as he was great, loving Christ as a little child, and pleading everywhere and always, often with tears for the work to which he had given up everything himself and for which his Master had given up all before him."[27]

Mr. Lowrie's devotion to missions meant more than the sacrifice of money, politics, fame, and fortune. It penetrated into the agonizing recesses of his soul. He gave three sons to Christ's service in faraway places. His oldest son, John, was among the first missionaries to go to India. The father shared the tragedy and heartache of his son as John's wife died a little over a month after her arrival on the foreign field and as ill health compelled John's fellow missionaries to turn back toward America, leaving John to work alone in laying the foundations of Presbyterian missions in India. Later his own health forced him home. He became assistant to his father and subsequently succeeded him as secretary of the Board of Foreign Missions.[28]

John was the first of three sons of The Honorable Walter Lowrie to heed the call to serve in pioneering for Christ on the foreign field. He alone was to return to the family fireside. A second son, Walter, a brilliant linguist, had gone to China where he was soon killed by Chinese pirates. The third missionary son, Reuben, also served in China. His brief career of six years on the field was closed by death in Shanghai.[29] Sorrow and sacrifice did not deter the father whose vision of Christ, calling the church to attempt great things in service, never faltered amid varied experiences of triumphs and trials. What Swift had begun, Walter Lowrie carried forward until he passed the torch of leadership to his son John who, in turn, continued to direct the policy of the Board of Foreign Missions until 1891. It is impossible to estimate the results of the Upper Ohio Valley's contribution to the cause of Foreign Missions in the service of this great trio of missionary leaders.

CONTRIBUTIONS IN MEN AND MONEY

To recount what has been done since 1837 by the churches and presbyteries of the Upper Ohio Valley in support of Presbyterian National and World Missions would take us far beyond the space limits imposed. Only some typical facts and features can be pointed out.

The establishment of the Board of Foreign Missions in New York was in the same year as the division into Old and New Schools. Each branch claimed to be The Presbyterian Church. Naturally, the New School branch continued to support the American Board. But several years before the church was reunited in 1870, some individual churches began to transfer their loyalty to the Board with the Presbyterian label. The New School branch was active and zealous in mission work. Its churches in this area were conspicuous for their zeal, pre-eminently the Pittsburgh Third Church.

At the division, the Presbytery of Athens had adhered almost solidly to the New School. So had practically all of the Western Reserve, a strong group of congregations in northwestern Pennsylvania, and another group in east central Ohio, which constituted the New School Presbytery of Pataskala. These in the aggregate represented a very considerable part of the New School strength in mission support. The total amount in funds contributed and missionaries recruited, we have not been able to compute.

Our Valley also contributed one notable leader, first of the home mission work of the New School branch, then of the Home Mission enterprise of the reunited church, Dr. Henry Kendall. After a three-year pastorate in Pittsburgh's Third Church, he was called in 1861 to serve as secretary of the General Assembly's Committee on Home Missions, New School. At the time of Reunion he became senior secretary of the Home Mission Board and served until his death in 1893. He was one of the farseeing statesmen of the church.

As for the Old School record, from the beginning the Pittsburgh area became known as the most dependable source of mission revenue, and has so continued to this day. It was and is also a nursery of missionary and ministerial leadership. Such facts and figures are not easy to compile completely and accurately. We have tried to find some answer to these definite questions, but with only partial success:

What and how many of our Upper Ohio Valley churches have sent men into the ministry?

What is the total ministerial product of our churches?

What churches have had missionary sons and daughters?

What is the complete roll of National Missionaries sent out, and of Foreign Missionaries?

What causes can be found for the fruitfulness of some churches and the barrenness of others?

How do we compare in these respects with other sections of our church throughout America?

Is the present trend upward or downward?

Does such a survey reveal any factors affecting life investment in the service of the Kingdom, of which the church of today and tomorrow should take account?

Results of Questionnaire on Missions

A questionnaire was sent to every church in our eighteen presbyteries, asking the pastor and session to list the names of all their members who had ever offered themselves for the ministry, for mission work, or for any other form of distinctively Christian service, with whatever facts were available about each. Included in these presbyteries are now eight hundred and twenty-six churches. Repeated appeals brought replies from only three hundred and forty-three churches. Of this number, ninety-four reported that they have never sent anyone into any kind of full-time Christian service. From a 41 per cent reply, no conclusions can be drawn, to be sure. But from the reluctance of those who reported "none," and from the apologetic tone of many of their replies, we can suspect that if all the others were reported, the percentage of those replying "none" would be still larger, probably much larger.

From these replies and from other sources, such as local church histories, alumni catalogues, personal knowledge and the like, we have compiled a list of two thousand, eight hundred and thirty-seven men and women who have been given by the churches of these eighteen presbyteries to the ministry and to home and foreign mission service, including a few who have entered such Christian callings as Christian education, Salvation Army, Y.M.C.A., and Y.W.C.A. We have added to the returns two or three churches now long out of existence but fruitful in their day. Among these are Old Salem in Blairsville Presbytery, which gave the four Boyd brothers and several more to the ministry; and the little Olivesburg Church in Wooster Presbytery, which never had more than a hundred members, but which sent out at least one home missionary and three ministers, one of whom, James Houston, spent a lifetime in Brazil under our Board.

The number of foreign missionaries included in the total list is two hundred and sixty-nine; of home missionaries, three hundred and eighteen. This means that more than 20 per cent of the candidates for Christian vocations lifted up their eyes to regions beyond. We have found no way of comparing this fairly with other sections of the country. But taking it church by church, a good many congregations have reason to be proud of their sons and daughters. Every community, and indeed every church takes pride in the men sent into the service of their country. Many proudly display bronze tablets carrying their names. But few are the churches that have thought such a tablet might be dedicated to the men and women they have sent into the army of the Lord. These, some of them, seem completely to forget. One church, which the writer knows to have been the spiritual home of a famous missionary of a century ago, put down "none" in answer to our inquiry.

In other cases men are claimed as sons of city churches because they brought their membership there while in college or Seminary, even though they received their call to service in the church of their fathers, down deep in the country. A case in point is David Thompson, who went to Japan in the early sixties and spent his whole life there. He spent his boyhood in Harrison County, Ohio, and graduated from Franklin College. While in Seminary he brought his membership to Pittsburgh's First Church, which claims him, while no Harrison County church remembers anything about him. Such situations as this make it hard to get at the exact facts.

Let us call the roll of some well-known names among the missionaries of our church, and write over against these their home churches:

NAME AND FIELD	CHURCH	PRESBYTERY
James McGready Alexander of India	Bridgeport	St. Clairsville
Edward Alexander of Persia	Bridgeport	St. Clairsville
Mrs. Edward Alexander (Gertrude Faris) of Persia	Forks of Wheeling	Wheeling
Roy M. Allison of Shantung, China	Hopedale	Steubenville
Isaac Boyce of Mexico	Center, Pittsburgh	Pittsburgh
Mrs. Daisy Campbell Bachtell of Siam	Concord	Butler
Howard Campbell of Siam	Grove City	Butler
Ira Condit of China	Sheakleyville	Erie
Hunter Corbett of Shantung, China	Leatherwood	Clarion
Elma Donaldson of India (58 yrs.)	Nickleville	Clarion
Herbert C., Mildred and Kenneth Downing of Kenya (Afr. Inland)	New Concord	Zanesville
John A. Eakin of Siam	Butler First	Butler
John Elder of Iran	Tidioute	Erie
J. C. R. Ewing of India	Saltsburg	Kittanning
Arthur H. Ewing of India	Saltsburg	Kittanning
John D. Frame, M.D., of China	Wooster Westm.	Wooster
Margaret Frame of China	Wooster Westm.	Wooster
Albert A. Fulton of China	Ashland	Wooster
Dr. Mary Fulton of China	Ashland	Wooster
William C. Gault of W. Africa	Pittsburgh 6th	Pittsburgh
Joseph P. Graham of W. Africa	Cove	Wheeling
Adolphus C. Good of W. Africa	Pittsburgh 6th	Pittsburgh
Watson M. Hayes of China	Unity	Shenango
Calvin Hazlett of India	Newark First	Zanesville

NAME AND FIELD	CHURCH	PRESBYTERY
William H. Hezlep of India	Swissvale	Pittsburgh
Mrs. Sophie Craighead H. of India	Swissvale	Pittsburgh
Samuel C. Henderson of Chile	Bethlehem	Beaver
Arthur Guttery of China (YMCA)	Upper Ten Mile	Washington
William C. Johnston of W. Africa	Bethel	Pittsburgh
John C. Lowrie of China and Bd. Sec.	Butler First	Butler
Calvin M. Mateer of China	Pgh. Central	Pittsburgh
Harry A. Rhodes of Korea	Slippery Rock	Butler
W. L. Swallen of Korea	Paris	Washington
Samuel C. Peoples of Siam	W. Fairfield	Blairsville
William Speer of China	W. Alexander	Washington
Herbert W. Stewart of Siam	Grove City	Butler
Dr. Norma Dunning Farmer of India	Beulah	Pittsburgh
Jonathan Wilson of Siam	Bethlehem	Beaver

These have been selected for conspicuous service, length of years on the field, and the variety of churches from which they came. The list might of course be greatly extended. Special mention should be made of missionary martyrs who came from our area, among whom are Walter Lowrie, brother of John C., a son of the First Church of Butler, who was killed by pirates in China; Maria Bigham Campbell, daughter of the Millersburg, Ohio, church, who with her husband was murdered in the Sepoy Mutiny of 1857; and Frank E. Simcox of Venango County, Pennsylvania (we have never determined which was his home church), who was slain at Paotingfu in the Boxer Uprising of 1900. Many others have died at their posts of exhaustion from overwork and bad living conditions, who equally deserve to be called martyrs.

We shall not attempt to compile any such roll of home missionaries. One needs only to remind himself that it would include practically every member of Redstone, Ohio, Erie, Hartford, Lancaster, Washington, and Steubenville presbyteries before 1820. On that roll would be placed such well-known names as Kerr, Bushnell, and Riggs among the Indians; Josiah Welch in the Mormon work; S. Hall Young of Alaska; Anna Belle Stewart among the mountaineers; Verner and Johnston and Hosack in negro education. Even Sheldon Jackson, though a New Yorker, prepared for college at Vermilion Institute within our bounds.

Leadership for the Whole Church

The nationwide leadership of the Upper Ohio Valley is strikingly revealed in the large number of men from this area who have served the entire church as General Assembly moderators, Board secretaries, and in other positions of honor and responsibility. The long list of moderators include Obadiah Jennings, son of Dunlap's Creek and pastor at Steubenville, who moderated the Assembly in 1822; Francis Herron, pastor of Pittsburgh First, moderator in 1827; David Elliott of Washington, Pennsylvania, moderator in 1837; William Swan Plumer, son of Mt. Pleasant Church of Darlington, Pennsylvania, moderator in 1838 (OS); David H. Riddle of Pittsburgh Third, moderator in 1850 (NS); Alexander T. McGill of Western Seminary, moderator in 1848 (OS); Francis McFarland, son of Cross Roads Church of Florence, Pennsylvania, moderator in 1856 (OS); Charles C. Beatty of Steubenville, moderator in 1862 (OS); John C. Lowrie, son of First Church of Butler, moderator in 1865 (OS); M. W. Jacobus of Western Seminary, moderator in 1869 (OS); as well as later and more familiar names to the number of seventeen, all sons of, or pastors of, churches within our bounds, or educators in our institutions. Nor should we overlook the fact that at least three moderators of the Cumberland Presbyterian Assembly were Western Pennsylvania men and that, with the exception of John Rankin, practically all the leaders of the Free Presbyterian Church were also from the Upper Ohio Valley.

These facts add up to a recognition by the church at large that this area, settled so predominantly by Scotch and Scotch-Irish of strong Calvinistic character, was producing for the need of later generations men of like stability, vision, and courage, as are still needed to possess the land for Christ and to carry the Cross to the ends of the earth.

The Response of the Present

We take in conclusion a quick look at the record of Upper Ohio

Valley presbyteries in their financial support of the world mission of our own church. Those six years of the work of the Western Foreign Missionary Society were in every way the day of small things. Yet they were large enough to amaze a visiting Englishman. Those first recruits for service were easier to find than was the money to send them. Yet the money did come. Churches and individuals gave sacrificially when they saw something tangible being done to answer the prayer, "Thy Kingdom come."

A seventeen thousand dollar budget looks pitifully small to us, yet there was no such holding back of eager volunteers for lack of funds as there has been many a time since. The Assembly's Foreign Board, formed in the very dust of the financial crash of 1837, has grown steadily in financial strength through one hundred and twenty years, until now it operates on a budget of more than eight and a half millions annually.

Since the receipts for foreign missions are no longer reported separately in the General Assembly minutes, we cannot tabulate the total amounts given to foreign and national missions by our individual presbyteries. We can only compare the giving of our eighteen presbyteries, member-wise, with the same record for the entire denomination. Such a comparison shows that, while the 2,809,603 communicants of our church gave in 1956 a total of $33,469,856 for all the Assembly-approved benevolences, or an average of $11.91 per member, the eighteen presbyteries in our area with their total membership of 300,551 gave $3,555,560 which averages $11.83 per member. That is somewhat below the denominational average and is not something of which we can boast, especially when we remember that ours is economically a favored section of our country. It would seem to show less zeal for the winning of the world to Christ than our fathers had in that far-off "day of small things." What of these nationwide calls to advance which have sounded out again and again across the church—the Men and Religion Forward Movement, the New Era Advance, United Stewardship drive, and the rest? Have they been heeded less in the Upper Ohio Valley than elsewhere? Perhaps we need to meditate prayerfully upon this "challenge of a heroic past," as Dr. McKinney has called it, so that it may reawaken us. We ought still to be in the forefront in furnishing both money and men to carry the Gospel to "the ends of the earth." In both points the Middle West and the Far West are gradually outstripping us.

Consecrated men and women in Pittsburgh and in smaller communities within our bounds have given generously for many home missions projects, and for the equipping and endowing of our struggling colleges as the next chapter will show in convincing detail. But in large individual contributions to the foreign mission enterprise, the New York and Philadelphia areas are ahead of us. Nearsightedness may be dangerous in times of rapid change.

The pioneering zeal of our forefathers throughout the Upper Ohio Valley has set historic standards of vision and consecration in the development of the ever-expanding missionary enterprise of our church. These standards should inspire us to re-examine the depth and drive of our present-day missionary convictions. They should stir us to respond with renewed enthusiasm, not only to the challenge arising out of a heroic past, but to the imperative needs of our own day with its revolutionary changes and its faith-testing uncertainties.

CHAPTER XX Gifts and Givers

THE PRECEDING CHAPTERS have discussed the development of special movements, traced unusual trends in the area, and noted the contributions made by leaders in this Valley in the fields of Education, Religious Journalism, Missions, and Church Unity. The decades since the Reunion of 1870 have indeed witnessed far-reaching changes in all these phases of Presbyterian activity in the Upper Ohio Valley. It is the purpose of this chapter to discuss the fruitage of the era to the Church and the nation only in the field of Benevolences.

Recently a capable and highly respected president of one of our area colleges visited New York City to interest a well-known philanthropic foundation in his institution. Before the interview had continued far, the representative of the foundation inquired, "From where did you say you have come?"

"From Western Pennsylvania," the visitor replied.

"Well, what are you doing in the East? Don't you know that the area from which you have come is the most sympathetic in the nation in supporting educational institutions, missionary projects, and benevolences generally?"

Whether or not the visitor succeeded in his mission of obtaining funds has not been revealed, doubtless for excellent professional reasons. But his own respect for the generosity of this Upper Ohio Valley, he reports, was considerably deepened by the experience.

Perhaps it might at first thought seem unusual that individuals or their descendants who came from the frugal, puritanic background of Scotland, North Ireland, or the Low Country should be benevolence-minded. These rugged pioneers were supposed to be constitutionally a phlegmatic, undemonstrative, hardheaded stock, lacking the *savoir vivre* or *gemütlichkeit* conventionally associated with extroversion in general or generosity in particular. In many instances their liberality has been concealed under the guise of anonymity, and many of them have discouraged, rather than sought, public recognition of their gifts. Who, for instance, is not familiar with the extreme concern of the late Mr. A. W. Mellon that his magnificent gift to the nation of the National Art Gallery, including with it his own invaluable collection of paintings and objects of art, should not be, if at all possible, associated with his name as donor.

Another specific instance of this aversion to publicity was revealed when the Communist invasion of China forced our missionaries to leave their well-established work there, resulting in the destruction of great numbers of hospitals and mission schools. Only then did it become known that a modest member of the writer's own Session had built, equipped, and endowed a hospital in China some years before, the existence of which was entirely unknown to his associates, his church, and his minister.

Or yet another instance concerning the self-effacement of some of our givers. Prior to his retirement a businessman and member of the Board of Trustees of a prominent college of this area had purchased a beautiful farm and stocked it with a herd of fine cattle, the care of which should be a labor of love and of continuing interest through the years. Already a generous contributor to the college, when he learned in a Board meeting that a contemplated building would have to be completed without the benefit of certain additional facilities he believed very desirable for the life of the students, he requested that the additions be included at his own expense, and that no mention be made of his gift—which was done. Few know that this special act of generosity and love was made possible by disposing of his valuable herd of cattle and by selling his lovely farm and country home.

These may be taken as typical instances of the sort of benevolences, known or even as yet unrevealed, that have established the reputation of the Valley for unselfishness and public service which neither receives nor indeed desires general publicity.

The boards and agencies of the Church have depended on its liberality. The disproportionately large number of independent Christian colleges that have prospered here through the years; the support almost alone (for the cause was not generally popular elsewhere) of work among the liberated Negroes immediately following the Civil War; the generous assistance to the presently great independent universities in Ohio and Pennsylvania, as well as many like Princeton and Yale in the East; the unusually large number of Young Men's and Young Women's Christian Association units built and supported in great part by funds from Presbyterian donors; the erection and equipping of numerous hospitals, clinics, and research institutions of the area; the maintenance of a large number of summer camps in addition to those supported by local churches and presbyteries, and the undergirding of theological education from the days of Dr. John McMillan's "Latin School" and the Washington Academy to the establishment of Western and Lane Theological seminaries; all these are fitting memorials to the generosity of Presbyterians of the Valley.

GIFTS THROUGH CHURCHES

A survey of the contributions made by the churches of the area since 1900 reveals that the presbyteries of Chillicothe, Columbus, Cincinnati, Dayton, Mahoning, Marion, Portsmouth, St. Clairsville, Steubenville, Wooster, and Zanesville, in Ohio; of Beaver, Blairsville, Butler, Clarion, Erie, Kittanning, Pittsburgh, Redstone, Shenango, and Washington, in Pennsylvania; and of Grafton, Parkersburg, and Wheeling, in West Virginia, comprising the geographic area of the Upper Ohio, have contributed the amazing total of $103,059,136 for benevolences through the churches since the turn of the present century. And, in addition, they have given an even more unbelievable total of $348,506,084 for the work of local congregations' self-support, and for such special projects as building funds, local extension undertakings, and synod and presbytery projects. Almost one-half billion dollars for the Kingdom in two generations from this Ohio watershed solely through the churches!

Though there have been realignments made from time to time in the administrative agencies concerned and the names of the activities changed, the projects supported have been principally the following: foreign missions; national missions; local missions and Americanization; church extension; theological seminaries and religious education; college activities under the auspices of the denomination; student loans and grants; fellowships for graduate study; ministerial relief and pensions for ministers and church employees; summer camps and conferences; young people's local, area, and national activities; women's and men's presbyterial, synodical, and national projects; Sunday-school work; appropriate denominational publications; temperance and moral welfare; evangelism; social education and action; relief of war-stricken areas and of refugee personnel; and conservation of significant records and shrines.

In the case of some of the foregoing, it has been necessary, in connection with their work, to erect and staff schools, hospitals, and institutions of higher education. In many instances both at home and abroad, the work has advanced far beyond the scope of activities of a board or agency, and has become a national project. And in the case of educational undertakings among the Freedmen, most of the institutions concerned have achieved complete academic accreditation and are functioning as do colleges generally.

Gifts for Service, not Display

When the tremendous inclusiveness of the foregoing program is appreciated, it can then be understood how vitally important the loyalty of the Presbyterians of the Valley has been to the Church. To be sure funds could easily have been hoarded and administered locally—as in a very few instances they unfortunately have been—and magnificent churches and educational facilities could have been provided first before the claims of others were considered. But it has been abundantly demonstrated by the happy experience of givers in this area that to those who are generous and liberal God makes available other and richer blessings.

The Presbyterians of the Upper Ohio have never coveted the reputation of being cathedral builders. They have not striven and saved from generation to generation that the fruits of their toil might be preserved in pretentious, even if beautiful, masses of stone, steel, and mortar. Perhaps they have rather preferred time-honored and familiar churches within the hallowed walls of which they and their fathers and fathers' fathers have worshiped God. They have sought to maintain dignified efficient churches and educational units. Except in the case of certain memorial institutions, the donors of which have always been at the same time generous in all the other vital areas of church or community responsibility for local buildings and programs, their concern might well be expressed in the familiar ideal—"Let All Be Done Decently and in Order."

No single method can be designated as having made possible this record of congregational generosity. Doubtless the oft-repeated emphasis upon the duty of youth and adults alike to give proportionately and, if possible, a tithe of their income to God has had a profound and cumulative effect as the years have passed. The spiritually and psychologically sound method by which every member, contributing weekly by special envelopes in which each

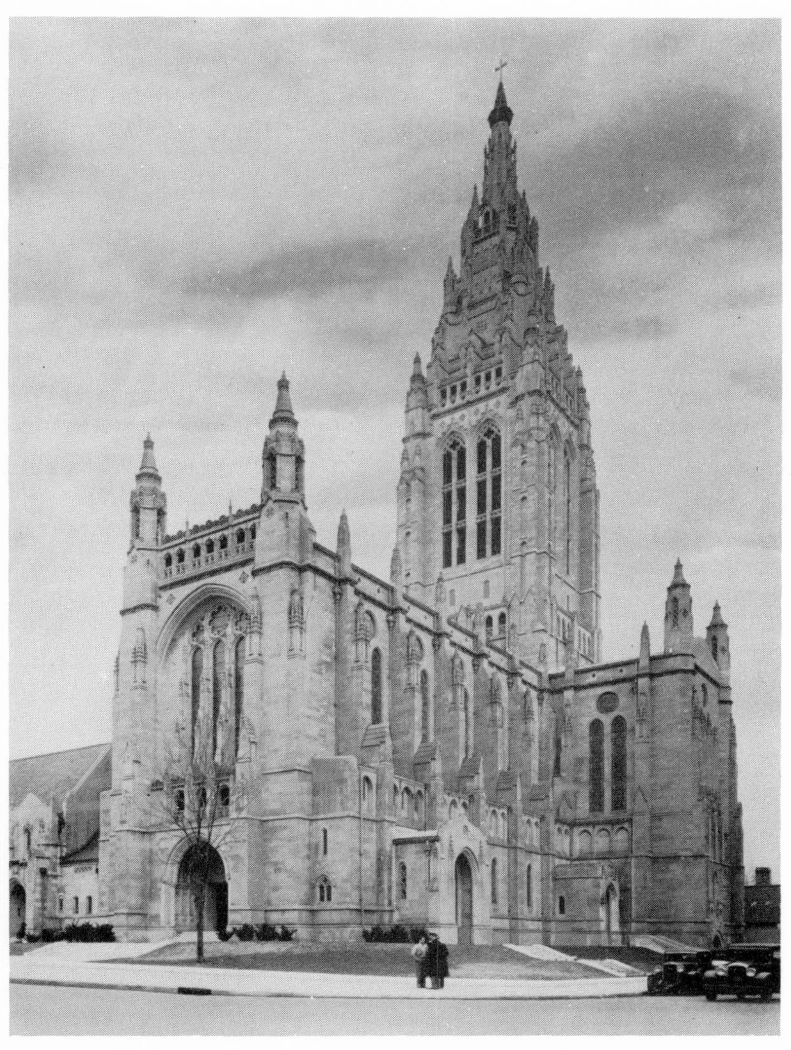

EAST LIBERTY PRESBYTERIAN CHURCH, 1935
The gift of Richard Beatty Mellon and Jennie King Mellon (Mrs. R. B.) as a memorial to their mothers, Sarah Jane Negley Mellon and Sarah Cordelia Smith King, who for many years were devoted members of this church.

COURTESY OF UNIVERSITY OF PITTSBURGH

THE HEINZ MEMORIAL CHAPEL

Presented to University of Pittsburgh by Henry John Heinz and his three children. Mr. Heinz was a leader in promoting Sunday-School teaching.

donor personally apportions his gifts, large or small, so that a definite share is devoted to the benevolence undertakings of the Church and only a part to the work of the local congregation, has without doubt kept before the membership the broader challenge of the world task of the Church. Certainly the consistent teaching of the children, from the nursery and kindergarten to young adulthood, to share through the Youth Budget with others even their smallest gifts has borne fruitage in the increasing generosity of young parents and homemakers.

Slight Variation in Ratio of Gifts

To return for a final moment to the combined benevolent and local church expense figures above ($451,565,220) an analysis of contributions of local presbyteries seems to indicate that, contrary to general opinion, the ratio in contributions in large urban and small rural presbyteries varies but little. It might be expected that in large presbyteries or large congregations, where local expenses are shared by a considerable number of contributors, or in churches and presbyteries having a backlog of endowments available to care for recurrent local needs, that the per capita benevolence-giving of such groups would be disproportionately greater than in the smaller presbyteries and in churches without sustaining endowments.

But a study of this situation in the twenty-four presbyteries referred to above reveals rather a remarkable similarity. For example, the average ratio of benevolence contributions to current receipts over the past fifty-six years is one dollar for benevolences to three dollars and thirty-eight cents for local expenses. But Pittsburgh Presbytery, with a membership of 85,629, contributed in the ratio of one dollar to two dollars and sixty-two cents; while Butler Presbytery, with a membership of but 10,917, contributed at the rate of one dollar to two dollars and seventy cents. Likewise, it is found that the average ratio in twenty of the twenty-four presbyteries is within seventy-five cents above or below the mean.

PRESBYTERY	BENEVOLENCES	CURRENT RECEIPTS	RATIO
Wheeling (Org. 1924)	$ 1,793,029.00	6,113,050.00	$1.00 to $3.41
Parkersburg	613,533.00	3,943,844.00	1.00 to 6.42
Grafton (Org. 1924)	909,728.00	3,421,509.00	1.00 to 3.76
Washington	2,456,972.00	9,478,753.00	1.00 to 3.85
Shenango	2,902,863.00	9,441,628.00	1.00 to 3.25
Redstone	4,183,175.00	16,298,090.00	1.00 to 3.89
Pittsburgh	34,535,635.00	90,788,539.00	1.00 to 2.62
Kittanning	2,255,008.00	8,511,329.00	1.00 to 3.77
Erie	7,071,870.00	24,381,465.00	1.00 to 3.44
Clarion	2,580,480.00	7,857,734.00	1.00 to 3.05
Butler	3,018,321.00	8,197,106.00	1.00 to 2.70
Blairsville	4,823,934.00	16,939,615.00	1.00 to 3.50
Beaver	2,393,593.00	9,535,814.00	1.00 to 3.98
Zanesville	2,123,169.00	7,812,730.00	1.00 to 3.67
Wooster	1,951,805.00	7,126,231.00	1.00 to 3.64
Steubenville	2,606,740.00	10,513,258.00	1.00 to 4.00
St. Clairsville	2,012,505.00	7,135,555.00	1.00 to 3.51
Portsmouth	1,348,032.00	4,970,407.00	1.00 to 3.68
Marion	1,134,784.00	6,852,952.00	1.00 to 6.03
Mahoning	5,091,085.00	20,506,465.00	1.00 to 4.02
Dayton	4,697,546.00	21,222,931.00	1.00 to 4.51
Columbus	4,468,813.00	18,053,566.00	1.00 to 4.04
Cincinnati	7,626,338.00	27,782,060.00	1.00 to 3.64
Chillicothe (Dis. 1935)	460,348.00	1,621,538.00	1.00 to 3.52
TOTALS	$103,059,136.00	$348,506,084.00	$1.00 to $3.38 (Average)

(For complete details, see charts, Appendix D.)

From this it may be concluded that, while other forms of special benevolences may be influenced considerably by large gifts, legacies, and endowments, most of what has been accomplished here in the Ohio Valley at the level of church benevolences has been made possible through a high general average of individual and family giving. These dour Puritan businessmen seem to have been rather cheerful and generous in supporting the work of the Kingdom of God!

This also seems to indicate among other things that the area's generosity in benevolences is not the result of having on the average more to share above the local needs of the congregation. Nor does it indicate that high pressure promotional methods and super organizations, which are more likely to be found in urban centers, are the explanation of the difference between casual and consecrated giving. It must rather be regarded as an evidence of the fact that generous, sustained benevolence is chiefly a matter of the soul's response to the divine challenge. Alike in wealthy congregations and those less affluent, in large city centers of population and productive industry and small rural areas alike, benevolence-giving through the local congregation is a matter of training and background, and that modesty and taste are regarded as preferable jewels to publicity.

GIFTS TO EDUCATIONAL INSTITUTIONS

Rather than attempt an exhaustive listing of the names of major contributors to every institution and the amounts given—which attempt would inevitably result in the omission of many worthy names, and would necessitate an examination of institutions' records quite unwarranted by such an undertaking as the present—perhaps it will suffice to mention only some of the rather well-known and honored givers of the presbyteries and their constituent communities.

Yet in doing so it will again be obvious that this will omit the recognition of literally thousands of donors of small amounts, whose devotion and loyalty are no whit less than that of the more generally recognized benefactors. These modest and faithful small givers continue to be the joy of the heart of an institution's president or of a board secretary. Often unsuspected as potential givers and certainly "uncultivated" according to the best promotional practices, these anonymous benefactors give important sums, often small, sometimes quite considerable.

One remembers how the late Dr. Hugh T. Kerr used to speak of an incident that occurred when he was President of the Board of Christian Education. During those years, when he was conducting his famous Sunday afternoon services over a local radio station, he received one day a brief letter from a man in a rather mountainous, inaccessible area south of Pittsburgh, requesting that he come down at his early convenience to visit the writer and suggesting in a general way that he might be interested in making a benevolence gift to the educational program of the Church. Accompanied by a representative of the institution concerned, Dr. Kerr, for the last stage of the journey using a horse and buggy, made the requested visit. He anticipated not so much a sizable gift as a new and interesting contact with a potential donor and a few hours of relief from the tension of city and parish duties in fellowship enroute with a brother minister.

As a result of the visit, the unknown and humble inquirer contributed a very large sum of money to the educational task of one of the institutions of the Church. Yet no record of this special and very personal gift appears in the reports of any local church or presbytery, nor does it, or thousands of others like it, appear in the inclusive chart above.

Without doubt the total amounts of these special benevolences to educational institutions and missionary undertakings cannot be estimated with any real measure of accuracy. Over a period of fifty years, they would doubtless be expressed in terms of hundreds of millions of dollars. Certainly to be included in this category would be the accrued endowments of our educational institutions, for who ever heard of such institutions retiring from operating receipts any considerable sums to be set aside for endowment purposes. Likewise, almost all the capital assets of an institution in real estate, buildings, and equipment may be assumed to have been obtained through funds provided by special donors. And in the case of many of the older local institutions, a number of the earliest buildings and developments already have been replaced and will therefore no longer appear as assets on their balance sheets.

But even on the basis of present investments in grounds, buildings, and endowments, the total benevolence contributions to those institutions that are, or have formerly been, affiliated with our Church is considerable. Included in the group are the present church-related institutions of Davis-Elkins, Grove City, Waynesburg, and Wooster colleges, and Western Theological Seminary; such other formerly church-related or Presbyterian-founded institutions as Washington and Jefferson College, the University of Pittsburgh, Marietta College, Allegheny College, Western College for Women, Chatham College, Miami University, and Lane Theological Seminary; institutions such as Carnegie Institute of Technology, founded for the most part by Presbyterian laymen, and supported through the years by many of the same persons who have sustained the University of Pittsburgh and many other local colleges; the considerable group of educational institutions provided for the education of colored people in the South, about which some brief comment should be made here.

Generous Support of Activities for Freedmen

It was by no mere chance that the Ohio Valley became the center of the Presbyterian church's participation in work among the Freedmen. This area was from the first the center of opposition to chattel slavery and the hotbed of abolitionist activities. Ohio and Pennsylvania, prior to the Civil War, were traversed by most of the Underground Railroad channels to Canada for fugitive slaves. Harriet Beecher Stowe at Cincinnati depicted scenes and stressed convictions shared by thousands in her vicinity. Chillicothe Presbytery early became a determined leader against slavery. It was joined by others, until the restlessness resulted in the organization of a Free Presbyterian Church.

To these crusading Free Presbyterians must go the credit for initiating missionary and educational work among the Freedmen. Before the end of 1863, they sent a few men and women to Mississippi to open schools among Negroes who had been gathered by the Federal Army into concentration camps to protect them against the violence of the whites. One of these was Elizabeth Welsh of Martinsburg, Ohio, who after her college years at Westminster and Oberlin offered herself for such service. Letters which she wrote home from Natchez in the early part of 1864 tell of her being within hearing of cannon fire as she carried on her work. Until emancipation, some of the southern states had made it a crime even to teach a Negro to read. Schools and evangelistic work which had been projected among them by people from the North were frowned upon everywhere.

In 1865 the New School Presbyterians voiced their sense of responsibility and almost immediately began some schools among the Freedmen. Except in the Pittsburgh area and eastern Ohio, the Old School branch was at first very lukewarm toward such undertakings. So after the war, and especially after the New School–Old School reunion, the Upper Ohio naturally became the energizing center of the Church's activities in behalf of the liberated Negroes of the South.

Within the Old School framework, two committees were set up, one at Indianapolis and the other at Philadelphia. These were merged the following year into the General Assembly's Committee on Freedmen. This Committee first met and was organized in the First Presbyterian Church of Pittsburgh. By 1882 it had grown into the Board of Missions for Freedmen with headquarters in Pittsburgh. Three years later the Assembly approved a special department of the Woman's Home Missionary Society to promote Freedmen work among the women of the Church with headquarters also at Pittsburgh.

The report of that Board to the Assembly in 1888 included this significant statement: "Among those consulted, it was found that only ministers and elders from Pittsburgh and its vicinity would agree to undertake the work. At the beginning, and for no inconsiderable time afterwards, the churches of Pittsburgh, Allegheny, and the surrounding country were the only ones freely opened in behalf of the Freedmen. It was with the greatest difficulty that the first secretary, Reverend S. C. Logan, D.D., succeeded in obtaining permission to present this cause to the churches of the larger cities and towns, in many places in the country."

Undaunted, this Board developed a broad-range program of establishing schools, churches, and evangelistic services for the millions of slaves and their families who had been set free by presidential proclamation and the subsequent triumphs on bloody battlefields. This humanitarian work of our Church benefited in no way from the largess of the postwar Federal "Freedmen's Bureau," as did Fiske, Atlanta, Hampton, and Howard universities, as well as hundreds of other educational institutions. The work of the Presbyterian church was strictly self-supporting with money contributed in large measure from the Pittsburgh area.

One of the first institutions to be opened was Biddle Memorial Institute in 1867. It has expanded into the Johnson C. Smith University located at Charlotte, North Carolina, and offers a comprehensive curriculum including theological education. Through the years Pittsburgh Presbyterians have made the original financial gifts for its early development and continued expansion and have devoted much time in helping to direct its enlarging program.

Among the colleges, universities, institutes, and academies of the Church that were established to carry on educational work, the following, among others, are noteworthy; and some of them, even by their names, commemorate the generosity of faithful men and women of the area:

Johnson C. Smith University (formerly Biddle)
Harbison Agricultural College
Boggs Academy
Swift Memorial College
Lorimer Academy
Lorimer Training School, at Petersburg, Va.
Barber Memorial Seminary and Scotia Seminary
(now Barber-Scotia College)
Gillespie Academy
Gillespie Hospital
Kendall Academy
Coulter Academy

All the foregoing colleges and institutions for work among Freedmen have drawn their resources, if not entirely at least in very considerable part, from Presbyterian donors of the Upper Ohio area. And in the case of some colleges, although no longer related in any way to our Church, the interest and support of families and of neighboring congregations in them have continued with little diminution through the years. It was reported, for instance, of one institution which is no longer Presbyterian that of a campaign a few years ago that provided approximately $1,250,000, at least $600,000 of it was given by Presbyterian donors and alumni.

Gifts to Other Institutions

In the case of Washington and Jefferson College—the oldest of our institutions in the area—its constituency, support, and capital funds have been characteristically Presbyterian. The University of Pittsburgh, founded in 1787 as Pittsburgh Academy, was chartered, staffed, and supported through the years for the most part by a similar constituency. Lane Theological Seminary was, until its union with McCormick Seminary in 1930, distinctly a product and active part of the area. Chatham College (formerly Pennsylvania College for Women) was founded by a group composed in considerable part of Presbyterian laymen and ministers, and its support has been received from similar donors. Western College for Women and Miami University, both in Oxford, Ohio, until their individual formal separation from this tradition, were for many years a part of its benevolent concern and support.

Taking into consideration the variable factors involved on the part of those fully supported and of those which have drawn partial support in later years from Presbyterian donors, and remembering also the recognized tendency to contribute outside denominational lines on the part of many of these donors, it would probably be a conservative figure to estimate the amounts contributed to endowments, capital funds, and special projects of all these institutions as in excess of *one hundred and forty-five million dollars.*

MANY GENEROUS CONTRIBUTORS

Now a final word regarding some of the honored names of the Ohio Valley that have been associated with educational benevolences, as well as benevolent undertakings in general. In the list below, they are included so far as is possible by presbyteries or communities. Due apology is made for the omission of many that should be included, and for areas from which no names are listed due to unavailability of necessary information. Yet the possibility—indeed the probability—of the inadvertent omissions of some most deserving and generous friends ought not to preclude entirely the recognition of scores of family and individual names that are remembered with gratitude for their loyalty and generosity.

Such an Honor Roll, with no attempt to estimate the amounts or equate in order their gifts, would be somewhat as follows:

PITTSBURGH PRESBYTERY

W. S. Arbuthnot
Charles D. Armstrong
Biddle Arthurs
George R. Aufderheide
Edward V. Babcock
Frederick R. Babcock
Alexander J. Barron
Davitt S. Bell
Frank B. Bell
Willis A. Booth
Roy G. Bostwick
Dr. W. A. Bradshaw
Charles A. Brooks
James I. Buchanan
John G. Buchanan
R. H. Buhl
A. P. Burchfield
J. Frederick Byers
C. William Campbell
Mr. and Mrs. R. D. Campbell
Mr. and Mrs. Wilson A. Campbell
Andrew Carnegie
Henry Carpenter
George H. Clapp
D. M. Clemson
W. L. Clouse
Mrs. Susan Pitcairn Crabbe
George R. Craig
J. S. Crutchfield
Charles L. Cunningham
Robert D. Dalzell
Mr. and Mrs. Allen S. Davison
George S. Davison

George H. Deike
Mrs. Elizabeth O'Hara Denny
Harmar D. Denny, Jr.
John Dalzell Duff
George D. Edwards
George C. Fisher
W. U. Follansbee and Family
Mr. and Mrs. David L. Gillespie
Miss Mabel Gillespie
Hon. James H. Gray
George W. Guthrie
James H. Hammond
Ralph W. Harbison
Samuel P. Harbison
W. A. Harbison
Mrs. Clifford Heinz
Howard J. Heinz
Howard J. Heinz II
Lewis W. Hicks
Wenman A. Hicks
Ray F. Hoffman
Mrs. Susan Lee Hunt
H. A. Johns
Harry W. Keller
George R. Laughlin
James H. Lockhart
George B. Logan
William A. Magee
S. S. Marvin
Dr. W. D. McClelland
Thomas D. McCloskey
Edward McDonald
Hugh K. McJunkin
Mrs. Virginia A. McKee
Mr. and Mrs. W. M. McKelvey
Andrew W. Mellon
Richard B. Mellon
Richard K. Mellon
Alexander Murdock
W. M. Murdock
John F. Miller
Dr. George B. Moreland
John E. Nelson
Edward O'Neill
Samuel T. Owens
Joseph R. Paull
Christy Payne
George L. Peck
Frank C. Pierson
Robert Pitcairn
Alfred C. Pollock
John E. Potter
Dr. W. B. Ray
James C. Rea
Alexander P. Reed
David A. Reed
W. A. Renshaw
A. C. Robinson
William M. Robinson
Alan M. Scaife
Mrs. Sarah M. Scaife
William H. Schuette
Wilson A. Shaw
S. M. Shelley
R. M. Sherrard
J. Hervey Shertz
G. Dixon Shrum
Mr. and Mrs. Johnson C. Smith

W. W. Smith
Dr. R. R. Snowden
Benjamin Thaw
Mrs. Mary Copley Thaw
William Thaw
James L. Thistle
Hon. A. M. Thompson
Mrs. Mary Thaw Thompson
Frank D. Thomson
R. R. M. Thorne
George Westinghouse
William P. Witherow

ERIE PRESBYTERY

E. H. Beshlin, Warren
Hon. George S. Criswell, Franklin
Kennedy Crumrine, Meadville
Richard Dresser, Bradford
Frank L. Fay, Greenville
Dr. Robert Kerr, Bradford
J. W. Kitchen, Warren
Chess Lamberton, Franklin
H. C. Markwood, Erie
John Z. Miller, Erie
Hon. S. H. Miller, Mercer
Calvin H. Payne, Titusville
William C. Pettit, Greenville
J. Howard Pew, Mercer
J. Newton Pew, Mercer
John G. Pew, Mercer
Arthur E. Pew, Jr., Mercer
J. H. Scheide, Titusville
S. S. Smith, Mercer
Miss Elizabeth Stewart, Greenville
Edwin S. Templeton, Greenville
Theodore C. Whiteman, Greenville
F. E. Whittlesey, Corry

BUTLER PRESBYTERY

W. D. Brandon and family, Butler
E. J. Fithian, Grove City
I. Lamont Hughes, Butler
Edward W. Humphrey, Butler
Weir C. Ketler, Grove City
James E. Marshall, Butler
Frank C. Reed, Grove City
George A. Spang, Butler
Joseph C. Trees, Mars
William V. Young, Grove City

BLAIRSVILLE PRESBYTERY

George H. Adams, Latrobe
Frank B. Andre, Blairsville
Mr. and Mrs. John Barclay, Greensburg
Gen. Richard Coulter and family, Greensburg
Hon. Joseph F. Guffey, Greensburg

George B. Hill, Blairsville
R. L. Jamison, Greensburg
Hon. Richard D. Laird, Greensburg
The Robbins Family, Greensburg
John C. Silsley, Greensburg
John B. Steele, Greensburg
Thomas Wallace, New Alexandria
Adam Wyant, Greensburg

KITTANNING PRESBYTERY

E. W. Allison, Indiana
W. E. Brown, Kittanning
Ellis and Amanda Caldwell, Kittanning
The Ewing Family, Saltsburg
T. D. Ewing, Kittanning
Miss Mary Henry, Kittanning
Gen. S. M. Jackson, Apollo
John H. Jackson, Apollo
William E. Jones, Apollo
The McKnight Family, Indiana
Vernon P. Taylor, Indiana
Dr. A. W. Wilson, Saltsburg

CINCINNATI PRESBYTERY

Norman P. Auburn
James Brown
Milton and Edith Brown (Foundation)
William E. Dean
A. O. Ring
Hon. Louis J. Schneider
Roe Walker
A. L. Whitaker

MAHONING PRESBYTERY

A. J. Gibbs
Dr. J. Edwin Purdy
Dr. Ralph K. Ramsayer
David Schaff
Walter Schaff
W. R. Timkin
J. L. Wick, Jr.

WOOSTER PRESBYTERY

Charles Annat
James R. Caldwell
Charles Collier, Jr.
Dr. C. R. Cutright
Charles W. Hochstetler
Ira Neeley
Stanley R. Welty

VARIOUS PRESBYTERIES

Mrs. George A. Breen, Emlenton
Hon. J. I. Brownson, Washington
Harry C. Crawford, Emlenton
Robert W. Darragh, Beaver
Sanford Fisher, Steubenville
J. A. Gelbach, Ellwood City
Hon. S. H. Hadley, Sharon
Homer P. Hartley, Beaver
Harry B. McDowell, Sharon
Harry B. Richardson, Beaver
J. V. Thompson, Uniontown

Benevolent Foundations

Notice must also be taken of the important place in benevolence activities today occupied by foundations, public trusts, and special funds. These are a comparatively recent development, springing in part from the personal limitations imposed upon donors of large benevolence sums in carrying out investigations of individual applications, in the mechanics of economical distribution, and in making adjustments with various taxing agencies. Most foundations include tremendous assets, only the income of which may be distributed in any given year. The investment, re-investment, and general administration of these assets so as to conform both to the desires of the donors and to the requirements of accepted "public policy" require administrative procedures and staffs unthought of a generation ago.

Furthermore, the tremendous sums involved in these funds make them a considerable factor to be taken into account by institutions needing assistance. Of course, an atmosphere of impersonality replaces the individual interest fundamental in previous giving, and sometimes strings are attached to grants that are not agreeable to grantees. But these characteristic limitations have become familiar in the raising and administration of community funds generally. Thorough investigation and soul-searching are increasingly indicated for both donors and recipients if they are to be regarded as benevolences and not business accommodations.

There are approximately sixty important foundations now available nationally, with an annual distribution of $413,863,000 reported for a recent year. Recipients included charitable and relief projects, scientific research, education and educational institutions, public health, recreation, specific arts and sciences, and certain professions like teaching, medicine, and dentistry.

The list of Foundations and Funds originating in this area, supported largely by Presbyterians or their affiliates, or established by persons or families originally from the Valley, would include:

The Buhl Foundation, 1928
The Carnegie Institute of Washington, 1902
The Carnegie Hero Fund Commission, 1904
The Carnegie Foundation for the Advancement of Teaching, 1905
The Carnegie Endowment for International Peace, 1910
The Carnegie Corporation of New York, 1911
The Sarah Heinz Foundation
The Virginia P. McKee Fund
The A. W. Mellon Educational and Charitable Trust, 1930
The Richard King Mellon Foundation, 1947
The Pew Memorial Foundation, 1948
The Pitcairn-Crabbe Foundation
The Sarah Mellon Scaife Foundation

From these foundations alone the income (not capital funds) made available each year for the support of benevolence projects is probably in excess of *forty-four million dollars.*

The foregoing list does not include, of course, the hundreds of smaller funds that have been established by individuals and industries for the purpose of assisting various projects, and that are to be administered in each case as determined by the donors. Neither does it include the many organizations, other than Federal Social Security, and individual commercial or business insurance plans that encourage the purchase of annuities for a number of benevolence purposes. Nor does it include the accumulated amounts of grants made by Mr. Andrew Carnegie to a large number of communities for public libraries, and of organs given to churches of many denominations, subject to certain conditions fixed by the donor. It is interesting to note, that among the large Foundations, certain of our local Carnegie group seem to have been the first established. They antedate by many years the imposition of the various Federal taxes that have been so discouraging to benevolences generally and have necessitated considerable readjustments in the entire field of larger gifts.

CHAPTER XXI Many Streams One River

MANY STREAMS of co-operative effort have formed the mighty river of Presbyterianism as it has flowed onward through "The Presbyterian Valley." Diverse contributions of self and substance have marked the creative leadership of our consecrated Presbyterians and have resulted in the development of numerous agencies of community and humanitarian service and in an increasing willingness to work in Christian co-operation in response to the growing ecumenical spirit.

THE PRESBYTERIAN BOOK STORE

One of the earliest and most effective means the pioneering Presbyterians used to extend the message of Christ was the distribution and sale of Bibles and other forms of religious literature. Out of this ministry has developed The Presbyterian Book Store which is now supported by eleven presbyteries in the Upper Ohio Valley.

If you had walked along the streets and wharfs of Pittsburgh in the decade following the year 1816, you would probably have seen a venerable-looking man, of medium height, squarely built, and with a pleasant voice. He was the Reverend Joseph Patterson who had closed a pastorate of twenty-seven years in the Montour and Raccoon churches. He was spending the sunset years of his life distributing Bibles and welcoming every opportunity for a pastoral ministry among the careless and unfortunate.[1]

Almost every day, when weather was favorable, he would enter

THE PRESBYTERIAN BOOK STORE

Located in Granite Building, Sixth Avenue and Wood Street, 1919–1948. A familiar gathering place for ministers on Monday morning. Incorporated, 1853, as Presbyterian Board of Colportage of Western Pennsylvania.

REVEREND JOHN MONTGOMERY GASTON, D.D.

President, The Presbyterian Book Store, 1922–1948. Secretary, Board of Missions for Freedmen, 1911-1938. Secretary and Treasurer, Board of Trustees, Johnson C. Smith University, 1938–

ROBERT J. GIBSON

Manager, The Presbyterian Book Store, 1906–1941. Prominent Presbyterian Layman. Clerk of Session, First Presbyterian Church, Pittsburgh, Pa., 1911–1914.

COURTESY OF PRESBYTERIAN HOSPITAL

FIRST BUILDING OF PRESBYTERIAN HOSPITAL, 1894

Hospital opened at 31 Sherman Avenue, North Side, Pittsburgh, Pa., with five rooms. Adjoining building soon rented, making total of twenty-four beds available.

MRS. LOUISE J. LYLE, M.D.
Founder of Presbyterian Hospital.
Superintendent, 1894–1902.

COURTESY OF THE PITTSBURGH PRESS

the boats along the river where dwelt families of immigrants. He had come to ask if they needed anything and to make sure they had a copy of the Bible. He was very hesitant to present a Bible without receiving some payment. He might sell it for a nominal sum, receiving as little as a cent a week. During his sixteen years' residence in Pittsburgh, Mr. Patterson received and distributed 3,920 Bibles and 2,943 New Testaments.[2] He was a man of bold and direct speech. Meeting a careless man upon the street one day, he asked painfully, "Is it true you believe you can go to Heaven without the Lord Jesus Christ?" "Why, no!" he replied. "Who told you so?" he asked indignantly. "I judged so from your actions," was Dr. Patterson's rebuking answer.

Dr. Patterson was the forerunner of a group of Presbyterian colporteurs who sought to evangelize Pittsburgh by the direct distribution of Bibles on a house-to-house basis. In 1852 the Synod of Pittsburgh organized this phase of religious service under a Board of Colportage. Headquarters and a Book Store were opened on Ferry Street. Here churchmen could meet and confer in fellowship and exchange ideas and good stories. Here were displayed and offered for sale Bibles, official books and pamphlets of the church, with helps for the Sunday-school lessons.

The original purpose of the Board of Colportage was "to carry the truth to such as are destitute and to supply such as are unable to buy" and to make available for sale "a sound and discriminating literature as one of the great necessities of the time."[3] As a non-profit agency of the church, this Board required for a number of years the voluntary contributions of the supporting churches.

Expands Into a Book Store

After twenty-three years of rather feeble service, the charter was altered to "give our store more of a miscellaneous character, hoping that it may thus become self-sustaining and that hence all church contributions may be sent directly to the Assembly's Board."[4] By that action the scope of the Board of Colportage was enlarged.

The activities of its Book Store were not to be limited to the mere sale and distribution of religious literature, which was the original meaning and intent of the word "colportage," but were to include the privilege of selling all types of helpful literature.

Control also passed from the Synods to the eleven presbyteries which continue to own the stock. Each of these presbyteries elects three representatives to form the Board of Directors. They shape the policy of what is popularly called "The Presbyterian Book Store." The legal name, however, is Presbyterian Board of Colportage of Western Pennsylvania. Unlike the Westminster Press book stores, it has never had any organic relation to the General Assembly nor to the Board of Christian Education. It has continued to function as an independently operated agency of the eleven sustaining presbyteries.

Throughout more than a century of service to the churches of the Upper Ohio Valley, this Board of Colportage has enlisted the leadership of some of the best-known clergymen of the Pittsburgh district. Dr. Elliott E. Swift, of the First Church of Allegheny, served as president during the early years of expansion as the work broadened into a prosperous book store. Upon the death of Dr. Swift in 1887, Dr. William Campbell, the Presbyterian pastor at Sewickley, gave much time and wise counsel during a long presidency of thirty-five years. He was succeeded by Dr. John M. Gaston, secretary of the Presbyterian Board of Freedmen.

He in turn was followed in 1949 by Dr. Joseph C. Stuart, who was also the executive of the Blairsville Presbytery. In that joint capacity he continued to serve until his death five and a half years later. Under his guidance the Book Store was transferred to its present location. Now the mantle of leadership has fallen on the shoulders of Dr. Frederick Speakman, pastor of the Third Presbyterian Church. His skill as an administrator is reflected in the further diversity of services that have made the Book Store an institution of helpfulness to many individuals, churches, and denominations.

When the Directors of the Board of Colportage expanded their Book Store in 1875, they selected Mr. William Webster Waters to be the superintendent. He was for many years an elder in the Presbyterian church at Sewickley. His previous experience in two other book stores had given him a thorough knowledge of books and the book business. He was a lover of books and a kindly gentleman of whom it was said: "He welcomed the patrons of the store with all the cordiality tendered a guest in the home rather than a buyer of books."[5] Soon he had enlisted the patronage of many other booklovers and had established the Book Store as a service agency of the church.

The annual report of 1882 could boast: "We are the largest distributors outside of Philadelphia of the publications of the Board of Publication in Philadelphia. They and the church generally would have occasion to rejoice if there were more distributing centers like our own, carefully managed and vigorously administered, in other sections of the country."[6] Mr. Waters, during his long service of thirty years, laid the foundations for the prosperous business which has made the Book Store at Pittsburgh perhaps the most successful of the Presbyterian denominational stores.

Mr. Robert J. Gibson Becomes Superintendent

He was succeeded as superintendent by his former chief clerk, Mr. Robert J. Gibson. Under his capable management, the Book Store was moved from the Fulton Building to the Granite Building, corner of Sixth Avenue and Wood Street and expanded in service. Sunday-school teachers found, on its well-arranged display tables, the suggestions and the helps they needed for improved teaching and special programs. Ministers used it as the convenient place to meet in fellowship and for suggestions in a wise choice of the best of newer books as well as older books of proved value. "Meet me at the Book Store" was the usual appointment. If delayed, the companionship of books or friends was sure to relieve any possible irritation caused by a tardy appointee.

Robert Gibson was followed by his son, Richard W. Gibson, whom he had trained as his successor and who inherited his father's love of books and skill in management. In its present location at 228 Oliver Avenue, with two floors of diversified books and helpful materials, it is well-equipped to serve an ever-enlarged group of satisfied customers. They find The Presbyterian Book Store an invaluable aid in all phases of religious study and service. Prosperity has rewarded the Book Store's successful service to the church. A substantial financial balance has been accumulated which assures the store's future and will enable it to keep abreast of changing opportunities to serve the church and the community.

As the Book Store developed into a prosperous business through the sale of religious literature and supplies, it did not forget nor neglect its original function of colportage. The unpublished minutes of official meetings record its unheralded gifts of materials to less prosperous churches, Sunday schools, hospitals, and institutions. Hymnals, Bibles, lesson helps, and other useful materials have been given without charge in response to requests or the suggestions of its management.[7]

During World War II, a suggestion from a visiting officer of the United States Navy presented a welcomed opportunity of service to the sailors leaving Pittsburgh. Mr. Gibson had offered his assistance as the officer was browsing over the books and pamphlets on the tables of the Store, seeking as he said, "something more helpful to the sailors than comic books." The happy result was an agreement between the Book Store and the library to make available a steady supply of literature. As a newly constructed ship was about to be launched from the docks of the Dravo Corporation at Neville Island, a careful selection of reading material was placed in the ship for the sailors' use on their voyage to the seas of international conflict.

The Book Store received many interesting letters of appreciation from these sailors overseas. The previous educational opportunities of some of these lads were apparently very meager. One of these boys, while stationed in the Mediterranean Sea, had finished reading for the first time Robert Louis Stevenson's *Treasure Island.* In the joy of a new discovery, he was eager for more adventure stories from the same author. "If Robert Stevenson has written anything else in the past few months, please send me a copy," he requested.

The Book Store has always been operated as a nonprofit agency of the church. Profits above a reasonable surplus were distributed annually throughout the years 1875 to 1955, as a dividend to the eleven presbyteries which own the stock. In 1956 the Directors felt that a more helpful service to these presbyteries would be the granting annually of scholarships to gifted Presbyterian students who needed financial assistance during their first year in college.

Accordingly, the Directors voted to offer five four-hundred-dollar scholarships a year; one to a worthy freshman in each of the five Presbyterian church-related colleges throughout the Upper Ohio Valley.[8] Those five colleges include Grove City, Waynesburg, Washington and Jefferson in Pennsylvania, Wooster in Ohio, and Davis and Elkins in West Virginia. The resulting service to the church of these scholarship-aided young people cannot be evaluated. Through the years, it may prove to be one of the most rewarding fruits of a service-minded agency of the Presbyterian church.

THE PRESBYTERIAN HOSPITAL

Christ's commission to His disciples was not only to preach and teach but also "to heal the sick." The ministry of healing, as well as the preaching and teaching of the Word, has marked the progress of the Christian Church throughout the centuries. Presbyterians in the Upper Ohio Valley have not been disobedient to Christ's command nor unresponsive to the cry of needy humanity. They have sought to help both the sick and the aged. The Presbyterian Hospital in Pittsburgh and the Presbyterian Home for the Aged in Oakmont are among the outstanding fruits of the spirit of compassion among Presbyterians in this area.

It required a woman's vision and consecrated determination to make the beginning in faith from which has developed the Presbyterian Hospital as it stands today at the heart of the University of Pittsburgh Medical Center, flanked on the left by the Eye and Ear Hospital and on the right by the Woman's Hospital.[9] "Despise not the day of small things" must have been the sustaining text of a determined Presbyterian woman. She started her hospital in a rented house with five dollars in cash and five available rooms for her prospective patients.

She, Louise W. Wotring, was born on her father's farm near the village of Buffalo in Washington County in 1842. Her public school education was supplemented at Washington Seminary, since she was the daughter of a prosperous Judge who could well supply the needs of his large family of eleven children.

As a labor of love, she engaged in missionary work under the guidance of the Reverend William Howard, pastor of the Second Presbyterian Church of Pittsburgh. The War Between the States was bringing wounded soldiers to Pittsburgh. Her natural love of medicine prompted her to seek opportunities of helpfulness in caring for the wounded and in making hospital supplies. While thus busy in labors of unselfishness, she met a student at Western Theological Seminary. In course of time, he graduated and she became the wife of the Reverend Joseph G. Lyle. She laid aside her interest in medicine to serve with devotion as a minister's helpmeet, first in Illinois, then at Homestead, and finally in the Third Presbyterian Church of Wheeling. A disastrous flood on February 7, 1884, destroyed the church building and the possessions of many of its members. This flood was the second highest in the entire history of Wheeling. Mr. Lyle overtaxed his strength amid those terrible days of difficult ministration to the needy. He died a victim of his zeal and consecration.[10]

Preacher's Widow Becomes a Physician

Mrs. Lyle remained in Wheeling long enough to rebuild the church and to raise the money necessary for its renovation. She also found time to serve as President of the Y.W.C.A. at Wheeling and to lead in temperance reform and in work among prisoners. Her continued love for medicine reasserted itself as the panacea for her own grief and the suffering of the poor who needed medical and surgical treatment. At the age of thirty years, she received the degree of Doctor of Medicine from the Presbyterian Woman's Medical College in Cincinnati. As a resident physician on the staff, she organized a free dispensary for women and children. Later she established and helped operate a hospital in Newark, Ohio.

With this experience she returned to Pittsburgh in 1893. Listen to her own story of the founding of the Presbyterian Hospital on the North Side of Pittsburgh: "After taking up the study of medicine, I became deeply interested in hospitals, especially denominational hospitals. I had been trying to solve the problem of the world's greatest needs. I was so sure I had found one of the greatest that I turned with enthusiasm to my own city. Why was it, in this great center of Presbyterianism, we could not have a hospital that would be a monument to that splendid type of men and women who lived and died in this great city of wealth and influence?

"The first step was to call upon our ministers, every one of whom was in hearty sympathy. I awaited the decision of a number whom I had interviewed and finally the verdict came: 'No money in sight.' I had been reading of a number of institutions founded on faith. I had sat in the pew of a beautiful church whose foundation stone had been laid through a little child's mite box, given just before she went to her final home. So I determined to commence with the five dollars available. I rented a three-story house at 31 Sherman Avenue at fifty dollars a month. With one of the five dollars, I hired a woman to help me set the house in order. I had already arranged for necessary furnishings on the installment plan.

"In a short time we had five rooms ready. Dr. Jane Vincent brought me the first patient who paid fifteen dollars a week. Soon the hospital was full and patients were turned away. At the end of the first year, 1894, all debts were paid and there were several hundred dollars in the treasury. I now felt the foundation of the Presbyterian Hospital had been laid."[11]

Yes, laid in faith and trust in God! The first annual report concluded with these words: "The success, which has attended the work, we love to trace to the hand of the Lord, our God, which had been with us from the first. The only discouragement has been the lack of room."

Presbytery Supported the Hospital

The success of that first year's venture kindled the glow of faith in the hearts of other Presbyterians. In December of that first year, the Presbytery of Pittsburgh pledged its cordial support to the hospital and authorized the use of the name, Presbyterian Hospital of Pittsburgh. Early in January a group of women accepted Dr. Lyle's invitation to meet in the Y.M.C.A. to organize and take steps to incorporate the Presbyterian Hospital Association of Pittsburgh.

On May 4 of that year, the hospital was incorporated with the following sixteen noble women from Pittsburgh, Allegheny, and Ben Avon as the charter members: Margaret H. Anderson, Gertrude L. Armstrong, Sallie D. Brown, Lydia I. Burchard, Kate M. Cadman, Mary O'Hara Darlington, Hannah W. Donnel, Emma M. Graham, Louise H. Herron, Fannie J. Logan, Dr. Louise J. Lyle, Sarah J. H. Mellon, Carrie S. Moore, Anna Jacobs Scott, Anna D. D. Shields, and Laura G. Shrom. The formal opening was an event of May 10, 1895. Within the same month, The School of Nursing was opened with six students.[12]

The object of the Presbyterian Hospital Association of Pittsburgh, as defined in the original charter, reads: "The establishment, support, and maintenance of an institution for the purpose of affording medical and surgical aid for sick and disabled persons of every creed and nationality." Originally it contained this further phrase: "And for the teaching of the Gospel." Later this was held likely to be sectarian by the state of Pennsylvania and so it was eliminated. Dr. Lyle was the first superintendent of the hospital which she had created.

Growth was rapid in response to pressing needs for increased capacity. The adjoining house was rented, making a total of twenty-four beds available. These were soon filled. More patients were turned away than could be treated. The report of 1896 stated that 388 patients were received and cared for, 133 being free patients, and the rest paying as their circumstances would permit. "Service to humanity in the name of Christ" was the cherished goal of Dr. Lyle.[13]

The more prosperous patients still preferred to be treated at home. They felt that there was quite a risk, and something of a disgrace, to have to go to a hospital for an operation. As a result, the doctor would come to the hospital to prepare his instruments for the operation, and secure the necessary supplies and then take with him a nurse or two to assist on the operative cases. Dr. Lyle sought to make available to the poor at the hospital the same benefits of surgery which had previously been available only to the rich and to those having fine homes where operations could be performed. She also sought to implant in the hearts of the nurses, during their period of training, her own ideals of sacrificial service and devotion to duty.

Miss Martha Swearingen, one of the six girls in the first class at the School of Nursing, related that Dr. Lyle would tell all the nurses that "their life as a nurse was about ten years and that in that ten years they must try to keep busy all the time because they would be worn out when that first decade was past." A nurse assigned to a case was on duty practically twenty-four hours a day and lived much in a few years. Nurses were paid ten dollars a month by the hospital. After six months' training, they could be sent out for private duty in homes. Whatever money they made in these private homes they were expected to return to the hospital. It was quite an exciting day when a nurse returned from private duty in a prosperous Sewickley home where she was paid twenty dollars a week for a five-week period. Dutifully she turned over to the hospital the hundred dollars she had received.[14]

Enlarged Facilities Become Necessary

With these goals of sacrificial service taught and exemplified, the hospital continued its service to the patients who crowded its facilities. In 1901 the hospital was removed to what was then the Sutton Building on Ridge Avenue. Instead of twenty-four beds, the opportunity of service was increased to ninety beds. Dr. Lyle now transferred the burden of administration to others whom she had trained and inspired. She continued to guide young nurses at the Nurses' Home on Arch Street where she served as directress for several years. Later she returned to Washington County to live her sunset years blessed with the joy of knowing that she had successfully carried her vision of a Presbyterian Hospital through three stages of its development.

At the age of ninety years, Dr. Lyle passed to her eternal reward, great in heart, mind, and soul and beloved by her family and friends who endearingly called her "Aunt Jane." Truly, as her pastor testified, "She was a Christian woman of great energy and zeal and real consecration." Shortly before her death, she was brought in a wheel chair to view the then uncompleted Presbyterian Hospital at the Medical Center in the Oakland area of Pittsburgh. She breathed in deep satisfaction as she viewed the elaborate structure of steel and stone for which her early faith and clear vision was largely responsible.

The fourth stage was the erection in 1911 of a four hundred and fifty thousand dollar hospital on Sherman and Montgomery avenues. It was planned as a fitting monument to the Presbyterians of faith and generosity who pioneered in the ministry of healing throughout Western Pennsylvania. The best of up-to-date equipment and the finest in medical science entered into its planning and construction. Another milestone in service to the sick and disabled persons of every creed and nationality had been passed.

But time prevents any complacent resting on past laurels. The facilities of the Presbyterian Hospital were taxed beyond capacity. The fifth stage of progress was reached in the completion and dedication on June 1, 1938, of the present Presbyterian Hospital. It stands as an essential part of the Pittsburgh Medical Center, operated as a separate entity, but with all the resources of the University of Pittsburgh School of Medicine to enable it to keep abreast of the rapid progress in modern medicine and surgical techniques.

PRESBYTERIAN HOME FOR THE AGED

Like the Presbyterian Hospital, the Presbyterian Home for the Aged in Oakmont had its day of small beginnings. It differed in origin from the Hospital where the women pioneered in an achievement that enlisted the co-operation of the men. The Home, on the other hand, had its creative beginnings in a sense of responsibility among the men which soon brought the women into sustaining support.

The first movement toward the establishment of a Home for the Aged Presbyterians became evident in 1921. Nine Western Pennsylvania presbyteries expressed an interest by appointing committees to investigate plans and possibilities. The following year Mr. William T. Wilson offered ten acres of land near Zelienople as a site for a Home. Presbyterians in Chicago, Philadelphia, and other cities had provided homes to take care of their older members. Pittsburgh Presbyterians, while supporting homes for other denominations, seemed strangely unaware that there was a similar need among their own church members.

As the need became more apparent, committees from the Pittsburgh Presbytery and seven adjacent presbyteries met to discuss the relative feasibility of a dozen or more places that had been suggested. No agreement was reached as to the most favorable location. A charter, however, was secured from the Court of

Common Pleas of Allegheny County for the establishment of "The Presbyterian Association for Care of the Aged and Orphans." The twenty-seven corporators included such prominent Presbyterian leaders as Reverend William L. McEwan, D.D., Reverend Clarence E. Macartney, D.D., Reverend Peter W. Snyder, D.D., Reverend Hugh T. Kerr, D.D., Reverend George Taylor, D.D., Reverend Stuart Nye Hutchison, D.D., Reverend Robert F. Galbreath, D.D., Reverend Michael M. McDivitt, D.D., William B. Ray, M.D., and Mr. Frank C. Pierson. Dr. George Taylor was chosen president of the new Association and continued in office until 1943 when he was succeeded by Frank C. Pierson.[15]

The necessary finances to begin on a small scale became available in 1930 with a bequest of ninety-five thousand dollars from Miss Martha Elma Kelly, a former missionary in China, and the willingness of Dr. Ray and his son William to sell their spacious home in Glenshaw to the Association for a very modest sum. Later they deeded to the Association without cost a cottage on the same property. Space was thus available for fourteen residents and the necessary staff. A small beginning, yes; but still a very inadequate provision to meet a need that was steadily increasing with the lengthening span of life and the changing conditions of family life that leave no available room to offer aged relatives.

A Splendidly Equipped Home at Oakmont

Necessity forced action. Early in 1944, with Frank C. Pierson a ruling elder in the Third Presbyterian Church as its president, the Association voted to survey the eight Western Pennsylvania presbyteries as to a possible response in a campaign for a much larger Home. The Reverend John C. Teyssier, D.D., a minister in the Washington Presbytery, was commissioned to lay the groundwork for a campaign for funds with a minimum goal of eight hundred thousand dollars. An estate of nearly fourteen acres on the outskirts of Oakmont was purchased for thirty thousand dollars. Success crowned the campaign. The enlarged Home was ready for occupancy on June 16, 1950.[16]

Dr. Teyssier, whose energy and determination were vital factors in enlisting the hearty co-operation of the eight presbyteries, was chosen to organize and manage the new Home. He continues to serve in that capacity where he has proved himself a devoted and capable manager, with a genius for administrative detail and a sacrificial concern for the welfare and comfort of the guests. With unfailing tact and patience, he aids the aged guests of varying dispositions and attitudes in meeting the inevitable problems of personal adjustment to community living. The Board of Managers continues to rejoice that Dr. Teyssier has been given those distinctive talents which have fitted him so admirably for successful service to the Presbyterian church in a difficult responsibility of ever-increasing complexity.

It is a delightful Home amid ideal surroundings of spacious lawns and gardens of flowers and vegetables where guests with "green thumbs" and sufficient strength can enjoy a healthful hobby. Other guests have less active hobbies and find fellowship and hours of pleasant pastime in the reading and recreational rooms. The beautiful chapel provides numerous worship opportunities both on Sunday and at stated times throughout the week. Every possible provision is made for the comfort and care of faithful Presbyterian church members whom the advancing years have left without means or ability to provide a home for themselves and who have a just claim upon the gratitude and generosity of the Presbyterian church. Those with adequate funds are asked to provide sufficient financial support to meet necessary expenses. But no one is turned away because of inadequate financial resources. All needy applicants are welcomed to the numerical capacity of the Home.

Following the sudden death of Mr. Pierson, Dr. Ray was asked to serve as president. He continued in office until 1956 when Mr. Alexander W. Dann, an elder in the Presbyterian Church of

Sewickley, was chosen to relieve Dr. Ray of a cherished but too onerous responsibility of leadership.

Further expansion soon became necessary. The mounting list of persons seeking admittance again challenged the sympathetic hearts of generous Presbyterians. Another successful campaign made possible a five hundred thousand dollar addition to the Home. This new wing was completed in June, 1956. It made available fifty-six additional single rooms and an infirmary with a capacity of twenty-five beds. The total capacity of the Home is now one hundred and sixty.[17]

Still the waiting list lengthens among those whose declining physical strength causes them to seek admission to this Presbyterian haven of maturity. Others who are mentally or physically impaired need similar care. Toward them the Presbyterian church has a further responsibility. With the growing need will come a growing response. Presbyterians never fail in the hour of challenge and service. Additional expansion appears on the horizon of responsibility. The unfortunate cannot be neglected by those who love and serve the Compassionate Saviour.

PRESBYTERIANS PIONEER IN SUNDAY-SCHOOL WORK

Nor did the Presbyterian pioneers fail to heed the Saviour's injunction: "Suffer the little children to come unto Me." What is generally recognized as one of the first Sunday schools in America was organized in 1800 in the First Presbyterian Church of Pittsburgh by the pastor, the Reverend Robert Steele.[18] It was the forerunner of the modern Sunday school and was another of the creative achievements of the Upper Ohio Valley.

It differed decidedly both in purpose and curriculum from the schools patterned after Robert Raikes's school at Gloucester, England. Unlike Raikes, Mr. Steele's purpose was not to impart the rudiments of education to pauper children on Sunday with the use of paid teachers. Rather, like the modern Sunday school, he depended on the volunteered services of his teachers and sought to impart religious instruction to the children of his church members and their friends. Every Sunday afternoon for an hour and a half, Mr. Steele gathered together the children of his congregation for religious training and instruction as a supplement to his preaching ministry. The program included Bible reading, prayer, explanation of the Scriptures, memorizing the Larger and Shorter Catechisms, and systematic instruction in problems of faith and conduct. Of the thirty-five or forty boys and girls enrolled in this first Pittsburgh Sunday school, several developed into very capable workers in the church.[19]

But Mr. Steele's pioneering efforts did not meet with the sustaining approval of the influential adults who felt their pastor was wasting with the children precious time which could be used more wisely in the adult program of the church. After several years this first Sunday school was discontinued temporarily, to be revived by Mr. Steele's successor, the Reverend Francis Herron. During his pastorate, the restored Sunday school became a permanent part of the program of that church and soon developed into an amazing agency of religious instruction and church extension. Similar schools were organized in neighboring churches.

A Sabbath-School Association Was Organized

In 1817 two Presbyterian and two Methodist churches joined in the formation of the Pittsburgh Sabbath-School Association.[20] This was the first interdenominational organization in Pittsburgh, attempting "to do together what can best be done unitedly." It may be regarded as the beginning of the ecumenical movement in Pittsburgh, and the germinal organization which was to develop slowly into the present Council of Churches of the Pittsburgh area. Within four years, the Association had expanded so rapidly that it included nineteen schools with a total enrollment of 1,513 pupils and 175 teachers.[21]

As this forerunner of the ecumenical movement in Pittsburgh developed further, it was renamed the Pittsburgh Sabbath-School

Union. The Reverend Joseph Patterson, whose zeal for the distribution of the Bible has been noted previously, gave much time to the Union and served as its president with Matthew B. Lowrie, an elder in the Second Presbyterian Church, the vice-president. Through their devoted leadership, more than any other factor, numerous missionary schools were organized and consecrated teachers enlisted and trained. Every other Sunday at sunrise, these volunteer teachers and officers met for prayer and discussion of methods for improving their work.[22] For them Sunday may have been a day of spiritual gladness, but certainly not a day of rest. Not one, but two sessions constituted the teaching program. The morning session opened at eight o'clock and continued for two and a half hours. A recess period enabled the teachers and pupils to attend the morning service of worship. Shortly after 1 P.M. school reconvened for another two-hour session previous to the afternoon preaching service.[23] The program was under the direction of the Union.

The annual report for 1823 listed a total of twenty-one schools, three hundred and twenty teachers and two thousand pupils. Another Presbyterian minister, the Reverend Joseph Stockton of Alleghenytown, was now the president. An observer at the annual meeting wrote in amazement: "There are assembling here persons from various religious denominations and churches in town, and harmony, peace, and love seemed to animate every countenance."[24]

Mission Schools of the First Presbyterian Church

But peace and harmony did not long reign over the united effort of Pittsburgh religious leaders. Presbyterians and Methodists could not agree as to which catechism should be taught. The inevitable separation resulted. The Pittsburgh Sabbath School Union languished to await some further impulse toward unity on a different organizational basis. Meanwhile, in 1825, the First Presbyterian Church organized its own Sabbath-School Association to foster the growth of Sunday schools under its own leadership and with its

COURTESY OF THE PITTSBURGH PRESS

REVEREND
CHARLES REED
ZAHNISER, D.D.

Executive Secretary, Pittsburgh Council of Churches, 1916–1928. Professor, Boston University, Massachusetts.

JOHN D. DUFF, L.H.D.

Elder and teacher, Edgewood Presbyterian Church. President, Pennsylvania State Christian Endeavor Union. Director of Allegheny County Council of Churches. Director at Western Theological Seminary, 1952–1957.

COURTESY OF DR. MOSER

COURTESY OF THE PITTSBURGH PRESS

REVEREND
THEOPHILUS M. TAYLOR, D.D.

Professor, Pittsburgh-Xenia Theological Seminary, Pittsburgh. First Moderator, United Presbyterian Church U.S.A.

REVEREND
J. CALVIN REID, D.D.

Pastor, Mt. Lebanon Presbyterian Church, Pittsburgh, Pa., 1945–. Vice Moderator, United Presbyterian Church U.S.A., 1958.

COURTESY OF
THE PITTSBURGH PRESS

own members as teachers. For twenty-seven years it continued to function with varied success and was sustained by the consecrated labors of many members of that church. The decade 1825–1835 was a period of rapid growth in Pittsburgh and vicinity, marked by prosperity and increased population and stimulated by the completion of the canal into Pittsburgh.[25]

The Sabbath-School Association of the First Church responded to the challenge of this new opportunity. Into the streets and alleys went its workers to enlist the interest of children who were not attending Sunday schools. They even called on Sunday mornings at unresponsive homes and assisted in dressing the children and washing their faces. Triumphantly they led them to some conveniently organized school in that neighborhood. Consecrated zeal of that type could not fail of expanding success. The crest was reached in 1833 when twelve schools were in full operation within a radius of five miles of the church.

The First Presbyterian Church at that time had a membership of only three hundred and eighty-nine. Yet from that comparatively small membership, a corps of nineteen superintendents and one hundred and three teachers was enlisted. Most of these schools had a morning and an afternoon session of one and a half hours. From among those consecrated workers developed some of the leaders of the church, including John C. Lowrie, the first missionary to India and, later, secretary of the Board of Foreign Missions. He was superintendent of two mission schools, one to the east at Arthursville and the other on Coal Hill, now Mt. Washington. New churches emerged from these schools, adding impetus to the moral quickening of Pittsburgh.[26]

As the years passed, sporadic attempts were made to draw Sunday schools together into an interdenominational organization. In 1826 a new union was formed as an auxiliary of the American Sunday School Union. Its membership of sixteen schools was drawn chiefly from Presbyterian churches. But by 1840 it faded out of existence. Denominational loyalties were strong. Distinctive doctrinal emphases were cherished. Ministers felt it was "their duty to God to win all men to their own theological opinions and ecclesiastical affiliations."[27] Laymen sought to lead where preachers hesitated. Teacher organizations were formed with some success in 1840, 1856, and 1863.

County Sabbath School Association

An Allegheny County Sabbath School Association was initiated in 1870. As usual, Presbyterians were in hearty support. J. D. Carlisle of the Bellefield Presbyterian Church was the first treasurer and T. J. Gillespie the corresponding secretary. A number of Institutes were held at various places throughout the county. The Reverend W. T. Beatty, pastor of the Shadyside Presbyterian Church, had been serving as president when the organization was discontinued in 1885.[28] The ecumenical spirit was developing all too slowly. Denominational leadership was mutually suspicious lest some denomination gain some possible advantage through co-operation. But Sunday school work was one thing which seemed both to require and to justify at least friendly exchange of ideas and methods of teaching. The adoption of the Uniform Lessons in 1872 had unified the curriculum and promoted the use of lesson helps which were prepared on an interdenominational basis.

The result was the organization of a Superintendents' Association for the purpose of discussing plans, comparing notes, devising ways to make Sunday school work more aggressive and to promote the spirit of Christian fellowship.[29] At that time there were twenty-five Presbyterian Sunday schools in Pittsburgh and fourteen in the city of Allegheny.

The first major project of this new Superintendents' Association was to act as host for the Sixth Triennial Convention of the International Sunday School Association in June, 1890. To make all necessary arrangements for feeding and housing some three thousand guests for four or five days, and to finance a large auditorium which would seat three thousand people was too great a project to handle alone. Necessity has always been the mother of invention. The pressure of an imperative need oftentimes hastens unanticipated progress. The dilemma resulted in a call to all the Sunday schools in Allegheny County to send representatives to a meeting in the Second Presbyterian Church on November 5. Delegates from eighty-five churches responded. The necessity of organizing a permanent county Sunday School Association was apparent.

At an adjourned meeting, representatives of fifty-three Sunday schools voted to proceed to organize. Sufficient resources thus became available to entertain the Triennial Convention. Enthusiasm was generated by this inspiring convention. The Allegheny County Sabbath School Association was thus launched on a successful program which expanded through the years.[30] The Association continued to function as an aggressive unity until 1943 when it was merged into the Pittsburgh Council of Churches. A venture by faith into the unknown had made possible the first successful functioning of the ecumenical spirit in Pittsburgh. Presbyterians throughout the years were in the forefront in sustaining this Association both by leadership and finance.

In numerous other ways Presbyterians were contributing to the spirit of unity "through deeds rather than through creeds." In co-operation with the Reformed Presbyterians, they helped organize, in 1863, the National Reform Association which has always maintained its headquarters in Pittsburgh. One of its early presidents was Dr. Henry Collin Minton, a former moderator of the General Assembly. In 1919 this Association brought to Pittsburgh the third World Citizenship Conference at Syria Mosque, with leaders from many countries in conference from November 9 to November 16 and with a total attendance exceeding fifty-eight thousand.[31]

Temperance agencies, such as the Washingtonian Societies, the Woman's Christian Temperance Union and later the Pittsburgh Anti-Saloon League were largely initiated and sustained by Presbyterians who believed Christians should crusade together to fight established evils and to lay the moral foundations for an improved community.

PRESBYTERIANS EARLY FOSTERED CHRISTIAN ENDEAVOR

A similarly hearty response greeted the organization of the first Christian Endeavor Society by Dr. Francis E. Clark at Portland, Maine, in 1881. Presbyterians in the Pittsburgh area welcomed it as another manifestation of the ecumenical movement and as an opportunity to draw young people of the various denominations into Christian fellowship and co-operation. Within eight years, fifteen Christian Endeavor Societies had been organized in Pittsburgh. Nine of these were within the Presbyterian family.

The first public meeting of the newly organized Allegheny County Christian Endeavor Union was held in the Second Presbyterian Church of Pittsburgh on November 25, 1889.[32] The next year the Union was host to the Annual Convention of the Pennsylvania Christian Endeavor Union. The eight hundred and eighty-two delegates represented twenty-three denominations. The speakers included John Willis Baer, the General Secretary of the United Society. Later he was honored as the first layman to be elected moderator of the Presbyterian General Assembly, U.S.A.

New societies multiplied rapidly in all the co-operating denominations. By the close of 1891, there were one hundred and four societies in the county. This rapid expansion made necessary the organization of Branch Unions the next year. Committees were organized to welcome young people who were moving into the county and to invite them to join the nearest society of the denomination of their choice and to crusade against the liquor traffic.

The first Intermediate Society was organized in the Knoxville Presbyterian Church in November, 1896. That same year an evangelistic committee was created with Dr. William A. Jones, pastor of the Knoxville Presbyterian Church, as chairman. He was succeeded by Dr. Hugh Thomson Kerr of the Shadyside Church. Meetings were held in homes for old folks, hospitals, enginehouses, at the Pittsburgh Association for the Improvement of the Poor, and wherever opportunities to testify for Christ were open.[33] In 1902 the Allegheny County Union was again host to the state convention, with headquarters in the Bellefield Presbyterian Church.

The twenty-first anniversary of the Union was celebrated on November 21, 1910, in the East Liberty Presbyterian Church. That year Dr. W. A. Jones was the president of the Pennsylvania Union and addressed the convention in his capacity as state leader.

When, in 1924, Pennsylvania Christian Endeavor Union again held its state convention in Pittsburgh over twenty thousand Endeavorers marched in a mammoth parade. The marching ranks formed at the Fifth Avenue High School, moved down Fifth Avenue and across the Sixth Street Bridge to the reviewing stand in the North Side Park. It was an impressive spectacle with banners and floats and distinctive county costumes. As they marched the young people sang Christian hymns. The next day one of the newspapers climaxed a glowing description of the event with the comment that "it will not soon be forgotten by people who never dreamed there were twenty thousand Christian Endeavorers in Pennsylvania." The Allegheny County Union by that time had grown into the fourth largest county union in the world.[34] In 1940 Allegheny was again host to the State convention with registrations exceeding five thousand five hundred. Capacity crowds attended the mass meetings each evening in Syria Mosque.

Leaders Developed for Presbyterian Churches

The real service of Christian Endeavor lay not in its spectacular parades and conventions, nor in the strength of its organizations, but in the spirit of brotherhood and Christian unity it engendered. Throughout all of its program it has remained Interdenominational, Interracial, and International. It has always stressed these four basic principles: Confession of Christ, Service for Christ, Loyalty to Christ's Church, and Fellowship with Christ's people. As a result, it has equipped for service some of the strongest leaders in many Presbyterian churches throughout the "Presbyterian Heartland."

Among the more prominent Presbyterian lay leaders who have served as presidents of the Allegheny County Christian Endeavor Union in more recent years were: William C. McClintock, Thomas S. Vates, Walter W. Pardee, Reuel B. Wolford, William S. Wise, Harry S. Scott, Howard W. Edgar, Ewing Lambert, D. Charles Davies, Grace L. Johnston, Ruth Clinton, and Lillian Wark. Mr. John Duff, a long-time elder in the Edgewood Presbyterian Church, served as a member of the Board of Directors of the State Union from 1937 until his tragic death in an automobile accident in August of 1957.[35]

The passing years have witnessed marked changes in the youth program of Presbyterian churches. Like other major denominations, the Presbyterian church has organized its own Youth Fellowship. The Westminster Youth Fellowship has been established as the official denominationally sponsored program for youth and so has largely replaced Christian Endeavor in most Presbyterian churches. Though maintaining its separate organization for interdenominational purposes, Christian Endeavor co-operates heartily with all the Youth Fellowships. It is also an organic part of the Youth Commission of the Council of Churches.

ORGANIZATION OF A COUNCIL OF CHURCHES

The present Council of Churches of the Pittsburgh Area came into being in 1943. It is housed in its own seven-story building at 220 Grant Street, which was purchased in 1956. There it stands as a symbol of Christian unity and co-operation and as evidence of the rapid growth of the ecumenical spirit throughout the present century. Within the Council's comprehensive program are enlisted the volunteered service of "one thousand two hundred active Christian men and women who serve on some forty departments, committees, and commissions which operate under the supervision of the Board."[36]

The Council was formed by merging into organic unity three organizations which were themselves the product of a developing spirit of co-operation among the Protestant denominations in the Pittsburgh district. The oldest was the Allegheny County Sabbath School Association, with a record of continuous activity in the field of Christian education since 1889. The youngest was the Council of Week Day Religious Education. It was formed in 1940 to develop a unified program in neighboring churches for the most profitable use of the one hour weekly of released school time granted by the Board of Education to high school pupils. The third was the Pittsburgh Council of Churches organized in 1916. It was the previous uniting of other organizations which had separately fostered evangelism, social service, and a program of comity to lessen the competition of denominations in establishing new churches in desirable places of expansion.[37]

The Leadership of Dr. Charles Zahniser

One Presbyterian minister in particular has been the guiding and inspiring personality behind the long and somewhat discouraging effort to persuade the Protestant denominations that additional strength and effectiveness could come only through co-operative endeavor. That pioneering personality was the Reverend Charles Reed Zahniser, a prophet both of unity and community betterment. As pastor of the Lemington Avenue Presbyterian Church, he was present when the Pittsburgh Ministerial Union was formed in 1900. He noted with amusement the zealous watchfulness lest some denomination might gain a tactical advantage in the drafting of the constitution.[38] He was active in the expanding work of that Union and was a member of some of the committees which dealt with the liquor traffic, prostitution, Sunday rest, indecent shows, and political corruption on one hand, and with rescue mission work, relief of poverty and similar services on the other. Gradually three of the committees developed into separate agencies to promote somewhat independently the causes of Evangelism, Christian

Social Service, and Church Comity.

Dr. Zahniser's special interest lay in the field of Social Service. He resigned his pastorate to become the General Secretary and directing head in campaigns on behalf of improved social conditions and against political conditions which were protective of social vices.[39]

Dr. Zahniser's experience soon convinced him that separate agencies of a volunteer nature could never accomplish results which a unified organization, supported and controlled by the church, could achieve. He discussed these convictions with Dr. Peter W. Snyder, at that time pastor of the Homewood Presbyterian Church and an active worker in all three agencies. Together they enlisted the advice of other denominational leaders. A plan for the organization of a Council of Churches, to be supported directly by the churches, was evolved. It was adopted by eight leading denominations, including the Presbyterian. The purpose of the Council was "to further co-operation among Protestant denominations in evangelism, social service, and comity in missionary work, as well as any other kindred work of an interdenominational nature within the bounds of Allegheny County."[40]

The Council of Churches emerged as a functioning organization on January 1, 1916, with Dr. Zahniser giving his full time to the Council as its executive secretary. In that position he continued to serve until 1929. Under his leadership, the Council pioneered in the first city-wide campaign of personal evangelism in America in 1920 with the Reverend Guy H. Black as the directing head. In succeeding years similar campaigns were carried forward under Dr. Black, Dr. Kernahan, and others. These campaigns reached a high point in 1928 when, at the Easter season, ten thousand new members were added to the churches.[41]

Dr. Zahniser was personally responsible for much of the planning and organization which resulted in the setting up of Pittsburgh's unique Morals Court in June, 1918.[42] His other notable achievements included a series of surveys of numerous districts and problem areas with suggestions for needed improvements and the drawing up of a "Comity Agreement," whereby the denominations pledged themselves to conference and co-operation in the location of new churches and in providing churches for overlooked areas. With the work well organized Dr. Zahniser resigned in 1929 to accept a professorship in Boston University.

He was succeeded by the Reverend J. W. Claudy, another Pittsburgh Presbyterian minister. However, Mr. Claudy served only until 1931. During the depression years feeble finances did not permit the employment of a secretary. The work was carried forward through the volunteer service of the different committees.[43] In 1943 the Pittsburgh Council of Churches merged with the Allegheny County Sabbath School Association and the Council of Week Day Religious Education to form the present aggressive and well-supported Council of Churches of the Pittsburgh area. Its budget for the year 1958 is $95,125. The Reverend Robert L. Kincheloe has recently succeeded the Reverend O. M. Walton as the Executive Secretary. The commodious building which houses the Council's activities is the fulfillment of a long-cherished dream of a united church center for the Pittsburgh area. The ecumenical spirit is beginning to pervade the churches.

ORGANIC UNITY WITHIN THE PRESBYTERIAN FAMILY

But deeper than these many efforts of Presbyterians to promote Christian unity in deeds and programs for community welfare has been the developing spirit of organic unity within the Presbyterian denominational family. Pittsburgh has the honored distinction of having been the scene of three important mergers. Perhaps God, in nature's symbolism of the uniting of the Allegheny and Monongahela rivers to form the mighty Ohio River, has been speaking parabolically and persuasively to the heart and conscience of a divided Presbyterian family.

Centennial of United Presbyterians

The first of the three mergers was the union on May 26, 1858, of the Associate Presbyterian and the Associate Reformed Presbyterian Churches to form the United Presbyterian Church. It was the happy fruitage of years of careful discussion of all possible points of disagreement. The inevitable conclusion followed that the differences were not hampering barriers which forebearance could not surmount in unity. In 1856 the presbyteries of both churches overwhelmingly approved the proposed Plan of Union. The following year both Synods ratified the action of the presbyteries and agreed to meet in Pittsburgh for the formal ceremony of union. Pittsburgh at that time was a city of only forty-eight thousand people and could boast of a few streets which were paved with cobblestones.[44]

The General Synod of the Associate Reformed church met in Allegheny City (now North Side) while the Associate Synod met in Pittsburgh. Only a river, to be crossed on the bridge of Christian compromise, separated them. That separating river was triumphantly crossed. The rain and clouds of the preceding day had cleared before the scheduled hour of union. The sun of God's favor seemed thus to be shining as the two groups met at the corner of Seventh and Smithfield streets. Arm in arm the moderators of the two Synods, followed by the Seminary professors and a long line of black-coated men, walked five blocks along Liberty Avenue to Market Street. Together the parading groups entered the old City Hall. It was the only building in Pittsburgh large enough to accommodate the participants and the crowd of three thousand which filled the Hall.

Very appropriately the Reverend John T. Pressly, D.D., pastor of the First Associate Reformed Church of Allegheny, and a long-time professor at Allegheny Theological Seminary, was chosen to serve as the first Moderator of the United Presbyterian Church of North America.[45] The union was as nearly unanimous "as Scotch-Irish are likely to achieve." The century of united advance which followed has been notable for unity of spirit and purpose and sacrificial zeal for missionary advance.

Old and New School Reunion

The close of the next decade witnessed the healing of a major breach in the Presbyterian church which had resulted in the separation into the New School and Old School branches. Again Pittsburgh was the scene of the reunion. A similarly prearranged agreement brought the Old School General Assembly to the First Presbyterian Church and the New School Assembly to the Third Presbyterian. Again the vote for reunion had been as nearly unanimous as "Scotch-Irish are likely to achieve." The New School had voted unanimously, while the Old School vote was 285 to 9. Only 9 out of 560 enrolled members of the two Assemblies in opposition! Five were ministers and four were laymen.[46] Previously all New School presbyteries had approved the Plan of Union while only three of the 154 Old School presbyteries had rejected it.[47]

The unity of the voting forecast unity in action. The merger was complete with no continuing minority to form a splinter denomination. Both General Assemblies then adjourned for the official ceremony of reunion. The New School left the Third Presbyterian Church on Sixth Street to march to Wood Street where the Old School commissioners were lining up on the opposite side of the street. At a given signal the two moderators crossed to meet each other in the middle of the street and to grasp hands as a token of uniting friendship.

The act of welcome extended through both marching lines. Arm in arm, amid tears of joy and cheers of approval, the two groups now united advanced to the Third Church for the official words and acts of reunion. The chilling November wind could not cool the enthusiasm of the marchers nor of the applauding crowds which lined the streets. This public profession of unity stirred the entire city. The hour was now 11 A.M. of Friday, November 12. The unfortunate schism of 1837 was healed in the reunion of 1869.

A NEW DENOMINATION IS BORN

A century of growth had lifted the United Presbyterian Church from a membership of 54,789, in 1858, to a total numerical strength of 331,000. Eighty-nine years of similarly united effort had increased the Presbyterian Church U.S.A. to an enrollment of 2,809,600. Amid impressive pageantry the two churches became one on May 28, 1958. A new and greater United Presbyterian church was created with a total membership of 3,240,000, perhaps the fourth largest Protestant denomination in the United States. Approximately one-fifth of that entire membership is enrolled in churches within a radius of two hundred miles of Pittsburgh. The Upper Ohio Valley becomes the great center of Presbyterianism where, as someone remarked, "Presbyterians are denser than any place in the world." The new Presbytery of Pittsburgh covers the entire Allegheny County with a membership of 370 ministers, 280 churches, and 131,000 members. It is, as *Presbyterian Life* defined it, "The Presbyterian Heartland."

This third historic merger in Pittsburgh was the expressed desire of the presbyteries of both denominations. A carefully prepared Plan of Union had been worked out in repeated conferences between negotiators officially appointed by each of the two General Assemblies. The Assemblies approved the Plan in 1956. A year later the ministers and elders of the different presbyteries had ratified the Plan. In the Presbyterian church, the vote by presbyteries had been unanimously in favor of union.

A number of United Presbyterians feared that their small denomination would be overwhelmed in the merger with a denomination almost nine times as large. In the United Presbyterian presbyteries, the final vote was only 57 per cent in approval of union. About the same proportional vote ratified the merger in their General Assembly. Faith triumphed over fear. The motion of

Dr. Cary N. Weisinger, of the large Mt. Lebanon United Presbyterian Church of Pittsburgh, was approved unanimously. "It is resolved by the 99th General Assembly that we enter the union of our Church and the Presbyterian Church U.S.A. with faith, hope, and love, and the prayerful purpose of making the union a happy and effective means of advancing the Kingdom of God, our Saviour and Lord."[48] That action was the command to go forward.

A year was spent working out the details of the consolidation of General Assemblies, Synods, Boards, and Agencies. Everything was in readiness for the ecclesiastical wedding on the morning of May 28. Somewhat the same ceremonial marked the creation of the new United Presbyterian church as had been followed in the two previous mergers in Pittsburgh. Separate Assemblies of the two denominations concluded all necessary business of the individual denominations on Tuesday. Wednesday at the appointed hour the United Presbyterians marched from the First United Presbyterian Church in the Oakland section of Pittsburgh to meet the Presbyterians who were leaving the nearby Bellefield Presbyterian Church. A continuous heavy rain, which the Commissioners may have regarded as symbolic of the promised "showers of blessing," did not daunt the enthusiastic marchers.

At the corner of Fifth Avenue and Bigelow Boulevard, the two groups met. Dr. Robert N. Montgomery, Moderator of the United Presbyterian Church, and Dr. Howard R. Martin, Moderator of the Presbyterian Church U.S.A., joined hands in symbolic unity. The Stated Clerks and commissioners of both Assemblies followed in a similar act of unity. Up Bigelow Boulevard the newly merged groups marched to enter Syria Mosque. There they joined in joyous worship under the leadership of the two moderators and partook of the consecrated elements of the Lord's Supper. The two denominations became one around the Communion Table. A new denomination was created in that act of consecration to the Master who had prayed "That they all may be one."

Just as a professor from the Pittsburgh Theological Seminary was elected Moderator a century ago at the formation of the United Presbyterian church, so on May 28, 1958, a professor from that same institution was chosen to serve as the first Moderator of the new United Presbyterian Church in the U.S.A. The man elected unanimously by acclamation to that unique honor was the Reverend Theophilus M. Taylor, D.D., professor of New Testament Literature and Exegesis at Pittsburgh-Xenia Theological Seminary in Pittsburgh. He had been a member of the committee which had drawn up the Plan of Union and had successfully advocated its adoption. For many years he has been an enthusiastic apostle of union.

The Historic Year of 1958

No more appropriate year for the Union could have been selected than the year 1958. It was the year the United Presbyterian denomination was celebrating the completion of one hundred years of service to Christ and His Kingdom. It was the Bicentennial year of the city of Pittsburgh and of Presbyterians in Pittsburgh. The city's celebration centered around the fall of Fort Duquesne in 1758 and the building that year of Fort Pitt. The Presbyterians were recalling the sermon preached in Pittsburgh on that occasion by a fellow Presbyterian minister, the Reverend Charles Beatty. It was the opening sermon in the subsequent two hundred years of expanding Presbyterian service in the Pittsburgh area.

In the providence of God, a great city was privileged to have its Bicentennial celebration made divinely unique by the official merging in Pittsburgh that year of the two great Presbyterian churches which for many years have had their greatest numerical and financial strength in and around Pittsburgh. A century of United Presbyterian history and two centuries of Pittsburgh Presbyterianism were gloriously climaxed by the merger which formed the new United Presbyterian Church in the United States of America.

The year 1958 can rightly be regarded as the focal point in the history of the Presbyterian church throughout the entire Upper Ohio Valley. That year looked backward in proud emphasis upon two hundred years of Presbyterian achievement in this Valley. That same year inspired Presbyterians to look forward with renewed hope and assurance to the greater task which confronts their new church in the years of unity which lie ahead.

Notes

CHAPTER I. The Organizational Foundations

1. *Minutes of the Presbytery of Redstone of the Presbyterian Church,* from September, 1781 to December, 1831. Cincinnati, 1878.

2. *Records of the Presbyterian Church U.S.A.* Embracing the Minutes of the General (First) Presbytery and General Synod (First) 1706–1788, p. 491. Philadelphia: Presbyterian Board of Publication and Sabbath School Work, 1904.

3. *The Founders of the Presbytery of Redstone,* Address by the Reverend W. F. Hamilton, D.D., Centennial Celebration, 1881.

4. John S. Bassett, *Short History of the United States,* p. 213. New York: Macmillan Co., 1914.

5. Joseph Smith, *Old Redstone or Historical Sketches of Western Presbyterianism, Its Early Ministers, Its Perilous Times, and Its Early Records,* p. 314. Philadelphia, 1854.

6. *Minutes of Redstone Presbytery,* p. 3.

7. Smith, *op. cit.,* p. 62. The author is a grandson of the Reverend Joseph Smith.

8. *Records of the Presbyterian Church U.S.A.,* p. 491.

9. Smith, *op. cit.,* pp. 225ff.

10. *Ibid.,* p. 229.

11. *Sesquicentennial of the Laurel Hill Presbyterian Church,* p. 10.

12. Dr. Power was born in Chester County, 1746. For an extended biographical sketch, see *Old Redstone,* pp. 225–250.

13. Cephas Dodd, "Memoir of Dr. T. Dod," written by his son and printed in the *Presbyterian Magazine,* Vol. IV, 1854.

14. Smith, *op. cit.,* p. 141.

15. *Ibid.,* p. 145f. Pages 139–151 contain biography of Dr. Dod.

16. D. M. Bennett, "Life and Work of the Reverend John McMillan," *Journal of the Department of History of the Presbyterian Church U.S.A.* Three installments: September, 1932; December, 1932; March, 1933.

17. Dwight R. Guthrie, *John McMillan, The Apostle of Presbyterianism in the West,* pp. 57ff. University of Pittsburgh Press, 1952, is a comprehensive and definitive study of Dr. McMillan.

18. Smith, *op. cit.,* p. 139.

19. *Ibid.,* p. 143.

20. W. F. Hamilton, *The Founders of the Presbytery of Redstone,* quoted by T. C. Pears, Jr.—*Journal of the Department of History,* Vol. XVI, p. 161, December, 1934.

21. The name Redstone Presbytery was given by the Synod since most of the country which lay west of the mountains, whether claimed by Pennsyl-

vania or Virginia, was referred to as The Redstone Settlement. It gets the name from Redstone Creek which empties into the Monongahela River below Brownsville. See Smith's *Old Redstone,* p. 311.

22. T. C. Pears, Jr., "This American Wilderness," p. 119, Stone Lectures for 1942. *Journal of the Department of Church History of the Presbyterian Church U.S.A.*

23. *Minutes of Redstone Presbytery,* p. 3. See Job 42:5–6.

24. *Ibid.,* p. 3.

25. Hamilton, *op. cit.,* p. 162.

26. *Records of the Presbyterian Church U.S.A.,* p. 10.

27. E. H. Gillett, *History of the Presbyterian Church U.S.A.,* Vol. I, p. 5. Philadelphia, 1864.

28. *Records of the Presbyterian Church, U.S.A.,* p. 60.

29. Alfred Nevin, *History of the Presbytery of Philadelphia and of Philadelphia Central,* p. 7. Philadelphia, 1888.

30. Charles A. Hanna, *The Scotch-Irish,* Vol. I, pp. 618–623. New York: C. P. Putnam Sons, 1902.

31. G. S. Klett, *Presbyterians in Colonial Pennsylvania,* pp. 3ff. Philadelphia, 1937.

32. W. W. Sweet, *The Story of Religion in America,* p. 178. New York, 1950.

33. W. W. Sweet, *Religion in Colonial America,* p. 275. New York, 1943.

34. G. J. Slosser, *They Seek A Country,* p. 42. New York: Macmillan Co., 1955.

35. L. J. Trinterud, *The Forming of an American Tradition,* p. 23. Philadelphia, 1949.

36. *Ibid.,* p. 29.

37. *Records of the Presbyterian Church U.S.A.,* pp. 231f, 282.

38. E. H. Gillett, *History of the Presbyterian Church in the United States of America,* Vol. I, p. 269.

39. J. S. Bassett, *op. cit.,* p. 125.

40. C. C. Beatty, *Record of the Family of Charles Beatty.* Printed for the private use of the family. A copy is available in the Library of the Presbyterian Historical Society in Philadelphia.

41. *Records of the Presbyterian Church U.S.A.,* p. 326.

42. C. Hale Sipe, *Fort Ligonier and Its Times,* pp. 141ff. Harrisburg: The Telegraph Press, 1932.

43. *Ibid.,* p. 222f.

44. Charles Beatty, *Journal of a Two-Months' Tour,* p. 30.

45. *Records of the Presbyterian Church U.S.A.,* p. 375.

46. Manuscript Minutes of the Donegal Presbytery, June, 1767; June, 1771, *et al. Records of the Presbyterian Church,* pp. 386, 389, 394, 405, *et al.*

47. C. W. Dahlinger, *Pittsburgh—A Sketch of Its Early Social Life,* p. 2. New York: Knickerbocker Press, 1916.

48. *Diary of David McClure,* with notes by Franklin B. Dexter, 1889, p. 56.
49. *Ibid.,* p. 47.
50. *Ibid.,* p. 100.
51. *Ibid.,* p. 47.
52. *Ibid.,* p. 104.
53. *Ibid.,* p. 112.
54. *Ibid.,* p. 41.
55. *Ibid., p.* 124.
56. Smith, *op. cit.,* p. 314f.
57. Sipe, *op. cit.,* p. 567f.
58. Smith, *op. cit.,* p. 250.
59. Sermon preached by the Reverend James Power on August 2, 1781. Sermon is in possession of a descendant, the Reverend George Fulton, D.D., Carlisle Presbytery.
60. Sipe, *op. cit.,* p. 650f.
61. *Minutes of Presbytery of Redstone,* p. 3.
62. Smith, *op. cit.,* p. 302.
63. *Minutes of Presbytery of Redstone,* p. 3f.
64. W. C. Degelman, *Historical Narrative of Bethel Presbyterian Church,* 1936, p. 12.
65. A biographical description of the Reverend James Finley, written by his son, Thomas Finley, states that Mr. Finley made his first visit to southwestern Pennsylvania in 1765. See also *Records of Presbyterian Church U.S.A.,* p. 417.
66. Smith, *op. cit.,* p. 131.
67. *Ibid.,* p. 340.
68. *Ibid.,* p. 342.
69. *Minutes of Redstone Presbytery,* p. 20.
70. *Ibid.,* p. 25.
71. *Ibid.,* pp. 30, 46, 66, 67, 87.
72. Smith, *op. cit.,* pp. 359–364, for biographical sketch of James McCready.
73. *Minutes of Redstone Presbytery,* p. 99.
74. Minutes of Ohio Presbytery, Vol. I, p. 1. (Typed mss.)
75. *Sesquicentennial of Lebanon Church,* p. 7., 1926.
76. *Ibid.,* p. 23.
77. Smith, *op. cit.,* p. 356.
78. *Presbyterian Advocate,* 1845.
79. Smith, *op. cit.,* p. 346.
80. *Ibid.,* p. 343f.
81. *Christian Herald,* March 17, 1832.
82. David Elliott, *The Life of the Reverend Elisha Macurdy,* which includes biographical sketches of other ministers, p. 309. Allegheny, Pennsylvania, 1848.

83. Obituary of the Reverend Joseph Patterson, *Christian Herald,* March 17, 1832.

84. *Centenary Memorial of The Planting and Growth of Presbyterianism in Western Pennsylvania and Parts Adjacent,* p. 193. Pittsburgh, 1876.

85. Minutes of Ohio Presbytery, p. 3. (Typed mss.)

86. *Ibid.,* p. 3.

87. *Ibid.,* p. 1.

88. *Ibid.,* p. 1.

89. *Ibid.,* p. 1.

90. *Ibid.,* pp. 40, 41.

91. *Ibid.,* p. 2.

92. *Centenary Memorial, op. cit.,* p. 215.

93. Sipe, *op. cit.,* p. 652.

94. S. J. M. Eaton, *History of the Presbytery of Erie,* p. 30. New York: Hurd & Houghton, 1868.

95. *Ibid.,* p. 31

96. *Ibid.,* pp. 183ff.

97. Agnes L. Starrett, *Through One Hundred and Fifty Years, University of Pittsburgh,* pp. 46ff. Pittsburgh: University of Pittsburgh Press, 1937.

98. Eaton, *op. cit.,* p. 195.

99. *Ibid.,* p. 28f.

100. *Ibid.,* p. 34.

CHAPTER II. Early Educational Development

1. Cephas Dodd (son of Thaddeus Dod), *The Presbyterian Magazine,* September, 1854.

2. Joseph Smith, *The History of Jefferson College,* p. 9. Pittsburgh, 1857.

3. Helen T. W. Coleman, *Banners in the Wilderness,* p. 11. Pittsburgh: University of Pittsburgh Press, 1956.

4. Smith, *op. cit.,* pp. 416, 417.

5. Dwight R. Guthrie, *John McMillan, the Apostle of Presbyterianism in the West,* Appendix C, p. 275.

6. Smith, *op. cit.,* p. 8.

7. *Ibid.,* p. 386, from a lengthy document written by Professor Robert Patterson.

8. *Ibid.,* p. 417, from "The McMillan Manuscript."

9. W. T. Doncaster, "Thaddeus Dod and the Pioneer Efforts of the Presbyterian Church in Southwestern Pennsylvania," p. 101, a Ph.D. dissertation at the University of Pittsburgh, 1952.

10. *The Works of John Witherspoon,* p. 349. Philadelphia: W. W. Woodward, 1801.

11. Joseph Smith, *Old Redstone,* p. 78.

12. *Ibid.,* p. 81.

13. *Ibid.*, p. 76.
14. *Ibid.*, p. 77.
15. Francis J. Collier, *Chartiers Church and Its Ministers,* p. 13. See also W. W. McKinney, *Early Pittsburgh Presbyterianism,* p. 214. Pittsburgh: The Gibson Press, 1938.
16. Johann David Schopf, *Travels in the Confederation,* 1783–1784, Vol. I, p. 244; quoted by Dahlinger in *Fort Pitt,* p. 49.
17. May Flower Hildreth, quoted by Killikelly, *History of Pittsburgh,* p. 108.
18. *Centenary Memorial,* p. 272.
19. University of Pittsburgh 125th Anniversary Celebration, *1912 Bulletin,* Vol. 8, No. 21, p. 107.
20. *Ibid.*, p. 108.
21. Agnes L. Starrett, *Through One Hundred and Fifty Years,* p. 23.
22. *Upper Ohio Valley Presbyterian Bulletin,* No. 2, September, 1946.
23. Starrett, *op. cit.*, p. 26.
24. *Centennial Volume,* p. 152.
25. S. J. Eaton, *History of the Presbytery of Erie,* p. 233f. New York, 1868.
26. *Ibid.*, p. 192.
27. Joseph Smith, *History of Jefferson College,* p. 18.
28. Coleman, *op. cit.*, p. 26f.
29. Minutes of the Board of Trustees, Washington Academy, November 25, 1788.
30. James Brownson, "The Educational History of Presbyterianism," *Centenary Memorial,* p. 75.
31. Minutes of Board of Trustees—January 20, 1789.
32. Dodd, *op. cit.*, p. 421.
33. Smith, *op. cit.*, p. 12.
34. *Ibid.*, pp. 18, 19; cf. The Minutes of Jefferson College, December 29, 1817.
35. James D. Moffatt, *Presbyterianism in Washington, Pennsylvania* (The Proceedings at the Centennial Celebration of the First Presbyterian Church of Washington, Pennsylvania), p. 64. Washington, 1893.
36. Joseph Smith, *Old Redstone,* pp. 147, 148.
37. Joseph Smith, *History of Jefferson College,* p. 17.
38. *Ibid.*, p. 12.
39. Robert Patterson, "Letter to Matthew Brown," *The Presbyterian Advocate,* September 1, 1849.
40. Smith, *op. cit.*, p. 25.
41. *Ibid.*, pp. 126, 127.
42. *Ibid.*, p. 26.
43. Patterson, *The Presbyterian Advocate, op. cit.*, September 1, 1849.
44. Smith, *op. cit.*, p. 29.
45. *Minutes of the Synod of Virginia,* Vol. I, p. 79.
46. Smith, *Old Redstone,* p. 439, quoting *Minutes of Redstone Presbytery.*

47. *Ibid.*, p. 449.
48. Smith, *History of Jefferson College,* pp. 31, 32.
49. *Ibid.*, p. 29.
50. Coleman, *op. cit.*, p. 56.
51. *Ibid.*, p. 54.
52. *Ibid.*, p. 55.
53. Smith, *op. cit.*, p. 63.
54. David Elliott, *The Life of the Reverend Elisha Macurdy,* pp. 283, 284.
55. Moffatt, *op. cit.*, p. 65.
56. Minutes of the Board of Trustees, Washington Academy, Washington and Jefferson College, Washington, Pennsylvania.
57. Moffatt, *op. cit.*, p. 65.
58. James I. Brownson, *Proceedings and Addresses at the Semicentennial Celebration of Washington College,* p. 37. Pittsburgh: J. T. Shryock, 1857.
59. *Ibid.*, p. 37.
60. "Letter of John Hamilton to Dr. Absalom Baird," written January 9, 1802 (Washington and Jefferson College, Washington, Pennsylvania).

CHAPTER III. Extension Through Evangelism

1. *Autobiography of Joseph Badger.*
2. *Minutes of Synod of Virginia,* Vol. II, pp. 68–72.
3. *Records of Redstone, Ohio, Erie, and Lancaster Presbyteries,* and of the *Synods of Pittsburgh and Ohio.*
4. Records of Synod of Ohio, Vol. II, pp. 24–25.
5. W. W. Sweet, *Religion on the American Frontier,* pp. 85ff.
6. *Old Redstone;* Life and Times of the Reverend Joseph Smith, pp. 51–92; especially p. 65, letter of Judge Edgar.
7. Gillies, *Historical Collections,* Vol. II, pp. 150ff.

CHAPTER IV. Upholding Moral Standards

1. Minutes of Dunlap's Creek Church Session, August 10, 1789.
2. *Diary of John Cuthbertson, Missionary to the Covenanters of Colonial Pennsylvania,* edited by William L. Fisk, Jr., Muskingum College, 1949.
3. Dunlap's Creek Minutes, *op. cit.*, May 19, 1795.
4. *Ibid.*, June 10, 1795.
5. *Westminster Confession,* Chapter xxx, "Of Church Censures."
6. Dunlap's Creek Minutes, *op. cit.*, June 10, 1795.
7. Joseph Smith, *Old Redstone,* containing summary of *Minutes of Redstone Presbytery,* p. 438.
8. *Ibid.*, pp. 452, 453, and 454.
9. *Ibid.*, p. 418.
10. *Ibid.*, p. 321.

11. *Ibid.*, p. 374.
12. *Ibid.*, pp. 325–326.
13. *Ibid.*, pp. 337–338.
14. Killikelly, *History of Pittsburgh*, p. 108.
15. Joseph Smith, *op. cit.*, p. 378.
16. *Ibid.*, p. 378.
17. *Ibid.*, p. 380.
18. *Ibid.*, p. 381.
19. *Minutes of the Synod of Virginia*, in Winchester, September 30, 1790.
20. Minutes of Ohio Presbytery, December 27, 1804. (Typed mss.)
21. *A Centennial Volume of Robert Burns*, p. 357.
22. *Pennsylvania Archives*, second series, 4:29–31, 230.
23. H. H. Brackenridge, *Incidents of the Insurrection*, 3:22.
24. R. T. Wylie, *The Whiskey Insurrection*.
25. *Pittsburgh Gazette*, January 17, 1789.
26. *The Planting of Civilization in Western Pennsylvania*, p. 471.
27. *Presbyterian Centennial Convention*, p. 396.
28. *Centenary Memorial*, p. 396.
29. Dwight R. Guthrie, *John McMillan*, p. 162.
30. *Centenary Memorial* quoting memoir of the Reverend Samuel Porter, p. 397.
31. *Minutes of the Synod of Virginia*, 1794.
32. Minutes of the Presbytery of Ohio, October 29, 1794.
33. *Ibid.*, 1795.

CHAPTER V. Competition for Converts

1. Matthew Clarkson, *Diary in 1776*, published in Henry R. Schoolcraft's *Information Respecting the History, Conditions, and Prospects of the Indian Tribes*, Part IV, p. 270.
2. Charles Beatty, *Journal of a Two-Months' Tour*, pp. 30ff.
3. G. J. Slosser, "A Chapter from the Religious History of Western Pennsylvania," *Journal of Department of History, Presbyterian Church U.S.A.*, September, 1934, p. 99.
4. *Journal of David McClure*, pp. 50–52.
5. Minutes of Ohio Presbytery, Vols. I and II. Leonard U. Hill, *John Johnston and the Indians*, pp. 186–187, 156.
6. Reconstructed Indian Village of Schoenbrun, and Moravian Archives at Bethlehem, Pennsylvania.
7. Slosser, *op. cit.*, p. 108.
8. Glasgow, *Manual of the United Presbyterian Church*.
9. Scouller, *Manual of the United Presbyterian Church*.
10. Slosser, *They Seek A Country*, Chapter v, "The Reformed Presbyterian Church," by David M. Carson, p. 109f.

11. S. J. M. Eaton, *History of the Presbytery of Erie,* p. 76f., 1868.
12. *Journal of David McClure,* p. 30.
13. Robert Reid, *The Seven Last Plagues,* a pamphlet in Western Theological Seminary Library.
14. Samuel Ralston, *On Baptism,* a pamphlet in Western Theological Seminary Library.
15. *Ibid.,* Preface, p. 4.
16. Minutes of Presbytery of Ohio, Vol. II, p. 31.
17. Minutes of Presbytery of Coshocton, Vol. I, p. 145.
18. Minutes of Presbytery of Ohio, Vol. VIII, p. 120.
19. Presbytery of Lancaster–Zanesville, Vol. IV, p. 5.
20. *Ibid.,* p. 160.
21. *Minutes of Presbytery of Richland,* Vol. I.
22. Minutes of Presbytery of St. Clairsville, Vol. I, p. 162.

CHAPTER VI. Emphases in Worship

1. Frederick Jackson Turner, *The Frontier in American History,* p. 176, 1920.
2. *Ibid.,* pp. 163–175.
3. George A. Chambers, *A Tribute to the Principles . . . of the Irish and Scotch, Early Settlers in Pennsylvania,* 1856.
4. Kenneth Scott Latourette, *A History of Christianity,* p. 1229.
5. Pliny's *Letters,* Ayer, p. 22.
6. Justin's *Apology,* Ayer, p. 34.
7. Arnold Wyclif, *Select English Works,* p. 480ff.
8. Joseph Smith, *Old Redstone,* 1854.
9. *History of Presbytery of Redstone,* p. 9.
10. John F. Schermerhorn and Samuel J. Miller, *A Correct View of That Part of the United States Which Lies West of the Allegheny Mountains.*
11. Solon J. Buck and Elizabeth Hawthorne, *The Planting of Civilization in Western Pennsylvania,* 1939.
12. Joseph Smith, *op. cit.*
13. *Ibid.,* p. 157.
14. *Ibid.,* p. 84.
15. *Ibid.,* p. 65.
16. *Ibid.,* p. 66.
17. *Ibid.,* p. 67.
18. *Ibid.,* p. 86.
19. Shakespeare's *Hamlet,* Act IV, Scene 2, line 128.
20. William Wilson McKinney, *Early Pittsburgh Presbyterianism,* 1938, pp. 161–188.
21. Joseph Smith, *op. cit.,* p. 295.
22. *Ibid.,* p. 291.

23. *Ibid.*, p. 291.

24. Clarence E. Macartney, *Right Here in Pittsburgh,* pp. 69ff.

25. *History of Presbytery of Redstone,* p. 40. Washington, Pennsylvania, 1899.

26. Macartney, *op. cit.*, p. 70.

27. Dwight R. Guthrie, *John McMillan, the Apostle of Presbyterianism in the West,* 1952, p. 65.

28. Macartney, *op. cit.*, p. 71.

29. *Presbyterian Banner,* January 31, 1866.

30. *Ibid.*

31. Gaius J. Slosser, editor of *They Seek A Country,* Chapter XI, written by James Hastings Nichols, pp. 239ff.

32. J. W. Nevin, *The Mystical Presence,* p. 3.

33. Joseph Smith, *op. cit.*, pp. 153–154.

34. *Ibid.*, p. 158.

35. *Ibid.*, p. 160.

CHAPTER VII. Westward Ho!

1. These include on Long Island: Hempstead, Jamaica, Huntington, Southampton, and perhaps others; in East Jersey: Elizabeth, Newark, Woodbridge, and Old Scots (Tennent). Some maintain that these were Congregational, but every one of them had a session, and full representative government on the local level. And every one accepted without demur the authority of Presbytery when opportunity came.

2. These include Rehoboth, Snow Hill, Pitts Creek, Manokin, Wicomico, Newcastle, and probably others whose founding date is still in dispute.

3. Ernest S. Craighead, *History of Craighead Family,* see sketch of Thomas Craighead.

4. *Diary of David McClure,* with Notes by Franklin B. Dexter, p. 100, 1899.

5. Journal of John McMillan, printed in Guthrie: *John McMillan,* p. 203.

6. *Records of the Synod of Virginia,* Vol. II, p. 74.

7. These are St. Clairsville, Mt. Pleasant, Crab Apple, Steubenville, Island Creek, and Two Ridges. Erie had Youngstown on the Ohio side.

8. McClure, *op. cit.*, pp. 103ff.

9. *Minutes of Presbytery of Redstone,* Vol. I, pp. 1, 3, 9.

10. Records of Ohio Presbytery, Vol. I, pp. 6, 51, 56, 62, etc. (Typed mss.)

11. James B. Scouller, *Manual of the United Presbyterian Church,* p. 173.

12. *Records of Synod of New York and Philadelphia.* Also *Minutes of Redstone Presbytery,* p. 1.

13. McClure, *op. cit.*, p. 114.

14. Journal of John McMillan from October 26, 1774 to August 6, 1776. (Typed mss.)

15. McClure, *op. cit.*, p. 41.

16. *Records of the Synod of Virginia,* Vols. I and II. At almost every meeting, Redstone, and after 1793, Ohio, were well represented.

17. *Ibid.,* Vol. I, p. 112.

18. Records of Ohio Presbytery, Vol. I, p. 1.

19. *Minutes of Redstone Presbytery,* Vol. II, and C. C. Hays, *History of Blairsville Presbytery,* p. 22.

20. *Records of Synod of Pittsburgh,* Vol. I.

21. *Records of Lancaster Presbytery,* Vol. I, pp. 1–3.

22. *Records of St. Clairsville Presbytery,* Vol. I, pp. 8–10.

23. *Records of Synod of Ohio,* Vol. I, pp. 1–4.

24. *Records of Synod of Western Reserve.* Records of Presbytery of Cleveland.

25. B. W. McDonnold, *History of the Cumberland Presbyterian Church,* p. 45, 1888.

26. *Records of Union Presbytery,* Cumberland Presbyterian, Vol. I.

27. *Minutes of General Assembly,* 1905, 1906.

28. *Minutes of General Assembly,* 1845, cf. Minutes, 1818.

29. E. B. Welsh's Chapter x in *They Seek A Country,* Slosser, editor, pp. 210ff.

30. E. B. Welsh, Unpublished History of the Presbytery of Athens. (Typed mss.)

31. W. W. Sweet, *Religion on the American Frontier,* The Presbyterians. New York: Harper & Brothers, 1936.

CHAPTER VIII. Into West Virginia

1. Thomas C. Pears, Jr., *Western Foreign Missionary Society,* 1931, p. 6.

2. Robert Woodworth, *A History of the Presbytery of Winchester,* p. 70. Staunton: McClure Printing Co., 1947.

3. *Minutes of General Assembly Presbyterian Church U.S.A.,* 1956, pp. 413ff.

4. *Inventory of the Church Archives of West Virginia—The Presbyterian Churches,* The West Virginia Historical Records Survey, 1941, p. 109. Charleston, West Virginia.

5. Gill I. Wilson, "History of Presbyterian U.S.A. Churches in West Virginia." Typed manuscript, pages not numbered.

6. James M. Callahan, *Semicentennial History of West Virginia,* p. 62. Charleston: Jarett Publishing Co., 1913.

7. *Inventory of the Church Archives of West Virginia,* p. 109.

8. For biographical sketch, see *Ibid.,* pp. 109ff.

9. Woodworth, *op. cit.,* p. 226.

10. Wilson, *op. cit.,* pages not numbered.

11. Woodworth, *op. cit.,* p. 60.

12. Wilson, *op. cit.*

13. Harry A. Strickler, *Forerunners.* Contains detailed sketch of the Ruffner family.

14. Charles H. Ambler, *A History of Education in West Virginia,* Huntington, 1951, for history of Mercer Academy, pp. 88ff.

15. G. I. Wilson, *A Sketch of Presbyterianism in West Virginia,* p. 14.

16. *Ibid.,* where he quotes from Minutes of Session.

17. Loyal Young, *From Dawn to Dusk,* 1884, p. 202.

17a. Wilson, "History of Presbyterian U.S.A. Churches in West Virginia."

18. *Inventory of the Church Archives of West Virginia,* p. 26.

19. *Ibid.,* p. 84.

20. Smith, *Old Redstone,* p. 318; also, p. 411 where there is additional information about Ohio Courthouse; also, *Minutes of Redstone Presbytery,* p. 5.

21. *Minutes of Redstone Presbytery,* p. 64.

22. Guthrie, *John McMillan, the Apostle of Presbyterianism in the West,* p. 112.

23. *Minutes of Redstone Presbytery,* p. 19.

24. *Ibid.,* p. 22.

25. "Minutes of Synod of West Virginia," which includes a historical sketch of the church written by Mrs. Mary A. Hervey.

26. *Minutes of Redstone Presbytery,* p. 37.

27. *Ibid.,* p. 65.

28. *Inventory of the Church Archives of West Virginia,* p. 83.

29. Minutes of Synod of West Virginia, 1940, incorporating "Origin and Early History of Three Springs Presbyterian Church."

30. *Minutes of Redstone Presbytery,* p. 71.

31. Minutes of Ohio Presbytery, August 28, 1800, p. 33.

32. Clarence Macartney, *Not Far from Pittsburgh,* 1936, p. 30.

33. *Minutes of Redstone Presbytery,* p. 71.

34. *History of Presbytery of Washington,* 1889, p. 128f contains biographical sketch of Dr. Hervey.

35. Minutes of Ohio Presbytery, p. 49.

36. In the May, 1950, issue of *Presbyterian Historical Society of the Upper Ohio Valley,* the question of date of church building is carefully discussed by the Reverend Martin Gerhardt, pastor of the First Church of Wheeling.

37. *History of Presbytery of Washington,* p. 327, which quotes from Minutes of Session of Wheeling, p. 41.

38. *The Wheeling Gazette,* July 5, 1826.

39. Wilson, "History of Presbyterian U.S.A. Churches in West Virginia," where their names are listed. (1957)

40. *Minutes of Redstone Presbytery,* pp. 18, 22, 27, 28.

41. *Ibid.,* pp. 41, 43, 60, 67, 90.

42. James R. Moreland, *History of First Presbyterian Church of Morgantown,* 1938, p. 3.

43. *Minutes of Redstone Presbytery,* p. 61.

44. *Ibid.*, p. 293.

45. Ambler, *op. cit.*, p. 81.

46. Bishop George W. Peterkin, *A History of the Protestant Episcopal Church in the Diocese of West Virginia,* p. 688.

47. *Minutes of Redstone Presbytery,* p. 326.

48. Moreland, *op. cit.*, pp. 28ff.

49. *Minutes of Redstone Presbytery,* p. 67.

50. *Ibid.*, pp. 85, 91, 102.

51. *Ibid.*, p. 154.

52. *Inventory of the Church Archives of West Virginia,* p. 60, where names of these New England settlers are listed with dates of settlement.

53. *Ibid.*, p. 60. Quotes in full the entire original commission.

54. *Ibid.*, p. 68, which quotes from Minutes of French Creek Church for 1820 as follows: "A church was also organized at Buckhannon with Martin Root and Dr. Elisha Barrett as ruling elders."

55. *Ibid.*, p. 61.

56. Wilson, Article on West Virginia Presbyterianism printed in *Journal of Presbyterian Historical Society of Upper Ohio Valley,* May, 1947, p. 6.

57. Minutes of Stewart's Run Church dated August 1, 1835. Now in possession of Mrs. Lena N. Brand and quoted by Dr. Gil I. Wilson.

58. Wilson, "History of Presbyterian U.S.A. Churches in West Virginia." Typed manuscript, pages not numbered.

59. *History of the Presbytery of Washington,* p. 103f, with biographical sketch. Philadelphia, 1889.

60. Young, *op. cit.*, p. 14f.

61. Alfred Nevin, *Encyclopaedia of the Presbyterian Church U.S.A.*, 1884, p. 1054; also, Young, *op. cit.*, p. 213.

62. Young, *op. cit.*, pp. 133 and 163.

63. Wilson, *op. cit.*, pages not numbered.

64. *Ibid.*

65. *Ibid.*

66. *Presbyterian Banner,* October 12, 1870, p. 3, col. 2.

67. *Ibid.*, October 12, 1870, p. 3, col. 3.

68. Young, *op. cit.*, p. 181.

69. Wilson, *op. cit.*

70. Ambler, *op. cit.*, p. 248.

71. Wilson, *op. cit.*

72. Minutes of Lexington (Virginia) Presbytery, October 13, 1897.

73. *Ibid.*, October 14, 1902.

74. Ambler, *op. cit.*, p. 470.

75. *Ibid.*, p. 733.

76. *Ibid.*, p. 471.

77. *Ibid.*, p. 472.

78. David Allen, "Report of the President." (Typed report.)

CHAPTER IX. Academies and Female Seminaries

1. S. M. J. Eaton, *A History of the Presbytery of Erie,* p. 34f. New York, 1868.
2. *Centenary Memorial,* p. 101.
3. Clarence Macartney, *Not Far From Pittsburgh,* 1936, p. 75.
4. Copy in Library at Zelienople, Pennsylvania.
5. *Centenary Memorial,* p. 102.
6. *Ibid.,* p. 102.
7. W. L. Young, "A History of Elders Ridge Academy," a special research project at Western Theological Seminary.
8. P. H. Sloan, *A History of the Presbytery of Kittanning,* p. 382.
9. "A History of Dunlap's Creek Academy." Typed manuscript by Sara C. Gorley from Trustees' Minutes.
10. *Ibid.*
11. Willis S. McNees, *History of Butler Presbytery,* p. 51.
12. *Ibid.,* p. 113.
13. *Ibid.,* p. 51.
14. Loyal Young, *From Dawn to Dusk,* p. 71.
15. Sloan, *op. cit.,* p. 406.
16. Rae, Bailey, *Old Keys,* a history of the village of Savannah, Ohio.
17. *Centenary Memorial,* p. 106.
18. *Ibid.,* p. 107.
19. "Centennial History," Martinsburg Presbyterian Church, 1908.
20. *Centenary Memorial,* p. 108.
21. Sloan, *op. cit.,* p. 406.
22. *Ibid.,* p. 402.
23. *Ibid.,* p. 376. The Kiskiminetas Springs School, despite its close connection with the Presbyterian church, has been omitted from the above review of academies in the Kittanning Presbytery. The school was founded in 1888, which is outside the period covered in this Chapter, and has had a distinguished record of service down to the present day.
24. *Ibid.,* p. 417.
25. Calvin C. Hays, *A History of Blairsville Presbytery and Its Churches,* p. 40.
26. *Ibid.,* p. 41.
27. Walter D. Cavert, "When Parochial Schools Failed," article in *Christian Century,* November 13, 1957.
28. *Ibid.,* November 13, 1957.
29. Price, *et al., A Survey of Religious Education,* p. 77.
30. L. J. Sherrill, *Presbyterian Parochial Schools,* p. 111.
31. *Ibid.,* p. 112.
32. "Presbyterian Parochial Schools," *Presbyterian Banner and Advocate,* January 3, 1857.

33. Sherrill, *op. cit.*, pp. 69, 70.
34. *Ibid.*, p. 144.
35. *Ibid.*, p. 128.
36. *Price, et al., op. cit.*, pp. 77, 78.
37. Sloan, *op. cit.*, p. 401.
38. Sherrill, *op. cit.*, pp. 80, 81.
39. *Christian Century.*
40. *Ibid.*
41. *Ibid.*
42. *Centenary Memorial,* p. 109. As early as 1812, Mrs. Ann Gazzam operated the Western Seminary for girls at Pittsburgh, teaching English grammar, arithmetic, geography, and some other academic subjects, in addition to needlework and the other graces of ladies of that era. Several other schools which taught some academic subjects also admitted girls. But in operating her Academy as a boarding school, and in her effort to give a complete education equal to that of men, Mrs. Olver appears to have been definitely a pioneer.
43. "The Steubenville Female Seminary," Richard Davis, S.T.M. Thesis at the Western Theological Seminary.
44. "Washington Seminary," Miss E. Margaret Alexander, *Bulletin, Presbyterian Historical Society,* September, 1957, p. 2.
45. *Ibid.*, p. 3.
46. *Ibid.*, p. 3.
47. *Ibid.*, p. 4.
48. *Ninth Annual Catalogue of Olome Institute,* 1853.
49. Helen Coleman, *Banners in the Wilderness,* 1956, p. 186.
50. *Presbyterian Banner,* July, August, September, 1870; March, 1871.

CHAPTER X. Changes Through Controversy

1. Charles Zahniser, "The Cumberland Presbyterian Church." Manuscript on file at Western Theological Seminary.
2. Joseph Smith, *Old Redstone,* p. 360.
3. *Ibid.*, p. 358.
4. Clarence Macartney, *Not Far From Pittsburgh,* p. 21.
5. For a more complete discussion of these evils, see Robert Davidson's *History of the Presbyterian Church in the State of Kentucky,* pp. 1–100. For a defense, see F. R. Cossitt, *The Life and Times of the Reverend Finis Ewing,* including a detailed reply to Davidson covering 150 pages.
6. William Speer, *The Great Revival of 1800,* p. 58.
7. *Ibid.*, p. 63.
8. B. W. McDonnold, *History of the Cumberland Presbyterian Church,* 1888, p. 48. Nashville, Tennessee.
9. *Ibid.*, p. 49.
10. *Ibid.*, pp. 66ff.

11. Minutes of Cumberland Presbytery, 1810–1813, p. 1, available at the Library of the Presbyterian Historical Society in Philadelphia. (Typed mss.)
12. McDonnold, *op. cit.*, p. 84.
13. *Ibid.*, p. 90.
14. Minutes of Cumberland Presbytery, p. 47.
15. Minutes of The Cumberland Presbyterian General Assembly, Vol. I, p. 1. (Typed mss.)
16. McDonnold, *op. cit.*, p. 273.
17. *Ibid.*, p. 274.
18. Report of Mr. Morgan quoted by McDonnold, *op. cit.*, p. 278.
19. *Ibid.*, p. 286.
20. *Ibid.*, p. 284.
21. *Ibid.*, p. 290.
22. *Ibid.*, p. 528.
23. *Ibid.*, p. 529.
24. *Ibid.*, p. 290, where McDonnold quotes the incident.
25. *Ibid.*, p. 289 (quoted from church paper February 12, 1883).
26. *Ibid.*, p. 292.
27. Minutes of the Cumberland Synod, 1839. (Typed mss.)
28. *Ibid.*, 1940, p. 4.
29. McDonnold, *op. cit.*, p. 533.
30. Printed in *Theological Medium*, Vol. XIV, July, 1878, and quoted by McDonnold, p. 536.
31. McDonnold, *op. cit.*, p. 537.
32. E. H. Gillett, *History of the Presbyterian Church in the U.S.A.*, Vol. II, p. 503.
33. *Ibid.*, pp. 513ff.
34. R. E. Thompson, *History of the Presbyterian Churches in the U.S.A.*, p. 117.
35. Gillett, *op. cit.*, p. 528f.
36. Thompson, *op. cit.*, p. 117.
37. Williston Walker, *A History of Congregational Churches in the United States*, pp. 316–317. New York, 1894.
38. W. S. Kennedy, *The Plan of Union:* or A History of the Presbyterian and Congregational Churches of the Western Reserve, p. 15. Hudson, Ohio, 1856.
39. *Ibid.*, p. 15.
40. W. T. Hanzsche, *The Presbyterians*, p. 100. Philadelphia, 1934.
41. R. B. Moore, *History of Huron Presbytery*, p. 98. Philadelphia, 1892.
42. W. W. Sweet, *Religion on the American Frontier*, Vol. II. *The Presbyterians, 1783–1840*, p. 47, quoting from "Memoir of Nathanael Emmons."
43. *Ibid.*, p. 47.
44. Gillett, *op. cit.*, p. 517.

45. *Records of the Synod of Pittsburgh,* September 29, 1802.
46. *Presbyterian Centennial Convention,* p. 164, Pittsburgh, 1876.
47. A. J. Brown, *One Hundred Years*—A History of the Foreign Missionary Work of the Presbyterian Church, p. 19. New York, 1936.
48. Records of the Synod of Pittsburgh, 1831, pp. 348ff.
49. Gillett, *op. cit.,* p. 493.
50. *Ibid.,* p. 494.
51. *Ibid.,* p. 514.
52. *Minutes of General Assembly of the American Presbyterian Church,* 1839, p. 24.
53. *Minutes of the Pittsburgh Presbytery,* Vol. I, p. 1.
54. H. E. Kline, Financial and Industrial Aspects of the Panic of 1837 (a Master's Degree thesis for the University of Pittsburgh, 1933).
55. *Minutes of General Assembly U.S.A.* for year 1947 listing all moderators of both Assemblies, pp. 433–435.
56. *Minutes of General Assembly* (New School), p. 292.
57. Gillett, *op. cit.,* p. 499.
58. James Wood, *Old and New School Theology,* pp. 252, 253.
59. *Minutes of General Assembly,* for years 1840 and 1860.
60. Samuel Baird, A *History of the New School.* Philadelphia, 1868.
61. *Minutes of New School,* 1859, p. 148.
62. *Ibid.,* 1869, pp. 173–174.
63. Gillett, *op. cit.,* p. 534.
64. *Minutes of New School,* 1860, p. 149.
65. *Ibid.,* 1840, p. 20.
66. *Ibid.,* 1849, p. 111.
67. *Presbyterian Reunion Memorial Volume,* pp. 254, 256f, 270f. New York, 1871.
68. *Ibid.,* pp. 380ff.
69. *Minutes of General Assembly U.S.A.,* 1870.
70. *Minutes of New School Assembly,* 1839; also *Minutes of General Assembly* (Old School), 1845.
71. *Ibid.,* (New School), 1849.
72. Slosser, *They Seek A Country,* p. 227. Chapter by E. B. Welsh.
73. *Ibid.,* p. 228.
74. *Minutes of Free Presbytery of Mahoning,* Vol. I.
75. Gillett, *op. cit.,* p. 557.
76. Morris, *Presbyterian Church—New School,* p. 142.
77. *Ibid.,* p. 142.
78. Hanzsche, *The Presbyterians,* pp. 105, 106.
79. *Ibid.,* p. 104.
80. *Minutes of Old School Assembly,* 1861.
81. Hanzsche, *op. cit.,* p. 113.

CHAPTER XI. THE GROWING EDGE OF CONSCIENCE

1. Henry Howe, *Historical Collections of Ohio,* Second Edition, 914–917ff. Cincinnati, 1888.
2. Elizabeth Custead, *Rose and Elza, Song and Stories of Bygone Days in Fayette County and Elsewhere*. New York, 1882.
3. Thomas Mellon, *Thomas Mellon and His Times,* Pittsburgh, 1886.
4. James G. Johnston, *Recollections,* 1929, p. 28f. Uniontown, Pennsylvania.
5. J. N. Boucher, *A Century and a Half of Pittsburgh and Her People,* Vol. I, p. 526. New York, 1908.
6. *Ibid.,* p. 526.
7. Elizabeth M. Davison, in *Annals of Old Wilkinsburg and Vicinity,* p. 94. Wilkinsburg, Pennsylvania.
8. Martha Graham Black, in above work, p. 203.
9. *Ibid.,* p. 203.
10. *Ibid.,* p. 204.
11. *Ibid.,* quoted by Elizabeth M. Davison, p. 93f.
12. *Ibid.,* p. 94.
13. *Ibid.,* p. 95.
14. Judge John E. Parke, *Recollections of Seventy Years, etc.,* p. 76f. Boston, 1886.
15. *Ibid.,* p. 316.
16. *The Presbyterian Advocate,* March 3, 1852.
17. Jacob H. Evanson, *Folk Songs of an Industrial City,* in *Pennsylvania Folk Songs and Legends,* Philadelphia, 1949, p. 432f.
18. *Presbyterian Advocate,* January 31, 1855.
19. *Presbyterian Banner and Advocate,* January 17, 1857.
20. *Presbyterian Banner,* July 28, 1865.
21. *Ibid.,* July 7, 1869.
22. Mrs. Thomas Carson and Mrs. E. W. Jones, in *History of the Pennsylvania Woman's Christian Temperance Union,* 1937, pp. 8–11. Quincy, Pennsylvania.
23. Mary Earhart, *Frances Willard and Others,* p. 59. Chicago, 1944.
24. Quoted by Carson and Jones, *op. cit.,* p. 11.
25. Pennsylvania *Laws,* 1700–1781, Vol. I, p. 492.
26. Wayland F. Dunaway, *A History of Pennsylvania,* p. 245. New York, 1935.
27. Robert W. Brewster, "The Rise of the Anti-Slavery Movement in Southwestern Pennsylvania," Western Pennsylvania Historical Magazine, Vol. XXII, No. 3.
28. *Pittsburgh Gazette,* May 26, 1787.
29. *Centennial History,* p. 137; Sarah H. Killikelly, *History of Pittsburgh,* p. 362f. Pittsburgh, 1906.
30. Boucher, *op. cit.,* p. 532.

31. Mrs. Sara C. Gorley, in Uniontown, Pennsylvania, *Morning Herald,* May 26, 1939.

32. Brewster, *op. cit.,* p. 16.

33. Boucher, *op. cit.,* p. 533.

34. Edward M. Burns, "Slavery in Western Pennsylvania," *Western Pennsylvania Historical Magazine,* 1925, Vol. VIII, p. 206.

35. Brewster, *op. cit.,* p. 4.

36. *Ibid.,* p. 5.

37. *Ibid.*

38. Boucher, *op. cit.,* p. 536.

39. Brewster, *op. cit.,* p. 16.

40. "Biography of Dr. Robert and Jane Mitchell." Manuscript compiled by Robert T. Mitchell, 1916.

41. Brewster, *op. cit.,* p. 16.

42. *Washington Examiner,* June 14, 1834.

43. Boucher, *op. cit.,* p. 537.

44. *Ibid.,* p. 537.

45. *Pittsburgh Gazette,* September 30, 1850.

46. *Pittsburgh Commercial Journal,* February 26, 1851.

47. Boucher, *op. cit.,* p. 539f.

48. *Presbyterian Banner,* July 19, 1862, p. 1.

49. *Ibid.,* September 6, 1862.

50. Burns, *op. cit.,* p. 209.

51. *Presbyterian Banner,* February 25, 1860.

52. *Ibid.,* February 25, 1860.

53. *Ibid.,* April 27, 1861.

54. *Ibid.,* October 14, 1863.

55. Brewster, *op. cit.,* p. 16.

56. *Pittsburgh Recorder,* November 22, 1825; *The Spectator,* February 7, 1828; *Pittsburgh Christian Herald,* November 23, 1833; *Presbyterian Advocate and Herald,* October 31, 1838; *Presbyterian Advocate,* May 24, 1848; *Presbyterian Banner and Advocate,* May 2, 1857; *Ibid.,* January 23, 1858.

57. Boucher, *op. cit.,* p. 285.

58. *Presbyterian Banner and Advocate,* June 28, 1856.

59. *Presbyterian Banner,* April 27, 1861.

60. *Presbyterian Advocate,* August 19, 1846.

61. *Ibid.,* December 16 and 23, 1846.

62. John Place, *Four Young Men,* Pittsburgh, 1954.

63. *Presbyterian Banner and Advocate,* June 14, 1856.

64. *Presbyterian Banner,* March 16, 1861.

CHAPTER XII. The Church's Fourth Estate

1. Title of Dwight R. Guthrie's definitive narrative of the life and labors of John McMillan, 1752–1833.

2. *Records of the Synod of Pittsburgh,* October 2, 1802, p. 13. Single volume from 1802–1832.

3. *Ibid.*, p. 13.

4. Issues of February, 1803, and January, 1804, are bound together as one volume and preserved in the Library of Western Theological Seminary in Pittsburgh. Unbound copies for years 1803–1804 not complete.

5. *Records of the Synod of Pittsburgh,* September 29, 1802, p. 8.

6. *Western Missionary Magazine,* Washington, Pennsylvania, 1803–1805.

7. *Ibid.*, Vol. I, February, 1803, p. 3 of Introduction.

8. *Ibid.*, February, 1803.

9. *Ibid.*, April, May, July, 1803.

10. *Ibid.*, May, 1803, pp. 125ff.

11. *Records of the Synod of Pittsburgh,* October 7, 1803, p. 21.

12. *Western Missionary Magazine,* February, 1802.

13. *Records of the Synod of Pittsburgh,* October 5, 1804, p. 26.

14. *Ibid.*, October 8, 1807, p. 34.

15. The last issue was dated December 13, 1937. At that time *The Banner* was merged into a new paper, *Pageant,* published as the official periodical of the Presbyterian Board of Christian Education.

16. *The Presbyterian Advocate,* December 12, 1849, which contains an extended biography following the death of the Reverend John Andrews, November 13, 1849, at the age of eighty-two years.

17. *Prospectus of The Weekly Recorder,* March 21, 1814.

18. *Ibid.*

19. *Records of the Synod of Pittsburgh,* October, 1821.

20. *Pittsburgh Recorder,* January 25, 1822.

21. *Records of the Synod of Pittsburgh,* October 4, 1821.

22. Erasmus Wilson, *Standard History of Pittsburgh,* p. 221.

23. *The Spectator,* January 3, 1828.

24. *Ibid.*, January 1, 1829.

25. *Pittsburgh Recorder,* March 1, 1825.

26. *Ibid.*, February 21, 1826.

27. *Christian Herald,* January 24, 1829.

28. *Pittsburgh Recorder,* July 4, 1826.

29. *Ibid.*, November 22, 1825.

30. *The Spectator,* February 7, 1828.

31. S. C. Jennings, *Recollections of Seventy Years,* p. 8.

32. *Ibid.*, p. 9.

33. *Ibid.*, p. 10.

34. *Christian Herald,* February 7, 1829.

35. *The Spectator,* November 20, 1828.

36. Jennings, *op. cit.*, p. 10.

37. *Ibid.*, p. 10.

38. *Christian Herald,* July 14, 1832.

39. *Ibid.*, May 26, 1832.

40. Copies of *Presbyterian Preacher* are available in the Library of the Presbyterian Historical Society in Philadelphia, and at Western Theological Seminary in Pittsburgh.

41. *Christian Herald,* December 31, 1831.

42. *Ibid.*, October 27, 1832.

43. *Ibid.*, July 21, 1832.

44. *Pittsburgh Christian Herald,* March 2, 1833, where at least half of the paper is filled with arguments pro and con and continuing throughout all issues to October 19, 1833, and then with less emphasis in subsequent issues.

45. *Ibid.,* September 28, 1833.

46. *Ibid.,* May 20, 1836.

47. *Presbyterian Advocate and Herald,* October 4, 1838.

48. *Ibid.,* May 14, 1845.

49. *Ibid.,* May 3, 1848.

50. *Ibid.,* August 1, 1855, September 5, 1855.

51. *Ibid.,* August 29, 1855.

52. *Cheap Religious Newspaper Adapted to General Circulation in the Presbyterian Church,* a pamphlet distributed as a circular throughout the church in 1851.

53. "Minutes of Huntington Presbytery," April 11, 1849, quoted in *Hollidaysburg Register and Blair County Inquirer,* March 1, 1850.

54. *Presbyterian Banner,* June 12, 1852.

55. *Presbyterian Advocate,* March 20, 1850; also, June 4, 1851.

56. *In Memoriam—David McKinney,* Pittsburgh Board of Colportage, p. 35f. Pittsburgh, 1879.

57. *Presbyterian Banner,* May 21, 1853.

58. *Ibid.,* October, 1854.

59. *Presbyterian Advocate,* October 31, 1855.

60. *The Presbyterian Banner,* November 3, 1855.

61. *Ibid.*, November 4, 1863.

62. *The Presbyterian Banner,* March 2, March 30, March 16, March 28, March 9, 1864.

63. *In Memoriam—David McKinney,* p. 37, quoting from *Presbyterian Banner.*

64. *Presbyterian Banner and Advocate,* October 11, 1856.

65. *In Memoriam—David McKinney,* p. 45, quoting from a personal letter. See also, *Presbyterian Banner,* February 3, 1864.

66. *Presbyterian Banner,* February 3, 1864.

67. *Presbyterian Banner and Advocate,* February 5, 1859, and January 13, 1864.

68. *Presbyterian Banner,* January 13 and February 3, 1864.

69. *Family Treasure*—An illustrated monthly, printed in Pittsburgh, first number dated April 2. Years 1864 to 1869 are bound together in a single

volume and preserved in Library of the Presbyterian Historical Society in Philadelphia.

70. *In Memoriam–David McKinney,* p. 39.

71. *Presbyterian Banner,* 1899.

72. *Ibid.,* December 31, 1936. Funeral sermon by Hugh Thomson Kerr. The entire issue was devoted to appreciative tribute of Dr. Snowden.

73. *Ibid.,* December 31, 1936.

CHAPTER XIII. Higher Education

1. Annual Catalogue of Washington and Jefferson College, 1890. Quarter-Centennial address by the Reverend Matthew Brown Riddle, D.D.

2. *Ibid.,* 1865–1866.

3. *Ibid.*

4. *Circulars,* on file in Library at the College, Washington, Pennsylvania.

5. Moffatt, *op. cit.,* p. 19.

6. C. M. Ewing, *Chronology,* College Library, Washington, Pennsylvania.

7. Moffatt, *op. cit.,* p. 21.

8. Ewing, *op. cit.*

9. *Annual Catalogue,* 1873.

10. *Ibid.,* 1874.

11. Ewing, *op. cit.*

12. Description of the College Buildings. A paper on file in College Library.

13. Ewing, *op. cit.,* 1901.

14. *Annual Catalogue,* 1950-1951.

15. *Ibid.,* p. 25.

16. *Ibid.,* p. 23.

17. *Centenary Memorial,* p. 95, cf. Presbyterian Historical Society of Upper Ohio Valley, *Bulletin,* No. 2, September, 1946.

18. W. L. Tobey and W. O. Thompson, *The Diamond Anniversary Volume of Miami University.*

19. James H. Brown, "Presbyterian Beginnings in Ohio." A typed Ph.D. dissertation.

20. Historical Society *Bulletin, op. cit.,* 1946.

21. *Centenary Memorial,* p. 98.

22. Letter from George J. Blazier, Librarian at Marietta College.

23. *Waynesburg College Bulletin,* 1957–1958, p. 8.

24. *Ibid.,* p. 9.

25. David A. Haines, "The Contribution of Waynesburg College to the Church," B.D. thesis, Western Theological Seminary. (Typed mss.)

26. *Bulletin, op. cit.,* p. 9.

27. Paul R. Stewart, letter to the writer.

28. *College Bulletin,* 1957–1958, p. 10.

29. *Bulletin,* Centennial Series, No. 1.

30. *College Bulletin, op. cit.*, p. 12.
31. Paul R. Stewart letter, *op. cit.*
32. *Waynesburg Bulletin,* Centennial Series, No. 1, quoting from *Who's Who in America.*
33. Stewart Letter, *op. cit.*
34. *Ibid.*
35. *Bulletin,* Centennial Series, No. 1.
36. Stewart Letter, *op. cit.*
37. Lucy L. Notestein, *Wooster of the Middle West,* p. 6.
38. *Ibid.*, pp. 9, 10, 21.
39. *The College of Wooster Bulletin,* 1956–1957.
40. Notestein, *op. cit.*, p. 38.
41. *Presbyterian Banner,* September 14, 1870.
42. *Bulletin,* 1956–1957.
43. Notestein, *op. cit.*, pp. 40, 41.
44. *Ibid.*, p. 75.
45. *Ibid.*, p. 134.
46. *Ibid.*, p. 213.
47. *Ibid.*, p. 214.
48. *Adventure in Education,* brochure, p. 89.
49. *Who's Who in America,* 1955–1956. See also, *Wooster Alumni Bulletin,* June, 1956.
50. *Ibid.*
51. *American Men of Science.*
52. *Who's Who in America.*
53. *American Men of Science.*
54. *Who's Who in America.*
55. *Ibid.*
56. Weir S. Ketler, *Adventure in Education,* brochure, pp. 10, 11. See also, *The College of Wooster Bulletin,* April, 1956.
57. Letter to the writer from Curt N. Tayler, Office of the Secretary, the College of Wooster.
58. *Pre-Centennial Development Program,* brochure, December, 1956–1966.
59. Weir S. Ketler, *op. cit.*, p. 8.
60. *Historical Sketch,* with Charter and Bylaws, p. 1.
61. *Ibid.*
62. *Pine Grove Normal Academy Catalogue,* 1876, 1877.
63. *Ibid.*, 1880, p. 27.
64. Lee McCandless, "A History of Grove City College," M.A. thesis, Grove City, 1925. (Typed mss.)
65. Marietta Dietrich, "The History of Grove City College," M.A. thesis, University of Pittsburgh, 1933, p. 23. (Typed mss.)
66. McCandless, *op. cit.*, p. 28.

67. Weir C. Ketler, *op. cit.*, p. 20.
68. Dietrich, *op. cit.*, p. 41.
69. Ketler, *op. cit.*, p. 18.
70. Dietrich, *op. cit.*, p. 58.
71. Ketler, *op. cit.*, p. 12.
72. Dietrich, *op. cit.*, p. 62.
73. *Announcement Booklet*, Bible Conference.
74. Ketler, *op. cit.*, pp. 9, 10.
75. *In Memoriam* (Joseph N. Pew and Isaac Conrad Ketler).
76. Ketler, *op. cit.*, p. 21.
77. *Biographical Catalogue*, Western Theological Seminary, p. 227.
78. Sir William Ramsey, *An Estimate of the Educational Work of Dr. Isaac C. Ketler*, pp. 7–22.
79. *In Memoriam, op. cit.*, pp. 30–33.
80. *Board Minutes*, December 20, 1915, and June 13, 1916.
81. J. N. Pew, "Letter to Isaac Ketler."
82. *College Catalogue*, 1958–1959.

CHAPTER XIV. The Mount of Sacred Science

1. *Bulletin of Western Theological Seminary*, 1956–1957.
2. Joseph Smith, *Old Redstone*, pp. 76ff. Philadelphia: Lippincott, Grambo & Co., 1854.
3. *Ibid.*, p. 76.
4. *Minutes of Redstone Presbytery*, p. 41, August 13, 1788.
5. W. N. Jamison, *The United Presbyterian Story*, 1958, p. 151.
6. Reverend Richard Lea, *Reminiscences of Sixty Years in Western Pennsylvania;* a sermon delivered at the opening of Pittsburgh Presbytery at Fairview, September 14, 1886.
7. *Minutes of Redstone Presbytery*, October 13, 1791, where the action of Synod of Virginia is quoted in full.
8. *Ibid.*, p. 81.
9. *Ibid.*, April 18, 1793.
10. *History of Jefferson College*, pp. 58–60.
11. *Old Redstone*, p. 209, which quotes Brown's unfinished life of Dr. McMillan. The handwritten textbook of Moses Allen, a student of Dr. John McMillan, is now in the possession of Mrs. Helen Allen Wragge of Pittsburgh, Pennsylvania.
12. Dwight R. Guthrie, *John McMillan, The Apostle of Presbyterianism in the West*, 1952, p. 75.
13. *Records of the Synod of Pittsburgh*, October, 1821, p. 178.
14. James I. Brownson, "Educational History," *Centenary Memorial*, p. 113.
15. S. J. M. Eaton, *History of Erie Presbytery*, pp. 7, 8.
16. Ashbel Green, *The Life*, prepared for the press at the author's request

by Joseph H. Jones, pp. 334ff. New York: Robert Carter and Brothers, 1849.

17. *Records of the Synod of Pittsburgh,* October, 1822, pp. 197ff.

18. W. W. McKinney, *Early Pittsburgh Presbyterianism,* Chapter x, for a more detailed narrative of the founding of Western Theological Seminary.

19. John McNaugher, *The History of Theological Education in the United Presbyterian Church and Its Ancestries,* Pittsburgh, United Presbyterian Board of Publication and Bible School Work, 1931, p. 39.

20. Slosser, Gaius J., "Western" in *Western Watch,* May, 1957, Vol. VIII, p. 4.

21. Elisha P. Swift, *Offices and Responsibilities of the Professorial Office in Theological Seminaries;* a sermon. Pittsburgh: Johnston and Stockton, 1828.

22. Published in *The Bulletin of Western Theological Seminary,* October, 1927, Vol. XX, No. 1.

23. In the Matriculation Pledge Book of Western Theological Seminary.

24. *Ibid.*

25. William H. Jeffers, *Occasional Addresses and Sermons by the late Reverend Samuel J. Wilson,* p. 15. New York: Dodd, Mead, & Co., 1895.

26. This story was told to the writer by Dr. Henry A. Riddle, president emeritus of Western Theological Seminary, who had received it from his father and grandfather, both of whom resided in Pittsburgh at the time of the fire.

27. In the Library of Western Theological Seminary.

28. John C. Hare, "The Presbyterian Church in Pittsburgh," Pittsburgh, 1951. Unpublished doctoral dissertation submitted to the Graduate School of the University of Pittsburgh, p. 202f.

29. *Ibid.,* p. 210.

30. *Ibid.,* p. 55.

CHAPTER XV. The Distaff Side

1. Massey Harbison, *A Narrative of the Sufferings of Massey Harbison, etc.* Pittsburgh, 1825.

2. S. J. M. Eaton, *History of the Presbytery of Erie,* 1868, pp. 219ff.

3. *Autobiography of Joseph Badger.*

4. Joseph Smith, *Old Redstone,* p. 226.

5. *News Standard Uniontown,* October 29, 1934. Reprint of history originally printed in *Uniontown Weekly Standard,* January 25, 1877.

6. Smith, *op. cit.,* p. 244.

7. *Ibid.,* p. 234.

8. *Bulletin of Upper Ohio Valley Historical Society*—reprinted from *Wheeling Intelligence.*

9. *Wheeling Intelligence,* 1867.

10. *Centennial Volume of the First Presbyterian Church of Pittsburgh,* 1884, p. 174.

11. Evangeline Metheny, *North and East of Musa Dagh,* 1950. Personal information from jacket of book.
12. *Reports of Bar Association,* Allegheny County Court, 1930.
13. History of Bethel Presbyterian Church.
14. *Weekly Recorder,* Chillicothe, Ohio, April 17, 1816.
15. C. M. Drury, *Presbyterian Panorama,* 1952, p. 37, where this action of General Assembly is quoted.
16. Florence Hayes, *Daughters of Dorcas,* 1952, p. 145.
17. *Ibid.,* pp. 149, 150.
18. *Centennial Volume, op. cit.,* p. 176.
19. *Ibid.,* p. 177.
20. *Pittsburgh Christian Herald,* February 8, 1838.
21. *Daughters of Dorcas,* pp. 152, 153.
22. *Pittsburgh Recorder,* April 11, 1826, p. 34.
23. *Presbyterian Banner,* April 8, 1868.
24. *Presbyterian Panorama,* p. 200.
25. *Ibid.,* p. 200.

CHAPTER XVI. Peace Through Conflict

No notes listed by writer.

CHAPTER XVII. Changing With Conditions

1. *Minutes of the Synod of Pittsburgh,* 1870. The Presbytery of Pittsburgh had previously been the name of the New School Presbytery, which was merged with the Ohio Presbytery under the more descriptive name, Presbytery of Pittsburgh. Allegheny City Presbytery was Presbytery of Allegheny and included the churches on the North Side. These two presbyteries were consolidated into the Presbytery of Pittsburgh in 1906.
2. *Minutes of General Assembly,* 1910.
3. *Minutes of General Assembly,* 1957.
4. *Presbyterian Reunion Memorial Volume,* p. 394. New York, 1871.
5. *Presbyterian Banner,* May 31, 1871, p. 5.
6. Erasmus Wilson, *History of Pittsburgh,* 1898, p. 938.
7. *Ibid.,* p. 956.
8. John Hare, "The Presbyterian Church in Pittsburgh," 1837–1870. A typed doctor's dissertation, 1951, pp. 94ff.
9. *Ibid.,* p. 115.
10. Quoted by Thomas C. Pears, Jr., in *Presbyterian Banner,* May 14, 1931, p. 12.
11. *Presbyterian Centennial Convention,* p. 5.
12. J. Ernest Wright, "Pittsburgh Seventies," *Western Pennsylvania Historical Magazine,* September–December, 1943, p. 137. It is a very interesting account of various aspects of life in Pittsburgh during the decade 1870–1880.

13. *Centennial Volume of the First Presbyterian Church*, p. 64. Pittsburgh, 1884.
14. Wilson, *op. cit.*, p. 964f., and *Centennial Volume of First Presbyterian Church*, p. 64.
15. *Minutes of General Assembly*, 1900.
16. Clarence E. Macartney, *Tell It To The Generation Following*, p. 28, Pittsburgh, 1934.
17. *The Pastorate of the Reverend Maitland Alexander*—Anniversary booklet, 1924, p. 22.
18. *Minutes of General Assembly*, 1926, p. 842.
19. *One Hundred and Twenty-Fifth Anniversary of the Second Presbyterian Church*, 1926, p. 29.
20. *Ibid.*, p. 30.
21. *Ibid.*, p. 30.
22. *The Third Presbyterian Church of Pittsburgh*, 1933, p. 25.
23. *Ibid.*, p. 26.
24. *Ibid.*, p. 25.
25. *Ibid.*, p. 28.
26. *Minutes of General Assembly*, 1931, p. 837.
27. Personal report from Dr. M. L. Best, associate minister, Third Church.
28. Georgina Negley, *East Liberty Presbyterian Church*, p. 21. Pittsburgh, 1919.
29. Private correspondence of Dr. E. P. Cuthbert, Titusville, Pennsylvania, a former member, who was present that Sunday.
30. *Minutes of General Assembly*, 1910.
31. *Presbyterian Banner*, May 14, 1931, p. 27.
32. Private correspondence of Dr. E. P. Cuthbert.
33. Georgina Negley, *op. cit.*, p. 145.
34. *Presbyterian Banner*, May 14, 1931, p. 27.
35. S. N. Hutchison, *The East Liberty Presbyterian Church*, 1935, p. 4. The book is a complete description of the church with many beautiful photographs.
36. Personal letter of Dr. Charles B. Robshaw to the author. It lists the church's program in detail.
37. Negley, *op. cit.*, p. 127.
38. History of the Shadyside Church, 1874. (Typed mss.)
39. *Ibid.*
40. *Ibid.*
41. Information furnished by James H. Blackwood, assistant pastor.
42. Minutes of Session, 1867, quoting charter granted September 29, 1866.
43. *Ibid.*
44. *Presbyterian Banner*, May 14, 1931, p. 25.
45. Information furnished by Blackwood as previously noted.
46. *Presbyterian Banner*, May 14, 1931, p. 25.
47. Blackwood, *op. cit.*

48. Mimeographed report prepared by the pastor, the Reverend Robert Young.

49. *Presbyterian Advocate*, January 25, 1854, p. 3.

50. *Presbyterian Banner and Advocate*, September 17, 1859, p. 2.

51. *Presbyterian Banner*, February 14, 1866, p. 2.

52. *Ibid.*, April 25, 1866, p. 2.

53. D. A. McKnight, *Historical Sketch of the Sabbath Schools of the First Presbyterian Church from 1800–1867*, pp. 29 and 37.

54. *Presbyterian Banner*, November 23, 1870, and October 23, 1872.

55. "History of the Presbyterian Missionary Training School"–Manuscript available in office of Presbytery of Pittsburgh, 1930.

56. *Presbyterian Banner*, May 14, 1931, p. 18.

CHAPTER XVIII. All Ye That Labor

1. Erasmus Wilson, *History of Pittsburgh*, Chicago, 1898, pp. 963ff.

2. *Presbyterian Banner*, July 25, 1877.

3. *Ibid.*, August 1, 1877.

4. *Ibid.*, August 8, 1877.

5. *Ibid.*, August 15, 1877.

6. *Charges and Addresses at the Inauguration of the Reverend W. H. Jeffers, D.D., and the Reverend S. H. Kellogg, D.D.*, Professors in the Western Theological Seminary, Pittsburgh, 1878, p. 47.

7. *Ibid.*, pp. 50ff.

8. *Ibid.*, pp. 51, 54.

9. Population statistics taken from *United States Census* reports.

10. J. E. Parke, *Historical Gleanings*, pp. 78–81. Boston, 1886.

11. *Pittsburgh Christian Herald*, May 29, 1830.

12. *Ibid.*, February 1, 1838.

13. *Presbyterian Banner and Advocate*, July 24, 1858.

14. *Ibid.*, April 5, 1856.

15. *Presbyterian Banner*, March 30, 1864.

16. *Ibid.*, July 20, 1892.

17. *Ibid.*, July 27, 1892.

18. *Ibid.*, August 10, 1892.

19. *Pittsburgh Dispatch*, August 4, 1901.

20. Quoted by Samuel E. Elliott, long head of Woods Run Settlement House, in conversation with the writer. Pittsburgh, 1955.

21. Conversations the writer had with many employees.

22. John A. Fitch, *The Steel Workers*, p. 229f. New York, 1910.

23. Lincoln Steffens, "Pittsburgh, A City Ashamed" in *The Shame of The Cities*, p. 165. New York, 1910.

24. These six volumes were: *Women and the Trades*, Elizabeth B. Butler; *Wage-Earning Pittsburgh*, Paul V. Kellogg, ed.; *The Pittsburgh District*–

Civic Frontage, Paul V. Kellogg, ed.; *The Steel Workers,* John A. Fitch; *Work Accidents and the Law,* Crystal Eastman; *Homestead–The Households of a Mill Town,* Margaret Byington. Most of the material was first published in *The Commons* (magazine) (later *Survey*) and the book publication was from 1909 to 1914. New York: Charities Publishing Co.

25. Daisy Lee W. Worcester, *Grim the Battle,* p. 96. New York, 1954.

26. *Ibid.,* p. 95.

27. Armstrong, Loetscher, and Anderson, *The Presbyterian Enterprise,* p. 278. Philadelphia, 1956.

28. Daniel L. Marsh, *The Challenge of Pittsburgh,* p. 260. New York, 1917.

29. *Ibid.,* p. 264.

30. *Religious Life In Pittsburgh And The Pittsburgh Spirit,* p. 299f. Pittsburgh, 1928.

31. Marsh, *op. cit.,* p. 113f.

32. Fitch, *op. cit.,* p. 223f.

33. *Ibid.,* p. 224f.

34. *Minutes, Presbytery of Pittsburgh,* December 14, 1948.

35. C. M. Drury, *Presbyterian Panorama,* p. 265. Philadelphia, 1952.

CHAPTER XIX. Unto the Ends of the Earth

1. *Diary of David McClure,* with Notes by Franklin B. Dexter, 1899, p. 27.

2. *Minutes of Redstone Presbytery,* June 23, 1785, pp. 17–18.

3. *Synod of Virginia Records,* Vol. I, p. 74.

4. *Ibid.,* Vol. II, p. 83.

5. *Records of the Synod of Pittsburgh,* Vol. I.

6. T. C. Pears, Jr., *A Brief Sketch of the Western Foreign Missionary Society,* p. 7f. Pittsburgh, 1931.

7. *Records of the Synod of Pittsburgh.*

8. Ohio Presbytery Records, Vol. I, p. 80. (Typed mss.)

9. *Ibid.,* Vol. III, p. 44. (Typed mss.)

10. Leonard V. Hill, *John Johnston and the Indians,* 1957, which quotes "Recollections" of John Johnston, p. 154.

11. *Ibid.,* p. 186f.

12. Ohio Presbytery Records, Vol. I, p. 25.

13. The first Presbyterian pastor installed in what is now the state of Ohio was James Kemper at Cincinnati and Pleasant Ridge, in 1792. These churches were a mission of the Transylvania Presbytery in Kentucky.

14. *Records of the Synod of Pittsburgh,* 1831, pp. 348ff.

15. Pears, *op. cit.,* p. 10.

16. Robert E. Speer, "Elisha P. Swift," *Centennial of the Western Foreign Missionary Society,* pp. 170–188.

17. *Memorial Pamphlet: Obsequies of the Reverend Elisha P. Swift, D.D.,*

Pittsburgh, 1865. Quoting from funeral sermon preached by Dr. S. J. Wilson. Pittsburgh: Wm. G. Johnston & Co.

18. Pears, *op. cit.*, p. 13.
19. *Ibid.*, p. 13f.
20. *Ibid.*, p. 14.
21. *Ibid.*, p. 15
22. *Ibid.*, pp. 24ff.
23. *Presbyterian Yearbook of Prayer*, Edition of 1957, p. 116.
24. Pears, *op. cit.*, p. 33.
25. *Ibid.*, p. 49.
26. Gaius J. Slosser, "Walter Lowrie, Mission Organizer"—*Journal of the Presbyterian Historical Society*, March, 1958, p. 7.
27. Robert E. Speer, *Presbyterian Foreign Missions*, which contains biographical sketch of Lowrie.
28. Pears, *op. cit.*, p. 41.
29. Slosser, *op. cit.*, p. 9f.

CHAPTER XX. Gifts and Givers

Materials used in this discussion are largely obtained from various statistical reports of the Presbyterian Church in the U.S.A.; from congregational and presbytery records; from catalogues and histories of area colleges; from reports of various Foundations and Funds; and especially from kind friends all the way from Bradford to Cincinnati, who have made available much local information to whom deepest personal gratitude is herewith expressed.

In some instances estimates—and consequently total amounts—are necessarily personally evaluated subjectively and doubtless flexible. But they are factual as nearly as possible and demonstrate the amazing generosity of The Presbyterian Valley. Had it been possible to have included a similar survey of the benevolences of the United Presbyterian Church in North America, the results would, of course, have been even more amazing.

Principle sources:

Minutes of the General Assembly of the Presbyterian Church in the U.S.A., 1900–1958.

The College Blue Book, 8th Edition, 1956. Edited by Christian Burckel.

The World Almanac, "Foundations, Public Trusts, and Funds." s.v.

Presbyterian Panorama—C. M. Drury.

CHAPTER XXI. Many Streams, One River

1. *Presbyterian Banner*, August 21, 1867.
2. *Christian Herald*, March 17, 1832, "Obituary of the Reverend Joseph Patterson.

3. *Diamond Anniversary, The Presbyterian Book Store,* 1927, where original charter is quoted, p. 6.

4. *Ibid.,* p. 7.

5. *Ibid.,* p. 9.

6. *Annual Report of the Presbyterian Board of Colportage of Western Pennsylvania,* 1882, p. 6.

7. For example, "Minutes of Executive Committee," October 16, 1916, p. 257; and March 20, 1918, p. 268.

8. *The Presbyterian Book Store Scholarship Program,* 1956.

9. "Faith And A Woman's Vision." Typed manuscript in historical records of Presbyterian Hospital, 1933.

10. "A Historical Sketch." Typed manuscript on file at Presbyterian Hospital.

11. Dr. Louise Lyle, "Founding of the Presbyterian Hospital of Pittsburgh," *Presbyterian Hospital Messenger,* 1911.

12. "A Historical Sketch"—*op. cit.*

13. H. D. Lindsay, "The Presbyterian Hospital," *The Presbyterian Banner,* February 16, 1898, p. 7. Mr. Lindsay was pastor at that time of the nearby North Presbyterian Church of Allegheny.

14. "Interview with Martha Swearingen." Typed manuscript on file at Presbyterian Hospital.

15. Typed abstracts from Minutes of the Association for the Aged.

16. *Ibid.*

17. Information furnished by Board of Managers in typed form.

18. D. A. McKnight, *Historical Sketch of the Sabbath Schools of the First Presbyterian Church from 1800–1867,* p. 10. Pittsburgh, 1867.

19. *Ibid.,* p. 11. Mr. McKnight's information is based largely on memory of Mrs. William Eichbaum who was one of the original pupils.

20. W. W. McKinney, *Early Pittsburgh Presbyterianism.* Pittsburgh: The Gibson Press, p. 152, 1938.

21. *The Pittsburgh Recorder,* May 9, 1822.

22. *Pittsburgh Gazette,* December 29, 1818.

23. McKnight, *op. cit.,* p. 3.

24. *The Pittsburgh Recorder,* August 8, 1822.

25. Erasmus Wilson, *Standard History of Pittsburgh,* p. 931. Chicago, 1890.

26. *Centennial Volume of the First Presbyterian Church of Pittsburgh, Pennsylvania,* pp. 109ff. Pittsburgh, 1884.

27. Charles R. Zahniser, *Pittsburgh Council of Churches, A Historical Interpretation,* 1944, p. 3.

28. F. A. Sharp, "The Development of Protestant Co-operation in Allegheny County," A Ph.D. thesis at University of Pittsburgh, 1948, p. 22.

29. *Constitution,* Superintendents' Association, 1889.

30. F. A. Sharp, *op. cit.,* pp. 24ff.

31. *The World's Moral Problems*—Addresses at the Third Christian Citizenship Conference, pp. 5ff.

32. *Forty Years of Christian Endeavor in Allegheny County, Pennsylvania,* 1889–1929, p. 10f. Pittsburgh, 1930.

33. *Ibid.,* p. 12.

34. *Ibid.,* p. 17.

35. *Fifty-Five Years of Christian Endeavor In Allegheny County, Pennsylvania,* pp. 10ff.

36. "An Adventure in Faith and Unity"—A brochure prepared by the Council, 1927, p. 1.

37. "In Glorious Tradition"—Mimeographed report to Council of Churches, September 25, 1953, pp. 2ff.

38. Zahniser, *op. cit.,* p. 2.

39. Sharp, *op. cit.,* p. 169.

40. *Constitution,* Pittsburgh Council of Churches.

41. Zahniser, *op. cit.,* p. 12.

42. "In Glorious Tradition," *op. cit.,* p. 3.

43. Sharp, *op. cit.,* p. 214.

44. Wallace N. Jamison, *The United Presbyterian Story,* 1958, p. 53f. Pittsburgh, Pennsylvania.

45. Gaius J. Slosser, (ed.) *They Seek A Country,* Chapter by J. H. Gerstner, Jr., 1955, p. 98. New York.

46. *Presbyterian Reunion Memorial Volume,* 1871, p. 354f., New York.

47. *Ibid.,* p. 374.

48. *Presbyterian Life,* June, 1957.

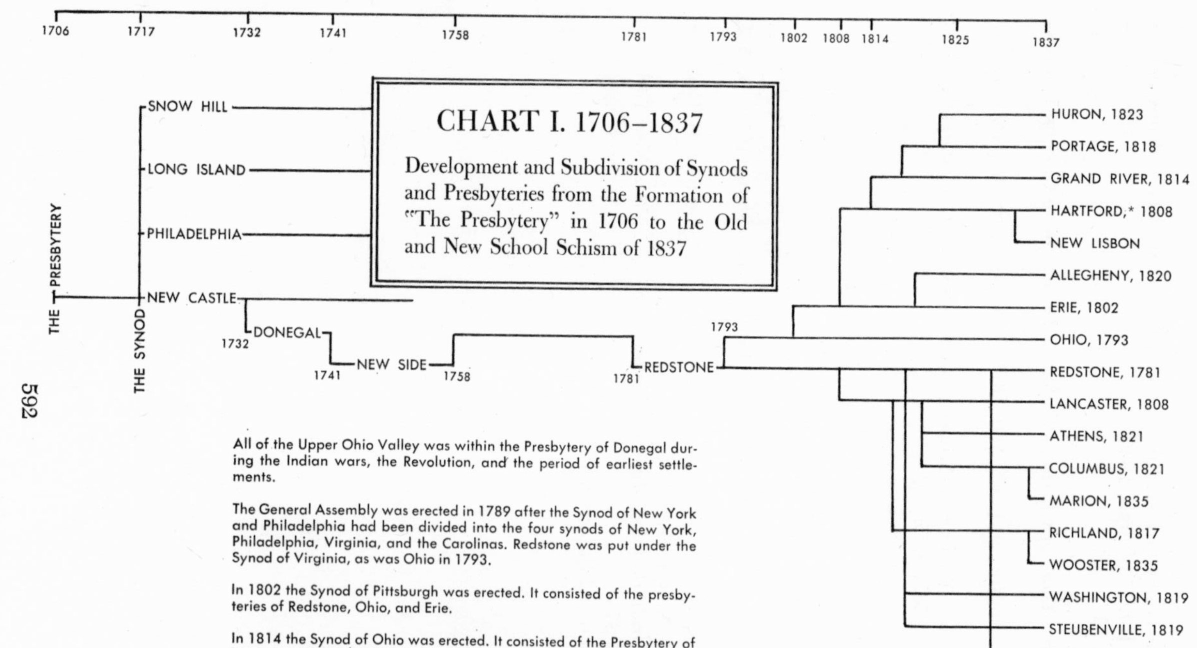

CHART I. 1706–1837

Development and Subdivision of Synods and Presbyteries from the Formation of "The Presbytery" in 1706 to the Old and New School Schism of 1837

All of the Upper Ohio Valley was within the Presbytery of Donegal during the Indian wars, the Revolution, and the period of earliest settlements.

The General Assembly was erected in 1789 after the Synod of New York and Philadelphia had been divided into the four synods of New York, Philadelphia, Virginia, and the Carolinas. Redstone was put under the Synod of Virginia, as was Ohio in 1793.

In 1802 the Synod of Pittsburgh was erected. It consisted of the presbyteries of Redstone, Ohio, and Erie.

In 1814 the Synod of Ohio was erected. It consisted of the Presbytery of Lancaster, with the presbyteries of Washington (in Kentucky and southern Ohio) and Miami, which were by the Assembly transferred to it from the Synod of Kentucky.

In 1825 the Synod of Western Reserve was erected. It consisted of the presbyteries of Grand River, Portage, and Huron.

Chart prepared by Dr. E. B. Welsh

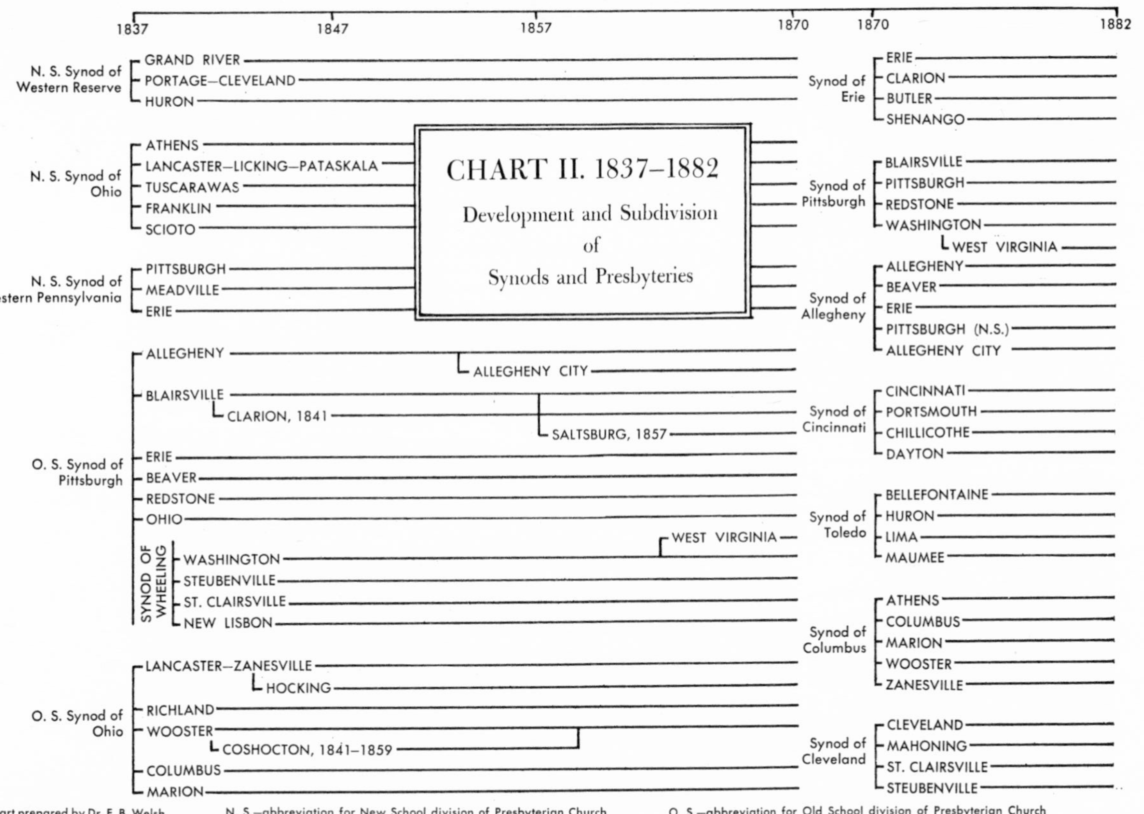

Chart prepared by Dr. E. B. Welsh N. S.—abbreviation for New School division of Presbyterian Church O. S.—abbreviation for Old School division of Presbyterian Church

CHART III. 1882–1958

Grouping of Presbyteries into Synods throughout Eastern Ohio, Western Pennsylvania, and Northern West Virginia

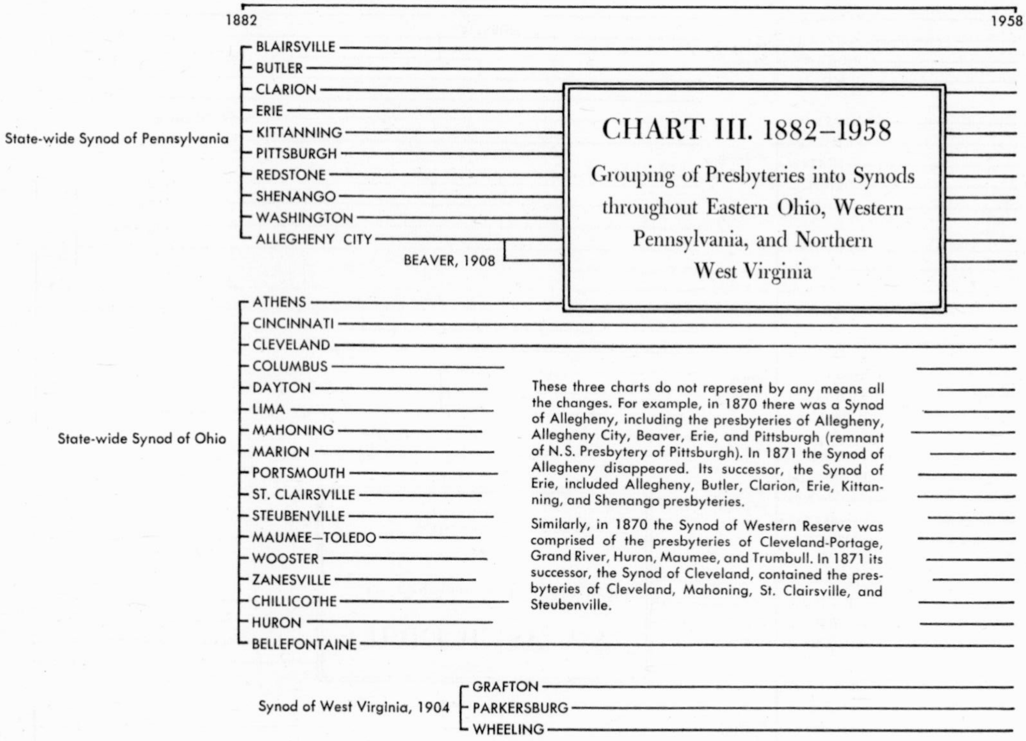

These three charts do not represent by any means all the changes. For example, in 1870 there was a Synod of Allegheny, including the presbyteries of Allegheny, Allegheny City, Beaver, Erie, and Pittsburgh (remnant of N.S. Presbytery of Pittsburgh). In 1871 the Synod of Allegheny disappeared. Its successor, the Synod of Erie, included Allegheny, Butler, Clarion, Erie, Kittanning, and Shenango presbyteries.

Similarly, in 1870 the Synod of Western Reserve was comprised of the presbyteries of Cleveland-Portage, Grand River, Huron, Maumee, and Trumbull. In 1871 its successor, the Synod of Cleveland, contained the presbyteries of Cleveland, Mahoning, St. Clairsville, and Steubenville.

Chart prepared by Dr. E. B. Welsh

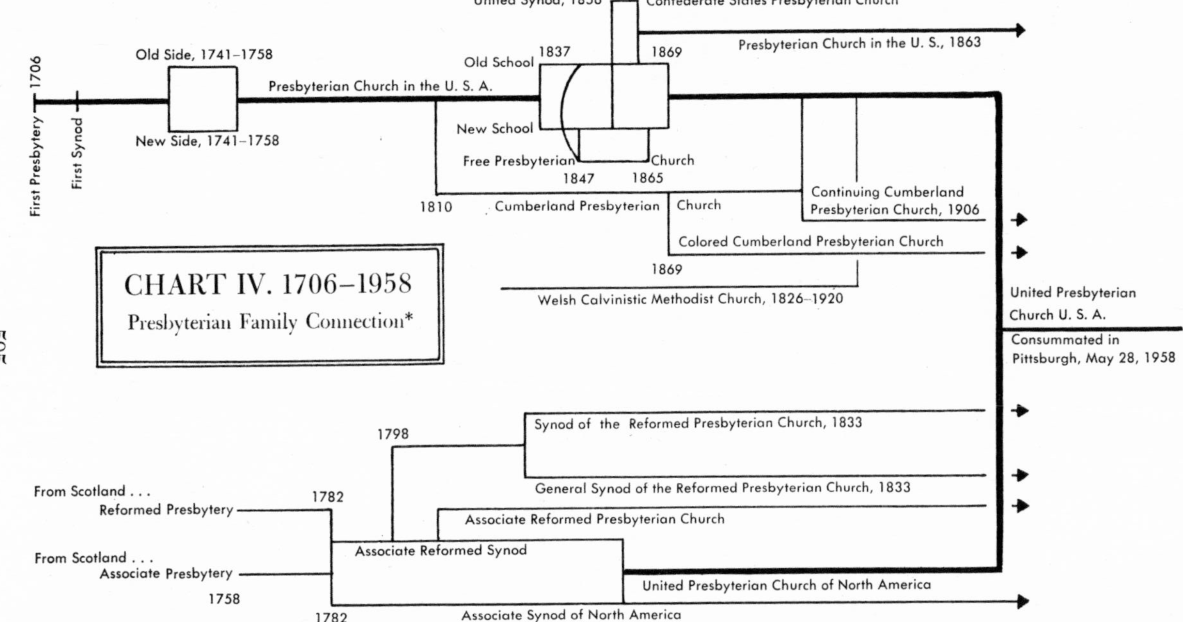

CHART IV. 1706–1958
Presbyterian Family Connection*

*Adapted by Dr. E. B. Welsh from a chart previously prepared by Dr. G. J. Slosser and printed in "They Seek a Country" (1955).

APPENDIX A

Churches Which Have Changed Their Names, or Have Developed from Churches of Other Names in Approximately the Same Location

PRESENT NAME	FORMER NAME OR NAMES
Armagh, Pa.	Wheatfield
Amity, Pa.	Lower Ten Mile
Aliquippa Pa. Mt. Carmel	White Oak Flats
Ashland, Ohio	Uniontown
Bakersville, Ohio	Evans Creek
Beaver, Pa.	McIntosh, Beavertown
Beech Spring, Ohio	Daniel Welsh's on Short Creek
Bethel, Pittsburgh, Pa.	West Congregation on Peter's Creek
Beulah, Wilkinsburg, Pa.	Bullock Pens, Penn Township
Beverly, Ohio	Waterford
Butler, Pa.	Thorn's Tent
Cambridge, Ohio	Wills Creek
Carmel, Pittsburgh, Pa.	Pipestown
Carnegie, Pa.	Mansfield
Chandlersville, Ohio	Salt Creek
Cheswick, Pa.	Deer Creek
Clarksburg, W. Va.	Harrison County
Cochranton, Pa.	Little Sugar Creek
Columbus First, Ohio	Franklinton
Connellsville, Pa.	Stewart's Crossings
Cooperstown, Pa.	Big Sugar Creek
Coraopolis, Pa.	Middletown
Coshocton, Ohio	Forks of Muskingum
Cove, Weirton, W.Va.	Three Springs
Crab Apple, Ohio	Cross Roads
Dalton, Ohio	Sugar Creek
Darlington, Pa.	Greersburg
Dunlap's Creek, Merrittstown, Pa.	Delap's
Elm Grove "Stone," Wheeling, W. Va.	Forks of Wheeling
Erie First, Pa.	Presque Isle, Colt's Station
Fairmont, W. Va.	Middletown

Fairmount, Sewickley, Pa.	Duff's
Fairview, Pughtown, W. Va.	Flats
Florence, Pa.	King's Creek, Briceland's X Roads
Franklin, Pa.	Mouth of French Creek
Fredericksburg, Ohio	Salt Creek
Fredericktown, Ohio	Frederick
Glenwillard Riverdale, Pa.	Shousetown
Grafton, W. Va.	Marion County
Granville, Ohio	New Granville
Hebron, Allegheny County, Pa.	Potato Garden, Hopewell
Herron Avenue, Pittsburgh, Pa.	Minersville
Huttonsville, W. Va.	Tygart's Valley
Jefferson, Pa.	South Fork of Ten Mile
Keene, Ohio	Mill Creek
Lancaster, Ohio	Hock-Hocking
Latrobe, Pa.	Proctor's Tent, Unity
Lebanon, Allegheny County, Pa.	East Congregation on Peter's Creek
Lisbon, Ohio	New Lisbon
Martinsburg, Ohio	Ebenezer
Monongahela, Pa.	Horseshoe Bottom, Parkinson's Ferry
Morgantown, W. Va.	Monongalia
Moundsville, W. Va.	Grave Creek Flats
Mount Eaton, Ohio	Paintville
Mt. Moriah, Fayette Co., Ohio	George's Creek
Mount Pleasant Middle, Pa.	Jacob's Swamp
Mount Pleasant, Ohio	Short Creek
Mount Vernon, Ohio	Clinton, Owl Creek
Neville Island, Pa.	Long Island
New Brighton, Pa.	Mouth of Big Beaver
New Castle, Pa. First	Lower Neshannock
New Concord, Ohio	Crooked Creek, Pleasant Hill
New Geneva, Pa.	Branch of George's Creek
New Providence, Pa.	Glades, Muddy Creek
North East, Pa.	Lower Greenfield
Old Washington, Ohio	Leatherwood, Washington
Outville, Ohio	Kirkersville
Paris, Pa.	Three Springs
Pataskala, Ohio	South Fork of Licking
Pleasant Grove, Pa.	Donegal
Putnam, Zanesville, Ohio	Springfield
Rehobeth, Belle Vernon, Pa.	Upper Congregation in "Forks of Yough"
Richmond, Ohio	Town Fork of Yellow Creek
Rock Hill, Ohio	McMahon's Creek
Round Hill, Elizabeth, Pa.	Lower Congregation in "Forks of Yough"

St. Clairsville, Ohio	Richland
Savannah, Ohio	Clear Creek
Sewickley, Pa.	Sewickleyville
Sharon, Coraopolis, Pa.	Flaugherty's Run
Smithfield, Pa.	Branch of George's Creek
Smithfield, Ohio	Centre, Tent
South Side, Pittsburgh, Pa.	Birmingham
Steubenville, Ohio	Fort Steuben
Utica, Ohio	North Fork of Licking, Concord
Utica, Pa.	Mill Creek
Warsaw, Ohio	Jefferson
Wellsburg, W. Va.	Charlestown
West Alexander, Pa.	Three Ridges
West End, Pittsburgh, Pa.	Temperanceville
West Liberty, W. Va.	Short Creek
Wheeling First, W. Va.	Wheelingtown
Yellow Frame, Fayette Co., Pa.	Branch of George's Creek

This list is not complete. Some congregations named repeatedly in early records have not been located, but are probably forerunners of churches now functioning under another name.

APPENDIX B

Associate, Associate Reformed, Reformed Presbyterian, and Presbyterian Churches of the Upper Ohio Valley, Organized Near Each Other in Time and in Location, and Apparently in Rivalry.

A.—Associate A.R.—Associate Reformed R.P.—Reformed Presbyterian

OTHERS	PRESBYTERIAN
Amity (Mill Creek) Coshocton Co., Ohio, organized 1818	Mill Creek (Keene) 1818
Barlow, Ohio, 1850	Barlow, 1835
Beechwoods, Jefferson Co., Pa., 1870	Beechwoods
Belmont, Ohio, 1827	Concord, Belmont, 1831
Bethel, Westmoreland Co., Pa., 1784	Long Run, 1772
Bethel, Monroeville, Pa., 1801	Cross Roads, Monroeville
Bethel, Lawrence Co., 1800	Mt. Pleasant, Darlington, 1798
Bethel, Indiana Co., Pa., 1810	Armagh, 1785
Bethel, Mercer Co., Pa., 1839	West Middlesex
Bethesda, Allegheny Co., Pa., 1780	Round Hill, 1778
Blairsville, Pa., 1831	Blairsville
Bloomfield, Jefferson Co., Ohio, 1871	Bloomfield, 1826
Brookville, Pa., 1840.	Brookville
Buffalo, Armstrong Co., Pa., 1812	Slate Lick, 1799, Worthington, 1850
Burgettstown, Pa., 1802	Cross Roads, 1798, Burgettstown, 1831
Butler, Pa., 1805	Butler, 1804
Cadiz, Ohio, Assoc., 1813, A.R., 1814	Cadiz, 1817
Calcutta, Columbiana Co., Ohio, 1815	Long's Run, 1802
Cambridge, Ohio, 1822	Cambridge, 1827
Canonsburg (Speers Spring) Pa., 1830	Canonsburg, 1830
Carrollton, Ohio, 1841	Carrollton, 1822
Center, Lawrence Co., Pa., 1820	Slippery Rock, Shenango Presbyterian
Chartiers Assoc., Canonsburg, 1775	Chartiers, 1775
Clarksville, Mercer Co., Pa., 1840	Clark
Claysville, Pa., 1809	Claysville
Clinton, Allegheny Co., Pa., 1797	Hopewell, 1820 (Potato Garden, 1800)

Clintonville, Venango Co., Pa., 1850	Clintonville
Cochranton, Crawford Co., Pa., 1815	Cochranton
Conemaugh, Indiana Co., Pa., 1798	Services in that vicinity, 1773 Bethel on Black Lick, 1790
Coraopolis, Pa., 1886	Coraopolis, 1882
Cross Creek, Brooke Co., W. Va., 1800	Three Springs, 1790
Dalton, Ohio, 1820	Dalton, 1815
Darlington (Brush Run), Pa., 1800	Darlington (Mt. Pleasant), 1798
Dayton (Glade Run), Pa., 1831	Glade Run
Deer Creek, Allegheny Co., Pa., 1802	Bull Creek, 1794
Deer Creek, Lawrence Co., Pa., 1795	Hopewell, New Bradford, 1800
Dunlap's Creek, Fayette Co., Pa., 1788	Dunlap's Creek, 1774
Fairmount, Westmoreland Co., Pa., 1801	Pleasant Grove, 1785
East Liverpool, Ohio, 1851	East Liverpool, 1817
East Union, Guernsey Co., Ohio, 1840	Beulah, Claysville, Ohio
East Unity (Scrubgrass) Venango Co., Pa., 1800	Scrubgrass, 1800
Elderton, Pa., 1845	Elderton, 1850
Erie, Pa., 1811	Erie, 1815
Evansburg, Pa., 1826	Conneaut Lake, 1817
Evansburg, Butler Co., Pa., 1838	Plains, 1806
Fairfield, Westmoreland Co., Pa., 1801	Fairfield, 1784
Fairview, Guernsey Co., Pa., 1824	Fairview, 1822
Frankfort Springs, Pa., 1790	Florence (King's Creek), 1798
Fredericksburg, Ohio, 1818	Fredericksburg, 1815
Freeport, Pa., 1820	Freeport, Pa.
Glade Run, Allegheny Co., Pa., 1812	Middlesex, 1802
Greenville, Pa., 1801	Greenville
Grove City, Pa., 1879	Grove City
Hanover, Beaver Co., Pa., 1825	Frankfort Springs, 1835
Harlansburg, Lawrence Co., Pa., 1854	Harlansburg
Harrisville, Harrison Co., Ohio, 1866	Mt. Pleasant, 1798, New Athens, 1835
Hartstown, Crawford Co., Pa., 1830	Atlantic
Haysville, Ohio, 1832	Haysville
High Ridge, Belmont Co., Ohio, 1824	Rock Hill, 1812
Hookstown, Pa., 1846	Hookstown

Iberia, Ohio, 1829	Iberia, 1836
Indiana, Pa., 1819	Indiana
Jamestown, Pa., 1853	Jamestown
Knoxville, Jefferson Co., Ohio, 1837	Island Creek, 1802
Latrobe, Pa., 1853	Latrobe
Laurel Hill, Fayette Co., Pa., 1791	Laurel Hill, 1776
Lebanon, Mercer Co., Pa., 1849	New Lebanon
Leesburg, Lawrence Co., Pa., 1859	Volant
Lexington, Richland Co., Ohio, 1821	Lexington, before 1823
Liberty, Trumbull Co., Ohio, 1805	Vienna, 1805
McMahon's Creek, Belmont Co., Ohio, 1827 (High Point, 1824)	Rockhill, 1812
Mahoning, Mahoning Co., Ohio, 1795	Poland, 1802
Mansfield, Ohio, 1819	Mansfield, 1815
Martins Ferry, Ohio, 1851	Martins Ferry, 1841
Mechanicstown, Carroll Co., Ohio, 1835	Mechanicstown, 1838
Mercer, Pa., 1802	Mercer, 1800
Mifflin, Allegheny Co., Pa., 1803	Lebanon, 1776
Millersburg, Ohio, A. 1825, A.R., 1841	Millersburg, 1827
Mt. Gilead, Allegheny Co., Pa., 1843	Sharon, 1817
Mt. Jackson, Pa., 1820	Westfield, 1802
Mt. Nebo, Allegheny Co., Pa., 1838	Fairmount
Hickory (Mt. Pleasant), Pa., 1795	Mt. Prospect
Mt. Pleasant, Pa., 1802	Mt. Pleasant Middle, 1776, Reunion, 1873
Nashville, Ohio, 1853	Nashville, 1846
Neshannock, Lawrence Co., Pa., R.P., 1814	Neshannock, 1799
New Alexandria, Pa., 1805	New Alexandria
New Athens, Ohio, 1851 (out of Free Pr.)	New Athens, 1835
New Bethlehem, Beaver Co., Pa., 1864	Mt. Olivet, 1867
New Brighton, Pa., A., 1803; A.R., 1825	New Brighton
New Concord, Ohio, 1812, R.P.	New Concord, 1804
Lisbon, Ohio, 1839	Lisbon, 1808
New Wilmington, Pa., 1809	Neshannock, 1799
Noblestown, Pa., A.R., 1792 Robinson Run Assoc., 1790	Oakdale

North Buffalo, Washington Co., Pa., 1778	Upper Buffalo, 1779
Norwich, Ohio, 1863	Norwich, 1828
Ohio, Beaver Co., Pa., 1820	Sharon, 1817
Oil City, Pa., 1864	Oil City, 1861
Ontario, Richland Co., Ohio, 1849	Lexington, 1832
Paris (Herman's Creek), Pa., 1805	Paris (Three Springs), 1790
Peter's Creek, Washington Co., 1795	Bethel, 1776; Center, 1830
Pigeon Creek, Washington Co., 1818	Pigeon Creek, 1775
Pine Creek, Allegheny Co., Pa., R.P., 1805	Pine Creek
Plain Grove, Lawrence Co., Pa., 1859	Plain Grove, 1798
Pleasant Hill, Guernsey Co., Pa., 1867	Birmingham
Poland, Ohio, 1804	Poland, 1800
Portersville, Pa., 1841	Portersville
Puckety, Westmoreland Co., Pa., 1795	Plum Creek (Puckety)
Scrubgrass, Venango Co., Pa., 1800	Scrubgrass, 1802, Clintonville
Savannah, Ohio, A.R., 1829; A., 1837	Savannah, 1833
Scroggsfield, Ohio, 1818	Carrollton, 1822
Service, Beaver Co., Pa., 1790	Mt. Olivet
Sewickley, Westmoreland Co., Pa., 1805	Sewickley, 1776
Sharon, Noble Co., Ohio, 1832	Sharon, 1821
Sharon, Pa., 1852	Sharon
Sheakleyville, Pa., 1825	Sheakleyville, 1799
Short Creek, W. Va., 1792	Short Creek, 1784
Smithfield (Short Creek), Ohio, 1799	Centre, 1814
Slippery Rock, Pa., 1809	Slippery Rock
Springfield (Summit Co.), Ohio, 1828	North Springfield, 1809
Union, Allegheny Co., Pa., 1793	Montours, 1778
Steubenville, Ohio, 1805	Steubenville, 1800
Stowe, Ohio, 1823	N. Springfield, 1809
Sunday Creek (Morgan Co.), Ohio, 1830	Sunday Creek
Tarentum, Pa., 1835	Tarentum
West Alexander, Pa., 1794	West Alexander, 1790
Tumlinson's Run, Beaver Co., Pa., 1834	Hookstown
Turtle Creek, Pa., 1798	Cross Roads, Monroeville
Union, Creekside, Pa., 1816	Center, Creekside
Unity, Harrison Co., Ohio, 1813	Crab Apple, 1798

Upper Piney, Clarion Co., Pa., 1821	New Rehoboth, 1802
Utica, Ohio, R.P., 1810; A.R., 1841	Utica, 1811
Utica, Pa., 1859	Utica, 1827
Washington, Pa., 1813	Washington, 1793
Waterford, Pa., 1812	Waterford, 1810
Waynesburg, Pa., 1821	Waynesburg CP
West Newton, Pa., 1850	West Newton
Calcutta, Ohio (Long's Run), 1815	Long's Run, 1803
Wheeling, W. Va., 1826	Wheeling, 1813
Wooster, Ohio, 1815	Wooster, 1815
Worthington, Pa., 1848	Worthington Free, 1850

Total of 141 communities where there is good evidence of rivalry.

APPENDIX C

Location in Church Cemeteries of Graves of Pioneer Pastors

No complete register has been compiled, but below is a partial list, with the places of their burial.

Joseph Smith, Upper Buffalo
Thaddeus Dod, Lower Ten Mile, Amity
James Power, Mt. Pleasant, Middle Church
John McMillan, Chartiers
John Clark, Bethel, Allegheny Co.
James Finley, Rehobeth
Jacob Jennings, Dunlap's Creek
Samuel Ralston, Mingo
James Dunlap, Abington, Philadelphia
James Hughes, Oxford, Ohio
Thomas Marquis, Bellefontaine, Ohio
Samuel Porter, Congruity
John McPherrin, Butler
Joseph Patterson, Raccoon
Samuel Tait, Mercer
James Satterfield, Moorefield, in Mercer Co.
Andrew McDonald, Mt. Carmel, Aliquippa
Reed Bracken, Mt. Nebo, Butler Co.
William Woods, Bethel, Allegheny Co.
Joseph Henderson, Bethel on Black Lick
George Hill, Fairfield, Westmoreland Co.
John Redick, Slate Lick
William Swan, Long Run
Matthew Brown, Washington, Pa.
Moses Allen, Crab Apple
John Rea, Beech Spring
Elisha Macurdy, Florence
Johnston Eaton, Fairview, Erie Co.
James Scott, Mt. Vernon, Ohio
John Watson, Chartiers
Robert McGarraugh, Concord, Clarion Co.
Boyd Mercer, Pigeon Creek
William Smith, Miller's Run
Absalom McCready, Neshannock
Francis Laird, Murrysville

APPENDIX D

CONTRIBUTIONS BY PRESBYTERIES: 1900–1957

(Current Figures Above; Benevolences Below)

Year	Wheeling	Parkersburg	Grafton	Washington	Shenango	Redstone
1900		28,444 3,796		69,265 33,993	46,207 11,802	70,002 15,729
1901		31,262 6,556		78,020 45,165	81,523 12,641	108,468 17,313
1902		36,602 5,409		66,927 31,111	71,551 13,227	106,621 22,911
1903		46,723 6,618		81,199 39,555	59,687 14,271	98,763 21,437
1904		24,610 3,984		97,040 46,671	75,452 14,957	91,556 19,165
1905		20,825 4,468		57,939 22,713	59,607 16,942	91,778 18,964
1906		20,894 9,433		45,413 18,980	60,403 18,407	75,404 22,420
1907		14,212 6,695		43,764 23,543	65,986 17,446	76,334 30,452
1908		21,561 5,538		62,008 28,391	64,370 17,968	131,389 26,973
1909		25,976 4,800		59,828 33,829	51,432 13,933	128,811 35,497
1910		27,136 5,156		69,151 27,395	52,223 14,661	110,732 39,049
1911		22,777 5,224		64,881 25,544	54,186 17,023	115,768 31,723
1912		22,775 6,399		80,904 37,713	56,638 17,325	113,458 30,983
1913		20,930 7,628		83,038 30,726	79,343 17,356	123,720 32,156
1914		19,620 6,284		79,974 35,041	68,401 20,381	152,625 37,329
1915		23,761 6,588		78,078 46,605	59,805 20,605	170,492 34,566
1916		23,999 6,324		86,124 35,186	64,289 22,879	130,407 29,728
1917		35,652 9,024		85,889 39,078	92,714 22,705	206,407 36,168
1918		27,928 10,653		94,697 42,669	69,831 31,659	156,345 45,132
1919		21,946 10,690		123,453 47,317	75,894 45,644	150,871 58,282

CONTRIBUTIONS BY PRESBYTERIES: 1900–1957 (Con't)
(Current Figures Above; Benevolences Below)

Year	Wheeling	Parkersburg	Grafton	Washington	Shenango	Redstone
1920		35,446 15,117		103,402 77,086	87,476 51,285	187,990 85,671
1921		44,029 17,858		118,018 79,444	113,288 78,568	193,542 102,689
1922		50,491 18,330		129,014 94,238	111,201 62,542	232,328 111,538
1923		50,410 31,261		125,327 65,505	103,524 177,902	234,947 103,274
1924	134,684 75,000	57,662 32,048	65,557 35,453	119,083 68,788	151,072 64,073	252,893 112,569
1925	147,857 77,033	81,768 29,282	86,371 132,624	137,397 66,376	145,979 75,435	329,968 112,505
1926	191,376 75,173	49,609 28,737	79,784 33,494	205,204 65,605	215,017 77,679	330,870 206,459
1927	157,914 63,266	62,874 23,194	83,824 30,697	189,289 68,475	228,621 86,493	323,069 105,705
1928	147,067 65,567	68,007 21,142	78,136 26,814	168,117 60,323	278,160 90,971	301,212 118,575
1929	145,344 60,041	92,369 18,110	78,145 23,502	202,046 58,019	219,584 91,528	376,076 81,363
1930	143,167 50,368	92,884 16,467	78,776 20,843	277,216 50,103	251,629 75,480	298,475 77,660
1931	158,447 45,119	61,056 16,247	83,087 13,298	254,356 49,367	199,725 70,618	272,336 63,030
1932	118,585 34,410	53,117 12,849	66,245 12,658	171,880 43,264	145,424 52,473	220,021 63,225
1933	96,822 24,691	46,621 9,725	52,345 10,792	135,065 33,135	112,167 35,291	166,938 45,626
1934	82,658 21,730	45,080 6,659	45,304 8,588	106,366 28,154	99,525 32,100	161,705 38,423
1935	89,486 20,585	44,709 7,680	48,930 8,400	105,158 29,864	108,725 30,142	183,418 32,126
1936	101,647 20,777	41,606 9,148	50,454 9,004	116,666 28,154	114,720 30,010	177,849 27,250
1937	114,852 20,554	54,467 8,397	48,424 8,606	164,525 29,416	151,956 36,954	266,783 41,045
1938	93,968 16,503	52,599 7,500	57,917 15,783	159,280 30,706	126,005 39,170	247,526 31,643
1939	96,632 23,300	45,699 7,700	60,315 15,565	139,970 28,777	133,318 39,811	226,161 32,544

CONTRIBUTIONS BY PRESBYTERIES: 1900–1957 (Con't)
(Current Figures Above; Benevolences Below)

Year	Wheeling	Parkersburg	Grafton	Washington	Shenango	Redstone
1940	129,912 26,449	50,776 8,532	55,520 15,522	146,768 31,441	133,169 40,071	251,714 34,959
1941	128,079 29,518	54,756 1,407	61,776 14,769	157,757 29,844	152,103 41,022	247,451 38,589
1942	115,162 32,813	51,368 8,066	65,070 15,764	151,845 32,814	180,342 47,568	257,737 40,123
1943	129,935 36,102	49,399 8,842	60,449 12,342	226,732 45,252	171,101 40,818	281,073 41,560
1944	122,874 38,412	53,351 8,978	74,711 14,949	188,448 35,813	179,137 42,167	291,180 48,085
1945	129,704 41,418	61,197 8,704	70,724 18,927	191,660 36,091	207,782 47,233	334,169 61,154
1946	185,440 48,202	68,247 9,456	100,941 19,532	209,151 50,981	192,259 50,913	356,386 73,388
1947	166,678 85,931	79,932 17,708	127,410 38,303	218,748 73,977	202,249 87,410	382,918 108,669
1948	140,079 48,632	65,380 16,580	76,680 26,504	195,120 50,631	167,712 49,545	281,157 80,029
1949	198,609 65,858	101,669 17,116	135,806 26,720	275,268 59,865	237,656 62,453	450,821 87,726
1950	213,477 63,882	116,450 16,295	135,243 32,538	317,743 57,763	277,856 64,155	475,272 96,791
1951	238,941 56,635	123,178 16,251	130,489 31,274	320,124 51,700	400,790 63,276	542,752 99,073
1952	259,134 63,995	130,422 17,640	151,753 24,280	324,431 57,302	392,895 69,927	629,141 104,373
1953	290,631 78,278	169,489 19,560	195,834 37,795	337,558 64,382	374,538 82,445	607,398 112,552
1954	295,889 90,342	216,188 24,293	248,173 37,146	389,541 71,730	394,883 96,043	664,636 135,886
1955	316,428 94,516	238,221 26,748	235,104 41,173	374,398 76,764	450,964 98,744	848,209 156,088
1956	485,826 97,933	236,752 28,357	215,246 43,808	428,657 95,952	540,843 114,626	943,312 170,636
1957	545,946 108,996	428,933 36,271	216,966 52,261	489,833 94,543	576,591 124,110	1,058,707 191,073
Totals	6,113,050 1,793,029	3,943,844 613,533	3,421,509 909,728	9,478,753 2,456,972	9,441,628 2,902,863	16,298,090 4,183,075

CONTRIBUTIONS BY PRESBYTERIES: 1900–1957 (Con't)
(Current Figures Above; Benevolences Below)

Year	Pittsburgh	Kittanning	Erie	Clarion	Butler	Blairsville
1900	355,695	37,356	116,682	49,905	30,726	101,773
	133,840	11,725	41,576	11,981	14,621	22,373
1901	374,806	31,131	155,466	49,219	37,536	86,210
	150,404	14,452	57,139	12,519	13,565	18,539
1902	457,125	44,908	131,817	45,591	32,326	115,257
	208,045	16,874	49,337	12,847	11,669	18,986
1903	570,682	56,179	121,941	48,789	40,171	95,715
	207,833	16,217	47,075	15,050	14,009	23,435
1904	542,170	39,547	123,815	59,722	58,686	107,461
	159,720	16,245	44,921	14,114	13,507	26,144
1905	482,282	45,477	147,862	64,916	40,752	108,214
	172,309	14,729	92,481	16,988	16,284	30,960
1906	442,375	72,293	128,520	68,554	43,160	106,667
	233,013	16,441	64,133	20,011	16,790	26,986
1907	663,194	83,124	106,469	57,985	55,595	97,968
	247,694	17,456	63,223	19,362	17,160	27,237
1908	692,077	117,025	162,799	56,749	53,292	116,394
	239,321	19,393	72,247	21,125	17,579	31,110
1909	685,776	58,477	130,312	63,977	45,687	117,619
	234,460	16,036	56,325	28,274	18,769	29,544
1910	628,461	56,190	146,138	85,169	48,090	127,679
	236,390	14,067	77,591	21,055	16,281	25,040
1911	660,442	127,722	160,904	90,342	56,853	130,023
	276,743	14,996	74,190	32,886	19,639	33,164
1912	761,900	71,860	160,818	78,711	57,195	242,001
	280,054	16,587	75,546	49,084	22,395	37,157
1913	805,220	59,086	163,738	82,812	69,394	179,668
	298,394	16,940	78,476	35,809	43,073	44,778
1914	714,271	67,399	184,901	125,316	58,285	177,512
	460,538	16,916	74,353	37,885	27,556	49,558
1915	795,129	68,199	197,510	115,642	59,347	188,305
	372,056	18,352	78,598	36,268	32,182	52,567
1916	840,224	71,487	183,013	96,241	62,128	180,804
	349,988	18,695	75,952	50,290	32,357	48,452
1917	910,159	75,048	203,188	95,582	80,154	181,899
	484,507	20,945	91,089	49,814	42,091	46,543
1918	982,889	67,097	254,561	87,160	71,030	268,735
	542,732	31,672	114,737	73,778	67,553	82,307
1919	942,891	78,994	238,790	89,809	65,318	187,706
	534,022	29,464	106,080	99,336	74,888	84,934

CONTRIBUTIONS BY PRESBYTERIES: 1900–1957 (Con't)
(Current Figures Above; Benevolences Below)

Year	Pittsburgh	Kittanning	Erie	Clarion	Butler	Blairsville
1920	1,038,638	85,235	390,130	115,861	76,292	274,900
	707,788	50,308	153,215	83,204	73,073	104,779
1921	1,473,449	102,253	279,980	106,890	104,386	268,046
	1,069,347	63,106	233,310	58,116	94,172	163,499
1922	1,193,412	107,916	316,547	135,588	106,153	265,494
	804,248	48,171	246,219	55,944	92,030	121,071
1923	1,300,626	133,768	324,924	127,658	101,846	266,021
	775,043	45,710	213,259	54,361	94,966	148,842
1924	1,408,305	155,210	380,453	178,763	132,314	305,239
	835,066	52,249	231,574	77,235	95,195	181,105
1925	1,528,987	170,199	407,029	192,273	174,998	288,805
	904,484	54,179	248,731	58,259	98,279	148,498
1926	1,589,030	139,981	431,112	158,166	190,981	271,049
	819,892	50,871	231,548	55,500	97,362	148,703
1927	1,573,528	146,592	392,234	144,220	370,593	361,821
	940,919	58,810	285,529	58,051	89,656	165,736
1928	1,833,574	140,118	662,012	147,731	211,305	360,087
	883,528	48,101	279,393	59,436	78,110	151,020
1929	2,003,357	148,664	679,954	134,277	183,020	365,400
	897,615	66,013	289,839	56,802	79,328	136,097
1930	2,011,687	143,594	631,111	133,894	173,921	368,537
	833,046	41,599	250,987	53,438	68,735	129,964
1931	1,710,677	149,459	674,753	135,612	158,648	328,107
	816,622	41,768	231,110	38,583	56,748	119,443
1932	1,457,568	119,805	429,377	113,807	116,719	270,392
	728,239	37,864	165,903	32,473	41,737	96,156
1933	1,109,216	102,632	320,552	91,869	107,907	206,192
	573,142	29,073	106,021	73,206	27,591	63,422
1934	1,094,529	99,072	350,850	85,077	91,546	189,810
	510,938	26,593	99,140	20,613	23,024	48,315
1935	1,055,552	101,885	287,583	87,497	98,626	212,909
	500,896	25,042	85,384	19,653	22,921	49,397
1936	1,169,691	109,131	271,834	89,413	119,504	214,684
	484,879	23,653	84,148	19,785	23,534	46,891
1937	1,296,152	111,127	295,396	101,530	99,457	242,677
	528,161	29,089	86,485	19,950	26,911	52,033
1938	1,526,161	115,152	337,505	99,664	107,106	244,855
	553,035	29,883	101,317	20,627	28,742	55,540
1939	1,393,411	128,125	309,166	99,384	103,853	255,702
	503,235	25,686	86,120	20,379	26,576	52,645

CONTRIBUTIONS BY PRESBYTERIES: 1900–1957 (Con't)
(Current Figures Above; Benevolences Below)

Year	Pittsburgh	Kittanning	Erie	Clarion	Butler	Blairsville
1940	1,337,586 510,271	127,685 27,235	338,976 94,133	108,498 20,478	199,188 28,375	283,257 51,998
1941	1,461,484 461,251	184,825 27,433	373,916 92,582	111,426 20,507	125,976 30,608	269,842 53,356
1942	1,631,737 479,028	147,407 28,099	323,056 91,628	123,848 21,659	135,302 31,196	292,911 54,556
1943	1,646,843 523,741	125,065 32,344	363,365 97,670	117,827 27,597	166,034 40,979	280,360 61,502
1944	1,661,655 523,992	156,600 36,831	755,464 107,375	148,591 34,948	158,304 46,263	292,300 64,312
1945	1,890,085 555,387	168,271 42,096	450,532 126,786	141,794 35,714	171,009 50,406	329,521 71,348
1946	2,134,440 712,243	187,297 50,829	481,465 140,222	154,464 42,021	182,395 66,039	383,218 74,456
1947	1,970,563 933,220	190,128 67,189	483,042 220,879	189,039 73,872	189,226 77,112	386,722 114,634
1948	1,817,795 654,425	160,521 44,693	459,268 145,269	159,030 50,033	168,920 60,794	325,998 81,711
1949	2,367,216 778,215	243,675 55,498	605,588 192,776	185,538 57,035	236,613 71,523	399,902 111,729
1950	2,548,252 794,814	229,542 64,460	872,486 192,369	220,677 57,764	277,684 71,629	441,472 104,966
1951	3,007,675 778,072	262,377 58,164	703,539 204,409	248,246 57,691	274,103 74,276	487,564 102,223
1952	3,204,569 831,312	273,205 64,411	762,240 221,471	292,022 60,142	276,057 77,178	490,683 172,898
1953	3,415,353 937,219	282,200 68,610	868,272 238,246	282,385 64,180	293,921 81,729	535,703 138,426
1954	3,974,208 1,021,687	459,990 71,620	941,986 271,442	309,001 79,949	276,257 93,501	594,515 145,704
1955	4,274,412 1,078,311	522,105 79,087	1,147,138 260,139	353,685 84,413	345,029 100,680	725,550 150,286
1956	5,040,103 1,193,150	417,674 91,844	1,394,475 286,839	339,927 93,925	373,062 117,591	898,779 152,225
1957	5,049,101 1,277,121	534,255 107,595	1,564,931 343,578	370,271 104,461	461,126 127,784	1,042,949 184,634
Totals	90,788,539 34,535,635	8,511,329 2,255,008	24,381,465 7,071,870	7,857,734 2,580,480	8,197,016 3,018,321	16,939,615 4,823,934

CONTRIBUTIONS BY PRESBYTERIES: 1900–1957 (Con't)
(Current Figures Above; Benevolences Below)

Year	Beaver	Zanesville	Wooster	Steubenville	St. Clairsville	Portsmouth
1900	118,591 46,221	40,031 8,920	40,013 8,960	53,972 11,292	50,947 7,810	27,245 3,248
1901	137,223 35,845	41,239 8,577	42,539 8,141	67,121 18,728	38,138 9,082	21,190 8,986
1902	195,526 38,814	43,175 10,087	43,970 13,950	66,578 32,476	41,219 16,407	23,188 6,648
1903	138,579 43,990	41,113 9,989	28,781 7,716	77,741 14,588	48,079 14,959	28,121 9,440
1904	190,708 46,292	46,059 10,619	42,441 17,205	63,906 13,688	64,372 11,076	26,175 7,328
1905	142,378 51,797	64,995 10,142	43,050 11,328	69,182 20,919	52,961 9,544	27,705 5,881
1906	183,450 43,157	63,108 12,116	72,643 9,799	74,339 21,104	55,700 10,656	31,941 8,623
1907	38,690 4,682	56,094 13,907	39,797 11,408	71,640 24,982	42,781 14,542	28,044 6,668
1908		53,479 13,643	46,790 11,085	80,286 35,317	39,831 17,511	33,631 7,684
1909	39,606 12,405	48,351 12,566	41,148 22,141	73,342 20,752	56,983 13,831	25,155 10,540
1910	40,405 11,169	64,051 10,515	48,357 12,064	70,259 18,040	47,699 16,134	28,092 6,111
1911	48,261 13,824	79,555 11,971	44,307 18,891	86,380 16,475	61,991 19,228	43,024 7,169
1912	55,279 13,999	83,676 13,034	44,625 16,387	77,514 29,085	52,729 18,551	124,807 7,427
1913	59,034 15,707	91,033 13,084	44,523 15,064	80,958 37,005	63,867 22,257	47,985 12,426
1914	58,821 19,093	142,891 21,888	57,145 13,534	81,433 36,954	89,720 22,004	54,985 8,532
1915	61,171 26,080	88,897 19,314	47,919 25,771	125,158 27,712	75,081 30,406	51,882 11,922
1916	54,157 20,578	81,675 21,862	57,448 68,289	93,683 31,275	83,610 22,272	36,200 40,910
1917	72,321 25,679	82,283 20,693	61,746 16,983	144,019 39,041	77,396 31,269	51,966 15,277
1918	66,416 26,420	76,334 85,538	58,818 27,237	146,410 30,388	75,705 44,612	35,548 24,989
1919	71,964 28,515	98,062 36,526	62,333 36,385	91,248 33,434	77,023 37,566	38,027 23,952

CONTRIBUTIONS BY PRESBYTERIES: 1900–1957 (Con't)
(Current Figures Above; Benevolences Below)

Year	Beaver	Zanesville	Wooster	Steubenville	St. Clairsville	Portsmouth
1920	84,555 53,966	97,668 60,085	68,982 48,948	121,104 54,969	83,429 56,180	48,312 32,833
1921	97,126 62,908	106,372 54,731	83,155 57,513	140,361 60,050	101,517 59,546	70,021 37,818
1922	90,591 56,190	126,408 63,064	81,509 54,075	155,030 62,609	95,250 54,140	71,500 58,590
1923	98,990 62,447	163,103 55,303	104,800 52,124	171,719 60,378	104,351 57,869	74,344 32,511
1924	114,819 68,382	128,815 60,171	136,728 51,317	257,875 63,396	136,000 71,520	77,924 36,090
1925	145,599 70,740	131,963 49,999	126,076 57,757	192,055 80,185	144,686 67,922	91,413 35,309
1926	132,386 63,230	138,337 53,800	139,090 51,057	106,832 61,600	135,185 60,199	85,821 34,050
1927	199,845 66,630	137,228 56,021	108,592 50,065	183,007 60,127	145,394 53,242	192,242 34,468
1928	365,106 60,401	158,538 46,520	111,105 47,581	199,809 56,698	186,656 53,567	109,851 26,394
1929	332,324 58,998	152,284 46,221	262,597 44,799	180,102 58,211	177,730 58,186	84,011 25,808
1930	422,267 51,403	160,872 44,617	268,405 41,479	205,484 60,283	136,258 55,768	80,610 22,419
1931	210,487 50,126	170,405 40,646	139,944 38,505	193,842 51,624	123,313 41,664	78,859 18,014
1932	167,208 41,631	145,001 35,194	106,897 30,793	152,728 48,850	108,937 32,927	64,996 17,502
1933	116,653 26,423	105,789 29,967	86,477 20,982	119,451 31,734	100,355 22,594	52,997 12,110
1934	99,023 17,932	95,697 22,392	78,281 20,590	104,670 30,280	106,332 20,551	52,649 10,467
1935	114,161 17,894	88,624 21,335	81,271 19,423	118,950 30,580	88,289 20,905	229,522 11,833
1936	113,397 17,601	96,733 20,156	179,401 18,655	119,870 33,401	94,084 20,547	67,852 15,562
1937	129,823 19,536	102,507 21,198	84,025 20,688	129,106 31,152	100,059 20,707	67,825 11,804
1938	140,421 20,570	100,844 24,396	114,538 22,905	128,561 31,921	104,976 23,672	75,152 14,363
1939	132,718 18,251	113,271 23,098	106,605 19,092	129,948 20,783	88,768 19,694	65,924 11,241

CONTRIBUTIONS BY PRESBYTERIES: 1900–1957 (Con't)
(Current Figures Above; Benevolences Below)

Year	Beaver	Zanesville	Wooster	Steubenville	St. Clairsville	Portsmouth
1940	127,425 18,081	108,850 21,799	114,445 20,235	136,993 33,187	104,989 21,445	77,167 11,942
1941	131,267 19,561	123,421 22,735	109,093 20,691	149,366 23,337	107,158 21,216	71,766 12,830
1942	149,447 21,077	139,498 24,642	121,254 21,587	169,013 26,442	101,637 21,901	79,568 12,602
1943	171,936 23,121	133,070 27,829	115,252 23,868	175,143 33,925	128,620 22,096	83,356 11,299
1944	167,423 25,917	29,847 27,555	118,572 25,426	175,504 33,482	128,038 25,920	77,406 13,660
1945	187,711 30,121	153,389 29,476	148,784 29,860	201,562 38,577	126,581 27,738	84,534 14,687
1946	199,763 40,851	146,572 32,673	45,703 31,645	225,429 55,587	144,143 24,769	95,750 13,836
1947	192,944 41,881	159,491 66,741	159,638 47,549	245,681 70,217	160,292 40,562	108,821 30,827
1948	170,961 41,396	149,432 37,472	128,195 48,209	206,000 52,748	126,154 28,460	88,223 19,468
1949	227,814 58,207	197,885 55,761	188,612 49,769	296,533 79,127	175,011 41,182	130,575 22,253
1950	239,655 58,552	218,936 50,634	212,705 49,208	340,684 63,249	198,537 43,653	138,234 23,051
1951	257,397 61,960	225,577 51,749	245,740 51,076	348,654 60,309	206,875 46,952	145,238 26,025
1952	252,390 68,528	278,787 57,025	247,711 53,411	369,311 64,135	224,524 50,143	175,069 27,403
1953	267,335 80,810	309,880 64,864	300,007 57,332	411,889 79,468	242,114 58,753	181,716 31,507
1954	342,359 85,200	318,151 77,511	305,582 62,332	483,487 89,752	282,890 64,386	189,241 34,497
1955	423,393 92,891	378,020 82,644	330,664 66,328	522,682 90,385	315,217 64,010	237,815 42,636
1956	428,044 94,714	399,115 93,284	370,942 80,911	534,749 104,011	421,161 70,519	249,522 50,925
1957	518,891 101,209	436,239 94,770	436,161 90,847	684,805 106,722	384,213 78,223	248,350 49,240
Totals	9,535,819 2,393,593	7,812,730 2,123,069	7,126,231 1,951,835	10,513,258 2,606,740	7,135,555 2,012,505	4,970,407 1,348,032

CONTRIBUTIONS BY PRESBYTERIES: 1900–1957 (Con't)
(Current Figures Above; Benevolences Below)

Year	Mahoning	Dayton	Columbus	Cincinnati	Marion	Chillicothe
1900	70,203 12,982	109,657 37,586	69,717 11,682	135,028 73,999	17,978 5,061	35,439 7,139
1901	87,278 17,790	103,553 45,064	68,590 9,090	207,750 41,845	19,816 3,882	27,882 7,026
1902	83,762 26,486	114,243 60,132	56,302 13,227	122,973 41,840	20,470 4,699	34,409 8,078
1903	72,673 14,397	114,449 38,176	48,321 15,564	170,010 51,830	26,411 4,048	37,117 9,683
1904	93,013 15,032	107,630 130,147	55,771 14,800	130,292 211,388	42,730 4,846	24,185 6,069
1905	124,789 21,979	105,314 227,422	45,037 22,969	130,802 35,487	33,165 5,052	28,575 7,964
1906	111,389 16,755	113,974 26,638	58,475 22,096	139,633 37,397	34,630 8,627	30,500 6,787
1907	84,930 21,621	134,528 30,318	64,985 13,587	142,488 43,311	28,048 6,675	37,383 5,786
1908	91,870 26,949	154,803 32,821	101,653 20,136	146,232 38,530	24,623 10,393	30,357 5,432
1909	78,601 24,722	110,667 40,644	113,642 19,985	140,210 38,159	25,425 15,701	49,459 8,251
1910	94,381 24,886	111,563 30,105	85,134 38,705	160,409 38,746	25,640 7,883	33,348 6,114
1911	103,796 19,103	125,951 49,897	84,979 29,327	191,786 45,522	30,698 10,892	29,983 10,362
1912	119,216 25,311	123,423 57,476	98,404 74,903	173,134 52,971	28,795 10,920	30,509 19,155
1913	138,742 30,319	110,147 50,048	100,275 55,334	181,871 56,617	77,459 15,737	36,882 12,954
1914	115,065 24,810	133,370 46,872	134,263 57,594	166,523 55,869	76,751 21,776	36,219 10,455
1915	104,238 31,983	143,715 42,432	163,460 64,665	208,754 69,925	73,547 19,145	45,282 10,869
1916	118,103 37,589	150,433 44,018	148,288 77,106	224,536 76,225	70,076 21,223	37,523 10,114
1917	131,871 48,683	142,327 57,225	158,826 85,996	199,382 70,653	71,203 18,166	36,156 14,019
1918	153,639 58,199	154,989 75,005	128,496 113,654	202,564 97,938	68,762 24,140	34,856 11,648
1919	155,606 58,265	148,242 74,236	129,917 113,033	187,291 84,305	72,696 23,742	43,649 12,801

CONTRIBUTIONS BY PRESBYTERIES: 1900–1957 (Con't)
(Current Figures Above; Benevolences Below)

Year	Mahoning	Dayton	Columbus	Cincinnati	Marion	Chillicothe
1920	213,163 102,305	166,655 82,221	149,032 154,050	250,550 111,710	87,455 43,752	47,835 22,522
1921	267,966 128,757	210,233 100,781	208,744 136,096	279,743 129,932	114,027 49,443	56,382 27,120
1922	245,660 121,702	239,255 100,001	239,881 79,930	342,414 124,564	103,251 45,429	63,658 22,162
1923	285,781 137,383	239,993 129,613	184,559 144,149	441,716 142,256	110,116 40,040	65,188 20,652
1924	265,596 130,421	272,049 111,257	208,301 144,029	651,070 140,528	118,697 46,301	71,267 25,968
1925	272,461 145,127	430,123 108,992	234,629 134,806	425,352 144,997	113,583 47,447	65,969 20,074
1926	275,896 141,546	1,063,312 126,469	256,360 85,509	498,960 157,297	149,922 45,496	69,354 16,572
1927	338,317 131,117	792,757 90,569	306,326 80,706	590,334 141,496	147,201 43,072	62,327 19,214
1928	339,477 128,897	478,038 89,456	307,518 85,130	652,199 162,761	133,924 42,823	52,298 17,911
1929	345,865 123,971	349,938 117,747	296,594 80,922	774,999 211,092	140,514 37,862	60,635 18,042
1930	331,987 111,906	334,276 88,424	285,308 69,160	704,196 170,812	133,318 35,422	55,993 18,430
1931	294,735 104,761	337,194 75,460	244,659 67,359	612,243 190,966	137,344 30,125	58,761 12,590
1932	212,809 67,410	266,711 60,205	221,435 52,334	586,716 118,733	110,618 22,379	47,601 8,348
1933	192,985 58,218	218,696 42,399	170,918 43,916	431,407 78,370	82,187 14,132	44,812 7,008
1934	180,132 41,698	221,590 35 633	147,813 36,141	352,038 75,497	81,365 11,767	40,964 6,535
1935	200,206 39,947	190,934 35,622	162,541 39,197	358,134 70,742	74,907 12,770	53,781 6,542
1936	206,543 42,519	266,113 37,485	215,711 46,349	372,756 75,011	81,799 12,429	
1937	248,353 44,754	211,695 42,660	249,173 46,997	404,733 81,925	85,168 13,335	
1938	252,793 40,338	218,949 42,885	309,367 46,480	473,534 81,027	98,517 12,843	
1939	260,155 46,890	252,507 40,741	273,074 44,663	440,017 75,439	92,181 12,388	

CONTRIBUTIONS BY PRESBYTERIES: 1900–1957 (Con't)
(Current Figures Above; Benevolences Below)

Year	Mahoning	Dayton	Columbus	Cincinnati	Marion	Chillicothe
1940	273,565 48,317	262,109 41,653	286,530 45,195	472,781 93,565	107,958 12,312	
1941	281,814 50,311	275,608 41,573	249,267 45,282	423,220 85,541	129,929 21,104	
1942	328,448 58,008	323,717 44,618	234,588 44,186	522,286 99,924	114,917 15,805	
1943	340,293 76,737	303,278 51,034	245,209 51,400	480,731 98,214	115,660 18,864	
1944	353,805 71,733	334,920 52,083	309,176 56,554	552,221 95,538	134,818 18,992	
1945	414,951 80,939	351,087 56,353	324,233 59,990	654,548 111,708	130,961 22,694	
1946	534,056 92,029	454,872 65,404	367,400 70,931	693,488 132,833	175,467 24,592	
1947	566,193 158,529	491,830 131,125	410,290 128,452	793,076 213,489	181,216 58,979	
1948	461,367 114,620	432,043 86,055	352,572 81,533	697,189 154,206	145,387 34,511	
1949	612,422 153,137	585,190 112,429	461,286 91,690	942,734 212,900	221,390 44,943	
1950	774,593 146,691	590,834 107,474	543,187 107,408	1,206,478 208,933	195,926 34,426	
1951	870,473 146,719	722,691 108,992	559,336 114,413	1,156,277 220,604	237,999 32,242	
1952	949,683 158,050	788,764 117,209	710,690 127,419	1,375,910 244,163	246,120 41,069	
1953	1,194,028 197,147	809,090 129,854	845,418 139,055	1,574,978 288,412	292,257 43,207	
1954	1,102,631 228,160	805,969 174,731	1,021,078 170,693	1,669,388 316,859	255,176 55,576	
1955	1,205,106 246,785	893,700 186,417	1,275,874 186,498	1,823,615 380,738	302,723 60,530	
1956	1,381,074 285,283	1,164,231 204,222	1,336,633 214,942	2,177,913 423,627	322,444 65,968	
1957	1,485,908 330,362	1,353,932 231,438	1,934,313 240,768	2,486,634 466,921	377,535 69,245	
Totals	20,506,465 5,091,085	21,222,931 4,697,546	18,053,566 4,468,813	27,782,060 7,626,338	6,852,952 1,134,784	1,621,538 460,348

Grand total for Current receipts.........$348,506,084

Grand total for Benevolence receipts.....$103,059,136

Bibliography

Listing Sources Previously Quoted

SECTION I. MINUTES

CHURCHES

Minutes of Dunlap's Creek Church Session, 1787–1804, typed by Jesse Coldren and available in Library of Western Theological Seminary.

PRESBYTERIES

Minutes of Allegheny Presbytery of the Cumberland Presbyterian Church, 1847–1907. A manuscript in the Presbyterian Historical Society, Philadelphia.

Records of Chillicothe Presbytery, Ohio, Vol. I.

Minutes of the Presbytery of Coshocton, Vol. I.

Minutes of Cumberland Presbytery, 1810–1813.

Minutes of the Donegal Presbytery, June, 1767, June, 1771, *et al.* Manuscript in Presbyterian Historical Society, Philadelphia.

Minutes of Lancaster Presbytery, Ohio, Vol. IV.

Minutes of Lexington (Virginia) Presbytery, 1897.

Minutes of Free Presbytery of Mahoning, Ohio, Vol. I.

Minutes, Presbytery of Ohio—Typed transcript by E. B. Welsh, 1935. Library of Western Seminary.
Vol. I, 1793–1806
Vol. II, 1806–1813
Vol. III, 1813–1817
Vol. IV, 1817–1822
Vol. V, 1822–1830

Minutes of Pittsburgh Presbytery (New School), November 20, 1839, to reunion in 1869. Complete in Library of Western Theological Seminary.

Minutes of the Presbytery of Redstone of the Presbyterian Church, 1781–1832. Printed in Cincinnati, 1878.

Minutes of the Presbytery of Richland, Ohio, Vol. I.

Minutes of the Presbytery of St. Clairsville, Ohio, Vol. I.

Records of Union Presbytery, Cumberland Presbyterian, Vol. I.

SYNODS

Minutes of Cumberland Synod, 1813–1828, Vol. I. Manuscript in Presbyterian Historical Society, Philadelphia.

Records of the Presbyterian Church in the United States of America—Embracing the Minutes of the General Presbytery and General Synod,

1706–1788. Presbyterian Board of Publication and Sabbath School Work, Philadelphia, 1904.

Records of Synod of Ohio, Vols. I, II, and III.

Records of Pennsylvania Synod of Cumberland Presbyterian Church. A manuscript in the Presbyterian Historical Society, Philadelphia. Vol. I, 1817–1827; Vol. II, 1838–1888.

Records of the Synod of Pittsburgh from its first organization September 29, 1802 to October, 1832. Pittsburgh: Luke Loomis, 1852.

Minutes of the Synod of Virginia, Vols. I and II.

Records of Synod of Western Reserve. Records of Presbytery of Cleveland.

GENERAL ASSEMBLIES

Minutes of the First General Assembly, Cumberland Presbyterian Church, 1829–1840, Vol. I; Vol. II, 1841–1847. Manuscript in Presbyterian Historical Society, Philadelphia.

Minutes of the General Assembly of the Presbyterian Church U.S.A. Old School.

Minutes of the General Assembly of the Presbyterian Church in the United States of America: with an Appendix: New York: John A. Gray, 1838–1850. New School. Subsequent Vols. I, 1851–1854; II, 1855–1858; III, 1859–1861; IV, 1862–1864; V, 1865–1867; VI, 1868–1869.

Minutes of the General Assembly of the Presbyterian Church in the United States of America.

SCHOOLS

Minutes of the Board of Trustees of Grove City College, 1915, 1916. Grove City, Pennsylvania.

Minutes of the Board of Trustees, Washington Academy, 1787–1806.

Minutes of the Board of Trustees of Washington College.

OTHERS

Minutes of the Association for the Aged. (Typed Abstracts.)

Minutes of Executive Committee of the Presbyterian Board of Colportage of Western Pennsylvania, 1878–1920.

Minutes and Documents of the Presbyterian Church related to Reunion 1866-1867 and Appendix 1869. Philadelphia, Presbyterian Board of Publication.

Minutes of the Faculty, Western Theological Seminary, Pittsburgh, Pennsylvania, 1829.

SECTION II. BOOKS

AMBLER, CHARLES H. *A History of Education in West Virginia.* Huntington, West Virginia, 1951.

American Men of Science. Lancaster, Pennsylvania, 7th Edition.

Annals of Old Wilkinsburg and Vicinity. Wilkinsburg, Pennsylvania, 1941.

ARMSTRONG, LOETSCHER, and ANDERSON. *The Presbyterian Enterprise*. Philadelphia, 1956.

BADGER, JOSEPH. *Memoir: Containing Autobiography and Selections from Private Journal and Correspondence*. Hudson, Ohio, 1851.

BAILEY, RAE. *Old Keys*. History of Savannah, Ohio.

BAIRD, SAMUEL J., D.D. *A History of the New School*. Philadelphia: Claxton, Remsen & Haffelfinger, 1868.

BASSETT, J. S. *A Short History of the United States*. New York: Macmillan Co., 1914.

BEARDSLEY, FRANK GRENVILLE. *A History of American Revivals*. American Tract Society, Boston, 1904.

BEATTY, CHARLES. *Journal of a Two-Months' Tour,* with a view of Promoting Religion among the Frontier Inhabitants of Pennsylvania. London, 1768.

BOUCHER, J. N. *A Century and a Half of Pittsburgh and Her People*. New York, 1908.

BRACKENRIDGE, HUGH H. *Incidents of the Insurrection in the Western Parts of Pennsylvania in the year 1794*. Philadelphia, 1795.

BROWN, A. J. *One Hundred Years*—A History of the Foreign Missionary Work of the Presbyterian Church. New York, 1936.

BROWN, JAMES H. "Presbyterian Beginnings in Ohio." Unpublished doctor's dissertation, University of Pittsburgh, 1952.

BROWNSON, JAMES I. "The History of the Western Theological Seminary" in *Centenary Memorial of the Planting and Growth of Presbyterianism in Western Pennsylvania and Parts Adjacent*. Pittsburgh: The Publishing Committee, Centennial Memorial Convention, 1876.

————. *Proceedings and Addresses at the Semicentennial Celebration of Washington College*. Pittsburgh: J. T. Shryock, 1857.

BUCK, SOLON J. and BUCK, ELIZABETH H. *The Planting of Civilization in Western Pennsylvania*. Pittsburgh: University of Pittsburgh Press, 1939.

BURCKEL, CHRISTIAN (ed.). *The College Blue Book,* 8th Edition, 1956.

CALLAHAN, JAMES M. *Semicentennial History of West Virginia*. Charleston: Jarett Publishing Co., 1913.

CARSON, MRS. THOMAS and JONES, MRS. E. W. *History of the Pennsylvania Woman's Christian Temperance Union*. Quincy, Pennsylvania, 1937.

A Centennial Volume of Robert Burns.

Centennial Volume of the First Presbyterian Church of Pittsburgh, Pennsylvania, 1784–1884. Pittsburgh: Wm. G. Johnston & Co., 1884.

Centenary Memorial of the Planting and Growth of Presbyterianism in Western Pennsylvania and Parts Adjacent. Pittsburgh, 1876.

CHAMBERS, GEORGE A. *A Tribute to the Principles . . . of the Irish and Scotch, Early Settlers in Pennsylvania,* 1856.

Charges and Addresses at the Inauguration of Reverend W. H. Jaffers, D.D., and Reverend S. H. Kellogg, D.D., Professors in the Western Theological Seminary, etc. Pittsburgh, 1878.

CHEESEMAN, LEWIS. *Differences between Old and New School Presbyterians.* Rochester: Erastus Darrow, 1848.

CLEVELAND, C. C. *The Great Revival in the West.* Chicago, 1916.

COLEMAN, HELEN T. W. *Banners in the Wilderness.* Pittsburgh: University of Pittsburgh Press, 1956.

COLLIER, FRANCIS J. *Chartiers Church and Its Ministers.* Centennial Celebration of Chartiers Church, August 25, 1875. Philadelphia: McLaughlin Bros., 1875.

CREE, JOHN, *et al. Evils of the Work now Prevailing in the U.S.A. under the Name of a Revival of Religion.* Washington, Pennsylvania, 1804.

CUSTEAD, ELIZABETH. *Rose and Elza, Songs and Stories of Bygone Days in Fayette County and Elsewhere.* New York, 1882.

Diary of John Cuthbertson, Missionary to the Covenanters of Colonial Pennsylvania, edited by William L. Fisk, Jr., Muskingum College, 1949.

DAHLINGER, C. W. *Pittsburgh—A Sketch of Its Early Social Life.* New York: Knickerbocker Press, 1916.

DAVENPORT, FREDERICK MORGAN. *Primitive Traits in Religious Revivals:* A Study in Mental and Social Evolution. New York: Macmillan Co., 1905.

DAVIDSON, ROBERT. *History of the Presbyterian Church in the State of Kentucky.* New York: Robert Carter, 1847. A preliminary sketch of the churches in the valley of Virginia.

DEGELMAN, WILLIAM C. *Historical Narrative of Bethel Presbyterian Church.* Pittsburgh, 1936.

Directory of American Scholars. Lancaster, Pennsylvania, 2nd Edition.

DRURY, CLIFFORD M. *Presbyterian Panorama.* Board of Christian Education, Philadelphia, Pennsylvania, 1952.

DUNAWAY, WAYLAND F. *A History of Pennsylvania.* New York, 1935.

EARHART, MARY. *Frances Willard and Others.* Chicago, 1944.

EATON, S. J. *History of the Presbytery of Erie, with Biographical Sketches of all Its Ministers and Historical Sketches of Its Churches.* New York: Hurd and Houghton, 1868.

ELLIOTT, DAVID. *The Life of the Reverend Elisha Macurdy,* with an Appendix containing Brief Notices of Various Deceased Ministers. Allegheny, Pennsylvania, 1848.

EVANS, LOUIS H. *The Third Presbyterian Church of Pittsburgh, Pennsylvania.* A Century's History, 1833–1933. Pittsburgh, 1933.

EVANSON, JACOB H. "Folk Songs of an Industrial City" in *Pennsylvania Folk Songs and Legends.* Philadelphia, 1949.

FERM, VERGILIUS. *The American Church of the Protestant Heritage.* New York: Philosophical Library, 1953. Chapter on Presbyterian Church was written by C. M. Drury.

FITCH, JOHN A. *The Steel Workers.* New York, 1910.

GERBERDING, G. H. *The Life and Letters of Dr. William A. Passavant.* Greenville, Pennsylvania: The Young Lutheran Company, 1906.

GILLETT, E. H. *History of the Presbyterian Church of U.S.A.* Vols. I and II. Philadelphia, 1864.

GILLIES, J. *Historical Collections,* Vol. II. Glasgow, 1754.

GLASGOW, WILLIAM M. *Cyclopedic Manual of the United Presbyterian Church of North America.* Pittsburgh: U. P. Board of Publication, 1909.

GREEN, ASHBEL. *The Life,* prepared for the press at the author's request by Joseph H. Jones. New York: Robert Carter and Brothers, 1849.

GUTHRIE, DWIGHT R. *John McMillan, The Apostle of Presbyterianism in the West.* Pittsburgh: University of Pittsburgh Press, 1952.

HANNA, C. A. *The Scotch-Irish; or, the Scot in North Britain, North Ireland, and North America.* 2 Vols. New York: C. P. Putnam's Sons, 1902.

HANZSCHE, WILLIAM THOMSON. *The Presbyterians.* Philadelphia: The Westminster Press, 1934.

HARBISON, FRANCIS R. *Flood Tides Along the Allegheny.* Pittsburgh, 1941.

HARBISON, MASSEY. *A Narrative of the Sufferings of Massey Harbison.* Pittsburgh, 1825.

HAYES, FLORENCE. *Daughters of Dorcas.* Board of National Missions, New York, 1952.

HAYS, CALVIN C. *A History of Blairsville Presbytery and Its Churches.* Pittsburgh: Pittsburgh Printing Company, 1930.

HILL, LEONARD V. *John Johnston and the Indians.*

History of the Pennsylvania Woman's Christian Temperance Union, various authors. Quincy, Pennsylvania, 1937.

History of Presbytery of Redstone, Washington, Pennsylvania, 1899.

History of Presbytery of Washington, 1889. Philadelphia: Jas. B. Rodgers Printing Co.

A History of Shady Side Academy. Pittsburgh, 1958.

HOWE, HENRY. *Historical Collections of Ohio,* 2nd Edition. Cincinnati, Ohio, 1888.

HUTCHISON, S. N. *The East Liberty Presbyterian Church,* Pittsburgh, Pennsylvania, 1935.

JAMISON, WALLACE N. *The United Presbyterian Story.* A Centennial Study, 1858–1958. Pittsburgh: The Geneva Press, 1958.

JEFFERS, WILLIAM H. *Occasional Addresses and Sermons by the Late Reverend Samuel J. Wilson.* New York: Dodd, Mead & Co., 1895.

JOHNSTON, JAMES G. *Recollections.* Uniontown, Pennsylvania, 1929.

JUSTIN, MARTYR. *Apology.* Ayer.

KENNEDY, W. S. *The Plan of Union: Or, A History of the Presbyterian and Congregational Churches of the Western Reserve.* Hudson, Ohio, 1856.

KILLIKELLY, SARAH H. *The History of Pittsburgh, Its Rise and Progress.* Pittsburgh: B. C. & Gordon Montgomery Co., 1906.

KLETT, GUY S. *Presbyterians in Colonial Pennsylvania.* Philadelphia: University of Pennsylvania Press, 1937.

KORSON, GEORGE (ed.). *Pennsylvania Folk Songs and Legends.* Philadelphia, 1949.

LATOURETTE, KENNETH SCOTT. *A History of the Expansion of Christianity,* 7 Vols. New York, 1943.

LINGLE, W. L. *Presbyterians–Their History and Beliefs.* Richmond: John Knox Press, 1944.

Diary of David McClure, edited with notes by Franklin B. Dexter. New York: Knickerbocker Press, 1889.

MCDONNOLD, B. W. *History of the Cumberland Presbyterian Church.* 2nd Edition. Board of Publication of Cumberland Presbyterian Church. Nashville, Tennessee, 1888.

MCKINNEY, WILLIAM W., *In Memoriam–David McKinney.* Pittsburgh Board of Colportage. Pittsburgh, 1879.

MCKINNEY, WILLIAM W., *Early Pittsburgh Presbyterianism. Tracing the Development of the Presbyterian Church in Pittsburgh, Pennsylvania, 1758–1889.* Pittsburgh: The Gibson Press, 1938.

MCNAUGHER, JOHN. *The History of Theological Education in the United Presbyterian Church and Its Ancestries.* United Presbyterian Board of Publication and Bible School Work. Pittsburgh, 1931.

MCNEES, WILLIS S. *History of Butler Presbytery.* Butler, Pennsylvania: Ziegler Printing Co., 1923.

MACARTNEY, CLARENCE E. *Not Far From Pittsburgh.* Pittsburgh: The Gibson Press, 1936.

———. *Right Here in Pittsburgh.* Pittsburgh: The Gibson Press, 1937.

MARSH, DANIEL L. *The Challenge of Pittsburgh.* New York, 1917.

MAXSON, CHARLES H. *The Great Awakening in the Middle Colonies.* Chicago: University of Chicago Press, 1940.

MELLON, THOMAS. *Thomas Mellon and His Times.* Pittsburgh, 1886.

METHENY, EVANGELINE. *North and East of Musa Dagh.* 1950.

MOORE, R. B. *History of Huron Presbytery.* Philadelphia, 1892.

Moravian Archives.

MORELAND, JAMES R. *History of First Presbyterian Church of Morgantown.* Morgantown, West Virginia, 1938.

MORRIS, EDWARD D. *The Presbyterian Church New School, 1837–1869.* Columbus: Champlin Press, 1905.

NEGLEY, GEORGINA G. *East Liberty Presbyterian Church, 1819–1919,* with Historical Setting and a Narrative of the Centennial Celebration, April 19, 1919. Pittsburgh, 1919.

NEVIN, ALFRED. *History of the Presbytery of Philadelphia and of Pennsylvania Central.* Philadelphia: W. S. Fortescue & Company, 1888.

NEVIN, ALFRED (ed.). *Encyclopaedia of the Presbyterian Church U.S.A.* Philadelphia, 1884.

NEVIN, JOHN WILLIAMSON. *The Mystical Presence.* Philadelphia, 1846.

NOTESTEIN, LUCY L. *Wooster of the Middle West.* New Haven: Yale University Press, 1937.

PARKE, JUDGE JOHN E. *Historical Gleanings and Recollections of Seventy Years, etc.* Boston, 1886.

Pennsylvania General Assembly—*Pennsylvania Archives.* (second series)

Pennsylvania Laws, 1700–1781.

PETERKIN, GEORGE W. *A History of the Protestant Episcopal Church in the Diocese of West Virginia.*

Pittsburgh and the Pittsburgh Spirit, addresses honoring the 75th anniversary of the Pittsburgh Chamber of Commerce. Pittsburgh, 1928.

The Pittsburgh Survey. New York: Charities Publishing Co., 1909-1914.

PLACE, JOHN. *Four Young Men.* Pittsburgh, 1954.

PLINY, THE YOUNGER. *Letters.* circum 100 a.d. Ayer.

Presbyterian Reunion Memorial Volume, 1837–1871. New York, 1871.

PRICE, CHAPMAN, TIBBS, CARPENTER. *A Survey of Religious Education.* New York: The Ronald Press, 1940.

RAMSAY, SIR W. M. *An Estimate of the Educational Work of Dr. Isaac Conrad Ketler, First President of Grove City College.* London: Hodder & Stoughton, 1915.

ROBERTS, W. H. *A Concise History of the Presbyterian Church.* Presbyterian Board of Publication. Philadelphia, 1917.

SCHOPF, JOHANN DAVID. *Travels in the Confederation, 1783–1784.* Vol. I. Philadelphia, 1911.

SCOULLER, JAMES B. *A Manual of the United Presbyterian Church, 1751–1887.* 2nd Edition. United Presbyterian Board of Publication. Pittsburgh, 1887.

SCHOOLCRAFT, HENRY R. *Information Respecting the History, Conditions and Prospects of the Indian Tribes.* Philadelphia, 1851.

SHERRILL, L. J. *Presbyterian Parochial Schools.* New Haven: Yale University Press, 1932.

SIPE, C. HALE. *Fort Ligonier and Its Times.* Harrisburg: The Telegraph Press, 1932.

SLOAN, P. H. (ed.). *A History of the Presbytery of Kittanning of the Presbyterian Church U.S.A. with Its Churches and Schools.* Pittsburgh: Barrows and Osborne, 1888.

SLOSSER, G. J. (ed.). *They Seek A Country—The American Presbyterians.* New York: Macmillan Co., 1955.

SMITH, JOSEPH. *The History of Jefferson College, Including an Account of Early Log Cabin Schools and the Canonsburg Academy.* Pittsburgh: J. T. Shryock, 1857.

———. *Old Redstone* or Historical Sketches of Western Presbyterianism, Its Early Ministers, Its Perilous Times, and Its Early Records. Philadelphia: Lippincott, Grambo & Co., 1854.

SPEER, WILLIAM, D.D. *The Great Revival of 1800*. Presbyterian Board of Publication. Philadelphia, 1872.

STARRETT, AGNES LYNCH. *Through One Hundred and Fifty Years*. The University of Pittsburgh. Pittsburgh: University of Pittsburgh Press, 1937.

STEFFENS, LINCOLN. *The Shame of the Cities*. New York, 1910.

STRICKLER, HARRY A. *Forerunners*.

SWEET, WILLIAM WARREN. *Religion on the American Frontier*. Vol. II. *The Presbyterians, 1783–1840*. New York: Harper & Brothers, 1936.

———. *The Story of Religions in America*. New York: Harper & Brothers, 1950.

———. *Religion in Colonial America*. New York: C. Scribner's Sons, 1943.

———. *Religion in the Development of American Culture, 1765–1840*. New York: C. Scribner's Sons, 1852.

SWETNAM, GEORGE. *Pittsylvania Country*—American Folkways Series. New York: Duell, Sloan & Pearce, 1951.

THOMPSON, ROBERT ELLIS. *A History of the Presbyterian Churches in the United States*. New York: C. Scribner's Sons, 1895.

TOBEY, W. L. and THOMPSON, W. O. *The Diamond Anniversary Volume of Miami University*. Hamilton, Ohio, 1899.

TRINTERUD, LEONARD J. *The Forming of an American Tradition: A Reexamination of Colonial Presbyterianism*. Philadelphia: The Westminster Press, 1949.

TURNER, FREDERICK JACKSON. *The Frontier in American History*. New York: H. Holt & Co., 1920.

United States Census

WALKER, WILLISTON. *A History of Congregational Churches in the United States*. New York, 1894.

Western Theological Seminary Biographical Catalogue, 1827–1927. Pittsburgh, 1927.

Westminster Confessions. Pittsburgh: The Westminster Press.

WHITEFIELD, GEORGE. *Journal of George Whitefield, 1739–1744*. London, 1744.

Who's Who in America. Chicago, 1955-1956.

WILSON, ERASMUS. *Standard History of Pittsburgh*. Chicago: Cornell & Co., 1898.

WILSON, GILL I. *A Sketch of Presbyterianism in West Virginia*.

WILSON, GILL I. "History of Presbyterianism in West Virginia U.S.A. Churches," 1958. (Typed mss.)

WOOD, JAMES. *Old and New Theology:* or The Doctrinal Differences which have agitated the Presbyterian Church. Philadelphia: Presbyterian Board of Publication, 1855.

WOODWARD, W. W. *The Works of John Witherspoon*. Philadelphia: W. W. Woodward, 1801.

WOODWORTH, ROBERT. *A History of the Presbytery of Winchester*. Staunton: McClure Printing Co., 1947.

WORCESTER, DAISY LEE W. *Grim the Battles*. New York, 1954.

The World Almanac, "Foundations, Public Trusts, and Funds."

The World's Moral Problems. Addresses at the Third Christian Citizenship Conference, November 9-16, 1919. National Reform Association, Pittsburgh, Pennsylvania, 1920.

WYCLIF, ARNOLD. *Select English Works.*

WYLIE, R. T. *The Whiskey Insurrection*. Elizabeth, Pennsylvania, 1912.

Yearbook of Prayer for Missions, 1957.

YOUNG, LOYAL. *From Dawn to Dusk—A Pastor's Panorama*. Claremont, New Hampshire: Claremont Mfg. Co., 1884.

SECTION III. PAMPHLETS AND THESES

"An Adventure in Faith and Unity." A Brochure prepared by the Council of Churches in Allegheny County, 1927.

BEATTY, C. C. *Records of the Family of Charles Beatty*. Printed for private use of the family. A copy is available in the Library of the Presbyterian Historical Society in Philadelphia.

The College of Wooster Bulletin, 1956-1957.

"Adventure in Education"—*The College of Wooster Bulletin,* December, 1956.

"Pre-Centennial Development Program"—*The College of Wooster Bulletin,* December, 1956.

Constitution of the Pittsburgh Council of Churches.

Constitution—Superintendents' Association, Allegheny County, Pennsylvania, 1889.

CRAIGHEAD, ERNEST S. *History of Craighead Family.*

DAVIS, RICHARD. "The Steubenville Female Seminary," thesis for the S.T.M. degree, Western Theological Seminary.

Diamond Anniversary, The Presbyterian Book Store, 1927.

DIETRICH, MARIETTA. "The History of Grove City College." M. A. Thesis, University of Pittsburgh, Pittsburgh, 1933.

DONCASTER, W. T. "Thaddeus Dod and the Pioneer Efforts of the Presbyterian Church in Southwestern Pennsylvania." A Ph.D. dissertation at the University of Pittsburgh.

EWING, C. M. *Historical Chronology of the College*. A circular in the Library of Washington and Jefferson College.

"Faith and a Woman's Vision." Typed manuscript in historical records of Presbyterian Hospital, 1933.

Charles G. Finney's Autobiography.

Fifty-five Years of Christian Endeavor in Allegheny County, Pennsylvania.

Forty Years of Christian Endeavor in Allegheny County, Pennsylvania, 1889–1929. Pittsburgh, 1930.

GORLEY, MRS. SARA C. "A History of Dunlap's Creek Academy." Brownsville, Pennsylvania: Clipper-Monitor Press, 1938.

Grove City Bible Conference Announcement Booklet. Library of Grove City College.

Grove City College Catalogue 1884–1958. Library of Grove City College.

HAINES, DAVID A. "The Contribution of Waynesburg College to the Church." Thesis, Western Theological Seminary Library, Pittsburgh, 1955.

HAMILTON, W. F. "*The Founders of the Presbytery of Redstone*." An address delivered at Centennial celebration, 1881.

HARE, JOHN C. "The Presbyterian Church in Pittsburgh, 1837–1870." Doctor's Thesis, University of Pittsburgh, 1951.

A Historical Sketch (probably written by Isaac C. Ketler). Grove City College Library.

"A Historical Sketch of Presbyterian Hospital of Pittsburgh." Typed manuscript on file at Presbyterian Hospital.

"History of the Presbyterian Missionary Training School." Manuscript available in office of Presbytery of Pittsburgh, 1930.

"History of the Shadyside Presbyterian Church." 1874. Manuscript.

"In Glorious Tradition." Mimeographed report to Council of Churches, September 25, 1953.

In Memoriam, The Life and Work of Joseph N. Pew and Isaac C. Ketler. Library of Grove City College.

"Interview with Martha Swearingen." Typed manuscript on file at Presbyterian Hospital.

Inventory of the Church Archives of West Virginia — The Presbyterian Churches.

The West Virginia Historical Records Survey, 1941. Charleston, West Virginia.

KETLER, WEIR C. *An Adventure in Education.* Published by the Newcomen Society, New York, 1953.

KLINE, H. E. "Financial and Industrial Aspects of the Panic of 1837." A Master's degree thesis for University of Pittsburgh, 1933.

Laurel Hill Presbyterian Church. Sesquicentennial.

LEA, REVEREND RICHARD. *Reminiscences of Sixty Years in Western Pennsylvania.* A sermon delivered at opening of Pittsburgh Presbytery at Fairview, September 14, 1886.

Lebanon Presbyterian Church. Sesquicentennial, 1926.

"Letter of John Hamilton to Dr. Absalom Baird," written January 9, 1802. Washington and Jefferson College, Washington, Pa.

"Letter of Robert Patterson to Matthew Brown," printed in *The Presbyterian Advocate,* September 1, 1849.

Letter of J. N. Pew to Dr. Isaac C. Ketler. In possession of Weir C. Ketler.

MCCANDLESS, LEE C. "History of Grove City College." M. A. Thesis, Grove City College Library, Grove City College, 1925.

McKinney, David. *Cheap Religious Newspaper Adapted to General Circulation in the Presbyterian Church.* A pamphlet distributed as a circular throughout the church in 1851.

McKinney, William W. *The Challenge of a Heroic Past; the Story of the Establishment of the Western Theological Seminary.* Pamphlet, 1939.

McKnight, D. A. *Historical Sketch of the Sabbath Schools of the First Presbyterian Church from 1800–1867.*

Macartney, Clarence E. *Tell It to the Generation Following.* Pittsburgh, 1934.

Martin, Vernon P., Sr. "Life of David Rice" (not published).

Martinsburg Presbyterian Church Centennial History, 1908.

Mitchell, Robert T. "Biography of Dr. Robert and Jane Mitchell, 1916." Manuscript in files of Indiana County Historical Society, Indiana, Pennsylvania.

Moffatt, James D. *Presbyterianism in Washington, Pennsylvania.* The proceedings at the Centennial Celebration of the First Presbyterian Church of Washington, Pennsylvania. Washington, 1893.

"Obsequies of Elisha Swift, D.D."—a memorial pamphlet. Pittsburgh, 1865.

Olome Institute's Ninth Annual Catalogue, 1853.

One Hundred and Twenty-fifth Anniversary, Second Presbyterian Church. Pittsburgh, 1926.

Pastorate of Reverend Maitland Alexander. Anniversary Booklet, 1924.

Pears, Thomas C., Jr. *Centennial History of the Western Foreign Missionary Society,* 1931.

Pine Grove Normal Academy Catalogues, 1876–1884. Library of Grove City College.

Power, Reverend James. A sermon preached August 2, 1781. In possession of a descendant, Reverend George Fulton, D.D., Carlisle Presbytery.

Presbyterian Board of Colportage of Western Pennsylvania. A report, 1882.

Presbyterian Book Store Scholarship Program, 1956.

Presbyterian Preacher. Available in Library of Presbyterian Historical Society in Philadelphia.

Ralston, Samuel. *On Baptism.* Pamphlet in Western Seminary Library.

Reid, Robert. *The Seven Last Plagues.* A Pamphlet in Western Theological Seminary Library.

Religious Life in Pittsburgh and the Pittsburgh Spirit. Pittsburgh, 1928.

Reports of Bar Association. Allegheny County Court, 1930.

Schermerhorn, John F. and Miller, Samuel J. *A Correct View of That Part of the United States Which Lies West of the Allegheny Mountains.*

Sharp, F. A. "The Development of Protestant Co-operation in Allegheny County." A Ph.D. thesis at University of Pittsburgh, 1948.

Speer, Robert E. "Elisha P. Swift." *Centennial of the Western Foreign Missionary Society.*

SWIFT, ELISHA P. *Offices and Responsibilities of the Professorial Office in Theological Seminaries;* a sermon. Pittsburgh: Johnston and Stockton, 1828.

University of Pittsburgh 125th Anniversary Celebration, *1912 Bulletin,* Vol. VIII, No. 21.

Washington and Jefferson College circular, referring to inauguration of Dr. Edwards and asking for support. Library, Washington and Jefferson College.

Washington and Jefferson College. "Description of College Buildings." Library, Washington and Jefferson College.

Washington and Jefferson College Annual Catalogue, 1865–1866, 1873–1874, 1950–1951.

Waynesburg College Bulletin. Waynesburg, Pennsylvania, 1957–1958; also, Centennial Series, No. 1, 1849–1949.

WELSH, E. B. Unpublished History of the Presbytery of Athens.

Western Theological Seminary—Matriculation Pledge Book.

YOUNG, W. L. "A History of Elders Ridge Academy," a research project for Western Theological Seminary.

ZAHNISER, CHARLES R. "The Cumberland Presbyterian Church." (Manuscript on file at Western Theological Seminary.)

ZAHNISER, CHARLES R. *Pittsburgh Council of Churches, A Historical Interpretation,* 1944.

SECTION IV. NEWSPAPERS AND PERIODICALS

ALEXANDER, E. MARGARET. "Washington Seminary," *Upper Ohio Valley Presbyterian Bulletin,* September, 1957.

BENNETT, D. M. "Life and Work of the Reverend John McMillan." *Journal of the Department of History of the Presbyterian Church U.S.A.* Three installments: September, 1932; December, 1932; March, 1933.

BREWSTER, ROBERT W. "The Rise of the Anti-Slavery Movement in Southwestern Pennsylvania" in *Western Pennsylvania Historical Magazine,* Vol. XXII. Pittsburgh, 1939.

BURNS, EDWARD M. "Slavery in Western Pennsylvania," *Western Pennsylvania Historical Magazine,* Vol. VIII. Pittsburgh, 1925.

CAMPBELL, ALLEN DITCHFIELD. "The Founding and Early History of the Western Theological Seminary" in *The Bulletin of the Western Theological Seminary.* Centennial number, Vol. XX, No. 3, April, 1928.

CAVERT, WALTER D. "When Parochial Schools Failed." *Christian Century,* November 13, 1957.

DODD, CEPHAS. "Memoir of Dr. T. Dod"—printed in the *Presbyterian Magazine,* Vol. IV, September, 1854.

ELLIOTT, DAVID. "Normal Schools." *The Presbyterian Banner.*

Family Treasure. An illustrated monthly, printed in Pittsburgh, first number dated April 2. Years 1864 to 1869 are bound together in a single volume and preserved in library of the Presbyterian Historical Society in Philadelphia.

FULTON, REVEREND J. P. "Early Presbyterianism in Fayette County, Pennsylvania." *Weekly Standard*, Uniontown, Pennsylvania. January-February, 1877.

GORLEY, MRS. SARA C. "Mary Power, First Lady of the Manse," from *The Morning Herald*, Uniontown, Pennsylvania. May-June, 1949.

Hollidaysburg Register and Blair County Inquirer, March 1, 1850, quoting "Minutes of Huntington Presbytery," April 11, 1849.

LINDSAY, H. D. "The Presbyterian Hospital." *The Presbyterian Banner*, February 16, 1898.

LYLE, DR. LOUISE. "Founding of the Presbyterian Hospital of Pittsburgh" in *Presbyterian Hospital Messenger*, 1911.

PATTERSON, ROBERT. "Letter to Matthew Brown." *The Presbyterian Advocate*, September 1, 1849.

PEARS, THOMAS C., JR. *Journal of the Department of History*, Vol. XVI, December, 1934, quoting from *The Founders of the Presbytery of Redstone* by Hamilton.

————. "This American Wilderness," Stone Lectures for 1942. *Journal of the Department of Church History of the Presbyterian Church U.S.A.*

"Pennsylvania College for Women." *The Presbyterian Banner*, July, August, September, 1870; March, 1871.

Pittsburgh Commercial Journal, February 26, 1851.

Pittsburgh Dispatch, August 4, 1901.

Pittsburgh Gazette, January 17, 1789.

Presbyterian Banner: Weekly Recorder (July, 1814–October, 1821), *The Pittsburgh Recorder* (1822–1827), *The Spectator* (1828–1829), *The Christian Herald* (1829–1832), *The Pittsburgh Christian Herald and Western Missionary Recorder* (1833—September, 1838), *Presbyterian Christian Advocate and Herald of the West* (October, 1838–1840), *The Presbyterian Advocate* (September, 1840–1855), *The Presbyterian Banner* (May, 1852–1855), *The Presbyterian Banner and Advocate* (November, 1855)—all formed lineage of *The Presbyterian Banner* (1860–1937).

Presbyterian Life, June, 1957. Witherspoon Building, Philadelphia. Semimonthly magazine of the Presbyterian Church U.S.A.

"Presbyterian Parochial Schools"—*The Presbyterian Banner and Advocate*, June 3, 1857.

SLOSSER, G. J. *Journal of Department of History, Presbyterian Church U.S.A.*, September, 1934.

————. "Walter Lowrie, Mission Organizer." *Journal of the Presbyterian Historical Society*, March, 1958.

————. "Western" in *Western Watch*, Vol. VIII, No. 2, May 15, 1957.

Theological Medium, Vol. XIV, July, 1878.

Uniontown News Standard.

Upper Ohio Valley Presbyterian Bulletin, No. 2, September, 1946.

Washington Examiner, June 14, 1834.

Western Foreign Missionary Society Annual Reports, 1833–1852.

Western Missionary Magazine. Issues February, 1803–January, 1804.

The Wheeling Gazette.

Wheeling Intelligence, 1867.

WILLIAMS, IRENE E. "Operation of the Fugitive Slave Law in Western Pennsylvania from 1850 to 1860." *Western Pennsylvania Historical Magazine*, Vol. IV, 1921.

WRIGHT, J. ERNEST. "Pittsburgh Seventies." *Western Pennsylvania Historical Magazine*, September–December, 1943.

SECTION V. AUTHORS' CORRESPONDENCE

CHURCHES

East Liberty Presbyterian Church, Pittsburgh, Pennsylvania. Letter of Dr. E. P. Cuthbert, Titusville, Pennsylvania, a former member.

Letter of Dr. Charles B. Robshaw, pastor of the church.

North Presbyterian Church, Pittsburgh, Pennsylvania. Mimeographed report to the editor from Reverend Robert Young, pastor.

Shadyside Presbyterian Church, Pittsburgh, Pennsylvania. Information furnished to the editor by Reverend James H. Blackwood, associate pastor.

Third Presbyterian Church, Pittsburgh, Pennsylvania. Letter of Dr. M. L. Best, associate minister, to the editor.

COLLEGES

Davis and Elkins College, Elkins, West Virginia. "Report of the President"; a typed report by Dr. David Allen.

Marietta College, Marietta, Ohio. Letter of George J. Blazier, librarian.

Waynesburg College, Waynesburg, Pennsylvania. "Hopes and Dreams for Waynesburg College," a letter of Paul R. Stewart, President of college.

Letters of Paul R. Stewart, President of college, information about Waynesburg, March 22, 1957, and December 30, 1957.

Letter of Paul R. Stewart, President of college, History of Waynesburg College between 1899 and 1921.

Wooster College, Wooster, Ohio; a letter of Curt N. Tayler, office of the Secretary.

Index